Corrections

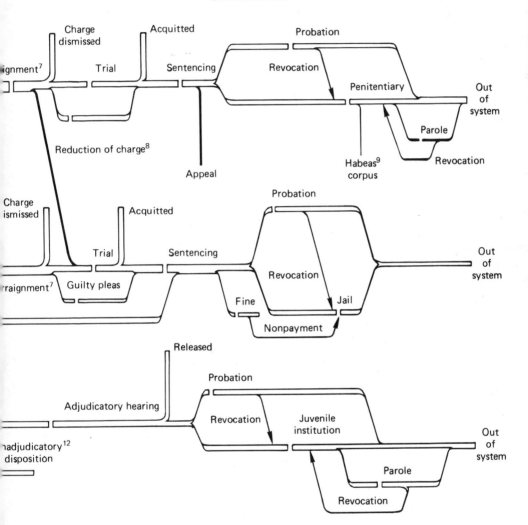

7 Appearance for plea. Defendent elects trial by judge or jury. If available counsel for indigent usually appointed here in felonies. Often not at all in other cases.

8 Charge may be reduced at any time prior to trial in return for plea of guilty or for other reasons.

9 Challenge on constitutional grounds to legality of detention. May be sought at any point in process.

10 Police often hold informal hearings, dismiss or adjust many cases without further processing.

11 Probation officer decides desirability of further court action.

12 Welfare agency, social services, counseling, medical care, etc., for cases where judicatory handling not needed.

DAVID DUFFEE

FREDERICK HUSSEY
Assistant Professor of Criminal Justice
The Pennsylvania State University

JOHN KRAMER
Assistant Professor of Criminal Justice
The Pennsylvania State University

CRIMINAL

JUSTICE:

Organization, Structure,

and Analysis

Prentice-Hall, Inc.,
Englewood Cliffs, New Jersey 07632

Library of Congress Cataloging in Publication Data

DUFFEE, DAVID. (DATE).
    Criminal justice.

    Includes bibliographical references and index.
    1.–Criminal justice, Administration of.   I.–Hussey,
Frederick, (date)   joint author.   II.–Kramer, John,
(date)   joint author.   III.–Title.
HV8665.D8   364   77–17292
ISBN 0-13-193490-2

Prentice-Hall Series in Law Enforcement
James D. Stinchcomb, *Editor*

Printed in the United States of America

10   9   8   7   6   5   4   3   2   1

PRENTICE-HALL INTERNATIONAL, INC., *London*
PRENTICE-HALL OF AUSTRALIA PTY. LIMITED, *Sydney*
PRENTICE-HALL OF CANADA, LTD., *Toronto*
PRENTICE-HALL OF INDIA PRIVATE LIMITED, *New Delhi*
PRENTICE-HALL OF JAPAN, INC., *Tokyo*
PRENTICE-HALL OF SOUTHEAST ASIA PTE. LTD., *Singapore*
WHITEHALL BOOKS LIMITED, *Wellington, New Zealand*

CONTENTS

part II

CRIMINAL JUSTICE AGENCIES: DEVELOPMENT, PROBLEMS, AND PRACTICES

part III
MODELS OF CRIMINAL JUSTICE
AND THE ANALYSIS OF THE CRIMINAL JUSTICE SYSTEM

PREFACE

There is considerable disagreement across the country about the proper curriculum for a university-level criminal justice program. There is not only disagreement among different programs, but there is apparent friction among the faculty of any one program—and among the students. Quite a range of possibilities exists for the study of criminal justice in an academic setting. Although the student can rarely go out and actually *do* work in the field simultaneously with studying, it is also possible to be so practical and specific that the program might more properly be located in a trade school, or a training academy, rather than in a university. And the academically inclined program could be so research-oriented that the mention of crimes and criminals would be too infrequent, and instead one would only hear about estimation, inference, and validity—which would be equally undesirable.

There are negative as well as positive aspects to the planning and the pursuit of education in the criminal justice field. The President's Commission on Law Enforcement and the Administration of Justice recommended, for example, that in the near future all policemen should have a college education.[1] One congressional response was the formation of the

[1] President's Commission on Law Enforcement and the Administration of Justice, *Task Force on the Police* (Washington, D.C.: Government Printing Office, 1967) pp. 125–128.

Law Enforcement Assistance Administration, which, along with other programs, has been responsible for increasing the opportunity for in-service personnel to gain a college education. The commission, however, was vague in describing what kind of education a police officer should receive and what a college education ought to do for police officers, or for the police department.[2]

As police work now stands—forgetting possible improvements for the moment—there is little personal reward for the struggle to get an educa-tion. The subject matter of a college education may have limited direct application to the role of a patrolman, and an academic degree may bring little financial reward, if any. It is also true that the educated policeman may have a problem fitting into the department, even if his degree is an aid to being hired. It is possible, in some areas, for example, that the supervisors of the college-trained recruit may have less education than the recruit would have had with just a high-school diploma. This is not to suggest that these supervisors are not performing adequately in a traditionally administered department. But they may not know how to redesign the organization to take advantage of the skills and capabilities that come with a college education or how to avoid some of the draw-backs. As a result, the college-trained policeman may end up doing what every other patrolman does; and, in time, the skills and knowledge that made him different in the first place may atrophy and be lost. Sooner or later he will become like everybody else.

On another front, there is little if any possibility to utilize a college education as a prison guard in a majority of contemporary prisons. Indeed, a little education with which to understand what is possible and what is ideal in the correctional area is quite likely to make the guard too dissatis-fied to continue in this line of work.[3]

Beneath these observations about college education and work in the criminal justice system, lie broader questions. For example: What can one get from any college education? What should a university offer to the crime problem? One answer came from Ronald A. Wolk, Vice President of Brown University:

> Useful as much increased emphasis on social science research may ultimately be, it is a somewhat sterile answer to society's desperate need for solutions to staggering social problems. . . . The great and unique contribution higher education could make to the social revolution which confronts us in the second half of the Twentieth Century is to produce a new breed of American . . . who will reassert a dying concept of individual worth. . . . Research on the phenomenon of racism (for example) will not accomplish

[2] Ibid.

[3] John J. Galvin and Loren Karacki, *Manpower and Training in Correctional Insti-tutions* (staff report, Joint Commission on Correctional Manpower and Training) (Washington, D.C.: Government Printing Office, December, 1969), pp. 61–66.

question, it would seem in comparing any one job to a university education that there is more choice within the university than at the job. Even if the individual likes his job, he is rather locked into a "role-set" or a particular set of relationships and anticipations about his behavior that will constrain his range of choices. He is not likely to thumb his nose at the boss in the morning and then sweep his secretary into his arms to establish good rapport. (It is because these things are not the normal way of behaving that we make jokes about them.) At the university, however, outside of the fact that a student has to play at being a student, the choices within that status are varied indeed. It is, for example, much easier to change one's professor than one's boss, assuming both parties want to continue in the same organization.

It would seem, then, to be a mistake to say, "I want to be a policeman, and therefore I will take 'Police Administration' and 'Principles of Criminal Investigation.'" *The decision ought to be made the other way around.* The student should take 'Police Administration' and 'Introduction to Urban Problems,' as well as 'French 1' and 'Hospital Administration,' and then decide from this variety of exposures which direction he wants to pursue.

More specifically, if the student approaches a course on introduction to the criminal justice system with a career already in mind, perhaps he should go out and be a policeman and get out of class. On the other hand, the policeman, or correctional officer, who returns to school to begin questioning the way things operate may be in the right place. The idea here is not to criticize the jobs in the field or the desire to get a job upon leaving college. Rather, this course of study and others will be most helpful to future plans if the student keeps those plans in the future and approaches the university course as an opportunity to study a subject matter from many different angles. Since there is more room to maneuver as a student than on the job, it is important to take advantage of that freedom.

The second question concerns what kind of decision—school or job—is irrevocable. Job mobility seems forever to be increasing, but it is hard to obtain a complete college education more than once. A worker can stay on a job six months, a year, or ten years; if he does not like it, he can go on to something else. Once his diploma is hung on the wall, however, he can't cash it in for a different one. He has to live with the formal education he has. Thus, it would seem much more important to get a good first education than a good first job. It may not be wise to allow the first potential job or career possibility to determine the kinds of material one confronts in school. Certainly a student will find himself *less* locked into a restricted career future if he lets his school behavior be governed by other criteria than the good first job.

How does all of this relate to an introduction to the criminal justice as much as enlightened curricula and teaching designed to liberate men from their prejudice and ignorance.[4]

Wolk may not be right, however. He asserts that enlightened liberal arts curricula will liberate men, but it is hard to assert that without researching the problem. Further, many so-called "enlightened" and expensive colleges have frequently been bastions of monied respectability rather than places of ferment and change.

But it is also true that most people entering criminal justice programs are *not* seeking a liberal arts education. They are not seeking to ask what social control means, or how social structures contribute to control, but rather they are seeking to find out how to join in the task of carrying out certain control functions. If this is a common orientation, then most people in such a program have already bypassed the most important criminal justice policy issues, because it is through the process of questioning the fundamental structure and operation of the system that change becomes possible.

There is a difference, however, between asking about certain American methods of social control and regarding those questions as an end in themselves. It is still the "in-thing" at some colleges for both professors and students to castigate the career-oriented student. An education, they say, should not be subordinate to practical matters. Education, the pursuit of knowledge, should be an end of its own. Although this text attempts to question processes and values to which many students might respond with "of course!" it does not go to this other extreme. It does not make sense to say, "Educate yourself now and do not worry about possible relationships in the future." It is ridiculous to suggest that there will not be some continuity between the individual as student and whatever that person may be doing five years from now. Indeed, the tradition of a liberal arts education was built in European society where the student did not have a great deal of choice about his prospective futures; therefore it is absurd not to plan that continuity and to make the most of it.

The opportunity for education to have a direct bearing on a future career also means the student should treat with some care the kinds of career decisions that are relevant to his education and, vice versa, the kinds of educational experiences that are relevant to his future career decisions.

One way of approaching the whole relationship between a college education and a possible career in criminal justice is to ask: (1) Where is there the most room to maneuver? and (2) Which decisions are irrevocable? These are really two very different questions. As regards the first

---

[4] Ronald A. Wolk, "The Reform of the University," in James S. Campbell, Joseph R. Sahid, and David Stang, *Law and Order Reconsidered* (staff report to the National Commission on the Causes and Prevention of Violence) (New York: Bantam Books, 1970), p. 254.

system? Regardless of whether or not the student's future plans involve the criminal justice area, what kind of learning experience and what subject matter can he reasonably expect to obtain in school rather than on the job? Putting it another way, we might ask, "Why are practitioners increasingly demanding academic instead of or in addition to practical experience?"

Douglas MacGregor, a management expert, tells the story of managers from private business who are very mistrustful of management training courses. They arrive at training conferences with a negative predisposition and insist that because MacGregor is a professor, rather than a manager, he cannot really have much to tell them. "There is no substitute for experience," they will say. MacGregor agrees that there is no substitute, but he points out that some executives learn from their experiences while others do not. Some people make the same mistakes over and over again, as if each disaster were totally unique and unavoidable. Others generalize from one situation to similar situations and learn to avoid problems.

A similar example comes from the area of music. Mississippi John Hurt, for example, could not read music. The inability to know the language of music did not stop him from being very good, but it did make him very dependent on tradition. By way of contrast, the improvisations of Jimi Hendrix came from knowing a great deal about music.

Knowing a subject matter academically does *not* guarantee that one will be a good manager or a good musician. But it should guarantee that the student does not start exporing *as new* an approach discarded by others long ago.

An education, even in a so-called practical or professional field such as criminal justice, cannot really prescribe what a student should do. It may, however, suggest the following.

1. What not to do.
2. What has been done before.
3. Who to see or where to look when he has questions about what he is doing now.

To move a bit closer to the substantive area of criminal justice, the student, the policeman on the beat, and the research director for a correctional department must all realize that the real world does not vary so much as the myriad perceptions about it. What a first-day student in an introductory course may think about metropolitan police arrest procedures may be very different from his perceptions of that same process six months or four years later. The way a student looks at the criminal justice system will depend a great deal, not on what that system really is or does, but on the angle of vision of the observer. The discussion of career plans and of approaches to university education becomes very important because this kind of decision will influence a person's outlook and, hence, his understanding of the criminal justice system.

The first substantive point we wish to make, then, is that there is no single or correct way to perceive, describe, or analyze the criminal justice system. Rather, in this book we have attempted to discuss related but different views of the criminal justice "system": the network of agencies and processes that are responsible for certain types of crime prevention, investigation, apprehension, prosecution, defense, conviction, and sentencing and the implementation of dispositional alternatives. Parts I and IV of this work place the descriptive and analytical sections within the contexts of community structure and the social system. Part II of this book takes a rather traditional and descriptive approach, presenting (1) the development of police, court, correctional, and juvenile justice agencies, (2) a description of their present operations, and (3) briefly identifying current issues, problems, and key policy questions. Part III presents a rather dramatically different view, an analytic one that concentrates on police, court, correctional, and juvenile justice organization. The four chapters in Part III build upon the descriptive material in Part II, but in doing so attempt to present a coherent system analytic model through which various criminal and juvenile justice operations can be understood and outcomes of various processes and structural arrangements can be predicted.

We intend that, taken together, the four parts of this work will allow any student of criminal justice to gain competence with the basic terminology, technology, and fundamental value issues in the criminal justice area as well as to gain competence in the application of social science theory to the operations and management of the current criminal and juvenile justice complex.

David Duffee
Frederick Hussey
John Kramer

THE SYSTEM AND
THE COMMUNITY

part I

chapter 1

Systems and the
Criminal Justice System

Under the assumption that what we are about to look at is a type of system, it will be important to have some notion of what a "system" is. For example, what does a series of high-fidelity components do that a series of law enforcement agencies also does? Although the similarity may occur on what seems to be a very general level, it is true that both the electronic components and the agencies *take something in, change it in some way, and give something off*. There is a sequence of input, through-put, and output.

What kind of system are these two? Each is an open or transactional system that interacts with an environment. There are also closed systems that do not interact with the environment. One such system is a theoretical triangle *A-B-C*. A closed system is a series or set of relationships in which what is important is the positions or statuses of the various components. The components of a closed system are identified in terms of *where they are*. The components of an open system are identified in terms of *what they do*.

By analogy, we can speak of open and closed social systems much as we would speak of open and closed physical systems. In introductory sociology, for example, we speak of *ascribed* and *achieved* status. A social system in which particular people behave in accordance with ascribed positions (such as race) is called a *closed class,* or *caste system.* A social system in which people behave in accordance with positions they achieve is called an *open class system.* A caste or closed system is pictured as changeless; regardless of a member's qualifications, he may do only certain things and will receive the privileges available to his caste. In an open class system, status is achieved or people are rewarded for their work. In the closed system, there is determination by unchanging position: *a design is upheld.* In the open system, there is determination by work produced: *a goal is upheld.*

An important thing to remember is that such open and closed systems are not real. They are models used by people for explaining, understanding, and predicting reality. Any real set of events will not conform exactly to the model. We generalize and simplify in order to understand, and we hope to catch the main, important variables. Hence, when we analyze some set of real operations as a system, and classify it as an open, closed, or other type of system, we are speaking just as much of the way it is easiest to see reality as we are speaking of that reality.[1]

For example, Kepler's universe located the planet Earth in the center, and all other bodies revolved around it.[2] This system was rejected not because it was not real but because it was clumsy and complicated compared to the explanation provided by Galileo. Galileo's explanation had the advantage of being simpler and therefore much more useful for scientific (rather than Christian) purposes.

In summary, the final evaluative criterion when we are analyzing any empirical phenomenon is whether or not that kind of analysis works well for our purposes. Therefore, our purposes, and our goals, in studying the criminal justice system must be decided upon *before* we start analyzing.

Just as it is all-important to determine our own goals in studying the system, determining the goals of the system is all-important to an analysis of its operations. If we are going to understand agencies of law enforcement, of judiciary, and of corrections, as they function as components in a system, we must first have a clear view of the kinds of goals these components are trying to achieve.

VARIETY OF GOALS AND THE SYSTEM

This introduction will include the following: (1) a discussion of the goals of criminal justice, (2) observation of the actual operations of the system,

---

[1] See Stafford Beer, *Decision and Control* (New York: Wiley, 1966); pp. 95–120.

[2] Johann Kepler, 1571–1630, German astronomer who constructed a mathematical model of the universe with the earth in the center.

and (3) a commentary on the divergence of operational results from the stated goals. In beginning this process, what kinds of goals should be considered? Is it possible that all goals are not of the same order? Is there a difference in the goals of the baseball spectator, the center fielder, or the general manager? Of the student, the parent, the teacher, or the principal?

It is obvious in the above examples that the goals of an activity may differ depending on the position from which that activity is viewed. The goals important to the police sergeant may not be important to the college student with a criminal justice major, or they may be important in a different way.

If a sergeant in the New York Police Department makes a speech to a college class in which he explains the goals of his department, should these goals be accepted at face value? And should the students automatically believe that the sergeant knows what is the best way to accomplish these goals?

The sergeant, as an employee, may have a commitment to a particular set of goals and to a particular angle of vision in his approach to the system. This doesn't mean that there is anything dishonest or hypocritical about his approach—to say that he is likely to explain police operations in a way that is favorable to his own image of himself. (*Note:* This does not tell us whether he is for or against the department.) But whatever explanation he gives, it is unlikely that this explanation would be equally advantageous to an operations research specialist. Similarly, the conceptual approach of this specialist, in terms of information and cueing theory, would have little relevance to the police sergeant. The same divergence in perspectives occurs at the other end of the criminal justice spectrum, where statisticians are now considering parole board decisions in terms of gaming theory. Although such a look at parole release decisions may help us predict final outcomes, the consideration of his job as a guessing game is not always welcomed by the parole board member!

What is the purpose of the student of criminal justice as he decides on the goals of the system? Should he consider the police department in the same way as a police academy instructor may later want him to consider it? In order to be an effective employee who wants to rise through the ranks and gain the respect of his fellow officers, a recruit may have to accept certain standard operating procedures such as the policy of traffic ticket quotas or the stop and frisk techniques used in high-crime areas of some cities. The recruit may accept these things, unpleasant or pleasant as they may be to his own taste, because he values membership in the organization. But the real question is how should an individual (perhaps the same recruit) consider the criminal justice system *as a student.* How one looks at the system, how one measures effectiveness and efficiency of the system, and what one considers professional behavior of the system employees will all largely depend on the angle of vision or the perspective one chooses in viewing the system.

An example of two very different approaches to the same system is suggested by Leslie Wilkins in a look at the game of pool.[3] First, he suggests that the game may be considered as a *closed system* in which the only question open to debate is how to hit the first shot. If there are no mistakes made—no violations from the plan allowed—then this first strike determines completely the outcome of the game. Second, he suggests that the same game may also be viewed as an *open system*. From this perspective it is assumed that the players are fallible and that the shots may not be hit properly. If this is so, then other things besides the angle of the first shot enter into the game strategy. For example, one may not want to make the first break because there is a chance of losing the turn immediately and leaving the opponent with an easy shot. To a mathematics professor, the closed-system approach may prove an interesting pastime. To the bettor, the system that allows for variation and probability makes more sense. The professor in this instance can afford to do things that the bettor cannot. The professor stands to be entertained whether or not he is successful treating his pool game as a closed system. But the bettor who wagers the outcome of the game on the first shot can lose a lot of money.

Now we can return to the police sergeant. Compared to what an outsider may do, he is not likely to take into account all alternatives to present police operations and all variables in the behavior of his men, as well as all possible goals in the administration of justice. The outsider can *afford* to consider more possibilities in the administration of justice because no organizational punishment will follow for ideas that are too conservative, liberal, or eccentric. Similarly, the sergeant will not consider taking a bribe openly, whereas a law professor might write an article about bribes. This is not to say that the law professor is more objective— but he has other goals, other reasons for looking at the system.

The question each individual student must ask himself is, In what ways can he afford to look at the system of criminal justice? If somebody has it irrevocably in mind to become a particular type of system official, then there are certain criminal justice alternatives that he may have to ignore. In certain agencies of justice, it would be an unhappy man who accepted the Supreme Court ruling regarding in-custody integration.[4] In other quarters, it stands to be a very frustrated person who leaves this course understanding that correctional organizations, to be effective, need

[3] This example is taken from Leslie Wilkins, *Social Deviance* (Englewood Cliffs, N.J.: Prentice-Hall, 1967).

[4] Miranda v. Arizona, 384 U.S. 436 (1966), landmark case that provides for notice of rights to defendant prior to questioning by police.

greater authority over intake and release decisions. The policeman who spends a great deal of time studying correctional systems may become ineffective according to his supervisors. He is undoubtedly aware that the police are often rewarded by the number of arrests they make and, in certain places, by the percentage of convictions following these arrests. But the more this policeman knows about prisons, the less he may want to arrest people. Even if his goal is protection of society rather than care for the offender, he will know that prisons often make offenders more dangerous, and thus he is not protecting society, in the final analysis, by arresting people.

A key dimension in the study we are about to undertake is not the goals of the teachers but the goals of the students. Students can shut teachers off and close textbooks whenever either of these sources disagrees with the students' own goals. Hence, it may be wise to postpone those personal goals that might interfere in the consideration of all the possibilities concerning all the issues. It will not do, however, to ignore or to suppress one's own goals entirely. It is more humanly possible to let personal goals and biases be known to oneself and to others, than to be unbiased. If someone is biased in favor of the way police do things now, because at some point he wants a job, he should let himself be aware of those feelings, and more importantly, he should let others know. In the same vein, if somebody is biased against the system of criminal justice because of personal experiences or observations, he should make these biases explicit in terms of his own study or in his discussions with others.

DIFFERENT METHODS OF IDENTIFYING GOALS

Although officials in the system are familiar with its operation, asking them what the goals of the system are presents several different kinds of problems.

1. Officials may express goals that will paint a favorable picture of the criminal justice system, or an unfavorable picture. Their perception may be filtered through a positive or negative "halo" created by their personal experiences that distorts what they see.

2. Officials who are paid for one particular job may not know the goals of the system as a whole. They may naturally assume that the system as a whole has the same purposes that they accomplish at their own jobs—for example, correctional officers might assume that the main job of correctional organizations is custody.

3. Different officials having different jobs and different perceptions will also have different ideas about the goals of the system. If in our study we do not ask all officials, we will get a biased view, or if we give all views the same weight, we may also bias the real situation.

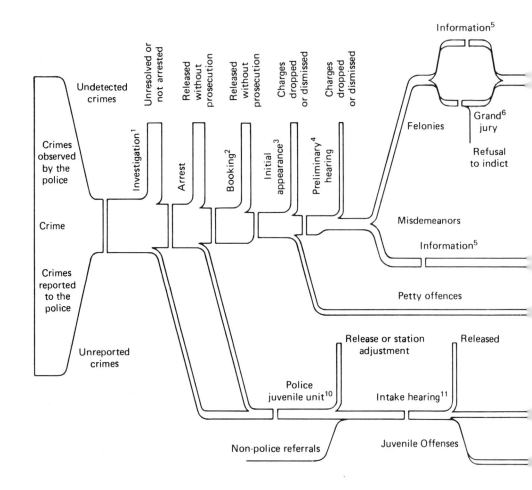

Police   Prosecution   Courts

1 May continue until trial.

2 Administrative record of arrest first stage at which temporary release on bail may be available.

3 Before magistrate, commissioner, or justice of peace, formal notice of charge, advice of rights, Budget Summary trials for party offenses usually conducted here without further processing.

4 Preliminary testing of evidence against defendent. Charge may be reduced. No separate preliminary hearing for misdemeanors in some systems.

Figure 1-1. A general view of the Criminal Justice System. This chart seeks to present a simple yet comprehensive view of the movement of cases through the criminal justice system. Procedures in individual jurisdictions may vary from the pattern shown here. The differing weights of lines indicate the relative volumes of cases disposed of at various points in the system, but this is only suggestive since no nationwide data of this sort exists. From President's Commission on Law Enforcement and Administration of Justice, *Challenge of Crime in A Free Society* (Washington, D.C.: Government Printing Office 1967, pp. 8–9.

Corrections

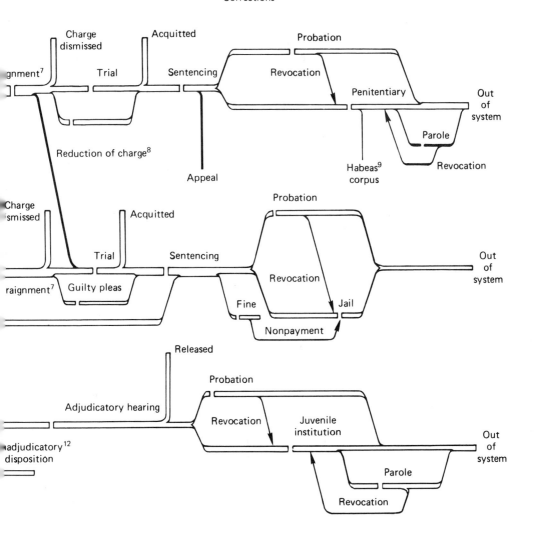

5 Charge filed by prosecutor on basis of information submitted by police or citizens. Alternative to grand jury indictment often used in felonies, almost always in misdemeanors.

6 Reviews whether government evidence sufficient to justify trial. Some states have no grand jury system, others seldom use it.

7 Appearance for plea. Defendent elects trial by judge or jury. If available counsel for indigent usually appointed here in felonies. Often not at all in other cases.

8 Charge may be reduced at any time prior to trial in return for plea of guilty or for other reasons.

9 Ghallenge on constitutional grounds to legality of detention. May be sought at any point in process.

10 Police often hold informal hearings, dismiss or adjust many cases without further processing.

11 Probation officer decides desirability of further court action.

12 Welfare agency, social services, counseling, medical care, etc., for cases where judicatory handling not needed.

What other ways are there of discovering what the goals of the system are? It may help simply to stand back and observe what the system does. A simplified but helpful picture of the criminal process is reproduced in Figure 1-1. Although it is an outline *of decisions about offenders* (rather than about staff members or buildings or community action groups), it may be considered an outline of something that we will later call the *production subsystem.*

There are a number of drawbacks with the outline presented in Figure 1-1.

1. The size of the lines representing the proportion of offenders handled at any one spot is occasionally inaccurate. For example, there are generally many fewer trials than guilty pleas, yet one would conclude the opposite from the diagram.

2. The diagram may give the beginning student the idea that the decision processes in felony, misdemeanor, and juvenile cases are equally orderly and formal. In actual fact, it may be much harder for the juvenile or the misdemeanant to distinguish different portions of the process than is the case with felons.

3. One must remember that the chart is limited to decisions about the offender. It is a charting of the *criminal process*; it is *not* a map of the *criminal justice system*. Much of the activity done in police, court, and correctional organizations has very little direct relationship to offenders. There are many decisions made in the bureaucracy and outside the agencies themselves that may affect the lot of the offender but are not made directly about him.

4. Also, in many of the decisions represented in the figure that are supposedly made about the offender, such as whether or not to charge or to accept a plea, the crucial variables are not the offender and his crime but relationships between agencies and between officials. In other words, the process supported by the bureaucracy has been fragmented into a series of highly formalized decisions. The victim and the offender have been deemphasized and replaced by an emphasis on the affairs of the state.

5. Lastly, the flow chart may give the impression that the process is an orderly progression from one decision to another. The chart deemphasizes the amount of time that comes between decisions. To understand the structure and motion of the system, the *time and duration* between recognized events are at least as important as the formal deliberations—particularly for our decision about its goals.

Now, let us examine the diagram in some detail. One could almost write a rough history of the development of the system by studying this outline. For example, what was the first area to be developed and what was the last? Notice that court decisions not only have their own name, time, and place but frequently their different authorized officials. An initial appearance involves a magistrate. The arraignment will involve a trial judge. In comparison police decisions are less distinguishable. Basically police decisions are differentiated by certainty of guilt and control over the suspect. Police can do only certain things to the suspected offender at first contact. They can do much more after an investigation and obtaining of a warrant for search or arrest.

However, the sequence of police decisions are often difficult to distinguish time-wise. An arrest often starts rather than completes an investigation. Arrest and investigation decisions are mutually supportive rather than sequential. If there has been an arrest, there will be an investigation to support the original decision; if there has been an investigation, the likelihood of a subsequent arrest may be related to the amount of energy exerted in the investigation. In many cases, police decisions are determined prior to the individual crime and the specific interception of a single offender. To some extent the decision is made prior to any crime or any suspicion—for example, a major variable in a police decision to arrest a juvenile is his *demeanor* rather than any specific illegal acts.[5] If the juvenile is belligerent and a challenge to authority, the police may find something to arrest him for; whereas if he is polite and penitent, they may overlook something wrong that he has done. In an "objective" view, both the belligerent juvenile and the polite juvenile may be equally guilty, but the probability of guilt is not the only factor in police decisions. Equally, if not more important, is the fact that the police may be uncomfortable (and reasonably so!) when their authority is questioned. Moreover, juveniles in some parts of a community are more likely to threaten police authority than juveniles in other parts of town.

It should be clear in the above examples that decisions are only clear-cut once they are made. While they are being made, they occur within a *framework of interaction*. Hence, the outcome of each decision, although it may be rigidly defined, is a matter of probability.

MAJOR DECISIONS IN THE CRIMINAL PROCESS

Keeping the probabilistic, variable nature of the decision in mind, we will find it helpful to know brief definitions of the major decisions of the criminal process. For the moment, we will concentrate on the adult process. The major police decisions vis-à-vis the offender are whether to investigate and whether to arrest.

   1. *Investigation.* Investigation is a variable process that may continue through a trial. It may, on the other hand, be quite short. But in all

[5] President's Commission on Law Enforcement and the Administration of Justice, *Task Force on Juvenile Delinquency* (Washington, D.C.: Government Printing Office, 1967), pp. 18–19.

cases, whether a crime is reported to the police or occurs within the sight of an officer, it is important to remember that the policeman has a decision to make. He can ignore a report, and he can decide not to interfere in an event that he witnesses.

2. *Arrest.* An arrest is made when an officer decides that he has probable cause to believe that a crime has been committed, and that the person in question committed it. An arrest takes place when an officer stops the person in question and restrains his liberty in some way. It is still debatable exactly to what degree a person's liberty must be interrupted to reach the level of an arrest, but there is now a consensus that the police do have the authority to stop and question short of an arrest and to do so on lesser grounds than probable cause.

Decisions that we should attribute to the prosecutor rather than to the police may not always be distinct because in some cases even an investigation is prompted by the prosecutor rather than by police suspicion. Depending on the importance of a case, or a particular offense, or the procedures of particular police departments and prosecutors' offices, the point at which the police consult the district attorney may vary.

3. *Charge.* The decision to charge is traditionally recognized as the prosecutor's rather than a police decision. When a prosecutor decides to charge the arrested person, he is deciding to continue the prosecution beyond the arrest. The process of prosecution itself occurs in different stages and involves several other officials.

4. *Initial appearance.* The initial appearance is the presentation of the suspect before a magistrate, federal commissioner, or justice of the peace. At this point there will be formal notice of the charge, and the judicial officer has the responsibility of reviewing the police decision to determine if indeed there was probable cause to believe a crime was committed by the suspect. The defendant will receive information about the rights he possesses. Very importantly, bail is set at this stage, or the defendant may be released on his own recognizance (R.O.R.). If he is not eligible for R.O.R. or cannot make bail, he will spend his pretrial time in jail.

5. *Preliminary hearing.* The preliminary hearing is a presentation by the prosecutor before a judge of sufficient evidence to show probable cause. A defense need not be made at this time. If there are "negotiations" to be made about the seriousness of the charge, they will often begin at this time. A defendant in most systems has a right to a preliminary hearing, but he often waives this right. If an indictment is returned before a preliminary hearing takes place, the issue of probable cause is moot, and the hearing does not take place.

6. *Information.* An information is the official document prepared by the prosecutor and sets forth a description of the offense and the relevant law or statutes. In the felony system the information is an alternative to a grand jury. In the misdemeanant system, the information is almost always used.

6(a). *Grand jury.* The grand jury usually consists of 24 citizens whose job is to review the prosecutor's evidence and decide whether there is sufficient proof of guilt to proceed to trial. The grand jury method is falling into disuse in many criminal justice systems as many people find that it offers few advantages and many disadvantages as compared to proceeding by information.

7. *Arraignment.* Arraignment is the appearance of the offender before the judge for the plea of guilty or not guilty. If there is a plea of not guilty, the defendant may usually elect trial by judge or trial by jury. If the defendant is indigent, counsel is usually appointed at this point, if one is appointed at all. If the defendant pleads guilty, a trial usually does not take place, although the judge is required to determine if the plea is intelligently and voluntarily made.

8. *Trial.* A trial is the determination of guilt or innocence by a judge or a jury after the presentation of evidence by prosecution and defense. In the United States, trials in most areas are much less frequent than guilty pleas.

8(a). *Guilty plea.* A guilty plea is, in effect, self-conviction. The defendant at arraignment pleads guilty to the offense as charged, or if some bargain has been struck in return for the plea, then the defendant may plead to some reduced charge in return for the prosecutor's recommendation on sentence.

9. *Sentencing.* Sentencing is the last appearance of the convicted offender before the judge for announcement (and perhaps determination) of the punishment for the offense committed. In the case of a guilty plea, particularly in misdemeanors, sentencing may occur directly after the guilty plea. In felonies the sentencing is usually scheduled for a later date, after the probation department has filed a pre-sentence report for the judge's consideration.

10. *Probation.* Probation is one sentencing option usually open to the judge. It is used most frequently with less serious offenses and with first offenders. When probation was first utilized, it was generally considered a demonstration of the court's mercy and was granted in lieu of a sentence. Today, probation generally involves at least minimum supervision from a probation staff and is definitely seen as a unique sentencing strategy during which the probation officer may exercise considerable control over the probationer.

11. *Incarceration.* Incarceration is the sentencing alternative in which the convicted offender spends a specified period of time in a jail or prison. A jail is usually a county facility that houses misdemeanants, and a prison is usually a state facility that houses felons. A felony is usually defined as a crime for which the punishment is more than a year, although the length of sentence differs according to locality. The authority to assign time for incarceration is delegated differently from place to place but in felonies usually involves a legislative decision about the outer limits of time to be received, a judicial decision about the actual minimum and maximum, and a parole board decision about how much of the maximum legal sentence will in fact be served.

12. *Parole.* Parole is the decision made by a parole board to release the offender from prison prior to termination of his sentence so that he may spend some time under correctional supervision after returning to the community. Parole is usually available in felonies and in some communities for misdemeanors.

13. *Revocation.* Revocation is the decision by the parole board that, because the conditions upon which the offender was released on parole have not been kept, he should be returned to prison. Revocation often occurs for the commission of a new offense by the offender, but it may also occur for "technical violations" of parole conditions or for acts that would not be crimes if committed by free citizens.

There are, of course, many other decisions made in the criminal justice system and many other decisions made about the suspect and criminal offender. The above items, however, are the decision points in which a major determination about the offender is made, and because of which he is likely to undergo a major change in status. There are a number of ways of looking at these decisions and at the processes and structures that connect them. One way would be completely formal. We could study the law governing each decision point. In so doing we would consider: (1) that officials must do certain things at each decision point, and (2) that offenders must have done particular things or have attributed to them certain criteria in order to move from one position to another. A second way might be a sociological study of the process of human interaction. We might compare arrest and conviction to other rituals of ostracism, and incarceration to other rituals of initiation. The most helpful way, however, would be a combination of these methods: to understand on the one hand what the process is supposed to do according to the law and to understand on the other hand how it operates as influenced by variables of human interaction.

THE IDEAL-LEGAL SYSTEM

From a strictly formal viewpoint, the system would be set in motion by the commission of a crime. The suspects who could have committed it would be investigated, a decision of probable guilt would be made, and a court test would be set up in which the adversaries argue for and against the probability that suspect X is the man responsible. Punishment would follow a finding of guilt in this model. It is particularly important to note that the officials are expected to be perfect—either more or less than human. They should be influenced only by factors related to the commission of the crime, and the relationships among officials and between officials and defenders are only those as prescribed by law or by administrative regulations.

The legal model of this process is *mechanistic* because there is no possible variation in the relationship between officials and offender and no variation among officials. The motion of the machine is started by some fact in the past and continues on to conclusion as originally determined by that fact.

Some problems of reality ignored by this approach include:

1. That the processing of one individual does not begin in isolation.
2. That it does not continue in isolation.
3. That it does not end in isolation, if it ends at all.

In other words, the process has undefined and changing origins somewhere in the community and ends in the same undefined and changing ways. Furthermore, common sense should tell us that since the process continues day after day, year after year, that the officials are involved with each other much longer and much more frequently than they are involved with a particular offender. Hence, many decisions that are made, even those ostensibly made about the offender, are often made for reasons rather unrelated to the offender and having more to do with how officials control each other. The study of the legal or formal process of the system is inadequate for an understanding of what really happens in the system.

THE INFORMAL SOCIAL SYSTEM

At the same time, we must be cautioned against a plan of study that starts by completely rejecting the influence of the legal definitions of the system. We could, for example, try to understand the process as a ritual of ostracism. We would then look for the following:

1. Cues of social disapproval.
2. Changes in offender status.
3. Reduction in citizenship.
4. Proscription of certain roles.

In doing so, we could find that, among other deprivations, the convicted offender loses the right to vote, loses the right to certain jobs, and loses freedom of movement. But, some offenders never were really "part of the society" that they are supposedly ostracized from. They may have been rejected by the dominant culture long before their introduction to the criminal justice system. Furthermore, the criminal process is invoked only for certain acts that result in social disapproval, not for all acts that result in disapproval. Conversely, the criminal justice system is only *one* means of ostracism in specific cases, not the only form of ostracism. In addition, one notices after a while that the process is used against some disapproved people and not against others, and occasionally it is used against socially approved people regardless of that approval. Therefore, although the legal-formal understanding of the system is not adequate by itself, law and legal constraints do have an effect on the system. The question is how.

Since the study of organization is a study of how the system operates, we will approach the criminal justice system *as one kind of organization*. We will talk about organizational systems in general, and then adapt the model to the criminal justice system. We will try to understand the criminal process—the series of decisions we have just reviewed—by looking at the organizations or the structures surrounding the process.

If one begins looking for the origins of the system in specific legislation, he will only get so far. He will find:

1. Statutes of substantive criminal law setting out those acts that are proscribed or required.
2. A mandate to proceed with their enforcement.

Hence we have:

Goal (Safe society)
Goals (Specific crimes)
Method (Agency of enforcement, administration of punishment)

The last part, the legislative directive on how to proceed, usually only goes so far. The law might state, for example,

In order to deter, punish, and rehabilitate criminal offenders, a Department of Correction will be established under a commissioner.

The commissioner may be given authority to set up the specifics of such a department. However, to set down the criminal justice system on paper, it will not suffice to write down the criminal and administrative law. The great majority of system activity is *extralegal*. The criminal law is carried out by *organizations* of people.[6] Each of these organizations at the moment is operationally independent of the other two. About the only thing these agencies have in common is (1) the criminal law and (2) a target population. But the agencies see different parts of the law as relevant, and they handle different parts of the target population. (See Figure 1-2)

The suggestion has been made in several places now that the system should have a common management. At the moment, however, centralized correctional management is still new (some states do not have state-

[6] For simplicity, we will here refer to courts as "organizations," but in Chapter Four we will identify and describe a variety of organizations that are court-related. Although we mention here police, court, and correctional organizations, it is obvious that many other organizations are involved in the criminal justice system.

Figure 1-2. Segmented Criminal Justice System

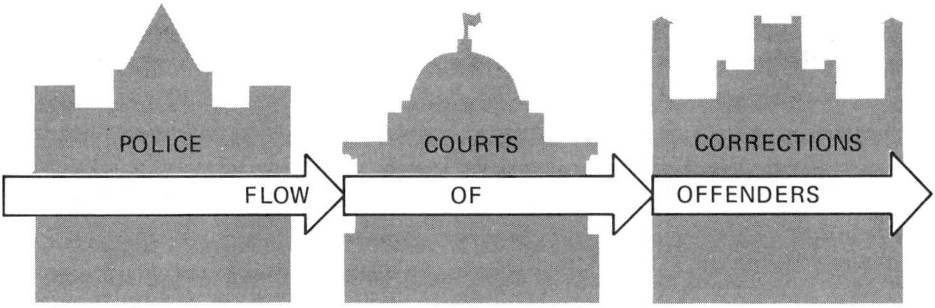

wide departments of correction), and unified court management has hardly been tried. Although it may be to our ultimate advantage to decide how all the components of the system fit or fail to fit together, and whether common management is desirable or not, let us look for a while at the organization as it stands, and see how it works.

A common current complaint about the administration of justice is the ponderousness of the bureaucracy. What is bureaucracy? We may think of bureaucracy in a variety of ways:

1. As a form of authority based on rules decided in advance, rather than on tradition or charisma.
2. As a form of organization divided into offices with specific, defined functions.
3. As an organization where division of labor and specialization of tasks are decided in relation to the easiest way to achieve some goals.
4. As an organization in which officers are hired not for personality or connections but for their ability to carry out certain functions.
5. As an organization in which people are regarded for what they achieve and are punished for what they fail to do in accordance with the rules.

All of these aspects of bureaucracy may be found in the organizations of the criminal justice system. The fact that the organizations of criminal justice are bureaucracies (about which people complain) presents us with a paradox:

People applaud rule by law, but people in the United States generally seem to dislike organizations known as bureaucracies that run on *legal* or bureaucratic authority or on the rule of law.

A key consideration for us then might be: Is there some alternative method for administering the law than by the present complex organizations structured by rules?

Many scholars have studied the operations of bureaucracies, although generally in other settings. James March and Herbert Simon generalized the findings of other scholars about the typical problem with bureaucracies as shown in Figure 1-3.[7] This figure summarizes the idea that bureaucracies are organized in such a way that a planned action not only has planned consequences, but that the planned or expected consequences yield unintended consequences that reinforce the original action. This phenomenon in itself is not damaging, but a frequent variety of this occurrence may be.

An example of the damaging phenomenon is pictured in Figure 1-4. In this case the unintended consequences are dysfunctional or work against the goals of the organization, but nevertheless they reinforce the original action. In the case of Figure 1-4, Peter M. Blau was studying employment offices, where the organization was to find clients jobs.[8] He describes the situation in which the demand for control over the employees is followed, rather logically, by the formulation of particular standards of operation and certain criteria of performance. By following the rules as established, employees may defend their actions before the evaluative eye of their superiors, and superiors may demonstrate their degree of control by the fact that they can reliably predict the procedure used by most employees in dealing with most clients. These relationships are represented by the solid lines in Figure 1-4. However, as depicted by the dotted lines, certain unintended and in this case unwanted things also occur when the demand for control is met with increased emphasis upon reliability of procedures. In order of their occurrence, the unintended series of events are: (1) increased rigidity of behavior as employees become more careful to follow rules, (2) increased difficulty with unemployed clients as employees become more interested in following rules

Figure 1-3. The General Bureaucratic Dysfunction

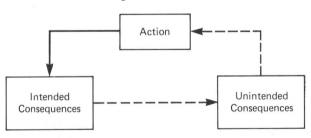

[7] James G. March and Herbert Simon, *Organizations* (New York: Wiley, 1958), p. 27.

[8] This case is taken from Ibid., p. 41.

Figure 1-4.   A Simplified Model of the Bureaucratic Dysfunction

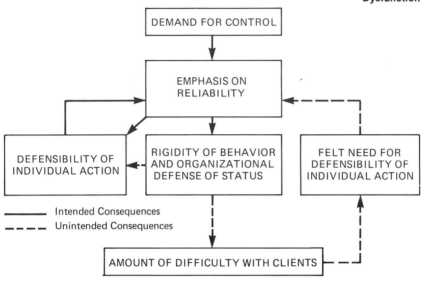

Source: Flow diagram from James G. March and Herbert Simon, *Organizations* (New York: Wiley, 1958), p. 41.

than in finding jobs, and (3) increased need on the part of employees to defend their actions as clients' complaints increase. Thus, the unintended consequences that are dysfunctional, if the goal of the organization is to maximize the number of clients placed, also tend to increase the emphasis on reliability and the defensibility of individual action. In other words, the general bureaucratic dysfunction, as we know it, is that the principles of bureaucratic authority, applied uniformly, produce unexpected as well as expected results, and the unexpected results produce problems that generate the same reponses that started the problematic behavior.

What can be done about this? What is lacking in such an organization that breeds such legal "revolt"? Discovering whether the behavior of bureaucracies is unalterable or manipulable is very important because the problems of criminal justice bureaucracies are reaching crisis proportions. A key to the discovery may lie in asking where the rules are decided upon. Do all people in the organization select the rules of operation, or are the rules manufactured and handed down from the officials at the top? Who in the organization is committed to achieve the goals intended by the rules? Are organizational participants on *all* levels committed to achievement of organizational goals, or just the few officials who made up the rules?

Usually we find that the lower echelons of the organization are not represented in the places where rules are made and goals are decided upon. University students, prisoners, and automobile assembly-line workers usually share in common the complaint that the organizational process is not democratic. None of them traditionally have had much power in deciding how they would be expected to behave in the organization.

When it happens that the population that is to follow the rules does not make the rules, it stands to reason that there is a higher probability that unintended consequences will follow. Rules and laws—criminal laws and rules of criminal procedure included—do not guarantee anything. They are only one way of expressing a number of goals that are to be obtained. Knowing the laws and rules will be a poor substitute for knowing the goals that those rules are supposedly related to, and knowing the behavioral consequences of those rules and laws as implemented, avoided, or overturned by the actors in the community and the criminal justice system.

Now let us look at what those rules help result in—and also what the rules may in part be a reflection of—that is, the actual operations of the system. It will be through understanding the actual operations of the criminal justice system, where the laws of society and the norms of bureaucracy meet, that we can decide what parts of the system should be abandoned and replaced by more worthwhile attempts at social control and what parts of the system should be saved and improved.

We will undertake that task in several incremental steps. In the next chapter, the issues concerning community development and community control are laid out. Where does the criminal justice system fit into the community? What other social organizations are related to it? What other community structures perform control functions? Do all members of a community perceive social control activities in the same way?

chapter 2

The Community and Criminal Justice

For years now, officials within the criminal justice system, legislators, judges, and concerned citizens have been calling for increased communication between executives in the criminal justice network and key individuals and agencies in relevant communities. Reasons for the absence of, or dysfunctioning of, communication links among all these parties have been variously stated in many different contexts. Although there have been almost identical pleas for mutual understanding and cooperation from both system executives and community workers, there are apparently different motives for these similarly stated requests. Undercurrents of frustration among system executives concerning apparent system ineffectiveness in achieving desired goals undoubtedly influence their requests for community support. In other words, the plea for cooperation and/or increased community involvement in criminal justice activity carries overtones critical to the current *lack* of such involvement, and carries undertones that assign responsibility for the deficiency to the community audience. Conversely, the various and conflicting demands by the community upon the criminal justice complex are influenced by the perceived unresponsiveness of the system and by the perceived lack of services in proportion to the costs of such a system.

The function of this chapter in addressing the general topic of community-system interrelationships is more narrowly circumscribed than is the coverage of other types of agency-community exchange, or other system outputs of the community. Community-agency relations have been covered specifically and in detail by several different texts and articles on police-community relations,[1] community-based corrections,[2] and system-community relations.[3] The broader topic, of what functions an idealized criminal justice system performs for the social system, has also been addressed, if perhaps vaguely, by social systems theorists such as Talcott Parsons and Robert Merton.[4]

In contrast, the particular task of this chapter is the presentation of a description of the community as a system, in such a way that community organization theory can be made relevant to the current concerns about criminal justice system integration, unification, decentralization, etc. We perceive this middle ground (the defining of community as a usable construct in criminal justice analysis) to be the weakest single topic in the developing study of criminal justice. Without strengthening the notion of community as used in criminal justice system analysis and planning, the down-to-earth practical expositions (i.e., police-community relations or anecdotal accounts of failures in such areas) will be without any theoretical mooring that can provide a solid base for improvements in this area. And, without a usable construct of community, the broader theories of social control will go untested because there will be no empirical validations possible.

CRIMINAL JUSTICE IN THE COMMUNITY

Previous attempts to define the concept of community in social and behavioral terms to be used in criminal justice administration have been tentative and abortive at best and sophomoric and useless at worst. To our knowledge, there is only one basic text that purports to define community as relevant to criminal justice.[5] An examination of this work (by Robert Trojanowicz and Samuel Dixon) demonstrates that these authors, like ourselves, are upset, worried, and dissatisfied with the inat-

[1] Paul F. Cromwell, Jr., and George Keefer, *Police-Community Relations* (St. Paul, Minn.: West, 1973); and Alan Coffey, Edward Eldefonso, and Walter Hartwiger, *Human Relations: Law Enforcement via Changing Community* (Englewood Cliffs, N.J.: Prentice-Hall, 1971).

[2] George G. Killinger and Paul F. Cromwell, Jr., *Corrections in the Community* (St. Paul, Minn.: West, 1974).

[3] Robert C. Trojanowicz and Samuel L. Dixon, *Criminal Justice and the Community* (Englewood Cliffs, N.J.: Prentice-Hall, 1974); and Robert C. Trojanowicz and Forrest M. Moss, *Community-Based Crime Prevention* (Pacific Palisades, Calif.: Goodyear, 1975).

[4] Talcott Parsons, *The Social System* (New York: The Free Press, 1951); and Robert Merton, "Social Structure and Anomie," in *Social Theory and Social Structure* (Glencoe: Free Press, 1947).

[5] See Trojanowicz and Dixon, *Criminal Justice and the Community*.

tention and/or sloppy thinking that has marked the criminal justice recognition and the accommodation of its interfaces with the external social environment. To aid in reducing this problem, these authors present an introductory chapter on the community that they hope will dispel some of the ignorance and cliché-ridden thinking that have dominated criminal justice approaches to the community. This discussion by Trojanowicz and Dixon is one of the few attempts at the basic level to introduce students to the complexity of community organization and its multifaceted and often contradictory relation to criminal justice administration. However, there is little if any attempt to integrate the material on community with the following chapters on criminal justice—community relations. Indeed, much of the remainder of the book could easily be classified as a traditional treatment of police—community relations on the agency level.

Although adequate coverage of system-community exchange certainly deserves volumes on its own, a rudimentary definition of the community as a social system should be clearly and explicitly related to the criminal justice system in an introductory text. Therefore, having described in the last chapter the bare bones of a criminal justice system, the next task before linking specific system and community functions is a theoretically based and current definition of community from the community rather than from the criminal justice literature.

THE COMMUNITY AS A SOCIAL SYSTEM

Many social scientists, particularly sociologists associated with Talcott Parsons, have been for many years active in describing large patterns of action of an identified body of people as a "social system." Ideally, there may be no limit to the numbers of people involved in a social system, beyond a sufficient number to form a small group. Generally, however, social systems analysis has been used to denote the study of very large and complex group patterns, such as those of a nation, state, or large geographical area. In a slightly different context, large bureaucracies and other organizations have been analyzed as social systems. One question that a leading student of community then poses is whether and in what ways can the social systems analysis that has been applied to larger and smaller social entities than the community also be applied to the community itself. Community is defined as *the arrangement of groups, organizations, and systems that provide locality-relevant social functions.*[6] In other words, a community is a certain social organization for delivery to people in one locality the activities and services necessary for day-to-day living.[7]

[6] Roland Warren, *The Community in America* (Chicago: Rand McNally, 1963), p. 9.

[7] Ibid., pp. 9–14.

The five social functions deemed to have "locality relevance" are: (1) production, (2) socialization, (3)social control, (4) social participation, and (5) mutual support.[8] These five social functions are very similar to the five "institutions" that other sociologists have labeled as essential to the endurance of any social system. These five institutions are: (1) economic, (2) education, (3) political, (4) religious, and (5) family.[9] The more generalized version of locality-relevant *functions* gets around the problem that several of the social insitutions, such as education, have secondary and tertiary functions as well as primary ones, and that other institutions, such as the family, do not any longer seem as strong as they once were, or as the only possible source of a particular social function (e.g., mutual support) thought to be provided by them.

The Production Function

A primary function that a community cannot do without is the production of goods and services and the mechanisms for their distribution and consumption. In some earlier studies of community that emphasized geographical location or political designation only, rather than the presence of community functions, it would have been quite possible to identify some unit of people regardless of whether that unit could supply its people with necessary provisions to sustain life. A functional examination of community, on the other hand, would study the economic linkages between people and groups in a particular locality prior to determining community boundaries. For example, a "bedroom" or residential suburb, in which all persons travel to a central city for employment, would be considered a portion of the large metropolitan community rather than a separate entity in its own right. On the other hand, some smaller suburban communities have been successful in luring business and industry from central city locations. It might be possible to consider these new industrial and business centers as communities on their own, at least to the extent that the production-distribution-consumption function is performed more or less independently of the larger central city.

The Socialization Function

The socialization function of a community includes all those activities that contribute to the transfer of community norms and values from dominant community groups to newcomers, particularly to children. Processes of socialization enable an organizational unit or complex, such

---

[8] Ibid., p. 9.

[9] Leonard Broom and Philip Selznick, *Principles of Sociology*, 4th ed. (New York: Harper & Row, 1970).

as a community, to remain stable over time by assuring that the values and desired end-states, and the valued or accepted ways of achieving them, remain intact over time. Probably the social units that have traditionally played the greatest role in socialization are public schools and individual families. Families inculcate children from their earliest stages with the broad values of a culture and with a particular moral sense that is to govern behavior within the family. The school not only educates children about accepted techniques and knowledge bases for performing properly in society, but also strongly emphasizes accepted behavior patterns, goals for achievement, and methods for cooperative group living.

It would be extremely difficult if not impossible for a social group that did not control its own socialization processes to be considered a community. This is one of the reasons for recent conflicts between large centralized city boards of education and smaller city units who are demanding "neighborhood control" of the schools.

Another important aspect of socialization is that performed by organizations other than schools and families upon adult members of a community, although some of these socialization forces are too organization-specific to be considered community socialization forces. For example, a high-school graduate may take on a highly technical job with a local manufacturing firm and in the course of his training not only learn the production techniques required on the job but also inevitably learn certain values and goals associated with doing that particular task or working for that particular company. However, in certain instances, at least in what may be considered well-integrated communities, organizational socialization includes indoctrination to values and goals of the community itself. For example, selling techniques that may work effectively in a large urban community may not be profitable in a small rural community where either different commodities or different retailer-consumer relationships are valued. Hence, organizations must become cognizant of local as well as general values and goals and must achieve the proper mix and the proper image on the local level in order to prosper.

The Social Control Function

An equally important function in community organization is that performed by activities and systems that control social behavior, or control the distribution of goals and means to achieve them. Institutional sociology traditionally referred to the "political institution" as carrying out this function of decision making and legitimating the power of decision makers. Within the context of functional community theory, it may not necessarily be the political system, in the traditional sense of parties and government, that always performs this function, or performs it unmodified by other groups and influences. The structural-functional analysis of organized crime, for example, has suggested that in certain localities the functions of legitimating power and controlling the distribution of resources are performed by an underworld elite who, in return for cooperation, provide services and goods to citizens who are not adequately served by the formal political groups in the areas where organized crime generally operates. Other examples of social control functions performed by nonpolitical or nongovernmental units are far less extreme than the one above. Recent advances in community power theory and research, for example, suggest that informal community "influence nets" exist in most communities and play strong roles in many community activities, policy decisions, and problem resolutions. Although this research has been marked by methodological and theoretical conflicts, as to whether power is exerted by stable elites or temporary, pluralistic influence groups, all such research demonstrates that the function of social control is considerably more complex and dispersed than would appear the case in analyses concentrated solely on political parties and formal governments.

The Social Participation Function

The concept of social participation has replaced, in the functional literature, the importance given to formal religions in the institutional literature. In all communities, there are a host of groups and organizations that provide avenues for citizens to participate in social activities with each other. The value of this function for community living may be considerably less clear and more difficult to state than the functions of socialization, social control, and production. Nevertheless, the opportunity for community members to congregate and share mutual interests, values, ideals, etc., provides a solidifying and mediating function for persons who in the normal course of daily activity frequently meet in the context of narrowly prescribed roles and special interests. In other words, the function of social participation, although it may be ritualistic and highly organized at times, as in a church service, or a voluntary action agency, provides at its core the opportunities for face-to-face primary group activity, in which performing a role is less important than being identified as a person belonging to an identifiable group.

Communities where the social participation system is weak may either be emerging or decaying. But in any case, it is unlikely that a strongly integrated community can exist for long without many and varied opportunities for relatively sanction-free, person-to-person sharing. Or, as Émile Durkheim described this function years ago, a community exists to the extent that the opportunity is present for the celebration of communal values.[10]

The Mutual Support Function

The last of the five locality-relevant social functions is the one of mutual support. Again, not many years ago, standard sociology texts would allocate this function as predominantly if not solely the province of the family. But, as we mentioned above, the single-unit family has not been the only source of mutual support in either historical or cross-cultural contexts, and it is not the sole source in America currently. Today, the numerous pressures placed upon the conjugal family have, in many instances and in many areas, seemed to sap the strength of the family unit. Sequential marriage partners for men and women are commonplace, as are communal and group arrangements, experiments in new "extended families," and the conscious decision by many persons to forego marital relationships altogether. Although it may be true that alternatives to the familial institutions are not emerging as rapidly as the family is decaying as a source of mutual support, it is true that many other alternative sources and auspices for mutual support functions currently exist. Religious groups frequently tend to needy members or those confronting crisis situations. A plethora of voluntary health and welfare groups has emerged, as well as more bureaucratized and formal alternatives such as medical and health insurance systems, various public welfare agencies, and so on. Whatever the structural pattern by which the mutual support function is implemented, it is fairly clear that communities, to last as such, must provide to their members those mutual support activities distinct from production, socialization, social control, and participation that enable their members to retain some autonomy and some of the culturally valued comforts that raise living beyond the subsistence level.

VERTICAL AND HORIZONTAL DIMENSIONS OF COMMUNITY

Equally important as the primary functions to understanding the community as a type of social organization is the examination of particular structural arrangements for performing those functions. Just as complex bureaucratic organizations may have different decision and control networks (e.g., a flat or a pyramidal hierarchical structure), communities differ in the way that production, socialization, social control, participation, and mutual support activities are carried out.

[10] Émile Durkheim, *Elementary Forms of Religious Life* (New York: The Free Press, 1955).

The functional theory of community suggests two dimensions upon which the structure of community may differ. The vertical dimension of community refers to the degree to which a local unit or community is tied to or dependent on the broader social system and larger government units for the performance of its locality-relevant functions. The horizontal dimension of community refers to the degree to which various groups, organizations, and systems within a community are interrelated for the performance of one function and the performance across functions.

The vertical dimension might be weak, for example, to the extent that most locally consumed goods and services are produced and distributed by local public or private organizations. The vertical dimension would be strong to the extent that members of a community are dependent on large corporations and state or federal government for the provision of goods and services. Similarly, the community has relative autonomy on the vertical dimension of the socialization function to the extent that local schools are independent of state or federal revenue and nonlocal policy and curriculum decisions. The vertical dimensions of social control might be considered weaker in a large city with a strong centralized political mechanism and its own police and regulatory agencies. Communities that are dependent on broader (or higher) governmental structures for the performance of social control functions (such as a town that contracts for police services from a state police agency) are influenced by a relatively strong vertical dimension.

The horizontal dimension of the various functions is strong to the extent that different community units interface and cooperate with each other. For example, a "company town" in which many if not all members are dependent upon one organization for production and look to the same organizational leaders for many socialization activities and many participatory and support services can be considered to have a strong horizontal dimension. Likewise, small, rich, and predominantly white suburban communities such as Winnetka, Illinois, and Brighton, New York, have a strong horizontal dimension because the population is relatively homogeneous, most persons in the community have the same values, and behavioral anticipations are generally consensual. There is usually little diversification in the community influence network: people influential in police policy, school-board decisions, and important church functions are either the same or know and cooperate with each other.

Although systematic research on community is skimpy, one can probably claim that all community social functions seem to be influenced to some degree by both horizontal and vertical structures. For example, on the vertical dimension, most city and town governments, no matter how powerful in their own right, are chartered and constrained by the state. And local school boards are dependent in some degree on state departments of education. Or county prosecutors and local police enforce state laws and are constrained by federal constitutional standards. On the horizontal dimension, even communities with fairly fragmented and dispersed participatory and support organizations may be integrated to some extent by central political mechanisms, school districts that overlap on other local boundaries, and so on.

The major conclusion from observing contemporary American communities is that the horizontal dimension of community functions has tended to weaken and the vertical dimension has tended to strengthen dramatically in the last several years.[11] What have been called the "master change processes" of the twentieth century—industralization, urbanization, and bureaucratization—are all powerful forces that have tended to make communities dependent on various vertical linkages for the performance of social functions. Corporations of national and international scope with diversified interests have tended to take on to a great extent the production-distribution-consumption functions that were once the province of individual and local entrepreneurs. State and federal governments have been increasingly responsible for support and operation of local schools and have concomitantly been more demanding of state and national standards to be met or implemented at the local level. Social control functions are increasingly state and federal concerns, as are many social participation and mutual-support activities. This trend has tended to mean that various local units charged with the delivery stages of different functional activities have less in common with each other and less loyalty to each other or to local citizenry, than to the superstructures at the state and national levels to which they belong. Health, welfare, and justice activities that may once have been performed by the same local units and informal groups are now performed separately, and policy decisions about each are now made at central headquarters far removed from local incidents and local problems.

How these different functions, and the horizontal and vertical dimensions of each, are related to the criminal justice system and its administration form the primary concerns of the rest of this chapter.

JUSTICE AS A COMMUNITY VALUE

One of the major difficulties, we would assume, in previous criminal justice treatments of the community is that the criminal process clearly cuts across most, if not all, locality-relevant functions, as well as varying at different decision points on both the vertical and horizontal dimensions. Several decades ago it may have been appropriate to consider the criminal process primarily as a set of activities within the social control function. Prior to the rise of systems analysis as an approach to criminal

[11] Warren, *The Community in America*, pp. 64–65.

justice study, police were generally considered ministerial agents who enforced socially approved laws in relatively stable, unvarying ways. Likewise, prosecutors were agents responsible for enforcing law, and by bringing criminals to justice were assumed to provide social control through deterrent action. Likewise, prison executives were perceived as "principal keepers" who simply implemented the dispositions of the court, which in turn pronounced punishment in accordance with legislated constraints.

Most criminal justice scholars now agree that the above mechanistic description of the criminal process was never very accurate. Furthermore, information and cultural revolutions in the 1960s have changed drastically the number and kinds of demands placed on the system by various community forces, and the goals and management practices within the system and any of its components have altered the ways in which all system officials perform their functions and are evaluated by themselves, their superiors, and various external groups.

One result of the multiplicative connections between different groups, cultures, and criminal justice agencies has apparently been the incapacity of the system or of any of its components to relate consistently or systematically to different communities or to conflicting groups within any one community. Whether we are analyzing police relations with citizens on the street, judicial conceptions of socially accepted standards of conduct, or correctional forays into the community for support and new resources, the tendency on all levels has been to conceive of "the community" as a rather vague, unknown, dangerous, but potentially valuable entity that can make or break any particular system program, but whose behavior in particular instances is extremely unpredictable.

Although this situation may continue for many more years to come, a careful examination of system activities in relation to community social functions, and the horizontal and vertical structure of those functions, is a logical first step in demythologizing the concept of the community held within the criminal justice system. As the criminal justice system is understood as a complex set of behavior patterns that contribute in different and perhaps conflicting ways to the necessary locality-relevant functions, more rational planning of criminal justice-community interchange may begin, and program implementation should become more effective.

INSTRUMENTAL AND TERMINAL VALUES

Students of culture and social values usually distinguish between values that are instrumental to the achievement of goals and terminal values that are perceived as an end in their own right. For example, in American society the value of freedom from undue constraints and governmental interventions is usually seen as a terminal value. The provision of equal opportunity for different groups of people, in contrast, might be conceived as an instrumental value in that its provision is necessary to the pursuit of "life, liberty, and happiness."

It is clear that the criminal justice process invokes, influences, and involves many different values, some instrumental and some terminal. The value, as vague as it might be for "justice for all" or "government of laws not men" may be a terminal value. As such, the criminal justice system is probably active in the fourth functional area: that of social participation. We will discuss that issue in some detail in a moment.

The problem to be addressed first is that the very strong, ideological values contained or manifested in criminal justice operations may tend to becloud the ways in which the system relates to other community functions and systems and by doing so probably renders the functional contribution in those other areas somewhat less effective.[12]

To provide some clear-cut examples, let us begin with an examination of the criminal justice contribution to the production-distribution-consumption function. Since economic analyses in the criminal justice area are in their infancy, particularly the application of cost/benefit techniques to criminal justice administration, the suggestion that criminal justice contributes to the production dimension may appear foreign and radical to many students. Not surprising in this context, then, is the fact that sociopolitical groups to make the most of this criminal justice function are socialist or Marxist, politically and economically. A Marxian economic analysis would suggest that the dominant entrepreneurial class can maintain control over production to the extent that it can maintain monopolistic control over legitimate coercive power. By doing so, the middle class can maintain control of the dispossessed proletariat. The criminal justice system, this philosophy would suggest, performs a very important function in this regard by interpreting all proletarian attempts to take or seize capital as revolutionary, and thus deals with revolt by placing criminals in prison, simultaneously undermining the political and economic interpretation of these revolutionary acts by labeling them as the pathological behaviors of bad or sick people. Invocation of the criminal sanction, therefore, strips the proletariat of political power and incarcerates the most impoverished workers, thereby eliminating or minimizing the chance of future complaints. In addition, stockpiling criminals in prisons and other coercive settings reduces the problem of

---

[12] See Thurmond Arnold, "Law Enforcement—An Attempt at Social Dissection," *Yale Law Journal*, 42 (1932), 1 ff.; and Jerome Skolnick, *Justice Without Trial* (New York: Wiley, 1966), pp. 12–13.

unemployment by periodically taking large numbers of the unemployed out of circulation.

A less Marxian interpretation of the same criminal justice activity is advanced by Parsons who suggests that the criminal justice system performs an "integrative function" for society by selecting out of the social system deviants and social dissenters, and thereby increasing the social solidarity of the remaining population.[13] We will discuss this view further under a discussion of the social control function.

Before moving on to the socialization function, we should mention that there are many more mundane and traditional ways in which criminal justice aids production. For some areas, or in some communities, these production functions may override all other criminal justice values. For example, in rural areas state prison facilities may be the principal employer in a small town. The importance of the economic contribution of the New York State Correctional Facility at Attica to the townspeople of Attica should not be underestimated in understanding the conservative operation of that prison or the physical reprisals taken upon Attica inmates after the 1971 uprising.[14] In many urban areas the criminal justice system is a primary employer of minority groups, and these groups find the newly expanding probation and parole professions to be some of the best available opportunities for upward mobility.

In another context, the concern of community entrepreneurs about competition with low-cost prison industry is one of the major reasons that state correctional industries have never been very profitable. Similarly, the concern of many unions about being flooded with stigmatized union members trained in prison has reduced considerably the vocational training and licensing opportunities available in correctional systems.

Throughout this discussion of instrumental criminal justice functions, the influence of the varying vertical and horizontal dimensions should be evident. Industries, corporations, and unions with strong vertical organizations have been successful in limiting the vertical strength of corrections in the production function, to the extent that prisoners' needs in the production function are sacrificed to the perceived production needs of other groups. On the other side of the coin, fairly strong horizontal ties between various rural communities have been powerful influences in the decision where to locate and staff correctional organizations. Ironically, correctional officials who have mobilized powerful vertical connections in order to relocate certain correctional agencies in urban communities have discovered that usually weak horizontal linkages in the inner city may

[13] Talcott Parsons, *The Social System* (New York: The Free Press, 1964), p. 36.

[14] The New York State Commission on Attica, *Official Report* (New York: Bantam Books, 1972).

strengthen rapidly over the issue of placing offenders in certain neighborhoods, and with negative consequences to the correctional plans.[15]

CULTURAL VALUES
AND COMMUNITY
DIFFERENCES

The contribution of the criminal justice system to the community socialization function is perhaps more difficult to observe and study than any other contribution. The principal difficulty here is that the weakening of the community horizontal dimension and the transfer of many socialization activities to vertically related organizations and bureaucracies have at this point in time left many diverse community subgroupings to be served by the same large social systems for socialization activities. However, the values and goals instilled by these large, complex state and federal systems may not be congruent with the values and goals of any particular community, subunit, or family.

Many social scientists, most notably Daniel Katz and Robert Kahn, have argued that the criminal justice system, or at least the correctional component of it, performs socialization or resocialization functions in terms of (1) identifying individuals whose behavior patterns manifest either rejection or absence of accepted community values and (2) working with these individuals to introduce acceptable values and attitudes.[16]

There are obviously many conceptual and administrative problems with the socialization function as performed by the criminal justice system. For one, even if a certain community or social system is rather homogeneous in the values of its constituent groups, and therefore there exists general community agreement concerning the identity of deviants, the fact that a local justice agency (the police) initiates remedial socialization, whereas a county or state agency usually carries out the "corrective" disposition, presents some difficult problems.

The police probably have the strongest horizontal linkages with other local agencies such as probation departments, schools, local political groups, businesses, and voluntary organizations. Therefore police identification of persons whose socialization is faulty will be influenced by their interpretation of these groups' reactions to deviant acts. Moreover, the police are likely to know many of the persons, or have information upon them, prior to any particular arrest. Given discretion to arrest or not to

---

[15] David Duffee, Kevin Wright, and Thomas Maher, *Refunding Evaluation Report* (Bureau of Corrections Community Treatment Centers Evaluation) (Harrisburg, Pa.: Governor's Justice Commission, January 2, 1975).

[16] Daniel Katz and Robert Kahn, *The Social Psychology of Organizations* (New York: Wiley, 1966).

arrest, the police are likely to believe, upon the event of arrest, that the suspect has been given all the latitude that community norms will allow.[17]

The courts, however, exist at a higher level in the vertical socialization linkages. Although the courts are responsible for the determination of wrong and the disposition of the wrongdoer, they are insulated to some extent from some of the horizontal linkages that influence police behavior, and these influences are replaced by countywide horizontal relationships (at least in the case of elected prosecutors and elected judiciary). In addition, the judiciary, whether or not they are elected, are attuned not only to cross-community concerns but also to the vertical linkages to appellate courts on both state and federal levels. Much of the current conflict between police policy and court policy might be understood through the examination of these conflicting vertical and horizontal pressures. Whereas police policy, in the eyes of many police experts, is essentially formulated on the street during police interactions with citizens, court policy in many instances descends downward from state and federal centers of authority. Thus, while the police may arrest a suspect after several previously undocumented brushes with the law, the judge passes on the appropriateness of police decisions in the individual case.

On a more abstract level, there is also a conflict between relatively specific community standards that the police seek to uphold and the relatively general cultural values that the courts are sworn to protect. Thus, we can see that there are conflicting cross pressures acting upon the criminal justice contribution to the socialization function, even, as we stated, when community values are relatively homogeneous.

When the community in question contains many cultural and value subgroups, the issues become even more complex. In a city with a relatively diversified political, ethnic, and economic base, with many pockets of power and influence, the problems confronting the criminal justice system frequently seem insurmountable. A centralized police force, for example, in a city with multiple cultural groupings, is faced with imposing a single set of laws and normative interpretations upon people who vary tremendously in their own norms and expectations of what is proper. For the police to apply the law, and the interpretation of it, uniformly across all groups may appear to some minorities like outright oppression by an alien force, whereas to discriminate about proper behavior from group to group may appear to be either favoritism or corruption.

Although the recent attempts at team policing,[18] the abortive attempts

---

[17] Skolnick, *Justice Without Trial*, pp. 182–203.

[18] John Angell, Raymond Galvin, and Michael O'Neill, *Evaluation Report on the Model Cities Team Policing Unit of the Holyoke Police Department* (Holyoke, Mass.: Massachusetts Model Cities Program, April 1972).

at civilian review boards,[19] and some pleas for neighborhood police headquarters or "mini city hall"[20] are all in one way or another accommodations if not solutions to the multiple-value one-city government problem, it must be remembered in evaluating all such decentralization plans that the modern centralized police administration was itself a reform reaction to clean up and standardize procedures of the old precinct headquarters.[21]

On the correctional end of the spectrum, the problems in performing socialization functions are somewhat different than for police, or have been until the most recent forays into "community-based correction." In contrast to police, prosecutorial, and judicial operations, the postconviction process became a state-level activity at a relatively early date. Initial reasons for this transfer of punitive authority from local governments to the state are many, including the fact that it was relatively difficult in the era before rapid transit and telecommunication for local agencies to keep track of and securely supervise offenders. But perhaps more important was the reform impetus provided by the Quakers and others who considered the local-level administration of punishment to be both brutal and wasteful. Moreover it was only when offenders were pooled from all localities of a state that an economy of scale was reached that made the implementation of the new penitentiary concept viable.

The problem is that what may have been both economical and more humane in a frontier society has become extremely costly and less humane in the twentieth century. Increased communications and more sophisticated supervision practices have made probation and parole no less safe than prison supervision while operating at roughly one-tenth of the expense. More to the point, the congregating of offenders from all parts of a state, or even from all parts of one city, has meant that offenders of different cultural and ethnic backgrounds, perhaps speaking different languages, and certainly interpreting similar behaviors in extremely different ways, are pushed together and forced to live in an organizational setting that increases their conflict rather than resolves their differences. Also, most prisons remain located in rural areas, at great distances from the cities that produce most offenders. Consequently, the values and attitudes of staff and inmates are quite foreign to each other. It is doubtful, under these circumstances, that socialization or resocialization can really take place. Indeed there is some evidence that incarceration, if not the whole correctional process, tends to deepen the rifts be-

---

[19] President's Commission on Law Enforcement and the Administration of Justice, *Task Force Report: The Police* (Washington, D.C.: Government Printing Office, 1967), pp. 199–202.

[20] Ibid., pp. 150–160.

[21] James Q. Wilson, *Varieties of Police Behavior* (Cambridge, Mass.: Harvard University Press, 1968), pp. 190–199.

tween offenders and the dominant groups who have control of the formal agencies of justice.

DETERRENCE OR RETRIBUTION

Weighing all the different philosophies of justice and schools of social thought, one would probably conclude that the most widely recognized or accepted function performed by the criminal justice system is one of social control. Although we would certainly not argue the opposite, it is difficult at this point in time to suggest that social control is the dominant function of the criminal justice system. To begin with, criminal justice system interventions into the lives of people are basically a retail business. Although the symbolic and cultural connotations of the system are certainly great, we doubt that those symbolic interactions should be discussed primarily under the heading of social control. Social control in community functional theory is not a "retail business" as much as it is the massive and sweeping control placed upon all people of a community because they have all consented to some degree to abide by decisions concerning distribution of resources and the means to achieve goals. Even professional criminals rarely reject all rules and norms. For example, a gang of bank robbers may pay for airline tickets out of the country, airplane hijackers and insurrectionists evidently hold some stock in the legality of amnesty, and an income tax cheater may pay his property taxes honestly. Criminals, in other words, are selective in breaking laws, whereas social control as a locality-relevant function is not selective in application. Social control does not refer to particular laws and particular ways of enforcing them so much as it does to the concept of rule of law and to the constraints placed upon people by less formal standards such as norms and anticipations of behavior.

It has been argued cogently by Edwin Sutherland,[22] Durkheim,[23] and others[24] that a certain level of deviant behavior is actually necessary to the concept of society and, by extension, to the "existence" of community. That is, a social "group" tolerant of all behavior is not really identifiable as a group, and a group whose standards are too rigid and whose tolerance is too low rejects so many innovative behavior patterns that it stagnates and ceases to exist.

In general, we would have to say that the social control function,

---

[22] Edwin Sutherland, ed., *The Professional Thief* (Chicago: University of Chicago Press, 1937), pp. 220 ff.

[23] Émile Durkheim, *The Rules of the Sociological Method,* trans. Sarah Solovay and John Mueller, ed. George E. G. Catlin (New York: The Free Press, 1950), pp. 65–75.

[24] Kai. T. Erikson, *Wayward Puritans* (New York: Wiley, 1966).

although perhaps assisted by the criminal justice system, is predominantly carried out by much larger and more powerful systems, such as general governmental and political organizations, private enterprise, and state or federal systems of health, education, and welfare.

Within the criminal justice contribution to social control, the major dilemma, as we see it, is the one between strategies for deterrence, in a very broad sense, and strategies for retribution. In order to clarify what we mean here, it is important to redefine retribution, and to relabel it in order to avoid the negative connotations that the term now possesses. Although few people would admit to retributive motives, most people can see the importance of supporting the norms of a community. The social condition that exists when group norms crumble and individuals are no longer aware of what standards govern their behavior is the condition of anomie. Émile Durkheim originally used the term to explain the type of suicide that frequently results when either natural or man-made catastrophe throws into flux very suddenly the conditions and constraints on social behavior within which individuals identified normality.[25] Since Durkheim's classic study, other behavioral scientists have added other kinds of conditions and social changes that might bring on a state of anomie, although the meaning of the term as a social state of existence has remained fairly stable.

We would suggest that the older term, *retribution,* which is defined as the punishment of an act because it is perceived as wrong, might now give way to the new concept of *punishment for the prevention of anomie.* It becomes clear, by this change in terms that punishment for moral justification is not a social act concerned with the past act of an offender, but on the contrary is a social act aimed at the present consequences of that offense, an offense that may, unless punished, create an anomic situation by detracting from the validity of the norm that was broken. In short, a community will seek to perpetuate its own stability and identity by invoking the criminal sanction against any acts that threaten to create a state of anomie.

Although modern penologists, reformers, and philosophers have criticized retributive punishment as either barbaric or wasteful because the act of punishment was conceived as performed against the individual offender, the focus in the prevention of anomie is clearly not the offender but the attitudes and values of the noncriminal (and nonpotential criminal) population who abide by group norms and whose regular behavior becomes impossible if others do not also conform. The criminal justice system may perform the function of preventing anomie to the extent that most community groups feel satisfied that offenders are apprehended and punished with some regularity and to the extent that the

[25] Émile Durkheim, *Suicide, A Study in Sociology,* trans. by John A. Spaulding and George Simpson, ed. George Simpson (Glencove, Ill.: Free Press, 1965).

criminal process as known to the public dramatizes the upholding of community norms. News media, the Supreme Court, and information sources play an important role in this regard, no matter what the particular outcome for the individual defendant—so long as the information and the portrayals demonstrate that important values and norms are upheld. The fact that Perry Mason can get innocent persons off is just as important as the fact that Sergeant Friday can apprehend culprits with machinelike efficiency.

Against this prevention of anomie function, criminal justice contributions to deterrence must be considered. Again, we wish to use the term *deterrence* slightly differently than it is defined in much research and jurisprudential literature. The late Herbert Packer defined *general deterrence* as the act of using one offender's punishment as an example by which to dissuade a potential offender from committing an offense, and he defined *specific deterrence* as the act of using one offender's present punishment as a means of dissuading the same offender from committing a similar offense in the future.[26]

In contrast, by deterrence, we mean *all intervention strategies that are effective in reducing the probability of future crime by the same and/or different persons.* Deterrence in this sense might be achieved by changing a man's psyche so that he no longer desired to offend, or by keeping him in constant surveillance by electronic devices so that he could no longer offend without being immediately detected and apprehended, or by providing sufficient jobs with desirable career mobility and sufficient training to perform the jobs that the opportunities presented by crime, *as perceived by the offender,* were no longer a desired alternative to legal behavior.

We would posit that the different deterrent tactics, such as the three just described, vary widely in cost and in effectiveness, but that all of them offer reduction in crime as an end result. Consequently, we reject the present debates over "punishment versus treatment"[27] as the basic and real dilemma confronting the community and criminal justice officials in the administration of justice. It would seem to us that the philosophical conflict between punishment and treatment is impossible to address logically, since punishment, if its benefits accrue to society, cannot be directly compared to treatment, if its benefits accrue to the offender. Moreover, we would perceive the suggestion that treatment must be of primary benefit to the offender as patently absurd, or society would not provide it.

A more recent discussion attempts to resolve the long-observed con-

---

[26] Herbert Packer, *The Limits of the Criminal Sanction* (Stanford: Stanford University Press, 1968), pp. 39–45.

[27] Leslie Wilkins, *Evaluation of Penal Measures* (New York: Random House, 1969) pp. 16–17.

flicts between treatment and punishment by examining simultaneously concern for the individual offender and concern for the community and determining how administrators can implement both concerns.[28] This is perhaps a more useful analytic framework, particularly when trying to examine and/or change the behavior of criminal justice executives who apparently make decisions based upon these two concerns.

However, we also think that singling out "concern for the offender" and "concern for the community" is too narrow a view when we are interested in determining how the criminal justice system is integrated into a community structure. To begin with, there is rarely "a community" that criminal justice officials can be concerned with. County, state, and federal officials must deal with so many different communities and conflicting groups from each that they are constantly taking from Peter to pay Paul. Local police also, at least in major metropolitan areas, must respond to many different community groups, and what may benefit one group may disadvantage another. Moreover, it is difficult from *outside* the criminal justice system to justify the orthogonality of the "individual offender" and the "community" concerns. Fifty years ago, perhaps, most offenders were isolated, dislocated, and communityless persons. But the vast majority of offenders processed today, in either the local misdemeanant system or the local-county-state felony system, are not homeless, rootless, or isolated.

Although some may suffer from psychopathologies or physical problems, most of them apparently suffer from poverty in a land of plenty, where all members of society are socialized to value certain physical and psychological end-states but where certain groups are systematically excluded from the means to achieve. As different dispossessed, disadvantaged, and deprived groups have gained the education to be aware of and to believe in these system differentials, they have gained considerable political, economic, and social power of their own. They may do so in cooperation with more traditionally powerful groups, or in opposition to traditional power networks. But in any event, in such a diversified and continually diversifying community structure, it is difficult to conceive that concern about some particular offender is not also concern about some particular facet of a relevant community. Ignoring an offender's legitimate and continual relationship with a viable community group may demonstrate disconcern about the future behavior of particular offenders.

Consequently, we demonstrate in the following diagram (Figure 2-1) a "new dilemma" (and hopefully not another false one) that juxtaposes two current and powerful *community concerns* relevant to the social control function. We have placed on the horizontal axis the demand for

[28] Vincent O'Leary and David Duffee, "Correctional Policy—A Classification of Goals Designed for Change," *Crime and Delinquency,* 17 No. 4 (October 1971), pp. 373–386.

Figure 2-1. Punishment and Community Structure

DEMAND FOR DETERRENCE		Low	High
	High	Community Vertical Ties High, Horizontal Ties Weak: Welfare Law Management	Community and its Values in Transition: Reeducation or Revolution
	Low	Lack of Community Formal Law Keeping	Community Horizontal Ties Strong, Vertical Ties Weak; Political Law enforcement

Low   High

DEMAND FOR RETRIBUTION

retribution (prevention of anomie), and we have placed on the vertical axis demand for deterrence. By dichotomizing each of the two dimensions, we are presented with four logical functional variations. Because of the lack of theoretical discussion and research in this area, the way in which we have filled in the boxes is tentative. Each box represents various structural relationships within communities as well as major operational trends for a criminal justice system in such a community, *on the social control function.*

Where the demands for deterrence and retribution are both weak, we would hypothesize that the community itself is weak, that little criminal justice activity of a formalized nature takes place, or that only very serious crimes meet community resistance. Basically, the system is charged with the ministerial duty of formal law keeping, but no groups are terribly vigilant about processes or outcomes.

When the demand for retribution is high and the demand for deterrence is low, we hypothesize that the community has strong horizontal ties and weak vertical ties. There may well be minorities or dispossessed groups in such communities, and it is principally keeping them and/or strangers "in place" that provides impetus to the criminal process. We suggest that the social control function of the criminal justice system in such a community might be considered "political law enforcement."

When the demand for deterrence is high and the demand for retribution is low, we hypothesize that the horizontal dimension of community functions is weak and that the vertical associations are strong. Such communities are likely to be highly diversified with multiple and conflicting power bases, and all groups might attempt to keep each other honest by calling upon separate, vertical structures or by calling upon one single vertical association, which for one reason or another all groups tend to trust and value. The result is a press for accountable government and "professional" managers, including officials in the criminal justice system. Such a system we might title "welfare law management," in that the system attempts to service all community groups, including those from which offenders come. The aim here is reduction in future crime, but concomitantly the system will only lend minimal support to the prevention of anomie for any of the particular and conflicting groups.

Lastly, there may be simultaneously high demands for both deterrence and retribution. Although it is particularly difficult without research to suggest the community characteristics that might prevail here, we hypothesize tentatively that the community is in rapid transition, that again there is a diversified power base, but that the conflict is not contained as it is in the "welfare law management" case. The criminal justice system can hardly be functional here. Either one group gains power successfully and reeducates certain units of the community into accepting the views of the other, or one group utilizes the criminal justice system and other systems to dominate conflicting groups, and those others retaliate with guerrilla warfare or open rebellion.

DRAMATIZATION OF COMMUNITY

The locality-relevant function of social participation is perhaps most strongly manifested in the symbolic overtones of criminal justice activity. Indeed, there are some criminal justice and social commentators who suggest that the primary contribution of criminal justice is in this area. To place a name on it, we might say that the criminal justice contribution to social participation can be described as a "dramatization of community," or a symbolic restatement of community norms, values, ideals, etc.

In a more traditional sociological analysis, this "boundary defining function" might be considered a social control function because the symbolic process of ratifying social support to laws and norms contributes, albeit indirectly, to minimizing the desire of community citizens to deviate from the values and behavior visibly supported by the operation of the justice system functionaries. This symbolic social control does indeed exist. Many of the activities we have discussed as "prevention of anomie" activities are symbolic, or have symbolic as well as practical dimensions and outputs. But in contrast to social control activities, which we consider as having more specific targets and more specific results, we are now attempting to delineate the contribution that criminal justice activity may make to a generalized sense of community, as perceived by the inhabitants of any particular community.

Many years ago, Émile Durkheim suggested the same functional output for "elementary forms of religion." He proposed that the gathering of a community, or a sect, or a tribe, ostensively to celebrate a particular religious belief, had the latent function of providing an opportunity for social participation.[29] Although Roland Warren posits that the same function for religious activity exists today,[30] it is true that separation of church and state in the United States as well as the diversification of religious organizations has lessened the horizontal scope of most formal religious associations.

Although we are certainly *not* suggesting that the symbolic content of the criminal justice system in any way replaces the function of religion in this area of social participation, we do suggest that it can have a very similar function. The moral content of the criminal justice drama is delivered during the interplay of roles that are archetypal to all American communities and many other cultures as well: the defendant, the defender, the accuser, the judge, and certainly a jury of peers are all important ritualistic representations of the community concerns for belonging or being cast out of a basic human group.

Whereas it may be difficult to measure criminal justice contributions to the social control function, it may be impossible to measure this contribution to social participation. It is probably more appropriate to suggest, as did Durkheim, that social deviance and the recognition of it are necessary to the concept of community.[31] And although the form and quality of that recognition may differ considerably, this symbolic manifestation of the individual in relation to the group is probably necessary in some forms for communities as we know them to exist.

PROVISION OF SERVICE

The fifth locality-relevant function is the provision of mutual support. This function is prototypically associated with health, welfare, and charitable organizations for which mutual-support goals are the primary reasons for being. In the past, the formally recognized service goals of the criminal justice system or of its separate components have been minimal. Within the last decade, however, goals of service have not only multiplied but have been identified as a major official responsibility.

It is well known that a major part of police work involves the provision of service as opposed to crime control. Authorities on police value this activity differently, although calls for strictly legalistic or crime-stopper

[29] Emile Durkheim, *The Elementary Forms of Religious Life, A Study in Religious Sociology,* trans. by Joseph Ward Swain (London: Allyn and Unwin, 1964).

[30] Roland Warren, *The Community in America* (Chicago: Rand McNally, 1963), p. 11.

[31] Émile Durkheim, *The Rules of Sociological Method,* trans. by Sarah A. Solovay and John H. Mueller, ed. George E. G. Catlin (Glencoe, Ill.: Free Press, 1958).

police forces have died down considerably in the last five years. No alternative systems for providing the 24-hour service availability of the police have been discovered.

The courts that value the provision of service most highly and most openly in the United States have been juvenile and family courts, where adjudicatory decisions have historically been flavored by the intention of the court to benefit the juveniles and families in whose lives it intervenes. Provision of service through formal dispositions has appeared a hypocritical claim ever since *Gault* and other major decisions documented the consequences of such dispositions and the lack of "client" participation in agreeing to them. With the start of the 1970s, however, service provision in both juvenile and adult criminal courts has appeared more sincere. Whether or not this sincerity is "real" is no longer a question of great importance, however. Belief in the sincerity and beneficence of intentions has meant for years that the negative consequences of those intentions have been ignored or covered up. In the future the intentions behind multiplying services and diversifying service sources and supportive resources will probably be modified and controlled by hard evaluative criteria applied to the outcomes of service rendered.

Perhaps the area where the service ideology is ascending most rapidly is corrections. Inmates are frequently called "clients," and there is evidence lately that client status will soon be replaced by a new consumerism, with offenders choosing from a variety of available services. Whether this change in language is less subterfuge or image-building and more critically evaluated than similar language and belief statements have been in the past is, of course, the important question here, just as it is in the courts.

To the extent that these new or reemergent tendencies are valid, and will become dominant trends, will depend greatly on community receptivity to this kind of purpose. As long as offenders are perceived as people whose deservedness is dubious, the strength of these trends must be questioned. If the community perceives purpose of service as desirable, it probably becomes less likely that the criminal justice system will remain for long the purveyor of these services, or that the service recipients will continue to become offenders in order to receive these services. Either the criminal justice system or the communities in which the system is imbedded will change drastically.

CRIMINAL JUSTICE AGENCIES: DEVELOPMENT, PROBLEMS, AND PRACTICES

part II

INTRODUCTION TO PART II

The term *criminal justice system* has been used so frequently that we may tend to overlook the fact that the perception of criminal process agencies as systemically related is a rather recent phenomenon and also that the use of the term *system* tends to becloud some issues. We, too, have utilized the term frequently, already, and will continue to do so throughout this book. In Part III, we will provide a more thorough definition of system and a more exhaustive examination of how the system, *as a system*, operates. In this part we will set the prerequisites for this analysis. In Chapters Three, Four, Five, and Six, the police, courts, correctional agencies, and juvenile justice agencies are described.

The major emphases in this part are (1) historical development, (2) current operating patterns, and (3) key issues and problems that confront practitioners, researchers, and citizens as they work in, analyze, seek service from, or are confronted by various portions of the criminal process.

chapter 3

The Police

In the last decade, the police have received more attention, more criticism, more outspoken support, a greater influx of college-trained personnel, and greater increases in financial support than any other agency of justice. This focus on the police is not surprising, since there are more police agencies and more police officers than any other type of criminal justice agency or official. Also more citizens are coming into direct contact with the police than any other representatives of criminal justice. The police are the frontline of the criminal justice system, as well as of the juvenile justice system. In the great majority of cases the police are the initiators of the criminal process. The police, however, do not operate merely as the initiators of the process. Police agencies have many other responsibilities *besides* law enforcement or in addition to the initiation of prosecution. Frequently the police are not so much a "component" of the criminal justice "system" as they are the sole arbiters of community problems and the sole purveyors of 24-hour service to the communities they serve. In the simple terms of *time spent* per activity, we might accurately classify the police as providers of "mutual support" rather than social control. It is, however, their social control function that has received the most public scrutiny, and it is in this area that there has been the greatest demand for increased effectiveness. Some of the contemporary factors that have contributed to this concentrated focus are discussed in the following section.

THE ASCENDANCY OF POLICING AS A CONTEMPORARY ISSUE

When Sir Robert Peel (British Prime Minister 1834–1835, 1841–1846) was arguing for the establishment of a London metropolitan police force, he encountered a counterargument that would seem strange indeed if sounded today in the United States. A parliamentary report of 1818 recommended *against* the police in order to maintain a lawful, peace-keeping society![1] With the gift of hindsight, we might credit this report with more of the gift of prophecy than it might deserve. And yet there would now appear to be some empirical validity to the parliamentary forecast. The responsibility for maintenance of the law, suggested the 1818 report, rested with the citizenry and with a competent and detached judiciary. Vesting *specialized* powers in a new, organized, law-maintenance force would inevitably mean the citizens would be divested of their rights to security—rights they had achieved through maintaining the law without resort to an internal, militaristic force.[2]

Certainly the social conditions in Great Britain at the turn of the nineteenth century and social conditions of the United States in the 1970s are vastly different. Although many critics in the last decade have decried lawless activity by the police, few persons have suggested the feasibility of law enforcement or maintenance of the peace without some special organization charged with *primary responsibility* for maintaining or regulating public order, surveillance, investigation, collection of evidence, and apprehension of suspects.

POLICE IN A SOCIETY OF DIVERSE CULTURES

One of the most marked differences between 1818 and 1977 is the tremendously greater complexity of society now than then. One aspect of such complexity is the diversity of culture. The police are responsible for upholding a single set of laws across a multiple and frequently conflicting range of cultures and subcultures. In rural areas, or within small police departments, this charge may not be terribly problematic. But in our large, sprawling, ethnically, economically, and politically fractioned cities,

[1] Charles Reith, *The Police Idea: Its History and Evolution in England in the Eighteenth Century and After* (London: Oxford University Press, 1938), p. 188.

[2] Ibid.

the duty of ministering *one* law may become a bewildering business—since different groups living within a few blocks of each other may interpret that law with widely ranging results, or may complain that the law, or its administration, or both, do not represent their values or interests, and that the police are, in effect, a foreign, occupying force.

Much criticism of police behavior has been spawned by the problem of diverse values within single legal jurisdictions. Of the many competing analyses of social structure, the two predominant models argue that (1) the law is a value-neutral mechanism responsible for the integration and stability of diverse elements, or (2) the law is a value-laden instrument wielded by the powerful in order to maintain disproportionate distributions of resources at the status quo.[3] In the first model, the police are perceived as one agency responsible for the impartial administration of law to all classes and segments of society. The suggestion here is that if the police could *effectively* identify deviants and control deviance, the remainder of society (e.g., all law-abiding elements) would be considerably more cohesive and unitary.[4] The other model suggests that the police are a partial agency of the executive charged with maintaining order against the rebellious claims of dissident and disenfranchised groups. The suggestion here is that the police are effective (in a democratic society) to the extent that this control function is masked by the *claim* that services are rendered impartially.[5]

Ironically, perhaps, the problems confronting the police officer may not be very different, whichever of these (or some other model) is chosen as an explanation of the police function. Whether the police function is integration of various social units toward the production of some consensual ideal, or the function is the control of conflicting groups in order to maintain an inherently unstable power and resource distribution, the police officer is confronted with frequent, fragmented evaluative decisions concerning particular courses of action. Although the officer may be provided with certain centrally imposed, management-made constraints, he is faced with short-fused, immediate decisions that involve balancing various payoffs and costs in any problematic situation. In the case of

[3] William J. Chambliss and Robert B. Seidman, *Law, Order, and Power* (Reading, Mass.: Addison-Wesley, 1971).

[4] See Talcot Parsons, *The Social System* (New York: The Free Press, 1955). The reader, however, should be cautious about identifying Parsons with the "conservatives" who support a unitary, integrated view of society. He at no place provides active support for that view, although he spends a great deal of energy analyzing the social system from that perspective. On the other hand, Parsons clearly points out that a social system heavily dependent on formal, coercive methods of social control is frequently caught in a deviance-amplifying cycle that will lead to system disintegration rather than stability. In other words, Parsons would see the police as inherently *ineffective* as primary agents of social control.

[5] Chambliss and Seidman, *Law, Order, and Power*, pp. 271–274.

diverse values confluent within an immediate physical space, he is weighing different and often conflicting interpretations of what is socially acceptable from the point of view of victims, suspects, himself, his superiors, and statutes.

This task has never been an easy one. But the conflicts inherent in balancing both *practical outcomes* (e.g., the victim wants reparation or revenge; the suspect wants to be left alone; the officer wants to go off duty on schedule) and *normative guidelines* (e.g., the suspect argues that the landlord has never made repairs and is deserving of the vandalism; the landlord argues that his tenants have always been careless of his property and are undeserving of greater responsiveness; the officer believes that neither the tenants nor the landlord are *his* kind of people)[6] are now less quickly resolvable conflicts. American culture *has* changed to the extent that many more diverse groups and leaders of different value sets have obtained access to forums of influential complaint (if not to forums of influential decision making).[7] Consequently, it is possible that the police may do an even better job presently than they did 20 or 50 years ago and still receive more criticism than used to be the case.

POLICING AND A DIFFERENTIAL
OPPORTUNITY STRUCTURE

Another social change that has contributed to the importance of policing as a social issue is closely related to the diversity of values and beliefs. Together with the aspect of growing social complexity is the increasing specialization in labor and in the sweeping bureaucratization of work. Such changes would affect the basic economic and social structure of society—even if our culture was more homogeneous. For example, orientations and objectives associated with any place of work, or any complex organization, differ even when general goals may be the same. The missions of colleges and universities differ, for example, in the kinds of students they select and in the kinds of faculty they prefer as well as in the kinds of knowledge and competencies they wish to instill in their graduates. Police forces also vary widely in terms of internal climate, managerial practice, and community relations, even if "enforcing the law" is a basic goal of every department. Thus, police work will be affected by the complexity of the occupational structure of society. Again, in communities with a fairly simple economic structure (e.g., all residents are

[6] On the simultaneity of practical and normative outcomes in criminal justice, see Thurmond Arnold, "Law Enforcement—An Attempt at Social Dissection," *Yale Law Journal, 42* (1932), 1–30.

[7] Roland Warren, *Community in America,* 2nd ed. (Chicago: Rand McNally, 1969), pp. 9–14.

farmers or dependent on farming, or most residents are white-collar workers on the outskirts of a city) this problem may not be terribly pressing: the kinds of crimes committed are generally similar, citizen attitude toward police may be similar, etc. However, in police jurisdictions that include widely disparate economic groups (e.g., New Haven is *both* an industrial town and a university town) the kinds of behaviors required of the police are considerably more varied.

On a broader scale, the complexity in the division of labor impacts upon police work in another manner; that is, where there is a highly differentiated opportunity structure, there are startling contrasts in the availability of both legitimate and illegitimate avenues toward valued social goals. Stated in gross terms, there is now a greater relative difference between groups with wealth, property, and power and groups without these resources than has ever been the case in the past. Whereas, in absolute terms, the conditions of the lowest economic groups in society have improved markedly in this century, the social conditions of the higher economic groups have improved even more dramatically. And the difference between these two groups seems to be increasing rather than decreasing. Regardless of whether social critics perceive the police as actively maintaining this situation or as neutral ministers trying to control the strains such a structure produces, the police will be criticized for prejudicial enforcement of the law. Because crime, like legitimate methods of achieving objectives, is differentially structured, some types of crime are more visible than others,[8] some kinds of crime are more easily prosecuted than others,[9] and some criminals have greater ability to avoid intervention than others.[10] Consequently, the police are probably involved in differential enforcement of the law, regardless of their own purposes or values.[11] And these differentials are becoming increasingly public, common information, thus providing additional fuel to current controversies about policing.

EXPLOSION IN THE CITIES

A more topical, less abstract problem confronting the police in the 1960s was the series of urban riots in 1967 and 1968. These were, of course, not the first riots in our cities, but their frequency and intensity in these two

[8] Michael Katz, "Patterns of Arrest and the Dangers of Public Visibility," *Criminal Law Bulletin*, 9, No. 4 (1973), 311–324.

[9] David Sudnow, "Normal Crimes: Sociological Features of the Penal Code in a Public Defender's Office," *Social Problems* (Winter, 1975), pp. 255–276.

[10] Leslie T. Wilkins, "Crime and Crime Prevention Measures of 1990," paper presented at the Annual Meeting, American Association for the Advancement of Science, San Francisco, February 25, 1974.

[11] Chambliss and Seidman, *Law, Order, and Power*, pp. 289–290.

summers seemed to stand out as bitter, violent, and expensive testimony of both racial conflicts and the impoverishment of our city governments. The explosion of the cities, as they were analyzed by the National Advisory Commission on Civil Disorders,[12] seemed to be clearly etched manifestations of both the problems of cultural diversity and differential opportunity structures. The profile of the "average rioter," constructed by the commission, pointed to a significant segment of the city populations who were young, black, better educated than their parents, and under- or unemployed.[13] An analysis of the social characteristics of cities that experienced riots clearly emphasized sharp differentials in power, in resource control, in occupational opportunity, and in social class between the areas in which riots took place and the surrounding areas of the metropolitan districts. In almost all the cities, the commission emphasized the long-range and long-festering problems, which city governments apparently either ignored or were incompetent to handle. Extreme differentials were noted in quality of education and in condition of educational facilities and in frequency and number of city services, including street sanitation, garbage and refuse collection, and availability of medical facilities and treatment. By and large, urban areas affected by riots were also the areas in which citizens paid the most money for the lowest quality of any important life supports. It was found that food in ghetto areas cost more than the same or better food in better areas of town, and that slum tenants paid higher rents for lower quality and more cramped quarters than would be the case in areas with more desirable housing.

In addition to these kinds of problems, it was generally found that these same areas also had the highest victimization rates and the largest number of complaints about lack of police protection and/or police unresponsiveness, as well as the greatest number of complaints about police brutality. Investigations of police hiring and promotional practices found that in almost all cities, blacks and other minority groups were vastly underrepresented on police forces, and that this underrepresentation became worse in the higher police management level.[14]

When the short-term or precipitating factors in the riots were analyzed, in most cases, the riots themselves seemed to have been touched off by a police incident. The precise nature of these incidents varied from city to city, but in general, the incidents involved an arrest situation in which there were many spectators, the arrest apparently involved questionable use of force, and the arrest was apparently preceded

---

[12] National Advisory Commission on Civil Disorders, *Report of the National Advisory Commission on Civil Disorders* (New York: Bantam Books, 1968).

[13] Ibid., pp. 127–135.

[14] Ibid., pp. 315–318.

and followed by faulty communication between citizens and the police.[15]

Interestingly, there are rather clear parallels between urban riot situations and prison riot situations. In both types of situations, the long-term factors causing dissatisfaction by the rioting group include poor and cramped living conditions, complaints of unresponsiveness by the officials of government, little participation by the rioters in the decisions that control their lives, and an increasing sense among the powerless group that they deserve more services or better conditions than are available.[16] In both of these situations, immediate precipitating factors seem to involve overt police action, questionable use of force, and poor communication made worse by mutual distrust.[17]

Although riots have decreased dramatically both in scale and number since the end of the last decade, they will doubtless reappear. Few of the underlying reasons for their occurrence have changed since 1967. And, as we said before, social differentials appear to be widening at ever-accelerating rates. But whether or not riots reoccur, they have served to change the face of policing in the United States. On the one hand, the 1967–1968 round of riots clearly emphasized the inability of modern, urban police forces to deal with massive civil disturbances. This discovery has resulted in some new tactical planning, police training, and equipment development. It has also contributed, at least partially, to new government legislation and vast increases in government spending for police departments. On the other hand, such disturbances, or the lack of significant social and political change in their wake, have demonstrated the alarming inability of urban political institutions to adapt successfully to new demands as well as the widespread belief of vast numbers of people that police forces are the martial pawns of the politically and economically powerful who use the police to keep other people "in their place."

LAW 'N' ORDER

It is not surprising that another sweeping social phenomenon closely paralleled, historically, the increasing conflicts in our cities. This phenomenon was the ideological concept symbolized in the call for "law 'n' order." This political catch phrase, in which the two concepts of law

[15] Ralph W. Conant, "Rioting, Insurrection and Civil Disobedience," *The American Scholar*, 37, No. 3 (Summer 1968), 420–433.

[16] See Richard McCleery, "Correctional Administration and Political Change," in L. Hazerigg, ed., *Prison Within Society* (Garden City, N.Y.: Doubleday, 1969), pp. 113–139.

[17] Ibid., particularly on the Attica riot.

and public order were slurred together into a new and single idea, became highly visible for the first time in Goldwater's 1964 presidential campaign. Although President Johnson's election victory was rather overwhelming, his political savvy suggested that his opponent's claim for improved social control should be incorporated into his (Johnson's) own administration. Consequently, the President's Commission on Law Enforcement and the Administration of Justice was convened in 1965, and in the aftermath of the commission's two-year effort, the Omnibus Crime Bill and Safe Streets Act became law in 1968. As part of that, the Law Enforcement Assistance Administration was established, a new executive branch organization that mushroomed through Nixon's first administration as one of the largest, most expensive, and most publicized forays of federal government into the improvement of local public services.

The major impact of "law 'n' order" has probably been on the police—both in terms of actual monies allocated and in terms of changes in belief patterns, ideologies, and methods of analyzing criminal justice functions and official roles and responsibilities. One telling change is visible in words alone; it was *after* 1967 that the term *law enforcement* began to supplant (or at least become synonymous with) the term *police*. The idea that the *primary* goal of police departments was law enforcement made great headway, and during the late sixties there were many serious police spokesmen and police analysts who argued that the police should be divested of all but their law-enforcement duties.[18]

The other important impact is evident in the one-breath utterance of "law *and* order," as if these were identical terms or that one was impossible without the other. This approach to the implementation of law and the maintenance of public order is rather foreign to the history of policing, and to discussions of law and order *prior* to 1967. Skolnick, for example, argued in 1966 that law and order tend to be mutually exclusive terms, or at least that they are rather uneasy bedfellows. The role of law, he suggests, requires that when officials intervene in citizens' behavior, their actions should follow rigorously preformed guidelines. One cannot intervene *by law* until some illegal act *has* been committed. Maintenance of order, on the other hand, frequently requires discretion on the part of officials who will intervene *prior* to the occurrence of legal violations.[19] Once a violation has occurred (one that will allow legal intervention), social order has already been disrupted.[20]

[18] Michael O'Neill, "The Role of the Police—Normative Role Expectations in a Metropolitan Police Department" (unpublished Ph.D. dissertation, State University of New York at Albany, 1974), pp. 44–52.

[19] Jerome Skolnick, *Justice Without Trial* (New York: Wiley, 1966), pp. 1–22.

[20] For the same dilemma between law and order in prisons, see Donald Cressey, "Contradictory Directives in Complex Organizations: The Case of the Prison," *Administrative Science Quarterly, 4* (June 1959), 1–19.

Consequently, there is some apparent irony in the rise of "law 'n' order" as a social and political issue. The emphasis on improvement in social control led to a marked increase in the study and analysis of criminal justice and to an emphasis on the utilization of systems analysis as an approach to such a study. The President's Crime Commission insists at every turn on the mutual influences of one agency or one decision upon previous or succeeding agencies and decisions in the criminal process. One might suppose, under these conditions, that the agencies might become more cohesive and might engage in more mutual planning and decision making. However, the reverse has frequently been true. The "law 'n' order" philosophy has functioned to some degree in separating the police from later phases of the criminal process. At least two reasons for this separation and heightened conflict are evident. "Law 'n' order" emphasized the importance, perhaps the centrality, of police work, for maintaining order or enforcing the law. In other words, instead of being integrated with prosecutorial and judicial aspects of law enforcement, many police have taken the position that they are fully responsible for law enforcement, and that they are hampered in their duties by prosecutorial or judicial perceptions of how a case should be handled. The police have apparently grasped the emphasis on "law 'n' order" as their own ideology, and have been able to use it as an independent value base by which to legitimize their criticism of other agencies in the criminal process. Attached to this growing sense of political power, the "law 'n' order" philosophy does much to confuse notions of how law is enforced with heretofore contradictory notions of how order is maintained.

THE POLICE AND THE COURTS

Another significant factor that has raised policing to its current controversial status has been the growing willingness of the appellate courts to review criminal cases in regard to constitutional and procedural adequacy. This trend is no longer new. Indeed, its origins predate both the latest urban crises and demands for "law 'n' order." Although many of the specific issues involving court intervention in police matters have now been resolved, we have placed this matter last in our discussion, because this is an ongoing relationship and one whose conflicts are best highlighted in the "law 'n' order" philosophy.

The first major intervention of the Supreme Court of the United States in local police operations occurred in *Mapp* v. *Ohio* (1961).[21] Although

[21] Mapp v. Ohio, 367 U.S. 643 (1961). This section will *not* review the principal procedural changes due to *Mapp* or subequent cases. We will save that discussion for the following section on the police and the criminal process. The emphasis in the present discussion will be on the apparent value conflicts between judicial and police functions and value systems.

the Supreme Court had intervened in the conduct of local police matters and state-level criminal procedure many times previous to *Mapp*, the *Mapp* opinion stands as a landmark in criminal procedure because of the *nature* of the intervention.

In the *Mapp* decision, the Supreme Court departed rather significantly from previous reviews of police behavior. First, the *Mapp* decision was the first occasion in which the Supreme Court applied the provisions of the constitutional Bill of Rights to local criminal process by providing a negative sanction, the "exclusionary rule," to improperly handled state criminal cases.[22] Second, this application of the exclusionary rule signaled some exasperation on the part of the Supreme Court with local law enforcement. The Court said, in effect, that given 12 years in which to do so, the states had been unable to find their own means of controlling improper police behavior. Third, this opinion in 1961 was a clear signal that the criminal process should be (and was about to be) standardized across jurisdictions to a greater extent than had previously been the case. In summary, this case was really the beginning of a decade-long attempt to bring about change in police behavior through external, judicially imposed controls.[23]

A large number of court cases following *Mapp* expanded this external intervention into many other areas including in-custody interrogations,[24] lineup and identification of suspects,[25] stop and frisk,[26] and the scope and occasions of proper search.[27]

These cases, in some quarters called the "due process revolution," have had a variety of consequences, many of which are still unfolding. Most of the major issues in the police phase of the criminal process had been considered by the end of the sixties. And some of the more recent Supreme Court decisions are apparently increasingly more supportive of the police-oriented version of criminal procedure. Furthermore, toward the tail end of this "revolution," the Court showed some signs of relenting in its demands for change, or in its demands for police compliance with the judicial interpretation of minimal criminal process standards. Perhaps one reason for this slowing down is best stated by the late Chief Justice Warren who observed in *Terry* v. *Ohio* that a great deal of police behavior cannot be controlled from the bench.[28]

[22] The development of search and seizure cases through *Mapp* is discussed in detail in Chapter Four, as an example of the relationship between the state and the federal court systems.

[23] O'Neill, "The Role of the Police."

[24] Escobedo v. Illinois, 378 U.S. 478 (1964); and Miranda v. Arizona, 384 U.S. 436 (1966).

[25] United States v. Wade, 388 U.S. 218 (1967).

[26] Terry v. Ohio, 392 U.S. 1 (1968).

[27] Chimel v. California, 23 L. Ed 2nd 685 (1968).

[28] Terry v. Ohio, see footnote 26.

To state the same observation more broadly, there is a great deal of police behavior that is not related to the criminal process itself, and other police behaviors that become related only because of some decision by the police to allow the relationship. In other words, the police frequently resort to other means to control situations than invocation of the criminal sanction. Indeed, the police go to the system so infrequently that they have difficulty understanding prosecutorial and judicial reactions to "normal police behavior" as if this behavior were just being invented for the first time when a hard or difficult case enters the system. If law enforcement, in a strict sense of the term, requires a formal and orderly progression of a case through the criminal process, maintenance of order in the community frequently requires (to the police) quite a different set of behaviors.

ORIGINS OF POLICING

For an adequate understanding of modern police functions, of the relationship of the police to the state and to its citizenry, of the values and beliefs of the police and about policing, and of the often confusing and frequently contradictory demands made of the police, an historical examination of the police is necessary. In tracing the development of policing, it is difficult, if not impossible, to separate a descriptive, chronological narrative of the various forms of policing from an analytical discussion of the notion of the state and the police functions(s). Although the terms *police* and *state* are both ancient and commonly used, it is perhaps a telling comment about the political and social organization of the police that the police themselves have seldom had the political acumen or the social background that would enable them to be either very sophisticated in their understanding of the power and structure of the state or very self-conscious in their performance of the police function.

In this and in the succeeding section, we will attempt to separate to a certain extent the analytical discussion of police function and power and the political construct of the state from a brief overview of the development of the modern police department. We shall take the history first, even though we may need to use in this overview a few terms such as *state* and *police power*, the definitions of which will be discussed some pages later on.

"Policing" Primitive Societies

An anthropological study of both contemporary and earlier societies should suggest that one basic distinction between various cultural mechanisms for handling issues of disorder, inequity, disagreements, and norm-breaking is the existence or absence of the state, and therefore of state officers who have responsibilities of governing and regulating group behavior. Contrary to some philosophical conjectures, there is evidence that even in stateless societies there are identifiable, patterned societal responses to social disorder and relatively stable, predictable means of returning the society to a condition of relative order when a disagreement occurs between two parties *within* that society. The Hobbesian argument—that, without subservience to law and the state, and without the individual waiving of some individual freedom in return for safety and protection, man would have to vie for himself against all others—is apparently empirically invalid. In other words, the juxtaposition of an individual's freedom and the requisites of group living (*sans* an official, legal order) is probably a false dilemma based on a faulty notion of the individual human being. Whereas stateless societies may deal with "offenders" or "troublemakers," or with "offenses" and "trouble" in a considerably different fashion than a modern industrial society, evidence is rather clear that social order, maintenance of the social group, and keeping the peace are all group values, the predominance of which is quickly emphasized when disputes and arguments arise among various social group members.[29]

The major characteristic of order maintenance and norm enforcement in stateless societies is the emphasis on dispute settlement by the social group itself rather than any resort to handling by officials of claims or complaints that are resolved in favor of one party vanquishing the other or gaining retribution for an act by the other party. In general, the disputants are not categorized as victim and offender, but as two equal members both of whom remain within the community (and continue to interact with each other after the dispute is settled). Dispute settlement generally involves compromise by both parties, with the primary group objective being return to peaceful living rather than a black and white determination of who was right and who was wrong.[30]

Under the conditions of statelessness, the role of police official obviously does not exist, nor is there any notion of executive leadership, delegation of authority, etc. There is no person or organization whose task is policing the other members of the group. There is, however, clear manifestations of what, in more complex, state-societies, would be termed the *police function*. This function, in the sense of maintaining social order or continuing observance of group norms, seems to rest in these societies as inherent in group living itself. In other words, prior to the evolution of states, administration of law, and regulation through formal organization, policing can be understood as the group provision for the welfare of the

[29] Chambliss and Seidman, *Law, Order, and Power,* pp. 251–257.
[30] Ibid., pp. 251–257.

group itself. It must be added, then, that in primitive, stateless societies, the battle for subsistence is so great and the requirement so strong for each group member to contribute to group subsistence that internal order must be maintained as the primary goal when any internal disorder emerges.

Policing in the Ancient State

The notion of policing and the focus of police behavior within states are considerably different from what takes place in stateless societies. Although the origins may be considerably more ancient, officials with the police function and the term *policing* were at least recognizable within the Greek city-states and were adopted, adapted, and made more complex within the Roman Empire. The Roman term *politia* was a crucial concept to the growth and administration of the Roman state. *Politia* translates as the "survival and welfare of the inhabitants of the city." It is the origin of our terms *policy* and *politics* as well as *police*.[31] Police *power* was at the very heart of the Roman state authority; it was the ability of the state to govern or to make policy concerning the welfare of Rome. Police *force* was the armed coercion that could and was used to enforce policy and therefore was seen as essential to maintenance of social welfare.[32] By the height of the Roman Empire, distinct roles had emerged for both the exercise of police power and the police force. There were administrators with responsibility for making policy and seeing to its implementation, soldiers with special duties to see to its maintenance (rather than with primarily military duties), and magistrates who would hear disputes. Within the Roman state, the administrative role was supreme, judicial officials were subservient to executive dictates, and the soldiers with police powers were primarily controlled by administrative policy without magisterial intervention. However, distinctions were made between violations of imperial policy and violations of civil laws and customs (i.e., dealing with crimes between individuals), and a criminal process consisting of apprehension by soldiers and trial by magistrate existed in these cases. Hence, a criminal justice network and a set of police actions quite similar to our own were operant for certain classes of crimes.

The Roman concept of police power and police administration was lost with the fall of the Empire and did not reemerge in Europe until the Middle Ages. In the interim centuries, peace-keeping and policing apparently reverted to the methods utilized in other stateless societies.[33]

---

[31] Brian Chapman, *The Police State* (London: Praeger, 1970), pp. 11–13.

[32] Ibid.

[33] Ibid., p. 14.

States again began to reemerge from tribal and simple, rural agrarian societies in the 1000s. With the emergence of states, police power and police officials inevitably reappeared. There were, however, two relatively distinct trends in policing now discernible: (1) centralized, nationalized, military police forces existed in France, Germany, and Austria, and (2) a community-controlled, constabulary developed in Great Britain. Although the fact is not arguable that the English rather than continental developments have had the greater influence in the United States,[34] it also is true that continental influences could be seen in England as early as the Norman invasion in 1066, and thus indirectly, continental developments also influenced policing in the United States.[35] The contrast between the English and European systems is important to an understanding of the notion of the state.

Brian Chapman has stated that there was a recognizable modern police force in France by the reign of Francis I (1494-1547). This system consisted of lieutenants and soldiers of the royal army who were under special assignment to patrol the countryside, keeping roads open and clear of thieves and robbers. These units clearly had some peace-keeping functions, but they were a military force rather than civil authority with police powers.[36]

By the end of the seventeenth century, however, the sophistication and complexity of state government had increased considerably. Means of internal and external control had been delineated, and there were clear specializations in financial administration, foreign affairs, and defense, and in running the internal affairs of state. "The word 'police' began to take on the connotations of internal administration, welfare, protection, and, in the more modern sense, surveillance."[37]

Major contributions to the development of modern policing in France included—first under Cardinal Richelieu (1585-1642) and after the Revolution under Fouché[37a]—the utilization of a "high police" who were responsible for the control and manipulation of politics and political groups. The high police were seen and used as protectors of the king's interests and the Empire's interests. This meant that the high police had both highly secretive spying and control duties over powerful groups and

---

[34] Ibid., p. 136.

[35] T. A. Critchley, *A History of Police in England and Wales 900–1966* (England: The Garden City Press, 1967), p. 1.

[36] Chapman, *The Police State*, p. 14.

[37] Ibid., p. 15.

[37a] Joseph Fouché, ᴅᴜᴄ d'Otrante, 1759–1820, French statesman in charge of police under Napoleon.

people as well as public and visible duties to enforce state policy and programs. In function and in relationship to state structure, the high police were very similar to the Roman administrators' utilization of soldiers to enforce decisions concerning public welfare. In contrast, the development of the "low police," whose duties included keeping order on the streets of Paris or arresting and prosecuting common criminals, was of much less interest to the state.

A distinctly different contribution to the development of the police occurred in Prussia, where the innovation of recognizable, contemporary bureaucracy as a means of governing created a distinction between the public and private roles of leaders and between the *person* of the executive and the implementation of law. Systems were devised for hiring and promoting officials on the basis of merit and for distinguishing between the desires (and whims) of bureaucratic leaders and what was best for the state and public welfare. Like the Roman political structure, the police in Prussia were perceived as responsible for mobilizing internal public policy as much as for, or more than, enforcing laws and capturing criminals. And judges were still not independent of the executive. But the idea of "civic duty" had emerged in a new sense, and the practice of public administration had advanced considerably.

A third characteristic of modern policing can be identified with the police system devised by the Hapsburg emperor Francis Joseph (1830–1916) who created a police subdivision that had the responsibility of policing officials (as well as the police), with the aim of assuring that imperial policy was carried out competently and fairly. Along with this development was the understanding of the police as an educative social force who instructed a less educated public in proper conduct and desirable social objectives.[38]

Compared to the English and American experience, perhaps the most important observation about European police history is the direct attachment of police to a centralized, autocratic rule. The emphasis on police control in the political sphere and the subordination of recognizable peace-keeping functions to more pressing state interests are a direct result of that relationship. The police were (and are) seen as more directly responsible for the administration of the state's internal affairs in a sweeping and (to our standards) very confining degree. The police are very much over, rather than of, the people, and the judicial function in the criminal process, as well as in state structure, is very weak. European police systems, as late as 1815, were apparently quite similar in function and organization to the police of the Roman Empire, perhaps the most efficient autocratic state of Western civilization. This connection of the

[38] For considerably more detailed discussions of the French, German, and Austrian developments, see Chapman, *The Police State*, pp. 15–29.

police to the executive branch (and consequently their freedom from judicially administered constraints) was severely limited in the nineteenth century, and the prosecution of crime became the specialty of a stronger and more autonomous judiciary by 1870.[39] Nevertheless, Raymond Fosdick's comparative study of European police systems in 1915 demonstrated continued freedom from public control that, said Fosdick, would have resulted immediately in riot in England.[40]

Police in England 1000–1829

The history of the English police, in contrast, shows considerably more similarity between the police function there and the peace-keeping functions of stateless social groups. Prior to the Norman conquest in 1066, the earliest example of English police is probably the Saxon "tythingman," who was responsible for collecting fines or apprehending criminals from within the "tyth" or "vil," the lowest social unit in Anglo-Saxon England. The tyths were organized into "hundreds," and a "hundredman" supervised all the tythingmen within his jurisdiction. Hundredmen, in turn, were responsible to the "shire-reeve," or sheriff, who had the responsibility of keeping the king's peace within the shire. Unlike the European systems—developing concomitantly—the pre-Norman system of policing was organized from "the ground up." It was each vil's duty (police duty) to maintain the peace, and to produce from within the local community any evildoer, or pay a collective fine. Although there was, through the supervisory position of sheriff, a connection to centralized government, the officials with peace-keeping duties were locally chosen, and each adult male had the duty to the community to accept his turn as tythingman.[41]

Immediately after the Norman invasion, the French influence on policing was felt, and the English sheriffs became repressive officials responsible for implementing Norman policy. But, by the twelfth century, police control in England had returned to the local level, and an official called a *constable* had appeared and was responsible for maintaining order in the manor or parish.[42] By 1400, each manor elected constables on a yearly basis, and all adult male citizens had to accept the election to office. There was a fine or other penalties for refusing the job, which, although quite time-consuming, carried no remuneration.

[39] Ibid., p. 40.

[40] Raymond Fosdick, *European Police Systems* (Montclair, N.J.: Patterson Smith, 1969, reprint of 1915 edition).

[41] Critchley, *A History of Police in England*, pp. 1–2.

[42] Ibid., pp. 3–4.

The two important laws that structured the constabulary, from the thirteenth century until the passage of the 1829 Police Act, were the Statute of Winchester of 1285 and the Justices of the Peace Act of 1361. The Statute of Winchester, the stated purpose of which was "to abate the power of felons" created the "watch and ward" to augment the local constable and defined the "hue and cry" as a community police duty. The watch clause provided for the formation of night watches in each village. Nightwatchmen had the duty of keeping streets clear and arresting criminals and strangers, etc. Those arrested were presented to the constable in the morning. The constable also took on the duties of organizing and staffing the watch. The "hue and cry" provided a procedure to deal with persons who resisted arrest by the watchmen or the constable. If resistance occurred, the constable was to raise the hue and cry in response to which all citizens in earshot were to drop what they were doing and join in the chase for the villain. Citizens who did not join in were penalized. The "hue and cry" later became formalized as a warrant issued by a magistrate to a constable who then had the power to arrest the sought individual.[43]

The Justices of the Peace Act of 1361 was somewhat contradictory to the Statute of Winchester, in that it centralized peace-keeping duties under a new official called the *justice of the peace,* whereas the Statute made police duties a town responsibility. The justices were originally knights of the manor, and later, the lords of the manor. The justices' legal relationship with the constables was not clear, but their higher social status and direct appointment by the king made them the constables' natural superiors. Furthermore, the justices first presided over and then frequently replaced the town courts, or liet courts, which had become, over time, the appointers of the constables. The introduction of the justices as supervisors of the king's peace throughout the manor was probably the first instance of police subordination to the judiciary (although clearly, the justices were subordinate to the royal executive).

Hence, by 1361, the English "old police" system was in place, and was to remain the peace-keeping machinery in England until 1829. Of course, a great number of operational changes in the system took place between 1361 and 1829, most of which were results of the commercialization, industrialization, and urbanization of English social and economic structure in the eighteenth century. The once honored station of constable was apparently in disrepute by Shakespeare's time, and the position of justice became degraded shortly thereafter.

By the late 1500s, the position of constable was apparently to be avoided at all costs, by the most powerful and respected town citizens. As

[43] Ibid., pp. 5–6.

farming gave way to business as the predominant way of making a living, prosperous civic and business leaders declined election to constable because the position usurped too much time from their shopkeeping. Consequently, it became the practice to pay a deputy to do the constable's work or to pay the fine for refusing election altogether. And, generally, it was only the unemployed, uneducated, and stupid who were willing to take on the constable's or deputy's duties for the pittance paid.

Likewise, individuals willing to take the position of justice slowly evolved means of making the position pay by charging fees for every action taken, or by taking bribes for letting well-paying criminals go.

By 1800, the English cities, and most notably London, were virtually unpoliced, and corrupt justices (or magistrates) had turned the administration of criminal law into a crime. With the exception of some notable experiments by Henry Fielding and a few others in the 1700s, the English police system had virtually crumbled away as the simple laws and simple structure of a feudal society unsuccessfully attempted to adapt to a new kind of social structure and a new type of state. The time was ripe for change when Robert Peel managed the passage of the Metropolitan Police Act in 1829.

The "New Police" in England

By the beginning of the eighteenth century, England was a far different place with far different problems than had prompted the medieval responses to community disorder. It was quite apparent by 1750 that the British dependence on the citizens' duty system of policing was not a sufficiently reliable mechanism for maintaining order in the streets, reporting and seeing to the removal of physical as well as social hazards, and apprehending and prosecuting criminals. Although most of the English cities had similar problems, the major focus was on London, where a trip through the streets, said one critic, was like going to battle.

Urbanized city life simply made it impossible to patch up the ancient principles of government that were still in use. In other words, there were cities long before there were city governments. The inability of the city to govern itself had many other manifestations beyond the corruption of the justices or magistrates, the impotence of the "hue and cry," and the absolute incompetence of the constabulary. Many other sorts of local civic functions had never existed before and now made city life a hazardous, dirty, squalid challenge. Between 1750 and 1829, several cities turned to the challenge of designing and implementing city government with some vigor. Spontaneous and voluntary citizens' groups sprang up in London, Manchester, and elsewhere. New, full-time employees, called *street commissioners, police,* or *safety commissioners,* sprang up. During these periods, real improvements were made, but there was a tremendous overlapping of efforts, competition between new commissions and the older night-watch and constable machinery, and, in the police area, considerable doubt over who had authority to do what.

The Metropolitan Police Act of 1829 established a full-time, unarmed, civilian police of 1,000 men. Although civilians, Peel's police wore uniforms and were organized in a military fashion. The police were supervised by two magistrates, Charles Rowan and Richard Mayne, who were later called *commissioners*. These magistrates, however, had only administrative duties rather than judicial powers. Much like the continental police forces, the police commissioners reported to the Home Secretary, the chief officer of state responsible for internal affairs. Unlike the home ministers of France, however, the Home Secretary was accountable to Parliament, rather than a strong monarch, and thus the London police were ultimately controlled by a democratic governing body.

The passage of the 1829 act had not been altogether popular in Parliament. Indeed, it had taken Peel seven years to garner sufficient support for the measure, despite the serious London crime problem. Opposition after passage did not immediately disappear. The more liberal members of Parliament were fearful of the possibility of police tyranny, and the aristocracy, although not worried on those grounds, were disappointed by the rigorously enforced personnel standards implemented by the two commissioners, who were from the start insensitive to the demands for a patronage system.

Despite opposition from the left and the right, the police were highly successful in reducing the problems of crime and disorder in London. Within a few years, the provinces and other cities in Great Britain were requesting police assistance. In 1839, Parliament empowered justices of the peace to initiate police forces in the counties, and in 1856, a similar act enabled all towns and boroughs to establish their own police forces.[44]

As the police became established, the justices gradually gave up their law-enforcement duties and functions and concentrated strictly on judicial functions. Although the laws that established the police had been written when the justices were responsible for investigative work, the laws were never revised to provide the police with authority for investigation. Thus, to the original front-line peace-keeping functions of the police have been added informally many detective and investigatory duties that legally rest with the magistrates.[45]

[44] J. Daniel Devlin, *Police Procedure, Administration and Organization* (London: Butterworth, 1966), pp. 3–16.

[45] Edward J. Barrett, Jr., "Police Practices and the Law—From Arrest to Release or Charge," *California Law Review*, 50 (March, 1962), pp. 17–18.

Early Policing in the United States

The police function in the colonies was, quite understandably, performed through the English constabulary and watchmen structures. Boston had a nightwatch prior to 1700, and other cities followed suit as they grew in size. Industrialization and urbanization created for the American cities the same problems found in London in 1800, and crime was equally rampant. Probably the first American police force was created in Philadelphia in 1833, and Boston followed in 1838. These early forces, however, retained the traditional night/day split, and conflicts between the night watches and the much smaller day police forces made these organizations ineffective. The New York legislature abolished the night-watch system and created the first unified police force in New York City in 1844. By 1870, most other police departments had followed this example.[46]

State police forces were established shortly before and after World War I, as substitutes for the sheriff system in the counties. On the federal level, law-enforcement agencies emerged in several federal departments, with the responsibility for regulating activity and enforcing laws that fell within the jurisdiction of these agencies. The Revenue Cutter Service was established as early as 1789 to prevent smuggling, and postal inspectors were employed in 1836. The origin of the Federal Bureau of Investigation was probably the authorization by Congress for 25 detectives in 1868. The F.B.I. itself was organized by J. Edgar Hoover as a division of the U.S. Department of Justice in 1924.

Unlike the situation in England, the early police forces in the United States were always hampered by, and controlled by, political interests. The police were perceived as an excellent opportunity for patronage, and chiefs or commissioners of police were appointed by local politicians, served at their whim, and rotated out of office at least as frequently as political power shifted from party to party at election time. Even in instances where front-line police hiring became immune to patronage shuffling, promotions and assignments were frequently controlled by the local political machines, and police officers were openly expected to help precinct or ward bosses control their territory.[47] Political control of the police has always been, then, more visible and perhaps more important in the United States than in England. Although the dangers of the European police states have, in both countries, been avoided, the police function in the United States has suffered from the opposite extreme: domina-

[46] President's Commission on Law Enforcement and Administration of Justice, *Task Force Report: The Police* (Washington, D.C.: Government Printing Office, 1967), p. 6.

[47] Cyril D. Robinson "The Mayor and the Police—The Political Role of the Police in Society," in George Mosse, ed., *Police Forces in History* (London: Sage, 1975).

tion by local, frequently changing, and often corrupt local government.[48]

By the First World War, and in some instances, sooner, the visibility of corruption in local politics and local police had led to attempted reforms. Civil service systems were instituted both to provide some permanency to a police officer's tenure, and to structure at least minimum standards for recruiting and promotions. Training academies were organized in a few cities in the early part of the twentieth century, and, for the first time, police were given some instruction in the laws that they were supposedly enforcing. The major attack on police corruption, however, came in the form of the first presidential commission on criminal justice. The Wickersham Commission reports lay bare the extent and severity of undesirable political influence; poor police standards, training, and personnel practices; on-the-street prejudices; and backroom brutality.[49] Although it has taken years to correct some of these problems, the widespread swing in the 1930s to local reform governments had a major impact on the environment of police organization and on police practices. The era of the modern police department had arrived.

THE POLICE AND THE STATE

The concept of the state as a social and political reality is relevant to the discussion of any criminal justice operation or component. Even a rudimentary discussion of the state becomes indispensable to the examination of the police because of the integral development of the police and the state, and the fundamental connections of the police with the concepts of policy, politics, and social welfare.

Perhaps it is because such an amorphous and confusing concept as that of the state can have such sweeping and ever-present influence on human behavior that issues of police policy and operations are at once so intriguing, ambiguous, controversial, and popular. The state is a difficult "thing" to pin down. It is an abstract, yet real, entity. It exists beyond the persons and organizations that maintain it and hold official positions within it. And it exists beyond the ability of those officials, or of the political power elites, or of the individual citizens who are influential in shaping its temporal quality. Amitai Etzioni points out, for example, that even totalitarian regimes must compromise and coopt in order to maintain control,[50] whereas the English and American experiences would suggest that even strong popular sentiment for little centralized control

[48] James Q. Wilson, *Varieties of Police Behavior* (Cambridge, Mass.: Harvard University Press, 1967), pp. 288–292.

[49] National Commission on Law Observance and Enforcement, *No. 14 Report on the Police* (Washington, D.C.: Government Printing Office, 1931).

[50] Amitai Etzioni, *The Active Society* (New York: The Free Press, 1968).

gives way over time to a demand for relatively stronger forms of coordination, integration, and governance.

Alexander d'Entreves suggests that there are three separate but related aspects or subconcepts operating within the larger notion of the state: (1) might, or force, (2) power, and (3) authority.[51] Primary to the notion of the state is *force,* or coercion itself. When people are organized in groups, it is the group rather than the individual that monopolizes the use of force. At least in any matters internal to the group, any other use of force is usually perceived as deviant and is quickly and negatively sanctioned. But, as we have seen, this appears to be the case in stateless societies, as well as in states.

The second aspect of the state is *power,* that is, the formalization or legalization of the monopoly on force. In other words, the state includes a mechanism that provides clear and consistent means for identifying the violation of norms surrounding the use of force. Unlike the problems caused in primitive societies by deviant manifestations of concern, in states there are laws that make the norms governing force explicit and that also routinize the procedures to be used when deviance occurs. It should be emphasized, however, that legalized force, or power, exists even in states that many people may not recognize as *desirable* governments. Autocratic and totalitarian regimes can operate legally, or can apply force in a predictable, controlled manner; but in doing so, these regimes can enforce laws the objectives of which are quite detestable. The problem posed by d'Entreves is the question of how the people in a state came to accept power and obey law so that force or coercion need not be used.

> We should not assume that we have fully unravelled the notion of the State unless we are able to explain how force, first legalized as power, becomes, in turn, legitimate as authority.[52]

The third aspect of the state, its *authority,* is perhaps the most difficult aspect to grasp. It involves the question of how and why states are stabilized as people within them begin to accept the objectives of law as desirable. Certainly, there is no single answer to this question. As we argued in Chapter Two, several social structures or institutions can produce similar or identical functions. Likewise, many forms of power are probably capable of achieving legitimacy. Although Hitler's Germany evidently did not achieve legitimacy in its legality, forms of state power as different as the United States and the U.S.S.R. apparently have.[53]

---

[51] Alexander Passerin d'Entreves, *The Notion of the State: An Introduction to Political Theory* (London: Oxford University Press, 1967), pp. 1–8.

[52] Ibid., p. 8.

[53] Etzioni, *The Active Society,* pp. 442–450.

Although there is not, then, any requisite form of policing, in order for a state to enforce its laws in a legal and an authoritative manner, there would appear to be some loose but important parameters. The two basic forms of policing (the English & continental) that apparently have the most survival value, or ultimate effectiveness, for the state, have been described, historically, above. The form in the Roman Empire, and later in continental Europe, utilizes the police on a very centralized basis as the coercive arm of executive policy implementation in matters of internal state affairs. This form of policing has been drastically tempered in Europe of the twentieth century, and an autonomous judiciary has evolved to intervene between executive policy making and the ability to coerce citizens. Nevertheless, there is a flavor, or style, to the strong, centralized government control of police. It is apparently quite viable and quite different from the second form of relationship between police and state.

This second form, epitomized by the "new police" of Great Britain, is also, although to a somewhat lesser extent, the situation in the United States. In contrast to the first form, Michael Banton argues, the London police established in 1829 did not act on or have the powers of the crown but possessed only the powers of every other citizen. They were "professional citizens."[54] The British and American police are indeed creatures of the state, who can act only under authority of the state, but the key difference in this relationship, compared to the continental form, appears to be in the cultural notions concerning the sources of power or the sources of social control. Unlike the European monarchs who, through police power, attempted to impose power in a relatively external fashion upon the populace, in the American and British democracies, "social control (is seen as) a property of states of social relations, not something imposed from outside."[55] By and large, then, the police are perceived as a secondary, and relatively minor means of achieving social control, when compared to "the extensiveness and intricacy of these other modes of regulating behavior."[56] In other words, the notion, evidently originating from the reign of the English king Alfred the Great (849–900?), that all citizens have police functions and must police each other, is a belief that has had sweeping and fundamental consequences for the administration of police in the United States.

Times, of course, have changed considerably since the appearance of the Bobbies in 1829, or the establishment of a full-time police force in New York in 1844. Social structure is markedly more complex, and the people policed in one American city are indubitably more diverse than the

[54] Michael Banton, *The Policeman in the Community* (New York: Basic Books, 1965), p. 6.
[55] Ibid., p. 2.
[56] Ibid.

people policed in all of England in 1850. Just as the ability to maintain the police function through an elected constabulary failed historically because of the division of labor and urbanization, so today the ability to maintain the police function through the employment of "professional citizens" has broken down in England and the United States.[57] For one thing, police technology has changed drastically. The neighborhood policeman began to disappear with the introduction of call boxes in the 1890s, and the introduction of radios and patrol cars began to tighten the boundary between police and citizens. Whereas police precinct stations of the 1890s were general-purpose social action and welfare centers, other governmental subdivisions have taken on such responsibilities. The police now serve much narrower functions than they once did and are isolated from other citizens by technology, bureaucracy, values, and stigma.[58] In many ways, bureaucratization and cultural diversification have placed the American police in much the same situation as the police of the European model: the people and the police have become separated, and many citizens frequently perceive themselves as coerced from without rather than policed from within.

The conflicts that this separation have caused are many and varied. But although there has been much discussion recently of police-community interaction, it may often be overlooked that this conflict between the police and the citizenry suggests new implications about the relationship of the police and the state. The existence of conflict between the police and community groups is usually perceived as either a problem in faulty police administration or as evidence of widespread community criminality. There is rarely any attempt to change the political and social structures of the communities that have fostered such confrontations. As one student of police puts it, "Simply stated, the political role of the police is to accept the punishment that might otherwise be received by their employers."[59] In other words, local government again seems deficient in structure and competence and unable to convince a large proportion of citizens about the social desirability of legal objectives. Under these circumstances, the police are used as a highly visible shield. As long as the animosity invoked by the wielding of unauthoritative power is directed at the police rather than at the state itself, state claims to legitimacy may remain in force. A great number of pressing social problems can be ignored or blamed on the inefficiencies of particular bureaucracies or individual officials, including the police. This situation

[57] Ibid., p. 7; and Leslie Wilkins, *Social Deviance* (Englewood Cliffs, N.J.: Prentice-Hall, 1965), pp. 65–71.

[58] See Mark Haller, "Introduction, The Nineteenth Century Police," (Philadelphia: Temple University, mimeographed, no date).

[59] Robinson, "The Mayor and the Police," p. 278.

does not mean that the police are blameless, or that all their acts are controlled by outside machinelike forces. But it does mean that many problems of policing are dilemmas, resolvable only on a higher level, in another alteration of coercion, power, and authority, which is the state.

POLICE RESPONSIBILITIES IN THE SYSTEM OF CRIMINAL JUSTICE

In the United States there are more than 40,000 federal, state, and local police agencies involving over 600,000 full-time law enforcement officers.[60] In 1975, budgetary expenditures on police in the United States amounted to $9,786 million, while the expenditures for the judicial system came to $2,067 million and corrections $3,843 million.[61] Policing is by far the largest and most expensive component in the criminal justice system.

The police are also the most visible, the most accessible, and the most pervasive criminal justice agency. Although the police are often perceived as crime control agents, only a relatively small proportion of most police officers' time is spent in crime control activities such as criminal investigation or arrest and interrogation of suspects. In fact, time studies of police activities have demonstrated that most activities of officers are not crime control at all, but represent service activities such as directing traffic, helping stalled motorists, providing emergency services for the sick and injured, licensing bicycles, searching for missing persons, and providing information to the public on a wide range of issues such as street locations, legality of events, etc. In light of such findings, the seemingly simple question, "What do the police do?" becomes extremely difficult to answer. Although most of the activities of police officers do not correspond to the traditional image of the policeman as crime fighter, the noncrime fighting activities have fallen to the responsibility of the police because no one else was willing or available to do them.[62]

In part, the expansive list of police activities results from the fact that the police are often the only government service agency available around the clock. Another contributing factor is the broad range of behaviors that are defined as "illegal," and the vagueness of some of these definitions. Given the structure of the criminal law, the police have either been

[60] U.S. Department of Justice, *Expenditure and Employment Data for the Criminal Justice System, 1975* (Washington, D.C.: National Criminal Justice Information and Statistics Service, 1977), p. 3.

[61] Ibid., p. 2–3.

[62] Donald J. Newman, *Introduction to Criminal Justice* (Philadelphia: Lippincott, 1975), p. 139.

granted or have assumed domain over a broad range of events and behaviors because some of these may be illegal. In 1967, the President's Commission on Law Enforcement and the Administration of Justice observed:

> . . . many of the complex problems of the criminal process could be solved by more narrowly defining the police function. If drunkenness were dealt with by medically qualified people, for example, police would not have to contend with the habitual drunk. If family problems were handled by social work agencies, police would not have to deal with the many domestic and juvenile problems which now confront them. If the substantive law were revised, police would not be confronted with the difficult decisions resulting from broad prohibitions against narcotics, gambling, prostitution, and homosexual activity. . . .[63]

Although there are many arguments for and against the legalization or decriminalization of various offenses referred to as "crimes without victims," such as narcotics, gambling, and prostitution, it is not important to review such arguments here. It is important to point out that attempts to regulate morality (i.e., the behavior of citizens in private) has the impact of expanding the police function both in terms of the types of behaviors they must attempt to regulate and the types of investigations that they must conduct in order to investigate "private" though illegal behaviors.

Frequently, engaging in "service" activities places the police in a position where they may prevent an offense from occurring or may respond to an offense observed during the service activity. For example, it may be a "service" for the police to require a drunk to take a cab, or to drive the drunk home, or to put him in jail, but it may also be viewed as a crime-prevention strategy as well. Drunks are susceptible to victimization by muggers, and thus officers may be preventing crime by getting drunks off the street. They may respond to a call about a "disturbance of the peace" and in so doing may be present when the disturbance becomes an assault. Thus, defining a wide range of activities as "service" may be misleading in that numerous service calls result in an officer's making an arrest or preventing an offense from occurring.

At this point our knowledge about what the police do by way of carrying out their responsibilities in the criminal justice system is still very inadequate. Most police behavior is neither reported nor studied. The police have been trained and accustomed to handling troublesome situations without resort to other agencies or reinforcements. Hence much police behavior is both discretionary and has outcomes (i.e.,*not* invoking the law) that make the activities difficult to observe. Therefore,

[63] President's Commission on Law Enforcement and Administration of Justice, *Task Force Report: The Police*, p. 14.

most of the material available on police behavior concerns those activities that relate the police to the rest of the criminal process, such as investigation and arrest.

CRIME INVESTIGATION

Criminal investigations are usually initiated in one of two ways. First, the investigation may be touched off by a citizen complaint. For example, a citizen returning home after an evening out finds his home has been entered and numerous items stolen. When he reports the burglary to the police, an investigation is initiated. Most criminal investigations are initiated by private citizens because police do not normally have access to the private places where most offenses occur. Investigations resulting from citizen complaints will be referred to as *reactive* investigations. It is estimated that 87 percent of the police arrests are a consequence of reacting to citizen reports.[64]

Investigations may also be initiated by the officer or the department. These police-initiated investigations can be termed *proactive*. Of the 13 percent of arrests not accounted for by citizen reports—the proactive investigations—there are two basic police methods for uncovering criminal violations. First, during their academy training, police recruits are frequently cautioned to be suspicious, and to note carefully the normal routines in their areas. They are told to interpret any departures from these normal patterns as an indication that an offense may be occurring.[65] Automobiles with engines running, two individuals exchanging money or goods, license plates too dirty to identify (especially on a clean car), or strangers to the area that are casting furtive glances, all suggest potential criminality to an observant police officer. Second, the officer may himself witness a crime in progress or behavior that appears to be a crime.[66]

Police abilities to investigate and to arrest are limited in most cases by the seriousness of the offense. Misdemeanants may be arrested *only* if the officer directly observed the offense or if a citizen who did observe the offense is willing to file a complaint. On the other hand, regarding felonies, the officer is provided with greater power to investigate and to make arrests. The officer's controlling standard for felonies is "probable cause" and is generally defined as

[64] Albert J. Reiss, Jr., *The Police and the Public* (New Haven: Yale University Press, 1971), p. 11.

[65] Richard Harris, *The Police Academy: An Inside View* (New York: Wiley, 1973).

[66] For a good discussion on police officer suspicion, see Jerome Skolnick, *Justice Without Trial* (New York: Wiley, 1966), pp. 45–48; and Newman, *Introduction to Criminal Justice*, p. 149.

facts or apparent facts, viewed through the eyes of the experienced police officer, which would generate a reasonable belief that a crime has been committed.[67]

There are several essential elements to the notion of "probable cause." First, the notion of "facts or apparent facts viewed through the eyes of an experienced police officer" suggests that behaviors that would not indicate criminality to the layman may do so for the experienced officer. For example, a police officer may observe a middle-aged male making or receiving numerous phone calls on a pay phone. This may not appear to be suspicious to the layman, but the officer may interpret these facts as indicative of a bookmaking operation. These facts alone would not support an arrest. However, they would support further investigation and might enable the police to obtain a search warrant if corroboration (such as by an informant) were available.

The notion that "reasonable belief that a crime has been committed" suggests the important point that "probable cause" does not mean "proof beyond a reasonable doubt," nor does it require substantiation through evidence that is legally admissible in a court of law.[68] Moreover, in order for there to be "probable cause" to make an arrest, there must be "a reasonable belief" that the person to be arrested committed the crime.

TYPES OF POLICE INVESTIGATIONS

Uncovering criminal offenses, linking an offender to an offense, and proving guilt or innocence often requires usage of various methods of investigation. In the following discussion we will cover field questioning and frisks, searches, use of electronic surveillance devices, and undercover operations. Each of these are complex legal phenomena. It is not the intent of these discussions to review the full range of police operations in these areas; rather, the intent is to present the reader with an overview that provides him with an understanding of police processes in investigating criminal activities.

Field Questioning

In an example mentioned previously, a police officer observed an individual receiving numerous calls at a pay phone booth. Persons acting in such a suspicious fashion may appropriately be stopped and questioned. Normally, these situations would not provide sufficient evidence to sup-

---

[67] J. Shane Creamer, *The Law of Arrest, Search and Seizure* (Philadelphia: Saunders, 1975), p. 7.

[68] Ibid., p. 15.

port "probable cause" to make an arrest or to obtain a search warrant. Earlier it was noted that "probable cause" is to be viewed through the eyes of an experienced officer. The street wisdom and suspicion that are an inherent part of the police role are best illustrated by the case of *Terry* v. *Ohio*.[69] A brief review of the facts of the case and the Supreme Court ruling will clarify police power to question and frisk suspicious persons in the field prior to an arrest.

A 39-year veteran of the police force observed two men standing on a corner. One of the men would walk past a store window, look closely in the window, walk on past, return for another look, and then return to the corner, whereupon his partner would engage in the same pattern. After doing this a dozen times, the men walked off together. The veteran officer, observing this pattern, interpreted the actions of the two men as "casing" the store for a possible robbery. Acting on his hunch, the officer followed the men until they stopped and joined a third companion, at which time he approached them and asked their names. The suspects responded with a series of mumbles, at which time the officer turned one of the men around and patted him down. In the suspect's coat pocket the officer found a .38 calibre revolver. Subsequently he also frisked the other two men and discovered another gun. The men were placed under arrest and charged with carrying concealed weapons.

The important sequence went as follows: (1) the officer suspected a possible robbery, (2) he stopped the men and frisked them, and (3) he found guns and charged them with carrying concealed weapons. Is this appropriate police investigation?

The question was raised in the United States Supreme Court because the prosecution argued that the evidence (guns) had been seized after a lawful arrest. The trial court admitted the guns into evidence, not because they were seized following a lawful arrest, but based on the court's belief that the actions of the officer were well within appropriate behavior since the defendants were acting suspiciously enough to warrant investigation by the officer. Moreover, the trial court held that the officer had the right to frisk these men for his own protection. The Supreme Court upheld the officer's actions and thus denied the petitioners' claim that the search was illegal because the officer did not have probable cause to make an arrest and, therefore, did not have the legal right to frisk the defendants. The Court found:

The officer need not be absolutely certain that the individual is armed; the issue is whether a reasonably prudent man in these circumstances would be warranted in the belief that his safety or that of others was in danger.[70]

[69] Terry v. Ohio, 394 U.S. 1 (1968).
[70] Ibid.

The Court, in specifying more clearly its definition of appropriate police procedure, stated:

> We merely hold today that where a police officer observes unusual conduct which leads him reasonably to conclude in light of his experience that criminal activity may be afoot and that the persons with whom he is dealing may be armed and presently dangerous; where in the course of investigating this behavior he identifies himself as a policeman and makes reasonable inquiries; and where nothing in the initial stages of the encounter serves to dispel his reasonable fear for his own or others' safety, he is entitled, for the protection of himself and others in the area, to conduct a carefully limited search of the outer clothing of such persons in an attempt to discover weapons which might be used to assault him.[71]

Most field stops do not result in a frisk as in the *Terry* case but involve the stopping of an individual to question what the individual is up to. For example, it is appropriate for an officer to check out whether an individual who is in a store after hours is legitimately there or is committing a burglary. In most cases, in checking, the officer will find no problem. However, occasionally his suspicion is rewarded by discovery of an offense. The crucial issue in police stops is their potential discriminatory use. Blacks and lower-class individuals are more likely than whites and middle-class individuals to be defined as suspicious, and therefore are more likely to be stopped. In some cases, such as that involved in the Zebra murders in the San Francisco area in which several people were murdered by black males, the police will have little information upon which to narrow down the possible suspects. In the Zebra murders all that was known for some time was that the murderers were black males. Consequently, the police, responding to public hysteria, undertook field questioning of any "suspicious" person—who happened to be any young, black male. Over 600 such persons were stopped and questioned before the process was stopped by civil rights leaders.

Search

As the case of *Terry* v. *Ohio* demonstrates, a significant aspect of many investigations is the search. In the *Terry* case, the search was a low-level investigation for weapons; however, a search of the person may involve a much more thorough investigation of the person or his property. A thorough search of an individual is permitted following an arrest, and a low-level search (pat down) for weapons is permitted when the officer reasonably fears "for his own or others' safety."

When he has the time to obtain a search warrant, or if he wants to

[71] Ibid.

search an entire building, an officer conducting an investigation is wise to obtain judicial clearance (search warrant) in his search of a person or property whenever he is unsure that he has "probable cause" to make such a search.[72] There are three basic conditions under which an officer may search without a warrant. First, as noted earlier, subsequent to a lawful arrest the officer may search the person, and he also may search the immediate area coming under the control of the person being arrested. The intent of this latter right to search the immediate area is to protect the officer and to prevent the possible destruction of evidence.[73]

Second, subsequent to the arrest of an individual operating a motor vehicle, the policeman has the right to search not only the person being arrested but also to search the entire vehicle in order to protect the officer and to prevent the loss or destruction of evidence. Third, and finally, under emergency conditions, the officer may search without a warrant. Examples of this would be an officer's attempt to save a life, or in "hot" pursuit of a dangerous criminal. Under these conditions the officer has greater authority to search than under more controllable circumstances.[74]

Although these guidelines may at first reading appear to be clear, their application to a particular circumstance is often vague. For example, what is the "immediate area coming under the control" of the arrested individual? In *Chimel* v. *California*, Justice Potter Stewart wrote that the arresting officer may search

> the area into which an arrestee might reach in order to grab a weapon or evidentiary items. . . . There is no comparable justification, however, for routinely searching rooms other than that in which an arrest occurs— or, searching through all the desk drawers or other closed or concealed areas in that room itself.[75]

The implication is that all other searches (in order to be legal) must be authorized by a search warrant, and this would appear to be a significant number of situations. However, in 1952 a study in Philadelphia showed that of a sample of 772 arrests, "the use of seach warrants in the cases examined was virtually nonexistent.[76] Moreover, the police often extend their legal boundaries by stopping and searching people in high-crime-rate sectors of the community in a relatively random fashion.[77] The

---

[72] Creamer, *The Law of Arrest*, p. 59.

[73] Ibid.

[74] Ibid.

[75] *Chimel v. California*, 395 U.S. 752 (1969).

[76] Paula R. Markowitz and Walter I. Summerfield, Jr., "Philadelphia Police Practice and the Law of Arrest," *University of Pennsylvania Law Review, 100* (1962), 1182–1217.

[77] Harry W. More, Jr., *Critical Issues in Law Enforcement* (Cincinnati: W. H. Anderson, 1972), p. 180.

intent of these extralegal stops and searches reflects attempts by the police to prevent crime by confiscating weapons and narcotics that may not be admissible in court for the prosecution of the possessor of the contraband, but are thereby seized and thus removed from the streets. The intent may be to prevent crime, but the actual consequence may be to cause "serious friction" with minority groups (the typical target of such searches) and thus to spur antagonism toward the police and to decrease the communities' cooperation with the police. The net impact may be an increase in crime.[78] The National Advisory Commission on Civil Disorders indicated that the "aggressive patrol procedures" initiated by the police department in an attempt to quell rising crime rates had in fact created tension through such procedures and actually fed the fires of civil disorder.[79]

Intelligence Gathering and Infiltration

Earlier it was indicated that most offenses are investigated in response to a civilian complaint. However, many offenses that the police are charged with investigating are unlikely to be reported and, thus, require different strategies of investigation. Political crimes, organized crime, and crimes without victims rarely come to the attention of the police through citizen reports or through police patrol procedures. Thus, if the police are to control these criminal violations, they must develop strategies whereby they can gather intelligence information on these offenses. Common techniques utilized include (1) undercover work whereby the police pose as susceptible victims or as willing offenders or agent provocateurs; (2) informers and spies; (3) electronic surveillance devices. We will briefly discuss each of these techniques.

UNDERCOVER OPERATIONS.   Police undercover operations involve police officers disguising themselves as potential victims or colleagues in crime in order to gain information and/or to gain legally admissible evidence. A major issue in undercover work is the role of the police officer as participant in and provocateur of criminal activity.

If the undercover officer induces an individual who would otherwise be innocent to commit a crime, the officer is guilty of *entrapment*.[80] For example, if the police officer approaches a suspected prostitute and requests from her certain sexual favors in exchange for $50, he has encouraged her participation, and evidence obtained in such a fashion

[78] President's Commission on Law Enforcement and Administration of Justice, *Task Force Report: The Police*, pp. 184–185.

[79] *Report of the National Advisory Commission on Civil Disorders* (New York: Bantam Books, 1968), pp. 304–305.

[80] *Sherman v. U.S.*, 356 U.S. 369 (1958).

would be suppressed because the officer entrapped the suspect. If, however, the officer just makes himself available to the suspected prostitute and she specifies the price and the favors, then no entrapment has occurred, and the evidence should be admissible. In effect, the police undercover role is to encourage potential criminals to engage in criminality in view of the officer, but not to overstep this passive position and actively encourage criminal behavior.[81]

Informers and spies. It is often difficult and dangerous for an officer to work as an undercover agent. Also, once his cover is blown, the officer is not likely to be an asset working undercover. Therefore the police fall back on street people who have ready access to suspected offenders. Since being a "stool pigeon" is not the most admired behavior in our society, the police normally provide some inducement for persons to act as informers. The informer and the police each have something to offer that forms the basis for a mutually beneficial exchange relationship. The informer can provide the police a privileged entrée to the activities of the underworld, including such offenses as drug-law violations, prostitution, and gambling. For example, the narcotic informant might provide information as to who is dealing, using, and if possible, the source of, drugs. In exchange, the police can provide the informant (who is often himself a law violator) protection from prosecution or from full prosecution, or they may provide the informant financial remuneration for his services. If the informer has made a significant contribution to a case or has the potential for making such a contribution in the future, the police and the prosecutor will protect the informer from prosecution as long as he cooperates and will hold the prosecution over his head to insure his cooperation.

Legally, evidence of information obtained from an informant is used at two phases of the criminal process. First, if the informant is reliable, his information may be the basis for obtaining a search warrant. For these purposes, a reliable informant is one who has provided accurate information in the past, has personal connections that permit his access to confidential information pertaining to criminal violations, or is known as a respected member of the community. Second, his testimony in court often is crucial in obtaining a conviction. One difficulty with informants appearing in court is that they lose their value as informants in the future, plus they may be placing themselves in a situation of extreme danger when they go back on the streets. Thus, the prosecution often attempts to protect the informant from being identified. If the prosecution's case is almost totally based on an informant's supposed testimony, it is incumbent upon the prosecution to produce the informant at the trial or suffer dismissal of charges.

[81] Newman, *Introduction to Criminal Justice*, p. 161.

The relationship between police and informants often reflects some interesting contradictions. For example, Skolnick observed that narcotic detectives often permitted their informants to commit burglaries, whereas the burglary detectives would permit their informants to commit narcotic offenses without arrest.[82] In this situation, organizational specialization created reward structures that encouraged permitting informants to commit certain offenses as long as they provided information on other criminal behaviors.

ELECTRONIC SURVEILLANCE.   Because the use of electronic surveillance techniques, such as wiretaps and other eavesdropping devices, when used by the police invades the privacy of an individual, the use of such devices has been closely regulated. In fact, the Omnibus Crime Control Act of 1968 delineated the conditions under which communication between individuals can be intercepted.[83] In this act it was specified that at the federal level, application for an "interception" order must be approved by the Attorney General, and at the state level, by the prosecuting attorney having jurisdiction in the area. Subsequent to this approval, approval must also be obtained from a judge who must determine whether there is probable cause to believe that the suspect has committed an offense defined as legitimate for interception such as espionage, sabotage, counterfeiting, gambling, and racketeering. In addition, the judicial officer must decide whether it is reasonable to expect to obtain information concerning the offense in question through the interception. If the judge decides that the pertinent information is unlikely to be obtained, it is his responsibility to deny the application. Many states have regulations similar to those of the Omnibus Crime Control Act. However, others, such as Pennsylvania, totally ban the use of electronic eavesdropping devices by state and local police. Though the Omnibus Crime Control Act specified certain restrictions on eavesdropping it is permissible for states to place more stringent requirements, but not less stringent. Therefore, some states such as Pennsylvania have totally banned electronic eavesdropping by state and local police.

Advocates for the use of electronic surveillance argue that it is an essential tool in investigations of organized crime activity. Because organized crime involves a complex organization, with the men at the top isolated from normal police investigation strategies by their subordinates, and since the planning of criminal activities takes place in private, the police have little chance for obtaining evidence against the upper echelons except through electronic devices.

There are serious objections to electronic surveillance. When viewed as

---

[82] Skolnick, *Justice Without Trial*, pp. 112–138.

[83] Jerry L. Dowling, *Criminal Procedure* (St. Paul, Minn.: West Publishing 1976), pp. 392–393.

a search device, it is claimed that since electronic eavesdropping is indiscriminate and all conversations are overhead, it is a violation of the individual's right to privacy specified in the Fourth Amendment. For example, if someone calls an individual whose phone is tapped, even though the calling individual is not suspected of any violation, his conversation will be overheard. Additionally, because searches are normally preceded by an announcement of what is being searched for, and by whom, electronic surveillance violates this aspect by its concealment. Another concern about electronic surveillance is that it may violate the First Amendment guarantee of free speech through its generating fear that conversations are being overhead and thus restrict individual freedom of expression.[84]

The constitutional concerns over electronic surveillance notwithstanding, it is unlikely that such surveillance will become a major police procedure in the near future. The investment of police resources in conducting a wiretap becomes expensive both in terms of economic expenditure and in terms of the loss of police manpower in more productive activities such as patrol, and therefore electronic surveillance devices are unlikely to become common police techniques particularly at the state and local level.[85]

Arrest

Arrest in criminal cases involves four aspects: (1) the police officer must intend to arrest the individual; (2) he must have "real or pretended authority to arrest"; (3) he must seize the individual; and (4) the individual being arrested must have some cognition that he is being arrested.[86] The officer has the authority to make a felony arrest if he has "probable cause" to believe that a felony has been committed and reasonable cause to believe that the individual being arrested is the offender. In the case of a misdemeanor, the offense must either have been committed in view of the officer, or a complaint must be filed by someone who did in fact observe the offense.

The typical arrest process involves the officer arresting the individual and transporting him to a place for booking, which is normally the county jail or police station. At booking, information is gathered on the name, address, age, occupation, and miscellaneous other factors. Prints and photographs are taken as well. This process is characteristic; however, for less serious misdemeanors, citations may be issued in lieu of arrest, requiring the accused to appear in court at a later date.

[84] Ibid., pp. 397–398.

[85] Ibid., p. 399.

[86] J. Shane Creamer, *The Law of Arrest, Search and Seizure* (Philadelphia: Saunders, 1975).

The time that the arrest occurs is a significant concern to the admission of evidence to court. If an officer investigates a suspect because he acts suspiciously, as in the *Terry* v. *Ohio* case, but the officer finds narcotics instead of weapons, the narcotics would not be legally admissible in a court of law. The officer, in such a situation, does not have "probable cause" to arrest, and thus would not be able to engage in the kind of thorough search (appropriate after arrest) that would discover narcotics. Also, the officer is only permitted a low-level search for weapons when he reasonably feels that either he or another person are endangered by the individual. Consequently, evidence of criminal behaviors other than possession of weapons is not legally admissible against the suspect in court, but of course the narcotics would be seized as contraband.

When arrested, a suspect has the right to remain silent and to have a lawyer present before undergoing interrogation by the police.

> . . . the prosecution may not use statements whether exculpatory or inculpatory, stemming from custodial interrogation of the defendant unless it demonstrates the use of procedural safeguards effective to secure the privilege against self-incrimination. By custodial interrogation, we mean questioning initiated by law enforcement officers after a person has been taken into custody or otherwise deprived of his freedom of action in any significant way. As for the procedural safeguards to be employed, unless other fully effective means are devised to inform accused persons of their right of silence and to assure a continuous opportunity to exercise it, the following measures are required. Prior to any questioning, the person must be warned that he has a right to remain silent, that any statement he does make may be used as evidence against him, and that he has a right to the presence of an attorney, either retained or appointed.[87]

It must be noted that arresting an individual does not necessarily mean that the officer has told the person that he is arrested. Legally, a person is arrested when he is detained for longer than the time involved in a street stop or when he is controlled by the officer such as when the officer orders him to get into the squad car for the ride to the station. As was indicated earlier, it is crucial that the officer intend to effect an arrest, and when the intent is coupled with any restraint, the reviewing court will infer that an arrest has occurred.

Arrests are not always made with the intent to prosecute. The arrest may be used as a sanctioning process itself. For example, *harassment* arrests are sometimes made of individuals for whom the police are unable to develop probable cause to make a legal arrest; however, in some cases the arrest may be used to get the individual off the street for a short time, or to indicate to the individual that the police are keeping an eye on him. Harassment arrests are most common for vice offenses because of the

---

[87] Miranda v. Arizona, 384 U.S. 436.

difficulty of obtaining substantial enough evidence to support a probable cause arrest. One of these vice offenses, prostitution, presents perhaps the greatest pressure for the officer to harass the violators because of the public visibility of the prostitutes and the citizen complaints concerning their open solicitations. Thus, officers may arrest prostitutes to get them off the streets, and to alert the prostitutes to the fact that such arrests will continue unless they reduce their visibility. In making these arrests the officer may ostensibly arrest for vagrancy or disorderly conduct; however, it is unlikely that the officer will arrest for prostitution. For example, one Detroit precinct had 2,942 arrests over a six-month period for "disorderly persons investigation," which was a cover-up for arresting prostitutes without sufficient evidence to prosecute.[88]

Drunk and disorderly conduct arrests, which account for over half of all arrests in the United States, are often used as camouflage to sanction the offender for behavior such as the prostitution example above. However, these arrests may also be used to protect the individual. In some cases, drunks are taken into custody not to sanction them but to protect them from possible muggings or from freezing in the cold weather. In such cases, often referred to as "golden rule" drunks, the drunk is released after he has become sober.

Although the police often misuse their arresting power by using the arrest as the sanction, they also misuse it to detain a person while an investigation is being conducted. In other words, an individual is arrested prior to the establishment of probable cause in order that the police may continue to search for probable cause. Obviously, this contradicts the legitimate use of arrests as defined previously. However, when one considers that in Detroit from 1947 through 1956 there were 219,053 arrests for investigation, of a total of 658,808 nontraffic arrests, it is apparent that the practice is common.[89]

Police Discretion

The public commonly perceives the police as engaging in full enforcement of the law; however, enforcement may extend beyond the legitimate authority of the police, as the previous example regarding prostitution and drunk arrests indicates, or enforcement may be less than full as when violations are ignored. An example of the police use of their discretion not to invoke the law is commonly found in the use of informants. If the informant can provide information to the police on more serious offend-

---

[88] Wayne R. LaFave, *Arrest: The Decision to Take a Suspect into Custody* (Boston: Little, Brown, 1965), pp. 455–456.

[89] President's Commission on Law Enforcement and Administration of Justice, *Task Force Report: The Police*, p. 186.

ers, then the police often will not charge the informant, or they will at least request that the charges against the informant be reduced.

Numerous factors may influence whether an officer makes an arrest in any particular situation. A particularly important factor is the demeanor of the offender.[90] Although the interpersonal factors are important, James Q. Wilson found that various departments oriented themselves to maintaining order and law-enforcement activities differently, depending on the policy of different police administrators and upon the political, economic, and social structure of the community.[91] Order maintenance and law enforcement are often not distinguished by the behavior of the offender as much as by the role of the police officer in the community. Obviously, offenses like robbery, burglary, auto theft, and rape are so serious as clearly to demand that an officer arrest the offender, thus making it a law-enforcement situation. However, most police contacts with the public do not *demand* arrest but only permit it. For example, behavior that is offensive to the public or disturbs the public peace, such as a barroom altercation or loud party, loitering in public places, and numerous other behaviors that are offensive to some of the public, may all involve law enforcement, but the officer is more likely to concern himself with "maintaining order" than with arresting those involved.[92] These situations often present difficulties in terms of who is to blame. For example, which of two or more barroom combatants is at fault? From an "order maintenance" perspective, the officer (encouraged by the department) might break up the fight and, if there was no damage to the bar, send the combatants home. On the other hand, a law-enforcement perspective would emphasize the arrest of the battling parties, which of course restores order but does it through formal police action.

Wilson found three styles of police departments: (1) watchman, (2) legalistic, and (3) service.[93] The watchman style occurred in Albany, Amsterdam, and Newburgh, New York. In these communities, there was a decided orientation to emphasize order maintenance rather than law enforcement. In the words of Wilson:

If . . . the public peace has been breached—creating a disturbance in a restaurant, bothering passers-by on a sidewalk, insulting an officer, causing a crowd to collect, endangering others, or publicly offending current standards of propriety, then the officer is expected to restore

[90] See for example, Irving Piliavin and Scott Briar, "Police Encounters with Juveniles," *The American Journal of Sociology*, 70 (September 1964), 206–214.

[91] James Q. Wilson, *Varieties of Police Behavior* (Cambridge, Mass.: Harvard University Press, 1968).

[92] Ibid., pp. 16–17.

[93] Ibid., pp. 140–277.

order. If order cannot be restored, or respect for authority elicited in any other way, an arrest is appropriate.[94]

Thus, arrest is appropriate only when order cannot be restored in any other fashion. Police departments operating in a watchman style utilize extralegal factors in their decision making more so than in the other style departments. The behavior of juveniles, blacks, and other groups will be judged not solely on the offense, but by criteria suggested by the standards of the membership group of the offender or offensive person. Watchman-style police departments will deal with juvenile offenders informally more than will the other types of departments, by taking the juveniles home or by sending them on their way without sending them to court. Characteristic of these departments was that officers were "locally recruited, paid low salaries, expected to have second jobs, given the very minimum in initial training and not rewarded for having or getting higher education."[95]

Departments in which officers were encouraged to deal with order maintenance situations as though they were law-enforcement situations were referred to as legalistic-style departments.

Whenever he (the officer) acts on his own initiative or to the extent he can influence the outcome of disorderly situations in which he acts on the initiative of the citizen, the patrolman is expected to take a law enforcement view of his role.[96]

Obviously, such departments would be likely to have a higher arrest rate, and since arrest is the appropriate decision for the officer, arrest rates for whites are close to that of blacks, whereas in watchman-style departments the police may display more deference to one race than to another when deciding to arrest. Wilson suggested that police departments in Oakland, California; Highland Park, Illinois; and Syracuse, New York were legalistic in style.

The third style of police enforcement style represents a moderate position between watchman style and legalistic style and is referred to as the service style. In this style, the police are less likely to treat a situation as law enforcement in nature than are the legalistic departments, but service departments are more serious about legal violations and consequently more prone to make arrest decisions than are watchman-style departments. Examples of service-style departments were found in Brighton, New York, and in the Nassau County Police Department.

94 Ibid., p. 142.
95 Ibid., p. 151.
96 Ibid., p. 172.

Wilson emphasizes that the style of policing a community receives reflects very strongly the political climate of that community. Communities having a strongly partisan political environment, such as Albany, with its Democratic machine, tended to be watchman in style. Promotion and entrance to the police department are controlled by the party. Service-style departments, on the other hand, seem to exist in communities in which local government tends to rest with local business and community leaders who demand service sensitivity to local class and status in police administration. Legalistic departments are characterized by the appointment of chiefs "strongly committed to 'police professionalism,'"[97] and are frequently found in cities that have recently undergone a transition to "reform" government in which cleaning up police corruption was an election issue. Hence, legalistic emphasis on "professionalism" is supported by political leaders who have been called in to provide professionalism to city government.

Local police agencies like those studied by Wilson manifest wide ranges in their enforcement patterns and maintenance of public order.[98] Furthermore, the variability of policing patterns reflects the discretion given to both the police department and the individual officer on the beat when dealing with less serious offenses.

In the book, *Target Blue,* Robert Daley indicates that Patrick Murphy, the former commissioner of the New York City Police Department attempted to curtail illegal payoffs to the police by issuing orders to stop enforcement of the gambling laws.[99] Even though gambling was stilll illegal behavior, the commissioner used his discretionary power to curtail its enforcement. Murphy's use of his discretion to stop gambling enforcement is peculiar because it involves "total nonenforcement." Normally, discretion involves decisions to enforce the law to a partial extent. Joseph Goldstein notes three situations in which officers typically decide not to invoke the criminal law:

(1) not to enforce the narcotics laws against certain violators who inform against other 'more serious' violators; (2) not to enforce the felonious assault laws against an assailant whose victim does not sign a complaint; and (3) not to enforce gambling laws against persons engaged in the numbers racket, but instead, to harass them.[100]

[97] Ibid., p. 259.

[98] Ibid., p. 259. See also "The Police on Skid Row: A Study of Peace-Keeping," *American Sociological Review, 32* (October 1967), 699–715.

[99] Robert Daley, *Target Blue* (New York: Delacorte Press, 1971).

[100] Joseph Goldstein, "Police Discretion Not to Invoke the Criminal Process: Low-Visibility Decisions in the Administration of Justice," *Yale Law Journal, 69* (March 1960), 546.

In most cases, assuming the officer has sufficient evidence, the police would arrest for the offenses mentioned by Goldstein; however, in particular situations, the officer (perhaps as an extension of department policy) may decide not to arrest.

CONTEMPORARY FORMS OF POLICE

Amendment X to the Constitution of the United States states:

The powers not delegated to the United States by the Constitution, nor prohibited by it to the states, are reserved to the states respectively, or to the people.

One of the significant responsibilities not delegated to the federal government by the Constitution was the power to develop and enforce criminal laws. Consequently, each state developed its own system of laws (although based on the English Common Law) and its own criminal justice machinery. Moreover, in keeping with the English tradition of police, within each state, the administration of the policing system was delegated to the local community. Thus, historically, we have had a decentralized system of policing.

The separation of state and federal government is well illustrated in the case of the assassination of President John F. Kennedy in 1963. Protection of the president is the responsibility of the Secret Service of the Treasury Department, yet since it was not a federal offense at that time to kill the president, it was incumbent upon the Dallas Police Department, within whose jurisdiction the crime was committed, to conduct the investigation into the assassination. Murder is a state offense, and thus investigation of murder, even of the president, was a state or local responsibility. In order to describe more clearly the delineation of jurisdictional responsibilities of the various law-enforcement agencies, we will individually describe (1) local police, consisting of township and municipal agencies, (2) county police (generally the sheriff's department), (3) state police, and finally (4) federal policing agencies.

In describing the various police organizations we begin with local agencies because they provide the basic enforcement responsibilities for state and local laws. Federal and state enforcement agencies account for less than 1 percent of the law-enforcement agencies in the United States. At the local level there are approximately 40,000 police agencies, but most of these (about 80 percent) contain less than five officers.[101] Since it

---

[101] Alvin W. Cohn, *Crime and Justice Administration* (Philadelphia: Lippincott, 1976), p. 218.

requires five officers to provide 24-hour, 7-day-a-week coverage, many local jurisdictions do not provide their own round-the-clock coverage. Such departments may obtain full coverage through agreements with the state police or by contracting with other local agencies.

It is to the local police agencies that the basic functions of policing fall. State and federal police usually do not have legal jurisdiction to become involved in local criminal matters, and are not available to respond to requests for assistance in situations such as barroom disturbances, delivering babies, or any other activities frequently carried out by local police officers. The importance of local police agencies is well summarized by Thomas Adams:

> The entire police and policing picture centers around the city or township police department. They are charged with crime prevention and repression, traffic law enforcement, protective patrol services, arbitration in neighborhood and family disputes, apprehension and arrest (or citation or warning) of criminal law violators, and recovery of stolen property.[102]

These various police activities are typically couched under the rubric of: (1) maintenance of order, (2) law enforcement, and (3) provision of general services. For example, in the above statement by Adams, "arbitration in neighborhood and family disputes" falls into order-maintenance activities, whereas "apprehension of criminal law violators" is a law-enforcement function. Adams fails to note that the police also assist motorists with disabled cars, give directions, and perform numerous other activities falling under the provision of general-services category.[103]

Structure of Municipal Police Agencies

The structure of the municipal police department varies considerably depending on the size of the community, which, in turn, largely determines the size of the department. As communities increase in size, the complexity of the law-enforcement tasks increase to the point that greater and greater specialization of function results. In small departments the patrol division is the only division in the department. Figure 3-1 presents the organizational structure for a large police department that is organized to carry out the wide range of responsibilities of a police agency. Moreover, within the police agency, the personnel are ranked along military lines to demarcate their formal authority in the organization. Accord-

---

[102] Thomas F. Adams, *Law Enforcement* (Englewood Cliffs, N.J.: Prentice-Hall, 1973), pp. 72–73.

[103] George P. McManus, "What Does a Policeman Do?" in Alvin W. Cohen and Emilio C. Viano, eds., *Police Community Relations: Images, Roles, and Realities* (Philadelphia: Lippincott, 1976), pp. 131–162.

Figure 3-1.   A Well-Organized Municipal Police Department

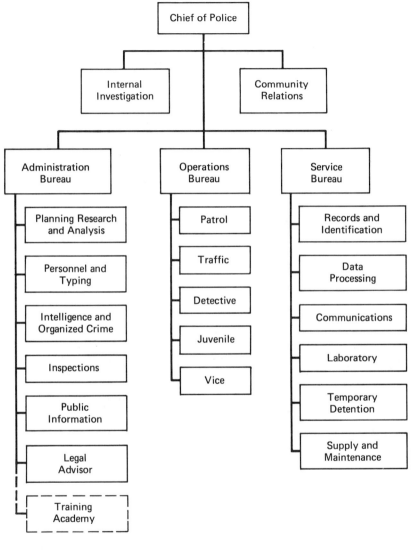

ing to George T. Felkenes, most commonly the chain of command in a municipal agency is as follows:

Chief of police
Deputy chiefs of police
Captains of police
Lieutenants of police

Sergeants of police

Patrolmen

Civilian employees

Special officers—includes jailers, custodial officers, matrons, vehicle inspectors, identification officers, and so forth[104]

Looking at Figure 3-1, we can identify the responsibilities of each of these functionaries in the department. For example, a deputy chief of police would be in command of each of the Administrative, Operations, and Service bureaus. The deputy chiefs are normally appointed by the chief (usually from men within the department) subject to the approval of the mayor of the city.

The captains are located in the organizational structure at the head of particular units of the department such as patrol, traffic, data processing, and inspections. In keeping with the military style of organization, captains are responsible to the deputy chief at the head of their respective bureaus. Below the captains in the chain of command are the lieutenants, who command particular police units or shifts. Felkenes describes this part of the organization:

> The captain of patrol would have a lieutenant in command of each shift; the captain in charge of intelligence and organized crime would have a lieutenant in charge of the detail on loan sharking, organized crime, and so on; and the captain in charge of vice might have a lieutenant in charge of the gambling, prostitution and illegal whiskey details.[105]

Sergeants are the operational supervisors who directly supervise personnel performing activities at the field level such as patrolmen. For example, the patrolmen on traffic detail are responsible directly to a sergeant, and normally receive their instructions prior to going into the field from the sergeant.

The quasi-military structure normally used as the format for local police organizations as well as for other police organizations has certain advantages. Officers know the authority structure, the rules are normally well specified, and as long as the officer can live up to the internal standards of the agency, he can expect good job security. However, as we will note in Chapter Nine, the formalistic command structure makes it more difficult for police officers to develop a definition of themselves as professionals, or to handle the discretion allotted them in a manner consistent with professional rather than military organizational structure. Professionalization necessitates self-leadership; military organizations

---

[104] George T. Felkenes, *The Criminal Justice System* (Englewood Cliffs, N.J.: Prentice-Hall, 1973), p. 20.

[105] Ibid., p. 21.

necessitate that people be led. Thus, there is an inherent contradiction between police organization and professionalism, or between police administration and the type of work that most police officers are expected to do.

The structure of the municipal agency has traditionally included such basic structural components as: (1) a patrol division, (2) a traffic division, and (3) a detective division. Less typically, the structure will include such an elaborate organizational setup as that represented in Figure 3-1. As can be seen from this figure, larger, more well-structured police departments may include administrative units such as planning, research and analysis, personnel, intelligence, legal advisors, and air inspections units. In the operations unit, optional units include tactical, juvenile, and vice units. Similarly, the service bureau may or may not contain speciality units like data processing, crime laboratory, and a communications unit. This discussion will not focus on the units defined as "optional" but will rather discuss the patrol, traffic, and detective units, which are common in all but the smallest police departments.

With the advent of more innovative command structures, the organizational structure illustrated in Figure 3-1 has changed considerably in many municipal agencies. The implementation of team policing might require an organizational structure considerably different than the specialized agency represented in this figure. For example, the team might have responsibility for all the functions in the Operations Bureau. Thus, the patrol, traffic, detective, juvenile, and vice units would often be eliminated in a particular sector where the team concept is implemented.

County Policing

The sheriff's office has been the major law-enforcement organization at the county level. Earlier in the history of our country, the sheriff's office was the major law-enforcement office. However, as society has become increasingly urbanized, the areas of the county that are unincorporated have decreased considerably, thereby diminishing the area for which the sheriff's office is the law-enforcement agency. When there is both a sheriff's department and a municipality with its own law-enforcement agency in one jurisdiction, the sheriff's office usually confines its patrolling to the unincorporated sections of the county.

The responsibilities of the sheriff's department involve providing baliff duties within the county courts and enforcing all lawful orders and directions of the courts.[106] The sheriff also conducts certain civil duties of the court, such as serving writs of the court, carrying out the sale of confiscated and unclaimed property, and certifying juror lists for the court. One other responsibility that the sheriff's office normally carries out is the

---

[106] Ibid., p. 56.

maintenance of the local jail facilities. Since jails serve to detain those awaiting trial and, in most cases, to incarcerate those serving sentences of one year or less, the sheriff must also perform certain correctional duties as well as law-enforcement duties. Consequently, the sheriff's role is one of the more complex and heterogeneous jobs in the criminal justice system.

In most counties in the United States, the sheriff is elected for two-, three- or four-year terms. The income to the position is usually a combination of a base salary plus fees for serving court orders and managing the county jail. For example, the sheriff may receive for each prisoner held in the county jail, a daily fee of $4, from which he has to pay for food for the inmate. If the sheriff can feed the prisoner on $3 a day, then he earns $1 a day per prisoner. Obviously, this may spur the sheriff to be miserly in his provision of jail services.

In any system in which the law-enforcement official is elected in the partisan political process, party control of the agency of justice function may result. Objective and fair law enforcement is an unlikely outgrowth of such a system. Furthermore, basing salary in part upon how cheaply an official can feed prisoners raises the possibility of mistreatment of the prisoners for the profit of the sheriff.

One rather rare form of county-level police agency is the county police department. Although in the traditional county policing system there is a county sheriff's office and then city or municipal agencies, in counties with police departments such as the Nassau County Police Department there is normally only one police agency, and it has total responsibility for enforcing the laws over the whole county.

Statewide Organizations of Police Services

There are numerous policing agencies at the state level. In this discussion we will focus on the state police and on the various forms that this organization takes. It is common for states to have special enforcement agencies such as a narcotics enforcement unit and an enforcement agency attached to the state department of justice. The major enforcement arm of the state is typically known as the state police or highway patrol.

In terms of responsibilities, there are significant differences between state police (such as in Pennsylvania) and the highway patrol department (such as in California). The highway patrol department is basically a traffic control agency for the state highways on which local sheriff and municipal agenies do not have traffic maintenance responsibilities. In contrast, state police agencies have broader enforcement responsibilities than is the case for the highway patrol. State police departments usually have statewide law-enforcement responsibilities as well as the traffic-enforcement responsibilities. Usually, the law-enforcement role by mutual agreement is limited to areas where no local enforcement agency is present, or during those times of the day when local enforcement is not available. Presently, 26 states have highway patrols and 23 have state police. However, there is a tendency for states to move in the general direction of broadening police powers at the state level to state police-type duties.[107]

The state agencies (both state police and highway patrols) have developed in this century for a variety of reasons, among which are: (1) increasing need for agencies with broader jurisdictions than municipal or county level organizations, to cope with mobility of criminals; (2) inability of local law-enforcement agencies to provide full police coverage (remember that about 80 percent of the law-enforcement agencies at the local level are five men or less); and (3) reluctance of law-enforcement agencies to enforce the law when they encounter severe political or community pressure.[108] Therefore, state-level agencies frequently fill in when no coverage is provided at the local level, and provide technical assistance such as forensic laboratories for processing evidence for local agencies. Additionally, state police agencies frequently maintain information assistance, such as central stolen-vehicle listings, which are available to local law enforcement officials.

ADVANTAGES AND DISADVANTAGES OF STATE POLICE. There is considerable conflict focused on the trend toward centralizing greater enforcement powers at the state level. Perhaps the basic contention centers around change in locus of enforcement power, because granting greater enforcement responsibilities to the state police usually results in local agencies relinquishing some of their authority. Arguments in favor of centralizing greater authority in the state police normally underscore the need for greater uniformity of enforcement by officers who are not enmeshed in the local community and, thus, are not pressured into overlooking offenses by the privileged and are not prone to clamp down on those in less advantageous positions. Further advantages enumerated for state policing are a strong budget base, higher salaries, better training, and greater opportunities for professional development.

Adversaries of state police point out that state police have greater social and physical distance from the public. Consequently, it is argued that the state police do not understand the particularities of the needs and desires of the local community, and thus would not be responsive to the local conditions. Furthermore, the state police, even though they are deployed throughout the state, have not normally been able to respond quickly to calls for assistance. Whereas municipal police attempt to re-

---

[107] Ibid., pp. 39–40.
[108] Ibid., pp. 38–51.

spond to emergency calls within three to four minutes, state police are usually deployed so that a 15-minute response is a quick one.

National Level

At the national level, a number of federal departments have various law-enforcement or regulatory responsibiltiies. In most cases, these police agencies enforce various bureaucratic regulations created by the federal government. They are not given power to enforce various state statutes, including robbery, burglary, murder, or other offenses most commonly thought of when we use the term *criminal*. Only when the commission of such offenses involves the violation of certain federal regulations as well, is a federal enforcement agency allowed to enter the case. For example, the F.B.I. has jurisdiction in cases involving assassinating federal officials, bank robbery (for federally insured banks), and kidnapping in which the victim may be moved across state lines.

In the Joseph Yablonsky murder case, the Federal Bureau of Investigation became involved in a murder case, which would normally be a state investigation, because Yablonsky was an office holder in a national labor union. As it happens, the federal government has no law against murder (unless it concerns the assassination of a federal official). Therefore, the federal government would not be able to prosecute the murder of Yablonsky, although they (the federal government) could federally prosecute for offenses such as violation of the civil rights of the victim (and murder would certainly violate the victim's civil rights). Or, the federal officials could turn over evidence bearing on the homicide to state officials.

DEPARTMENT OF JUSTICE.   The Federal Bureau of Investigation (F.B.I.) is located within the Department of Justice and is the most well-known federal enforcement agency. The responsibilities of the F.B.I. include investigation of all violations of federal laws except those explicitly delegated to other federal agencies. Among those offenses coming within the investigatory powers of the F.B.I. are auto theft across state lines, interstate transportation of stolen goods, other crimes involving interstate transportation, robbery or theft from agencies whose funds are federally insured, and crimes on government property and Indian reservations. The authority of the F.B.I. also extends to the internal security of the United States, including surveillance of activities by spies and subversive groups.

The activities of the F.B.I. are not limited to law enforcement. The F.B.I. also provides assistance to local law-enforcement agencies through training of local officers, maintaining a crime laboratory that is available to local agencies, and maintaining the central clearing house for fingerprint and arrest files. Furthermore, the F.B.I. collects crime statistics from local agencies, compiles the statistics, and then disseminates them in the *Uniform Crime Reports*. The *Uniform Crime Reports* provide local, state, and national information on reported criminality.

Other agencies located within the Department of Justice are the Immigration and Naturalization Service, which has jurisdiction over immigration and naturalization laws, including the deportation of undesirable aliens, and the Drug Enforcement Agency, which is entrusted with the enforcement of the registration provisions of federal drug laws. Also included within the Justice Department is the Bureau of Prisons, Border Patrol, and United States Marshals.

DEPARTMENT OF THE TREASURY.   The Department of the Treasury includes such well-known enforcement and regulatory agencies as Alcohol, Tobacco, and Firearms (A.T.F.); Bureau of Customs; Internal Revenue Service; and the Secret Service. In carrying out their duties, the Secret Service guards the president and presidential candidates and investigates counterfeiting activities; the A.T.F. investigates illegal transportation and sale of firearms and illegal distilleries; and the I.R.S., of course, investigates violations of federal income tax laws.

Urban versus Rural Policing

Historically, societies have progressed from small rural communities to industrialized, bureaucratized conurbations. Society in the United States today is perhaps the most technologically advanced in the world. One impact of technology has been the concentration of production in centralized factories. Around these factories congregate the workers, and service and distribution networks span out from the centers of production. Vast megapolitan networks are now established on both the east and west coasts and on the Great Lakes. Urbanization has provided increased opportunity for criminal activity in part at least because of the increased population upon which to prey, and the increased social distance between members of the urban community. Urban settings are also more complex in culture, and therefore there are greater conflicts between local values and the criminal law than is the case in more homogenous settings. Consequently the academic study of crime has focused on metropolitan crime and metropolitan police systems.

It is interesting to consider, however, that in states such as Pennsylvania, New York, Illinois, and California that are noted for their urban centers, a sizeable proportion of the state population lives not in cities but in small, rural, or rural-oriented communities. In addition, many states such as Idaho, Mississippi, Vermont, South Dakota, and numerous others do not possess large metropolitan centers. Certainly, law enforcement is a significant factor in these areas.

The 1960s were a time when a national commission was established to study crime in America, followed by a commission investigating the civil disorders of the last half of the sixties, and by the Walker report on the "Chicago Police Riot" at the 1968 National Democratic Convention.[109] Each of these was a response to a national "crisis" and laid the groundwork for change in the criminal justice system and for the police in particular. Heretofore, the police had been subject to procedural scrutiny by the courts, but in terms of their role within the criminal justice system and within the community, the police had previously been largely ignored. However, increasing crime rates and the role of the police in civil disorders during the late sixties focused attention on the quality of policing in America.

In this section we shall briefly discuss a few of the more pressing issues in policing today. We have identified recruitment and hiring, new models of police organization, training (both recruitment and upgrading), community relations, and policing the police as the areas in which we would like to review some current trends. In closing this chapter these trends will be dovetailed with the controversial and complex issue of police professionalism.

Recruitment and Hiring

Debate focuses on whether the individual creates and adapts the police role to himself, or whether the police role molds the individual into a policeofficer. If the police role dominates the individual officer to the extent that his values, social relationships, and behaviors are dictated by the fact that he is a policeofficer, then we would argue that attempts to change the department by recruiting and hiring are unlikely to be successful. Arthur Niederhoffer, for example, takes the view that policeofficers are extremely cynical, and that this cynicism emerges as a consequence of socialization while on the police force, not prior to entering police work.[110] Neither Neiderhoffer, nor any other exponents of the socialization view, however, argue that the type of person recruited has no impact on police performance. Rather they believe that on-the-job experience influences police behavior and attitudes more than prior experiences. In contrast, the National Advisory Commission on Standards and Goals argues as follows:

---

[109] National Commission on the Causes and Prevention of Violence, *Rights in Conflict* (New York: Bantam Books, 1968).

[110] Arthur Niederhoffer, *Behind the Shield* (Garden City, N.Y.: Anchor Books, 1967).

The initial selection process is particularly important because entry into the police service traditionally begins at the lowest level. The quality of personnel selected for the police service determines the character of police performance and ultimately the quality of police leadership. Too frequently the people who possess the necessary qualities do not apply for the job on their own.[111]

The essence of any discussion is suggested by the commission's phrase: "the people who possess the necessary skills." What are the necessary skills? There is some controversy over whether the police role is essentially law enforcement or social service in nature. The literature on the police often focuses on the police officer's enforcement of law, and gives only minimal attention to noncrime fighting activities. One study discovered that of over 700,000 calls to the police, almost 70 percent were noncrime related.[112] If it is accepted, as traditionally has been done, that the police are basically crime fighters, and that fighting crime requires the imposition of physical authority, then it is easy to understand the "common sense" belief that the police job is a male job, and, in particular, a job for men of imposing stature. This results in two perspectives that are currently being challenged. One, it defines the job in physical terms, thus diminishing the interest in college-educated individuals whose training focuses on philosophical issues. Second, it eliminates the likelihood that many women would be thought of as capable of carrying out the full line of police duties. Both the role of the college-educated officer and women in policing are worthy issues of further discussion, and it is to them that we will now turn our attention.

College Education and the Police

In 1967 the President's Commission on Law Enforcement and Administration of Justice made the following recommendation.

The ultimate aim of all police departments should be that all personnel with enforcement powers have baccalaureate degrees.[113]

Shortly thereafter, universities and colleges across the country benefited from federal expenditures on college education for current and potential police officers and other criminal justice personnel. By 1972–1973, 505

[111] The National Advisory Commission on Standards and Goals, *Police* (Washington, D.C.: Government Printing Office, 1973), p. 320.

[112] Franklin G. Ashburn, "Changing the Rhetoric of 'Professionalism,'" in *Innovation in Law Enforcement* (Washington, D.C.: Government Printing Office, 1973), pp. 6–7.

[113] President's Commission on Law Enforcement and Administration of Justice, *Task Force Report: The Police*, p. 107.

associate degree programs and 211 baccalaureate programs in law enforcement and criminal justice were available. Many of these were partly supported by the Law Enforcement Assistance Administration (LEAA) funds to hire faculty, build buildings, and generally assist the development of criminal justice programs. But another stimulant for colleges to provide criminal justice education was the Law Enforcement Educational Program (LEEP), which provides in-service personnel with financial aid to assist them in attaining a college education.

With this extensive expenditure of money, it may be assumed that a college education must have some positive impact on a police officer. But does it? Does the fact that an individual has taken philosophy, sociology, psychology, mathematics, etc. in college make him a better police officer? Solomon Gross indicates that he believes the purpose of higher education is:

> . . . to clothe them (the police) in a broad moral and ethical coat with a capacity for flexibility and breadth to enable them to cope with the diversity and rapid change that characterizes today's society.[114]

There has been little research done on whether a college education actually fulfills these goals. Alexander Smith, Bernard Locke, and William Walker in 1968 reported that when they compared college and noncollege police officers they found that the college-educated police officer was less authoritarian than the noncollege policeofficer.[115] Other studies have found that higher-educated officers have fewer incidents of misconduct, and fewer complaints by civilians.[116]

The utility of college education is not without its detractors. One potential concern about an influx of college-educated officers is that the senior, noncollege educated officers may develop hostility towards the new standards and the new officers.[117] The consequence of this as well as the result of boring routine police work may create a second problem, job dissatisfaction among the college-educated officers. There are some indications that college-educated officers are more likely to move on to other jobs, thus negating the investment in their training, and requiring that the training process be initiated once again. This is supported by Ruth Levy's findings that length of service decreased as groups increased in education.

[114] Solomon Gross, "Higher Education and Police: Is There a Need for a Closer Look?" in *Journal of Police Science and Administration, 1,* No. 4 (1973), 479.

[115] Alexander Smith, Bernard Locke, and William Walker, "Authoritarianism in Police College Students and Non-Police College Students," *Journal of Criminal Law, Criminology and Police Science, 59* (1968), 440–443.

[116] Cynthia L. Sparling, "The Use of Education Standards as Selection Criteria in Police Agencies: A Review," in *Journal of Police Science and Administration, 3,* No. 3 (1975), 332–335.

[117] Ibid., p. 333.

A third argument suggests that college-educated officers are not "street wise." This argument suggests that college-educated individuals have been isolated from the criminal environment and are thus not familiar with the types of people and neighborhoods in which an officer must operate. As the results of the evaluations to date would indicate, the college-educated officer does not seem to be the liability that this argument would suggest, although there has been no evaluation of the social environment of nurturance on the individual's performance as a police officer.

Women in Policing

As mentioned earlier, the police job has traditionally been defined as a male job, and thus women, with few exceptions, were excluded from participating in patrol and other dangerous activities. In defining the police job as a job for physically tough individuals, police departments created tests of physical agility and physical size that for all intents and purposes eliminated the likelihood of many women going into police work. Significant challenges are being made to the appropriateness of these selection criteria. As many women have questioned: If the physical criteria for acceptance into police work are so crucial, why is it that once an individual becomes a police officer, he is allowed to deteriorate in height to weight ratio and in physical abilities? For example, police agencies normally have a weight range that an individual must fall within in order to be eligible. The Pennsylvania State Police have a rather typical standard that a male six-feet tall must be between 155 and 175 pounds.

A more significant hurdle to the recruitment of women has been the physical agility and strength tests. A study of male and female performance on physical tests revealed that 11 percent of the males and 91 percent of the females were unable to pass the physical abilities part of the examination.[118] On one of the tests, the applicants were to surmount a six-foot fence without any assistance, and they were permitted 15 seconds in which to complete the test. Four percent of the males and 50 percent of the females failed the test. The issue that confronts the courts and police administrators is whether or not it is an essential ability for police officers to surmount a six-foot wall. If not, then it should not be an important selection criterion; if it is, then the officers should be expected to maintain that capability as long as they are performing duties for which such capability is important.

In 1970 the Supreme Court handed down the landmark case of *Griggs* v. *Duke Power Company*, 401 U.S. 424 (1970), which held that employ-

---

[118] Richard C. Wilkie, Jr., "Job-Related Physical Tests for Patrol Officers," *The Police Chief* (May 1974), pp. 42–44.

ment selection criteria must be nondiscriminating, job-specific, and that those criteria must be validated. Furthermore, in 1972 the Equal Employment Opportunity Commission (EEOC) was given the authority to enforce Title VII of the Civil Rights Act of 1964 in terms of employment discrimination against women.[119] Under Title VII, all jobs must be available to both males and females unless sex "is a bona fide occupational qualification necessary to the normal operation of that particular business or enterprise."

Fortunately, because of research conducted during the last few years, we are in a better position to assess whether certain police jobs are too physically demanding for a woman to perform. The most detailed study of women in patrol work (the most physically demanding role) was conducted by the Police Foundation in Washington, D.C.[120] Beginning in 1972 women were assigned to patrol in Washington. In the experiment, 86 women were assigned patrol duties and, as a control group, they were compared with 86 men who entered the department at the same time as the women.

Performance comparisons between the men and women led the researchers to conclude that the experiment supports the contention that "sex is not a bona fide occupational qualification for doing police patrol work."[121] In general, there were small differences between men's and women's performances. Exceptions to this were that women made fewer arrests and gave fewer traffic citations; men were more likely to engage in unbecoming conduct; and women were more likely to be injured, but were no more likely to be absent from work than men because of injuries. There were no differences between men and women officers in handling angry or violent citizens, resignations, arrests resulting in convictions, calls for back-up or assistance, and number of driving accidents. Interestingly, the Washington, D.C. study also performed a survey of police officials and rank-and-file officers' attitudes toward women patrols. Since the performance levels between men and women officers indicated basically no differences, we might expect that patrolmen would rate the women officers equal with men. However, the responses indicated that patrolmen did not believe that patrolwomen were as capable as patrolmen, and their attitudes did not improve over the duration of the study. Police officials, although being critical of patrolwomen's ability to handle violent situations or disorderly males, did have a more positive attitude toward patrolwomen after one year.[122]

[119] The National Advisory Commission on Standards and Goals, *Police*, p. 343.

[120] Peter B. Bloch and Deborah Anderson, *Policewomen on Patrol: Final Report* (Washington, D.C.: The Police Foundation, 1974).

[121] Ibid., p. 3.

[122] For an overview of the findings, see Ibid., pp. 5–7.

Evaluations by independent observers who rode along in the squad cars, and by interviews assessing citizen satisfaction, rated policewomen and policemen as equals. The citizen interviews are especially revealing because in these interviews it was found that citizens were not only satisfied with the service received from the patrolwomen, but they felt just as safe when a patrolwoman responded as when a patrolman responded.

In spite of negative feelings from fellow officers and officials, it is clear that women are capable of carrying out patrol functions. In addition to the Washington, D.C. study, one performed in suburban St. Louis comparing women and men working alone in squad cars found that women were as effective as men.[123] This should only be surprising to those who continue to define the police job in unrealistic "cops and robbers" terms. Moreover, even within the infrequent violent confrontations, women may act as a defusing mechanism, whereas a male officer may stimulate violence because of the competition not to "lose" face to another male. Another "common sense" belief is that taller men are more capable of deterring violence because of their imposing stature. Cheryl Swanson and Charles Hale, in studying height and assaults on the police, found no evidence to substantiate this belief. In fact, their findings indicated that taller officers were more likely to be the victim of multiple assaults.[124] This finding suggests that physical stature does not act as the deterrent to violence that so many believe it does. Louis Sherman, in reviewing research on women, suggests that: "women may be more effective than men in avoiding violence by defusing potentially violent situations."[125]

The Police Officer: An Organizational Man

The police officer operates as a middle man in a system over which he has minimal control. The legislature creates the laws he is to enforce; the courts and prosecutor decide whether and how much punishment is to be administered, and whether the officer conducted himself in a procedurally legitimate manner in making the arrest; and the community often expresses discontent and distrust of police actions. A recent study of stress among police officers found that over 50 percent of the respondents indicated that the courts were a serious source of stress. Specifically, they felt that the court's leniency with offenders and lack of concern for policemen in scheduling their court appearance were the major sources of

[123] Lewis J. Sherman, "An Evaluation of Policewomen on Patrol in a Suburban Police Department," *Journal of Police Science and Administration*, 3, No. 4 (1975), 434–438.

[124] Cheryl Swanson and Charles Hale, "A Question of Height Revisited: Assaults on Police," in *Journal of Police Science and Administration*, 3, No. 2 (1975).

[125] Sherman, "An Evaluation of Policewomen."

stress.[126] Another major source of perceived stress was the police relations with the community. Officers indicated that public apathy and the public's negative attitudes were stress-producing aspects of the police job.[127]

If external relations are a problem, then the leadership and management provided by the administrators of the organization should provide the support necessary to overcome the stress provoked from outside. Such support does not appear to be forthcoming. In one study, the officers indicated that the administration of their department only contributed to their difficulties because the administrators failed to utilize the patrolmen's talents or to support them against outside criticism.[128] Other studies suggest that administrative pressures on officers occur because of reliance on negative sanctions,[129] attempts to organize officers into specializations and organizational military hierarchies,[130] and emphasis on increasing professionalism (by definition this emphasis implies the incompetence of many current officers) through college education and increased training.[131] Because of the increasing concern about police alienation, many feel that perhaps the most significant issue in contemporary policing is the changing styles of management. The most noteworthy trend is a move away from the traditional bureaucratic organization with its specialization of job function and military style of chain of command, which restricted participation of line officers in the decision-making process. Team policing is one strategy to break down the traditional bureaucratic structure (see Figure 3-1).

Team Policing

Team policing attempts to increase the individual officer's responsibilities by enlarging the police job by having officers take full responsibility for the policing of a particular sector of the city. Team policing is not a recent innovation. Aberdeen, Scotland, in the mid-1940s started a team policing program "to counteract the low morale and boredom of single

[126] William B. Kroes, Bruce L. Margolis, and Joseph J. Hurrell, "Job Stress in Policemen," in *Journal of Police Science and Administration, 2,* No. 2 (June 1974), 145–155.

[127] Ibid., p. 147.

[128] Ibid., pp. 148–149.

[129] See for example, Niederhoffer, *Behind the Shield,* p. 189; and Tom Denyer, Robert Callender, and Dennis L. Thompson, "The Policeman as Alienated Laborer," *Journal of Police Science and Administration, 3,* No. 3 (September 1975), 251.

[130] Georgette Bennett Sandler and Ellen Mintz, "Police Organizations: Their Changing Internal and External Relationships," in *Journal of Police Science and Administration, 2,* No. 4 (December 1974), 458–463.

[131] Niederhoffer, *Behind the Shield.*

officers patrolling quiet streets."[132] Although the team policing concept was adopted by a few small cities in the United States by the early 1960s, it was not until after its recommendation by the President's Commission on Law Enforcement in 1967 that experimentation with it became extensive. Currently cities such as Holyoke, Detroit, New York City, Los Angeles, and Cincinnati have tried team policing with various degrees of success. But prior to examining what we know to date concerning the success or lack thereof, we shall describe generally how team policing functions.

Team policing has been heralded as a possible mechanism through which officers can participate more actively in what has traditionally been decision-making authority reserved to supervisory personnel. Additionally, it has been hoped that by giving this authority to patrolmen, team policing will raise the morale of the officers and increase the respect that the community has toward the police. Although the structure of team policing varies considerably among the cities that have adopted it, there are certain goals that most team policing projects attempt to achieve. One goal of team policing programs is *unity of supervision*.[133] Unity of supervision in team policing means that one supervisor has responsibility in a particular area at all times. Thus, the officer who is on a particular team is commanded by only one supervisor, whereas under more typical command situations there is constant changing of supervisors for a particular area with each shift.

A second goal of team policing is to decentralize certain operational decisions by placing the responsibility for these decisions in the hands of the team.[134] This is commonly referred to as *participative management.* Within this management form, officers who have usually not been given any input into decisions such as style of uniform or the manner in which they want to provide protection to the community are given the opportunity to participate in the decision-making process. This particular aspect of team policing focuses on permitting those officers working a particular area and who should know the policing needs of that area best to make significant decisions about the manner of policing the area. An additional benefit of this participation in decision making might be increased morale of the officers because of the increased self-respect gained from input into the management process. The intent of team policing is obviously to manage people so that they will be more productive workers.

Job enlargement is a third characteristic of team policing. Team policing attempts to redefine police roles that are often specialized by such classifications as "detective" and "patrolman" and to unify them in a

---

[132] Lawrence Sherman, Catherine Milton, and Thomas Kelley, *Team Policing* (Washington, D.C.: Police Foundation, 1973), p. xiii.

[133] Ibid., p. 5.

[134] Ibid., pp. 5–6.

"generalist-specialist" function. The generalist-specialist is an officer given responsibility and (hopefully) training to be capable of carrying out investigative duties from the initiation of the investigation to its disposition in court.[135] Under typical patrolman duties, a patrolman may be dispatched to the scene of a crime; however his role in the investigation of that offense terminates when a detective arrives on the scene. Under the team policing concept, the responding officer would conduct the investigation with the authority to call in specialists if needed. In order to illustrate more specifically how one department instituted team policing, we will describe the project implemented in one of the original team policing cities.

DAYTON'S TEAM POLICING.[136]   Dayton, Ohio, is a city with a population of approximately 250,000, but it has a metropolitan area of almost one million. Dayton's original team policing design included three basic goals: (1) to test the generalist-specialist police officer role; (2) to produce a more community-oriented police department; and (3) to move the traditional quasi-military police structure toward a "neighborhood-oriented professional model."[137]

In attempting to carry out the team policing project, the department planned to assign a team of 40 volunteer patrolmen, 4 sergeants, and a team leader to a particular district of Dayton. Although each officer would be a generalist-specialist, each member of the team would also have specialty training such as in working with youths, particular aspects of investigation, or crisis intervention.[138] Furthermore, specialists from the department could be called in at the discretion of one of the team members. Other planned aspects of the Dayton project were for each team member to live in with a family in the neighborhood in order to develop better understanding of community values and behaviors, to eliminate preventative patrol, and to permit greater discretion in working hours and uniform style.

Unfortunately, many of the planned aspects of the program were never accomplished. For example, team officers were able to live in with some members of the community, but not enough black families accepted police officers as live-in guests. Therefore, this aspect of the program was dropped. Moreover, although officers were given greater decision-making authority, the teams continued military rank and uniforms traditional for

[135] Robert Koverman, "Team Policing: An Alternative to Traditional Law Enforcement Techniques," in *Journal of Police Science and Administration*, 2, No. 2 (1974), 16.

[136] The following description is based on Sherman, Milton, and Kelley, *Team Policing*; and Koverman, "Team Policing."

[137] Sherman, Milton, and Kelley, *Team Policing*, p. 15.

[138] Ibid.

the rest of the department. Despite these problems, Dayton's team policing project was able to develop a police system more responsive to the community, and one in which the officer participated in a broadened generalist-specialist role.

Other departments have developed some form of team policing with various degrees of success. For example, New York City instituted such a program but was unable to maintain either the geographical stability or the generalist-specialist role so important to team policing.[139] In Detroit, another problem surfaced. Detroit started the Beat Commander Program in 1970 in which a sergeant was given the responsibility to schedule tours of duty, assign officers as "he" desired and in general run the police operations in one of Detroit's busiest areas. However, when a new commissioner was appointed, he did away with the program.[140] The failures of team policing projects do not seem to reflect problems with the conception, but rather with the difficulties of changing an organization that has a long tradition of operating as a quasi-military organization, and in which the police role is already clearly defined. Team policing requires extensive change, and change is often met with suspicion or even hostility. Team policing programs are experimenting with involving additional officers in the planning so that they will be able to contribute more to the planning and to understand better the rationales for the change. Certain cities such as Los Angeles and Holyoke were apparently more successful in overcoming resistance to change by their involving more officers from various levels of the organization in the planning process.[141]

Policing the Police

One of the crucial issues confronting not only law enforcement, but society as well, is the use of police power. Police power manifests itself most strongly through the policemen's privileged use of force to enforce the law. In this area, concern focuses on police abuse of their authority in terms of their use of force. The essence of the issue is how much force should an officer be permitted to use in order to carry out an arrest, or to obtain evidence or information. Consider, for example, whether or not it is appropriate for an officer to use deadly force in subduing a person thought to be an escaping felon. Should a different level of force be appropriate when the suspect is involved in murder than when involved in auto theft?

A second issue regarding police power centers on police corruption. The police are given the privilege of enforcing the law and thereby have

---

[139] Ibid., pp. 28–33.
[140] Ibid., pp. 23–27.
[141] Ibid., p. 64.

access to information that, when combined with their discretion, enables them to engage in corrupt activities. For example, if an officer stops a motorist for speeding, he may give a warning or a ticket. If the individual happens to offer $10 for the officer to forget it or to give only a written warning, the officer may accept the bribe if he legitimates it to himself. The officer's belief that he is underpaid, coupled with the belief that the offense was not very serious anyway or that the courts will not punish the offender even if he issues a citation, may be used by the officer as an excuse to legitimate acceptance of the bribe. Similarly, if an officer goes into a store that has just been burglarized and decides that no one will miss an electric toaster, in part because the owner will be able to receive compensation through insurance, then he may well pick up the toaster and put it in his trunk.

In any discussion of the problem of policing the police, it is important to consider the issue of control. The following sections will elaborate more thoroughly what police abuse and corruption are, and will explore ways in which various departments have attempted to control these problems.

POLICE ABUSE OF AUTHORITY. Abuse of authority may include the illegal search and seizure of evidence, the planting of evidence on an accused, the use of excessive physical force in making an arrest or obtaining information, or the verbal mistreatment of members of the public. A study conducted in the late 1960s for the President's Commission on Law Enforcement and Administration of Justice documented numerous cases of unnecessary and illegitimate use of violence by police officers.[142] During the seven weeks in which observers monitored police contact with citizens, 37 cases occurred in which force was used. The following are three examples of cases observed during this study.

The watch began rather routinely as the policemen cruised the district. Their first radio dispatch came at about 5:30 p.m. They were told to investigate two drunks in a cemetery. On arriving they found two white men "sleeping one off." Without questioning the men, the older policeman began to search one of them, ripping his shirt and hitting him in the groin with a nightstick. The younger policeman, as he searched the second, ripped away the seat of his trousers, exposing his buttocks. The policemen then prodded the men toward the cemetery fence and forced them to climb it, laughing at the plight of the drunk with the exposed buttocks. As the drunks went over the fence, one policeman shouted, "I ought to run you fuckers in." The other remarked to the observer, "Those assholes won't be back; a bunch of shitty winos." . . .
. . . [A]s the two [officers] were moving across the precinct shortly after 10 p.m., a white man and a woman in their 50's flagged them down. Since they were obviously "substantial" middle-class citizens of the

[142] President's Commission on Law Enforcement and Administration of Justice, *Task Force Report: The Police,* p. 182.

district, the policemen listened to their complaints that a Negro man was causing trouble inside the public-transport station from which they had just emerged. The woman said that he had sworn at her. The older policeman remarked, "What's a nigger doing up here? He should be down on Franklin Road." With that, they ran into the station and grabbed the Negro man who was inside. Without questioning him, they shoved him into a phone booth and began beating him with their fists and a flashlight. They also hit him in the groin. Then they dragged him out and kept him on his knees. He pleaded that he had just been released from a mental hospital that day and, begging not to be hit again, asked them to let him return to the hospital. One policeman said: "Don't you like us, nigger? I like to beat niggers and rip out their eyes." They took him outside to their patrol car. Then they decided to put him on a bus, telling him that he was returning to the hospital; they deliberately put him on a bus going in the opposite direction. Just before the Negro boarded the bus, he said, "You police just like to shoot and beat people." The first policeman replied, "Get moving, nigger, or I'll shoot you." The man was crying and bleeding as he was put on the bus. Leaving the scene, the younger policeman commented, "He won't be back." . . .

White officers responded to a man with a gun . . . and heard three shots fired. Then the white man with the gun got a drop on the officer— somehow they got the gun away and handcuffed him (gun was a 12 gauge 1905 musket). When they got him to the station garage, they kicked him all over, but the principal one was the officer who had been in danger when the man had the drop on him. He beat him as the others held him up. I got to the scene and the lockup man whistled for them to stop but they didn't. The Lieutenant arrived with everyone else and said there's going to be a beef on this one so cover it up and go find the empty shells. Someone call an ambulance (he needed it badly). Then the Lieutenant took complete control. They got the shells, got a complainant who said the three shots were an attempt to kill the officer, and he would sign a complaint, said he called an ambulance, etc. They wrote a cover for the incident. The officer who beat the man most was shaken by then but the others gave him support, telling him how brave he was and how wise he had been not to kill the guy at the scene, etc. They then set about to put all the stories in order and I was carefully notified of it in detail so I would have it straight. I had enough rapport with these officers that they talked about it even after. The man was in pretty bad shape when he got to the hospital.[143]

These observations document police brutality, but the importance of these observations perhaps lies in the fact that the officers performed these activities in front of outside observers.[144] It can only be assumed that the officers involved believed that their behavior was morally appropriate, and thus were not prone to conceal it from nonpolice observers. Any discussion of policing the police must concern itself with officers'

---

[143] Ibid.

[144] William Chambliss and Robert Seidman, *Law, Order, and Power* (Reading, Mass.: Addison-Wesley, 1971).

acceptance of the use of excessive violence. William Wesley's study in 1951 queried officers as to when they thought an officer was justified in "roughing a man up." Interestingly, 37 percent of the officers indicated that disrespect for the police warranted roughing up.[145] Legitimation for abusive conduct by officers may be due to lenient treatment of offenders by the courts. The police officers may believe it is not only appropriate, but necessary, that they punish the offender. Also, the courts, and the procedural restrictions that they place on the officers (see *Mapp* case discussed earlier), may serve as a possible legitimation of officers planting evidence (flaking) on an individual that they "know" is an offender in order to substantiate a conviction they have been unable to prove previously. This is particularly true of narcotics violations because of the ease of concealing and destroying narcotics, thus making it difficult to obtain legally admissible evidence.

POLICE CORRUPTION. The police are societies' "upholders of law," yet investigations of police officers in various metropolitan areas have invariably disclosed extensive corrupt activities on the part of police officers. The most famous of recent investigations of police corruption, the Knapp Commission in New York City, found corruption to be widespread.[146] In their investigation, the commission discovered that plainclothesmen collected regular payments biweekly or monthly "amounting to as much as $3,500 from each of the gambling establishments in the area."[147] The payments from all gambling places were then divided into equal shares each month (called "nut") for the officers. The "nut" in midtown Manhattan was normally about $300 to $400, whereas in Harlem it reached $1,500.

However, the police corruption uncovered by the Knapp Commission was not limited to gambling. Narcotics, prostitution, construction trade, parking and traffic enforcement, Sunday Blue Laws, and many other areas of enforcement became means whereby officers could take advantage of their position to obtain illegal payoffs. Police corruption in narcotics include: (1) retaining money and/or narcotics collected in a raid; (2) "flaking"—planting narcotics on an individual to build a case; (3) "padding"—adding narcotics to that found on a person to raise the seriousness of the offense; (4) exchanging narcotics for stolen goods; (5) "financing heroin transactions"; and numerous other abuses.[148]

In New York, police corruption even extended to the tow truck busi-

[145] William Wesley, *Violence and the Police* (Cambridge, Mass.: Massachusetts Institute of Technology Press, 1970).

[146] The Knapp Commission, *Report on Corruption* (New York: George Braziller, 1972).

[147] Ibid., p. 1.

[148] Ibid., pp. 91–92.

ness. Because automobile repair can be a lucrative business, and because the towing company that towed the car away usually got the contract to repair the auto, the tow truck companies enlisted police help both in making them (the tow company) aware that an accident had occurred and in "encouraging" the operator of the damaged car to have a particular tow truck remove his vehicle. For example, an officer may observe an accident, and before broadcasting it over the police radio, he would call a particular tow truck company so that no other company would be cognizant of the accident. For such service, the officer would receive $20 to $30. In one instance, a driver was refusing to sign a contract at the scene of the accident for repair of his vehicle. However, he quickly gave in and signed when the officer indicated that if he did not sign, he could be issued summonses for drunken driving and driving without a license.[149]

The May 6, 1974 issue of *Time* magazine reported that in Houston, Texas, nine officers were awaiting trial for various forms of corruption, including dealing in heroin. In Indianapolis, police corruption was uncovered in the enforcement areas of prostitution, narcotics, and stolen goods; and in Philadelphia, the Pennsylvania Crime Commission uncovered "systematic, wide-spread corruption at all levels."[150] Thus, police corruption is not solely a New York City phenomenon, and although the focus has been on major metropolitan areas, patterns of corruption are discovered from time to time in police agencies of all sizes.

FACTORS SUPPORTING POLICE ABUSE AND CORRUPTION. We have treated police abuse and corruption as somewhat separate phenomena, as is typical of the literature. However, police corruption and police abuse extensively overlap. Moreover, the impact that each has on the society that the police serve is similar. The toll of police corruption and police abuse is perhaps most noticeable in the diminished faith and respect that the public has toward the police. The ironical twist that those empowered to enforce the law make use of that power to abuse citizens and to "pad" their pocketbooks cannot but hurt the public perception of the police. In reality, the public that is most harmed by these police violations is the lower-class individual who is most likely to be the victim of both criminal and police violations. A democracy such as our own bases itself on the presumption that all men are equal before the law, and all men will be treated justly. A system that tolerates, and perhaps encourages, violations such as those previously described can lay small claim that it treats all fairly and equally.

Regardless of the inconsistency of these violations with our conception of justice, the criminal justice system has taken few steps to stop these

[149] Ibid., pp. 158–162.
[150] "Making Police Crime Unfashionable," *Time*, May 6, 1974.

violations from occurring. It has been widely discussed that police officers develop strong ties to one another. It has also been argued that these ties develop because the police believe the public neither trusts nor respects them, and because they work odd hours, thus reducing their opportunity and desire to interact with the public. The imact is to create a public service agency that is socially isolated from the public it serves and in which a strong allegiance develops among the officers. Part of this allegiance involves a code of secrecy and protection of offending officers and, in some cases, strong normative supports for engaging in corrupt and abusive behavior.[151]

Jonathan Rubenstein notes that not only does the informal system encourage and protect violations, but that many of the violations by police officers are a result of pressures from the department to make arrests of vice offenders, particularly of drug violators.[152] Because of the difficulty of obtaining legally admissible evidence in vice activities, the pressure from the department to make arrests encourages the officers to do such things as "flaking" or "padding" in order to make a bust. According to Rubenstein, only "the money hungry" would engage in illegal activities if it were not for the pressures in vice enforcement.

In summary, the social isolation of police officers and the concomitant development of strong ties with other officers indirectly can encourage violations by officers. Furthermore, the police are responsible, and bureaucratically pressured, to enforce the law which ironically encourages corruption and abuse by the officers concerned. The issue for contemporary police departments is how to rid themselves of this problem.

REDUCTION OF POLICE VIOLATIONS.   Perhaps the most popular reform measure centers on the professionalization of police forces. It can be argued that since police officers are given considerable discretion, it is next to impossible to set up an enforcement mechanism strong enough to act as a deterrent to officers engaging in activities such as those previously described. The police unit that is given the responsibility to enforce departmental rules, as well as state codes on violating officers, is variously known as the "internal affairs division" or "internal investigation division." However, the officers manning such units are often identified as "rats" or "stooges" and are not respected by their fellow officers. Therefore, the pressure on an internal affairs officer makes it almost impossible for him to carry out his assigned tasks.

In the conception of professionalism, internal affairs officers would not

---

[151] Ellwyn R. Stoddard, " 'The Informal Code' of Police Deviancy: A Group Approach to 'Blue-Coat Crime,' " in *Journal of Criminal Law, Criminology, and Police Science*, 59, No. 2 (1968), 201–213; and Knapp Commission, *Report on Corruption.*

[152] Jonathan Rubenstein, *City Police* (New York: Ballantine Books, 1973), p. 377.

be the main enforcement mechanism, but rather the identification of the officer with his profession would serve as the main control mechanism. Attempts to instill more professionalism, and thus more self-control, generally focus on recruiting officers with higher educational qualifications and on providing in-service training to officers in special professional emphasis areas such as crisis intervention, criminal investigation, and management strategies.

The development of professionalism is also encouraged through the development of an awareness among officers that their job is more than a law enforcement one. In fact, most police tasks are service in nature, and many areas of law enforcement such as intervention in family crises involves more social work abilities than law-enforcement abilities. The goal of emphasizing the service aspect of police work may provide the officer more positive contacts with citizens, thereby perhaps discouraging police misbehavior.[153]

However, not all attempts to eliminate or reduce police misbehavior have been internal mechanisms. There have been commissions such as the Knapp Commission, external to the police department. Additionally, some cities have flirted with the use of civilian review boards, which are intended to act as outside receivers and reviewers of complaints against the police. Few review boards exist in the United States because police agencies have actively opposed review boards, and the majority of the public has, upon occasion, been sympathetic to the police position, or at least, has remained apathetic to the establishment and maintenance of review boards. The most notable experience with civilian boards occurred in New York City, where the civilian review board lasted only six months before it was voted down in a public referendum.[154] Furthermore, those boards that have operated have been only minimally successful.

Most review boards are composed of elected or appointed officials. In most of the ineffective or short-lived attempts to implement these review panels, the boards' review powers were so severely limited that some original supporters of civilian review complained that the actual boards had no effective sanctions at their disposal, or were sufficiently stacked with pro-police members that objective review was not feasible. Most review boards were exactly that: they could review complaints, but their sanctioning power was limited to making recommendations to police administrators. Their effectiveness, also, has been hampered by their use of regular officers as investigators, the unwillingness of officers to appear when subpoenaed, and the filing of civil suits against the board by police officers. Consequently, civilian review boards have not attained their ob-

---

[153] George Berkley et al., *Introduction to Criminal Justice* (Boston: Holbrook Press, 1976), p. 217.

[154] See Paul Chevigny, *Police Power* (New York: Vintage Books, 1969).

jective of policing the police, nor have they satisfied the civilian complainants that their case was objectively heard.[155]

No easy solutions present themselves for controlling police deviations from prescribed rules of criminal or departmental procedures. Present methods have not proven adequate, yet disappointingly we have not undertaken any systematic attempt to try alternative strategies, besides those few started at the local level. It appears that suggestions for civilian review boards and the like divide people into those pro- and those anti-the police. Obviously, such side taking obscures the crucial issue—that the police officer sometimes violates the law and the civilian has little recourse against his action. The police department may yet be able to create adequate internal control mechanisms, and police procedure certainly has improved since the Wickersham Commission's exposures of corruption and brutality in 1931. However, there are numerous difficulties and many unresolved and even unaddressed questions concerning the roles and functions of police within complex urban communities.

We will return to these difficulties in Chapter Nine, wherein we shall conduct an in-depth analysis of factors that shape present police operation and organization.

[155] See John Culver, "Policing the Police: Problems and Perspectives," *Journal of Police Science and Administration*, 3, No. 2 (June 1975), 134.

chapter 4

The Court System:

Prosecution and Defense

THE COURT SYSTEM IN THE UNITED STATES

Apparent in our description of the police are the complexity of the governmental arrangements for the provision of police services and the problems that may arise in the coordination of such services. The court system in the United States is no less complex. The complexity begins, perhaps, with the constitutional relationship of the states to the federal government. The federal Constitution established a dual court system in which particular offenses were the concern of the federal courts, whereas most criminal matters were reserved for the states.

The Dual Court System

The states and the national government are related federally, which means that whereas the federal government regulates or controls interstate activities and relations with foreign powers, most intrastate activity is controlled by the state governments. Since most criminal offenses are offenses against state law (about 85 percent), it is the state court systems that determine much of the quality of justice in this country. The state and federal systems are said to be a "dual court system" because they operate independently of each other in most matters. Criminal matters that originate in state courts are reviewed in the federal system only rarely, and generally only when the question involves a federal constitutional issue or the administration by a state agency of federal civil rights.

The Federal Court System

The only court established in the Constitution is the Supreme Court of the United States. Article III, Section 1 of the Constitution states that "[t]he judicial power of the United States shall be vested in one Supreme Court, and in such inferior courts as the Congress may from time to time ordain and establish." The Supreme Court has original jurisdiction in cases affecting ambassadors and other representatives of foreign governments and in cases in which one of the states is a party (i.e., as when one state attempts to sue another). Congress exercised the power granted in the Constitution to form a federal court system in the Federal Judiciary Act of 1789. It created two levels of inferior courts under the Supreme Court—the *United States district courts* and the *United States courts of appeals*. The United States district courts are the trial courts in the federal system. They are the courts of original jurisdiction in cases where a defendant is accused of breaking a federal law. Above the district courts are the United States courts of appeals (which were known until 1948 as the United States circuit courts of appeals). The federal court system is divided into 11 circuits, with each circuit comprising three or more states, with the exception of the 11th Circuit, the District of Columbia. Each state is divided into one or more federal districts, depending on the size and population of the state. New York, for example, is divided into four federal districts, whereas Arizona and New Mexico each have a single district court.

Congress has made appeal to the U.S. Supreme Court from the federal inferior courts largely a matter of discretion for the Supreme Court. Among the appeals that the Supreme Court must hear are cases from state courts in which a federal statute has been interpreted as unconstitutional or in which a state statute has been challenged as unconstitutional. Most cases coming before the Supreme Court come up on *writ of certiorari*. This is a request for review issued by the Supreme Court asking a lower court to send up the record for consideration. In most instances, the Court has chosen to review the case, but has not been required to do so.

Below the trial courts (district courts) on the federal level are the United States magistrates. The U.S. magistrates have functions very similar to justices of the peace or district magistrates. They issue search warrants, they "arraign" the defendant on the charges after a federal arrest, inform him of his rights, and fix bail. They may hold preliminary hearings on the issue of probable cause, and they may hold trials for minor crimes if the defendant waives a right to trial in a district court.

The State Court Systems

Every state court system is different, but there is enough similarity that we can discuss a generalized "state system" rather than discuss all 50 systems separately. Usually, the state courts are divided into *lower courts, courts of general jurisdiction,* and *appellate courts.* In most states, there is a lower level of appellate court and then a state supreme court (although the exact name may change from state to state).

The lower courts in large cities may be called *magistrates' courts, recorders' courts, municipal courts,* etc. In rural areas, the lower courts are generally called *justice of the peace courts.* In states such as Pennsylvania, the justice of the peace has been replaced by magistrates who then run magistrates' courts. Whatever the particular name of the court, it is the lower court judicial officer or magistrate who is usually responsible for issuing search warrants and arrest warrants. After an arrest, the defendant, in an initial appearance, is notified of charges, informed of his rights, and admitted to bail in the lower courts. In petty offenses and most misdemeanors, the lower courts are also the place of trial (if there is one) and the place of disposition. (In most states, dispositions for misdemeanors are limited to under one year in jail and under a certain fine—perhaps $1,000.) In felony cases, the lower court may hold the preliminary hearing, and in some states a magistrate may hear pleas to a felony, but in all cases jurisdiction of a trial for a felony remains with a court of general jurisdiction.

The *superior courts, general trial courts,* or *courts of general jurisdiction* have felony jurisdiction for a particular geographical area (usually a county). Unlike most magistrates, the judges of superior courts are lawyers admitted to the bar. The trial courts may hold preliminary hearings, usually hear the plea at arraignment, and always conduct the trial in felony cases. The trial court judge is also responsible for sentencing felony offenders and for holding probation revocation hearings.

The state appellate courts are frequently organized into two levels, as is the federal system, but some states only provide for one appeal court. Although there is no federal constitutional right to appeal, all the states have established some appellate mechanism. Generally, an appellate court hears a case on the record. In other words, no testimony is taken in the process of an appellate review. Courts of general jurisdiction are courts of record, but the lower criminal courts generally are not. Since no record of a trial is kept in the lower courts, lower court decisions on appeal are heard *de novo* in the higher trial courts—that is, as if they were being heard for the first time. Appeal in either the state or the federal system will then be on the record.

THE RELATION OF FEDERAL AND STATE COURTS

It is important to understand that the supreme court of a state is not under a federal district or federal circuit court. The state and federal systems are dual or parallel rather than sequentially related. The only federal court that is superior to the state supreme court is the U.S. Supreme Court. When the U.S. Supreme Court issues an opinion interpreting the Constitution or a citizen's federal civil rights, it is controlling in all courts. In contrast, the decisions of a federal court of appeals are controlling *only* for federal district courts within that circuit. These decisions do not control other federal circuits or the state courts that fall within that geographical area.

The appellate process is very important to the development of the law in the United States. When an appellate court hands down an opinion on a question of law, it settles the law for all courts within that appellate court's jurisdiction. Thus, when a state supreme court issues an opinion, it is binding on all courts in the state. When a federal court of appeals issues an opinion, it is binding in all federal district courts in only that circuit. When the Supreme Court issues an opinion, it is binding in all federal *and* all state courts. The U.S. Supreme Court, in its supervisory capacity, also may issue rules binding on federal courts that have nothing to do with the state systems.

In order to look at some of these court relationships, it may help to have an historical account of a case law development. A particularly interesting set of cases involves the "search and seizure" issue of the Fourth Amendment.

The Fourth Amendment of the United States Constitution protects, "[t]he right of the people to be secure in their persons, houses, papers, and effects, against unreasonable searches and seizures. . . ." The Fourth Amendment, of course, only refers to such a protection in federal courts. Thus, in *Boyd* v. *United States* in 1886, the Court stated that citizens were protected from "[a]ll invasions on the part of the government and its employees of the sanctity of a man's home and the privacies of life."[1] In 1914, in the case of *Weeks* v. *United States*, the Supreme Court dealt

---

[1] Boyd v. United States, 116 U.S. 616 (1886).

with the issue of evidence unconstitutionally seized and used to convict Weeks in a federal court. The Court decided there that if such evidence was admissible at trial, that the Fourth Amendment offered little protection. The Court then devised for the first time the "exclusionary rule," deciding that unconstitutional evidence would be excluded from trial.[2] This decision governed all federal prosecutions but did not govern state prosecutions. The traditional interpretation of the *Weeks* case was that the exclusionary rule, while of constitutional origin, was a federal remedy to the use of illegal evidence in the federal system. At any rate, since that case was a federal one to begin with, the holding restricted the exclusionary rule to federal cases. A state prosecution was not at issue.

The relationship of the federal Constitution to state prosecutions was highlighted in the 1949 case of *Wolf* v. *Colorado*. In this case, illegally seized evidence was used to convict Dr. Wolf in a state court. Although the court of last resort in Colorado admitted that the evidence was illegally seized, it did permit the conviction to stand. Thus, the Supreme Court considered the question of whether the *Weeks* case excluding unconstitutionally seized evidence should be applied to the states. The Court, in that instance, handed down a complex, compromise decision, stating on the one hand that the Fourth Amendment right to privacy applied to the states through the Fourteenth Amendment, but that the exclusionary rule was not "an essential ingredient of that right." The Supreme Court, in essence, was recognizing that it had no general supervisory powers over state courts, and argued that the states should devise their own methods of controlling law-enforcement procedures to protect the right to be protected against unreasonable search and seizure.[3]

In the years that followed *Wolf,* the Court slowly and sequentially continued to close the door to the use of illegal evidence. The Supreme Court applied the exclusionary rule to instances where federal prosecutions were built on evidence illegally seized by state agents.[4] And in *Rea* v. *United States* (1956) the Court forbade in state court the use of evidence illegally seized by federal agents.[5]

But in the several cases following *Wolf* that involved state use of illegal evidence obtained by state agents, the Court held to the distinction made in *Wolf* between the application of the Fourth Amendment through the Fourteenth and the remedy for official misbehavior called the *exclusionary rule*. Then in 1961 the Court was confronted with the case of *Mapp* v. *Ohio* in which Cleveland policemen had illegally seized evidence

2 Weeks v. United States, 232 U.S. 383 (1914).

3 Wolf v. Colorado, 338 U.S. 25 (1949).

4 Elkins v. United States, 364 U.S. 206 (1960).

5 Rea v. United States, 350 U.S. 214 (1956).

of pornography during an illegal search. At this point, the Court reconsidered *Wolf*, in the light of the experience of the states in dealing with illegal searches since the 1949 decision. The Court, for example, pointed out that before *Wolf* nearly two-thirds of the states opposed the exclusionary rule, whereas after and in spite of Wolf, by 1961 nearly half the states had adopted an exclusionary rule.[6] The California Supreme Court, for example, adopted such a rule in 1955 in *People* v. *Cahan*, stating that the court was "compelled to reach that conclusion because other remedies have completely failed to secure compliance with the constitutional provisions."[7] (Hence, since *Cahan*, the exclusionary rule has applied in all California courts, since the highest court in California had rendered the decision—regardless of what the U.S. Supreme Court would do.) Finally, in *Mapp*, the Supreme Court also concluded that the only feasible way of protecting the federal right in state prosecution was to reissue, in a sense, the *Weeks* rule, not as a supervisory ruling to federal courts, but as a constitutional rule applying to all courts.

In summary, the relationship between state and federal courts is never clear-cut in operation. And as in the search cases, the relationship is delineated over several years' time. Also clear in the above examples, the Supreme Court was highly influenced by the actions of the appellate courts of the states, although these courts have no legally binding relationship over the Supreme Court. Another general trend evidenced increasingly over the years is the expansion of the Supreme Court's interpretation of the Constitution, and particularly the Amendments, so that now almost all rights due to citizens in federal prosecutions are also enjoyed by citizens in state prosecutions. The application of the Fifth, Sixth, and Eighth Amendment rights followed relatively quickly after the *Mapp* case broke the ice for the first time.[8]

THE CRIMINAL PROCESS FROM INITIAL APPEARANCE

Before we go on to look in some detail at each of the officials in the court system and describe each of their roles, it may be helpful to describe briefly once again the criminal process from the stage of initial appearance. Our concern is to point out that, unlike the police activities in a municipality, or the prison supervision in a state, the judicial phases of the criminal process involve *many* separate organizations.

[6] Mapp v. Ohio, 367 U.S. 643 (1961).

[7] People v. Cahan, 44 Cal. 2d 434 (1955).

[8] Malloy v. Hogan, 378 U.S. 1 (1964); Escobedo v. Illinois, 378 U.S. 478 (1964); Miranda v. Arizona, 384 U.S. 436 (1966); Robinson v. California, 370 U.S. 660 (1962).

1. Initial Appearance

This hearing, generally following very quickly upon arrest, may involve the prosecutor in districts where the prosecutor makes the initial charging decision. In many other districts it involves merely the magistrate, the police, and the defendant. The defendant receives notice of the charges, is informed of his rights, and may request the provision of a lawyer if he cannot afford one. The magistrate is responsible for setting bail, which is usually based on the seriousness of the charges rather than on information about the defendant. And importantly, but usually merely a formality, the magistrate examines the arrest report to ascertain if indeed there was probable cause to arrest.

2. Decision to Charge

Officially, the decision to charge is made by the prosecutor. If the district attorney is not present to consult with the police prior to the initial appearance, however, then the official decision to charge is really the decision to continue prosecution.

3. Preliminary Hearing

The preliminary hearing involves not only a court and judicial officer, but a prosecutor who must display a prima facie case, and a defense attorney. In states where a grand jury is the usual procedure for processing felonies, the grand jury indictment will obviate the need for the preliminary hearing.

4. Indictment/Information

In major cases (felonies) the defendant must be arraigned on the charges and plead to them in a trial court. In most eastern states and in the federal system, the prosecutor presents evidence to a grand jury who return an indictment if they believe that there is probable cause. In some western states, particularly California, the grand jury system has been replaced by the formal filing of charges by the prosecutor in a bill called the *information*.

5. The Arraignment

The arraignment involves the prosecutor, a trial judge, and a defense lawyer if the defendant has not waived his right to counsel. The arraignment is the stage at which the defendant must plead to the charges, and it is also the scene of the guilty plea conviction, which is the most typical kind of conviction in the United States.

6. The Trial

Defendants who plead not guilty put the state to the test. Frequently defendants waive a full jury trial and are tried before the judge. If the right to a jury trial is not waived, the prosecutor and defense lawyer must go through the often agonizing selection of a jury prior to the actual trial.

7. The Conviction

The conviction occurs after the judge accepts the defendant's guilty plea or after he accepts the verdict of guilty from a jury. Conviction is the pronouncement of guilt by the judge. The prosecutor, of course, is present, as is the defense lawyer.

8. Sentencing

Sentencing in felonies usually occurs after a probation officer has investigated the convicted offender and has presented all facts to the judge that might be relevant to sentencing (regardless of whether these facts were presented or were admissible at trial). The prosecutor also makes a recommendation to the judge concerning sentence. This recommendation is generally followed, particularly in guilty plea cases where negotiation for the guilty plea included the promise by the D.A. to recommend a particular sentence. Although a judge may sentence the defendant to any sentence within the statutory limits, the judge, like the prosecutor, is usually very concerned that bargains are kept.

9. Appeal

When a defendant appeals his case, other organizations come into the process. A defendant in a misdemeanor or petty offense may appeal a case to a superior trial court, where the case will be heard *de novo* (since no record is made at the magistrate's court). In felonies, appeal may be available to a state appellate court, or immediately to the state supreme court (if there is no lower appellate court).

10. Probation Revocation

Probation in most states is considered an alternative to or a suspension of sentence, which the defendant may enjoy as long as he obeys whatever probation regulations are imposed upon him. When a probationer violates probation (by breaking these rules or by committing a new crime), he may be sentenced on the original charge after a probation revocation hearing. At such a hearing the judge will consider whether the offender's behavior warrants revocation, and whether the probation officer can justify the case for revocation. The judge can then sentence the defendant to the original sentence that he had suspended during probation, or make the original pronouncement of sentence if he has not done so.

It is clear that the judicial phases of the criminal process involve a great many organizations and a great many different actors. The office of the prosecutor, the office of the defense attorney or the public defender, the lower court, the trial court, and the probation office are all involved in most felony prosecutions.

OFFICIALS IN THE COURT SYSTEM

In this section, we will be describing the significant officials in the court system. As much as possible we will delineate the roles as they are normally played out, without much attention to role dysfunctions, or the criticisms that are currently being raised concerning each of these positions. The advantages and disadvantages of current operating patterns will be addressed in the concluding section. In addition to describing the major officials in the system, we will also look at the grand jury and at the jury trial process. One major court role will be held back from this section—that of the court administrator. Court management specialists are so new to the scene that it makes more sense to discuss this emerging role in the context of the next section, as we review current issues in court operations.

The Prosecutor

One of the most important officials in the court system is the *prosecuting attorney*. The district attorney is in many ways the prime mover of the criminal process. It is he who makes the decision whether to prosecute— whether or not to pursue the state's interest manifest in the police arrest of a suspect.

The administrative arrangements for prosecution differ widely from jurisdiction to jurisdiction, the greatest difference being whether the office is rural or urban. On the local level, the prosecutor is an elected official, usually operating with countywide jurisdiction. In large metropolitan counties, the elected district attorney is the supervisor of a great number of appointed subordinates, usually called *assistant district attorneys*. In these large offices, all the prosecutors are full-time workers who obtain salaries generally competitive with private law firms and corporations. Large county offices are also well staffed with investigative support, composed of individuals who will either be county detectives or city detectives on special assignment.

In small rural counties, the office of district attorney is rather different. The position is frequently a part-time post, and the salary is commensurate with the expectation that the elected D.A. will also maintain his private practice. This circumstance frequently leaves the rural D.A. overworked, understaffed, and occasionally in conflict with his role as private attorney.[9]

In both urban and rural counties, it is a general American tradition that the prosecutor is not a career official. The elected D.A., as a politician, usually perceives the office as a stepping stone in a political career. Although he may be a competent lawyer, it is fair to say that he generally does not see the prosecutorial role as his goal, or as his specialty. Assistant district attorneys are also frequently politically ambitious. They see the prosecutorial role as a good way to make the contacts that will enable them to run for office. In large urban offices the many assistant positions may be civil service appointments, or, if not, it is still likely that the assistants can, if they desire, outlast their elected superior. The elected D.A. in large offices will rarely try cases himself. The elected position is generally a policy and political role. It is the assistants who become skilled trial lawyers. Since the assistants also use the office as a stepping stone to a career, in the large office there is generally a high turnover of personnel.[10] Nevertheless, there will be a sufficient number of assistants who decided to remain so that in the urban offices rather narrow specialties may develop. One assistant, for example, may become known for his skill with burglary cases, whereas another may develop great expertise with murder or rape cases, etc. In the large offices, the bottom-level jobs are usually parceled out to the new recruit. He serves as the liaison with the police department, where an unskilled assistant prosecutor will make the initial decision either to charge (and what to charge) or to drop prosecution. In the rural, one-man offices, the special functions cannot, obviously, develop. The elected prosecutor must become skilled in all phases of the criminal process.[11]

The relationship of the prosecutor's office with the police differs widely from place to place. The layman's common assumption that the prosecutors and the police have a close, continual, and good working relationship

[9] See President's Commission on Law Enforcement & Administration of Justice, *Task Force Report: The Courts* (Washington, D.C.: Government Printing Office, 1967), p. 73.

[10] On urban prosecutor's offices, see Abraham Blumberg, *Criminal Justice* (Chicago: Triangle, 1967), pp. 57–63.

[11] See David Sudnow, "Normal Crimes: Sociological Features of the Penal Code in a Public Defender Office," *Social Problems* (Winter 1965), pp. 255–276.

is probably not a safe generalization. Frequently, the staff in the prosecutor's office are too busy to develop good working relations with the police. At any rate, both the prosecutors and the police tend to have different perspectives on the criminal process that frequently produce disharmony rather than mutual understanding and cooperation. The prosecutor, for example, tends to view each particular case in terms of how it stacks up against other cases that have been prosecuted successfully and in terms of the rules of evidence and criminal procedure that dictate which cases are provable in court. Even if the prosecutor in urban offices is fighting a large case backlog with dependence on the guilty plea process, he will view each case for how "bargainable" it is. If the police have made an obvious procedural error during an arrest, for example, it becomes very difficult to bargain for a guilty plea successfully since the defense knows that the D.A. cannot go to trial. Plea bargaining is most successful from the prosecutor's viewpoint when he knows that he can prove a case in court, even if he does not want to. Thus, even in plea bargaining cases, the evidential quality of the case is very important to the prosecutor. The police, on the other hand, generally do not possess such a thorough understanding of the rules of evidence, so they cannot always identify the prosecutor's motives in picking and sorting through arrests for cases that he cares to prosecute. There are, of course, many instances where the policeman feels rewarded when his "good pinch" is followed by a successful conviction. But, as we have seen, the police emphasis is frequently on the *arrest* rather than on the conviction, or, even more so, frequently on the street situation rather than on the technicalities of arrest. Thus, the police and the prosecutor can often be at odds even though they must cooperate in the successful prosecution of a case.

The prosecutor is frequently on better terms with the judge (or the judges in an urban court) and with the small number of regular defense attorneys and public defenders than with the police. Although there is not, in the "ideal" model of the adversary system, any particular reason why the state's attorney should be on cordial terms with his opponent or the judge, in the daily life of the criminal court, it is these three men who must come to terms on case after case, day in, day out. Hence, it is usually they, rather than the prosecutor and the police, who comprise the cooperative court group.[12]

The major exception to this situation might be the case in which the D.A. has been cooperating with the police from the initial stages of the investigation on a very complex or important case. It is, of course, in these cases that the police (and the prosecutor, of course) very much desire that a good, clean pinch be made, followed by a short, successful

[12] Blumberg, *Criminal Justice,* pp. 110–115.

prosecution. Hence, the prosecutor may work closely with a squad of detectives for the duration of a case. Or, as Jerome Skolnick points out in *Justice Without Trial,* large city vice squads frequently have this kind of close working relationship with the D.A. all the time, because vice cases are frequently the most difficult to prosecute and the most complex and intricate to investigate properly.[13]

Above the local level of prosecution stands the state attorney general. He is generally appointed by the governor, and is usually thought of as the first law-enforcement officer in the state. Whether or not the state attorney general has actual supervisory power over county district attorneys is another matter. Some states have statutory or constitutional provisions that give the state attorney general authority to intercede in county prosecutions or to post policies that must be followed on the local level. It is more frequent, however, that the local prosecutor, as an elected official, is completely independent of his state counterpart. In these instances, the state attorney general is the chief law-enforcement officer in cases that involve the state. However we are beginning to see increasing cooperation between state and local prosecutors, or perhaps seeing greater exertion of state power in what used to be local matters, with special state task forces to investigate and prosecute particular types of crime. In New York State, for example, there is a state prosecutor's task force to deal with organized crime, partly because it is thought that the local officials do not have sufficient jurisdiction to deal with a widespread or highly mobile criminal operation, and partly because it is thought that a state official is freer of criminal or corrupt influences.

A recent Pennsylvania controversy highlighted, if it did not clarify, the relationship between the state and the county levels. After the Pennsylvania Crime Commission released its report on corruption in the Philadelphia Police Department, Attorney General Israel Packel announced that he was appointing a special state's prosecutor to conduct the state's case against the individual city policemen. This maneuver brought immediate objections from the Philadelphia county prosecutor's office, which claimed that it had already done a tremendous amount of investigation, that the state was interfering with the administration of the law, and that the removal of the county prosecutor would cast doubt on the entire Philadelphia criminal justice system. Packel responded that he did not doubt the competence of the county office, but pointed out that the county prosecutor had to cooperate daily with the Philadelphia police and that this needed cooperation would be hampered by the intrusion of the prosecution. Although Packel may have had a valid point, his authority to take over the case rested on a little used nineteenth-century

[13] Jerome Skolnick, *Justice Without Trial* (New York: Wiley, 1966), pp. 139–163.

statute, the activation of which highlighted the infrequency of state-local relationships.[14]

Prosecutors in the federal system are all appointed. The U.S. Attorney General, is of course, a cabinet member chosen by the President and approved by the Senate. The Department of Justice is a highly complex bureaucracy in which there are many prosecutorial specialties. On the district court level, prosecution of cases is handled by U.S. district attorneys. They are, of course, only responsible for offenses against laws passed by Congress. Roughly 15 percent of the criminal offenses in the country are prosecuted in U.S. district courts. About the only federal court (and federal prosecutor's office) that closely resembles a county court, in terms of case load and type of case, is the court of the 11th Circuit, in the District of Columbia.

EDUCATION AND TRAINING OF THE PROSECUTOR.   The education of prosecutors in the United States is very similar to the education of defense lawyers and trial and appellate judges. They are all lawyers, who, consequently have been through law school and have been admitted to practice following the successful completion of a bar examination. It is generally surprising to the layman to discover that this professional training is usually not considered adequate within the criminal justice system for satisfactory performance of the prosecutorial role.[15]

There are many reasons for this traditional inadequacy, not the least of which is the very uneven quality of training from law school to law school. More relevant, perhaps, is that most law schools place little emphasis on criminal law, and even less emphasis on its administration. Future prosecutors in most law schools will probably be required to take only one course in substantive criminal law, and another in constitutional law. There may, in addition, be a widely attended course in criminal procedure, but there was not, until 1968, much attention paid to the matter of criminal justice administration, or to the ways in which the various components of the justice system interrelate and influence each other. There is even less attention paid to the daily issues and dilemmas that confront a practicing prosecutor, such as his role in the decision to charge, his concern with the setting of bail, or release on recognizance, and certainly not with his very important influence on the judicial decision of sentence.[16]

---

[14] This controversy has continued and has amplified since Packel resigned and Attorney General Robert Kane was appointed. The special prosecutor's source of funds has been attacked, so far unsuccessfully by the state legislature.

[15] Blumberg, *Criminal Justice*, pp. 44–45; and John Kaplan, "The Prosecutorial Discretion—A Comment," *Northwestern Law Review*, 60 (1965), 174–193.

[16] President's Commission on Law Enforcement & Administration of Justice, *Task Force Report: The Courts*, p. 74.

In addition to these oversights, there is the tradition in most law schools that any interest shown in criminal law is denigrated to a certain extent. Generally, the law professors with the best reputations as legal scholars and teachers are not in the criminal law field, and most top law students follow in their teachers' footsteps.[17]

Abraham Blumberg, for example, points out that most criminal lawyers in the Manhattan court system have been graduated from the law schools with the poorest reputations or have graduated in the bottom of their class. There are several reasons for this situation. First, it is the city law schools, usually with night-school programs, that are closest to the political establishment in any particular jurisdiction. Hence, it is frequently to these law schools that politically active students gravitate, or it is the law students in these schools who begin to value the political advantages of a prosecutorial appointment. Moreover, as Blumberg states, politically active law students, who may be interested in governmental positions upon graduation, typically have less time to devote to academic study and for this reason end up on the bottom ranks of their law-school class. Last, the traditionally valued rewards for a legal education center on acceptance in private or corporate practice. It is widely held, and generally true, that the financial reward in the criminal field is rather restricted—since county governments typically cannot compete financially for the best law-school graduates, and criminal defendants are rarely well paying or dependable clients.[18]

Thus, in terms of formal education, future prosecutors are generally ill-equipped to deal with the administrative intricacies and the ethical issues in criminal prosecution. Since the President's Crime Commission report of 1967, many law schools have attempted to deal with these problems. Furthermore, the great increase in the national concern for human services in general and for criminal justice in particular has changed the values of many law students and increased the prestige and importance of criminal law and the provision of legal services to clients confronted with state intervention. A number of law schools have experimented with summer intern programs in which students with sufficiently high law-school averages are permitted to participate in field projects dealing with such things as release on recognizance and bail reform, court reform, and provision of legal services to the poor, to minority groups, and to incarcerated offenders. One idea behind many of these programs is that better quality law students can be redirected toward the criminal law and its administration if they have, prior to graduation, first-hand experience with the criminal justice system in placements and projects supervised by

---

[17] Blumberg, *Criminal Justice*, pp. 99–103; and President's Crime Commission, *Task Force Report: The Courts*, pp. 61–63.

[18] Blumberg, *Criminal Justice*.

experienced law professors who are active in the field.[19] Furthermore, government agencies such as the Office of Economic Opportunity and private agencies such as the Vera Foundation of New York City and various legal aid societies have developed placements for law students within the system and simultaneously have organized the provision of legal services to disadvantaged groups that provide new opportunities for recent law graduates in the criminal and social law areas.[20]

Nevertheless, the basic legal education still leaves much to be desired in the preparation of public prosecutors. New recruits to district attorney offices and most newly elected district attorneys have their first real confrontation with the realities of the criminal justice system during their first day on the job. Perhaps the most important aspect of the prosecutorial role that is not covered in law school to any great extent is the exercise of the vast amount of discretion that the prosecutor can and must deploy daily. We will speak of that issue at length in the last part of this section.

After law school, there are two types of training that prosecutors receive: (1) the formal training available to practicing prosecutors, and (2) the informal socialization and evaluation process that takes place on the job. Formal prosecutorial training, beyond the law degree, is increasingly available across the country. There is now a national college for prosecutors in Washington, D.C., and an increasing number of training programs and conferences across the country that are relevant to the assessment and improvement of the prosecutorial role. But there are few prosecutors' offices that offer or provide substantial on-the-job training, even in large urban counties.[21]

The informal training or the on-the-job, learn-as-you-do pressures that influence every new worker in any organization are somewhat stronger. In large offices, for example, new assistants are frequently relegated to some kind of police liaison and charging duty, where they are responsible for ascertaining which arrests are worth pursuing further and what specific charges ought to be filed. At this level, new prosecutors learn from their elder and more experienced associates in a typical apprenticeship role. It seems doubtful, however, that young prosecutors are given enough supervision, or the right kind. Where it is a practice, for example, to divide the large prosecutorial office into specialty functions, younger and less experienced men are frequently confronted with very important charging decisions without the support of trial experience or the knowledge of what criteria to use in evaluating the police report in order to

---

[19] Private communication from Professor Donald J. Newman on strategy behind Wisconsin Law School intern program.

[20] Lee Silverstein, *Defense of the Poor* (Boston: Little, Brown, 1965).

[21] President's Crime Commission, *Task Force Report: The Courts*, pp. 71–73.

128

select the triable cases. In this situation, more experienced policemen frequently go "prosecutor shopping," trying to find an assistant who knows when poor police procedure can be covered in the prosecution process, when an apparently strong case has hidden weak spots, or when a careful investigation after arrest can bolster a weak case.

Prosecutors on any level, and with any amount of experience, are soon confronted with the intricate facts and behind-the-scenes dealings that are a part of the guilty plea system. Assistants in large offices come face to face with the divergence between the adversary model of the criminal process as it might be presented in law school and the cooperative, marketplace climate of the operating criminal court. Chronic underbudgeting in urban court systems and chronic case overload make the speedy way through prosecution appear the best method. Prosecutors become attuned to which judges are most careful in accepting guilty pleas and which are lax; which judges are cognizant of police misprocedure and which are not; which private lawyers and public defenders will insist on trial, or bargain on a mass basis for guilty pleas, or continually threaten trial only to back off at the last instant; which type of defendants are likely to object wholeheartedly to the criminal process and demand full exercise of their rights; and finally, which defendants because of ignorance, poverty, or prior record are in no position to drive hard bargains.

At the heart of much of this learning process are two key issues: (1) the fact that prosecutors in most offices are evaluated in terms of the efficiency of their operation (e.g., how many defendants they can induce to plead guilty quickly); and (2) the fact that, contrary to textbook prosecution, each case is related to every other case.[22] In other words, it is valid from the prosecutorial perspective in most overloaded jurisdictions (at any rate) to bargain light on one case, by dropping charges below the level that could be substantiated in court (or to recommend probation or a short prison term in a serious case) in return for not bargaining down in cases that might actually be weak and challengeable in court. Many prosecutors tend to feel that over the long run, these kinds of negotiations even out. (Hence the public interest might be short-changed in one case and overemphasized in another.) But of course, this view of justice can rarely "even out" in the individual case. It can be fairly said that prosecutorial discretion, particularly as to charge and to recommendation on sentence, is not generally explainable when each case is considered on its own merits. It only makes sense when all cases are viewed together.[23]

Coupled with this dependence on the mass of cases to balance the

---

[22] Jonathan D. Casper, *American Criminal Justice* (Englewood Cliffs, N.J.: Prentice-Hall, 1970), pp. 128–134.

[23] For an excellent discussion of the influences and objectives in a prosecutor's office, see Kaplan, "The Prosecutorial Discretion."

scales of justice, the prosecutor is typically confronted with ratings of his skill based on his "batting average" (e.g., the prosecutor is judged on the proportion of cases he successfully prosecutes, or on the number of convictions over the number of prosecutions). Generally, the most reliable and fastest way of obtaining a high batting average is by successfully negotiating a large number of guilty pleas, since when a defendant agrees to plead guilty, there is no question of outcome at the trial.[24]

John Kaplan summarizes this pressure as the belief of most prosecutors that they should only prosecute cases where they are firmly convinced of the guilt of the defendant, or when they are firmly convinced that they can obtain a conviction. Although this belief is unassailable on its face, a consequence of this operating tactic is that the more complex cases are least likely to be tackled, whereas the run-of-the-mill cases with undistinguished attorneys and uncomplaining defendants are the most likely to be prosecuted.[25]

ROLE OF THE PROSECUTOR IN THE PRECONVICTION PROCESS. The prosecutor is generally the chief architect of the preconviction process from the point of initial appearance to the pronouncement of verdict. To say this does not mean that the prosecutor is free to do as he pleases. But if the prosecutor decides not to prosecute, there is, in operation, little that any other person can do to force the issue because the prosecutor is the elected official with the statutory or constitutional authority to decide whether or not the state should intervene in specific instances. Correlatively, if the prosecutor does decide to prosecute, then generally, the most that can be done to combat this decision is to ask that the state meet the full burden of proof in court.

Exactly how or where the prosecutor's role begins in the criminal process varies, as we have pointed out above. One major constraint on the prosecutor's exercise of power is that he cannot go out and select his own suspects. In cases where the police choose not to arrest, the prosecutor has few significant decisions to make. It is likely, however, that even the police decision to arrest is influenced by policy guidelines or standards that the prosecutor can issue formally or informally about the kinds of cases that he considers most important, about the quality of procedures that he considers sufficient to justify continuing prosecution, and in general, about the priorities he sets for the spending of the prosecution dollar.

In some jurisdictions, and in all jurisdictions for particular kinds of cases, the prosecutor's relationship with the police is a fairly close and continual one. He may, for example, suggest which suspicious circum-

---

[24] See Donald J. Newman, *Conviction: The Determination of Guilt or Innocence Without Trial* (Boston: Little, Brown, 1967), pp. 45–99.

[25] Kaplan, "The Prosecutorial Discretion."

stances should be investigated further. He will probably let it be known how vigorous the police must be in observing statutory and constitutional procedural restrictions. He may even suggest kinds of police training commensurate with those goals. By prosecuting speedily in particular instances, and by refusing to proceed on other arrests, he indirectly sanctions various police behaviors and the distribution of police resources. By refusing to prosecute in some instances, he can probably cut down to some extent, police interest in certain matters, and by manipulating the decision to charge, he can change the size of the caseload in every segment of the system dependent on his decisions.

If his role with the police is one responsibility, then another is his duty to investigate crime and to develop cases to the extent that they are ready for trial. In large urban offices, there may be many prosecutors active in this role. In rural districts, investigative support may be nonexistent.

In a broader view, this second function becomes the larger one of managing all the cases from the decision to charge onward. The prosecutor is responsible for deciding how the state's interest will be best protected in each individual case. In some instances, he may opt for a pretrial informal disposition. In others, he must manage the case through the presentation of the state's case in court. If a case is going to court, the prosecutor must ascertain what charge is the most appropriate one, and whether there is sufficient evidence to demonstrate every element of the crime charged. In doing so, he must assess the capacity of state witnesses to convince a jury that their testimony is complete and accurate. He must make sure that all subpoenas have been issued on time and must have some reasonable assurance that all parties to a case and all witnesses are going to appear in court on the specified date. Where there are problems with these matters, he must coordinate the activity of warrant servers and make sure that incarcerated defendants are delivered to court on time by jail personnel.

In major cases, where the state proceeds by way of grand jury, the prosecutor is responsible for presenting evidence sufficient to demonstrate a prima facie case. If the defendant does request a preliminary hearing, the prosecutor must present the same amount of evidence in court to convince the judge that probable cause exists. If the defense chooses to put on a defense at the preliminary hearing (which is rare), the prosecutor must be prepared to cross-examine witnesses and rebut the defense.

In cases where the defendant can afford an attorney or has been provided with one, the prosecutor will usually have close contact with the defense counsel. In minor cases, in the lower courts, this contact is actually minimal, perhaps a few minutes' conversation prior to the hearing. In major cases, this contact may be quite extensive and drag out over several months.

The major issues in negotiation with the defense counsel generally revolve on (1) the level of the charge, and (2) the recommendation for sentence. In these discussions, prosecutor and counsel are seldom enemies, although they may be adversaries. But even the adversary relationship is tempered (or even fundamentally structured) by the fact that the adversaries are seldom at equal strength (as they might be in an ideal model) and that their strengths frequently lie in different directions.[26] In most cases, the prosecutor has more information, more investigative support, and a greater number of resources. But he also lacks direct access to the crucial factor: the decision of the defendant on how to plead. In essence, then, the defense counsel approaches the prosecutor as a mediator between all the state resources and the decision maker, upon whom the prosecutor wants his influence to bear.[27]

Defense attorneys who fail to cooperate in these negotiations soon learn that they have paid a heavy price for their staunch defense of one particular client. The counsel who refuses to cooperate and to bring to his client offers of leniency in return for the guilty plea will find that the desired access to police and prosecutorial files is suddenly closed, that the prosecutor will not cooperate on other cases when the defense does have some reason to bargain, and, in the long run, that the client convicted at trial generally suffers stiffer sentences than the one who pleads guilty.[28]

This kind of negotiation is of course more frequent in congested urban courts than in rural areas. There may even be particular jurisdictions where the prosecutor may want to go to trial, even when his case is so strong that he might not need to do so. But in most cases, the prosecutor is a man who must decide how far below the optimum level of law enforcement he can operate without incurring the wrath of his constituency and without upsetting a very precarious balance among all the agencies and interests who come together in the administration of the criminal process.

ROLE OF THE PROSECUTOR IN SENTENCING.   Certainly, the major role of the prosecutor is in the preconviction process. But since the prosecutor's preconviction tactics typically involve a decision on his desires about disposition, should conviction occur, the role of the prosecutor in sentencing is also very important to understand. The prosecutor in this phase of the process is in much the same boat as most judges and defense attorneys;

[26] Abraham Goldstein, "Balance of Advantage in Criminal Procedure," *Yale Law Journal,* 69 (1960), 1149–1194.

[27] Abraham Blumberg, "The Practice of Law as Confidence Game: Organizational Co-optation of a Profession," *Law and Society Review, 1,* (June 1967), 115–139.

[28] See Stephen Bing and S. Stephen Rosenfeld, *The Quality of Justice in the Lower Criminal Courts of Metropolitan Boston* (Boston: Governor's Committee on Law Enforcement and the Administration of Justice, 1970).

that is, the formal education of all of these individuals is very likely to have been devoid of sentencing concerns, or to have covered the various sentencing alternatives only in the briefest fashion. Major criminal law texts, such as Monrad Paulsen and Sanford Kadish, *Criminal Law and Its Processes*,[29] do not discuss sentencing or the correctional process. And as major a jurisprudential work as Herbert Packer's *Limits of the Criminal Sanction*[30] does not mention the postconviction process except as the logical consequence of conviction.

In contrast to the lack of interest given to the postconviction process in law schools and in legal literature, the concern for sentencing in the operating system is crucial. As we have seen, much of the prosecutor's preconviction activity and many of the relationships that he forms with the defense counsel and the defendant are concerned either with the particular charge or the number of charges (which will determine the statutory limits to the sentence), or with the prosecutor's promise to recommend a particular sentence (a promise usually followed by the judge.)[31]

When plea bargaining has occurred, it becomes the duty of the prosecutor to make sure that the bargain is fulfilled. Thus, if it becomes impossible for a prosecutor to recommend a particular sentence, or if the judge is not willing to follow the recommendation, the prosecutor must suggest to the judge that the guilty plea be set aside and the case scheduled for trial.

The relationship between sentencing and the preconviction process is perhaps most clearly highlighted in the lower courts, where the entire business might be compressed into one hearing. It has been common in the Manhattan lower courts, for instance, that counsel and prosecutor will approach the judge together in open court to settle the matter of charge and the issue of probable sentence at the same time.[32] If in return for stated concessions, the defendant does plead guilty, the judge will pronounce the promised sentence on the spot. Although this sort of practice has normally been condemned in any number of legal circles (and by prosecutors as well); the charges of insensitivity and hypocrisy that arise are frequently unfairly placed on the shoulders of the judge or the prosecutor. Generally, all the actors in these situations are sincere in their effort to work out an agreeable compromise. What is hypocritical, perhaps, is

[29] Monrad Paulsen and Sanford Kadish, *Criminal Law and Its Processes* (Boston: Little, Brown, 1962).

[30] Herbert Packer, *The Limits of The Criminal Sanction* (Stanford, Calif.: Stanford University Press, 1968).

[31] Failure to follow such a recommendation may be used to argue that the plea of guilty was not obtained constitutionally; see Newman, *Conviction: The Determination of Guilt*, pp. 36–37; and see *Santobello v. New York*, 404 U.S. 257 (1971).

[32] "I Have Nothing to Do with Justice," *Life*, March 12, 1971, pp. 56–58.

the legislative budget for the court that makes such marketplace justice commonplace.[33] Under these circumstances, the responsibilities of the prosecutor are really quite different than we have described them above. Although he will have a police arrest report to go on, and a rap sheet, he will not have had time for intense contact with the police, or time to conduct an investigation, or much time to worry about preparation of evidence or the selection of witnesses. In essence, he takes the police report at face value, assumes the defendant is guilty of the crime as described, and then racks his conscience to decide whether the state in this case can afford to lose the disposition that would be most probable for the particular criminal event, in return for whatever disposition can be worked out in return for the plea. In Manhattan and other busy lower courts, this may mean that the convicted defendant is released on the day of hearing because he will serve as his entire sentence only the time he has already spent in jail awaiting the hearing. (This waiting time still approaches a year in many jurisdictions.)[34]

In the higher trial courts, considerably more time may intervene between conviction and sentencing, and a probation officer may conduct a pre-sentence investigation into the character of the defendant, his dangerousness, and his eligibility for probation. But even with such a report, the prosecutor's recommendation carries considerable weight and may frequently override the probation recommendation. This is particularly true when a plea has been obtained on the basis of the prosecutor's promise to drop certain charges or to recommend a certain sentence prior to a probation investigation about the offender. If the pre-sentence investigation (P.S.I.) demonstrates that the offender has a long past record, or is a poor risk in the community, the prosecutor is still bound by his promises. If because of the P.S.I., the judge is unwilling to follow the prosecutor's recommendation, the prosecutor should give the defendant opportunity to withdraw his plea and to stand trial.[35]

THE PROSECUTOR'S DISCRETION. Throughout this section we have pointed to many decision points and many issues about which the prosecutor has considerable discretion. In some ways the prosecutorial discretion is less controversial than police discretion or judicial discretion because there is general consensus that the prosecutor has the right to exercise it. This right extends from the fact that, in most states at least, the prosecutor is an elected official whose actions are assumed to repre-

[33] See *People* v. *Byrd*, 162 N.W. 2nd 777 (1968), concurring opinion of Judge Levine.

[34] See *Life* article mentioned in note 32; and Bing and Rosenfeld, *The Quality of Justice*.

[35] On this particularly embarrassing kind of conflict, see John Kaplan, *Criminal Justice* (Mineola, N.Y.: Foundation Press, 1969), pp. 454–477.

sent the desires of his constituency. If the prosecutor fails to perform to community standards, he can be removed from office at the next election (usually every four years). However, it should be noted that the most frequent exercise of prosecutorial discretion is invisible to the community because it involves the processing of cases internal to the system and in which there is little public interest.

Except for the ballot box, there are few real checks on the prosecutor's power and his use of discretion. The most constraining one, in reality, is probably the fact that the prosecutor must operate within an on-going, complex system. And complex systems, as we shall see in Part III of this text, have operating patterns of their own that are difficult for any particular individual or group to change. A prosecutor who was continually unwilling to bargain, for instance, would be confronted with an unmanageable caseload and would come under severe criticism from politicians, judges, and the bar. Or a prosecutor who severely abused his discretion, such as refusing to prosecute major cases or refusing to investigate widely publicized corruption in the system, could be removed from office.[36]

More difficult to deal with are the instances when the prosecutor attempts to extend his power or use it arbitrarily against the many poor and ignorant offenders who have no voice in the community. In systems that utilize grand jury indictment, the grand jury can (but rarely does) check prosecutorial power by refusing to indict. The trial jury is of course another check built into the system, although few cases go to trial. The judge, of course, has the final say as to whether or not there is a trial, and the judge has the power to dismiss a case in the interest of justice even if the prosecutor desires to prosecute.

In some systems there has been increasing attention to the decision not to prosecute. When the prosecutor does not desire to bring a case to court, he may file a *nolle prosequi*, a statement that the state will not ask the defendant to answer the charges. In many systems, the prosecutor's discretion to *nolle pros* a case is virtually unchecked. But in some jurisdictions, the prosecutor is now required to file a statement explaining why he desires to drop the case. Although there has been some criticism that the district attorney's response to this requirement has been as routine and uninformative as the nolle pros itself, it is probably some improvement over systems that require no answer at all.[37]

The factors that the prosecutor may take into consideration in deciding whether to prosecute or not are many and varied. Several common conditions for not prosecuting are as follows:

[36] There is, however, apparently wide flexibility or tolerance for this behavior in others. The reticence of some bar associations to disbar the convicted lawyers in the Watergate cover-up is a case in point.

[37] Frank Remington et al., *Criminal Justice Administration* (Indianapolis: Bobbs-Merrill, 1969), pp. 568–570.

1. When the offense is *de minimis*, or the defendant a first offender who, in the prosecutor's view, will not reoffend.

2. When the case is one in which an alternative to prosecution is available, as when counsel promises that the defendant will undergo private therapy or will commit himself to a mental institution.

3. Where one partner in a consensual vice crime is particularly young and inexperienced, and the prosecutor does not wish to subject him to the criminal sanction.

4. Particularly in assault cases, when the complaining witness appears to have a change of heart, or in cases where the witnesses do not seem straight in their stories and the testimony may be unconvincing to a jury.

5. When restitution is made and the victim seems satisfied.

6. When prosecution would necessitate uncovering a police informer who is valuable to other investigations, or when identification might endanger the life of the policeman or the informer.

7. When the victim is of such an age or mental state that the prosecutor feels that prosecution would be more damaging than ignoring the offense would be.

8. When the prosecutor is convinced that prosecuting the offender would cause severe damage or hardship to him or his family, and the benefits to the state of conviction are not great.[38]

An important issue in relation to prosecutorial discretion is the code of ethics that govern, or that certain people have argued *should* govern, the conduct of the prosecutor's activities. The district attorney is, of course, a member of the bar and is governed by the professional code of ethics of the bar association. This code will be covered in some detail in our discussion of the defense counsel role in the next section. There are ethical constraints above and beyond the codes of such professional associations, however, that are relevant to judging the performance of the prosecutor as a public official and as an agent or representative of the court. The prosecutor, when elected or appointed, is sworn to uphold and enforce the laws of the state or the federal government, which, of course, is a duty the implications of which a private attorney does not confront. There is implied in this relationship, for example, the duty of the prosecutor to decide how the interest of the state will be manifest in the administration of criminal law. Hence, whereas one can decide whether or not to negotiate in return for a plea of guilty, or whether or not to charge, relying simply on administrative criteria such as whether the cost savings to the state are substantial or whether the strain of the present caseload merits leniency at *this* particular time, from the ethical standpoint these considerations are tempered by whether the possible prosecutorial alternatives are *proper* in light of the merits of the present case, and whether the selected alternative is *fair* compared to how other de-

---

[38] Newman, *Conviction: The Determination of Guilt*, pp. 131–173.

fendants in the same class or other cases of similar circumstances were handled in the past. For example, the prosecutor is bound by the constitutional restriction of the Fifth and Fourteenth Amendments that state citizens have a right to equal protection of the law. Therefore the district attorney in a particular jurisdiction cannot single out one suspect or one violator for special attention when it is clear that other persons are equally suspicious or equally in violation of the law. This constraint does *not* imply that the prosecutor cannot prosecute one case because of the high probability that other offenders acting in the same manner have not been apprehended. It is unreasonable to demand that the police must apprehend all burglars, for example, in order for the burglar caught to be prosecuted. But such a restraint would mean, for example, that the prosecutor cannot single out one large discount store open on Sunday in violation of Sunday Blue Laws when he permits the small novelty shop or grocery to remain open in clear violation of the same law.

Or, as we discussed in the beginning of this chapter, the prosecutor cannot ignore due process violations by the police by using illegally obtained evidence, for example, in order to obtain a conviction. Some spirited debate has focused on this particular issue, in relation to the prosecutorial duty. How intensely, for instance, must the prosecutor examine the arresting police officer in order to ascertain for himself that due process has been observed? It is a demonstrated fact that the police have on occasion has been known to lie or fabricate an arrest report to make the events surrounding search and arrest conform to constitutional guidelines. Can the prosecutor use such evidence as reported by the police over vociferous contradiction by the arrested suspect? Can he use it if he has doubts but is not sure? And if he *does* examine police or complaining witnesses thoroughly prior to accepting their version of events, what risk is he incurring that these witnesses will refuse to cooperate in future cases or will lie even more convincingly?

Two major spokesmen for rigorous prosecutorial ethics in such matters were Justice Brandeis and Justice Holmes in the case of *Olmstead* v. *United States.* In this wiretap case, a conviction was allowed to stand based on evidence obtained by police in violation of a State of Washington statute forbidding interception of telephonic communication. Although the chief thrust of Brandeis' dissent is aimed at the narrow interpretation of the Fourth Amendment, certainly his conclusions are also directed at the prosecutor who is willing to use evidence that he knows was obtained in an illegal manner.[39]

Decency, security, and liberty alike demand that government officials shall be subject to the same rules of conduct that are commands to

[39] Olmstead v. United States, 227 U.S. 438 (1928).

citizens. In a government of laws, existence of government will be imperiled if it fails to observe the law scrupulously. Our government is the potent, the omnipresent teacher. For good or ill, it teaches the whole people by its example. Crime is contagious. If the government becomes a lawbreaker, it breeds contempt for the law; it invites every man to become a law unto himself; it writes anarchy.

Justice Holmes' briefer dissent was even pithier:

It is desirable that criminals should be detected, and to that end that all available evidence should be used. It also is desirable that the government should not itself foster and pay for other crimes, when they are the means by which the evidence is to be obtained. . . . We have to chose, and for my part, I think it is a less evil that some criminals should escape than that the government should play an ignoble part.

In short, the prosecutor has a duty not only to uphold the law but to do so in such a way and by bringing such an example that respect rather than contempt for the process is fostered. If the prosecutor condones illegal activity as a means to apprehension of criminals, or if he utilizes the fruits of police misprocedure, or takes advantage of perjured testimony, he may uphold one law in a particular instance, but he is defeating his goal as an official of the state.[40]

The Defense Attorney

The defense attorney in the criminal justice system has been a figure of considerable controversy since 1963. Particularly during the last years of the Warren Court, the expansion of the role of counsel has been rapid, and this expansion has required rapid adjustment by the agencies who administer criminal law.

The landmark case governing the entrance of the defense attorney into criminal system is *Gideon* v. *Wainwright* (1963).[41] Defense attorneys were, of course, active in the criminal justice system prior to 1963. The Sixth Amendment of the Constitution has always provided citizens in federal prosecutions with the right to counsel at trial, and, traditionally, the right to counsel in state prosecutions has generally been provided in particular instances as implicitly required by the Fourteenth Amendment due process of law. Thus, in the 1932 case of *Powell* v. *Alabama*, it was decided that, ". . . in a capital case an indigent defendant would be provided with counsel, if he could not adequately present his own de-

---

[40] For a fictional rebuttal of the Holmes-Brandeis ethic, the reader might compare Joseph Wambaugh, *The Onion Field* (New York: Delacourte, 1974). This book effectively demonstrates that the balance of advantage is with the criminal—at least in celebrated cases, or at least from the policeman's point of view.

[41] Gideon v. Wainwright, 372 U.S. 335 (1963).

fense."[42] After *Powell,* a series of cases followed in which the question was addressed as to whether the defendant had provided an "adequate defense." The case-by-case approach to whether or not counsel was necessary was formalized in the 1942 case of *Betts* v. *Brady.*[43] It was held there that in order for a case to be revised because of violation of due process, the defendant would have to demonstrate that the special circumstances of his social or personal situation resulted in prejudice because of the absence of a lawyer. From *Betts* v. *Brady* onward, a long series of opinions were delivered by the United States Supreme Court, in which a large variety of special circumstances were reviewed in order to determine, retrospectively, whether the defendant had been able to provide an adequate defense, without the aid of counsel. This review process soon became laborious and confusing, much like the situation in the search and seizure area between *Wolf* v. *Colorado* and *Mapp* v. *Ohio.* Finally, in 1963, in *Gideon* v. *Wainwright,* the Supreme Court, in a surprisingly brief opinion written by the late Justice Black, reversed *Betts* and stated that absence of counsel, without clear and convincing demonstration of knowing and willing waiver of counsel by the defendant, would in and of itself be grounds for claiming lack of due process.[44] In other words, the court reversed the conditions under which proof of due process was required. Under the *Betts* ruling, the burden fell on the defense to demonstrate that due process required a lawyer. Under *Gideon,* the burden fell on the state to prove that it did not.

THE EXPANSION OF THE ROLE OF COUNSEL. *Gideon* settled the issue of right to counsel *at trial,* at least in cases where there was a possibility of incarceration for a year or longer. That in itself was a major change. Suddenly, courts across the country had to provide counsel and establish the mechanisms for provision, and had to provide the funds to make the right a reality. In fact, *Gideon* went further than simply establishing the right at trial because Black made mention of the right at any "critical stage" in the prosecution. Hence, the case opened the door to the exercise of the right at many other stages of defense. But it did not address the issue of which decision points or events were indeed critical stages.

Thus, a series of cases followed rapidly upon the heels of *Gideon* that clarified the language of that case and, in so doing, expanded the role of counsel considerably. The most famous of these, perhaps, is *Miranda* v. *Arizona* (1966).[45] *Miranda* is a complex case that covers a variety of issues and interprets both the Fifth and Sixth Amendment rights. This

[42] Powell v. Alabama, 287 U.S. 45 (1932).

[43] Betts v. Brady, 316 U.S. 455 (1942).

[44] See note 41.

[45] Miranda v. Arizona, 384 U.S. 436 (1966).

case has already been mentioned in the chapter on police, and it will receive considerably more attention throughout the text relative to particular issues. Of concern here, of course, is the most controversial part of the holding in *Miranda;* namely, that all defendants prior to the beginning of in-custody interrogation must be told that they have the right to see a lawyer and that a lawyer will be provided if they cannot afford one. In other words, police station or in-custody interrogations were deemed a critical stage of the criminal process, and thus in any case in which the penalty imposed might exceed one year, counsel had to be provided.

In the case of *United States* v. *Wade*, it was decided that a lineup in a police station is another critical stage, and hence the defendant has a right to the presence of counsel at the lineup.[46] This case was even more of a departure from the "strict constructionist" or conservative line than *Miranda* represented, although it did not come as such a surprise. But in *Miranda*, for example, the role of counsel is still one of advising the client. This means counsel can speak to the defendant prior to police questioning, can be present during questioning, and at any point in the questioning process can request that the interrogation be terminated.[47] In contrast, in *United States* v. *Wade*, counsel at lineup has little that he can tell his client, nor is his client generally expected to answer any questions concerning the crime (although he may be asked to give a voice sample). In reality, the presence of counsel at lineup is not to provide advice to the defendant, but strictly to guard against a biased or weighted presentation at the lineup by the police. (For example, he can make sure that his defendant is not the only black man in the lineup, or not the only man over six-feet tall in the lineup, or not the only man to wear a blue coat similar to the one observed at the scene of the crime, etc.)

In *White* v. *Maryland*, it was decided that the preliminary hearing, where there is a right to one, is also a critical stage.[48] Here, the more traditional role of counsel is evident. There are many things that can occur at the preliminary hearing that only a lawyer could know how to use properly. For example, a lawyer can check that testimony given by state's witnesses at the trial matches testimony at the preliminary hearing; he can prepare to meet the testimony or other evidence given at the preliminary hearing in time for the trial; he can cross-examine witnesses; he may gain knowledge of and prepare to raise motions concerning police procedure; and so on. If the defendant insists on a preliminary hearing but is not represented, the hearing is fairly meaningless, at least in terms

[46] United States v. Wade, 388 U.S. 218 (1967).
[47] See note 45.
[48] White v. Maryland, 373 U.S. 59 (1963).

of preparation for trial. The prosecutor is put through the paces of showing a prima facie case, but that is fairly easy to do.

In the case of *Mempa* v. *Rhay,* the Supreme Court examined a Washington state case involving a sentencing after a probation revocation.[49] The case has been variously interpreted, but it definitely states that right to counsel at sentencing follows from the *Gideon* critical stage language—even though the defendant has already been convicted. There are, of course, a variety of alternatives open to counsel at sentencing that a defendant by himself would not think of or be competent to handle. For example, motions for appeal must be filed at sentencing, or shortly thereafter. Defense counsel can also protect his client from a sentencing decision based upon pre-sentence investigation information that is inaccurate factually or is based upon conclusions not grounded upon facts. Very importantly, of course, counsel can make sure that a plea bargain, if made, is kept, or, if it is not, that the defendant has an opportunity to reconsider his plea. Equally important, defense counsel, when he has been active in defense of his client, probably knows more about the defendant than anyone else in court. (There are, of course, few chances for a busy public defender or overworked criminal lawyer to be very active in defense.) At any rate, counsel who is concerned enough to present before the judge his own recommended disposition is likely to have some influence, particularly if he can suggest an alternative to the typical disposition. Counsel is at a disadvantage during sentencing, however, in that the judge has already read the pre-sentence report (if there has been one), or has already determined in his own mind the most likely disposition.[50]

Counsel in corrections is a much more current topic than counsel in preconviction stages. *Mempa* v. *Rhay,* in granting the right to counsel at sentencing, did so in the specific instance of a probation revocation. In the state of Washington, however, sentencing is delayed until probation revocation (rather than pronounced and suspended). Thus, some jurisdictions have interpreted the case to refer to *sentencing* itself rather than to *probation revocations* (an interpretation that is very doubtful in view of the sweeping but vague language of the opinion).[51]

Within institutional settings, counsel has been generally excluded under a number of theories, but the case of *Johnson* v. *Avery* (1969)[52]

[49] Mempa v. Rhay, 389 U.S. 128 (1967).

[50] See Michael Feit, "Before Sentence Is Pronounced," *Criminal Law Bulletin,* 9, No. 2 (March 1973), 140–157; and Kaplan, *Criminal Justice,* pp. 463–477.

[51] On the various possible interpretations of *Mempa,* and an argument for the more liberal interpretation (i.e., that *Mempa* refers to probation itself), see Fred Cohen, "Sentencing, Probation, and the Rehabilitative Ideal: The View from Mempa v. Rhay," *Texas Law Review,* December 1968, pp. 1–59.

[52] Johnson v. Avery, 393 U.S. 483 (1969).

guarantees inmates the right to lawyers or equivalent legal services (i.e., cell block lawyers or law student assistance) as a means of ensuring open access to the courts. Note that there is a considerable difference between this issue and the issue in *Gideon*. One can, of course, imagine many instances of incarceratory practices that would parallel the issue in *Gideon* or in *Mempa*. For example, right to a lawyer at prison disciplinary hearings might be argued as a critical stage of the criminal process. The Supreme Court has recently rejected the need for counsel in such instances, in *Wolff* v. *McDonnell*,[53] but the recent report of the National Advisory Commission on Criminal Justice Standards and Goals recommends just such an extension of the basic right, regardless of what the Supreme Court may hold.[54]

The case of *Morrissey* v. *Brewer*[55] as well as *Wolff* v. *McDonnell* suggests that the *current* members of the Supreme Court are not willing to extend the right any further than they have. *Morrissey* is a case concerning the rights of a parolee during the parole revocation process. The Court held (1) that the defendant had a right both to a preliminary hearing and to a dispositional hearing on the parole officer's complaint, and (2) that the parolee could cross-examine witnesses and call witnesses in his own behalf.[56] But, unlike all the similar cases in the past from *Miranda* to *Mempa*, the Court did not address the issue of counsel. And one would think that if the Court is not willing to grant counsel in a case where a man stands to lose his liberty and be returned to prison, that the Court would not think of opening the prison door itself to counsel.[57] (Lawyers of course, can visit inmates in prison about nonprison matters, such as appeals, suits, and other pending prosecutions. But the right to counsel in operations of prison administration has not been established.)

Lastly, there is also right to counsel on first appeal if appeal is a matter of right (*Douglas* v. *California*, 1963).[58] After the *Douglas* decision, there followed an interesting series of cases in which several courts considered how the appointed counsel for an indigent appellant might withdraw from the case if he felt the appeal was frivolous, and how he might do so without arguing the case against the appellant. In the 1967 Su-

---

[53] Wolff v. McDonnell, 418 U.S. 539 (1974).

[54] National Advisory Commission on Criminal Justice Standards and Goals, *Task Force on Corrections* (Washington, D.C.: Government Printing Office, 1974), pp. 253–257.

[55] Morrissey v. Brewer, 408 U.S. 471 (1972).

[56] Ibid.

[57] In *Wolff* v. *McDonnell*, the Court left open the possibility of granting the right to counsel for internal prison matters, at a future date. In other words, this *Wolff* decision would not have to be *overturned* in order to make counsel available. But at present, the prospects look dim.

[58] Douglas v. California, 372 U.S. 353 (1963).

preme Court case of *Anders* v. *California*,[59] Justice Clark issued the opinion that appointed counsel could not withdraw simply by writing to the court that he found no merit in the appeal. The Court said that such procedure was not good enough because simply filing such a letter did not provide the appellant with the aid of an advocate as required in *Gideon.* Later, the California Supreme Court responded in the case of *People* v. *Feggans* (1967) with the precise duties of appointed counsel for appeal:

> Counsel must prepare a brief to assist the court in understanding the facts and the legal issues in the case. The brief must set forth a statement of the facts . . . discuss the legal issues . . . and argue all issues that are arguable. . . . If counsel concluded that there are no arguable issues and the appeal is frivolous, he may limit his brief to a statement of the facts and applicable law. . . . Counsel is not allowed to withdraw from the case until the court is satisfied that he has discharged his duty to the courts and his client. . . .[60]

In summary, the role of counsel has expanded tremendously since 1963. The effort is clearly to provide the poor man with a defense equal to that available to the rich man, and to provide all men with some assistance or advantage in the battle against state interventon. What is not so clear at times is how that should be done. The *Miranda* case has not stopped many defendants from speaking (or police from interrogating).[61] The *Wade* case had a very clear intent but made the lawyer a policer of the police. And a case such as *Feggans* depicts the lengths to which the court must go in an attempt to even out or reduce some social inequities as they are reflected in the invocation of the criminal sanction.

ORGANIZATION FOR THE PROVISION OF COUNSEL. *Gideon* and its progeny have made sweeping changes in the organization of defense lawyers. Prior to *Gideon,* a lawyer who dealt strictly with the criminal law was a rarity. For instance, it was estimated that in 1968, 25 criminal lawyers handled 80 percent of the criminal cases in the city of Philadelphia. And Blumberg speaks about the number of "regular" criminal lawyers in the Manhattan courts to be a handful—all known to each other, and to the judges, and to the prosecutors.[62] A few criminal lawyers earn a national reputation for getting people off, but these men are not available to the defendants who frequent the lower courts and the felony courts, day in, day out. Most of these defendants do not know any lawyers and certainly cannot afford to retain one.

[59] Anders v. California, 386 U.S. 738 (1967).

[60] People v. Feggans, 432 P2d 21 (Supreme Court of California, 1967).

[61] See materials in Livingston Hall et al., *Modern Criminal Procedure* (St. Paul, Minn.: West, 1969), pp. 552–557.

[62] Blumberg, *Criminal Justice,* pp. 103–109.

Although there were means for providing legal assistance to the indigent prior to *Gideon,* the demand has certainly increased tremendously since then. There are basically three alternative plans for provision of counsel.[63] First of all, the judge may simply *appoint counsel* from a list supplied by the bar association in the jurisdiction. This approach is used frequently when and where the demand for appointed counsel is not too great. In many instances, lawyers who are so appointed are expected to perform without pay, as a duty owed the court. In certain jurisdictions, there is some provision for payment, although it ranges from the barely adequate in the federal system to the ridiculously meager in some state systems. Another disadvantage of this system of counsel for the indigent is that counsel appointed may be utterly unfamiliar with criminal law and may be completely inexperienced at trial procedure. Judges in some jurisdictions may then appoint only lawyers known to them as experienced—but in many cases this may simply mean that the appointed counsel is a friend of the judge who hangs about the court house waiting for cases to be thrown his way. In other words, the criterion of appointment is availability, not competence.[64]

Two other mechanisms for provision of counsel have arisen as options to the straight appointment system. One is the *Legal Aid Society* or other organized groups of lawyers who defend indigents as a regular, full-time vocation. Funds for such societies may be supplied through private donations or through some mix of public and private funds. This form of provision of counsel is evidently fairly successful, except that funds available are often inadequate. Legal Aid Societies vary in quality from place to place, and only certain areas seem able to provide support for them. There is also the criticism (raised more often about the public defender type) that the salaried Legal Aid lawyer is not bound financially in regard to the outcome for the clients he defends and consequently is not bound to provide a terribly rigorous defense.[65]

The third form of provision of counsel is most frequently found in larger metropolitan areas, that is, the *public defender.* As the name implies, the public defender is a government official, generally appointed, to defend indigents within a particular jurisdiction. In rural areas, there may be one public defender, or one part-time public defender, for an entire county. In cities like Los Angeles, Chicago, and Philadelphia, public defenders' offices are large complex organizations with many full-time lawyers, clerical staff, and investigative support. There are many

[63] See Casper, *American Criminal Justice;* and Richard Harris, "Annals of Law" (Boston Criminal Courts—I and II), *New Yorker,* April 14, 1973, and April 21, 1973.

[64] President's Commission on Law Enforcement & Administration of Justice, *Task Force Report: The Courts,* pp. 59–60.

[65] *Ibid.;* and Casper, *American Criminal Justice,* pp. 118–122.

advantages to the public defender system—at least in areas large enough to support one. A large defender's office, for example, probably pays well enough to attract and retain competent lawyers who become as experienced in criminal trial work as the prosecutors. Also in large offices there will be sufficient resources to do adequate investigative work in order to prepare a case for trial. An experienced public defender, unlike the appointed private attorney, and perhaps unlike a Legal Aid lawyer (who may have civil cases as well), the public defender probably knows his way around the court house, the prosecutor's office, and the police station as well as anyone else. On the negative side, it is difficult to find an indigent defendant who is satisfied with the defense provided by a public defender. The most general claim is that the public defender is a county official, paid from the same source as the prosecutor. Indigent defendants naturally have difficulty trusting in the motivations of such a person. There is also the similar claim that a salaried person who does not get paid on the outcome of the case cannot have great incentive to be an adversary. More pointedly, there is the claim that the public defender bargains too often and too easily, pleads all his cases guilty, and is actually working for or with the prosecutor.[66]

There is, in other words, no unequivocal answer to the issues raised in *Gideon, Mempa, Anders,* and the like. It is a certainty that in most cases, indigent defendants provided with counsel receive a poorer quality defense than the rich man can buy. It is also a certainty that the forms of provision so far invented have not satisfied the indigent (irrespective of the quality of the defense) because it is hard to convince an indigent defendant that the same persons about to prosecute him will simultaneously provide him with a defense.[67] Vice versa, it is hard to convince many publics to vote adequate money for indigent defense for the same reason—people ask why at the same time that taxes pay for prosecution should public funds go to the cost of defense. Ironically, it is doubtful that any indigent defendant has had better counsel than the day *Gideon's* appeal was argued before the Supreme Court by a lawyer named Fortas!

EDUCATION AND TRAINING OF DEFENSE COUNSEL. Most topics relevant to the education of defense lawyers have been discussed above under the "legal education of prosecutors." These problems will be covered from a different viewpoint in Chapter Ten when we are analyzing the organizational structure of the court system. An issue that is perhaps even more pressing, when discussing training and informal socialization processes in a court setting, is the general lack of attention to the training of lawyers that counsel defendants in the criminal justice system. There is, of course,

[66] Casper, *American Criminal Justice,* pp. 106–114; and Bing and Rosenfeld, *The Quality of Justice,* pp. 30–34.

[67] This point is highly emphasized in Casper, *American Criminal Justice.*

an ongoing socialization process. Lawyers recruited by law firms with a certain amount of criminal cases and lawyers who work for Legal Aid Societies or public defenders' offices are immediately confronted with pressures similar to those experienced by new prosecutors. There is the pressure to bargain, and there are the clear but unofficial messages that a lawyer who does not cooperate will lose information open to court regulars—such as access to files. Lawyers learn which judges sentence leniently and which do not, which judges have particular biases for certain kinds of cases or defendants and which do not.

Equally important to new defense counsel, as to new prosecutors, is the discovery that competency in criminal law and competency in maneuvering about the courthouse are not necessarily the same thing. They may learn, for example, that in one courthouse a particular clerk is a good source of information, and that in another a chief probation officer is extremely influential. They learn that the official relationships mandated by the criminal law or administrative law are either strengthened or subverted by the daily interaction among particular officials in particular settings.

A concern of current importance in assessing the strategies of defense is the difficulty of evaluating the work of defense counsel. This problem is particularly important, and perhaps most difficult, in assessing the work of public defenders. The public defender's office receives, generally, the greatest number of cases and the greatest majority of cut-and-dried cases where the fact of guilt seems least in doubt. It is true that defenders bargain more frequently than other kinds of defense counsel, and that a greater proportion of their cases result in convictions. But the criticism that is often levied against defenders, that they are only another branch of the prosecutor's office, is unfair if there is no way to control for the type of case handled, because it is probably true that defenders have the fewest cases that can be defended successfully.

There is another aspect of the argument that is harder to dismiss. One would suspect, for example, that defenders, who, day in, and day out, defend the indigent, friendless, ignorant, suspicious, and uncooperative, are the most likely counsel to give up on cases, to be bureaucratic in their approach, and, critically, to fail to provide these defendants with a sense of defense or support that would make some semblance of justice apparent in the system. It is likely in metropolitan defenders' offices for example, that defense tasks are divided into bureaucratic specializations so that a defendant does not even have one defender familiar with his problems and his case for the duration of defense. There may be a certain number of defenders assigned only to initial appearances, another group only to lower courts, and another group only to felony court. Thus a defendant whose case proceeds through four or five hearings may have four or five different defenders, and a defendant who receives only one short hearing in lower court may see his assigned counsel for only a few minutes prior to the hearing. In this kind of situation, it may be hard to convince a defendant that he has received his "day in court." If the Sixth Amendment right to counsel is, as it is always interpreted, a right to *adequate* defense, the present system for provision of counsel to indigents may need serious overhaul.

One apparent consequence of the present system, at least for defendants who end up incarcerated, is the feeling that they have been short-changed, that the system speaks of principles of fairness and balance of advantage but operates on principles of speed, routinization, and insensitivity. If there is any corrective value in having the convicted defendant contemplate his punishment as a natural consequence of an illegal act, the present system is likely to divet his attention from the moral justification of the punishment to the shabby process in his case, and to all the contingencies such as poverty, ignorance, and so on that play such an influential role in determining the kind of defense that he received.

ETHICS OF DEFENSE. The ethics of defense are somewhat different from the ethics of prosecution. The prosecutor is bound not only by the cannon of ethics of the bar association but also by the ethics of his public office. He has a responsibility not only to the state in the short-term case, but also to the administration of justice over the long haul. And we have seen how these long- and short-term interests can conflict. On the other hand, it is fairly evident that the long-term responsibility of defense is manifest or congruent with the manner in which each case is handled.

The theoretical function of the defense attorney is to act as an advocate for his client, and to provide the best defense possible. Without an active and concerned advocate for the defendant, all the resources, information, and power reside with the prosecution. Supposedly the goal of an adversarial system is to arrive at the truth in each case through a balancing of evidence presented by two partisan actors—the counsel for the state and the counsel for the defense. If defense counsel does not attempt to examine, challenge, and refute evidence introduced by prosecution, theoretically the validity of the process is damaged because the evidence presented by the prosecution tends to take on a neutral, face-value quality rather than evidence as perceived from the prosecutorial perspective. Thus, in order for the adversarial system to work as it should, the defense counsel is bound *not* to acquiesce but to protect his client in any manner possible—short of obstructing justice (i.e., by actually hiding evidence). The differences in duty, then, between the defender and the prosecutor have raised much debate, particularly in an era that has been colored by "law and order" politics and by the claims (more myth than fact within the daily operations at the trial level) that the defendant has the state at bay, unable to protect itself.

One of the scholars who has thought through these differences at greater length than most other people, Monroe Freedman, has suggested that it is a prosecutorial duty to disclose evidence negative to prosecution, whereas it is a duty of the defense counsel *not* to disclose evidence negative to defense.[68] To his critics, this suggestion seemed to imply that the defense counsel had license to commit fraud and countenance perjury, but this was not what Freedman actually had in mind. He would argue, for example, that a prosecutor must disclose to the defense the information that the police procedure in obtaining a confession was of doubtful constitutionality. It is not, however, a defense duty to disclose to the court that the defendant or a defense witness has given perjured testimony (although counsel should certainly point out to the witness the consequences for perjury). In other words, the defender has a duty to protect, to the utmost of his ability; whereas the prosecutor's zeal to prosecute must be subordinate to his greater interest in maintaining a just and fair procedure and the entire institution of justice. Freedman argues, in conclusion, that to ask otherwise of defense counsel, is to ask that, in operation, he argue against his client and weaken the foundations of the accusatorial system.[69]

A last ethical consideration that we wish to mention here might also be placed under the discussion of the role of defense counsel, except that the ethical underpinnings are so important. And that issue is the duty of counsel to the defendant *after* conviction. As we have seen, a few law schools, few prosecutors, and indeed little of the criminal justice process emphasize the postconviction stages. It is clear from cases such as *Mempa* v. *Rhay* and *Morrissey* v. *Brewer*, however, that as a constitutional concept, defense does not stop with conviction. And since so many cases are decided by guilty plea, the sentencing decision becomes critical, not only for the judge but also for defense counsel who has little actual preconviction defending to do if a guilty plea is the chosen alternative. To state the principle briefly, defense counsel has the duty to see the case, and more importantly his client, *through*. Of ultimate importance to the defendant, if not to the state's officials in the system, is what is going to become of him? What is the disposition? The defense counsel who takes an active role in this part of the process can have considerable influence on the ultimate outcome, largely because sentencing is the least studied and most ambiguous decision of the criminal process. It is at this point that judges have the least information to guide them, and consequently are most willing to listen to any suggestion with arguable merit. Counsel, for example, must ascertain that a bargain struck in plea nego-

[68] Monroe H. Freedman, "The Professional Responsibility of the Prosecuting Attorney," *Georgetown Law Journal*, 55 (1967), 1034–1045.
[69] Ibid.

tiations is carried through. He must also ascertain that a probation presentence investigation, if conducted, is accurate. And although the probation department operates on the claim of neutrality to the case, the defense counsel must ascertain that the probation recommendation is made in his client's best interest.

On a broader but perhaps more important level, the defender's role at sentencing is crucial to convincing the offender that *someone* has taken his interest to heart and that the disposition, whatever it might be, is tempered by this concern. Unless the defendant can be convinced of this fact, there is little reason to hope that the defendant will ever come to terms with his actions and with the disposition, and concentrate on what he can or should do in the future.

chapter 5

The Court System:
Judiciary and Probation

THE JUDICIARY

The judge is one of the central figures in the administration of criminal justice. A judge is responsible for all judicial duties within the jurisdiction of his court. This jurisdiction may be established by state constitution or by statute, and is usually limited to a particular geographical area, such as a county, municipality, district, or state. An exception is the federal system, wherein a mechanism exists that judges may sit in any district for a specified period of time, to share duties or take over duties for another judge. It is not uncommon, for example, for one of the justices of the Supreme Court to hear an appeal in a U.S. Court of Appeals. In state and local systems, a judge's jurisdiction is defined by the geographical area over which he presides, as well as by the type of case he may hear or the duties he may perform. A district magistrate, for example, may issue warrants and try petty offenses, but a felony case must go to the county court of general jurisdiction for trial.

A judge's duties are many and varied, such as issuing warrants, deciding on probable cause at initial and preliminary hearings, deciding on motions such as change of venue or admission of evidence, trying cases, charging the jury, sentencing, and overseeing the administration of justice in his jurisdiction, formally through his supervisory powers, and informally through his "central" position in the criminal process.

To a large extent, the quality of justice in any particular system depends on the quality of the judiciary. Frequently the terms *judge* and *court* are used synonymously, symbolizing the crucial role the judge plays in determining the operations of the court. In many decisions, the judge has virtually autonomous power to do as he sees fit. This independence is important in order to isolate the judge from the many powerful and conflicting interests that are confluent in the criminal court. But this autonomy also raises serious problems when a judge makes a mistake or incompetent decision, or when he is no longer able to perform the duties of his demanding office.

Selection of Judges

In the United States, unlike many European countries, judges receive no special training prior to entering the judiciary. They are elected or appointed. Trial and appellate judges must be members of the practicing bar, but lower court and district magistrates frequently are not lawyers. Thus there are many judicial officers without formal legal training.

The most common form of selection for judgeships is election for a specified time. The emphasis on election was most common in the states entering the union in the latter half of the nineteenth century. The concern was that judges should be responsive to the will of the people. The election of judges is unusual in Western societies, however, and has peculiar disadvantages, especially in the urbanized society of the twentieth century. For example, it is unlikely that the electorate responds to the qualities of competent judgemanship rather than to the qualities of demeanor, personality, and image that are common in legislative and executive elections. Also, it is difficult to get competent lawyers and judges to make the kind of effort that pays off in popular elections, such as politicking for support at local clubs and seeking support from local political parties.[1]

There are basically two forms of election operating in different parts of the country today. The more common form is *partisan election,* in which candidates for judgeships are chosen by each party and candidates run against each other. The problems in this system are generally those just mentioned above, plus the additional difficulty that selection of judicial candidates by party leaders normally includes other influences and considerations than the merits of a particular lawyer for the judicial position.

[1] President's Commission on Law Enforcement and the Administration of Justice, *Task Force Report: The Courts* (Washington, D.C.: Government Printing Office, 1967), pp. 66–68.

A frequent criterion, for example, is whether the candidate had been active politically in the past or has supported other party activities. Very frequently the selection of party candidates for judicial positions becomes one area where political deals, negotiated elsewhere about other matters, become finalized. In other words, the party agreement on a candidate frequently becomes a favor to someone who has compromised on some other issue, or who has lost his argument and needs to be soothed.

In contrast to the selection of judges through party politics, the *nonpartisan election* process is considered even worse. In some states, judges run for election without a party designation, on the basis of their being issued a spot on the ballot by some designated means, generally a petition. Critics point out that, regardless of all the flaws in the partisan system, at least the parties retain some interest in presenting respectable candidates who will do a more or less competent job in office. However, when the election is nonpartisan, no organized political body retains interest in the selection of competent judges. Although only candidates who meet certain minimum qualifications may be eligible to run, the candidates in nonpartisan elections are generally self-selected persons who for one reason or another desire to be judges. And although some may be good judges, there is ample room in this sort of system for a man to run for any number of reasons that have no relationship to his competence for the job. Thus, most critics conclude that the nonpartisan election is the worst method of selecting judges.[2]

Another selection process is based on what is alternately known as the *merit plan* or the *Missouri plan*—after the state that first adopted such a plan. According to the Missouri plan, there is (1) a group of persons who nominate qualified judicial candidates; (2) this is followed by appointment of judges from the nomination list by the executive; and (3) there is final approval of the appointed judges by the voters. In Missouri, which adopted such a selection process in 1940, there is a nonpartisan nominating committee chaired by the chief justice of the state supreme court. This committee of seven investigates the qualifications of all prospective judges when a judicial vacancy occurs. After much investigation, the commission submits to the governor a list of three lawyers whom they feel would be excellent replacements. The governor fills the vacancy from that list. Then, at the next general election, the appointed judge runs unopposed. If the majority of the votes are affirmative, the judge completes his term.[3]

There have been some objections to the Missouri plan; for example, it is argued that the nonpartisan committee is not representative of the electorate, and that the nominees are rarely from minority groups, infre-

---

[2] On partisan and nonpartisan election of judges, see ibid.
[3] Ibid.

quently have criminal law experience, and are likely to be corporate counsel in large firms. To date, statistics on the persons nominated and persons appointed to judgeships have not borne out these criticisms. On the contrary, the Missouri plan apparently emphasizes criteria of selection that are generally correlated with the judicial duties, brings competent men into office, and yet retains some participation of the electorate to the extent that they either ratify or veto the appointment.

The other common form of judicial selection is straight executive appointment. This method is also open to nonjudicial motives as in the appointment of two justices who were recently rejected by the Senate.[4] Appointment of lower-court judges is considerably more routine, and is usually done after the president has conferred with the senators from the state in which appointments will take place.

Removal of Judges

There are infrequent but important occasions when judges cannot or will not perform the duties of their office properly. At such a time, the issue of removing a judge from office is raised. Any process of removal is expensive, time-consuming, and costly in the social sense that judges are the most respected members of the criminal justice system, and even raising the question of removal casts doubt on the integrity of the entire system. Somewhat paradoxically perhaps, the inability of most U.S. systems to come up with an effective removal procedure also casts doubt on the integrity of the system itself when it is evident that incompetent judges remain in positions of power where they influence in irrevocable ways the lives of many people.

There are four systems for discipline and removal of judges that are in effect in different parts of this country: (1) there are states with constitutional provisions for removal procedures (including impeachment); (2) there are states that convene a special court process to consider the issue of removal (New Jersey); (3) there are commission plans (as in California); (4) one must also consider aspects of retirement plans, particularly involuntary retirement, as a type of removal plan. Although each of these systems has advantages and detractions (and apparently more of the latter), one general criticism (although in varying degrees depending on the particular system) is that it is very difficult to discipline or censure a judge or in other ways to call attention to and ask for changes in his behavior short of removal. Hence only the most drastic cases of judicial misbehavior and incompetence are generally subject to review and action. In many cases where there is a consensus that something should

---

[4] Ibid.

be done short of removal, appropriate mechanisms simply do not exist.[5]

There are, of course, many judicial mistakes that cannot and should not be subject to either disciplinary action or impeachment. No system can require that all judges be perfect, and a system, for example, that in some way negatively sanctioned a judge for a reversible error (other than the sanction of reversal of his judgment on appeal of a case) would place all judges in constant jeopardy and make them wary of exercising the judgment and discretion commensurate with the proper functioning of their office. While appealing the processes or outcome of a particular case is the most frequent means of correcting errors in the judicial processes, appeal on a case by case basis is not always an appropriate remedy for judicial error. Furthermore, the appeal process is itself an expensive and time-consuming mechanism that generally culminates in an appellate decision several years after the original trial. Given such a time lag, it is unlikely that the reversal carries the same sting or the same instructional value as it would if the corrective were applied closer to the error. Also, the appeal process is not an available corrective in many instances. In many cases, a guilty plea covers up what would have been a reversible process if the case had gone to trial. In the great majority of cases, no one considers an appeal. Lastly, when judicial error caused by incompetence results in a mistaken acquittal, the state had no recourse to appeal.

In the federal system, the constitutional remedy is one of impeachment. The only way to remove a Supreme Court justice is through an indictment in the House and a conviction in the Senate. No justice has ever been impeached, although impeachment proceedings have been initiated against a justice. The same procedure is necessary for the removal of lower-court judges. It would seem unlikely for either congressional body to allow its calendar to be disrupted for weeks simply to try one judge. The impeachment process is also the constitutional remedy in several states, such as Florida, where it has proven to be an equally unworkable mechanism.[6]

The process in New Jersey is somewhat different. The state constitution gives the chief justice of the state supreme court administrative power over all courts in the state. Under his supervisory authority, the chief justice is empowered to have his administrative staff investigate all charges of judicial misbehavior. If the investigation turns up evidence to warrant discipline or removal, the chief justice can certify to the governor that a judge ought to be removed. Because the legislation necessary to have the chief justice use his constitutional removal power, has not been

---

[5] Ibid., pp. 69–72.
[6] Ibid.

enacted, the remedy to judicial misconduct in New Jersey is always informal. The chief justice wields considerable power as head of the court system, and he has been able to call for resignations in some instances, and to demand changes in behavior in others. Although the New Jersey system is the cheapest and one of the most effective, it does have the limitation that the informal proceedings cannot be raised to a formal level.[7]

In the states of California and Texas, another form of disciplinary plan exists. In California, a permanent Commission of Judicial Qualifications, consisting of five judges, two lawyers, and two nonlawyers, assisted by a full-time staff, receives complaints about judges, conducts investigations, and can take disciplinary action. At present, the only formal sanctions are removal and involuntary retirement, but more frequent than these options are voluntary retirement or resignation of judges under investigation, or a promise by a judge to change his behavior after a discussion with the commission.[8]

Lastly, another mechanism with different variations in different districts is the retirement system. Retirement salary is generally high for judges, and should be maintained at that level so that older or incapacitated judges can step down and allow younger judges to take their place without losing dignity or incurring serious financial problems. Some states have compulsory retirement plans for disabled judges, and frequently a judge's peers can bring sufficient pressure to have a judge retire if the retirement system is flexible enough. In states where judges must serve a minimum number of years before retirement, the judiciary may be reluctant to pressure that a judge step down prior to his serving the minimum number of years.

Training of Judges

Increasingly important to the proper functioning of the judiciary is judicial training. Law-school programs have traditionally treated criminal law in cursory fashion, although the attention to criminal law and criminal justice administration has increased in the last several years. Another problem is that except in large cities, judges usually have both civil and criminal law responsibilities. Since the largest caseload is civil, it is difficult for judges to specialize in criminal law. Moreover, judges are rarely experienced in criminal law before coming to the bench. Most judges prior to election or appointment are civil lawyers, often from large law firms or corporations. It is not uncommon that a new judge has never acted as a defense counsel for a criminal defendant, and he may be thoroughly

[7] Ibid.
[8] Ibid.

unfamiliar with criminal law procedures. A goodly minority of judges, however, have had some prosecutorial experience.

Given this situation, the training of practicing judges becomes all the more important. In most states, in-service training for judges prior to their taking over judicial responsibilities is meager or nonexistent. Since 1962, in the federal system, new judges have attended an institute on sentencing and have had available a series of seminars in which the problems of judging are discussed with more experienced associates.

In 1964, the National Conference of State Trial Judges established the National College of State Trial Judges with permanent facilities at the Nevada Law School in Reno, Nevada. The college runs a four-week summer session annually. The faculty consists of experienced judges, law professors, and social scientists who cover the important issues that confront judges daily. Many state judges have expressed willingness to use some of their vacation time for such training, but the college has been unable to accept all applicants.[9]

Judicial Functions

We have discussed briefly the number of decisions over which a judicial officer presides. In this section we wish to look at each of these decision points again in relation to the general judicial role, the education and training of judges, and other characteristics that we have outlined above.

Usually, the first chance of byplay between judicial authority and the other officials in the system occurs in regards to police investigatory procedures. The Fourth Amendment governs searchers and seizures, either of material in evidence or of persons. The Fourth Amendment states that no warrant shall issue except upon probable cause. Warrants may only be issued by a judicial officer, typically a district magistrate or lower-court judge (although all judges are magistrates). Of course, most arrests occur without a warrant when an officer apprehends an offender on-site. When an offender is arrested without a warrant, then the police must present the arrested person before a magistrate quickly at the initial appearance, and the formal warrant is issued then. Most searches occur without a warrant, incident to arrest. However, the case of *Chimel* v. *California* limits the scope of such searches to the person of the arrested and the area within his immediate physical control.[10] Hence, search warrants are now required frequently after an arrest in order to search the house of the suspect or another area that the police have probable cause to believe contains evidence relevant to the crime.

Frequently, however, the police in the investigation of a crime, or the

---

9 Ibid., pp. 68–69.
10 Chimel v. California, 23 L. Ed 2d 685 (1968).

pursuit of a suspect, have occasion to seek a warrant that empowers them to arrest a suspect who is not in the act of committing a crime. At such time, the police officer must appear before a magistrate and sign an affidavit certifying to the facts that lead him to believe the suspect has committed a crime, or lists the materials he believes will be found at a particular place, and why he thinks so. It is the duty of the judicial officer to ascertain whether the police have sufficient cause to seek such a warrant or whether the police are acting on mere suspicion. The case law concerning warrant procedure has become particularly detailed in vice crimes, where the law-enforcement officers typically have conducted an investigation of some duration or are proceeding on the information provided by an informer. When police do seek a warrant for search or arrest based on an informer's tip, in order to establish probable cause it is now necessary that the police can certify to the magistrate the reliability of the informer by stating the number of reliable tips he has provided in the past or in some other manner. This procedure is difficult when the police wish to protect the identity of the informer, or when a tip is given anonymously but appears believable on the face of it. The other areas of most controversy have been in regard to wiretap and electronic eavesdropping. In instances where such investigation is allowable, the police must seek a warrant and must be able to state with some specificity the kind of information they are seeking and the reasons they expect to find it through that particular search technique.

Warrant procedure has frequently been criticized for becoming too routine, as when the police or the court system, or both, find ways of subverting the intent of the warrant requirement while adhering to formalities. It has been discovered in some instances, for example, the magistrates sign warrants without inquiring about the facts, or that signatures have been rubber-stamped by a court clerk or other lower officer acting on behalf of the magistrate. A particularly costly result of such official subversion (or bureaucratization) has been the discovery that the then Attorney General John Mitchell's initials were signed by his assistant in his absence. Since federal warrants for wiretap were only to be issued on approval of the Attorney General or a designated Deputy Attorney General, the illegal warrants and resulting illegal arrests will apparently adversely affect some 600 federal cases.[11]

The second instance of judicial responsibility is usually at the initial appearance of the arrested suspect. At this time it is required that a judicial officer inform the suspect of his rights, review probable cause, and set bail. Generally this fairly important prosecutorial step devolves

---

[11] This apparent "oversight" seems typical of the "Law 'n' order" approach to prosecution.

on the magistrate in a police court, municipal court, or justice of the peace court, etc. It is still common that such judicial officials are not lawyers, and it is doubtful that many of them have an adequate legal understanding of probable cause or a properly judicial commitment for providing the suspect with adequate and clear information about his right.[12] It is also common that magistrates have a deficient understanding of the right to bail, or use bail improperly. We will discuss the bail problem in considerable detail under "Current Issues in Criminal Courts" at the end of this chapter.

An important issue involving the initial appearance concerns *when* it occurs. In the federal system under something called the "Mallory Rule" (after the Supreme Court decision affecting federal practice—*Mallory* v. *United States*),[13] all arrested suspects must be brought *immediately* before a U.S. magistrate for the initial appearance. This requirement raised considerable criticism in some circles on the grounds that since the magistrate admits the suspect to bail, the federal law-enforcement officer would never have a chance to interrogate a suspect after arrest. This fear has not been borne out in practice, nor have the federal law-enforcement officers appeared overly hampered in their investigative work.

In the state court system, there is generally some provision that a suspect must be brought before a magistrate "with all possible speed" or some other such phrase that generally seems to mean within 24 hours. The Supreme Court decided *not* to require the state to follow the federal procedure in *Miranda* v. *Arizona,* which allows the police to announce the rights prior to questioning. It is clear from a case such as *Mallory* that the Supreme Court views it as very important that a judicial officer intervene between the arrest and the continuation of prosecution. The Court emphasized that the magistrate is a neutral figure who stands between the suspect and the forces mobilized for prosecution. Without such a hearing immediately after arrest, the Court felt that the defendant could be overwhelmed by the superior power of the state. That the Court later did not demand that magistrates in state prosecutions intervene at precisely the same time is perhaps no more than another manifestation of the usual caution the Court displays in intervening in state criminal justice. But it may also have been some indication that the Court no longer had such confidence in the beneficient effect of the magistrate's neutrality or in his ability to control more than figuratively the tendency toward

---

[12] There has been a recent move in some states to improve the minor judiciary through legal or related training. In Pennsylvania, for example, magistrates are required to undergo a specified number of hours of training within a specified curriculum, provided through the continuing education branch of the Pennsylvania State University.

[13] Mallory v. United States, 354 U.S. 449 (1957).

prosecution. At any rate, police practice has generally improved over the years in this regard, and seldom is the delay between arrest and initial appearance very great.

A judicial officer also presides over the preliminary hearing, when one is not waived by the defense, or when an indictment is not returned by the Grand Jury prior to such a hearing. In some jurisdictions the preliminary hearing may be heard by a lower-court judge, and in others by a trial judge. In any event, the basic function is simple. The prosecution must present before the judge a prima facie case, that is, a case of sufficient merit to warrant further prosecution. It is not typical for a defense to be mustered at this time because counsel generally does not want to disclose his defense to the prosecutor before trial. After the evidence is presented, counsel will generally move that the case be dismissed because a prima facie case has not been demonstrated, and generally this motion is denied and the judge sets the date for an arraignment. The judge may have important duties in this hearing in respect to · decisions about the quality of evidence and the quality of police procedure. The judge has the discretion at any point in the preconviction process of dismissing a case because he does not feel that the case warrants prosecution or because he feels the prosecution is likely to falter for constitutional or other reasons.

Usually, the last preconviction judicial stage is the arraignment because most defendants plead guilty at this stage. The judge then has the important duty at the arraignment to ascertain whether the plea is intelligently and voluntarily given. However, a judge usually has some difficulty in assessing these constitutional requirements because his judicial station removes him from the actual deliberations among defense counsel, client, and prosecutor that may have taken place. Typically the judge asks some standardized questions as to whether any inducements have been offered, or whether coercion has been applied, and whether the defendant knows the possible consequences for pleading guilty to the charge. Many judges are now also conscientious enough to examine the facts of the case sufficiently to decide for themselves whether the defendant actually has committed the crime. A few judges may be rigorous enough to inquire into police procedure or other matters that may raise questions about whether a trial would result in conviction. When the judge is convinced that the plea is both an informed one and willingly made, he accepts it and schedules a date for sentencing. If the plea is not guilty, a date is set for trial. It is not unusual for a defendant to enter court several times for the arraignment before a plea is actually taken, either because the counsel is still working on a defense, or because plea negotiations are still under way. It is also common in larger lower courts for the judge to accept a motion for continuance when the defense counsel is seeking payment prior to entering of the plea. Although such delay is strictly speaking not proper, many judges and lawyers have come to an unspoken understanding that such prepayment is the only effective method counsel has of collecting his fee.

Judicial responsibilities at trial are fairly well known. The judge presides over the selection of jury and may hear a variety of pretrial motions before trial actually begins. During trial he is responsible for monitoring the adversary process, for deciding what testimony should be entered, and what evidence is acceptable and what is not. He must control how both the prosecutor and defense counsel question witnesses, to make sure, for example, that on direct questioning the lawyer is not leading the witness. When the presentation of the evidence is complete, the judge accepts from both parties their written versions of how he should charge the jury. After reading these, he writes his own, summarizing the facts as presented and explaining to the jury exactly what they must decide concerning each count on the charge. After the jury deliberates, the judge accepts the verdict, and will schedule a sentencing hearing, as he does in the case of a guilty plea. He is also responsible for accepting motions from appeal then or shortly thereafter. In many cases, defense may waive a jury trial. In these cases the trial is before the judge, who decides the verdict for himself.

SENTENCING. Many persons now consider sentencing to be the judge's crucial decision. Given this consensus, it is surprising how little is known about the sentencing decision, about the consequences of various sentences, and about ways of improving the sentencing decision. Very little is written about sentencing, and very little information exists concerning sentencing. The law school and scholarly interest in sentencing has been almost nonexistent, and consequently most of the bar, most judges, and most legislators have little understanding of this very important decision.

The judge's role in sentencing differs from state to state, and from crime to crime. The sentencing decision has generally two components: (1) what the type of sentence will be, and (2) how great the sentence will be. The legislature states what kinds of punishments are allowable for certain crimes. In some petty offenses, it is possible that only a fine is required. But generally the legislature allows for a fine of some amount, probation, incarceration, or some combination of these, and it also allows the judge to select which type of punishment he thinks proper in a particular instance. In a small number of cases, the legislature may not give a choice to the judge, demanding that he pronounce a fixed mandatory sentence upon any person convicted of a certain type of crime. (E.g., all of the state death penalties initiated after *Furman* v. *Georgia*, which did away with the discriminatory invocation of the death penalty, list certain crimes for which the death penalty is mandatory. And under the new drug control legislation in New York State, conviction of certain drug offenses carries mandatory incarceration as a punishment.)

Not only does the judge generally have some decision about the type of sentence, he also usually has a decision to make about the quantity of punishment given. Fines generally can be fixed at any amount below a certain maximum. The length of time that probation supervision is required can be varied. But the most familiar choice a judge has is in setting the length of the incarceratory period. Again, when the state mandates a particular type of sentence, it might also mandate a particular duration of sentence. For example, armed robbery carries a mandatory 20-year sentence in Michigan (one consequence being that few people were ever convicted of armed robbery). In most cases, however, discretion in fixing the sentence is usually shared in some combination by the legislature, the judge, and an administrative body, generally called the *parole board.*

In a few states, notably Washington, the judge has no discretion once he decides to send an offender to prison. He merely sentences the offender to the proper administrative authority which then has complete sentencing discretion within the maximum imposed by the legislature. In other states, the judge is mandated to a certain prescribed maximum, but may alter the minimum time that a man must serve. In a few states, the judge may increase the minimum so that it is almost equal to the maximum statutory sentence, but in most states the judge can only raise the minimum to some fraction of the maximum. In states that have this sentencing arrangement, the judge uses this discretion in cases where he does not desire that a man be paroled from prison until relatively late in his sentence. In other states, the legislature does not give the judge permission to alter the legislative minimum, but may allow the judge to adjust the statutory maximum downward. Where this practice is allowable, a judge will exercise his discretion when he does not want the parole board to keep a man in prison an extremely long period of time. In the federal system and several states, there has been increasing use of the indeterminate sentence. Although any sentence in which there is some flexibility between the minimum and maximum might be, strictly speaking, indeterminate, this term is generally reserved for instances in which the judge sentences an offender from a minimum of one day to a maximum as prescribed by statue. In this situation, the paroling authority has complete discretion.[14]

Many persons have championed the indeterminate sentence, which for all practical purposes takes most of the sentencing decision out of the

[14] For the best general discussion of sentencing and its variations, see Robert Dawson, *Sentencing* (Boston: Little, Brown, 1969).

judge's hands. The indeterminate sentence until recently has been most widely used in California, and it was hailed there as a rehabilitative revolution—until the state had some experience with it. Currently the finding is that inmates serve more time in prison per type of crime in California than in any other state in the union. Moreover, there have been many inmate complaints that the paroling authority and prison officials hold the indeterminate sentence over the inmates like a club—refusing to release until the inmate behaves.[15] For this and other reasons, California changed its sentencing structure on July 1, 1977. California now uses a "presumptive model" of sentencing, in which the judge must sentence within a three year range for each offense as presented by the legislature. It would appear that the heyday of the indeterminate sentence is over.

Although the indeterminate sentence became popular as a tool *against* improper or uninformed discretion being used by a judge, other people have argued that there are more issues to be considered than simply the future behavior of the offender. It has been suggested in New York, for example (by the Governor's Special Committee on Criminal Offenders),[16] that a judge be allowed to sentence a man to a flat term (e.g., five years in prison, with no parole possible) if the crime committed was a particularly heinous one or one that aroused the community in a particular way. If the attitude of the community is not at issue, and the offender does not appear very dangerous, then he should be sentenced with rehabilitation as a goal (i.e., with a low minimum sentence). But the New York Committee made it clear that it would leave up to the judge the decision whether support of community norms or concern for the individual offender was the most important concern in each instance. It is this kind of decision for which the committee felt the judge had a special aptitude, and for which a distant administrative board would not be suited.[17]

APPELATE JUDGE'S ROLE. The appellate judge's role in considering appeals is considerably different from any judicial task that we have discussed so far. An appellate judge is responsible for reviewing the decisions of other judges. He does so on the record sent up from the trial or lower appellate court. Decisions made by an appellate judge "settle the law" on that particular issue in similar cases for the entire jurisdiction of the appellate court. Obviously, then, the role of the appellate judge is a

---

[15] For the variety of opinions on the indeterminate sentence, see John Irwin, *The Felon* (Englewood Cliffs, N.J.: Prentice-Hall, 1970); George Jackson, *Soledad Brother* (New York: Bantam Books, 1970); Jessica Mitford, *Kind and Usual Punishment* (New York: Knopf, 1974).

[16] New York Governor's Special Committee on Criminal Offenders, *Preliminary Report* (New York: Governor's Office, 1968).

[17] Ibid.

crucial one—he is establishing the law for that particular area. He does not of course draft legislation, but his interpretation of statutes and cases determines how the law should be implemented within that particular jurisdiction.

It is quite possible, upon first glance at the awesome responsibility, that the appellate judiciary fails to estimate accurately the consequences of the appellate task. Even on the Supreme Court level, what justices say often does *not* go—and the justices are increasingly aware of this fact. In the *Miranda* decision in 1966, the court handed down a 100-page decision governing police procedure, and they did so with attention to minute detail. Indeed, some of *Miranda* reads like legislation. Two years later, in the stop and frisk case of *Terry* v. *Ohio* (1968), then Chief Justice Warren stated point blank early in the opinion that there is much police behavior that cannot be touched from the Supreme Court.[18] Likewise, there is much of any behavior that cannot be touched from the appellate court. This is not to belittle the appellate task, but rather is an attempt to put it in perspective. A complete study of criminal justice administration clearly demonstrates the truth of Francis Allen's remark that the law is only 10 percent of criminal justice.[19]

SUPERVISION OF CRIMINAL JUSTICE SYSTEM.   The last judicial task we wish to consider is the judge's role in the supervision of the criminal justice system. There is, of course, for each court a judge, often called the *president judge, presiding judge,* or *chief judge,* etc., who is responsible for the administration of the court. We will discuss that task in the next section. The supervision we are concerned with here is really more fundamental. The judge, because he sits central in the system, and because of the nature of the decisions that he makes from that position, can have tremendous influence over the entire system. What the judge decides to do or not to do can send shock waves of influence both forward through prosecution and defense offices to the police, and backward from probation offices and diagnostic centers to parole boards, parole officers, and halfway houses. A trial judge may have this influence directly by refusing to pass certain types of cases through the system (and thereby eventually changing police practice) or by constantly accepting certain cases (and thereby establishing the correctional response). On an indirect level, the appellate judiciary now feel free, in most areas, to inspect not only police practices but correctional practices as well. The judge is important, in other words, not only in the determination of who is selected for the system, but he is also important in the determination of how selected offenders will be treated once convicted. It is a job, as we shall see in

---

[18] Terry v. Ohio, 392 U.S. 1 (1968).

[19] Francis Allen, *The Borderland of Criminal Justice* (Chicago: University of Chicago Press, 1964), pp. 1–25.

Chapter Ten, that the judges and the judicial structures have difficulty in fulfilling.

THE PROBATION OFFICER

Most persons would agree that another chief figure in the court organization is the probation officer, and the probation organization makes the last major addition to the criminal court structure. The probation officer in a criminal court system has two distinct functions. On the one hand, he aides the judge in a determination of sentence, at least in important cases, by conducting a pre-sentence investigation. On the other hand, he is responsible for the supervision of persons convicted and placed on probation in lieu of punishment (or as a punishment, depending on one's point of view).

The administration of probation differs from state to state and even within states. Generally, however, probation is a county operation, and the judge is seen as the chief administrator of the probation office. Typically, under the judge there is a chief probation officer who supervises the field staff. In smaller offices the same probation officers may be responsible for both adult and juvenile probationers (and the same judge may hear criminal and juvenile cases at different times). In larger offices, there may be different officers under the chief probation officer for juveniles and for adults. And in large metropolitan counties, where there is a specialized juvenile or family court, juvenile and adult probation are also handled separately. A full description of juvenile court and probation practices will be given in Chapter Eight.

In some states, such as Connecticut, probation is an autonomous state operation: the probation staff works closely with the judges of various courts, but they hold civil service positions and are part of a separate state bureaucracy. In other states such as Wisconsin, and in the federal system, all field services of probation and parole are combined in one state organization. In this case, the same officers have both probation and parole responsibilities, and must work closely with both judges and prison officials. In other states, such as Pennsylvania, there is a state organization of probation and parole for serious offenders (generally felonies), whereas separate county probation offices handle misdemeanant cases. (County parole is a rarity.)

Selection and Training of Probation Officers

Generally, probation and parole work carry the highest entrance requirements for front-line workers (with the exception of trial judges and lawyers). The history of probation and parole will be covered in the next chapter. Meanwhile, in relation to selection and training of probation offices, it is relevant to note that probation work began in the nineteenth century as a voluntary philanthropic mission of well-intentioned volunteers who had few or no special qualifications other than their zeal and good intentions. When probation became a statutory position in Boston in 1871, the opportunity for specifying entrance qualifications arose. The real thrust toward specialized training and professional development took hold at the turn of the century with the ascendancy of social work as a profession.

It is now generally required that probation officers have a bachelor's degree in one of the social sciences, and in many states a master's degree is preferred, in social work, psychology, criminal justice, or some related area. Clinical practice, separate or in conjunction with the degree, is also frequently sought. However, the shortage of trained manpower in the social service areas is still critical, and many probation offices settle for personnel with entrance qualifications far short of the ideal. In many areas, persons with any college degree are eligible for front-line positions, regardless of the relevance of the degree to their work.

Training in probation and parole work is an established activity, in contrast to other areas of criminal justice. Beginning before the Second World War, there were probation and parole institutes run by the National Probation and Parole Association, which is now a nationwide group known as the National Council on Crime and Delinquency (N.C.C.D.). The N.C.C.D., L.E.A.A. (Law Enforcement Assistance Administration), and other groups have been active in probation and parole training. In addition, many of the larger probation and parole offices, particularly those operated on a statewide basis, have training divisions.

One of the major issues in correctional field work concerns the question of what kind of training and college curricula will be the most productive of effective field supervision and service. To a great extent, this kind of issue can only be addressed within a policy context. It makes no sense to decide on an educational and training design that is not compatible with the goals and policies of particular field service offices. Although there are certainly mixes of various policies in operation, as we will see in the next chapter, there are basically three policy modes that would suggest different training thrusts. And of these three, the probation and parole emphasis on surveillance and apprehension of re-offending probationers is presently not actively urged as a training goal, in and of itself. But there is some conflict between the so-called policy of reintegration and the policy of rehabilitation. Within the training context, adherents of a reintegrative policy are more likely to favor training that emphasizes teamwork, active advocacy of client needs in the community, and frequent use of referral services and volunteer aid. In a rehabilitation model, on the other hand, the training emphasis is on developing good officer-client relations, developing therapeutic counseling skills, practice of effective case management, and the use of the general social-work model of social intervention.

By far the most common model of training, and consequently the most common probation organizational scheme, the rehabilitation policy, emphasizes the social casework approach. This model is running into problems, however, in meeting large caseload demands. It is not uncommon, for example, for a probation officer to have a caseload of 100 or even 200 persons. And it is unrealistic for a probation worker with this many charges under his supervision to be expected to provide active social counseling for most of his clients. As a result, much probation supervision amounts to little more than periodic phone calls or office visits, during which the probationer verifies his status or reports any changes and receives a couple of hopeful words from the caseworker, who remains inundated with paper work.

In addition, people have recently argued that the casework model is too costly, and is not effective with many of the clients most frequently placed on probation. Many experts have argued that the one-on-one counseling setting may be counterproductive, particularly where the probation officer is a young, white college graduate and the client is poor, black, and uneducated. Hence, the reintegration model of teamwork, use of ex-offenders, and volunteers, with practical emphasis such as job training and job placement, is now the ascendant model.[20]

Pre-Sentence Investigations

A major responsibility of probation officers is the pre-sentence investigation (P.S.I.). In many offices, probation officers spend up to 50 percent of their time on pre-sentence investigations, and in some larger offices, certain probation officers specialize in P.S.I.s, doing nothing else. In areas where this is the case, pre-sentence investigation work is sometimes seen as more prestigious than probation supervision, and as requiring more qualified personnel. Whether or not this is true, many organizations do place tremendous emphasis on the intake decision (which the P.S.I. influences). Also, the officer responsible for pre-sentence investigation work must be attuned to the requirements, desires, prejudices, and whims of the judiciary, regarding sentencing. A probation officer may supervise many probationers without too much contact with the judge, but he may have to testify in court on the pre-sentence investigation. For all those reasons, if there is specialization in an office, the more experienced officers will generally handle P.S.I.s. On the other hand, many probation supervisors have resisted separating their staff into such functional specialties

[20] Dennis C. Sullivan, *Team Management in Probation, Some Models for Implementation* (Hackensack, N.J.: National Council on Crime and Delinquency, 1972).

and instead may assign P.S.I.s to the officer most likely to handle the offender on probation if it is granted.[21]

Pre-sentence investigations are made routinely in some areas and only at the request of the judge in others. They are rarely available in minor cases that may be heard and disposed of in one day in lower court. But in felony courts it is common practice in many systems to assign the case to a probation officer after conviction so that the officer can report on the character and condition of the offender relative to sentencing prior to the sentencing hearing.

The information included in pre-sentence investigation reports also differs widely from area to area. In some places the P.S.I. is nothing more than a cursory interview with the offender in jail and a review of the police rap sheet. In other areas the officer may add a few phone calls to verify information, to check on educational history, employment status, etc. In other areas a thorough background investigation is conducted in which the probation officer may interview family and employer, codefendants (if any), teachers, friends, etc., and hold several meetings with the convicted offender.

Whether the pre-sentence investigation is thorough or cursory, it can, of course, have several different goals. Abraham Blumberg contends that probation officers merely try to justify the conviction of the offender by hunting up every negative aspect of his life that may now be used collectively to seal the offender's doom. Certainly some probation officers may have a policy of recommending for probation, or presenting facts favorable to probation, only when they consider the offender a good probation risk. Other probation organizations may take an opposite stance, attempting to screen out of prison all but the worst risks. But no matter how conservative or liberal the probation staff, it has been argued by some that all the probation officer does is try to guess the judge's feelings or inclinations and then build the case to support that sort of sentence.[22]

There are also many different kinds of information that probation officers might seek during the course of a pre-sentence investigation. Until recently, many reports were very clinical in orientation, frequently with a Freudian or quasi-Freudian twist. In these cases, the field worker might interview any number of people, and gather any sort of information, but always with an eye to using the material as symptomatic of some inner state of the offender, about which it is the officer's duty to express and inform the judge. Although some judges may see this as good

[21] Abraham Blumberg, *Criminal Justice* (Chicago: Triangle, 1967), pp. 143–167.

[22] Ibid.; and see National Advisory Commission on Criminal Justice Standards and Goals, *Report on Corrections* (Washington, D.C.: Government Printing Office, 1974), pp. 184–190.

probation work, or as the kind of justification they personally need in order to sentence an offender, it seems in general a social-work affectation that, regardless of its merits elsewhere, has little to do with the realities of whether a particular offender might be maintained in the community or should be incarcerated. Recently, then, there has been more attention to social background and social conditions, to the offender's definition of his goals, to the appraisal of those goals by the officer, and to strategies of achieving them. Lest this sound ideal, it should be remembered that the offender is in a poor position to negotiate with the officer, or to open up with the truth, and even very real goals may simply be staying employed for three months or refraining from beating up the wife for six months.

Probation Supervision

Probation supervision has already been discussed to some extent in the context of training, and the development of field work will be discussed in the next chapter. For now we should like to point out that supervision techniques are beginning to change after roughly 50 years of the case-work model. There needs to be much change, however, before most probation departments will be able to meet the ever-growing caseload demand, or before any significant indications of effectiveness will be frequently forthcoming.

Probation supervision begins, some would say, with the pre-sentence investigation. But without philosophizing about the importance of that part of the process, it might be fair to say that in a formal sense, probation supervision begins with the judge's pronouncement of probation as the consequence of conviction. Probation has two general legal variations: (1) sentence pronounced but unexecuted and probation imposed, or (2) sentence suspended and probation imposed. In the first case, a revocation decision may be an administrative matter that need not return to the judge; whereas in the second case, upon revocation the probationer must return to the judge for sentencing to be decided.

Probation supervision always begins with a list of probation rules, adherence to which will lead to satisfactory termination of probation, and violation of which can mean incarceration. General supervision rules are more or less the same in all states. They include provisions for law-abiding behavior, for cooperation with the probation officer, and for notification of change of address or loss of job. They may include permission to drive a car and to marry. Prohibiting the use of alcohol or the frequenting of bars is common. In addition to such general provisions, the judge may specify particular conditions for particular offenders. Making restitution is common, and cooperating with police or grand jury investigations may be another stipulation. In states where the probation office is not organized under the judge, the judge's power to make certain conditions may be limited and may be transferred to the probation agency. In such cases the judge would order the probationers to follow such conditions as set out by the probation officer.[23]

One problem with probation supervision is that there is not too much control over who becomes a client. There is much greater control in felony cases than in misdemeanor cases, but probation is more frequent in the latter type.

As we have said, supervision is often constricted by severe overdemands on the manpower of the system. Frequently supervision is a monthly phone call or a five-minute visit. Often probationers are not seen or heard from until they are picked up on a new charge or until they are released from supervision. Supervision, in other words, is often nonexistent; but nonexistent supervision is frequently all that is necessary. Many first offenders placed on probation never return to crime. On the other hand, it has also been found that reducing caseload size or increasing staff competency or training can result in *more* violations and revocations, either because there is more client contact or greater expertise in predicting and detecting misbehavior.

Some agencies have in the last five or ten years begun experimenting with supervision organization and with supervision goals. For example, under several new career programs, ex-offenders have been hired as probation officers or as officer-aides.[24] Also, job specialties have been added or developed, or specialists have simply emerged. Often such varied specialists will work in teams with a common caseload. But instead of managing men, they try to manage problems.[25]

Although effectiveness of probation supervision has probably increased over the last decade, and although one southwestern state has recently claimed probation recidivism as low as 15 percent,[26] it can probably still be said that, in general, probation has proven no more but no less successful than incarceration as a method of reducing future crime, when type of offender is controlled.[27] Given this standoff on effectiveness, the major advantage of probation is its cost. Maintaining an offender in the community generally costs about one-tenth of what it costs to incarcerate him. And although recidivism rates might be equal, prison affords few

[23] Frank Remington et al., *Criminal Justice Administration* (Indianapolis: Bobbs-Merrill, 1969), pp. 796–807.

[24] Sullivan, *Team Management in Probation*, pp. 33–35.

[25] Ibid., pp. 22–35.

[26] The claim of a 15 percent failure rate was apparently either overconfident or premature. Later examinations of the same offenders found rates had doubled.

[27] Leslie T. Wilkins, "Information and Decisions Regarding Offenders," in S. A. Yefslay, *Law Enforcement, Science and Technology* (Washington, D.C.: Thompson, 1967).

positive alternatives for people under supervision, whereas probation allows a job or vocation to be maintained and family life to continue.

OTHER ACTORS AND GROUPS
IN THE COURT

To this point, we have discussed the primary actors in the complex of organizations that are typically referred to as the "court" component of the criminal justice system. These major actors (the prosecutor, the defense attorney, the judge, and the probation officer) are supported and integrated by numerous other officials and groups in the court phase of the criminal process. Of course, specific actors differ from jurisdiction to jurisdiction, and from one type of court to another. There are, however, some other key personnel and court subsystems that are fairly typical. With the exception of the actors involved in the juvenile justice system (who will be discussed in Chapter Six), the other important court actors are briefly discussed in this section.

The Trial Jury

The trial jury, or petit jury, is an ancient institution. Trial by jury is guaranteed in the Sixth Amendment. Like other rights, a jury trial can be waived. A plea of guilty, of course, is a waiver of the right to jury as well as of other rights.

The trial jury is a key ingredient in the American adversarial system. The defense attorney and the prosecutor must establish their cases before the jury, who decides whether the state or the individual has the strongest case. The jury represents the people of the state whom the defendant, if guilty, has wronged. But the jury also represents the defendant's peers, who stand between him and the power of the state.

Given the relative infrequency of jury trial, one might suppose that its major effects are symbolic rather than practical. However, the practical influence of the jury trial is wider spread than its direct use would imply. Most plea bargaining, for example, is based to some extent on the knowledge that a jury trial *could* be demanded.

There are currently a number of criticisms of the jury. Perhaps the most common is that the jury is an exceedingly costly and cumbersome device to determine facts. Many critics suggest that a judge could do as adequate if not a better job, and at much less expense. Others claim that the complexity of the law has increased to such an extent that proper fact finding requires the education and training possessed by a judge.

It is possible that some of these complaints, particularly about expense, would be reduced if the courts could manage jury selection and management more efficiently. Other problems caused by poor management involve insensitivity to and low pay for jurors, and consequently considerable reluctance by citizens to serve as jurors.

Trial juries usually have 12 members, and usually require a unanimous decision. Some states are now experimenting with smaller juries in misdemeanor cases or at the agreement of both defense and prosecution. In other instances, less than unanimous decisions are now acceptable, at least for some kinds of cases.

Jury selection is a complex procedure. Potential jurors are usually selected from the tax rolls of the county. Jury panels are selectd for varying lengths of time. In some smaller jurisdictions, there may be only one or two jury sessions a year. In larger courts, new panels may be chosen quarterly or monthly. Once a panel has been selected, persons who have valid excuses are replaced by other persons from the jury list. When a jury trial is scheduled, prospective jurors are chosen randomly from the jury panel. When a person is selected, he is examined by both the prosecutor and the defense attorney. Prospective jurists can be challenged for cause or preemptorily. Some causes would be that the juror is a witness, or related to the victim or the defendant, or had been a witness to a similar crime, etc. A preemptory challenge dismisses a juror without need to state or show cause. The number of such challenges is limited, either by statute or from trial to trial. The defense usually has more such challenges than the prosecution.

The Grand Jury

The grand jury is another institution of rather ancient origin. The grand jury was apparently an English innovation, in which 12 lords, and eventually 23 citizens, had to vote in favor of prosecution. And indictment is still one major function of a grand jury, thereby certifying to the strength and quantity of evidence presented by the district attorney.

Some critics of the grand jury system argue that this long and expensive method of establishing probable cause is without concomitant advantages, because most grand juries simply go along with whatever the prosecutor wants. Other critics tend to agree about the expense, but point out that the grand jury does not always acquiesce to the prosecutor's desires—and that these instances of refusing to prosecute are difficult to evaluate in cost terms.

Grand juries have other functions, however, besides passing on probable cause. The function that is most often cited as unique to the grand jury is its independent investigatory and watchdog role. A grand jury may initiate its own investigations, about disposition of public funds, the conditions in public institutions, corruption among public officials, etc. It is quite possible that the grand jury may be the only public investigative body with sufficient anonymity and sufficient independence to examine certain kinds of crime, particularly crimes involving public officials.

Other Roles in the Court Organization

There are many other offices and roles within the court and related organizations. Bailiffs are responsible, among other things, for the physical management of the courtroom, calling and protecting witnesses, sequestering of the jury, and maintaining order in the courtroom.

Court reporters are a specially trained group responsible for maintaining a written record of courtroom transactions. Until recently most court reporters used a special stenographic machine in order to maintain a record of testimony. Some courts are now tape-recording hearings, and it is the court reporter's responsibility to record, maintain, and transcribe the tapes.

Court clerks have the general responsibility of coordinating the written documents required for hearings with the scheduling of hearings. They must make sure that all the legal documents are available when and where they are required. They must, for example, file and distribute the information with written notice of charges (the complaint) and accurately record and file the disposition of each case.

Because the criminal process is so entirely dependent on *written* notice of charges, and *written* record of proceedings and findings, an extremely important component of the court system is the stenographic pool. If the variety of formal reports are not accurate and timely, the entire process can bog down. Thus, although the textbooks may focus great attention on the major actors, one should not forget that the more mundane aspects of operation may be equally important.

CURRENT ISSUES IN CRIMINAL COURTS

There are a variety of current issues in the criminal court system that warrant fuller discussion than a book such as this can provide. Therefore we will only briefly mention here some of the most important issues that are of current concern in the courts. These are (1) release pending trial, (2) the conditions of the lower courts, (3) judicial discretion and its control, and (4) court management and information systems.

Release Pending Trial

There are few court experts who have not been clamoring for reform in the bail system of the criminal process. Bail reform and alternatives to bail have been "hot issues" for at least ten years, and yet little seems to be changing. A few large cities have made some major innovations, such as release on recognizance and the 10 percent bail system, for a certain portion of the offender group subject to pretrial detention. But surveys of nationwide release practices reveal little in the way of a major shift in this area of the criminal process.[28]

Whether or not bail is a constitutional right has been a matter of academic debate for years. The Eighth Amendment prohibits excessive bail but says nothing about the right to bail itself. Some people have argued that it is absurd to prohibit excessive amounts of something that itself is not available, but other persons have argued that the Eighth Amendment clause means that *where bail* is available, it cannot be excessive. This latter argument, has, one must agree, won out in the practical realm, because indeed people are denied bail every day. On the other hand, this argument really makes little sense, since when the officials can delimit where or to whom something will be available, they may automatically make it excessive to other groups. In other words, if *somebody* can afford bail, it is hard to argue that it is not excessive to the person who cannot afford it. That is, persons who argue for detention of somebody, in fairness ought to argue to detain everyone. Clearly they do not do that, and clearly it is the poor, disenfranchised, uneducated, and jobless who will remain in jail pending their hearing, while a rich man, regardless of his future danger to society, can go free.[29]

A common complaint about the bail system is the bonding procedure most commonly employed. Usually the court sets bail at a certain figure, which the defendant cannot afford. For a fee that ranges from 10 to 20 percent, a professional bondsman will post a bond with the court, which supposedly guarantees that the bondsman will pay the bail fee if the defendant absconds. Often the court does not require proof that the bondsman has such money, and frequently the court does not seek to collect anyway. But in most jurisdictions, the person just as responsible as the judge for the decision of who stays in jail and who gets out is the professional bondsman.[30]

In some states, notably Illinois, an attempt has been made to combat this system with the "10 percent bond system." In this system the defendant pays 10 percent of the bail directly to the court. Then, if he returns for his hearing, his money is returned except for 2 to 3 percent that is kept to pay for the expense of running the bail system. Although jurisdic-

[28] Paul B. Wice, "Bail Reform in American Cities," *Criminal Law Bulletin, 9,* No. 9 (November 1973), 770–797.

[29] Legal Aid Society of New York City, "The Unconstitutional Administration of Bail: Bellamy v. The Judges of New York City," *Criminal Law Bulletin, 8,* No. 6 (July/August 1972), 459–506.

[30] President's Commision on Law Enforcement and the Administration of Justice, *Task Force Report: The Courts,* pp. 37–41.

tions that use this plan can do away with the bondsman, there have been no more people released to the community since people who cannot pay a bondsman 10 percent cannot pay it to the court either.[31]

Increasingly common as an alternative to money bail is a personal bond, or release on recognizance (R.O.R.). The first large-scale R.O.R. program was instituted by the Vera Foundation in several selected precincts in New York. It was demonstrated that release on recognizance subjects had a lower absconding rate than persons released on money bond, and after several years the Vera bail project became a citywide operation that has since been initiated in other cities. The object of R.O.R., unlike the 10 percent bail plans, is the release of persons who could not afford money bail. There are, however, some limitations. Release on recognizance status can be achieved by persons who have been resident in the city for a certain period of time, have family and other community ties, or are steadily employed. In other words, defendants at the bottom of the economic barrel, without a job or family, are unlikely to be selected as R.O.R. candidates. Also, release on recognizance is usually not open to persons who have committed particular crimes (regardless of the fact that such offenses may be bailable offenses). The information used to determine R.O.R. eligibility is usually gathered while the defendant is awaiting his initial appearance. Usually law students do the interviewing and then make a few phone calls to verify the information. If the defendant scores so many points, according to the weighting for different kinds of information, the interviewer passes along an eligibility notice to the magistrate, who then may follow the release on recognizance recommendation or demand that bail be met. In New York, most magistrates now comply fairly regularly with the R.O.R. interview scores. In some other cities there may be less cooperation.[32]

One major data discovery that accompanied the R.O.R. evaluation in New York City is the tremendous importance of the released/incarcerated status of the defendant pending the outcome of his case. When the Vera Foundation compared outcome of case to the pretrial status, it found that about 15 percent of released defendants were incarcerated as a disposition, whereas about 85 percent of incarcerated defendants were later given a jail or prison sentence.[33] A later study by the New York Legal Aid Society found approximately the same results, even when the type of crime and other variables were controlled. In other words, whether a man is free or jailed pending the disposition of his case is a

[31] Ibid.

[32] Ibid.

[33] Charles E. Ares, Anne Rankin, and Herbert Sturz, "The Manhattan Bail Project: An Interim Report on the Use of Pre-Trial Parole," *New York University Law Review*, *38* (January 1963), 67–95.

major determinant of whether the defendant becomes a prisoner after disposition of his case.[34]

Another important issue in pretrial release is the one of preventive detention, or of holding a defendant pending trial on the grounds that he would be dangerous if released on bail or by some other method. Preventive detention became an important political issue during the first Nixon administration, although the practice of preventive detention is probably as old as bail itself. Prior to the Bail Reform Act of 1966 for Washington, D.C., however, preventive detention was always accomplished in a subterraneous fashion, since there had been no provision for preventive detention in state or federal statutes. Ordinarily, a judge who desired to retain a defendant, for whatever reason, could do so by setting bail so high that it could not be met. In some cases, as with civil rights demonstrations in the South in the 1960s, southern magistrates would set bail at exorbitant rates in order to punish the demonstrators. But in many other cases, magistrates might set high bail in order to hold an offender who might reoffend while on bail. The facts often cited in support of this practice are cases in which a defendant commits another crime while on bail in order to pay for his legal fees. How frequently such events occurred is uncertain, but these cases provided impetus for the legalization of preventive detention in Washington, D.C. The federal statute sets out in complex and somewhat ambiguous terms the occasions when a judge may invoke the preventive detention provision. Early findings about the practice in Washington suggest that the provision is not as necessary as legislators may have thought. In the first seven months of the program, the clause was used seven times. In most cases where the judge may have thought that preventive detention would have been necessary, the offender was usually poor enough that he could not meet normal bail anyway.[35]

The Conditions of the Lower Courts

Another extremely important issue is the improvement of the lower courts in the United States. Justice of the peace courts, magistrates courts, police courts, recorders courts, and so on, have the greatest volume of cases in the system and affect the greatest number of people, and yet these courts operate with the poorest budgets, the least trained judges, and the least semblance of justice. It has frequently been suggested that these lower courts should be abolished and their functions taken over by trial judges. Of particular concern has been the quality of justice dis-

[34] Legal Aid Society of New York City, *Unconstitutional Administration of Bail.*

[35] President's Commission on Law Enforcement and the Administration of Justice, *Task Force Report: The Courts,* pp. 39–40.

pensed by justices of the peace and other such judicial officers who are often without legal training.[36]

Although figures are not very reliable, it is frequently the case that an offender will have several contacts with the lower court system as the consequence of several petty offenses or misdemeanors before he commits a felony. The President's Crime Commission, reviewing this situation, asked why it was that so little attention was given to an offender until he committed a major crime, at which point whatever attention rendered is probably of the wrong type and too late.[37]

This kind of problem is compounded by the guilty plea process and by lack of concern in the lower courts about provision of counsel. For these reasons, many judicial indiscretions probably go unnoticed, unappealed, and uncorrected. It is common, for example, for a lower-court judge to sentence a dozen drunks at a time as they are herded before him, or to complete a trial in a matter of moments, or to threaten a defendant who asks for counsel with a stiffer sentence when he is convicted.[38]

The remedies for this dysfunctional and immoral situation are at this point unclear. It is possible that modernized court management practices might improve the situation somewhat, but there appear to be undeniable needs for many more qualified judges, or for creating alternate means for dealing with the problems of the offenders who most frequently end up in lower courts. In some states, for example, public drunkenness has been decriminalized if the drunk can be certified as an alcoholic. In other states, programs such as "preconviction probation" or "accelerated rehabilitative disposition" attempt to unclog the courts by placing certain defendants under voluntary probation in return for a waiver of prosecution.[39]

Discretion and Its Control

The use of discretion by criminal justice personnel has been a major policy and research issue for at least the last dozen years. The importance of the police decision not to arrest was highlighted in the 1965 American Bar Foundation survey of criminal justice practices, and the impact and

[36] Samuel Dash, "Cracks in the Foundation of Criminal Justice," *Illinois Law Review, 46*, No. 3 (July/August 1951), 385–406.

[37] President's Commission on Law Enforcement and the Administration of Justice, *Task Force Report: The Courts*, pp. 29–36; and Stephen Bing and S. Stephen Rosenfeld, *The Quality of Justice in the Lower Criminal Courts of Metropolitan Boston* (Boston: Governor's Committee on Law Enforcement and the Administration of Justice, 1970).

[38] Bing and Rosenfeld, *The Quality of Justice.*

[39] Nicholas N. Kittrie, *The Right to Be Different* (Baltimore: Penguin, 1971), pp. 261–296.

variability of the patrolman's discretion were basic research foci in the now classic studies by Skolnick and Wilson.[40] In the court phases of the criminal process, discretion also holds sway as a major variable in the determination of case outcome. The usual distinction between police discretion and the variability of decision making in the courts is that police are legally bound to administer statutory provisions, whereas prosecutors and judges have constitutionally or statutorially delegated discretion in a number of areas. For example, we have seen that magistrates have discretion in the setting of bail; they have a range of bail levels that are presumably "not excessive." Furthermore, prosecutors have legal discretion to file a nolle prosequi; that is, they may decide for a variety of reasons not to prosecute even if evidence of guilt seems strong. Judges also have discretion to dismiss a case at any point in the proceedings, or to process a case in an alternate manner. Very important is their discretion to accept or reject pleas of guilty and their discretion in the setting of sentence both as to type of sentence and as to amount of punishment prescribed within certain legislative constraints.[41]

Important issues in studying the use of discretion include the reasons for its use (and misuse), the constraints upon its use or the variables that influence its direction, and the consequences of discretion for the administration of justice. A crucial problem in any of these facets is the fact that discretion and the conditions under which it is exercised all tend to inhibit the study of it. For example, the entire guilty plea process is riddled with decision nodes at which discretion is used and cannot be avoided. And yet the conditions that spur the use of the guilty plea route, such as the overload of cases, the avoidance of the provision of counsel, the poor education and low social class of most guilty plea offenders, frequently result in conditions of secrecy, low visibility, and lack of decision factors, and also make it difficult even to identify when decisions have been made or discretion exercised.

The few studies that are available generally agree that officials tend to create situations in which they have discretion and to avoid or restructure situations in which it is not available. Hence, offenses with mandatory sentences are usually avoided by prosecutors and judges. The use of guilty pleas is influenced by the official's desire to have room to negotiate and to avoid open, adversary proceedings where discretion is less often available or more visible to scrutiny.[42]

Contrary to the studies of business, industrial, or public administration

[40] Jerome Skolnick, *Justice Without Trial* (New York: Wiley, 1966); and James Q. Wilson, *Varities of Police Behavior* (Cambridge, Mass.: Harvard University Press, 1968).

[41] Frank Miller, *Prosecution* (Boston: Little, Brown, 1970); and Dawson, *Sentencing.*

[42] Remington, *Criminal Justice Administration,* pp. 413–473.

bureaucracies, there seems to be a direct relation in the court system between the bureaucratization of procedures and the availability of discretion. In other words, officials tend to routinize and standardize work flow (as in the guilty plea process) in order to gain some decision room that is *not* available in an adversarial setting. Although many critics of court bureaucratization such as Blumberg and Harris generally bemoan the displacement of goals when standardization and routinization set in, these critics usually emphasize the influence of the "work ethic" or "production ethic" on the emergence of bureaucratic structure.[43] Equally important, it would seem, is the flight by officials from a combative situation and their move toward a cooperative system, such as a bureaucracy. We will discuss this trend at greater length in Chapter Ten.

Court Management and Information Systems

Stemming directly from the observation of the tendency of officials to create discretionary situations, there is now recognized need for improved court administration. Blumberg, for example, sees the criminal courts as emergent bureaucracies, in which the adversary model is slowly being displaced with a bureaucratic model both for the production in the system and for the general structure of organizational relationships in which this work takes place. Although Blumberg then criticizes the new structure for its propensities to create conditions in which constitutional rights may be violated, other experts have taken the different tack of suggesting that the bureaucratic trend, being unavoidable, should be completed or reinforced with *new* methods of controlling discretion and controlling work flow. In other words, since the adversarial controls do not work in a bureaucratized, cooperative court system, then information and control methods must be introduced that will provide this function within the new structure.[44]

THE NEED FOR COORDINATION.   One basic need for better court management is simply the need to coordinate the work of the many different groups that come together within the court phases of the criminal process. As we have noted earlier, the court is not *one* organization but the result of many interacting organizations, including the judicial orga-

---

[43] Blumberg, *Criminal Justice,* pp. 169–188; and Richard Harris, "Boston Criminal Courts-I," *New Yorker,* April 14, 1973 pp. 45–88; and "Boston Criminal Courts-II," *New Yorker,* April 21, 1973, pp. 44–89.

[44] *Ibid.*—compare with the approach taken by the Supreme Court in *Alford* v. *North Carolina,* 400 U.S. 25 (1970), and by the National Advisory Commission on Criminal Justice Standards and Goals, *Report on the Courts* (Washington, D.C.: Government Printing Office, 1974), pp. 42–65. See also James A. Gayell, "The Future of State Court Management," unpublished manuscript, San Diego State University, San Diego, Calif., 1976.

nization, the prosecutor's office, the defense office, and perhaps a separate probation office. There is no "boss" or overall supervisor of all these agencies. These agencies have many autonomous sources of power and influence, and as each organization gets more complex, the chances of interorganizational conflict increase.

There have been a variety of suggestions made for improving cooperation, and almost all of them include the injection of modern planning and management practices into each organization, or providing a *common* management and information system. For example, in the federal courts, a computerized information system called *PROMIS* has been developed for the use of federal prosecuting offices for the scheduling of cases; for the location, notification, and monitoring of witnesses; for the evaluation of individual prosecutor's records; and so on. This system is an example of a management component for one organization that then must be coordinated with separate systems for the judicial system and federal probation and parole. In contrast, in the St. Louis area, a system called *JURIS* has been structured that provides information and evaluative data for all agencies connected with juvenile justice in the region. On the adult level, *REGIS* is the counterpart system for the same geographical area.[45]

The largest and most ambitious such undertaking is known as *Project SEARCH, Inc.*, a L.E.A.A.-funded activity originally managed by the California Crime Technological Foundation. SEARCH has several different project goals, two of the largest being the computerization of criminal histories on a state and national level, and a project called Offender-Based Transaction Statistics (O.B.T.S.), which for the first time would provide a systematic monitoring of each offender's passage through all phases of the criminal justice system, from arrest through correctional release.[46]

Such programs offer many advantages over the present state of affairs, such as their ability to delineate how many offenders "fall out" at each decision point in the system, or how long it takes to process different kinds of offenders through the system, or how many times original charges are reduced before trial, and when in the processing such reductions take place. Given the operationalization of such systems for a number of years, accurate data will finally become available on the workings of the system in its entirety and the relationships among operations in different functional components.

Of course, this kind of management trend also raises some new issues

---

[45] SEARCH Group, Inc., *SJIS State Judicial Information Systems: State of the Art* (Sacramento, Calif.: SEARCH Group, Inc., technical report No. 11, June 1975).

[46] SEARCH Group Inc., *OBSCIS Offender-Based State Corrections Information System* (Sacramento, Calif.: SEARCH Group, Inc., technical report No. 10, May 1975).

of concern, such as who should have access to such data, how such access can be controlled, and how violations should be punished.[47]

TYPICAL MANAGEMENT PROBLEMS. There are a variety of different problems that need to be addressed in the contexts of these managerial developments. Some typical ones are: (1) the management of court delay, (2) the management of jurors and witnesses, (3) liaison between organizations, and (4) evaluation of effectiveness.

COURT DELAY. Court delay is an age-old problem. Discussions now generally revolve around the right to speedy trial and the financial cost of delay. Major problems include sorting out the kinds of delays into those that are avoidable and those that are necessary, then analyzing how to eliminate the avoidable delays, and predicting how such action might impact on other parts of the system.

WITNESSES AND JURORS. A major criticism of courts as they now operate is the terrible waste and inconvenience caused to both jurors and witnesses because of poor selection practices, poor notification procedures, and so on. The computerization of information about cases such as hearing dates, names and addresses of witnesses, prosecutors' decisions about cases, etc., can have beneficial effects both on the kinds of witnesses selected and on the kinds of cases prosecuted (i.e., whether witnesses are trustworthy and cooperative or not), as well as on the notification of witnesses about when and where to appear for a case. Similar computerization of data on prospective jurors can ease tremendously the tedious procedures prior to trial, by extracting from jury panels the most ineligible prospects prior to courtroom examinations.

LIAISON. Also important is the facilitation of interaction between different court organizations by providing each organization with a common set of data, or by removing much of the manual paper work involved in interorganizational or interunit communication. We can predict improvements, for example, both in very busy public defender offices in which one lawyer defends a client at the initial appearance and another at trial, or in easing communication between prosecutors' offices and the police regarding investigations or court appearances.

EVALUATION OF EFFECTIVENESS. Lastly, computerized management devices such as PROMIS may allow officials for the first time to gather information about the differential effects of alternate processing routines. Judges may finally receive information about the differential effectiveness

[47] SEARCH Group Inc., *Standards for Security and Privacy of Criminal Justice Information* (Sacramento, Calif.: SEARCH Group, Inc., technical report No. 13, October 1975).

of different dispositions in different types of cases. If officials are sophisticated in the analysis of such information on system outputs, they may finally have the data base from which to take strategic action in modifying system operations. All of these technologies, however, will not reduce the need for good decisions by qualified people. But such technologies may reduce daily operations to a workable level so that decision makers finally have enough time to consider the variety of issues implied in any policy decision.

chapter 6

History and Current Problems in Corrections

Traditionally, the prison and parole process has been the least visible and least understood part of the criminal justice system. Since the establishment of a maximum security prison in the early 1800s, a prison has been visible to the public as a massive stone wall, hiding activities that were filled with mystery. The worn cliché, "Out of sight, out of mind," is an inaccurate statement of the relationship of prisons to the community. What was in sight was an impenetrable fortress that functioned not only to keep people in, but equally important, to keep the public out. As we shall see later, this forbidding image was originally designed as a therapeutic device. The prisoner was shut away as a punishment, but an integral part of that punishment was the belief that reform was possible only if offenders were isolated from the evils of society. In other words, if "out of sight, out of mind" refers to the public response to the condition of incarcerated offenders, the strategy originally was to keep society out of the offender's sight and out of his thoughts.

We frequently forget the fact that the stone wall was an implied criticism of the community. The wall and the internal custody precautions were, in their first years, a statement that crime is generated by community conditions, by the social evils of the emerging eastern cities, by social institutions that fostered crime and rewarded criminals, and by an apparent lack of concern by political and social leaders for correcting these problems before they would lead to crime.[1]

Perhaps more than any other major factor, it was the reformers' basically pessimistic view about society and their basically optimistic view of the potentials of the individual human being that created the kind of correctional organizations we have today. This concept would also seem to be a major reason for the despair and cynicism that exist in and about prisons and parole today. This reliance on the concept of individual potential goodness and the distrust of concerted group or community activity has proven to be rather unadaptable to the complexity of urban twentieth-century living.

This theme, on a broader scope, becomes one of the basic reasons why the coverage of the criminal justice system is organized as it is in this book: namely, that the emphasis on individual rights vis-à-vis the politically organized society is one of the major underpinnings of our federal system of government. The framers of the U.S. Constitution took exceeding care in the regulation of organized power so that state rights were not usurped by the national government. Behind this famous political design problem there were analogous interests in preserving community control from state domination and, ultimately, of guarding the individual citizens from coercion from any level of organized government.[2]

This political design has had some important consequences for the "criminal justice system." On the most general level, the check and balance system of three branches of government, combined with the complicated arrangements between federal, state, and local political entities, has meant that we do *not* have *one system* of criminal justice. Rather, we have complex and often contradictory relationships among legislatures that write laws, executive agencies that apprehend criminals and punish offenders, and judicial organizations that are to pass judgment on the outcome of legislative and executive actions for any given individual. In short, there historically has been as much interest in who (under what authority) was performing the criminal justice tasks as in whether the task itself was completed effectively.

We have seen some of the consequences of this political arrangement for the police, courts, and probation. The organization for the accomplishment of correctional tasks has been equally fragmented. Indeed, although people frequently speak of sentencing and probation as *correctional* processes, these functions are usually carried out by organizations

---

[1] David Rothman, *The Discovery of the Asylum* (Boston: Little, Brown, 1971), pp. 84–88.

[2] Nicholas Kittrie, *The Right To Be Different* (Baltimore: Penguin, 1973), pp. 45–50.

that have many other preconviction responsibilities. And although some states and the federal system have combined probation and parole services, it appears to be more common among the states to combine prison and parole services, and to keep probation under the authority of the courts and local government.[3]

THE CURRENT STATE OF PRISON AND PAROLE

The average convicted offender is subjected to many competing penal philosophies and many contrasting demands on his behavior. One reason for this is the fragmentation of his correctional experience into the functional responsibilities of different organizations with different constraints and little common policy.

The Fragments of the Correctional Task

SENTENCING AS A CORRECTIONAL DECISION. We have discussed sentencing structures and sentencing policy basically in relation to the courts and the judiciary. Crucial to the understanding of the prison and parole process is to see sentencing from the other side of the prison door. Many of the judge's reasons for sentencing a person to prison are irrelevant to the behavior of the incarcerated offender. As many wardens say (but don't quite mean), the offender arrives at prison "with a clean slate." Although prison officials obviously do make distinctions among incoming offenders, with this statement they are recognizing that a prisoner's behavior is frequently unpredictable in terms of the police and judicial perceptions of the man. Wardens are quick to use the example that the offender who commits one heinous murder, although treated as an extremely dangerous quantity prior to conviction and sentenced to a long number of years, is frequently a model inmate, remorseful about the act and cooperative with officials. Conversely, the "bad actors" within the prison are frequently relatively minor offenders who went through the preconviction system in a routine manner.

Regardless of the frequency of the examples given above, they are a useful demonstration of the relationship between court-sentencing practice and correctional operation. Sentencing is the *intake decision* for the prison and parole process, but the prison officials have little formal control over sentencing practices. Judges and prison officials *do* communicate. For example, when a prison is extremely overcrowded, judges are

---

[3] President's Commission on Law Enforcement and the Administration of Justice, *Task Force Report: Corrections* (Washington, D.C.: Government Printing Office, 1967), pp. 35–37.

more likely to sentence to probation. On the other hand, some of the problems that eventually lead to the prison conditions of which judges have taken notice are probably generated by poor court-prison communication in the first place. For example, in one northeastern state the department of corrections has offered a standing invitation for judges to visit the prisons and learn more about the facilities, their potentials, and their problems. In the first four years of that invitation, no judge took advantage of it. In the same state, one particular judge continually sentenced felons "for psychiatric care" to a prison that had no psychiatric personnel or facilities.

Perhaps the critical difference between the judge's perspective and prison officials' perspective in regard to sentencing is that the prison officials have to find some way of controlling the offender, whereas the judge does not. Sentencing disparity, for example, frequently occurs because the judge sentences each offender in relation to immediately prevailing court conditions, rather than in relation to other offenders or prevailing prison conditions. Although the pressures that influence the judge's sentence may be legitimate concerns, they are not always functional from a prison official's point of view.[4]

Ideally, most prison officials would like to have some sort of formal control or at least an advisory status in sentencing. The most common argument in favor of correctional sentencing is that the judge cannot predict the future behavior of offenders as well as correctional officials can. Although this may be true, judges have other reasons for sentencing besides the future behavior of the offender. The counterargument is that the judge is more directly in contact with the community than the correctional officials, and therefore he can more adequately sentence, taking all factors into consideration.[5]

A few states have taken much of the sentencing discretion away from the trial judge and placed it in the hands of a sentencing board. California is perhaps the most famous of these. This innovation was heralded as a major improvement in sentencing practice, because the board would have at their disposal, prior to their decision, a complex diagnostic report. The sentencing board also is in closer contact with prison officials and, theoretically, can adjust the sentence, based on more up-to-date observations of the offender's prison behavior. Moreover, the personnel on the board were supposed to be highly trained behavioral experts whose decisions would be clinically, rather than judicially, oriented.[6]

---

[4] Robert O. Dawson, *Sentencing: The Decision as to Type, Length and Conditions of Sentence* (Boston: Little, Brown, 1969), pp. 215–222. See also Orland and Ryler, (eds.), *Justice in Sentencing* (Mineola, N.Y.: Foundation Press, 1974).

[5] New York Governor's Special Committee on Criminal Offenders, *Preliminary Report* (New York: State of New York, 1969).

[6] John Irwin, *The Felon* (Englewood Cliffs, N.J.: Prentice-Hall, 1970), pp. 50–60.

The California system and others like it, however, have come in for sharp criticism lately by prisoners and by behavioral scientists. One problem seems to be that the political pressures on the board are as severe as those on the judge. Second, the board has never had the clinical expertise that was planned for it. A third problem is that, from the prisoner's point of view, it is an extremely uncomfortable situation not knowing how much time must be served when one enters prison. In Washington this problem is not so great as it is in California, because the sentencing board there announces its sentence within six months after receiving the prisoner. However, both the Washington system of the definite date for sentencing and the flexible California procedure place the offender in an exceedingly ambiguous position for a long period of time. Since his time is about all a prisoner has left at that point in the criminal justice process, most inmates would prefer a definite pronouncement from the trial judge to a delayed reaction from a special board.[7]

The fourth problem with the sentencing board is related to the third, that of delayed sentencing, and is perhaps even more important from the inmate's point of view. This problem has to do with the supposed purpose of the sentence—particularly when the sentence announcement is delayed as it was in California. The delayed decision by a special board is supposed to allow sentencing to be more congruent with whatever treatment the inmate is diagnosed as needing. The counterclaim, however, is that the indeterminate sentence is used as a punishment if the offender misbehaves, or as a threat to keep him in line. The inmates argue that sentencing by the board is governed by custodial rather than therapeutic motives. They claim that they are coerced into obeying any and every whim of their captors and that the expense of disobedience is an additional delay in the pronouncement of sentence. Although the validity of such claims would certainly be denied by officials, it is true that incarcerated inmates in California spent more time in prison than in other states. But it is also true, as the officials point out, that California uses probation more liberally than many states and that, consequently, it is only the more dangerous offenders who reach prison.[8]

The settlement of such arguments is well beyond the scope of this book, but the argument demonstrates the pros and cons of different sentencing procedures. It should be of particular interest how quickly the questions of *who* sentences and *when* the sentence is announced become issues of in-custody control. The selection of which offenders will go to prison and how long they will spend there cannot be separated from how

[7] Ibid. California abolished this sentencing system in 1977.

[8] George Jackson, *Soledad Brother* (New York: Bantam Books, 1970); and Jessica Mitford, *Kind and Usual Punishment* (New York: Knopf, 1973), pp. 86–87.

the offenders behave in prison. Thus the notion is gaining strength that corrections should be able to influence the sentencing process.

PROBATION WORK AS A CORRECTIONAL DIAGNOSIS.   Just as the actual sentencing decision is usually made independent of prison and parole officials, probation work is also usually separate from the prison and parole process. The variety of probation administrative forms were discussed in Chapters Four and Five. What is of interest here, is how the separation of probation decision making and probation supervision affects the prison and parole operation. Perhaps of greatest relevance are the preparation of the pre-sentence investigation and the decision to revoke probation and to impose a prison sentence.

Usually the first person with the reputation as a "correctional worker" to come in contact with the offender is the probation officer. In those cases where a pre-sentence investigation is ordered, the probation officer's first contact concerns whether or not the convicted offender will land in prison. Surely, the reliance that the judge places on the recommendation of probation reports differs from jurisdiction to jurisdiction, but there is every reason to suppose that the pre-sentence investigation (P.S.I.) is a significant piece of information in the eyes of most judges.

Pre-sentence reports also differ greatly from probation department to probation department. Generally, however, the probation officer is one of the first officials in the system who is openly and admittedly concerned with more about the offender than the crime he committed. It is a probation tradition, by now, for the officer to emphasize "character" and "condition" as well as "acts." Since probation usually operates under some sort of treatment ideology, this interest in more than the criminal act is justified on the grounds that the man, rather than the crime, is the focus of treatment.[9]

What is important to prison and parole, but something we know very little about, is what conditions of character, as perceived by the probation officer justify to him the recommendation to incarcerate the offender or to place him on probation? The answer to this question is much more complicated than one might think. Certainly, some facts or assumptions about the offender are influential. For example, was it a violent crime? Does he have a history of past crimes? Has he stable family or community relationships? Does he have a job? and so on.

But some studies have shown that data about the offender *are not the most relevant information* in the decision as to whether someone should be placed on probation or be incarcerated. In California, for example, the state subsidizes the county for offenders retained in the community, and this procedure has reduced the number of felony incarcerations. Con-

---

[9] Abraham Blumberg, *Criminal Justice* (Chicago: Quadrangle Books, 1970), pp. 143–154; Dawson, *Sentencing*, pp. 35–41.

versely, the requirement in Pennsylvania that the county pay most probation costs for offenders, but that the state assumes the burden of state
institutional costs, seems to have increased the use of incarceration. Thus
one important criterion in the choice between prison and probation has to
do with the legal and financial relationships between a local probation
system and a state prison system.[10] There are some other agency-centered (as opposed to offender-centered) influences on the probation decision. One might be the size of the community in which the probation
office is supervising offenders. In a small town, even if the chances of
adequate supervision are good, the visibility of the probationer might be
high enough that the probation office is cautious about accepting responsibility. In a large city, even if adequate supervision is infrequent, the
visibility of the offender might be low enough to allow the probation staff
to take some risks. Another factor, of course, is the size of the probation
office itself. For example, how many offenders can the office handle?
Another factor might be the elapsed time since the last notorious probation revocation; that is, is the heat on the agency or is it off?[11]

Exactly how any or all of these factors influence the pre-sentence
investigation and the subsequent recommendation on sentence is unknown. But certainly these kinds of factors influence the probability that
probation will be recommended. We can assume that most of the variables that influence the probation investigation have the general tendency
to make things easier for the probation department. Correlatively, we
could expect that the probation officer who concludes that an offender
should be incarcerated has, in essence, *rejected* a man as a probation
possibility rather than *selected* him as a desirable candidate for imprisonment.

Although many of the probation officer's considerations are valid,
given our presently fragmented system, his primary consideration is not
what can be done for the offender in prison. If we view the pre-sentence
investigation as the first correctional diagnosis of the offender, we should
probably conclude that the pre-sentence reports that recommend incarceration are really justifications for not maintaining control of the
offender in the community. If this is true, the prison is really viewed as a
dumping ground for persons who are not viewed as satisfactory (for
whatever reasons) to some other agency. This kind of decision-making
procedure is a far cry from the optimal route of deciding what is the best
available program for any given offender. Instead of sending to prison

---

[10] The Pennsylvania subsidy arrangement is a recent change. Previously, counties
had to pay per diem charges for offenders sentenced to state institutions. Under this
older system, the counties tended to rely on county jail facilities even for serious
offenders—because the county jail costs per man were less.

[11] Blumberg, *Criminal Justice,* pp. 154–161; Dawson, *Sentencing,* pp. 79–100.

Figure 6-1.   Prison Selection as Incremental Default

persons for whom prison is seen as a positive value, or even from whom society needs particular protection, we are really sending persons for whom no one has been willing to make a positive program decision.

We can state this problem in another way with the help of two figures. In Figure 6-1, present prison selection is depicted. It might be characterized as a process of incremental default. The offender is passed by a number of officials in sequence. Each of them might decide to do something with him. As each official decides that the offender is unfit for a particular alternative, the offender is cast deeper into the prison bin as undesirable.

The major point of Figure 6-1 is that prison is not, in reality, one of several equally probable alternatives for the handling of convicted offenders. Prison is the only alternative remaining when no other way out of the system is adopted before the offender reaches the end of the disposition process. The extremely fortunate offender, regardless of his guilt, is the one who is informally handled by the police on the street. If the police see no way to handle a situation informally and invoke the criminal justice process, the offender is then passed from one decision point to the next. The farther down the funnel the offender travels, the more stigmatizing and disruptive the disposition will probably be. But it is only the small minority of defendants who are not screened out prior to the prison door. The key is that offenders are selected *away* from prison rather than for it.

Figure 6-2 presents an alternative to the present sequential pattern of disposition. In this type of disposition pattern, the variables significant to maintaining the prison and parole process are also considered in relation to each offender.

Figure 6-2.   Prison Selection as a Planned Alternative

The feasibility of such a pattern would depend on devising ways in which officials in the latter stages of the criminal process would have an equal voice in the determination of sentence. A mechanism such as state sentencing boards obviously does not accomplish this goal, because the boards make decisions only about offenders who have already been rejected by probation officials and other community alternatives. Precisely what kind of organizational mechanism might be used is unclear. It would probably include staff of private agencies and police and prosecutors as well, so that preconviction as well as postconviction alternatives would be clearly open to consideration.

The other probation decision directly relevant to prison and parole is the revocation decision. To suggest the number of factors influencing this decision would be redundant, but again it should be noted that agency-centered as well as offender-centered variables are important.[12] It should also be clear that such a decision is made independently of the probation revokee's probable future behavior in prison. As we have already seen, the time a probationer spends under community supervision before revocation is frequently ignored when a prison sentence is subsequently imposed. Regardless of the logic or fairness of this practice, it highlights the fact that probation is often treated as a substitute for a sentence rather than as a "correctional" (punitive) device in its own right. Or, to reverse our focus, prison is often seen as the exhaustion of alternatives rather than a positive correctional strategy in its own right. And, given the place of prison in the current sequence of decisions, prison has little chance of harboring a more positive value.

THE AUTONOMY OF THE PAROLE BOARD.   Just as the correctional task is fragmented in its initial phases, it is also fragmented in its final phases. Again, there are historically valid reasons for the fragmentation. But understanding the reasons for the present situation should not color our perception of the negative consequences.

[12] John P. Scheurell, "Valuation and Decision Making in Correctional Social Work," *Issues in Criminology, 4,* No. 2 (Fall 1969), 101–108.

Parole, unlike incarceration, is really an invention of this century. Its origins go back farther than that, and its history will be discussed later in this chapter. Our focus at this point is still the fragmentation of the correctional task, and we want to concentrate briefly on the number of agencies with intertwined responsibilities for shaping that task.

Parole is a broad term referring to the release of inmates from prison prior to the expiration of sentence. The major attraction of parole has always been that it gives the state supervisory authority over the offender in the community while there is still the chance of returning him to prison for misbehavior. If an offender were not released on parole, he would be released at the expiration of his sentence, a completely free man. The ex-offender still with criminal intent would be free to return to his criminal activity; and the ex-offender desiring to behave legally would have to face the community without help or guidance—possibly a forbidding prospect to a person who for a number of years has been accustomed to total custodial regimentation of his needs and wants.[13]

The parole proecss is broken into at least two important parts. First, there is the decision to release on parole. Second, there is the parole supervision itself. When parole began, the different states struggled with a variety of administrative decision mechanisms. Many states placed the release decision in the lap of the governor. Others allowed institutional officials to make the decision. In most states today, the parole decision for adults is usually made by a parole board. The autonomy of the board from the rest of the correctional organization is usually viewed, particularly by the board members, as sacrosanct. There is good reason for this. If the release decision was actually made by the governor, claims of political interference in the release decision could hardly be avoided. And although board members are generally political appointees, the release decision as the product of a committee does provide something of a cushion, both from political interference and from claims that such interference exists. On the other hand, if the release decision was made by institutional officials, claims from inmates that the decision was just another custodial tool would be more or less justified. Parole board members, although they ask for recommendations from the institutional staff, are quick to rebuff institutional control over the release decision. Thus, in some ways, the parole board has a relationship to the prison process analogous to the judge's relationship to the prosecution. The board reviews the everyday operations of a criminal justice bureaucracy but attempts to remain aloof from the pressures of day-to-day administration. Like the judge, the board also falters under the weight of its own respon-

[13] Frank Remington et al., *Criminal Justice Administration* (Indianapolis: Bobbs-Merrill, 1969), pp. 884–895.

sibilities, strays from its ideal position, and frequently discovers that effective decision making demands entering into a fray it is trying to oversee.[14]

Of prime importance here is the consequence of a legally autonomous parole board for the continuity of correctional activity. We have suggested that one crucial component of an organization is the right to select the people who will be members of it. And we have seen that prisons have little access or planned influence over the selection of inmate members. Another crucial component of an organization is the selection of people who will leave. Once again the prison organization is frustrated since the parole board is independent of the prison, which places another major organizational decision in the hands of outsiders.[15]

Although we must still emphasize that good reasons for the autonomy of the board exist, this situation again opens up the possibility that factors extraneous to internal operation and control will exert major influence in the decision.

Ideally, the criteria for the parole decision include the past behavior of the offender and/or predictions of his future behavior in the community. But, as with sentencing, the argument can be conceded in relation to parole that the decision is made by personnel with poor command of the most relevant information. It is common for a parole board to be composed of nine men with three of them sitting at any particular parole hearing. The pressure of the volume of cases to be decided usually dictates only a cursory review of the crime record and prison record, and a short interview with the parole applicant. Generally the real parole decision is made by one man, as the other two are usually reviewing other scheduled cases. Under these conditions, it is doubtful whether an optimal decision can be achieved, even if adequate information were available. It is frequently the case, however, that the offender's file is poorly organized, incomplete, and inaccurate. Due to the above factors, parole officials are now searching for other mechanisms with which to make a decision. At present, however, prison officials usually complain of poor liaison with the board and of no information on why a particular decision is made.[16]

Prison officials naturally reach the conclusion that they are better equipped to make the decision themselves because they have greater access to information for considerably longer periods of time. As we shall see later, however, these officials are also frequently in the dark about

---

[14] Ibid., p. 884.

[15] Daniel Katz and Robert Kahn, *The Social Psychology of Organizations* (New York: Wiley, 1966), pp. 85–100.

[16] Donald Jackson, "Parole Board," *Life,* July 10, 1970, pp. 54–64.

prisoners because accurate information does not flow freely within the current prison climate. Prisoners are naturally guarded in their communications with staff, but equally damaging is the fact that different segments of the prison staff are very close-lipped in communicating with each other. The safest conclusion is probably that no effective information channels exist in prison, and therefore, no effective decision-making pattern exists.[17]

We cannot escape the fact, though, that prison administrators feel singed because their candle burns at both ends. They have little power over who comes in and not much more over who leaves. Although such a situation can spur people to action, it is also a situation that generates simple, paniclike solutions to very complex problems. In other words, the structure of the decision process is such that the cooperation necessary for concerted planning and problem solution is usually lacking.[18]

THE TRANSITION TO PAROLE SUPERVISION.   Roughly 98 percent of the inmates in prison today will be released at some point in the future. A good many of these men will leave the prison completely free men, and completely alone, to do as best they can in the community. Roughly 60 percent of felony inmates released from prison, however, are transferred to some form of parole supervision. The number so released can be expected to increase steadily in the future. Parole, then, is the single most important reentry route for serious offenders, and it offers some advantages for both parolee and community when compared to release at expiration of sentence. A much more infrequent method of release is executive pardon, which, unlike other release processes, implies forgiveness for the crime, or innocence of the crime, and restores the prisoner to full citizenship rights.[19]

Unlike the felony situation, parole for misdemeanors (i.e., release from a local jail) is a rarity. Regardless of the fact that the misdemeanant may be just as much in need of community supervision as the felon, and regardless of the fact that a three-month jail sentence may be just as disruptive as a year sentence, most counties do not provide supervision for offenders released from local jails. A jail inmate is usually sentenced to a flat term by a judge, serves all of it, and leaves the jail without aid or supervision. (The peculiar characteristics of the American jail system will be discussed in greater detail later.) Again, let us concentrate on the

[17] Donald Cressey, "Contradictory Directives in Complex Organizations: The Case of the Prison," *Administrative Science Quarterly, 4* (June 1959), 1–19.

[18] Harold Bradley, "Designing for Change: Problems of Planned Innovation in Corrections," *The Annals of the American Academy of Political and Social Science, 381* (January 1969), 89–98.

[19] President's Commission on Law Enforcement and the Administration of Justice, *Task Force Report: Corrections*, pp. 185–190.

consequences of having yet another agency responsible for part of the correctional task.

There are, as we might expect, a variety of administrative structures for parole supervision in operation across the country. Because parole became popular after prisons were well established, most prison and parole administrations are separate entities.[20] As the professionalization of correctional administration was emphasized during the last decade, there has been a move in many states to centralize prison and parole administration. But even when institutional and field operations fall under the same department of state government, they are operationally separate entities in most cases.

Parole was originally formulated to accommodate in some degree the difficulty with the transition from institution to community. Because prison and parole supervision is separate, there is also a problem of transition to parole. In other words, not only is the offender returning to the community likely to be jarred by the change in his physical status, his new freedom, his new responsibilities, and so on; but the offender is also likely to be jarred by the change in penal philosophy as he moves from the hands of prison officials to the hands of parole officials. Again the offender begins with a "new slate," and again he must reorder his perceptions of reality, his frame of reference, and his understanding of what is right and what is wrong vis-à-vis his supervisors. One example of the drastic nature of this change is the following. An offender in a moderately progressive institution might be required to attend group-counseling sessions. If he is at all attentive in these sessions, he learns that he is to depend in some degree upon his fellow offenders in order to achieve his reformation. He learns that he should seek the advice of concerned peers because they have had experiences similar to his own, and therefore their criticism of his behavior may be more valid than the criticism of a professional. Once this offender reaches parole status, he is likely to find in many states a rule forbidding his consort with ex-offenders and other parolees. Thus the correctional philosophy to which the offender must respond has changed as abruptly as the agency itself. Suddenly the offender who has been rewarded for seeking out peer support can be severely punished for doing the same thing!

The more frequent transitional problems are probably more subtle than this but the extreme case is representative of the *kind* of experience the offender faces as he moves from the "unwanted bin" back toward the community. According to John Irwin, because the parole process involves loyalties to a separate bureaucracy, much of the parole officer's supervision seems to be the presentation of hurdles that the offender must clear

---

[20] Charles L. Chute, "The Development of Probation," *National Probation Association Yearbook* (New York: National Probation Association, 1941), pp. 29–40.

to remain free rather than the presentation of steps that the offender can use to remain free.[21]

In summary, the correctional task is a fragmented one in which several agencies play a part. The part they play generally has the tendency to emphasize the needs of the particular agency rather than the completion of the entire correctional task. It is much as if a motorist traveling from Philadelphia to Camden, New Jersey, went by way of Wilmington, Delaware, because he possessed only a Delaware map.

The Current Crisis in Corrections

The conditions sketched above have been characteristic of corrections for many years. Only lately have they reached the proportions that allow us to speak of crisis. By crisis we mean that the current assumptions and operating patterns are simply *inadequate even for the task of maintaining* the present system. Either the system will find some way of drastically changing itself, or it will collapse completely and society will find something else to take its place. We are not in a position to value one of these alternatives over the other. Many people will be taking sides (since even doing nothing is, in a crisis situation, taking a political position). It would seem quite likely that the people committed to changing the system from the inside will be as revolutionary, if judged by our present standards, as the people who attempt to bring change from outside the system.[22]

Rather than argue the merits of one outcome or another, our present goal is to clarify the conditions that contribute to the present situation so that as people opt for one kind of change or another, their choices might be more informed. In the last section we saw some of the reasons why the correctional task is fragmented. It may be a broad, but perhaps accurate, generalization that for the value we place on federalism and the freedom of the individual, one of the prices we have paid is the price of being rather "incompetent" in dealing with deviance. A more positive way of stating this, although it may sound strange next to the ring of "Law 'n' order!" is that in a democratic society, conformity of the individual is not of prime importance, and the social devices for keeping order are not effectively developed.[23]

In the following section we will investigate why the conditions described are now perceived as leading to crisis. For example, have Ameri-

---

[21] Irwin, *The Felon*, pp. 1–3.

[22] David Duffee, "The Use of Organizational Variables in the Periodic Assessment of Correctional System Effectiveness," *Proceedings,* Second International Symposium of Project SEARCH (Sacramento, Calif.: SEARCH Group, Inc., 1974), pp. 643–655.

[23] Leslie Wilkins, "Crime and Crime Prevention Measures of 1990," paper presented to the American Association for the Advancement of Science, San Francisco, February 1974.

can values been reordered? Or has the environment of the prison and parole system changed so that an ineffective punishment system can no longer be considered a positive American value?

INCREASE IN INFORMATION.   Perhaps the most drastic change in the environment of the prison and parole process has been a technological one. More people receive more information about more things than ever before. The amount of information we receive increases at geometric, rather than arithmetic, rates. The advent of computers, for example, increased our capacity to process information so rapidly that the increase of a few short years was equal to a hundred previous years. Professor Wilkins has suggested that as the information flow changes, so will the dominant values, and the concept of a generation of people will continually shrink. That fathers and sons have difficulty communicating is old hat—soon older and younger brothers will confront the same sort of generation gap![24]

The power of the influence of changes in information is hard to overemphasize. The Vietnam War was the first one fought by America in which both blunders and heroics could be reported within moments of their happening. It was the first war in which the dead victims could be viewed daily at dinner on the evening news program. Surely public attitudes about the war were directly related to the greater quantum of information that was available about it. And it seemed to be the attitudes of the public strengthened by such information that brought one American president to his knees.

It is not surprising that increased information has had similar effects on prison and parole. The walls of the prison are no longer an effective barrier between the public and the prisoner. For example, two of the most widely read recent contributions to revolutionary literature were written by inmates.[25] And the riot at Attica prison in New York received more coverage than any other riot in history.[26]

An important aspect of the information we now receive is that it differs from older information, not only in amount, but in *source*. The public was shocked that the Attica hostages had died in police fire rather than at the hands of inmates. The public also listened to people such as William Kunstler talk about Attica, when in previous years these voices might not have been heard. Equally important to the increase in quantity of information, then, is the increase in the origins of information. Official spokesmen for prisons or parole systems are no longer the only people likely to

[24] Leslie Wilkins, "The Information Explosion and Social Control," (mimeographed paper, School of Criminal Justice, SUNY-Albany, February, 1970).

[25] See Eldridge Cleaver, *Soul on Ice* (New York: Dell Publishing Co., 1968); and Jackson, *Soledad Brother.*

[26] New York State Special Commission, *Attica* (New York: Bantam Books, 1972).

be heard on a particular issue. Neither are they likely to be the only spokesmen sought out. As more information is transmitted from more sources, the listeners have a more confusing time interpreting what they hear. The probability that only one side of a controversial issue will be taken as the valid side is greatly reduced.

BROADER DISTRIBUTION OF POLITICAL POWER. Developing considerably after the technological increase in information, but becoming very noticeable by the time of the 1972 Democratic convention, is the broadening of political power. There has been considerable attention lately to the radicalization of inmates. Eldridge Cleaver and George Jackson wrote about the California prisons as indoctrination grounds for political radicals. At Attica, the concerted radical action of inmates, black and white, versus a commonly perceived suppressor, was vividly presented. It is probably not true, however, that radicalism begins within a prison and works outward. It is more likely that politics in prison is following the trend in the nation—a trend that indicates the traditional means of achieving power and the traditional means of maintaining power are breaking down. Although it may still be true that the rich and well-heeled control the legislatures, legislators are now listening to a differently structured constituency. The poor, the young, women, blacks, chicanos, and other previously powerless groups now count at the ballot box. More importantly, the representatives of these groups, in growing numbers, are reaching positions of power in local, state, and federal government. A startling characteristic of these new leaders is an apparent lessening concern for the traditional methods of maintaining and distributing power. There *does* seem to be a greater cohesiveness in "people's politics," less emphasis on low-profile, behind-the-scenes control, and more willingness to include dissenting opinions within the group.

Exactly where this trend will lead on the broader political level is not our concern. For us, the implications of this trend in politics predicates important changes in the prison and parole process. The first such change relates to the organization of the criminal justice system. One factor that has been important in the functioning of the fragmented system has been the dominance of the will of officials over the will of the offender. The offender has been told indirectly, but in no uncertain terms, that doing "easy time" in prison requires cooperation with officials. The question of who is making the correctional decisions has been more important than the consequences of these decisions for the offender. And as the power to make decisions has turned from one official authority to another, the offender has been required to spin like a top and to adjust quickly to the new ideology and new organizational constraints that have accompanied each change in authority. This demand upon the offender's behavior, at least in the correctional area, has usually been officially justified on the grounds that the offender is guilty, that he has lost his rights to participation in decision making, and that he is untrustworthy or incompetent to second-guess the expertise of officials in the field.

The dominance of *who* is to make decisions and the requirement that the offender do most of the adjusting are two factors that are likely to change as political power becomes more evenly distributed among various social groups. Many new political leaders do not perceive a conviction as a justification for loss of decision-making power.

Many new political groups understand criminal behavior as partly explained by the political motives of the people in power, rather than as evidence of the psychological noncomformity of the individual.[27] Many offenders are finding newly powerful groups in society who accept criminal behavior as one reasonable alternative to certain social circumstances. Although most of these political groups do not favor criminal activity as an effective problem-solving alternative, they are also unlikely to discuss the criminal as untrustworthy, sick, or evil. Thus, as a consequence of the changing distribution of political power, many offenders are finding firm philosophical and social foundations from which to object to their inconsiderate treatment by officials. In other words, offenders are discovering an anchor *outside* the prison and parole process that helps them to stop spinning and to challenge the decisions that are made about their welfare. Although most of the officials in the criminal justice system have political ties to the traditional political powers in America, the simple self-interest of prison or parole officials requires that they accommodate to some of the desires of the new emerging political groups, some of which sympathize with the demands of prisoners. Thus, one major contributing factor to the current crisis in corrections is that the offenders are beginning to see themselves as representatives of *legitimate* political power.

Contrary to some explanations of internal changes in prison and parole, we can conclude that the perceived legitimacy of criminal activity *itself* may not necessarily be changing. What is changing is that the criminal can now support his demands for participation in decisions on the basis of his affiliation with noncriminal social groups. He can justify his noncooperation with officials on the probability that his future behavior is linked to viable power groups who *also* espouse challenge, rather than cooperation, with the present political establishment.

BREAKDOWN IN CREDIBILITY. The increase in information from different and independent sources and the broadening of political power interact to produce a third crisis-provoking factor in the prison and parole process. This factor is that the official explanations and justifications of the operat-

[27] David Gordon, "Capitalism, Class and Crime in America," *Crime and Delinquency* (April 1973), pp. 163–186.

ing patterns of prison and parole have lost much of their credibility. They have lost credibility not only with inmates and powerful outside minorities but also with prison and parole staff and ordinary citizens. If for a moment we can suspend the fact that the quailty of different social conditions is relative, we might be able to say that prison and parole conditions today are much more humane and effective than they were in 1930. But even if this is true, the changing social and political forces are such that prison and parole officials had to confront less question and less challenge to the value and the correctness of their decisions in 1930 than they do today. Major reasons for this are that there were fewer information sources that would contradict public statements by officials, and there were fewer politically relevant groups that had to be satisfied about the value and effectiveness of prison and parole activity.

As we have already seen in talking about fragmentation, very important to the internal operation of any organization is the ability of the organization to influence its environment and, hence, to control the behavior of its members. Thus, since the public bases its behavior on the information available to it, it is obviously crucial to the organization to be able to send out messages about its operation that will be believed and responded to in the anticipated manner. Wardens and parole supervisors, for example, want to gain support for what they do by explaining to the public their intentions, their problems, and the consequences of their operating procedures. They want these explanations to be accepted at face value so that they can anticipate support rather than hindrance from the community.

Because there are now other sources by which the public can learn about prison and parole operations, the messages from official sources have to compete for public acceptance. And because alternate views of prison and parole are supported by viable political interest groups, the dissent to the official view cannot be easily dismissed as the revenge of convicted felons.

There is a similar loss of credibility within the organization. Staff members and prisoners obviously have access to information that the public does not possess—and these two groups have always possessed it. But the effect that a superior's public statements have upon organizational members is probably underestimated. Although staff members and offenders may know that certain things their superiors say are not accurate, the organizational superiors have at least one area where the staff, at least, look to them for guidance. This area has to do with explaining how the various activities of the organization are integrated to produce an overall result. Although the man on the front line may have more immediate and detailed information about organizational activities than his superiors, his superior has a broader perspective, as well as information about other aspects of the organization and the environment, that is not visible to people lower down in the organization. Perhaps for this reason, staff (and sometimes inmates) often believe in the essential validity of their superior's messages about the organization. For staff, at least, the ability to believe that the organization is functioning effectively and serves a good purpose eases somewhat the frustrations of everyday realities. When organizational spokesmen begin to lose credibility with the outside world, and when they begin to admit that there are problems with the organization, staff find themselves in a much more ambiguous and tentative position.

DEMAND FOR EFFECTIVENESS. As people inside and outside the system have increasing doubts about the value of prison and parole, there will be increasing demands that prison and parole systems be able to demonstrate their effectiveness in reducing crime. For many years it seemed sufficient that prison and parole systems were good because it was their purpose to protect society and to reform the individual offender. As long as the public was satisfied with the good intentions of the system, there was little demand for particular consequences. Now that public confidence in the goodness of the system has decreased, the alternative justification for the existence of the system would be that it actually accomplishes some important tasks. (People might say, "Well, if it is not a moral enterprise, at least it has utility!")[28]

As the dependence on moral explanations decreases, it is frequently replaced with an interest in the facts of the situation. Science has replaced religion as the justification of many social enterprises. The system of corrections, however, is now at that point where the demand for effective social action has preceded the techniques by which to achieve it. The system is therefore ill-prepared for demonstrations of fact. Facts are only as useful as the theories that interconnect them, but theory building has frequently been disregarded in prison and parole work.

Perhaps the most ironic thing about the demand for effectiveness is that there seems to be a contradiction between an effective prison and parole system and the willingness of society to accept offenders returning from prison to the community. Perhaps one of the reasons that society has taken so long to demand effective correctional action is that ineffectiveness is a reflection of society's attitude toward deviance. Any systematic and complete evaluation of prison and parole activity is bound to point out not only deficiencies in prison and parole organization but also the correlative dysfunctional aspects of the broader social structure.

Although the demand for effective action is now conflict-provoking for the system, this demand is also a reflection of broader social and political

[28] George Dession, "Psychiatry and the Conditioning of Criminal Justice," *Yale Law Journal*, *47*, No. 3 (January 1938), 319–340; and Leslie Wilkins, *The Evaluation of Penal Measures* (New York: Random House, 1969), pp. 3–11.

changes. Some of these, such as the increase in information and alterations in the political structure, we have mentioned. If this trend continues, prison and parole activity might actually have a chance of
becoming corrective. Perhaps society will be willing to give up its retributive tendencies in order to effect rehabilitation. It is likely that this sort of
trend is more dependent on improvements in social conditions than on
improvements within prison and parole itself.

OLD RIGHTS NEWLY APPLIED.   Another way in which increase in information and new political powers affect corrections is in the change in the
judicial perception of prison and parole. The Constitution of the United
States is not an immutable document. The interpretation of the Bill of
Rights changes, for example, as the Supreme Court learns of new facts or
as the political climate of the country changes. For years the constitutional constraints on the criminal justice procedure stopped at the prison
door. Long after the Supreme Court had intruded into police operations,
correctional administrators were free of these court constraints "because
of the need for discipline." As the information contradicting the purported goals of corrections has increased, and as prisoners have become
identified with legitimate social groups, the court has seemed more willing to grant prisoners the rights of citizens. The most sweeping changes
in correctional law at this point would seem to involve the Sixth, the
Eighth, and the Fourteenth Amendments.

The Sixth Amendment, which guarantees rights to notice, hearing,
confrontation, and counsel, is perhaps the most formidable right in terms
of making the defendant an active participant in the criminal process.
Gideon v. *Wainwright* answered the question of right to counsel at trial.[29]

Since *Gideon* a series of cases have broadened the right to other "critical stages." The first crack in the correctional facade came in *Mempa* v.
Rhay,[30] concerning the right to a lawyer at a probation revocation. Some
people expected that the Supreme Court would also insist on lawyers at
parole revocation decisions. The case of *Morrissey* v. *Brewer*, however,
shied away from the issue of counsel.[31] Nevertheless, *Morrissey* is significant in that it clearly stated that with the exception of the presence of
counsel, the parole revocation decision must be a clear and orderly
process in which the revokee has the opportunity to challenge the case
against him and offer a defense. Within the prison itself, these methods to
assure due process and fairness have not been systematically applied, but
the argument is strengthening that inmates facing serious disciplinary

[29] Gideon v. Wainwright, 372 U.S. 335 (1963).
[30] Mempa v. Rhay, 389 U.S. 128 (1967).
[31] Morrissey v. Brewer, 408 U.S. 471 (1972).

charges should also be protected by an orderly and open proceeding (see *Wolff* v. *McDonnell*).[32]

The Eighth Amendment, protecting citizens from cruel and unusual punishment, is the amendment most obviously applicable to corrections. The cruel and unusual punishment clause, however, has generally been a weak guarantee. Prison disciplinary procedures, for example, usually had to be extremely rare and harsh in order to be considered cruel and unusual. Moreover, cruel and unusual punishment has normally been interpreted to mean specific acts within the penal organization. In other words, inmates had to demonstrate the existence of particular, out-of-the-ordinary acts in order to find relief in the courts. This interpretation of the Eighth Amendment has recently shown signs of breaking down. In the landmark case of *Holt* v. *Sarver,* the federal judge declared the entire Arkansas prison system a violation of the cruel and unusual punishment clause.[33] He said the decision was based on the *entire climate* of the prison system rather than on any *particular* aspect of prison operations. Shortly thereafter, the same broad interpretation of cruel and unusual punishment was applied to the three Philadelphia county prisons. Again, the decision said that the normal everyday prison conditions, rather than their extreme manifestations, were a violation of the Eighth Amendment (*Jackson* v. *Hendrick*).[34]

The third key amendment would seem to be the Fourteenth. It is through the due process clause of the Fourteenth Amendment that the Sixth and the Eighth Amendments are applied to the states. A more significant and interesting aspect of constitutional law may involve the equal protection clause of the Fourteenth Amendment. According to recent court interpretations of equal protection, the government may not discriminate between citizens or groups except for an overriding purpose, and the purpose and discriminating categories must be related. Given our present information about prison and parole and our changing attitude toward the political establishment, it might be possible to argue that the incarceration of most inmates occurs in violation of the equal protection clause. One might say that the discrimination between guilty people in prison and guilty people free in the community is not based on any overriding social purpose, or if there was some overriding purpose, that a relationship between the purpose and the criteria for incarceration cannot be demonstrated.

Although the specific changes in the legal structure of corrections may not be predicted yet, it is certain that the trend is toward increasing the

---

[32] Wolff v. McDonnell, 418 U.S. 539 (1974).

[33] Holt v. Sarver, 309 F. *Supp.* 362 (E.D. Ark. 1970).

[34] Jackson v. Hendrick, 40 *Law Week* 2710 (Ct. Comm. Pls. Pa. 1972).

rights for prisoners and increasing the demand on the state to articulate the reasons for its custodial and treatment decisions. This change fits in with the changes in information, the broadening of political power, the breakdown in the protective cover of corrections' custodial and treatment ideologies, and the breakdown generally of corrections' traditional isolation from the communities where crime originates.

THE HISTORY OF THE CORRECTIONAL ENTERPRISE

We have seen some of the long-standing organizational problems with prison and parole and some of the current external pressures that have turned those problems into a crisis. Before we go on to look at prison and parole operations in some detail, it may be helpful to review briefly the history of prison and parole. It is easier to understand the contradictory goals of today's prison, for example, if we can see the traditions behind each set of goals and the reasons why none of them has disappeared. Although the correctional component of the criminal justice system is a much younger social institution than the judicial component, prison and parole organizations change very slowly. The current interest in changing them and the desire to make them more effective may be energy misspent unless proper attention is given to their historical development.

The Goals of the Criminal Sanction

Although it is a vague generality, we can talk about the adjudication process as a rough attempt to achieve justice. We can talk also about police work in terms of community service and law enforcement without paying much attention to what happens to people who are apprehended. But it really seems impossible to speak for long about postconviction processing without asking *why* it is being done. The motivation or rationale for punishment has been extremely important, whether or not it makes any difference to the offender or to society. It is easy to be misled by such an interest—to be satisfied by the rationale for the punishment and to ignore the all-important consequences. But social scientists who would ignore official or public motivations completely and would explain the reasons for social activity totally in terms of consequences are also making a mistake. The scientist who pooh-poohs notions such as deterrence, for example, because the punishments in vogue simply do not deter, may be missing an important aspect of the complex social interaction. It *may* be that society does not really want to deter crime and merely utters the word in order to assuage public guilt. But it may also be that society really does expect to deter crime and simply has not taken a good look at the consequences of punishment. If social desire to achieve deterrence is sincere, then other ways of achieving it may be shown that are more effective than the usual punitive devices. A scientist who finds no validity in the traditional "motivators," "goals," or "purposes" of the criminal sanction, has forgotten that even the illusions of a social group are real in their consequences.

RETRIBUTION. Perhaps the best known and, at this point, the least popular purpose of the criminal sanction is retribution. Retribution has frequently been defined as doing something to a man because of his past wrongdoing. In other words, retribution is a reaction of society to a crime already completed. Retributive punishment does not portend changing the offender's *future behavior*. It has nothing to do with the future behavior of the offender. This traditional understanding of retribution is logically awkward. It is hard to think of society continuing to act in a particular way because of something that happened in the past and is now completely done with. A more complete definition of retribution might be that it is a response to a past crime in order to correct the present social disturbance caused by that crime. In other words, retribution has to do with the victim and/or the social group achieving some satisfaction after being severely disturbed. But retribution is not geared to changing the offender's future acts. The focus is on the present effect of the crime on society, rather than on the offender.

INCAPACITATION. Another common purpose of punishment is merely to stop the offender physically from doing any more damage. For example, the habitual criminal with whom chances of rehabilitation seem slim may be sentenced to an additional sentence merely to keep him incarcerated and out of society. In Elizabethan England, incapacitation was literally achieved. A pickpocket would lose his hand or a gossip her tongue. Corporal punishment has now been outlawed in all states, and the attempt to control the offender is limited to incarceration. John Kaplan points out that incapacitation through incarceration merely limits a dangerous offender's victims to the inmate population.[35] A few years ago society may have been satisfied with so limiting the victim population. The courts now are more rigorous in demanding that custodial care also mean that inmates are protected from their fellow inmates.

Beyond the hypocrisy of limiting a criminal's crimes to victims who have also committed crimes, perhaps the greatest limitation to incapacitation as a motivating factor of the criminal sanction is that it is rarely indefinite protection. Unless the death penalty is reinstated or unless dangerous inmates are not paroled, even dangerous and recalcitrant in-

[35] John Kaplan, *Criminal Justice* (Mineola, N.Y.: Foundation Press, 1973), pp. 25–26.

mates who are committed to returning to crime will be released some day to do just that.

DETERRENCE. Deterrence, unlike retribution or incapacitation, purposes to affect the behavior of criminals in the future even when there is no physical contact between officials and the offender. Deterrence is usually broken down into two types. First, *specific deterrence* refers to punishing a man so that he will not commit the same act in the future. *General deterrence* refers to punishing one offender for a crime so that potential offenders will not commit similar acts in the future. Specific deterrence is an attempt to have the offender use the consequences of his past behavior as an example governing his future decisions. General deterrence is the use of one offender as an example to other potential offenders.

Deterrence has become increasingly popular as a justification for punishment as the popularity of retribution has declined. Some critics, such as Justice Holmes, were suspicious of this inverse relationship and argued that deterrence is merely a cover-up for retributive motives.[36] However, most people who have taken deterrence at face value have found it a more promising conceptual foundation for punishment because it holds some utility for the future safety of society. On the negative side, there have been few studies that demonstrate the effectiveness of deterrent measures. In order for deterrence to be effective, the potential criminal must know of the possible consequences, and the actual probability of apprehension and conviction must be high so that the threat carries weight. Many studies have suggested that potential offenders do not take possible punishment into consideration, and furthermore, that our system of justice is so ineffective that the threat of actual punishment is weak. Besides, in order for deterrence to take effect, the potential offender must perceive the possibility of punishment as sufficiently costly relative to his other opportunities. For many of the offenders whom we would wish to deter, the threat of punishment is negated by the fact that the opportunities of legal activity are even smaller than the opportunities for illegal gain.[37]

This last set of data raises an interesting point that is frequently ignored in the criminal justice system. Most people seem to be more effectively controlled by the promise of positive reward than by the threat of negative reward. Since there are few positive rewards available to convicted offenders, it is probable that the most effective deterrent strategy involves changes in other social institutions such as in the educa-

[36] Herbert Packer, *The Limits of the Criminal Sanction* (Stanford, Calif.: Stanford University Press, 1968), p. 44.

[37] Gordon, "Capitalism, Class and Crime in America," pp. 170–177.

tional system or the labor market. But this kind of deterrent effort is generally beyond the scope of criminal justice authorities.

REHABILITATION. The last traditional, and, at this point, perhaps the most popular, purpose of punishment is rehabilitation. Rehabilitation is the act of changing a man's perceptions of the world or changing his behavior so that he no longer wants to commit a crime. Rehabilitation is distinguished from deterrence in that, theoretically, it does not involve a constant threat for a wrongdoing but changes instead the offender's perception of what is valuable, so that no threat or surveillance is needed to control his future behavior. Rehabilitation might be further distinguished from general deterrence on the grounds that it is available only *after* a man has been apprehended for a crime. Presumably, general deterrence is also effective against people who have committed no crimes.

It is important to understand that rehabilitation like incapacitation and retribution is a *punishment* rather than an alternative to punishment. Offenders rarely come banging on the prison door seeking rehabilitation. The state has the authority to intervene in order to effect rehabilitation only after the adjudication of guilt. Because it is a response to crime and the person to be changed is coerced, rehabilitation has the legal status of punishment, and it is most generally perceived by offenders as punishment. There is, however, a tendency in correctional officials to contrast rehabilitation with punishment, perhaps because it makes their job of coercing offenders psychologically and socially more palatable.

As with deterrence, there are few studies that demonstrate the effectiveness of rehabilitative measures. A common argument used by officials to excuse their ineffective attempts is the fact that successful rehabilitation frequently conflicts with other legitimate goals, such as retribution and deterrence. One aspect of this argument is, however, rather inaccurate. Officials frequently claim that their duty to society for the implementation of deterrence or retribution conflicts with their interest in the offender's rehabilitation. This perceived conflict, as stated, seems invalid. It is unlikely that rehabilitation would take place at all if the sole motivation behind it was the interest in the offender. The fact of the matter is that society places a value on rehabilitation for its own sake. It is not an effort undertaken out of some altruistic concern for the downtrodden offender. In order, then, to see how the usually stated goals of the system have evolved together, it is necessary to examine the development of our prison and parole operations.

Punishment in the New Republic

Punishment in seventeenth- and eighteenth-century England was largely capital and corporal. Either people were executed or they were disfigured, branded, or banished. Prisons, although they existed, were generally reserved for political prisoners, debtors, and persons awaiting trial. This kind of punishment was sure and swift, but to many people it began to seem cruel and harsh, and in addition, it did not seem to do much to protect the cities from further harm.

Even before 1800, there were some signs of the operations that would later become prison and parole, but they were the exception rather than the rule. Henry Fielding, for example, as a magistrate in London in the 1740s, experimented with probation and with detention homes or houses of refuge for youthful offenders. Fielding undertook such steps under the idea of crime prevention. Workhouses also developed for healthy beggars and charities for the poor, to prevent these individuals from turning to crime. In other words, the idea of *housing* deviants and the idea of *reforming* them were both present prior to the American innovation of the penitentiary.[38]

Another factor influencing institutionalization in the United States was the work of utilitarians, notably Jeremy Bentham.[39] Corporal and capital punishments usually seemed to be based on the idea that the offender was wicked and beyond control. Bentham, on the other hand, saw criminal activity as a conscious calculation on the criminal's part that the fruits of the crime were worth its costs. Therefore, he suggested that punishments for crime should be great enough, but no greater than necessary, to dissuade the offender from the criminal act. Maiming and execution were rough punishments that did not lend themselves to a utilitarian calculus. Imposing a variable time in prison as a sentence did seem a handy way of increasing the cost to benefit ratio, and therefore the popularity of utilitarian philosophy was another impetus to the innovation of the prison.

In the colonies and through the Jacksonian era, prisons in the United States were rather haphazardly constructed and haphazardly managed. The prisons of the early states, although they were seen perhaps as reforms when compared to punishments often meted out in Europe, were careless combinations of reform impulse, utilitarian logic, and meager budget. Within these prisons, vice of all kinds was common—the prisons were run by the offenders, who lived and slept together in what must have seemed at times to be a retreat between arrests. Although crime within the prison was common, escapes were also common, and so the early jails had problems both inside and out.[40]

The reformation of these early jails perhaps had roots in several accidental developments arising from the early lockups. The first such devel-

---

[38] Charles L. Chute, "The Development of Probation."

[39] Jeremy Bentham, *Panopticon Postscript* (London: printed for T. Payne at the Mews-Gate, 1971), pp. 498–501.

[40] Rothman, *The Discovery of the Asylum,* pp. 88–94.

opment had to do with *separation*. In the early, unseparated institutions, such as the Walnut Street Jail in Philadelphia, the warden was basically at a loss to control unruly inmates. Then, in Pennsylvania and New York, the officials stumbled upon the idea of locking the worst disciplinary problems in separate cells. This action was definitely viewed as a punishment, and something not intended for all prisoners. The second more or less accidental development was the institution of labor in the jails. This was done with some hope of saving money but also with the idea of demonstrating to the community and to the offender that being locked up was, indeed, a punishment.

Thus the two techniques of labor and isolation in cells were already known to the Quaker reformers in Philadelphia. Meanwhile, the Quakers had decided something was drastically wrong with the prison system. To the two available techniques they added the rationale that allowed their systematic use. That rationale was basically a religious one—a belief that an evil man could be reclaimed if, through penitence and sober habits, he became free of the criminogenic pressures that surrounded him. Thus the reformers of the early jail argued for complete separation of the offender from the outside world *and* from other offenders. They suggested that in the solitude of his cell the offender could reconsider his crime, read the Bible, repent his sins, engage in industrious labor, and eventually be released as a useful citizen. Based on this theory, there was erected in the courtyard of the Walnut Street Jail in Philadelphia the first cell block in 1797. The inhabitant of each cell remained alone for the duration of his stay. This system of complete isolation became known as the "Pennsylvania system." The system was developed further and was implemented on a full-blown scale at the Pittsburgh penitentiary in 1826, and at the Philadelphia penitentiary in 1829.[41]

In the interval between the construction of the Walnut Street Jail cell block and of the Pennsylvania penitentiaries was the development of somewhat different models in Auburn, New York, in 1819 and in Ossining, New York, in 1823. Hence, contrary to common belief, the Auburn system, as it is called, in some way predates the contrasting Pennsylvania system. The difference between the Auburn and Pennsylvania systems had to do with the lack of *physical* isolation at Auburn. Inmates of the Auburn prison ate together and worked together during the day—although they were to remain in absolute silence—and then returned to single cells during the night. Adherents of the Auburn system claimed that complete physical isolation, as in Pennsylvania, was contrary to the human condition, and that the congregate plan allowed for cheaper construction and management and more profitable labor. Pennsylvania proponents retorted that it was really impossible to shut off all communi-

[41] Ibid., pp. 94–101.

cation in the congregate system and that the punishments needed to maintain discipline were too harsh.[42]

Both systems had in common the concepts of isolation, industriousness, and obedience. The Auburn system placed less emphasis on isolation and more on obedience; the Pennsylvania system more on isolation and, hence, less on obedience. Both systems also had in common, when they began at any rate, the fundamental interest in reformation of the offenders. Although there are not any records to show whether reformation actually took place, there was the ever-present (and somewhat gigantic) assumption that institutionalization was *the* means to reformation.

The reasons for this assumption are those stated in the introduction to this chapter. The reformers evidently placed little faith in the social institutions of the community and considerably more faith in the potential of the individual to return to a sinless condition if he were isolated. There were probably at least two additional reasons for the emphasis on institutional treatment rather than on some community alternative. One had to do with the extremely mobile nature of a frontier society. Community ties were nonexistent in the case of many offenders, and the developing cities themselves were not stable enough to offer much hope of some sort of commmunity control. Thus, placing all offenders within a state in one or several central locations was advantageous to the state. Second, the nineteenth century saw the rise of an industrial society, with its basic unit being the factory. Perhaps the same forces that tended to make economic entrepreneurs emphasize routine, uniform, and disciplined factory operations also influenced the prison reformers to model the prison as a punishment factory.

The Pennsylvania system, largely through the writings of de Tocqueville and other European visitors, became the major American export to Europe. Within the United States, however, the promise of cheaper punishment and more profitable prison industry made Auburn the most copied model.[43]

IDEOLOGIES AND REALITIES OF IMPLEMENTATION. The penitentiary system spread quickly from New York and Pennsylvania to other states of the eastern seaboard. By 1864 there was a state penitentiary in Kansas. As the innovation spread westward, and as the eastern penitentiaries ran into shortages of money, personnel, and space, the ideology of the prison and its implementation became noticeably divergent. In 1835 the inspectors of the Auburn prison pronounced it perfect, but by 1850, inspectors of

[42] Ibid.

[43] Gustave de Beaumont and Alexis de Toqueville, *On the Penitentiary System in the United States* (Carbondale, Ill.: Southern Illinois University, 1964).

Auburn and its offspring in other states were complaining of poor discipline, lack of silence and isolation, and little, if any, financial benefit. By the time the innovation found its way to Kansas, the prison was much less than a promise of reformation. In reality, the prison by the time of the Civil War seemed little more than a place of restraint. It functioned to keep offenders out of society, but the original intent of reforming criminals through rigorous internal discipline seemed to be a bankrupt concept.[44]

Post-Civil War Reform—Rehabilitation Again

After the throes of the Civil War had passed, and after the original hopes for reconstruction had faded, burgeoning economic and industrial development became the dominant characteristic of the last third of the nineteenth century. Although many people may not realize it, it is during times of rapid economic growth—when there is a generally high standard of living—that people turn toward the reform of welfare, crime, disease, and other social problems as worthy pursuits. The welfare rolls swell when the gross national product is increasing. When the rich begin to feel the pinch, there is usually no money or interest in welfare. Conversely, it seems that it is generally when the rich feel snug and beneficent that people turn their attention to crime and reform of the criminal system.

The great reform movement in the United States arrived in the 1870s and grew progressively stronger, climaxing perhaps in women's suffrage (19th Amendment passed in 1920) and Prohibition (1920–1933). It was during these years that the corrections system made its greatest advances until the President's Crime Commission in 1967. The beginning of this reform era can probably be marked by the founding of the American Correctional Association in 1870. At the first meeting of the association in Cincinnati, the members drew up a set of resolutions, almost visionary in scope, that have yet to be achieved today. The association's major tenet was that reformation, not vindictive suffering, was to be the object of punishment. The decade of the seventies also saw the passing of the first probation statute in Boston and the first formal parole from the Elmira Reformatory in New York State.[45]

To the extent that parole supervision is similar to probation field work, parole probably has its roots in the work of John Augustus in Boston in 1840. Augustus, a cobbler by trade, is generally known as the "father of probation," and his motivation, again, was rehabilitation (specifically of

---

[44] Rothman, *The Discovery of the Asylum*, pp. 100–105.

[45] Howard B. Gill, "A New Prison Discipline, Implementing the Declaration of Principles of 1870," *Federal Probation* (June 1970), pp. 29–33.

the drunkard).[46] Probation is different from parole, however, in that it was imposed *before* sentence. Therefore, the more direct origin of parole probably comes from the practice in Australia of giving an offender a "ticket of leave" so that he could find employment and lodging in the Australian colonial settlements prior to the actual expiration of his sentence. If the person on leave did not behave properly, he could be returned to the chain gangs to complete his time at hard labor.[47]

Another innovation that sparked the idea of parole was the granting of "good time" to prisoners who were obedient in prison. When so much good time was accumulated, the prisoner was released, a free man. In other words, good time reduced the actual sentence expiration date. Meanwhile, someone made the suggestion that not only could good time be used as a means of obtaining early release of men from prison, but that it could also be used to allow the state to maintain custody of the offender in the community.[48]

A third factor that influenced the initiation of parole at Elmira was the juvenile court movement (which will be discussed in detail in Chapter Eight). Although probation and parole gained impetus independent of the juvenile court movement, it is doubtful that these correctional concepts would have come so far if it had not been for the presence of the juvenile in the criminal court and, hence, in probation and parole caseloads.

As we have mentioned, the 1870s and 1880s saw the rise of many reform movements. And one of the strongest was the attempt to obtain better living conditions for juveniles. Restraints were placed on the use of children in coal mines and factories; the importance of education for children was emphasized. Also during this period grew the idea of saving the children from the foul places called prisons.[49]

As we shall see in Chapter Eight, the reformers became interested in treating rather than punishing youth, and they could see nothing but punishment available in the prisons. This new interest in treating juveniles, and in rescuing youth from the poor social environment of the industrial city, was strengthened by the development of social work as a professional activity with considerable substance behind it. Perhaps the

[46] John Augustus, 1784–1859, Boston cobbler reputed to be first probation officer in The United States, see David Dressler, *Practice and Theory of Probation and Parole*, (New York: Columbia University Press, 1959), p. 11.

[47] Edwin Sutherland and Donald Cressey, *Criminology*, 8th ed. (Philadelphia: Lippincott, 1970), p. 585.

[48] Ibid., pp. 580–581.

[49] Anthony Platt, "The Rise of the Child-Saving Movement: A Study in Social Policy and Correctional Reform," *The Annals of the American Academy of Political and Social Science, 381* (January 1969), 25–28.

greatest contribution of social work to probation and parole was the idea of casework. John Augustus attempted to rehabilitate the people he bailed by making sure that they did not drink and that they had regular employment, and they had his concern and sincere support.[50] But systematic casework, in which the problems of an individual are analyzed, strategies for change are planned, and steps are implemented and evaluated, was something that had to wait for the development of the behavioral sciences in the tail end of the nineteenth century.

It was a new idea, born in the social science and social work, that rehabilitation of an individual was *progress* rather than a reversion to a former sinless state. The new idea was that change was actively *induced* by an outside agent, and that the client was actually going in a direction or toward a state that he had never experienced before. Thus, although social work had its origins in volunteer philanthropy, the former seems proactive and the latter comparatively reactive and passive.

The use of social work and casework at the same time that probation and parole were statutorily recognized provided probation and parole with some of the methodology necessary in order for release in the community to become a change-producing force in its own right, rather than a merciful substitute for the perils of the prison. The idea that work with the offender in the community could be a correctional strategy (rather than a reward or a grant of mercy) also suggested that a fundamental shift in the perception of the community was taking place.[51]

The use of parole as a correctional force in a person's life after he left prison implied two major changes in penological philosophy. The first was that institutionalization by itself was insufficient to produce (or, in reality, antithetical to) law-abiding behavior in the offender. The second was that an agent working with the offender in a community context *could* effect change.

Exactly how revolutionary this philosophy was can probably not be appreciated by the student newly introduced to the field, but it may be helpful to have an understanding of some of the underlying dimensions of this change in correctional approach. The original move to institutionalization in 1820 was based primarily on the belief that crime was caused by an evil environment. Classical notions of cause-effect relationships would demand that such relations are irreversible. A cause can never be an effect. If the community caused crime, it certainly could not cure the criminal! On the contrary, the idea of parole was based on some implicit conception of mutual causation, or of system relationships. Underlying the idea of parole, in other words, is the notion that the same set of

---

[50] David Dressler, *Practice and Theory of Probation and Parole,* pp. 13–19.

[51] Duffee, The Use of Organizational Variables," p. 645.

factors that lead to crime, also may lead away from it. Thus, parole from the very beginning was a fundamental change in correctional philosophy.

It is important to note, however, that this concept of community-based correctional change did not present itself as an alternative to the institution. Rather, it was tacked on to the institution in the form of parole. It is rather ironic that one operation based on pessimism with the community should be placed together with another operation based on optimism with the community and that together the two should become one correctional process!

ATTICA, 1931 AND 1971.   On September 9, 1971, the largest prison riot in American history broke loose in the New York correctional facility in Attica, New York. A brief look at the history of Attica (rather than the specific incidents leading to the riot) provides a clear and harsh example of the divergence between the goal of rehabilitation and the realities of corrections today. It is really of small consequence that the revolt took place at Attica rather than in some other New York prison or in some other state. Yet there is a sense of historical symmetry in that it was the oldest prison system in the United States that should manifest most clearly the cancerous social structure and bureaucratic dry rot that infest all our correctional systems.

Attica was built in 1931 as a response to the criticism of the Wickersham Commission's investigation of the prison facilities in the state.[52] Attica, like Auburn a hundred years previously, was hailed as a new invention, a final answer to the troublesome realities of penological activity. Despite these claims for the innovations at Attica, the prison was essentially no more and no less than the same model first implemented at Auburn. It was the same, that is, with perhaps one exception: there were no idealistic claims as Attica opened that it was a rehabilitative facility. Rather, it was hailed as the most secure prison ever built.

Between the 1870 movement that formalized the practices of probation and parole and the opening of Attica in 1931, it seems that for most purposes, the interest in rehabilitation of the criminal had died. About all that Attica could claim is reported in a *New York Times* item from August 2, 1931:

ATTICA PRISON TO BE CONVICT'S PARADISE

Condemned by the Wickersham Commission for its maintenance of Auburn and Clinton prisons, New York State will have an answer to charges of inhuman penal conditions when the new Wyoming State Prison [Wyoming County, N.Y.] opens at Attica within the next few months with its full quota of 2,000 convicts. Said to be the last word in modern prison construction, the new unit in the State's penal system

---

[52] New York State Special Commission, *Attica*, p. xiii.

will do away with such traditions as convict bunks, mess hall lockstep, bull pens, and even locks and keys.

In their places will be beds with springs and mattresses, a cafeteria with food under glass, recreation rooms and an automatic signal system by which convicts will notify guards of their presence in their cells. Doors will be operated by compressed air, sunlight will stream into cells and every prisoner will have an individual radio.[53]

This kind of praise is considerably different from the promises for reformation with which Auburn opened. On the other side, if rehabilitation is impossible within a maximum security prison, perhaps it is simply more honest to praise the cleanliness and efficiency of the cages than to say anything about changing people. However, the claims made in the *New York Times* never came true. The New York State Special Commission on Attica comments:

Perhaps because of the depression economy, perhaps for other reasons as well, no Attica inmate has even seen the institution described (in the *Times* report). When Attica opened, there was no cafeteria with food under glass, no recreation room, no automatic signal system, and no sunlight streaming into the cells. There was, in fact, nothing but another huge, foreboding prison. With the unprecedented emphasis on security visible in every brick and every door, this "last word in modern prison construction," far from doing away with locks and keys, made them the focal point around which all life revolved.[54]

We can conclude that Attica was Auburn all over again—except that Auburn was built and defended by dedicated reformers who had made a mistake, whereas Attica was built by keepers of men who had neither the money nor the dedication to fulfill the promise of clean cages.

When Attica erupted on September 9, 1971, the direct precipitating incident was rather trivial, but the grievances beneath the surface were long-festering, explosive issues voiced by the most desperate of men. When the New York Police retook the institution on September 13, 1971, 43 people had died; most of them, including hostages, fell before the bullets fired by officials of the state government. Since this revolt, there have not been many significant changes, except that personnel have changed—including most of the inmates, who have been transferred to other institutions or been paroled.

Whatever changes do eventually take place in the New York prison system, the fact that Attica of 1971 was virtually unchanged from the Attica that opened in 1931, and the fact that Attica of 1931 was virtually unchanged from the Auburn of 1819—these facts are what are significant.

[53] As reprinted in ibid., p. 15.
[54] Ibid.

It is true, as Ramsey Clark has said, that America knows better. The social, psychological, administrative, and architectural skills exist by which to do better than Attica, and yet Attica is symbolic of similar inertia, stupidity, or just plain indifference found in other parts of the country.[55]

The California Experience

The California prison and parole system has long been regarded as the best in the nation. California is one of the few states with the foresight to spend any substantial money on correctional research; it is also one of the few states to experiment with a variety of treatment and custodial alternatives. In many respects California offers many contrasts with the New York correctional system. it is therefore somewhat surprising to find that the California system is also under attack for its basic inhumanity and its ineffectiveness. Just how progressive a state correctional system can be and still fail is something worth noting.

California corrections is notable for more program variations than can be reviewed here. Some of the best-known innovations are:

1. A probation subsidy program that functions to keep more offenders in the community and to divert funds from the institutions to the improvement of probation programs.[56]
2. Accurate record keeping, both of incoming inmates' characteristics and of parolees' subsequent behavior on parole.[57]
3. Comparatively sophisticated classification systems enabling more effective diagnosis and the matching of offenders to programs.[58]
4. More systematic and complete educational programs than most state prison systems.
5. Innovative group and individual counseling programs involving both staff and inmates.
6. The constant generation of research projects that have included evaluation components and have even used inmates as coresearchers.
7. A variety of parole programs, involving various combinations of offenders, parole officer types, size of caseloads, etc.

Probably more is written about the California corrections system than any other, and certainly the California system has contributed as much as

[55] Ramsey Clark, *Crime in America* (New York: Pocket Books, 1971), pp. 214–218.

[56] Robert L. Smith, "A Quiet Revolution: Probation Subsidy," *Delinquency Prevention Reporter*, May 1971, pp. 3–7.

[57] Donald M. Gottfredson, *A Shorthand Formula for Base Expectancies*, California Department of Corrections, Research Division, Research Report No. 5 (July 1962).

[58] Marguerite Q. Warren, "The Community Treatment Project: History and Prospects, *Law Enforcement and Technology, 1* (1967), 191–200.

any other system to our knowledge of crime causation, correctional programming, and the evaluation of correctional activity.

Unfortunately, in spite of these innovations, or perhaps because of them, the California institutions are gaining a reputation equal to New York's. The average amount of time served in prison is longer in California than in any other state.[59] The California prisons have also gained a reputation for their violence, and some critics doubt if the most violent incidents have been fully reported. The official explanation for the increased difficulties within the maximum security prisons is a good one (theoretically)—that the increased use of probation and parole has meant that the population left in prison have increasingly been the poorer risks.

Nevertheless, most of the inmates in California's maximum security prisons are not there because of their dangerousness. Many of the prisoners who are left in maximum security units are there simply because the new and innovative programs have not included them. Even highly rated educational and vocational training within prisons has reached only a minority of inmates. In short, there seems to be something wrong with the entire design of even our best correctional systems. Innovative community-based programs are offered as options to incarceration only for the best-risk offenders, and the potential of the institutions themselves for treatment rather than for restraint is usually ignored. What a correction system needs, in other words, is less dependence or less focus on institutions in the first place. Although it is true that the probation subsidy, among other things, has reduced the California institution population, we seem to be prepared to house a sizable core of the offender population within prisons. This core population is generally made up of the poor, the black, and the uneducated—that is, people who have received no benefits from any other part of society before their incarceration.

Progress and Two Commissions

There have been two major commissions appointed in this century to investigate the state of law enforcement and judicial and correctional agencies in the United States. The first, commonly called the Wickersham Commission, reported in 1931.[60] The second, commonly known as the President's Crime Commission, reported in 1967, 36 years later.[61] A brief

[59] Donald M. Gottfredson et al., *Four Thousand Lifetimes: A Study of Time Served and Parole Outcomes* (Davis, Calif.: National Council on Crime and Delinquency, June 1973), p. 30.

[60] National Commission on Law Enforcement Observance and Enforcement Report No. 9 (Montclair, N.J.: Patterson-Smith, 1971).

[61] President's Commission on Law Enforcement and the Administration of Justice, *Challenge of Crime in a Free Society* (Washington, D.C.: Government Printing Office, 1967).

comparison of the two correction reports of these commissions provides us with a conclusion to the history of corrections and a good introduction to present correctional operations.

A rather ambivalent, but accurate, conclusion is that the two correctional reports are both alike and different. They are alike in that the essential components of corrections have remained the same. The maximum security institution was the focal point of corrections in 1931, and it remained the focal point in 1967. Probation was the major means of escaping from the system in 1931, and probation was used even more often in 1967. Parole was the major way out of prison in 1931, and it was still the primary means in 1967. The system was impoverished in 1931, and the personnel were poorly trained if they were trained at all. The situation was much the same in 1967. And in 1931, the academic and professional consultants hired by the Wickersham Commission seemed to have plausible theories of correctional behavior—and data of some quality to support them—that, taken together, suggested knowledge of humane and therapeutic correctional activity far in advance of the correctional realities of 1931. In 1967, the recommendations of the Task Force on Corrections again demonstrated that our knowledge was far in advance of our willingness to implement our ideas.

Regardless of these similarities, there are some significant differences between the findings of the Wickersham Commission and the findings of the President's Crime Commission. The Wickersham report on corrections begins with a review of the physical dimensions of prison cells across the country. The report continues in well-controlled, but undisguised horror, particularly concerning the conditions at Auburn and Clinton prisons. Without a doubt, the overriding concern of the Wickersham report was the physical deterioration of the prisons. Although the President's Crime Commission reported that, in 1967, 62 operating prisons were built before 1900, the commission does not seem to be as upset at physical conditions as the Wickersham Commission. Although the 1967 report is concerned with the same kinds of problems as the 1931 report, the terror and flavor of the report have changed considerably. The more recent report is concerned with increasing the effectiveness of corrections, but there seems to be a conviction that there is a core of valid activity for the present correctional agencies to undertake.

Perhaps the greatest difference, and a rather significant one, has to do with the conception of the criminal justice system in its entirety. The Wickersham Commission was aware of certain interconnections among the components of the system of criminal justice. The first commission, however, did not use a system model in order to examine the interrelations of the parts or to analyze the dysfunctions of the system. (We will introduce a system model for our own use in Part III of this book.) Although it has not been suggested frequently, one possible reason for the more optimistic tenor of the second report is that the President's Commission had discovered a more powerful means of analysis than the Wickersham Commission had at their disposal.

Very noticeable in the 1967 report of the Task Force on Corrections is the knowledge of the interactions of sentencing, probation, in-prison treatment, and parole. Although the 1967 commission is not at all satisfied with the present state of corrections, there is some optimism in the recommendations for the future. Perhaps the optimism has faded since 1967, but the power of the new analytical tools remains as one principal advantage of modern criminal justice study.

A second major difference between the two reports is the presence in the 1967 report of a chapter on alternatives to incarceration. Among these alternatives are foster and group homes, guided group interaction, reception center parole, prerelease or halfway house programs, and intensive community treatment programs. (These programs will be discussed in the next section.) Many of these innovations have involved juveniles rather than adults, but they do point to some changes in correctional alternatives. Furthermore, it has seemed to be a tradition in correctional evolution that what it first applied to juveniles is later adapted to adults.

In conclusion, although 36 years have not taken us far, we may have arrived at the threshold of change.

chapter 7

Current Programs

and Issues

in Corrections

We have now seen the development of corrections from approximately 1820 to the present. Some of the stated goals as they have been idealized and as they have been implemented were discussed, along with the agencies of the criminal justice system as they have developed in relation to our traditions of federalism and the balance of power between federal, state, and local government. We have also seen that, from the very beginning of our present correctional system, the goal of rehabilitation has been paramount. Treatment is not a new idea developed in this century. Indeed, the concept of rehabilitation in its present form is at least 150 years old. It is quite understandable, under these conditions, that the officials responsible for implementation may be suffering more from the frustration of faulty implementation than from the frustration of lacking new ideas.

In this section we will examine the current state of the art; we will review briefly the various practices and operations in the correctional area, concentrating on prison and parole. By this time it should be obvious, though, that concentration on two aspects of corrections must be a matter of emphasis. We cannot limit our discussion to prison and parole. We will also have to cover diversion, pretrial release and detention, sentencing, and postconviction alternatives to incarceration. We will try to cover these aspects as they affect the primary prison and parole process. Other aspects of diversion, detention, and sentencing are covered in other chapters of this book.

Major sources for this section are the President's Crime Commission and the National Advisory Commission on Criminal Justice Standards and Goals. The President's Crime Commission report was the largest and most systematic survey ever made of the criminal system. It was published in 1967.[1] The National Advisory Commission on Criminal Justice Standards and Goals released its report in January of 1974.[2] It serves a considerably different purpose than the *Task Force Report.* The 1974 *Report on Corrections* is a series of systematic recommendations that to the commission seem feasible for implementation in the near future.

The Commission on Criminal Justice Standards has taken a hard line on corrections. For example, the standards on legal rights of prisoners go far beyond court decisions. If there are any major faults with the standards as recommended in the 1974 report, they would seem to involve the purposive shortsightedness and the emphasis on feasibility. Unless the standards are implemented forthwith, the timelag between the statement of them and their implementation may prove dysfunctional. States that are slow to implement the recommended standards may, by the time they do so, create more problems than they solve by forcing outmoded correctional systems to adapt to outmoded recommendations. If there are negative repercussions, these departments may continue to blame inmates for their ingratitude rather than focus on the problems of lackluster state government. Despite this kind of problem, the *Report on Corrections* is a novel reference work in that the commentary to the actual recommendations, when compared to the 1967 *Task Force Report,* becomes the most current survey of corrections.

DIVERSION

Diversion is the act of channeling an offender out of the criminal justice process somewhere between arrest and conviction, regardless of the fact that the defendant appears to be guilty. It is an activity that includes the police, the prosecutor, the defense attorney, the judge, and the probation staff rather than the traditional correctional workers. But it is a *correc-*

---

[1] Full name for their commission is the President's Commission on Law Enforcement and the Administration of Justice, *Task Force Report: Corrections* (Washington, D.C.: Government Printing Office, 1967), pp. 38–44. Shortened title henceforth to read *Task Force Report.*

[2] National Advisory Commission on Criminal Justice Standards and Goals, *Report on Corrections* (Washington, D.C.: Government Printing Office, 1974), pp. 73–97.

tional activity in that it deals with people who, except for diversion, would become intake for the correctional system.

The practice of diversion is not new. People have probably been diverted from the criminal justice process as long as there has been formal prosecution. The *concept* of diversion, however, is new. Diversion implies a *planned* redirection of offenders, rather than a haphazard redistribution.

To date, diverting offenders from the criminal process has been basically haphazard. The police, for example, have always made the decision *not* to arrest in certain cases involving extenuating circumstances. For example, if the suspect is inexperienced, extremely young or extremely old, or if his crime is accompanied by a plausible explanation of extreme circumstances, the police may decide that arrest is not in the interest of community order or law enforcement. Another common reason for police diversion has to do with the use of informers. The police informer is frequently threatened with arrest and then promised leniency if he cooperates with the clearing of other cases.[3]

The prosecutor also has reasons for diverting. Fundamental to the prosecutor's sense of his effectiveness is his ability to gain a conviction. If a particular case seems difficult to win at trial, or if the normal pressures for a plea of guilty do not seem effective, the prosecutor may settle for informal alternatives to prosecution, such as warnings, plans for psychiatric care, a parent's promise for private schooling, and so on.

The judge, too, has reasons for seeking diversion. He is pressed daily by the sheer weight of the cases on the calendar. According to recent studies of urban criminal courts, the judge is at least as interested in moving the cases in the docket as he is with specific outcomes. If the judge is approached by the defense attorney or by the prosecutor, or by both, with some suggestions for alternative processing, he is quite likely to consider them. And he has been more willing to look for alternatives lately as the traditional incarceration process appears increasingly ineffective.

The fact that preconviction officials utilize diversion to solve (or get rid of) difficult cases should not be overemphasized. As we have seen in terms of the operation of bail and plea negotiation, maintaining a steady flow of cases is very important to the system. But it is not the only concern. Police, prosecutors, judges, and other officials may be sincerely interested in the outcome of the criminal process for any particular defendant, and they may make the decision to divert a guilty person in what they consider to be the best interests of rehabilitation, justice, or community safety. This kind of decision is made, however, with a dearth of formalized alternatives to fall back on. And it is made after a more or less

---

[3] Jerome Skolnick, *Justice Without Trial* (New York: Wiley, 1966), pp. 112–138.

subjective compromise among the many conflicting interests and goals that meet head on in the criminal process.

To state this problem in another way, whatever criteria officials have used in the past as reasons for diversion, these criteria have not been studied in relation to their effect on the correctional process.

By and large, we can assume that the present practice of diversion is too subjective and haphazard to ensure safety or rehabilitation, and it has had insufficient visiblity to allow proper planning and interagency coordination.

Therefore, one important aspect of the new emphasis on diversion is that the decision to divert should be an articulated and defensible decision. In order for this to occur, criminal justice officials must rid themselves of the idea that diversion is a necessary evil that must be hushed up in some way. If part of the pressure on officials derives from the feeling that the community will object to their diversion of offenders, then the policy of open diversion also calls for the reeducation of the community. This undertaking is a weighty one. Changing public opinion about the proper handling of offenders may be necessary to the achievement of effective criminal justice. But there is also the danger that persons with the power to manipulate correctional programs will do so without consulting and informing the public.[4]

This ethical issue becomes even more important because the Commission on Criminal Justice Standards and Goals recommends not only open and articulated diversion decisions, *but also that diversion become the preferred alternative* in cases that do not require strict supervision. In essence, the commission has stated (and accurately) that the correctional system is handling more cases than it can handle and is handling cases that it is not competent to handle. It particularly recommends diversion of the mentally ill, the retarded, alcoholics, and drug addicts. It views these social problems as more effectively addressed by other agencies of government. Most importantly, it considers the explanation that the social alternatives for these cases do not exist . . . an inadequate excuse.[5] Therefore correctional organizations will begin to speak out and seek influence in order to see that behavior problems tangential to criminal justice are handled elsewhere.

PRETRIAL RELEASE AND DETENTION

The practice, the problems, and the constitutional issues in relation to bail have already been discussed in Chapter Five. However, the pretrial re-

---

[4] Ibid., pp. 12–15.
[5] See footnote 2.

lease decision also affects corrections, because if a defendant is detained rather than released, he will be imprisoned in a local jail. Local correctional facilities are probably the most infamous penal institutions in the United States. If the maximum security prison has not changed substantially since Auburn was constructed in 1819, then the local jail has not changed substantially from the penological mockeries that *preceded* Auburn! Local jails now have cells, and most of them are constructed along maximum security lines; nevertheless, the contemporary jail is still very often a den of vice, where convicted and unconvicted offenders mix freely, and the custodians have little control.

The physical conditions of jails by themselves make pretrial detention one of the most significant phases of the criminal process. If a defendant cannot afford bail or is not eligible for release on recognizance (if such a program exists), he may be forced to spend weeks or even months in jail. He may lose his job, his family, his ties to the community. Of equal significance, he may also find himself branded with the stigma of convict or jailbird even though he has been convicted of nothing.

These kinds of conditions are pernicious in and of themselves. They breed more crime, disrespect for the law, and hatred for the officials of government. In addition to this type of problem with pretrial detention, another crucial problem is the relationship between pretrial detention and the postconviction disposition of incarceration.

The data from the evaluation of the Vera Bail Project, perhaps more than any other single variable, demonstrated that the conviction and disposition decisions were determined by the type of pretrial assignment—that is, detention or release pending trial.[6] In the Vera Institute study, 30 percent of people released pending trial were convicted, whereas 60 percent of the people detained were convicted. Second, only 16 percent of the convicted people released pending trial were eventually incarcerated, whereas 98 percent of the people who were detained were eventually incarcerated. Although the Vera Institute data were not representative of the total number of offenders (for example, very serious offenders were not included), additional data collected by the New York Legal Aid Society support the Vera findings for other categories of crimes, and for offenders released on bail rather than on recognizance.[7]

We can conclude that all the data presently available demonstrate that the chance of incarceration (and thus also of parole) is influenced to a greater degree by the presence or absence of pretrial detention than by a

[6] Charles F. Ares, Anne Rankin, and Herbert Sturz, "The Manhattan Bail Project: An Interim Report on the Use of Pre-Trial Parole," *New York University Law Review*, 38, (January 1963), 67–95.

[7] Legal Aid Society of the City of New York, "The Unconstitutional Administration of Bail: Bellamy v. The Judges of New York City," *Criminal Law Bulletin*, 8, No. 6 (July/August 1972), 459–506.

particular kind of criminal offense or particular kind of deviant pattern. The implications of this conclusion for corrections is immense. First of all, it means that almost all the goals that correctional organizations are supposedly structured to accomplish are tangential to the main reason for an offender's presence in prison. Most of these goals normally have something to do with crime reduction. Certainly the inmate or the parolee has probably committed a crime, but there are evidently many equally or more serious offenders who did not reach prison because they were not detained pending trial. Since the most direct reason of incarceration seems to be the relative poverty of the offender, rather than his commission of a crime, much correctional activity seems to be directed at the wrong characteristics of the offender.

Perhaps if we reverse the emphasis of this conclusion, it will make more sense. Considering that correction of criminal behavior is the *legitimate* goal of prison and parole, we would need to conclude that the primary selection criteria for corrections (i.e., pretrial detention) are not directly related to the recognized correctional goals. Offenders are not selected for prison and parole on the basis of prison and parole services from which they might benefit or on the basis of dangerousness or some other criteria that correctional officials are supposedly competent to judge. Rather, the offenders are selected on the basis of poverty, and (we would suspect) other criteria that would indicate that the real concern of the preconviction process is the reduction of pressure on the system, rather than the achievement of crime-reduction goals.

A second very important issue in relation to pretrial detention concerns the administration of detention programs. Certainly we are aware that the practice of pretrial detention should be reformed, but meanwhile we should not overlook what is happening to people who have been detained. In most cases, they sit in abject idleness and suffer stricter supervision and regulations than the convicted population in the jail. Furthermore, persons who have been bound over for trial and the convicted misdemeanants are not supposed to come in contact with each other. However, in reality, most jails do not have sufficient facilities or security precautions to make complete segregation possible. In many jails, the only operational distinction between a detainee and a jail inmate is the color of the uniform they wear.[8]

Concerning the programs themselves, one would suspect that there is much that could be offered to the detained population that is not presently available to them. The scope and depth of treatment programs are also sadly lacking for the convicted misdemeanants. (This subject will be covered later in the chapter.) When we discuss programming for de-

---

[8] On these and other jail problems, see Henry Burns, Jr., "The American Jail in Perspective," *Crime and Delinquency*, 17, No. 4 (October 1971), 446–455.

tainees and convicts simultaneously, one important distinction must be recognized. There is no legal authority for asking the detainee to do anything in the jail. The situation may be absurd, but he is not there for punishment; he is merely awaiting trial. Under such circumstances, extra precautions should be taken to ensure voluntary participation. Furthermore, we can assume that many detainees could benefit from the social services of various agencies, such as job and family counseling, and that providing such services is small recompense for the indignity and inconvenience of detention. A final note of caution, however, might be that the improvement of detention facilities and programs can never be an adequate substitute for pretrial release and criminal justice diversion procedures.

One mechanical, but rather effective, means of improving services for detainees is the unanimous recommendation of the President's Crime Commission and the National Advisory Commission on Criminal Justice Standards and Goals that detention facilities be run by correctional officials rather than by the police.[9] Most jails are county facilities, but even a county department of corrections with a jail run by a warden is likely to structure a better jail program than one that is run by a sheriff or the local police department. Several states, such as Vermont and Connecticut, have done away with county facilities and have turned the local jails over to the state department of corrections. This arrangement enables the state to use the facilities with considerable flexibility. For example, they can use the jails as work-release centers for convicted felons, and they can transfer misdemeanants to prisons with better vocational training facilities. The strength of county government in other states precludes this arrangement, but states like Pennsylvania are seeking flexible cooperative arrangements between county jails and state correctional authorities.[10]

SENTENCING

In the view of the two commissions and of most experts in the field, sentencing should remain a task performed by the trial judge. From time to time it has been argued that sentencing should be taken away from the judge and should be turned over to correctional officials. Some states such as Washington have done this—so that the actual sentence decision is made by a board. In these states, all the judge does is sentence the offender to

[9] President's Commission on Law Enforcement and the Administration of Justice, *Task Force Report: Corrections,* pp. 79–81; and National Advisory Commission on Criminal Justice Standards and Goals, *Report on Corrections,* pp. 126–127.

[10] Pennsylvania Crime Commission, *Corrections in Pennsylvania* (Harrisburg, Penn.: Office of the Attorney General, 1969), pp. 20–27.

the maximum allowable period of incarceration. However, this kind of sentencing structure has run into other criticism, such as the claim that the board "retries" the offender when they are considering him for release, and that the board treats more harshly offenders who have poor prison conduct records. Most states have retained the traditional tripartite sentencing structure, in which legal limits are set by the legislature, the range for a particular crime is set by the judge, and the actual release date is set by the parole board.

Within this traditional structure, many improvements are possible. Some factors, such as the pre-sentence report, have been discussed either in Chapter Five, or above in our discussion of the fragmented correctional task. Perhaps the most important factor in relation to sentencing as a correctional task is the development of information systems by which to inform the judges about the results of particular sentences. As Judge Marvin Frankel has said, one of the greatest problems with judicial sentencing is the essential isolation of the judge.[11] When making a decision about the type and length of sentence, the judge is like a blindfolded man throwing darts in a silent room. He never receives any information back about how accurate his tosses in the dark have been, unless he receives extremely biased information about a particularly lenient sentence that later proved to be a disastrous mistake.

Two kinds of activity (among many others) are needed to improve a judge's conception of what sentencing should be and to evaluate whether the sentencing actually accomplishes its purpose. First, legislative reform of sentencing codes is drastically necessary. At the present time most state legislatures have dealt with the punishments for individual crimes in piecemeal fashion as bits of legislation have reached the floor for action. Legislatures should reconsider this kind of sentencing legislation, and should turn instead to a unified sentencing code in which classes of crimes are grouped and sentencing options are provided for classes of crimes. Models for this kind of code are provided in the Model Penal Code[12] and the Model Sentencing Act.[13] Either model provides a simple and rational set of alternatives in which the responsibilities of legislature, judge, and parole board are clearly defined.

This kind of relegislation cannot be accomplished, however, without considerable legislative expertise about the interrelationships within the system of criminal justice. For example, the New York legislature, in an effort to deal more sternly with drug crimes and to deter plea negotia-

---

[11] Marvin Frankel, "Lawlessness in Sentencing," *University of Cincinnati Law Review, 41,* No. 1 (1972), 4–24.

[12] American Law Institute, *Model Penal Code,* 1962.

[13] National Council on Crime and Delinquency, *Model Sentencing Act* (Hackensack, N.J.: 1965).

tions has probably given judges and prosecutors so little discretion that the entire criminal justice system will be upset. Some defenders have estimated that the number of trials will increase 100 to 200 percent because the new sentencing code makes it impossible for offenders to gain anything by pleading guilty. Another possibility is that bargaining, rather than being effectively curbed, will be pushed back earlier in the procedure. Most negotiations will take place in the station house prior to the filing of charges. The result will be lower visibility of discretionary decisions—which is the precise opposite of the goal recommended by the President's Crime Commission and the National Advisory Commission on Criminal Justice Standards and Goals.

A second kind of activity that could improve a judge's sentencing decision would be a more active part taken by correctional organizations in sentencing. Rather than mutter behind closed doors about insensitive, misinformed, and even stupid judges, correctional authorities should actively seek out interaction with judges to discuss sentencing policy and inform judges about actual correctional practices. This kind of interchange is now occurring in sentencing institutes in which trial judges come together for several days' or weeks' training on current sentencing issues.[14] Correctional officials who can take an active role in institute presentations and discussions are reducing some misapprehensions that have led to sentencing disparity and faulty sentence options. A problem, however, with such training institutes is making sure that what a judge learns, he carries back with him into his operational sentencing policy. The chances of this learning actually being implemented are probably increased if correctional officials and judges from the same jurisdiction have the opportunity to meet together in training sessions.

CLASSIFICATION

After a prisoner is received from the sentencing court, he will be classified in some manner. The sophistication and purpose of the classification depend on the correctional system. In jurisdictions where each institution is still independent of a central correctional authority, the judge may sentence a prisoner to a particular prison. Classification in such cases is limited to the security precautions taken at that prison and to the programs available in that prison. In most states, however, a judge may sentence a prisoner to the department of corrections, and the actual institution for incarceration is chosen by the department. In this situation, classification is usually more sophisticated and lengthy, because the range

---

[14] For example, "1969 Sentencing Institute for Superior Court Judges," *California Reporter*, 85 (1969), 31–40; and F. Remington and D. Newman, "The Highland Park Institute on Sentence Disparity," *Federal Probation*, 26 (March 1962), 3.

of custody and of treatment option is much broader. Even in these cases, unfortunately, it is not unusual for the classification tests to be sensitive to more options than the system can accommodate. In other words, much of the information that may be gathered about the inmate during the classification period is subsequently useless because the personnel programs or facilities do not exist to cover the options in the diagnostic report.[15]

Under the most complete classification procedure, all inmates received from court are sent to a diagnostic and reception center. Within this center the new inmate will spend his first weeks in prison while he is being tested, interviewed, and observed. Regardless of the exact methods used in any particular center, the actual operative goals of diagnostic centers are to identify (1) extreme custody or behavior risks, (2) good choices for any current experimental program, (3) general program possibilities that might be suggested by the inmate's file (such as remedial education or Alcoholics Anonymous), and (4) first prison living and work assignments.[16]

From the point of view of prison officials, the important classification decisions are those involving housing and work assignments. These two decisions establish the location of the inmate in a particular institution for the majority of his time. These two decisions are also of greatest significance to the inmate because they determine whom he lives with and what kind of prison labor he must do. The job classification itself can be important because it generally carries a wage of varying amount (always small), and it opens or closes the opportunity structure of the prison. For example, inmate clerks, runners, and janitors have access to information not obtainable by other inmates, and they generally have more relaxed relationships with prison staff. Research findings have also indicated that the work supervisor and the custodial officer attached to work assignments develop more intense and significant relationships with inmates than do other staff members. Thus, it would seem that regardless of decisions about experimental programs, different counseling relationships, and so on, the work and housing decisions carry the greatest weight with inmates and custodial staff.[17] Consequently, a proper manipulation of these arrangements might offer the greatest classification contribution to treatment, although generally the housing and work decisions are based on institutional need.

An important classification issue raised by the National Advisory Com-

[15] National Advisory Commission on Criminal Justice Standards and Goals, *Report on Corrections*, pp. 197–220.

[16] American Correctional Association, *Correctional Classification and Treatment* (Cincinnati, Ohio: Anderson, 1975), pp. 1–25.

[17] Daniel Glaser, *The Effectiveness of a Prison and Parole System* (Indianapolis: Bobbs-Merrill, 1969), pp. 90–94.

mission on Criminal Justice Standards and Goals concerns the underlying dimension upon which the offender will be classified. Many different classification schemes exist, but most of them would seem to fall into two general types: (1) a custodial or security classification and (2) a treatment classification. The National Advisory Commission recommends that all departments should move to a security classification because this dimension seems more conducive to a guarantee of fairness. The commission argues that treatment classifications (i.e., classifying an inmate as to some psychological type on some maturity level) are not sufficiently exact so that inmates are reliably classified, nor are the programs based on treatment classifications effective enough to justify segregation in terms of treatment types. Furthermore, the commission suggests that housing and work assignments are so important to inmates that, in fairness, the inmates should be able to understand why they receive the classification that they do. Also the inmates are more likely to understand some gradient of the security-risk factor, particularly when it is based on the inmate's past record, than they are to understand a complex treatment classification based on theories of deviance. The commission further suggests that classifications should be appealable if the inmate is dissatisfied, and that appeals are more reliably argued in terms of security risk than treatment diagnosis. In essence, the commission is saying that it is better to run a fair and open custodial institution than to claim to run a hospital and to use this claim as justification for punitive decisions.[18]

LOCAL ADULT INSTITUTIONS

One kind of institution where sentencing institutes and more sophisticated classification procedures have made little difference is the local jail. The jail situation has not changed considerably since de Beaumont and de Toqueville studied the American prison system in 1831. Indeed, many jails still in use have not changed physically since 1831. Although some improvements have been made in major adult institutions (which will be discussed in the next section), the emphasis on the serious or dangerous offender and on felony offenses has meant that conditions in local institutions for misdemeanants have been largely ignored.

Perhaps more than any other correctional problem, the plight of the offenders in local institutions demonstrates the slowness of the democratic process and the conflict of interest at the local level. State institutions are financed by state taxes, and at the state level, partisanship and factionalism have occasionally given way to rational correctional legislation. These advantages are not found at the local level. The administration of the local jail is an integral part of local government, and city and

[18] National Advisory Commission on Criminal Justice Standards and Goals, *Report on Corrections*, pp. 213–214.

county organization has traditionally lagged behind state and federal organization for effectiveness and accountability in many areas. It is not surprising that the local jail suffers from the same mismanagement, poor personnel, and poor financing that have characterized local schools, health services, and recreation facilities.

Unfortunately, the local jail is an unavoidable experience in the correctional process for the great majority of offenders. Detainees experience jail prior to trial, and misdemeanants experience jail as their punishment. We do not know how many minor offenders (graduates from the local jail system) later commit serious felonies, but it is likely that most offenders who reach state prisons have suffered a jail term somewhere along their criminal career track. Because of the position of jails in the correctional system, one might expect them to receive a major amount of attention; but as it does in other matters, local government often ignores dysfunctional operations until they reach emergency proportions, and then symptoms rather than causes of disorder are attacked. Hence, the problems of the misdemeanant and the detainee in local jails are usually ignored. Only when the commission of a felony provides the possibility of a state prison term does someone take the problems presented by an offender seriously.

In 1966, the National Council on Crime and Delinquency conducted a survey of correctional institutions operated by states and counties throughout the United States. The survey found that for the year 1965, 1,016,748 offenders had served sentences in local jails and that the average daily population in all jails was 141,303. Annual operating expenditures for the custody of jail inmates came to $147,794,214, so that the average daily cost per inmate was $2.87. In comparison, the amount of money spent on a felony inmate in a federal or state penitentiary for each day of incarceration was three to six times that amount.[19]

Given the financial situation of many local governments, particularly of large cities, we are unlikely to see much improvement in the jail situation in the near future. The local taxpayer does not want the increase in taxes that an improvement in local jails would undoubtedly require, and there is no politically powerful voice from inside the prison that might wage a battle for reform. When many local school systems are facing bankruptcy, it is probably too much to expect civic concern for the local jail. Thus, while local economic and social situations militate against improvements in jails, at the same time local political forces are countering suggestions that the state should take on responsibility for local jail administration. Among the reasons given are: (1) disilke of state officials interfering in local affairs, (2) the desire to retain political patronage jobs that the jail

---

[19] President's Commission on Law Enforcement and the Administration of Justice, *Task Force Report,* p. 162.

often offers, and (3) the feeling that jail prisoners are not worthy of relief anyway.

While these conflicts maintain the inertia of local corrections, conditions are getting worse. The overcrowding, the viciousness, the indignity to the human spirit of places like the Cook County Jail in Chicago or the Washington, D.C. jail are infamous. In 1972, conditions in the three jail systems of Philadelphia County became so miserable that a federal judge declared the entire system a violation of the prohibition against cruel and unusual punishment.[20] Among the conditions that reached court attention were the fact that "consensual homosexual relations" in the prison were not punished. Officials claimed they had not sufficient control within the overcrowded and understaffed structure to maintain proper supervision. Investigations by the county district attorney and others revealed that most of the homosexual relationships classified as consensual by the staff were actually rapes of which the victim was too intimidated to complain. In June 1973, the warden and deputy warden of the Holmsburg prison in Philadelphia were stabbed to death. The immediate reaction of Mayor Rizzo and others was for the reinstitution of the death penalty. The Pennsylvania legislature followed these suggestions in short order. Hence, the backlash to violent crime was immediate but improvement of the living standards and of the rehabilitative capacity of Holmsburg was again ignored. (Governor Shapp vetoed the death penalty.)

Although improvements in the jail situations are hard to come by, Henry Burns and others have suggested three steps that might alleviate the situation to some degree.[21] The first of these is an adequate program of diversion for petty offenders and alcoholics. Chronic minor offenders and drunks do not find any help in the local jail, and they take up space that is sorely needed for more adequate treatment of more serious offenders. Group houses and other community-based alternatives for these offenders should be investigated.

The second suggestion involves increased use of programs of work release, which might at least reduce some of the hardships imposed by a jail sentence. Work release is a program that enables offenders to continue their jobs in the community as long as they spend their nonworking hours in jail. Offenders who can continue to work as they serve a jail sentence can maintain support of their families and thus retain one of the social roles crucial to their stability in the community. Many jails have initiated work-release programs of some sort, and although sophisticated evaluations of these programs have been lacking, their greater effectiveness when compared to other jail alternatives has been assumed. Prob-

[20] Jackson v. Hendrick, 40 *Law Week* 2710 (Ct. Comm. Pls. Pa. 1972).

[21] Burns, *American Jail in Perspective*.

lems associated with work release include: (1) lack of transportation to distant work centers, (2) antiquated state laws that forbid intermittent confinement, and (3) the hesitancy of business leaders to provide jobs for convicted offenders. Nevertheless, work release seems promising, and the concept of mixed confinement and community release might be expanded to include other release purposes.[22]

One last suggestion is the regionalization of jail and detention facilities. Local governments have created combined organizational structures for the administration of transportation, sewage, recreation, and education services. Certain localities are now exploring the possibility of regionalized police forces, and the suggestion that jail services be regionalized seems a natural development. Such a plan may bypass some of the objections to state control of the jails and still provide a sufficient financial base for improvement in personnel, facilities, and programs. Problems with regionalization are also numerous. One major drawback is that many of the jails that would benefit most from the increase in personnel and services are so distant from other jails that regionalization would require the construction of a new facility equally distant from main population centers. However, it may be possible to regionalize the organization and management of local jails without centralizing physical facilities and services. These kinds of possibilities need still to be investigated.

STATE AND FEDERAL ADULT INSTITUTIONS

In contrast to the local jail situation, most institutions for serious adult offenders (generally those serving one year or more) have seen some improvements in the past generation. The federal government and most state governments have established centralized correctional administrations that govern policy and top management decisions for all the institutions in the system. These centralized correctional administrations have also made possible greater coordination between institution and probation and parole operations, and frequently parole and institutional administrations have been combined. In addition to improved coordination and planning of correctional services, the central administration of corrections and the generation of unified policies for all institutions have seemed to facilitate the formation of new correctional structures such as halfway houses, group houses, and work-release centers.

Unlike the nineteenth century, the major trend in adult institutionalization has been away from large maximum security units toward smaller minimum security institutions. The National Advisory Commission on Criminal Justice Standards and Goals has recommended that this trend

---

[22] Elmer H. Johnson, "Work-Release: Conflicting Goals Within a Promising Innovation," *Canadian Journal of Corrections, 12,* No. 1 (1970), 67–77.

should be drawn to its ultimate conclusion by deemphasizing institutions altogether and placing the majority of felony inmates in small community-based correctional centers.[23] This goal will not soon be implemented. The mere fact that the isolated correctional institutions are useless for any purpose except incarceration has often been an important reason for their continuance. Even if legislatures admit that prisons are ineffective for most present correctional goals, budget-conscious lawmakers do not wish the institutions to be a complete waste. What they generally fail to realize is that even burning the institutions down is probably less wasteful than maintaining their present operation.

Hopefully the ultimate ineffectiveness of isolated penal institutions will someday be recognized, but in the meantime someone must deal with institutions. On the state and federal level, most correctional officials, particularly top institution and central administrators, are concerned individuals dedicated to change. It is also true that many correctional managers have suffered as a result of isolation from other departments of government, have been confused and simplistic in their solutions to prison problems, and have been defensive about their administrations and wary of outside intervention.[24]

Reasons for this isolated stance are not just physical. The prison has traditionally been an island fortress. As much as possible, it has been a self-sustaining community. Since the construction of Auburn, inmates have been used as cheap labor for the maintenance of the physical plant, for growing of food, and for manufacture of goods for use in the prison. Custodial officers in many prisons have traditionally been ordered to keep prison secrets in prison. Evidence that prison personnel were even describing prison operations to outsiders has been considered enough grounds for a reprimand, and at some institutions, grounds for dismissal. In addition, correctional personnel, particularly the custodial forces that make up the largest bulk of prison personnel, were supposed to manifest unquestioning loyalty to the warden. What he said, went, and no questions were asked. In return, an inmate's word was never accepted over the word of an officer. The staff suffered long and grueling hours at boring and frustrating work. But many correctional personnel with poor training and little education recognized the pay as equal or better than what might be available elsewhere, and they saw security in state retirement plans.

This kind of interlocking, mutually supporting social structure has been difficult to change. The behavioral patterns and social traditions

[23] National Advisory Commission on Criminal Justice Standards and Goals, *Report on Corrections*, pp. 73–97, 221–246.

[24] Elmer K. Nelson and Catherine Lovell, *Developing Correctional Administrators*, final research report, Joint Commission on Correctional Manpower and Training (Washington, D.C.: Government Printing Office, 1969), pp. 33–35.

built up over the years are not easy to break down. One of the most difficult stumbling blocks to change in traditional prisons is the interaction between the staff and inmates that is usually recognized as "the inmate culture." Whether or not there is a strictly inmate culture is now a matter of debate. Classic prison studies such as the works of Donald Clemmer and Gresham Sykes make much of the uniqueness of the prison experience and the consequences of that experience for the foundation of norms and values unique to the inmate group.[25] Another body of prison literature has questioned this approach, pointing out that many norms and values found among inmates are also found in the ghettos of our urban centers where people, although not in prison, feel equally oppressed.[26]

Whichever explanation of the inmate culture is accepted, there seems to be a consensus that the inmates as a group act to protect their solidarity against encroachments from the staff and to reject the validity of staff perceptions of them as being morally worthless and/or in need of rehabilitation. There also seems to be a consensus that as the staff and inmates interact as polarized groups, the result of the inmate culture is to entrench further the traditional prison climate of caution and inertia. The inmate culture produces this effect because the inmate feeling against talking to the staff or cooperating with staff plans means that only socially recognized inmate leaders have the status that allows them to maintain contact with the staff. Inmates in leadership roles receive rewards from both the inmates and the staff and develop a vested interest in their position. Given this interest in the status quo, the inmate leaders oppose changes in prison structure and program because these changes threaten current reward systems. Hence, although neither the inmates or staff are happy with prisons the way they are, change threatens long-established social sanctioning patterns and is usually rejected.[27]

In the last two decades, if not earlier, many states have found that the inmate culture and custodial resistance to change are much less evident in smaller, less secure institutions. Although there are many ways of classifying penal institutions, one common method is in terms of the security precautions taken. In this classification scheme, it is common to talk about maximum, medium, and minimum security prisons. Although farming activities may actually take place at all three kinds of facilities,

[25] Donald Clemmer, *The Prison Community* (New York: Holt, Rinehart & Winston, 1958); and Gresham Sykes, *The Society of Captives* (Princeton, N.J.: Princeton University Press, 1971).

[26] John Irwin and Donald Cressey, "Thieves, Convicts and the Inmate Culture," *Social Problems, 10,* No. 2 (Fall 1962), 142–155.

[27] Richard A. Cloward, "Social Control in the Prison," *Theoretical Studies in Social Organization of the Prison* (New York: Social Science Research Council, March 1960), pp. 20–48.

states that have two or three grades of prisons usually emphasize farming at the minimum security institutions. Maximum security institutions usually have the largest population and concentrate on activities that can be accomplished within the confines of the prison. Hence, it is frequent that vocational training and educational programs are more developed at maximum security institutions than at less secure facilities.

In addition to institutions for adults, most correctional departments also have a reformatory to house youthful offenders. Some states have a statutory definition of youthful offender (i.e., someone who commits a crime between the ages of 16 and 18). Other states and the federal system have looser restrictions, using reformatories for adult offenders under 30, or for offenders for whom schooling or vocational education is required, or for offenders of a particular security grade. In general, however, a state reformatory is a maximum security institution for youthful offenders with a heavy emphasis on vocational training.

PAROLE

Parole is the process by which offenders are released from institutional custody prior to the expiration of sentence and are placed under the supervision of a parole staff. Parole officials have the two somewhat conflicting responsibilities of facilitating the offender's reintegration into society and at the same time protecting the community by ensuring that certain parole standards are maintained or that the parolee is returned to the institution if the standards are violated.[28] The size of parole caseloads and the standards of supervision vary widely from state to state, but generally parole caseloads are much smaller than probation caseloads, and parole officers are usually civil service employees of a statewide parole system.

The decision to parole is usually made by a parole board who hears evidence about the parole applicant's past record and prison behavior and decides whether, in light of those, the proposed parole plan offers a satisfactory chance of success. Criteria that parole boards use in deciding to parole vary widely depending on particular local conditions, the makeup of the parole board, relationships with the institutional system, and relationships with the state and local political forces. In many states, written articulation of reasons for denial or granting of parole has not been required, and consequently we lack adequate data about the significance of different variables for the board's decision. A nationwide study of parole board decision processes is now under way, and we will

[28] Glaser, *Effectiveness of a Prison*, pp. 289–315.

shortly have clarification of the factors to which a board is most likely to respond.[29]

Generally, we can expect the nature of the parole decision itself to make the board conservative about release. Basically there are two ways in which a board can make an error in the release decision: it can hold a man who should have been released, and it can release a man who should have been held. The chances of these two errors do not have equal influence on the board since the mistake that retains a parolable man in prison is rarely visible, whereas the mistake of paroling a man who misbehaves is all too visible. Consequently, in terms of risk of error, it pays the board to err on the side of holding men in prison who might succeed on parole. To counterbalance this tendency, however, there is the growing public awakening that institutional treatment is both costly and often unwarranted. There is also the increasing sophistication of parole field supervision that allows for release of poorer risks.

The use of parole varies widely from state to state. New Hampshire and Washington for example, parole almost all felons, whereas Mississippi and some Rocky Mountain states only parole 30 to 40 percent of offenders. In general, the use of parole has increased about 50 percent from 1931 to 1967. The Wickensham Commission reported that parole was the method of release from prison in 43 percent of reported cases, whereas the National Council on Crime and Delinquency survey for the President's Crime Commission found parole used in 62 percent of releases.[30]

Parole supervision varies as widely as the use of parole, but parole is generally administered on a statewide basis in a department of parole, or in some combination, with institutional or probation services. A single, unified authority for all correctional services does not exist even on the federal level, where there is a separate Bureau of Prisons as well as the Federal Probation and Parole Board.

Generally parole supervision, like probation supervision, is based on a casework model with a one-to-one relationship between the parolee and a particular parole officer. Officers are usually assigned cases according to geographical areas, but some states have experimented with matching particular offender types to particular parole-officer styles, or classifying parolees into categories requiring differing amounts of supervision. Even these innovations, however, have generally retained the casework model, so that one officer is responsible for meeting the needs of, and keeping

[29] The parole decision studies were directed by Don Gottsfredson, National Council on Crime and Delinquency Research Center, Davis, California.

[30] President's Commission on Law Enforcement and the Administration of Justice, *Task Force Report,* p. 61.

under surveillance, every individual in his caseload.[31] Parole officers are then usually organized in typical pyramidal fashion, with one parole supervisor over half a dozen or so officers, and a chief supervisor responsible for the entire parole operation.

An alternative organizational plan that is being tried out in a few places is to organize the staff into teams with a varied membership whose skills and competencies are complementary. One example of such a team would be a parole officer with a graduate degree, two parole officer aides–perhaps ex-correctional officers, and two ex-offenders or indigent street workers. The idea behind team organization is to manage the parolee's problems rather than the parolee himself. Much of the fieldwork involved, such as contacting employers and locating a suitable residence, does not require the formal educational training for which the parole officer is paid. Thus officer aides can be utilized for the very important and demanding community contacts, while the officer can maintain a supervisory role or concentrate on serious clinical problems. The employment of ex-offenders is increasing as correctional professionals discover that selected ex-offenders, with proper aptitude and training, develop quicker rapport with parolees, develop more productive relationships in some instances, and are less easily "conned" by a parolee who has returned to criminal activity. The advantages of the team are the different resources and skills that team members with varied backgrounds bring to bear on the problems that a parolee encounters in a community. Although the team approach is still very new, it seems to be the trend in departments that decide the basic parole function is to marshall community resources and change community structure so as to provide the optimum chances of reintegration for the greatest number of offenders. Departments that decide the parole function is primarily treatment of the individual offender, particularly on a clinical basis, or departments that decide the parole function is primarily protection of the community from the parolee, will probably retain the casework, one-to-one model.[32]

A major controversy involving supervision policy centers on the quality of the relationship between the parolee and the state. Three basic arguments exist concerning this relationship. First, and perhaps historically oldest, is the idea that parole is a grant of mercy from the governor or his designated officials. Second is the idea that parole is a contractual arrangement in which the parolee gains his freedom in return for a specified performance. Third is the idea that parole is simply a change in the place of custody, but that the state has the same total control over the

[31] Ibid., p. 70.

[32] National Advisory Commission on Criminal Justice Standards and Goals, *Report on Corrections,* pp. 435–436.

offender on parole as when he was institutionalized.[33] Frequently such varied explanations of the parole relationship have been used to justify the lack of a clear and open decision-making process—either at the initial granting of parole, or at the decision to revoke. A recent Supreme Court case, *Morrissey* v. *Brewer*, has ended much of the argument, at least in regard to revocation. Although the Court did not decide on the right to counsel, it clearly required a hearing on the merits of the revocation recommendation, a hearing upon revocation itself, and opportunity for cross-examination and confrontation of witnesses. In other words, it seems clear at this point that parole is constitutionally a state of relative freedom that cannot be infringed upon without due process of law.[34] The National Advisory Commission on Criminal Justice Standards and Goals recommends that the granting of parole be viewed in the same light.[35]

POSTCONVICTION ALTERNATIVES TO INCARCERATION

The majority of felony convictions proceed from reception to prison to parole. Lately, however, there are a growing list of postconviction innovations that substitute for institutional treatment, or at least for part of it. Very similar if not identical programs are also found in the preinstitutional phase of the process, as alternatives to, or as conditions of, probation. People frequently object, however, to mixing inmates returning to the community from prison with offenders who have never been to prison. Hence, a probation staff may manage a "halfway-in" house for offenders who need more supervision than is available on probation and who yet should not be institutionalized; meanwhile, down the street, the correctional department may run a "halfway-out" house for parolees who need group supervision and time to make the transition to parole status. This segregation of offenders often means a duplication of services, but it is doubtful that there will be a sufficient number of such facilities in the near future that the supply will exceed the demand or that the waste from duplication will be substantial.

As was mentioned earlier, many of the alternatives to incarceration first appeared in the juvenile justice system. As such, they will be dis-

---

[33] Model Penal Code, Comment Section 305.21, American Law Institute, Tentative Draft No. 5, 1956.

[34] Morrissey v. Brewer, 408 U.S., 471 (1972).

[35] National Advisory Commission on Criminal Justice Standards and Goals, *Report on Corrections*, pp. 422–424; and Fred Cohen, *The Legal Challenge to Corrections* (Washington, D.C.: Government Printing Office, 1967).

cussed in the next chapter. These innovations are now adapted to the adult system in a growing variety, and the existing programs are the harbinger of the apparently irreversible trend toward community-based corrections.

Community-based corrections is a new concept that will undergo many changes in the future. The most ambiguous points at this time are: (1) the issue of who will control the community-based centers and (2) the concept of community that is implied in much of the literature in this area.[36]

The first point seems to be the most controversial, but it would appear to be the underlying confusion about the conception of community that is causing much of that controversy. Reintegrating offenders into the community is presently the most popular of correctional policies. It is based on the idea that criminal activities are learned as problem-coping mechanisms by persons who have difficulty in achieving their personal goals or maintaining their personal values within the communities in which their crimes are committed. Theoretically, the reintegration policy is founded on Edwin Sutherland's theory of differential association[37] and/or Robert Merton's paradigm of deviant behavior.[38] Briefly, Sutherland's theory is that crime is committed by persons who are socialized into groups where the positive definitions of illegal behavior outweigh the negative definitions. Merton's paradigm is a model for classifying the types of deviant behavior based on a conflict between an equal distribution of socially acceptable goals and a social structure that reduces the opportunities for certain segments of the population to obtain those goals legally. Considering this thoery and paradigm, we might predict that bank robbery is more likely among groups who perceive the legal opportunities for gain as small and for whom the social prohibitions against bank robbery have been neutralized through group processes that approve toughness or violence or other such values as acceptable means of achievement. The theory of reintegration would accept such an explanation and would reject institutionalization as a means of control, because incarceration will reinforce the group perception of criminality as favorable and will reduce still further the probability of legal alternatives.[39]

[36] David Duffee, "Community Structure and Criminal Justice Change," paper presented to the Association of Criminal Justice Researchers—Northeast and Canada, April 1975.

[37] Edwin Sutherland and Donald Cressey, *Criminology*, 8th ed. (Philadelphia: Lippincott, 1970), pp. 75–91.

[38] Robert Merton, "Social Structure and Anomie," *American Sociological Review*, (October 1938), 672–682.

[39] Vincent O'Leary and David Duffee, "Correctional Policy: A Classification of Goals Designed for Change," *Crime and Delinquency*, 17, No. 4 (October 1971), 373–386; and Elliott Studt, *The Reentry of the Offender into the Community* (Washington, D.C.: Government Printing Office, 1967).

Thus community-based corrections reverse the traditional assumptions of change in offenders by postulating that criminal behavior can only be unlearned in the same community context in which it was learned.

Most community-based programs have a two-pronged attack to the reduction of criminality. First, there is the attempt to guide the social interaction of the offender group within the community so that peer pressure will militate against criminal values. Second, there is the attempt by the staff and the offender group as a unit to change the actual opportunities for legal achievement available in the community.

Although the theoretical work for such programs seems fairly valid at this point, most of the correctional literature does a shoddy job of defining the "community" that is to be affected.[40] Some programs seem to take the conservative viewpoint that the community is whatever social entity exists in close proximity to the commission of crimes and that, rather than change it, the program should merely locate opportunities that have previously been ignored by offenders. At the other end of the spectrum are programs that take the radical approach that "community" is a conflux of social functions that should serve the needs of all members of a certain locality. The implication of this concept is that the community as such does not exist except as a goal to strive for, and that the correctional program should take an active part in developing existing structures in order to obtain that goal.[41]

These two views of community are polar opposites. One view implies that correctional change should focus on the offender in order that he may better adapt to the status quo. The other view implies that correctional changes should focus on existing social structures in order to change them in a specified direction. Both of these views are probably more extreme than any particular program director would actually adopt in operation. Hence, between these extremes, there exists a host of compromises that would essentially define community operationally in terms of the social leaders and political groups that the program interacts with in order to get particular services for returning offenders. A few of the programs which are most important and widely used are given below.

Work Release

Work release is an increasingly popular program; it is found in county jail systems as well as at the state and federal levels. Establishing these programs on the higher government levels is more complex than on the

---

[40] For example, in a graduate seminar at the Pennsylvania State University, a survey of the most frequently cited works in police, court, and corrections that purportedly analyzed criminal justice, community interaction failed to define community.

[41] Roland Warren, *Community in America* (New York: Rand McNally, 1963), pp. 9–14.

local level because most state and federal institutions are located in areas distant from job centers. Hence the state and the federal government have established small residential centers in urban areas and transfer work-release inmates to these centers. Another option is to utilize local jail facilities by contracting with the county correctional agencies to supervise work-release inmates.[42]

Halfway Houses

Halfway houses are small residential units located in the areas to which most inmates will be returning. Halfway-house programs usually provide room and board for offenders until they adjust to the new responsibilities of community freedom and until they can locate suitable living arrangements of their own. Halfway houses may also provide jobs for a limited number of inmates who have not been able to obtain employment, or who have been so institutionalized by a long period of incarceration that traditional parole supervision does not seem practicable. In addition to these practical arrangements, halfway houses usually provide, or require of newly-released inmates, participation in group-counseling sessions, in which problems with community adjustments are discussed and peer support is focused on offenders who show tendencies of returning to criminal behavior.[43]

Drug and Alcoholic Centers

Drug and alcoholic centers are very similar to halfway houses but usually include concentrated counseling programs aimed at offenders with past histories of alcoholism or drug use. Because of the nature of these problems, these centers usually provide for more extended residential periods than the average halfway house.[44]

Volunteer Centers

Volunteer centers are becoming more numerous. They are generally not residential facilities, but are meeting places in a given area for ex-offenders and parolees who can come together with business leaders or other

[42] Glaser, *Effectiveness of a Prison*, pp. 285–287.

[43] Oliver J. Keller, Jr., and Benedict S. Alper, *Halfway Houses* (Lexington, Mass.: Lexington Books, 1970); and David Duffee et al., *The Evaluation of State-Delivered Community-Based Correctional Services* (Harrisburg, Pa.: Governor's Justice Commission, June 1975).

[44] Lewis Yablonsky, *Synanon: The Tunnel Back* (New York: Macmillan, 1965); Joseph A. Shelley and Alexander Bassin, "Daytop Lodge: Halfway House for Drug Addicts," *Federal Probation, 28*, No. 4 (December 1964), 46–54; and Nicholas Kittrie, *The Right to be Different* (Baltimore: Penguin, 1973), pp. 278–296.

concerned citizens to discuss the problems of reentry and to receive the additional practical help and concern that such volunteers can often provide. Such centers are often run on a minimum budget with a core staff of professionals who can coordinate volunteer efforts and provide more in-depth counseling when it is required.[45]

Guided Group Interaction

In its original form, guided group interaction (G.G.I.) referred to residential facilities for juveniles established at the Highfields project in New Jersey, and a similar program in Provo, Utah. Guided group interaction is essentially a group-counseling technique that seeks to organize peer pressure and support for legal, rather than criminal, values. Such a technique has seemed transferable to other settings, however, and it is now also used, for example, by parole officers who convene parolees within a district several times a week during the night, or at other times that fit into work schedules.[46]

Reception Center Parole

The reception center parole is a device for releasing offenders back to the community shortly after they have been received by the correctional authority. There may be a residential facility supervised by the correctional department or by the parole staff, or there may simply be a meeting place for offenders living in the community.[47]

MANPOWER DEVELOPMENT AND ORGANIZATIONAL CHANGE

Changes in correctional programs and changes in what people expect from corrections have increased considerably the demands placed on correctional personnel and have made the existing organizational structures even more inadequate. Two separate issues are involved here: manpower development and organizational change. The first issue of manpower development deals with changing the way in which personnel,

[45] Vincent O'Leary, "Some Directions for Citizen Involvement in Corrections," *Annals of the American Academy of Political and Social Science,* 381 (January 1969), 99–108.

[46] Lloyd W. McCorkle, Albert Elias, and F. Lovell Bixby, *The Highfields Story: An Experimental Treatment Project for Youthful Offenders* (New York: Henry Holt, 1958); and Presidential Commission on Law Enforcement and the Administration of Justice, *Task Force Report,* pp. 38–39.

[47] President's Commission on Law Enforcement and the Administration of Justice, *Task Force Report,* pp. 42–43.

services, and physical settings are arranged and coordinated, in order to achieve the goals that have been chosen by the organization—that is, to achieve the second issue of organizational change. In organizations where operating patterns are entrenched as much as they usually are in correctional organizations, the activity of organizational development ordinarily begins with a considerable amount of manpower development. Indeed, many development programs that had structural change as a goal never really got beyond the training of individuals, and thus, our present notions about organizational change in the correctional area are basically conjectures about what has worked in other kinds of organizations.

The qualifications of incoming personnel were so low and the correctional training they received so poor that, in 1967, the Joint Commission on Correctional Manpower and Training was established to study the problem. The Joint Commission had a broad interpretation of their charge and took an innovative approach to the issues involved in manpower and training. The legacy of the commission has been some of the most usable papers and reports in the correctional area—including about the only available survey information concerning public attitudes toward correction and characteristics of correctional personnel. The most important of these reports was one by Elmer K. Nelson and Catherine Lovell, *Developing Correctional Administrators*,[48] probably the first systematic examination of correctional managers. Some of their most significant findings were that correctional administrators are, by and large, long-term correctional careerists, with little or no training as managers. Most of them are "locals" rather than "cosmopolitans," and their perception of the kinds of groups significantly related to correctional management is rather narrow. Managers of correctional institutions, for example, spend most of their energies dealing with internal organizational affairs, although (according to Daniel Katz and Robert Kahn) top management roles in other organizations usually involve more contact with the community than with internal operations.[49] On the other hand, Nelson and Lovell found that most correctional administrators have managerial styles rather similar to those displayed by managers in other kinds of American organizations. Perhaps most significant was the finding that almost all correctional managers across the country are committed to change rather than maintenance of the status quo. Parole and probation managers seemed to be the most conservative.[50]

Central to Nelson and Lovell's research was the question of what kind

---

[48] Nelson and Lovell, *Developing Correctional Administrators*. See footnote 24 above.

[49] Daniel Katz and Robert Kahn, *Social Psychology of Organizations* (New York: Wiley, 1966).

[50] Nelson and Lovell, *Developing Correctional Administrators*, pp. 85–95.

of manager would be needed for correctional organizations of the future. In order to answer this question, they polled managers about their correctional goals—both those that they now have and those that they would like to implement in the future. The administrators were given three options:

1. *Reintegration,* or providing offenders with the skills and opportunities to established noncriminal behavior patterns.
2. *Treatment,* or working with the offender's individual psychological problems or with his difficulties in social interaction.
3. *Restraint,* or the punitive control of the offender in order to protect the community or to punish for an offense.

The correctional managers generally chose reintegration as the most desired goal in the future.[51]

The survey results that Nelson and Lovell present, suggest that there are probably not many correctional managers presently available who could implement the reintegration goal effectively. According to Vincent O'Leary and David Duffee, reintegration would call for a professional manager skilled in coordinating people and in facilitating communication among others. He would have to be flexible, open to having his decision challenged, and desirous of having decisions made in the most democratic manner feasible. He would also have to be oriented toward the correctional environment rather than toward internal operations, and he would depend heavily on the expertise and resources of his subordinates in order to get tasks completed. He would also have to be open to a variety of leadership structures, as the integration goal would probably require that different group members act as leaders for different aspects of the reintegration process.[52]

Nelson and Lovell conclude that this kind of manager will have to be developed rather than found. It is fairly certain he will not spring up automatically from the kind of correctional organization that is presently most common. Therefore, the research on development of correctional administrators also addresses the issue of organizational change.

The typical organizational structure is terribly rigid. Generally, there are three separate hierarchies in a prison. As Donald Cressey puts it, there are in the normal prison three separate organizations for the guarding, serving, and using of inmates.[53] Officially, these hierarchies are known as custodial, treatment, and maintenance divisions. The difficulty

[51] Ibid., pp. 77–79.

[52] Vincent O'Leary and David Duffee, "Managerial Behavior and Correctional Policy," *Public Administration Review,* 31 (November/December 1971), 603–616.

[53] Donald Cressey, "Contradictory Directives in Complex Organizations: The Case of the Prison," *Administrative Science Quarterly,* 4 (June 1959), 1–19.

with this arrangement is that the three separate groups of staff are usually in competition for power and resources, they rarely achieve consensus, and they rarely share a common interest in the inmates. Problems in this kind of structure are difficult to solve, and changes are difficult to bring about. Obviously, if corrections is going to move to the community, and to small residential units, this kind of administrative structure cannot be carried over. New organizational structures and management patterns must be developed that are better able to cope with the changing needs of different individuals and the changing face of the community.[54]

Executive development is a popular enterprise in all kinds of organizations these days. Managers are continually being sent away to "T-groups" (training groups), sensitivity sessions, and management training seminars. The constant danger in this activity is that it rarely seems to achieve its purpose, unless its purpose is simply to entertain the executives. In correctional development, the goal, presumably, would be to achieve more effective results for (or with) inmates. In order to accomplish this, training cannot stop with top-level managers. Generally, inmates are going to be affected the most by the nonprofessional, frontline staff. It is also usually this level of staff that receives the smallest amount and the poorest kind of training. For this reason, some correctional departments have already opened training academies. But training academy curricula often suffer from the same problems that have long plagued police academies. Instruction is often poor, materials and resources are in short supply, and content is often irrelevant to the actual day-to-day operations.[55]

Training in the parole area is generally somewhat better than that in corrections, since it is often a requirement that parole officers have a college education. However, many states have not been able to enforce a requirement for social science degrees, and at this point, many correctional experts are uncertain of the kind of college training that would be most efficacious. On the organizational development side, parole organizations do not seem to be much more flexible than many prisons. Parole organization is, of course, different, but parole agents seem to be as committed to their established operating patterns as institutional staff are to theirs.[56]

Perhaps one major development to expect in regard to both institutional and parole training and organization is the blurring of the boundaries between these two phases of the criminal process. Correctional insti-

---

[54] David Duffee, *Correctional Policy and Prison Organization* (Beverly Hills, Calif.: Sage-Halstead, 1975), pp. 186–204.

[55] David Duffee, "The Correctional Officer Sub-Culture and Organizational Change," *Journal of Research in Crime and Delinquency, 11,* No. 2 (July 1974), 155–172.

[56] Nelson and Lovell, *Developing Correctional Administrators,* p. 80.

tutional staff are developing small community-based centers by which to transfer inmates gradually into the community, while parole staff are gradually developing meeting places and halfway houses to reduce the need for revocation and further institutionalization. In other words, correctional goals are now changing to the extent that the primacy of change in the offender is highlighting the ineffectiveness of fractionalized correctional services. Thus, in the future, we should expect both more unified training programs and more unified organizational structures.

RESEARCH AND INFORMATION

Learning is a change process in which the learner uses stored information about past results in order to pick the most satisfactory alternative of action when confronted with similar situations in the future. A complex learning process should include "learning how to learn" experiences, so that new problem situations, when confronted for the first time, would be analyzed in the manner most likely to produce solutions. And it is a fact that correctional systems have long suffered from both a lack of information and a lack of learning experiences.

Correctional research has long been ignored. Many prison and parole organizations function effectively to suppress information rather than to promote its flow. Donald Cressey has suggested one major reason for the lack of information flow and/or the flow of inaccurate information in prisons has been the traditional punitive reaction by management about information that indicates problems. Cressey suggests that there are two basically different ways in which management can act toward mistakes. On the assumption that mistakes are purposive, the response is punitive. On the assumption that mistakes are unintentional, the response is educative. Most prisons have been run on the assumption that the inmates and staff alike should obey rules to the letter and that any variation from directives was purposive misbehavior. If information had to be passed on from the staff to superiors about problems, someone was likely to suffer. Therefore, the staff would frequently ignore situations that should have been reported, or, if requested to apply information, they might report inaccurately. Under these conditions, management decisions are based on hunches, or upon an independent source (often the managers themselves or their own separate lines to the inmates), or upon tradition.[57] The idea of *research* as a problem-solving activity is rather foreign to this kind of environment, and it does not fair very well when it is introduced.

An exception to this overall set of antiresearch conditions has usually been recognized to exist in the California juvenile and adult correctional

[57] Cressey, "Contradictory Directives in Complex Organizations."

organization. California corrections is perhaps the only one, other than the federal system, to spend regular and significant amounts of money on research. Many of the most innovative experiments in correctional programming have sprung from this research, and California is one of the few states to support systematic evaluations of correctional efforts.

California can be proud of this tradition. Federal funding programs and the increased interest of private foundations in the correctional area are both responsible for the wide distribution of correctional research at the present time. Equally important is the tremendous growth in criminal justice programs at universities. Most of this expansion has occurred after the President's Crime Commission made crime respectable for study and the Safe Streets Act made research in the area financially rewarding. How long and how deeply universities will be interested in corrections is uncertain. If it lasts, the research activity in criminal justice is certain to expand and become more sophisticated.[58]

Research in the correctional area has been so sporadic, disconnected, ill-conceived, and poorly implemented that it is unwise to generalize about its findings.[59] However, there is one observable trend that promises to have significant impact on correctional activity. This is the trend from research about the individual offender, to research about the *system* that is organized to punish offenders. For years, the prisons, the bars, the machinery for punishment, the decisions to parole or to revoke, and whatever else *now* seems important to the understanding of a criminal justice system were apparently invisible to the researchers who were studying criminality. For example, 20 years ago, it was common (and today it is still possible) for researchers to treat offenders in prison as representative of the entire offender population or to see the low affect, suspiciousness, and opportunism of the incarcerated inmate as characteristic of an "offender personality," rather than as a normal and expected reaction to prison life. In other words, even in the best criminological research, there seemed to be particularly tenacious underground assumptions about the nature of offenders as bad or different people; and, as a result, these assumptions obscured the significance of the system interaction with offenders and provided answers to crime problems that were not terribly practicable even if they had some validity.

The traditional complaint of correctional managers about research has been that it was irrelevant. In many ways, the essential correctness of this complaint has been borne out—although perhaps not for reasons that the managers would have anticipated. Much correctional research focused on the individual offender. However, analysis of prison and parole decisions

---

[58] Kenneth Polk, *The University and Corrections, Potential for Collaborative Relationships* (Washington, D.C.: Government Printing Office, January, 1969).

[59] For a general review of criminal justice research, see Chapter Thirteen.

that have been undertaken in the last five years demonstrates that the individual offender has *not* been a top priority item in decisions made about him. The offender is treated in this or that way because of *other* things, external to him, making him an important commodity to the system when treated in that way. In bold language, correctional researchers were interested in offenders when correctional officials were not. Thus, the irrelevance of research![60]

Thus, although research since the President's Crime Commission has not demonstrated anything startlingly different or new, much of it does seem sensitive to the interaction between offenders, treaters, and programs. These three variables (any many more) must be considered simultaneously in order for research to be valid and useful.[61]

THE FUTURE OF CORRECTIONS

According to a recent paper by Leslie Wilkins, the future of criminal justice is not bright. It seems unlikely that the legislative process can make the needed changes soon enough in the scope and use of the criminal sanction that it will appear to be a useful form of social control by the year 2000.[62] (Indeed, Wilkins predicts that the entire legislative process will be breaking down by 1985.) Major reasons for this pessimistic point of view include the whole tendency among criminal justice planners to resist revolutionary changes in the system that are needed to catch up to the rapidity with which new problems are developing.

To some degree, the corrections task force of the National Advisory Commission on Criminal Justice Standards and Goals seemed cognizant of this dim future. The corrections recommendations go far beyond the innovations suggested by the police and court task forces. However, despite the willingness of the National Advisory Commission to take what they called a "hard-hitting" approach to corrections, many of the recommendations continue to be "more-of-the-same" as Wilkins has put it. The Commission, for example, took an advanced stance on the rights of offenders—to the extent that they suggested that matters of internal prison discipline should become an open and visible procedure complete with due-process safeguards. Their reaction went far beyond immediately foreseeable demands from the Supreme Court, which has recently re-

---

[60] See also the discussion in Duffee, *Correctional Policy and Prison Organization.*

[61] The key article on the interaction of those variables is still J. Douglas Grant and Marguerite Grant, "A Group Dynamic Approach to the Treatment of Nonconformists in the Navy," *The Annals of the American Academy of Political and Social Science,* 322 (March 1959), 126–135.

[62] Leslie Wilkins, "Criminal Justice at the Turn of the Century," *The Annals of the American Academy of Political and Social Science,* 408 (July 1973), 13–20.

fused an opportunity to require counsel in parole revocations. But their reaction went in the same direction as the Court, to the ultimate conclusion of the due process trend that started in the 1950s. The "due-process revolution," as some commentators have called it, changes to some extent the balance of power between the state and the individual and probably implies a changing perception of the *worth* of individuals such as offenders who are now gaining the right to challenge official decisions that are made about them. But this kind of thinking is squarely entrenched in outmoded, perhaps dying, tradition of legal change. Unless commissions, correctional officials, academicians, inmates, and other concerned parties can advance fundamentally different ways in which correctional goals can be achieved, the entire enterprise is likely to be given up as a waste of time.[63]

In the short run of the next dozen years or so, we can expect certain changes in the organization of prison and parole and in the way in which correctional tasks are perceived and performed. There are too many of these changes to discuss all of them individually, so instead of that, we will examine briefly three of the most important trends and their relationship to each other. These three are: (1) the decentralization of services and the unification of tasks, (2) a switch in the target of change from people to problems, and (3) the change in the perception of management from one of strict control to one of research and facilitation.[64]

Decentralization and Unification

It is likely that two complementary processes will become visible in correctional organizations in the near future. The first is decentralization of services. One of the original advantages of bringing all offenders in a state together for punishment had to do with the geographic and demographic characteristics of the early United States. The population was not only mobile, and the major eastern cities just emerging, but it was also relatively easy for offenders to disappear simply by going west. Communication networks were poor, governmental structures were still being built, and concerted correctional action would have required some centralization of facilities, services, and personnel. And perhaps most important, correctional programs began with the assumption that isolation of the offender from the vices of society was necessary in order to promote rehabilitation. Communication networks are now quite vast and relatively efficient; centralized governmental structures have come into

[63] David Duffee, "The Use of Organizational Variables in the Periodic Assessment of Correctional System Effectiveness," *Proceedings*, Second International Symposium of Project SEARCH (Sacramento, Calif.: SEARCH Group, Inc., 1974), p. 655.

[64] Duffee, *Correctional Policy and Prison Organization*, pp. 194–198.

being; and our assumptions about rehabilitation have changed. Under these conditions, facilities will become smaller, services can be decentralized and modified to meet the varying specifications of different communities, and personnel (staff) can be managed more efficiently (and perhaps more effectively) since they will be distributed across a broad geographical area and can make certain policy and administrative decisions on the basis of local program development.

Tied to this trend of decentralization will be the trend to unify correctional tasks. The first section of this chapter dealt with the fragmentation of the correctional task. Sentencing, probation, institutional programs, parole, and community programs are now run by different officials with different organizational goals and a host of conflicting vertical loyalties. As services and personnel are decentralized, we will also see an increasing emphasis on unification of the correctional tasks that are required for the change of any particular offender. Professionals will develop attachments and commitments to completing a task or a particular problem rather than commitments to agencies or organizational divisions that are responsible for only parts of tasks. For example, Harold Bradley has suggested that correctional staff should be organized so that one set of treaters could follow one set of offenders throughout the different phases of the criminal process. A team of officials would be assigned to the institutional treatment of a small group of offenders housed in a community-based facility. As the need for institutional custody decreased, this staff would also perform the tasks of community supervision, such as employment counseling, location of residences, and so on. Thus one staff team would guarantee a continuity of effort for the rehabilitation of one set of offenders.[65]

Another way of visualizing this trend is to think about the requirements of changing an individual. Change of any sort implies a learning process. And learning in its earliest stages, requires the opportunity for trial and error, and for testing different alternatives and comparing their consequences. A change process also requires risk. The opportunities for undesirable action will increase along with the opportunities for desirable action. In short, an organization that has a goal, the change in offenders will also need to change itself, and to do so frequently. And correctional organizations that are committed to the achievement of change in offenders will be less committed to any particular organizational structure. Thus the unification of tasks will mean that the correctional organization can change as the offender changes, and as the needs of new groups of offenders change.[66]

---

[65] Harold Bradley, "Community-Based Treatment for Young Adult Offenders," *Crime and Delinquency, 15*, No. 3 (July 1969), 359–370.

[66] Stafford Beer, *Decision and Control* (New York: Wiley, 1966), pp. 345–350.

Related to the emphasis on task commitment will be a reduction in the deference paid to the individual offender as a unique, troublesome, and deviant personality. In place of the concentration on the offender will be an emphasis on the problems of offenders. The offender himself is less likely to be perceived as the object that is to change. Rather than changes in individuals, the correctional system will emphasize changes in the interfaces between individuals and among organizations. One important consequence of this shift will be the tendency to take offenders' values and goals as valid, and to encourage participation of the offender in the formation of change plans.[67]

Feedback from the offenders about the impact of correctional action will be sought, and negative feedback from offenders will not be taken as a sign of insubordination or insurrection, but as a sign that adjustments must be made in the program for that individual.

Concomitant to this kind of change will be a decrease in the importance of organizational status. Personnel will be assigned to solve problems rather than to put in eight hours in some particular organizational division that may not have a direct bearing on offender change or that may be in conflict with other organizational activities.[68]

Management as Research

A third major trend involves a change in the basis of decision making and organizational control. Most prison and parole organizations are presently arranged in a pyramidal, bureaucratic fashion, and managers are reluctant to distribute discretionary power or to accept inputs from subordinates on key decisions about correctional policy.

As correctional organizations became community-based, and as the emphasis on problem solving increases, managers will tend to seek accurate information as the basis for decisions and as the means of evaluation. The manager will be valued less for his knowledge about particular correctional operational procedures and valued more for his ability to gather, analyze, and distribute information that will facilitate program decisions made by other people.

In a sense, this trend is analogous to the concepts implied by the term "corrections" in the first place. If correctional activity of a government is a

[67] Leslie Wilkins, *Social Deviance* (Englewood Cliffs, N.J.: Prentice-Hall, 1965), pp. 71–74.

[68] Donald Cressey, "The Nature and Effectiveness of Correctional Techniques," *Law and Contemporary Problems,* 23 (Autumn 1958), 754–771.

planned reaction to social disruptions and dysfunctions, the correctional manager's ultimate responsibility is to relay, in an operational manner, information to society about its structural faults. The correctional manager is a facilitator of social integration. For years we have understood that job as one of taking out of society its disruptive people. In the future, we will understand it as one of resolving problems in society that produce conflicts among its people.

chapter 8

The Development
of the Juvenile
Justice System

The field of juvenile justice is undergoing change today at a faster pace than ever before in its history. This is exemplified by the dramatic steps taken in Massachusetts, where all institutions for juvenile delinquents were shut down in the early 1970s. The trend to closing institutions, or "deinstitutionalization," continues to flourish—particularly in Pennsylvania under the direction of Jerome Miller, the person responsible for deinstitutionailzation in Massachusetts. Short of closing down institutions, many are calling for the development of alternatives to institutional incarceration and for diversion from "the system." Calls for diversion from the juvenile justice system seem particularly paradoxical since what is essentially being called for is diversion from the original diversion—the juvenile court. Originally, the juvenile court was developed as an alternative to incarceration so that youths would not be exposed to "the enduring stigma . . . of having been committed."[1] Although this rationale for developing a juvenile court as an alternative to incarceration was offered nearly 100 years ago, it is still a current and rational argument against present-day institutionalization.

[1] Homer Folks, "The Care of Delinquent Children," *Proceedings: National Conference of Charities and Correction* (1891), pp. 137–140.

In considering the juvenile justice system, we must go beyond just the juvenile court or just institutions to present the full picture. It may be helpful to briefly discuss the kinds of behaviors or conditions that are likely to bring a juvenile to the attention of the juvenile court. Many people serve as gatekeepers to the system, including juvenile police specialists, schoolteachers, welfare workers, clergymen, parents, and even victims. The people occupying these roles play a commanding role in determining who will, and who will not, be processed by the system. Once the juvenile has come to the attention of the system, probation officers, judges, masters (nonjudges who serve in judicial roles in some courts), and institutional staff are likely to play significant roles in managing the individual through the system. Finally, if the juvenile is contained for a period, sometimes until the age of majority, he will be involved with an authority that has the power to grant or deny parole. Once parole has been granted, the youth may be supervised by an aftercare worker or parole officer. Thus it can be seen that many more facets of the juvenile justice system become involved with a youth who has been selected or screened into the system than just the courts of institutions. An attempt will be made in this chapter to describe not only where the justice system is today, but how it got there as well. By understanding historical trends and developments of the past, we can begin to put into perspective the trends and developments of today. Even though it may seem that we are living in an era of tremendous change and modification in the social order and in the justice systems, a look at the past will help us to better understand the present and future.

In examining the development of the juvenile court, it is necessary to understand the Classical and Positive schools of criminology. Not only did these schools play a central role in the development of the adult and juvenile systems, but our tendency to try to mix them together and to have the best of both worlds leads to ambiguity and confusion in treating offenders. Because one must understand these positions, the first part of this chapter will be devoted to briefly describing them.

From 1066, personal wrongs were considered transgressions against the state and only the state had the right to punish such acts.[2] The forms that punishment took in these early times included banishment, death, torture, mutilation, and fines. However, cultural and economic factors in the sixteenth, seventeenth, and eighteenth centuries led to a new attitude of preserving life, in part to augment the limited labor supply. And in the late eighteenth and early nineteenth centuries, criminals came to be seen as not possessed by evil, but as people who deliberately chose to violate the law because it gave them pleasure or profit. This utilitarian idea of

[2] William J. Chambliss, *Crime and the Legal Process* (New York: McGraw-Hill, 1969).

free will and the ideas of Beccaria formed the basis for the Classical School of criminology. The principles of the Classical School are often viewed in an oppositional manner to those of the Positivist School, which developed in the middle and latter part of the nineteenth century. The Classical School can be represented by the positions of Bentham and Beccaria, and the Positivists by Lombroso, Garofalo, Ferri, and Goring.[3]

THE CLASSICAL SCHOOL AND BECCARIA (1738–1794)

Beccaria wrote his treatise on penology, *Dei Delitti e Delle Pene,* when he was 26 years old.[4] It was published in 1764 and was a devastating attack on the repressive, uncertain, and barbaric system of criminal law. In that system, the treatment accorded a person depended solely on his station in life and power he could exercise with the law. Furthermore, no distinction was made between the accused and the convicted in the treatment they received. The principles of the Classical School as elucidated by Beccaria are as follows:

1. Social Contract Theory holds that the basis for punishment lies in the necessity to restrain men from encroaching upon the freedom of one another. The basis for all social action must be the utilitarian conception of the greatest happiness for the greatest number. The right to punish transgressors is an essential consequence of the nature and scope of the contractual relations of men in society.[5]

2. Punishment for crime is established only by law, and it is the "legislator" who determines penalties and the magistrate who inflicts them exactly as prescribed. The essential end of punishment is deterrence, or to prevent offenders from doing further harm to society and to prevent others from committing crimes. It was the certainty of punishment that rendered it an effective deterrent.

3. Crimes must be considered an injury to society, and the only measure of the seriousness of crimes is the amount of harm done to society. Crimes were classified into three categories based on the varying degrees of injury done to society by their perpetrators.

4. In criminal trials, Beccaria was unilaterally opposed to secret accusations and the use of torture. He maintained that a man should be tried by his peers.

5. It is more important to prevent crimes than to punish them. The prevention of crime was to be accompanied by rewarding virtue and through extending knowledge through education.

[3] Clarence Ray Jeffrey, "The Historical Development of Criminology," in Carl Manheim, ed., *Pioneers in Criminology* (London: Stevens and Sons, Ltd., 1960), pp. 364–394.

[4] E. Monachesi, "Cesare Beccaria," in *Pioneers in Criminology*, pp. 36–324.

[5] See Harry Elmer Barnes and N. K. Teeters, *New Horizons in Criminology* (Englewood Cliffs, N.J.: Prentice-Hall, 1959), pp. 322–324.

6. Imprisonment should be more widely used but improvements should be made in physical conditions, and by separating and classifying prisoners according to age, sex, and degree of criminality.[6]

Extensive reform took place in Austria, Prussia, France, England, and America under the influence of Beccaria's essay. By 1800, a wave of reform had spread over the European continent.

Bentham (1748–1832)

Perhaps the greatest leader in the reform of criminal law in England at this time was Jeremy Bentham.[7] Bentham was involved in the abolition of injustices and of the vindictiveness of punishment. He believed that punishment was solely to deter. Perhaps illustrative of the Classical School's emphasis on the legal ramifications of crime, in the introduction to Bentham's volume, *The Theory of Legislation,* reference is made to crime, offense, and criminality, but none is made to criminals nor offenders.

The elements of Bentham's criminological thinking can be summarized as follows:

1. *Motivation*—All men pursue their ends deliberately, after rational consideration of the divergent elements involved. All behavior is reducible to the pursuit of pleasure and the avoidance of pain. Bentham believed that it was not the individuals but situations that vary, and that without adequate deterrence (pain), anyone would act criminally.

2. *Social Control*—Sanctions (physical, political, moral, and religious) serve to bring the individual's pursuit of his own happiness in line with the best interest of the society as a whole.

3. *Deterrence and Punishment*—(a) The aim of punishment is to prevent others from committing similar offenses and to prevent recidivism. (b) Punishment should not be an act of anger, resentment, or vengeance. (c) The less certain the punishment, the more severe it must be to have the possibility of deterrence. (d) Overtly equal punishments are not equal, because of the variations among offenders.

4. *Prisons*—The use of prison in Bentham's time was novel. In its stead, capital punishment, the pillory, fines, transportation, and assignment to prison hulks were normally employed. Bentham did feel the need, however, for an intermediate stage for releasing the offenders into society.

Reforms that have been attributed to Bentham's influence include: (1) lessened severity of criminal punishment, (2) abolition of transportation that involved shipping offenders to far-off places including America, and

---

[6] Ibid., p. 323.
[7] See Gilbert Geis, "Jeremy Bentham," in *Pioneers in Criminology,"* pp. 51–67.

(3) adoption of a prison philosophy that stressed making an example of an offender and reforming the offender.

The views that Bentham and Beccaria held toward punishment were basically similar. They both saw punishment as a deterrent, felt that punishments should fit the crime and that no one type of punishment was suitable for all crimes. It is important to note that the emphasis of the Classical School is on the legal aspects of crime and that the offender is seldom mentioned as a unit for individual study. With few exceptions, present-day criminal justice practices are based on a study of the individual and reflect an orientation to the Positive rather than the Classical School.

THE POSITIVE SCHOOL

The Positive School seeks to understand an individual's criminality by studying the character and background of the offender. It is essentially a deterministic approach, meaning then if individual X has Y set of traits, there's a high likelihood that he will be a criminal. It is focused on prediction of future criminality based on possession of certain variables, and, in that sense, it is a scientific approach.

Cesare Lombroso (1835–1909)

Lombroso has been called "the father of modern criminology."[8] In contrast to the belief of Beccaria and Bentham, Lombroso said that criminals represent a distinct anthropological type. Lombroso divided the criminal population into the multiple categories of the epileptic criminal, the born criminal, and the insane criminal, but assumed a common epileptoid base.[9] Despite the several variations of criminals elucidated by Lombroso, he theorized that criminals may be identified by multiple physical anomalies that were either atavistic or degenerative.

In terms of punishment and correction, Lombroso emphasized the principles of reformatory treatment of all offenders except born criminals. He maintained that the first object of punishment was to protect society, and the second was to improve the criminal. A fundamental Lombrosian principle was that we ought to study and treat the criminal rather than focus on the crime or its legalistic ramifications. He demanded individualization of treatment, which consisted of applying "special methods of

[8] See Marvin E. Wolfgang, "Cesare Lombroso," in *Pioneers in Criminology,* pp. 168–227.

[9] Richard Knudten, *Crime in a Complex Society* (Homewood, Ill.: Dorsey Press, 1970).

repression and occupation adapted to each individual."[10] He felt that penalties should be indeterminate and that the differential use of an indeterminate sentencing structure would depend on whether one was dealing with a born criminal, an occasional criminal, or a criminal by passion.

Lombroso, then, is responsible for the wide diffusion of the notions of a deterministic approach to crime and individualization of treatment. Although our present criminology does not relate criminality to anthropological differences, its multiple-factor approach to seeking the influence of instituional, social, structural, and personality characteristics is in the Lombrosian tradition. According to Wolfgang, "in penology, his [Lombroso's] emphasis on the importance of understanding personality traits of the offender and of individualization of treatment has long been academically accepted and is increasingly employed in the administration of diagnostic centers, probation, parole, and classification system."[11] We continue to see the influence of Lombroso's ideas in the therapeutic treatment of criminals and, more particularly, with the placement of psychiatrists in the courts to make recommendations to judges regarding sentence disposition.

ESSENTIAL POINTS OF
THE CLASSICAL AND POSITIVE SCHOOLS

The essential elements of these two schools can be summarized as follows:

Classical School	*Positive School*
1. Attempted to protect the accused against the harsh treatment of the state and was interested in reforming the legal system.	1. Attempted to apply scientific methods to the study of crime.
2. Define crime in legal terms.	2. Rejected a legal definition of a crime.
3. Focused on crime as a legal entity.	3. Focused on act as a psychological entity.
4. Emphasized free will.	4. Emphasized determinism.
5. Maintained that punishment had a deterrent effect.	5. Maintained that punishment should be replaced by a scientific treatment of criminals calculated to protect society.

[10] Marvin Wolfgang, "Cesare Lombroso," in *Pioneers in Criminology*, p. 213.
[11] Ibid., p. 223.

The development of the juvenile court can be understood best in a historical context that focuses on perceptions of how to maintain social order and the various methods developed to do so. The several broad ideologies that characterize recent penological history reflect essential definitions of deviance and dependency, and their management. To use a dramatic example of how people differentially define deviance, consider the case of a murderer who is definitely mentally ill. In such a situation, the person accountable for the murder is not held responsible by reason of insanity. The definition of the same act is clearly different in the case of a gangland-style killing or the "legitimate" killing of a soldier in war.

Historically, America has not interpreted the meaning of criminal actions consistently but, rather, has interpreted criminality in different ways. For instance, prior to the 1800s, there were very few institutions per se, and those that existed served a limited, short-term nonrehabilitative function. However, during the late 1700s, attempts were made to revise the penal code in an effort to implement the ideas of Beccaria and others who represented the Classical School of criminology. This effort resulted in the zealous advancement of institutions and institutionalization as reform attempts to deal with deviance and dependency. The use of institutions as mechanisms of social control snowballed during the first half of the nineteenth century; and during the last half of the nineteenth century and into the twentieth, institutions began to adopt the medical (Positivist) model that was concerned with the offender per se and his rehabilitation. Moderate interest was also generated in noninstitutional measures, such as probation and parole, during the middle to late twentieth century. The development of the juvenile court can be seen as a basic manifestation of the Positive thinking of the late nineteenth century and illustrates the certainty and righteousness characteristic of the reformers of the day.

Responses to deviance and dependency can be understood to some degree by determining the imputed source of the social problem that social programs attempt to ameliorate. For instance, although some feel that social problems are the result of imperfect social structures, others feel they are the result of individual pathologies. The difference between an individual pathology interpretation of a problem and a social structural interpretation deserves mention. In cases where middle-class people are confronted with violent, aggressive, and "unexplainable" actions of lower-class youth, those adopting an individual pathology explanation may assert that the youths are sick, nuts, or crazy and are in need of extended psychotherapy to "cure their problem." On the other hand, those adopting a social structural interpretation might interpret the situation entirely differently. They might say, for instance, that the observed behavior resulted from economic and class oppression and that to rectify the problem, the economic and class structure must be altered. In the first case, the solution was seen as residing with altering the individual, and in the second case, the solution involves manipulating the external environment. Clearly, representatives adopting the social structural orientation would offer different solutions to social problems than those offered by representatives of an individual pathology orientation. Thus the evolution in the way that deviance and dependency were dealt with from the eighteenth to the nineteenth century can be seen as representing a shift from the social structural to the individual pathological orientation.

Basically, eighteenth-century thinking on crime and dependency reflected the colonists' ideas of the proper functioning of society. It was felt that poverty and crime did not reflect a defect in community organization, nor were they unexpected or deemed to be a problem that should be addressed through ameliorative action. Therefore there were no reformatory efforts because crime eradication was not an issue. During this period, which was characterized by the notion of an appropriate social hierarchy, it fell upon the shoulders of the rich or to one's neighbors to offer philanthropy to those in need. Although the prevalent notion of localism or local responsibility made it incumbent upon neighbors to render assistance when needed, philanthropy by the affluent agreed well with Protestant ideology, which interpreted the conditions of poverty as necessary and just but to be alleviated by the charity of the church. In this scheme, the wealthy were to serve as the stewards of God in alleviating poverty, while retaining their proper and wealthy position in the social order. In essence, three social institutions were involved to combat temptation and misconduct during this era. They were the family, in which parental authority was stressed in the maintenance of order; the church, through which the relationship between God-fearing behavior and lawful behavior was established; and the network of community relations, through which stability of residence served the social order. David Rothman indicates that: "Under these conditions, non-institutional mechanisms of relief and correction seem logical and appropriate, and social realities did not compel a re-examination or revision of the program."[12]

Although neighbors were expected to serve those among them who were in need, and the affluent were to act as philanthropists, the stranger, rogue, or vagabond was not defined as an appropriate target for their benevolence. Ignoring or even rejecting a stranger served as a measure to insure residential stability and a stable social order. In addition to

[12] David Rothman, *The Discovery of the Asylum: Social Order and Disorder in the New Republic* (Boston: Little, Brown, 1971), p. xix.

stringent laws that made it difficult for strangers to remain in town, the colonists adopted, to a small degree, the workhouse or almshouse of England as a preventive measure. The almshouse took in and provided shelter to those who were unable to care for themselves or who could not be cared for by neighbors. It also took in destitute strangers, but for short periods only. Essentially, stringent laws and the threat of incarceration at hard labor were designed to keep the stranger from entering the community. Thus the almshouse served as a deterrent to strangers; it provided food, lodging, and employment to the town's needy; and it was used, but only as a last resort, to fulfill the needs of the exceptionally burdensome case. Almshouses were organizationally and physically structured around the family-life model, exemplifying the noninstitutional thinking characteristic of the era.

Although poverty and dependency were addressed with a certain air of egalitarianism in the colonial period, responses to criminal acts ranged from telling a stranger to leave town, to capital punishment in case of multiple offenses. In general, the measures used by the colonists fit well into their perception of the self-policing community. If holding the offender up to the public ridicule of his neighbors through the use of whippings, the stocks, or pillory failed to deter criminal acts, the offender could expect execution. At this time, jails were used to hold men caught up in the judicial process, and not as corrective measures.

At the turn of the century, several factors operated to force a critical reapproaisal of the notions concerning the cause of crime, poverty, and dependency. Rapidly growing cities and the attendant problems of urban growth, the advancement of Classical ideas concerning crime and punishment, increased manufacturing, and the expanding horizons involved in nationhood all contributed to the disruption of the complacency of colonial thought. Increasing geographic movement along with social and economic mobility challenged the notion of social hierarchies and localism. As the result of these forces and others, Americans came to believe that traditional methods of social control were obsolete. Faced with such perplexing and frustrating changes occurring in the social order, reformers came to believe that if they could understand the origins of poverty, dependency, and criminality, the social order could be strengthened.

Reveling in their new-found independence, Americans came to believe that the origins and persistence of deviant behavior could be found in the nature of the colonial criminal codes[13]—clearly a Classical notion. With the spirit of freedom stoked by revolutionary rhetoric and ideology, America came to be seen as the ideal place to implement Beccaria's thesis that stated that for punishment to be effective, it had to be unavoidable.

---

[13] Ibid., p. 59.

Classical ideology stated that criminals were not only to be punished, but it also assumed that punishment would lead to eradication of crime. Quite obviously, this was something that was not even seen as problematical during the previous century. By the second decade of the nineteenth century, Classical thinking resulted in changes in the penal codes of most states. As a result of these changes, incarceration was substituted for corporal or capital punishment. In the early years of the nineteenth century, incarceration was seen only as a humane measure, and correcting the offender was not a relevant notion. In substituting a rational system of corrections in which punishment was swift but humane, the cause of deviancy was located in the legal order. If colonial codes encouraged deviant behavior, then changing the laws should end the problem.

The penal codes of many states were revised, based on the location of the source of deviance in the relationship of the deviant to the legal order. By the 1820s, however, it became apparent that such moves failed to have the desired effects. Undaunted in their fervor and still believing that crime could be eradicated, reformers in the 1820s to 1830s turned to the life history of the offender to establish the cause of deviance. In search for the roots of deivant behavior, the most time and effort were devoted to the offender's upbringing. Consequently, the family was identified as the key variable for deviance causation with rampant vice and environmental temptation playing a supporting role. The family was seen as a frail institution cast in a rowdy sea of deviance where taverns and houses of prostitution posed serious threats.

In essence, the fluidity and mobility of the nineteenth century were causing grave concern to a generation weaned on the stability of the stable community. Although Americans of the 1830s looked to environmental and family variables as the causes of deviance, they tended to overemphasize the magnitude of the problem. In essence, they are using an outmoded orientation from a prior century to comprehend current social issues. Thus, the frailty of the family and an almost paranoid perception of environmental influence were moved to center stage as causes of deviance.

As a result of seeing poor family life and a detrimental environment as the causes for deviance, people adopted a firm belief that environmental modification would lead to offender reformation. It is apparent that a change occurred, not only in the perceived origin of deviant behavior, but also that correction or offender reformation was seen as possible and desirable. Since it was felt that strengthening family ties would be insufficient to the great task at hand, the offender was presented with a small, artificial environment in which there would be no chance of external influences while he mended his ways. The environment created to make these changes was the penitentiary. America thus embarked on a continuing institutional "binge" as a solution to the problem of deviant behavior.

In addition to believing that the environment and the family were the sources of criminal behavior, there was a strong belief that if the causes of crime could be determined, a cure would be found. This was true of adult criminality as well as juvenile delinquency. Thus, as soon as the first House of Refuge, a reformatory for juveniles with a variety of problems, opened in New York in 1824, case histories were collected and published. In the eyes of the refuge managers, parental neglect and the rampant vice in the community were the sources of deviant behavior of juveniles.

Thus, in the nineteenth century, Americans reversed their earlier position and proposed with fervor the eradication of deviance. They departed from the notions of localism and ultimately decided that people could be best helped if they could be removed to more controlled environments. The answer of course was to remove the deviant and place him in the penitentiary where the daily routine and the internal and external arrangements were all designed to isolate the offender from the scourges of society. The penitentiaries of the day became the pride of the nation, and few visitors to this country failed to visit them.

Two competing penitentiary systems were to develop in the first quarter of the nineteenth century, leading to a sort of national and international competition in which the number of converts to each system were used in evaluating its desirability. The institutions that were the focus of so much attention were the Auburn State Prison in Auburn, New York, and the Western Penitentiary in Pittsburgh, Pennsylvania. Each system attempted to isolate the offender as much as possible, and although an extraordinary amount of intellectual and emotional energy was absorbed by each, they were basically similar. It was expected that offender isolation from the vices and temptations of the external world and a daily regimen of regular steady work would lead to offender reformation. An almost incredible belief developed in the reformative power of the penitentiary and was reflected in the degree to which people believed that the social order would benefit over the long term. Such incredible faith in reformatory treatment can be illustrated by the comments of Reverend James Finley, Chaplain at the Ohio penitentiary:

Never, no never shall we see the triumph of peace, of right, of Christianity, until the daily habits of mankind shall undergo a thorough revolution. . . . Could we all be put on prison fare, for the space of two or three generations, the world would ultimately be the better for it. . . .

As it is . . . taking this world and the next together . . . the prisoner has the advantage.[14]

THE EMERGENCE OF THE JUVENILE COURT

The emergence of the juvenile court can be accounted for in part by a change from the Classical thinking characteristic of the late eighteenth and early nineteenth century to Positive thinking which took hold in the late nineteenth century and is still the dominant ideology.

The ideas of Lombroso and the tenets of Positivism in general appeared at a time in our history that coincided with a general dissatisfaction with the way that juvenile offenders were being processed. The force of these and similar ideas gave rise to the juvenile court, a reform measure that emerged in Illinois at the end of the nineteenth century that sought to deal with children apart from adults in the correctional process. The reformers who gave impetus to the movement were firmly based in Positivistic doctrine and felt that knowledge of the antecedent causes of behavior permitted planful intervention. Firm in their belief that knowledge of antecedent causes gave them power to change the resultant behavior, the reformers argued for a court based on the rehabilitative ideal—individualized treatment seeking to relieve the offender's shortcomings.[15]

Although the juvenile court was a natural outgrowth of a belief in *positivism*, several earlier events prepared the way for the emergence of juvenile court. These included the initiation of probation services in Boston in 1841, which highlighted some of the special problems of dealing with youth, and the establishment of special institutions for children like the Houses of Refuge in 1825.[16] Houses of Refuge received money from municipalities, state legislatures, and from philanthropic sources. These institutions dealt with juveniles convicted of petty crime, and disobedient and wandering children. They provided philosophical examples for the forthcoming juvenile court because they diligently trained their clientele to cope with the disordered community life, as they sheltered, disciplined, and reformed the child. In a broader sense, a growing humanitarianism also influenced the formation of the court. The reformers were ardent in their desire to separate children from "hardened"

---

[14] J. B. Finley, *Memorials of Prison Life* (Cincinnati, Ohio: 1851), pp. 41–42. Cited in Rothman, *The Discovery of the Asylum*, pp. 84–85.

[15] See Daniel Katkin, "Children in the Justice Process: Reality and Rhetoric," in D. Gottlieb, ed., *Children's Liberation* (Englewood Cliffs, N.J.: Prentice-Hall, 1973).

[16] H. W. Dunham, "The Juvenile Court: Contradictory Orientations in Processing Offenders," *Law and Contemporary Problems, 23* (1958), 512–525.

criminals in the judiciary process but were often frustrated by the fact the judges were hesitant to find a child guilty if it meant incarcerating him with adults.[17] This problem led Julia Lathrop, one of the Chicago women influential in the creation of the juvenile court, to observe that children "were often let off because often justices could neither tolerate sending children to the bridewell [house of correction] nor bear to be themselves guilty of the harsh folly of compelling poverty-stricken parents to pay fines."[18]

All of these problems were exacerbated by the rapid growth of cities during the nineteenth century. In 1800, there were no cities of 100,000 people; but in 1900, there were 37. The growth of cities can be largely attributed to the influx of rural Americans and European immigrants. The culture shock encountered by the children of these immigrants often led them to respond in delinquent ways. And in view of the difficulty with the English language and American values experienced by the parents of these children, the emerging juvenile court came to perform many unforeseen functions, including aiding immigrant family adjustment, providing an education in American values, and protecting the child from demoralizing home situations.[19]

The Legal Basis of the Juvenile Court

The justification for the early intervention in the lives of those who are unable to care for themselves was derived from the *parens patriae* doctrine. This doctrine, based in English common law, held that the king was responsible for the protection of those who were unable to care for themselves. More specifically, the *parens patriae* principle evolved in the case of *Eyre* v. *Shaftsbury* in 1772 and paved the way for the court to act in lieu of parents who were deemed unwilling or unable to perform their proper parental functions.[20]

In the formation of the juvenile court, it was thought that the state would undertake the tutelage of a child in the same way that his parents should have done. Judge Julian Mack, in 1927, summarized the *parens patriae* power of the state this way:

There is a finer and nobler legal conception hidden away in our history that has never been brought forward or invoked for the purpose of

[17] Von Stapleton and Lee Teitlebaum, *In Defense of Youth: A Study of the Role of Counsel in American Juvenile Courts* (New York: Russell Sage, 1973).

[18] Julia Lathrop, "The Background of the Juvenile Court in Illinois," in Jane Addams, ed., *The Child, the Clinic, and the Court* (New York: New Republic, 1927), pp. 290–291.

[19] Dunham, "The Juvenile Court," p. 510.

[20] Ibid., p. 508.

dealing with the youngster that has gone wrong. That is the conception that the State is the higher parent; that it has an obligation, not merely a right but an obligation, toward its children; and that is a specific obligation to step in when the natural parent, either through viciousness or inability, fails so to deal with the child that it no longer goes along the right path that leads to good, sound, adult citizenship.[21]

The Nature of the Court

Zealous reform idealism, coupled with Positivistic thinking and an appropriate justification, contributed to the court's focus on individualized treatment of the child, rather than on penal exactitude, because "juvenile offenders were not to be punished but treated as helpless children in need of care and attention" as well as socialization.[22] Since the emphasis was to be on diagnosis and treatment, the delinquent was seen as in need of compassion and salvation, rather than rights and punishment.

Consonant with Positivistic thinking, delinquency proceedings were to focus, not on whether a specific violation of criminal law had occurred, but rather on whether the child's *condition* is such as to require intervention.[23] Judge Mack, an early incumbent of the Chicago juvenile court, emphasized the rehabilitative nature of the court in saying:

The problem of determination by the judge is not, has this boy or girl committed a specific wrong, but what is he, how has he become what he is, and what had best be done in his interest and in the interest of the state to save him from a downward career.[24]

The task of the court was not to try a child for a crime and to sanction his behavior but to change the child and his condition so that undesirable behavior would not continue. The enthusiastic support of reformers converged with advances made by psychology and psychiatry in the individual treatment of children, giving rise to the notion that every action taken by the juvenile court can be regarded as treatment. The persuasive nature of the treatment ideology is exemplified by Dunham who said:

Whether the juvenile court sends the child to the reformatory or the clinic, places him on probation or in a foster home, dismisses him with a lecture or without a lecture—all is rationalized as treatment, especially

[21] Julian Mack, "The Chancery Procedures in the Juvenile Court," in *The Child, the Clinic, and the Court,* pp. 311–312.

[22] Nicholas N. Kittrie, *The Right to Be Different* (Baltimore: Johns Hopkins, 1971), p. 111.

[23] Stapleton and Teitlebaum, *In Defense of Youth,* p. 8.

[24] Julian Mack, "The Juvenile Court," *Harvard Law Review, 23* (1909), 119–120.

> by those professionals who have a deep need to view the juvenile court as an agency for treatment and never for punishment of the child.[25]

The therapeutic role of institutions and the ways they serve the best interests of the child can also be seen in the following:

> [P]roceedings under this law are in no sense criminal proceedings, nor is the result in any case a conviction or punishment for crime. They are simply statutory proceedings by which the state . . . reaches out its arm in a kindly way and provides for the protection of its children from parental neglect or from vicious influences and surroundings, either by keeping a watch over the child while in its natural home, or where that seems impracticable, by placing it in an institution designed for that purpose.[26]

The Lack of Procedural Safeguards

Because the juvenile court was interested in the child's condition and adopted the parental model—where the court proceedings were supposed to be therapeutic—traditional constitutional safeguards were not incorporated into the juvenile justice system. The juvenile court operated under the assumption that children enjoyed a special status but at the same time lacked the rights and privileges accorded to adults. Thus, participation of an attorney in juvenile proceedings was infrequent at best, in part because the juvenile court appearance was held to be nonadversarial and noncriminal in nature. Also, because the role of an attorney was to challenge the state in an adversarial manner, it was generally felt that a lawyer could play no helpful role in the court. In keeping with its therapeutic orientation, neither jury trials nor the privilege against self-incrimination was accorded to the youth in a delinquency hearing.

Similarly, because of the civil nature of the juvenile court, the rules of evidence were significantly relaxed. In place of "proof beyond reasonable doubt," the notion of the "preponderance of the evidence" was substituted. Ben Lindsey of the Denver juvenile court justified this, saying:

> The whole proceeding is in the interest of the child and not to degrade him or even to punish him. We do not protect the child by discharging him because there is no legal evidence to convict, as would be done in a criminal case when we know that he has committed the offense. This is to do him great injury, for he is simply encouraged in the prevalent opinion among city children . . . that it is all right to lie all they can,

[25] Dunham, "The Juvenile Court," 516–517.

[26] State v. Scholl, 167 Wis. 504, 509, 167, N.W. 830, 831, (1918).

to cheat all they can, to steal all they can, so long as they "do not get caught" or that you have "no proof."[27]

Other rights and privileges accorded to adults were moderated in various ways by juvenile court proceedings. These included the admissibility of hearsay evidence and the use of unsworn testimony.

Thus, in an attempt to keep the relationship between the court and child unencumbered, procedural safeguards were ignored. In spite of the fact that the child was supposed to enjoy a special status, the lack of due process requirements led Justice Fortas to observe

> that the child received the worst of both worlds: that he gets neither the protections afforded to adults nor the solicitous care and regenerative treatment postulated for children. . . .[28]

Critics of the court asked why a youth charged with delinquency was not protected against illegal search and seizure, was not accorded the right to be released on bail pending trial, the right to a timely notice of the charges, the right to counsel, the right to confront and to cross-examine witnesses, the privilege against self-incrimination, and the right to a court transcript and appellate review.[29]

It was the lack of justice, combined with doubts about the extent to which rehabilitation had actually been realized by the juvenile courts, that occasioned the landmark decision of the Supreme Court in *In re Gault*.[30] The decision involved Gerald Gault, who had been adjudicated delinquent by the juvenile court for making obscene phone calls. If the offense had involved an adult, the maximum punishment would have been a fine of $5 to $50, or imprisonment in jail for not more than two months, instead of the commitment to a state industrial school for a maximum of six years (until adulthood) received by Gault. In calling into question the degree to which the juvenile court fulfilled the rehabilitative ideal, the Supreme Court of the United States reflected on the rationale for the juvenile court as follows:

> The early conception of the Juvenile Court proceeding was one in which a fatherly judge touched the heart and conscience of the erring youth by talking over his problems, by parental advice and admonition, and in which, in extreme situations, benevolent and wise institutions of the

---

[27] Ben Lindsey, "The Juvenile Court in Denver," in S. Barrows, ed., *Children's Courts in the United States* (Washington, D.C.: Government Printing Office, 1904), p. 107.

[28] Kent v. United States, 383 U.S. 541, 556 (1966).

[29] Kittrie, *The Right to Be Different,* p. 115.

[30] Katkin, "Children in the Justice Process."

state provided guidance and help "to save him from a downward career."[31]

In regard to *Gault,* the Supreme Court held that juveniles must be accorded "the essentials of due process and fair treatment."[32] Perhaps equally important was the commentary directed at the degree to which juvenile court philosophy had fallen short of its rehabilitative ideal.

Ultimately, however, we confront the reality of that portion of the Juvenile Court process with which we deal in this case. A boy is charged with misconduct. The boy is committed to an institution where he may be restrained of liberty for years. It is of no constitutional consequence . . . that the institution to which he is committed is called an Industrial School.The fact of the matter is that, however euphemistic the title, a "receiving home" or an "industrial school" for juveniles is an institution of confinement in which the child is incarcerated for a greater or lesser time. His world becomes a building with whitewashed walls, regimented routine and institutional hours. . . . Instead of mother and father and sisters and brothers and friends and classmates, his world is peopled by guards, custodians, state employees, and "delinquents" confined with him for anything from waywardness to rape and homicide.[33]

Based on this review of the development of the juvenile court, it can be said that the juvenile justice process is interested in determining the child's condition and giving treatment appropriate to his needs, and, until recently, it did so in the absence of procedural safeguards. Perhaps the most prevalent view that others hold of the juvenile court, and indeed the court holds for itself, is its image as a social service agency designed to meet the needs of the child. Because the court was influenced, and continues to be influenced, by the medical model and developments in psychology, psychiatry, and social work, it is easy to see why juvenile court proponents assert that the interests of the child will be served by these disciplines whether the child is in his own home, a foster home, or an institution.

SUPPORTING AGENCIES AND FUNCTIONS

Although the juvenile court (and its development) is central to understanding the administration of juvenile justice, it is but one element of the juvenile justice system. The handling of a youth who is held to be delin-

---

[31] In re Gault, 387 U.S. 1 (1967), 6.
[32] Ibid.
[33] Ibid.

quent, that is, has committed a crime or is referred to court because of a "status" offense, such as truancy, neither begins nor ends with the court itself. If we think of processing a juvenile through the system as constituting the "deviant career" of the youth, the police clearly serve an important gatekeeping function in determining when and if an individual youngster will embark on his career as a delinquent. Even if the police decide to pick up a youth, the youth will not necessarily end up in juvenile court. The police frequently make judicial decisions on the spot and may refer the youngster to his parents, to a clergyman, or to a social service agency that may be able to help the youngster. The role of the juvenile police officer will be discussed later, but it is important to note that the police are often encouraged to divert youngsters from the juvenile court or to informally dispose of the case.

Even if the police decide to refer a case to juvenile court, it will not automatically result in the youth being "petitioned" into court for an appearance before the juvenile judge. The probation department is frequently empowered to screen cases and to decide which cases they feel must be seen in court and which cases may be resolved by either informal probation or referral to another social agency. If the case is brought before the court, the child has the right to an attorney and other due-process rights resulting from the *Gault* decision. It has been said that the attorney may or may not be an asset in a juvenile hearing. For instance, the rhetoric of the juvenile court is treatment, and the attorney is not a specialist in treatment. Prior to *Gault* it was felt that lawyers had no place in the juvenile court setting, and after *Gault* there is evidence to suggest that this may still be true in some places.

If the child is brought before a judge, the probation department plays a significant role in managing his deviant career. Much of the information provided to a juvenile court judge is compiled by the probation officers, who are employees of the court or essentially subordinates of the judge. If the case is sufficiently severe to warrant an adjudication of delinquent, then the judge has available several response alternatives: (1) he may place the child on probation, (2) he may remand the youth to an institution, (3) he may suspend the sentence and place the youth on probation, or (4) he may refer the child to a private care facility or a public institution. If a child is referred to a public facility, several types of alternatives are available. These include training schools, ranches, forestry camps, farms, and halfway houses. If the youth is institutionalized, he may at some point be paroled from the institution and may receive after-care or parole services. If the child is not deemed to be delinquent, the individual may still be referred to probation supervision as a person or child "in need of supervision." A final adjudicatory alternative available to a judge is to declare a child a "dependent or neglected" child, which is likely to happen in cases where the parents are unable or unwilling to care for the child. A child who is considered to be dependent or neglected may also have committed a crime, in which case he may be adjudicated delinquent.

The Role of the Juvenile Police Specialist

Thus, even though the development of the juvenile court has been emphasized, several other segments of the system must be considered. It was pointed out earlier that the juvenile court developed as a specialized response to the needs of children. Just as the court, in particular, and social services, in general, have specialized in handling juveniles, so have the juvenile police specialists. The first juvenile police specialists were appointed in Detroit in 1877 and were charged with "watching juvenile offenders and enforcing compulsory school laws."[34] Women were appointed to the Women's Bureau in Cleveland in 1922 and attempted preventive work with women and children, while also handling all cases dealt with by the police involving women and children. Other major cities such as Boston, Cleveland, Baltimore, and Louisville followed suit in developing specialized police services for children.

It is difficult to single out the task of many of these early juvenile units, but their job is frequently described in general terms such as "handle," "prevent," "follow-up," and "investigate." Although many agree that the juvenile court was developed as a treatment-oriented rehabilitative social agency, it is interesting to note that the Crime Prevention Bureau established in Boston in 1943 was charged with initiating rehabilitative programs for maladjusted children.[35] Whether juvenile police specialists perform a rehabilitative function or a law-enforcement function, it is obvious that both juvenile officers and other police officers perform a similar role in decision making. The juvenile police specialist and other officers act to select out those that will and those that will not become involved in the official justice system. The general screening process for the criminal justice system was illustrated by a President's Commission report, the *Challenge of Crime in a Free Society* (1967), but the police filtering of juveniles, in particular, has been highlighted by Norval Morris and Gordon Hawkins in their book *An Honest Politician's Guide to Crime Control.*[36] They state that, of every 500 "arrest situations," only 100 youths will be arrested; 40 will be processed through intake; one-half of these 40 will be dealt with by the court; and fewer still will end up in the

[34] Richard Kobetz, *The Police Role and Juvenile Delinquency* (Gaithersberg, Md.: I.A.C.P., 1971), p. 5.

[35] Ibid., p. 162.

[36] Norval Morris and Gordon Hawkins, *An Honest Politician's Guide to Crime Control* (Chicago: University of Chicago Press, 1970).

correctional system. It is clear that the police play a very commanding role in paring down the large number of youths who could become involved in the system.

Several studies have focused on the characteristics that officers use in this decision-making process but have not produced consistent results. Irving Piliavin and Scott Briar[37] find that blacks are more likely to be stopped and interrogated, and Donald Black and Albert Reiss[38] indicated that black youths are more likely to be arrested. However, Jerome Skolnick,[39] Edward Green,[40] and Black and Reiss[41] concur that police decisions do not reflect racially biased responses. In addition to the race variable, police use a youth's demeanor, prior record, and seriousness of the offense in making decisions.

It was mentioned previously that the police are frequently encouraged to divert youngsters from contact with the juvenile court and to utilize community agencies in dealing with troublesome youth. Recent survey research indicates that the frequency of referral may be less than one would expect and that the juvenile officer may be in a tenuous position as regards his fellow officers.[42]

As is true so frequently in the juvenile justice and criminal fields, the ideal established for juvenile police officers may not be wholly carried out. Although juvenile police specialists are supposed to be specialists in dealing with youthful offenders, they are also charged with protecting the public through enforcement of the law. These two charges are likely to lead to conflicts, and it is the treatment and referral functions that are likely to suffer from this conflict. Hopefully, juvenile specialists will focus on preventative and diversionary efforts to minimize the involvement of youths in the official system.

Courtroom Dynamics

Involvement of the police in the deviant career of a youth is an official first step in invoking the juvenile court to respond to delinquent behavior.

[37] Irving Piliavin and Scott Briar, "Police Encounters with Juveniles," *American Journal of Sociology,* 70 (1964), 206–214.

[38] Donald Black and Albert Reiss, "Police Control of Juveniles," *American Sociological Review,* 35 (1970), 63–77.

[39] Jerome H. Skolnick, *Justice Without Trial: Law Enforcement in Democratic Society* (New York: Wiley, 1966).

[40] E. Green, "Race, Social Status, and Criminal Arrest," *American Sociological Review,* 35 (1970), 476–490.

[41] Black and Reiss, "Police Control of Juveniles."

[42] Fred Hussey and John H. Kramer, "An Exploratory Analysis of the Police Role in Diversion and Treatment of Juveniles" (unpublished manuscript, Pennsylvania State University, 1976).

Robert Emerson's study of the entire process of a large metropolitan juvenile court aids us in understanding how the juvenile court responds to delinquency.[43] His book deals with court organization, relationships with enforcement and treatment agencies, and the management of the youth through the system, focusing particularly on the various disposition alternatives available to the judge. Emerson found that the court operates on the basis of minimal working concepts in that assessments of individuals are made based on the dimensions of "trouble" and the necessity of "doing something." Cases in which there is "real" trouble are separated from those where "trouble" is "mild" or "normal," and which require little attention.[44]

Furthermore, the severity of offense, as well as patterns of behavior preceding serious criminal activity, contributed significantly to the development of the notion of trouble. Not only were severity of offense and degree of perceived deviance invoked in the judgment process, but the notions of trouble and moral character were used to justify various court dispositions. "Normal" kids received routine handling, "hard core" or criminal-like delinquents were more likely to receive incarceration, and "disturbed" kids required special care and treatment, usually being referred to the court's psychiatric clinic. Emerson also found that incarceration followed if one was unable to mobilize resources as upper-class children were able to do.[45]

In spite of the rehabilitative ideal held for the juvenile court experience, Emerson found that the courtroom experience is designed to impose a discreditory self-concept and status. Questions are asked in such a way that it is clearly implied that there is "no legitimate reason or justification of the act. . . ."[46] The incident is recast in terms of the individual's responsibility and guilt, which rejects the delinquent's framework and rationale. Emerson's findings are directly opposed, of course, to traditional court philosophy. Although every act, including sentencing to a training school, is held to be rehabilitative, Emerson's discussion of the process invoked when a delinquent is sentenced to a "training school" lends credence to the notion that "training schools" continue only to manage deviance, and not to rehabilitate. Prior to adjudication, the youth is threatened with reform school—as if it were the worst possible fate, occupied by the worst possible people imaginable. If the youth is in fact sentenced there, then he is "cooled out" or told that it's not the end of the world, and that he can make it. The process of "cooling out" the delin-

---

[43] Robert Emerson, *Judging Delinquents* (Chicago: Aldine, 1969).

[44] Ibid., p. 84.

[45] Ibid., p. 98.

[46] Ibid., p. 187.

quent is invoked to facilitate a quiet and cooperative departure from the courtroom, and to insure cooperation before being delivered to the institution. In the process, the youth may receive apparently favorable treatment as he is redeemed from "social death" by assurances that he still shares some human qualities.

> While this reincorporation [of the youth into normal social order] may only be temporary and may collapse before the realities of institutional life, it effectively secures the delinquent's cooperation in the initial process of his own incarceration.[47]

The conclusion to be drawn from the "cooling out" process and of the need for such a procedure, is that training schools do not operate in the spirit of traditional juvenile court philosophy.

Essentially, the Emerson study confirms some of the hypothetical concepts advanced to explain the processing of deviance. From this study, it can be concluded that at least some juvenile courts operate from a prestance of guilt and that the system operates to support that presumption.

To complete the picture of courtroom interaction, we must consider the role that an attorney can play. It will be recalled that the treatment and rehabilitative philosophy of the juvenile court tended to lessen the likelihood of a lawyer playing a significant role in the juvenile justice proceedings. Although we have no evidence that there are courts that are not interested in rehabilitating children or in alleviating their condition, there is evidence to suggest that even before the *Gault* decision, there were differences in the degree to which juvenile court judges permitted or adopted an adversarial stance in their courtroom.

In order to better understand the role of the lawyer in the juvenile court, Stapleton and Teitelbaum conducted an "experiment" in which lawyers were randomly assigned to selected juvenile cases in two cities.[48] A control group in each city was comprised of similar youngsters who were not offered the service of an attorney. The main finding of the study was that represented youngsters fared better in one city than in the other, and the study suggests that differences in the operational procedures of the courts and the attitudes of the judges in the two cities were the primary determinants of case outcome. In the city identified as Zenith, youngsters represented by lawyers were more likely than unrepresented youngsters to win acquittals, or at least to have the case continued without a formal declaration of delinquency ever being entered. In the other city—identified as Gotham—there was not a statistically significant difference between the experimental and control groups; there was, how-

---

[47] Ibid., p. 211.
[48] Stapleton and Teitlebaum, *In Defense of Youth.*

ever, a slight trend indicating that unrepresented youngsters had a better chance of avoiding an adjudication of delinquency.

Although the assistance of a lawyer made a significant difference in Zenith at the adjudicatory stage, it did not make any difference at all in the dispositional stage. Youngsters were 3.7 times more likely to be placed on probation than to be institutionalized, regardless of whether they were represented. In Gotham, however, lawyer assistance at the dispositional stage seems to have been unhelpful. The study showed 85½ percent of the unrepresented youngsters received probation as opposed to 79 percent of the youngsters who were assigned a lawyer. Conversely, 21 percent of the represented youngsters were committed to institutions as opposed to only 14½ percent of the boys in the comparison group.

Their conclusion—that lawyer effectiveness is determined primarily by the dominant judicial attitudes on a particular bench—is well grounded. Most of the judges in Zenith were new to the juvenile court bench and were comfortable with the adversary model common to most branches of law. On the other hand, the judges in Gotham had all served for a long time and were all firmly committed to the *parens patriae* approach that involves the state as "wise parent." These philosophical differences were manifested in the procedures adopted by the courts in those many areas not regulated by *Gault*.

Decision Alternatives in Juvenile Justice

It should be clearly understood that not all juveniles who appear before a juvenile court are offenders of the criminal code or of local ordinances. Consistent with the intentions of those who developed the juvenile court, youths who have inadequate support, education, and other necessities as well as youths without parental guidance may appear in the juvenile court. Furthermore, youngsters who have done nothing other than offend the sensitivities of adults by smoking, drinking, or using vulgar language may also find themselves before the juvenile court. Youths who offend by virtue of the offensiveness, but not criminality, of their acts are frequently referred to as *status offenders*—offenders by virtue of their status as juveniles. As one might assume, these different categories of youths are not treated equally in terms of disposition by the juvenile court.

Although the purpose of this section is to speak briefly about institutions for juveniles and the trend toward deinstitutionalization, mention must be made of the several ways in which various categories of children are dealt with. In an attempt to lessen the stigma, and hence negative labelling of being adjudicated delinquent, New York (1963) developed the additional category of "person in need of supervision" (PINS). According to New York law, there are two categories of juveniles.

(a) "Juvenile delinquent" means a person over 7 and less than 16 years of age who does any act which, if done by an adult, would constitute a crime.

(b) "Persons in need of supervision" means a male less than 16 years of age and a female less than 18 years of age who is a habitual truant or who is incorrigible, ungovernable or habitually disobedient and beyond the lawful control of parent or other lawful authority.[49]

As mentioned above, the purpose of this act (N.Y. Family Ct. Act S 712) was to remove the stigma accruing to those judged to be in need of supervision but not judged to be delinquent. The paradox of creating non-stigmatizing categories for youths is that they, that is persons in need of supervision or neglected/dependent children may still be institutionalized.

In addition to dealing with unlawful or offensive behaviors, the juvenile court handles cases of dependent and neglected children. Neglect cases involve children whose parents have abandoned them or refuse to provide proper care, education, or a fit environment. The cases of dependent children involve the complete absence of a legal guardian or the lack of proper care as a result of physical, mental, or financial inability.

Although the above two classificatory schemes—neglect and dependency—are representative of those used in many states, Pennsylvania's revised juvenile court act only separates children into delinquent and deprived categories. In Pennsylvania, a delinquent act is a violation of local, state, or federal law, *or* "a specific act or acts of habitual disobedience of the reasonable and lawful commands of his parent, guardian, or other custodian committed by a child who is ungovernable."[50] Concomitantly, a delinquent act involves a child whom the court has found to have committed a delinquent act and is in need of supervision or rehabilitation. On the other hand, a deprived child refers to a child who is without proper parental care or control, subsistence, education, or other care necessary for physical, mental, or emotional health morals; or has been placed for adoptions in violation of the law; or has been abandoned by parents or other guardians, or is without a legal custodian; or is habitually and without justification truant from school.[51] In terms of disposition, a deprived child may be placed anywhere the court deems appropriate, including the parental home, except that he or she, unless the child is found to be delinquent, may not be committed to an institution or other facility operated for the benefit of delinquent children. Children who are adjudicated delinquent may be put on probation, com-

---

[49] N.Y. Family Ct. Act S 712 (1963).

[50] Penn. Act 333, S.B. 439.

[51] Ibid., p. 2.

mitted to an institution, to a young development center, or to some other appropriate facility.

Nature of Juvenile Incarceration

It is in keeping with the purpose of this chapter, portraying the historical development of juvenile correction and identifying trends, to consider the nature of incarceration. Training schools and correctional centers for youngsters are the result of faith in the rehabilitative ideal and the feeling that a child, at times, must be removed to a more secure and less tempting environment than that of the street. The belief that a positive change will occur in such an environment may be as prevalent now as it was in the early 1800s, and probably no less naive as well.

Perhaps one of the most potent reasons for not removing a youth to a correctional or treatment center is the self-fulfilling prophecy that was used when applying the "delinquent" label to a youth. As pointed out in our discussion of the role of juvenile police officers, the simple fact that we call a youth a deviant may be enough to elicit further deviant, delinquent, or criminal actions. When we place a youth in a secure training school, our actions go beyond merely labelling him: we begin to treat him as if we had redefined him and now view him as a person outside the norms of society. It should be of no surprise that one whose essence has been redefined acts in ways that are consistent with the new definition of self. Not only is the incarceratory process itself likely to result in a new definition of self, it almost requires a new definition of self if a youth wants to be released from the correctional center or training school. If a training school is to treat a youth's condition or rehabilitate a youth before he can be released, then the youth must present a problem that is treatable. In a sense, the youngster must ask for help. That a youth must assume a receptive stance and be "treated" is clear from the comments of A. E. Elliott who asserts that boys will be paroled from training schools when they have: (1) come to grips with who they are; (2) are able to maintain stable and productive relationships with others; and (3) have shown improved social functioning and have made constructive use of the resources of the training school.[52]

There are many arguments that could be made against the use of training schools for delinquent youth, and even against prison for criminal adults. However, the purpose here is to portray trends more than to present arguments. The trend in juvenile corrections seems to be toward deinstitutionalization and the development of alternative strategies for dealing with youth. The clearest example of deinstitutionalization occurs

---

[52] A. E. Elliott, "Parole Readiness: An Institutional Dilemma," *Federal Probation*, 28, No. 1 (1964), 26–30.

in Massachusetts, where all traditional institutions, except for a few secure facilities for extremely dangerous youth, have been closed. Although all the reasons for taking such a dramatic move are beyond the scope of this chapter, suffice it to say that the change has not been easy.[53] Jerome Miller, the former Commissioner of the Department of Youth Services who closed down the institutions, had no intention of doing so when he took over the system in 1969. His original goals of establishing therapeutic communities within the walls of traditional institutions were scuttled when he found that the staff, programs, and ideas were so entrenched that anything short of fundamental change was nearly impossible. Thus, the traditional training school system has been replaced in Massachusetts with a network of foster homes, group homes, nonresidential programs such as Neighborhood Youth Corps, and other social services delivered on a purchase of services basis. Although other states have moved toward deinstitutionalizing their juvenile justice systems, none has gone as far as Massachusetts.

Juvenile Parole

Discussions of the juvenile justice system often fail to take proper notice of parole release or aftercare.[54] Just as adults frequently do not serve the maximum prison term allowable by law, neither do juveniles always stay institutionalized until the age of majority. A juvenile who is released from an institution before the age of majority may be released to the supervision of a parole officer who frequently serves as both a probation officer for kids who are not sent to an institution and as a parole officer for those who have been institutionalized. In both the juvenile and adult systems of juvenile justice, we as a society, have spent much time and energy focusing on what should happen to people in institutions and have spent far fewer resources on examining the processes by which they should be released back to the community.

It was not until the last quarter of the nineteenth century that America began to focus on the process of releasing the offender to the community in a way that enhanced his chances of making it on his own. The delay in our considerations of the parole problem may have been the result of our firm belief in the institutionalization process, or it may have resulted from several other factors. Whatever the reason, the first "parole" system in America was developed at the Elmira reformatory in 1876, the design of

---

[53] For a rather complete accounting of this change, see L. E. Ohlin, R. B. Coates, and A. B. Miller, "Radical Correctional Reform: A Case Study of the Massachusetts Youth Correctional System," *Harvard Educational Review, 41*, No. 1 (1974), 74–111.

[54] This discussion draws heavily from F. A. Hussey, "The Decision to Parole: A Study of the Parole Decision Process with Juveniles," Doctoral dissertation, Brandeis University, 1975.

which was influenced by the Croften system in Ireland and the Macon-cochie's system at Norfolk Island, an island about 1000 miles northeast of Sydney, Australia, developed in the 1840s. Even after a long time lag between early conceptions of parole systems and implementation in America, the notion of a parole system was slow in "taking hold" in this country. By 1901, only 20 states had parole laws.

Although parole in general has received little systematic study, the paucity of research dealing with juvenile parole is even more apparent. One fairly comprehensive study of juvenile parole, by William Arnold, is largely a descriptive study that reviews relevant parole information and attempts to relate it to empirical data about juveniles on parole[55] Arnold's study was justified on the grounds that the parole phase of juvenile corrections is relatively crucial to the overall corrections process and because the failure rate for juveniles on parole is much higher than that for adults.

The adult and juvenile parole systems overlap significantly in purpose, origin, and even the criticism leveled at each. As with adult parole, one finds both "mechanistic" definitions and "treatment" definitions of the juvenile parole process. For instance, Arnold presents a mechanistic definition of juvenile parole, seeing it as "a mechanism to guide their [the parolees'] activities after their release from a residential treatment center,"[56] whereas the President's Crime Commission indicated that "each juvenile must have a carefully planned, expertly executed, and highly individualized program if he is to return to life outside the institution and play a constructive role there."[57]

After-care, or juvenile parole, has its origins in the practice by the Houses of Refuge (1825) of indenturing children to work for several years in private homes where the daily regimen indicated very little except hard work.[58] It was the responsibility of the receiving family to feed and clothe the indentured youngster, and it was also the family that decided when he had earned his complete freedom. The general stay in the House of Refuge was short, and an attempt was made to release juveniles to the status of indentured servitude where there was some feeling that the host family was not depraved. Apparently, faced with the same present-day problems of placing difficult children, delinquents demonstrating no improvement were often sent on whaling voyages, which "at least would keep them out of the community if not out of

---

[55] W. R. Arnold, *Juveniles in Parole: A Sociological Perspective* (New York: Random House, 1970).

[56] Ibid., p. 4.

[57] President's Commission on Law Enforcement and the Administration of Justice, *Task Force Report: Corrections* (Washington, D.C.: Government Printing Office, 1967), pp. 149–150.

[58] "Juvenile Aftercare," *Crime and Delinquency, 13* (1967), 97–112.

trouble."[59] The status of juvenile parolees as indentured servants was somewhat analogous to the status of prisoners who were sold as indentured servants in the 1700s by shippers who were transporting them to penal colonies. Prisoners who were indentured signed an agreement accepting certain conditions, some of which were similar to present-day conditions of parole.

Some of the concerns of the early days parallel those of today. For instance, in the early and middle nineteenth century, little thought was given to the quality of after-care placement. It has been said that the officials of Houses of Refuge

> devoted a minimum of attention and energy to the problems of release. They did not diligently investigate the households to which they apprenticed inmates or make a sustained effort to facilitate adjustment back into society. They, like their contemporaries, focused almost exclusively on the organization of the institution. . . . Asylum care, and not after-care, monopolized their interest.[60]

In recent times, this same problem regarding the influence of relevant information on parole decision making has been characterized as follows:

> Far too typically, overworked institutional caseworkers must attempt to gather information on a prisoner from brief interviews with him, meager institutional records, and letters to community officials. This information is often fitted into a highly stereotyped format. Frequently the sameness of reporting style and jargon makes it very difficult for board members to understand the individual aspects of a given case and assess them wisely. This can lead to decisions which are arbitrary and unfair as well as undesirable from a correctional standpoint.[61]

Basically, parole for juveniles faces many of the same problems and has many of the same potentials as the adult system. Perhaps the most demanding job of the juvenile parole worker is the effective remobilization of an individual who has withdrawn from his home, family, friends, and familiar institutions and has been placed in an institution that has imposed a whole new social order. The youth who has gone through this system is faced with reintegrating into a society with which he formerly had trouble, and which, upon return, may view him more negatively than before because of his involvement with the juvenile correctional system. In a system that is more in tune with dealing with children on the streets, the youthful parolee (who has been institutionalized) may find himself at a disadvantage.

[59] Rothman, *Discovery of the Asylum,* p. 225.

[60] Ibid.

[61] President's Commission on Law Enforcement and the Administration of Justice, *Task Force Report: Corrections,* p. 63.

MODELS OF CRIMINAL JUSTICE AND THE ANALYSIS OF THE CRIMINAL JUSTICE SYSTEM

part III

INTRODUCTION TO PART III

This part of the book is a rather marked change from our coverage of the criminal justice system to this point, and it represents as well a rather significant departure in coverage and organization from other introductory texts. Most introductory courses in criminal justice follow the flow of the criminal process, describing in detail and analyzing in a rudimentary fashion the police, the courts, and the correctional agencies. We have also recognized the need on the introductory level to place first things first. Hence, there is a detailed description of the criminal process, of the community in which criminal justice operates, and of the specific agencies charged with carrying out particular criminal justice functions. But at this point most texts end, and most courses end too. In contrast, this book is obviously only half complete. Depending on whether the college course in which the book is used is organized on a semester or a quarter basis, depending on the desires of the instructor, and depending on the student's academic status when he enrolls in an introductory course in criminal justice, the following two parts of this book may be treated as a separate course or as the continuation of one in-depth introduction.

Our goal in this part of the book, as the title indicates, is to present a model of the criminal justice system in toto, and to analyze the internal operations of each component of the justice system and the way in which these operations fit together in the criminal process, for the achievement of agency and systemwide goals. Following this, we will return in Part IV to the community context of criminal justice to look systematically at different kinds of evaluation and at the possible future of social control in a rapidly changing society.

Each chapter in this part counterpoints one chapter in Part II. There are, in other words, chapters on the police, the courts, corrections, and the juvenile system. It is possible that some instructors or some students may prefer to read these chapters in relation to the parallel chapters in Part II. However, the reason that we have reserved coverage of the organizational analysis of each component for this section of the book, rather than incorporate each of these chapters into Part II, is that we personally prefer to emphasize the commonalities in the four models we will present here. Moreover, we hope that by thus extracting the use of models from the description of the system in Part II, students who are having a first brush with criminal justice will be less confused and less dependent on our own analytical framework should they prefer another framework. But now that the students do have a fairly detailed picture of the flow of the criminal process and at least a preliminary understanding of the labyrinth of agencies that come together in this process, it is time to attempt some generalizations in order to examine what all police departments have in common, what characteristics are common to all courts, etc., and to analyze how these functions and structures facilitate or militate against the systematic organization of criminal justice in its entirety.

There may be several ways of doing this. For our purposes, organizational theory seemed most beneficial since one of our overall goals is the positing of an organization for justice that may or may not be manifest in the operations of the components of the system. We would like to emphasize, however, that organizational systems analysis is only one method of proceeding, that it has peculiar advantages and concomitant disadvantages. We will seek to suggest alternate models and means of analysis in Part IV.

Our starting point in this section is with the concept of complex organization. Since different police, court, and correctional operations all take place in the context of complex bureaucratic structures, we feel that a full understanding of the criminal process is only possible through an examination of the human agencies organized around this process.

SIMPLE AND COMPLEX ORGANIZATIONS

Let us think for a moment of possible distinguishing characteristics of things simple and things complex. As we look at criminal justice operations we must be very careful of this distinction because a simple solution to a complex problem can be a waste of resources and can lead to a reduction in the public and administrative confidence in the use of criminal justice as a problem-solving strategy.

Many people have been introduced to simple explanations—for example, in the search for single causes of juvenile delinquency. They have sought to reduce delinquency to a simple phenomenon:

If A, then B; or,

If broken homes, then delinquency.

But research has shown that not all juveniles from broken homes are delinquent, and not all juveniles from intact families are law-abiding.

People then sought to control other variables such as education, economic condition, intelligence, race, and what have you. Finally, there was the discovery that no single cause existed, and no single variable was present in all cases. Discovery has been made, rather reluctantly, that it may be a set of factors that produces delinquent behavior. An example is given in Table 4-1.

When configurations of variables produce an effect, or are more likely to produce an effect than other configurations, and where none of the individual factors have such outcomes, then we are dealing with a complex situation.

The same kind of principle distinguishes complex from simple organizations. A simple organization may be two people who go fishing together because they enjoy each other's company or can share the rowing of the boat. Both people know all there is to know about that particular kind of fishing, and if either of them remained behind, the job of catching fish could still be carried out.

Table 4-1   Factors

Juveniles	A	B	C	D	Outcome
1	+	−	+	+	and delinquent
2	+	−	−	+	and not delinquent
3	−	−	−	+	and not delinquent
4	+	+	+	−	and delinquent
5	−	+	+	+	and not delinquent
6	+	+	−	+	and delinquent

Notes: + = factor characteristic of juvenile.
       − = factor not characteristic of juvenile.

The organization becomes complex when one of the fishermen changes into a builder of boats, while the other does the actual fish catching. Now if the fisherman is sick, the builder is stuck with an unused boat, and both men go hungry. And if the builder is sick, the fisherman is stuck with a leaky boat, and both men go hungry.

In other words, a complex organization is one in which there must be a simultaneous functioning of all components in order to accomplish one task, and in which, without all parts working together, the task will be left undone. If we are to consider a complex organization as a system, we are looking for those distinguishable tasks or functions that must all be completed for the organization to achieve its goals. In the short run, we may speak of this simultaneous, cooperative functioning as necessary in order for the organization to be effective (i.e., to achieve its goals more completely). But in the long run, such cooperation is necessary for organizational survival.

The chief categories of organizational behavior are listed below.

1. There are those people in the organization directly acting upon the thing or service produced: suspects are apprehended, categorized, processed, and, in one way or another, released. There are many officials in the criminal justice system directly concerned with the handling of offenders, such as policemen, prosecutors, and correctional officers.

2. Then there seem to be some officials who never come in contact with the thing produced. They spend their time keeping track of staff, or of the organization: new organizational members are trained and socialized. There are many officials concerned with hiring, promoting, setting standards, training, and developing new organizational structures.

3. Then there are other people who seem to spend most of their time dealing with the outside world rather than with staff or product: public opinion is sought and manipulated for support of the organization. There are some officials, usually near the top of their organizations, who are responsible for relating to other agencies of government and the general public.

Social scientists who have specialized in the study of organizational behavior have categorized these three kinds of behaviors, which they say are common to all complex organizations. By using these three major functions it is possible to build a model of organizational systems that will allow us to differentiate types of organizations and analyze effectiveness of goal achievement within types. Therefore, understanding the three major functions, or subsystems, of the organization becomes crucial to understanding the operations of the criminal justice system and assessing its effectiveness.

The three core activities are:

1. The main work of "transformation," "change," or "production" that the organization is responsible for.

2. Work that controls internal affairs, or regulates the activities among members in order to produce stability and predictability in operations.
3. Work that controls external affairs, or regulates the ways in which the production material is gathered, products are disposed of, and the community reacts to the organization as a whole.

For our purposes we will label these three subsystems as follows: (1) *the production subsystem:* concerned with reducing crime, or changing the behavior of people who have committed crimes; (2) *the maintenance subsystem:* concerned with relationships between organizational members and between members and the goals of the organization; (3) *the boundary subsystem:* concerned with the environment and links with other organizations, or with integrating the organization into its environment.

(We could also speak separately about a *managerial subsystem.* However, speaking separately about management might confuse the issue, since there are managers in all three subsystems, as well as managers supervising all three activities together.)

The three components of organization are known as *subsystems* because they all have individual input-output complexes. They are also called *subsystems* because they support each other and would collapse in the absence of one another. It is only in their coordination that we achieve a total system output.

THE PRODUCTION SUBSYSTEM

The production subsystem is usually called the *primary subsystem* because the organization in most cases evolves about the task or problem that is represented in production. In our fishing organization, the shipbuilder, although he may be skilled, has nothing to do unless there is the primary task of fishing to be done. It is because of the production of fishing that maintenance and boundary supports come into existence. Hence, the first production subsystem was simply a series of similar problems such as foodgetting, or shelter finding, handled in a similar way.

In the case of criminal justice, an act is committed and meets with common disapproval. Consensus about the value of the act makes it a social, rather than an individual, problem. The original handling of the problem was probably spontaneous and was probably handled by the person who had been wronged. But gradually the righting of wrongs becomes the task of one man—a chief of some sort. As laws become more complex and formalized, and righting of wrongs becomes a much more complicated matter, the task of hearing disputes is delegated by the community leader to another person, and it becomes that person's sole task. It is when the task can no longer be handled by the leader and an assistant (a judge) takes over, that division of labor and job specialization really begin. It is then that the possibility of complex organization first appears.

There is something of a paradox involved here. The main social leader will function as the judge or dispute adjuster only as long as deviant behavior is so rare that each occurrence is seen as a major disaster. However, as crime becomes more common, reactions to it become routine, and *then* responsibilities for decisions about crime are delegated to an assistant. One reason that crime is handled by secondary bureaucracies in our society is because individual crime is less of a problem for our society than it was for more rigidly structured primitive societies.

Various social tasks, including reactions to crime, became the domains of specialized units as society evolves. As a task is broken down further and further into parts, it will become more and more a standardized operation. Certain people develop a vested interest in a particular way of handling things.

1. The once-new officials gather an interest in remaining officials.
2. Other people in the community forget how to do the job.
3. All similar cases are lumped together and sent to the officials so no one else gets any practice.
4. Skill in handling similar interactions develops in the specialists.
5. Perception of alternative means of handling these problems diminishes.

Hence, a production system emerges as a set of people responsible for doing a particular task well, over and over in return for money, power, prestige, and any number of personal motivations.

Whatever the special, personal motivations of the specialist, some rewards seem to attach to the job itself. As Jerome Skolnick constantly emphasizes about the police, the policeman's major goal as a policeman is to be known as a *good* policeman as judged by his peers. He wants to be known as a craftsman.[1] Thus we can consider the major *value* of the production subsystem to be *proficiency,* or a *decided quality with a given frequency.*

In the three main components of the criminal justice process, where is there the most opportunity to be proficient? A clue to this answer is available in Figure 1, which consists of a flow chart of decisions in the criminal process. The police area is marked only by decisions to investigate and to arrest, and the correctional area is just as simply demarcated. In the prosecution and court area, however, there are many separate decisions, some of which are made by separate officials. The magistrate

---

[1] Jerome Skolnick, *Justice Without Trial* (New York: Wiley, 1966), pp. 196–199.

who rules on probable cause at the initial appearance, for example, is not the judge who will later accept the guilty plea or preside at the trial. This specialization of function is the basis of proficiency in the court area. Proficiency is most possible in the court for a number of reasons:

1. There is greater formalization of requirements for decisions—there is something to be proficient about.
2. The major participants—the judge, defense lawyer, and prosecutor—are all members of one profession.
3. This part of the system was historically first and therefore has had the greatest amount of time to develop.

The important point is that proficiency means a high standard of performance, but the definition of that standard belongs to a particular group. A "job well done" is defined primarily by the people who do that job, the people who work in the courts have higher status than people who work at police and at correctional tasks. Furthermore, the court job may be defined in terms of dealing with a nonhuman entity because lawyers and judges manipulate the law, whereas police and correctional officials have to manipulate the behavior of people. And finally, achievements with the law are easier to measure and keep track of than achievements with people. The law stays put, whereas people move around. In order to be proficient, there must be criteria met, and criteria are much easier to set for judges and lawyers than for policemen and correctional officers.

Exactly what it is that the criminal justice system is producing is a matter of some debate. Everything the system produces is in some way a social response to crime, but there are probably several different responses involved, only some of which are responsibilities of the police, court, and correctional agencies. For example, most "crime prevention" activity is in reality the proper functioning of different community systems. If political, educational, health, and welfare institutions, considered in their broadest terms, were satisfactorily maintaining the quality of life in the community, there would probably be less crime, if crime is an innovative response to social problems. Crime prevention to the people usually means stopping individual events but not changing the community structures that generate those events. Likewise, correctional organizations are responsible for preventing by rehabilitating, but it has only been very recently that correctional organizations have thought that their responsibility might go beyond the control of individual offenders.

Since the criminal justice system is usually activated in response to or in anticipation of individual events and individual perpetrators, its major productivity may be said to center on offenses and offenders. And although it may not always be the case, offenses are usually dealt with only in terms of the particular offenders arrested and processed for those offenses. Therefore, we can usually define production as the activity of the system known as the criminal process. What this process is supposed to accomplish however, is another matter. It would be possible to treat the offender as if the only interest in him were for his past behavior. He would be punished for the act for which he was arrested. One way of labeling this activity is retribution—exacting payment from the criminal for his transgression. A further analysis of this act, however, demonstrates that the real interest is not in the past act of the offender but in the future acts of the victim or of other groups. A state punishes or exacts retribution because either (1) law-abiding citizens would feel unsafe and anxious without such punishment, or (2) potentially law-breaking citizens would feel safe in committing crimes without the visibility of a punitive social response. In either case, the individual offender is processed *as an example*. What happens to the offender, for his own sake, is usually of little consequence.

Although we cannot underestimate the time and energy that go into treating the offender as an example, it is rare these days for society to claim that it is not interested in the offender for his own sake, or at least for a social goal not represented by retributive or deterrent motivations. Society is sophisticated enough to realize that the offender usually returns to the free community sooner or later and, therefore, that the offender's future behavior has made many people concerned about the durability of retributive or deterrent responses to criminal acts. Furthermore, it is true that American society in the second half of this century places much more value in the potential of the individual than many foreign cultures have done or would do. Thus, there seems to be some validity in the social goals of changing an offender's behavior, rather than in punishing past transgressions. Since society seems desirous of viewing the criminal justice system as a place where individual offenders are changed from lawbreakers to responsible citizens, the model of the criminal justice system that we shall use here is built on assumptions about the production subsystem as involving activities that are supposedly geared to changing the behavior of individual offenders in socially desirable directions.

THE MAINTENANCE SUBSYSTEM

A proficient production subsystem must be supported in a number of ways. Production input must remain the same or change in specified and predictable ways; otherwise, changes in output will be unspecified and unpredictable. In the case of criminal justice, it appears that a paramount *maintenance* activity is the regulation of operations so that offenders must plead guilty. The selection process (basically, the rules of arrest and the priorities of crimes to be investigated) is such that only suspects likely to be "convictable" are likely to be arrested. Why? Will a white upper-class matron be usual production material? No, because she is likely to have a lawyer and is likely to complain. And she is also likely to feel very deprived if she is treated like an offender. Such a person is less "role ready" for the offender role than someone who is poor and uneducated and without a lawyer. As John Irwin has pointed out, the usual person processed through the criminal justice system was at the bottom of the social hierarchy before the arrest took place and before investigations of specific crimes were even contemplated.[2] Traditionally, such an offender has perceived himself and has been perceived by others as having less to lose by undergoing the changes in status and the degradations that are a part of the criminal process.

What is wrong with this method of gathering input for the system? Basically, it has less to do with who is guilty or innocent or who in the eyes of society needs control, than it does with the organizational need for a certain type of cooperative offender. When the police, court, and correctional officers are trained and socialized to cooperate with each other in processing this type of offender and in concentrating on the kinds of violent or property crimes perpetrated by such an offender, the results have usually been the maintenance of stability and predictability in the system because the offender is powerless to disrupt the process and the officials are less likely to perceive alternate means of handling the offender and his problems than would be true in cases of offenders committing less visible and more complex middle-class crimes. But the maintenance activity based on processing such offenders does not facilitate changes in the system to accommodate the changing political and social awareness of this group of offenders, or the changing of social awareness about the types of social disorder that are most important to the function of social control. This type of stability or predictability, for example, discourages the investigation of crimes such as consumer fraud, corporate violations of environmental ecology, or organized crime.

As poor people and minority people become more politically active and more socially aware, and as society tends to emphasize the value of the individual rather than certain categories of people, and as people in general become more educated and more aware that "something is wrong with the criminal justice system," then fewer and fewer defendants will be "role ready." It is becoming gradually apparent to lower economic strata of this society that many times they are shuttled into this system because of their relative powerlessness in the socioeconomic order, rather than their relative guilt in the legal order.

This type of selection process is really the reverse of entry into systems

---

[2] John Irwin, *The Felon* (Englewood Cliffs, N.J.: Prentice-Hall, Inc., 1970).

where membership is valued rather than abhorred. For example, less intelligent, rich students occasionally gain entrance into colleges with rigorous academic standards, particularly if their fathers are alumni, when more intelligent but poorer students cannot enter. The production unit of a university system is the student, and the major criteria for selection is intelligence, past scholastic record, and other indices of academic potential. But since the university needs alumni support to maintain itself, these essential production criteria are sometimes over-looked to please a rich alumnus and thereby gain essential maintenance needs.

These mechanisms work in reverse in the criminal justice system. The poor get in on the wrong criteria. The selection differential for system admission is frequently *not* guilt, since there are many rich people who are guilty but unprosecuted, and many white-collar and organizational crimes that are not investigated. Frequently the criteria that make the difference contribute to the ease with which the system has traditionally been able to control the suspect, the defendant, or the convicted offender.

As universities (both public and private) have increasingly become publicly supported institutions, the visibility of the entry decision has increased, and it becomes less and less possible to allow entry under maintenance, rather than productive, criteria. The same is true in the criminal justice system. As the system becomes more visible, it will be much more difficult to retain the same admissions requirements. White-collar crime prosecutions and consumer-related crime prosecutions should increase.

What really are "maintenance," as distinguished from "production," admission requirements? What happens when a system consistently sub-stitutes one for the other? In the university setting, the maintenance perspective emphasizes membership, not of the student, but of his par-ents in the organization. This perspective is *not* interested in how the person admitted might perform as a student.

In the criminal justice setting, how can we tell maintenance from production criteria? The concept of production would be that something can be turned out or *changed*; the concept of maintenance is that some-thing will be a stabilizing influence and will help support the status quo. In the criminal justice case, a stabilizing influence is an offender who co-operates and moves along quietly. He does not invoke all his rights, and he does not insist that officials spend much time with him. *He probably is guilty of something because an innocent man would object and disrupt the process. But he is good material, not because of guilt, but because of his potential cooperation* when compared to an equally guilty, but more powerful, defendant.

There are many people committing crimes or guilty of something who qualify under production admission requirements. But many of these guilty people do not appear to be socializable as offenders and are not so likely: (1) to be investigated; or, if suspected, (2) to be found out; or, if discovered, (3) to be prosecuted; or, if brought to court, (4) to be convicted; or, if convicted, (5) to be incarcerated.

It must be emphasized that maintenance is *not* totally separated from production, but the emphasis becomes cooperation rather than guilt. Guilt, itself, is presupposed. Legally speaking, the offender who waives his right to trial and pleads guilty (as about 90 percent of convicted persons do) does not have to admit the crime charged; rather, his guilty plea legally means that he agrees that the state's case is strong enough that he would probably be found guilty if he went to trial and the state had to prove its case.

In many cases during the course of events prior to acceptance of a guilty plea by the court, a "deal" is made. In this case, the prosecutor and the defendant or his lawyer usually agree to exchange a guilty plea for a reduction of the charge, dropping of some of the charges, and, in some cases, a recommendation by the prosecutor to the judge about the length of the sentence. What is interesting about this common process in regard to maintenance is that the guilt itself plays only a small role in such negotiations. In fact, the important part of the negotiation involves length and type of punishment. *The principal argument involves membership in the organization* (e.g., how long the offender will serve), not the kind of crime the offender committed or the kind of activity the offender will engage in as punishment.

In the plea negotiation, the end product of the "system" is *not* considered. The consideration is time served and not what will be done with that time. In other words, *most of the considerations are nonsystematic* because there is no concern for function or activity but merely concern with static relationships. A systematic consideration of admission would proceed from the agreement on the goal or end state that is to be ultimately achieved. There would be a policy for system operation that must be followed in order to increase social control or reduce criminal behavior.

Police and court officials frequently seem preoccupied with *efficient* motion in the system and defend such a practice as plea negotiation because it is efficient. However, *a strict definition of efficiency* might entirely destroy the notion of police or court work as efficient. Efficiency is a ratio of output/input. Either or both output and input may vary, but efficiency *does* involve the relationship between intake and final result. If, from a systemic point of view, the efficiency ratio was some form of discharge/arrest, then efficiency is rarely considered in this system because the ratio of criminal behavior changed/criminal behavior intervened is not considered. In other words, the relationship of correctional output to police input is not an issue.

The efficiency that does exist is *agency specific*—that is, specific to arrest and conviction—and completely avoids the correctional end of the system. In most official perspectives and in many research perspectives, the final output of the criminal justice system is seen as the sentencing of the offender to prison. A very different and rarely used perspective would see final output as the release of the offender to the community at the end of sentence. These are two fundamentally opposed views of the criminal justice system. The first we can call the vanquish, or *Battle Model*. In it, the offender is "exiled" as the result of the process. The second we can call the *Integration Model*. In it, the offender is returned to the community as a result of the process.

It is really only with the Integration Model in mind that we can accurately speak of a *system* of criminal justice. It is only in that model where the output has been acted upon or changed, and where the output, in turn, has had an opportunity to act upon the system in terms of people returning to or staying away from additional criminal activity. In the Battle Model, the "system" is really a collection of agencies that very rarely work together and very rarely have to cooperate significantly because the goal is to shunt the offender off to prison where he will not harm anyone else or bother anyone by concerning them with his future criminal activity (except such crimes as he may commit in prison or exile). In the Battle Model, the agencies in the system do not have a mutual responsibility to change the offender. It is only when the goal is to return an offender to the community that the agencies must cooperate extensively and integrate their agency-specific goals.

It is unfair to ask which of these models is most "accurate" because they both are accurate in relation to different things. A judge or a police officer may behave as if the offender is exiled, or as if the system ends at conviction. In a way, even correctional officials operate this way. The planned influence of the correctional organization on police and courts is minimal, whereas courts and district attorneys regulate police activity every day. In other words, the court officials frequently behave as though the sentencing process ended matters and that the goal was to release the offender from court. While correctional agencies presently do very little to influence the behavior of agencies that preceed them in the criminal process, police activity, in contrast, is rather strictly regulated by requirements that the court has set for admission of offenders to the court process. If the Integration Model governed the behavior of officials, then police and court action would be governed by the requirements of achieving satisfactory correctional release.

The entire preconviction understanding of incarceration is jail-bail time. Prisons are conceived as dead-end by nature or as fairy-tale places where the end products of the police-court system receive "treatment" *in an entirely separate system.* Almost all prison troubles are attributed, not to previous procedure in the preconviction system, but to the inherent or presystem characteristics of offenders or to the prison system itself.

If the police and the courts had correctional goals in mind, they would have to behave differently. Many of the indices that the system uses to gauge "production," such as number of guilty pleas or ratio of arrests/ crimes known to police, are productive only in terms of the Battle Model. These indices only measure the speed and frequency with which offenders are withdrawn from society and remain inside the criminal justice system. From the point of view of the Integration Model, many of these indices are maintenance ratios, not production ratios.

THE BOUNDARY SUBSYSTEM

So far we have discussed briefly organizational production and organizational maintenance. There is a great deal more to be said about both, but a more complete picture of the specific activities of the individual areas of the system will have to wait for the following four chapters. Presently a general picture of the system as an organization will have to suffice.

So far we have a production subsystem that does the work that is given priority, and a maintenance subsystem that makes internal organization more predictable. Surrounding the system is the environment: in this case, a highly social and political environment. Part of boundary activity includes procuring input and dispensing output for the organization. In this text we want to emphasize one particular segment in organizational boundary activity: the regulation of information in and out of the system concerning purpose and place of the organization in the community (the criminal justice environment).

The kind of information by which an organization explains itself to the community is usually the function of someone such as a college president, a chairman, or a commissioner. This information is regulated in such a way as to integrate the organization and its surrounding organizations, its clients, its competitors, and so on. The gathering of loyalty, respect, and support on the general level is important. This is generally the level where there is the most rhetoric and where high ideals are most frequently verbalized. It is on this level that profit-making companies explain their role in terms of community service. Talcott Parsons calls this kind of activity the "institutional function," because it is through this function that an organization attempts to present itself as a necessary social institution.[3]

Where is this kind of activity most evident in the criminal justice

---

[3] Talcott Parsons, *The Social System* (New York: Free Press, 1964), pp. 36–45.

system? Where, and at what level, and with what messages does the system do most of its relating to the general public and try to gain the most respect? Although perhaps less now than formerly, most of the public considers the Supreme Court of the United States as the final voice of the system. It is here that we find so much pomp and ceremony, and it is here that the system, regardless of its faults, is presented as a great institution. How much effect do Supreme Court opinions have on the system itself? Not as much as one might first expect. For example, the famous case of *Mapp* v. *Ohio* (1961) gave defendants in state prosecutions protection against unreasonable searches and seizures and implemented the protection by applying an "exclusionary rule."[4] In other words, from *Mapp* onward, it became possible for defense to move that evidence be excluded from the deliberation on guilt because it had been seized illegally. Although the protection is undeniably important, the ruling can be said to control the police only in cases where the police are interested in a conviction as a reward for their investigatory efforts. Although the police do express an interest in having the court convict a person that they bothered to arrest, most of the organizational rewards for being a policeman hinge on the conduct of investigations and arrests. Convictions per se are viewed as the responsibility of the prosecutor. Thus it is usually only in cases where the prosecutor and the police are working very closely together (i.e., vice crimes) that the police feel governed in thier operations by the requirements of conviction. Usually searches occur incident to an arrest, without a warrant, and in the split-second world of street confrontations. In these majority of cases, it is unlikely that constitutional restrictions are a primary constraint on police behavior.

Perhaps the clearest example of the difference between the effect of a Supreme Court ruling on the environment (boundary function) and the effect of the same ruling on the police processing of offenders (producing function) is the case of *Miranda* v. *Arizona* (1966).[5]

It was *Miranda* that provided for the "warnings" of certain constitutional rights prior to police interrogation of an arrested suspect. In brief, the provisions were that the suspect must be informed of (1) his privilege against self-incrimination; (2) his right to counsel prior to questioning; and (3) his right to the appointment of counsel if he cannot afford his own. Surprisingly (to some people), this decision did not do much to change the number of interrogations conducted or the number of confessions obtained. Furthermore, as Albert Reiss pointed out, the number of

[4] Mapp v. Ohio, 367 U.S. 643 (1961).

[5] Miranda v. Arizona, 384 U.S. 436 (1966).

cases in which a confession was necessary to the prosecution of the defendant turned out to be rather minimal.[6]

Although *Miranda* might not have done as much to change actual police operations, or the behavior of the suspect confronted in the station house, it did have a great effect on the general public—on the image of the kind of system that citizens thought we had. As such, it is quite possible that the decision will have much greater secondary effects on the operations of justice than it first had. As the public, in light of its revised conception of the system, begins to respond differently to agents of the system, system operations are indeed going to change. But certainly this circuitous pathway was not the change strategy that motivated the original *Miranda* decision.

The effects of this kind of boundary activity are several. To a certain extent the "institutional message" from the Supreme Court protects the system even as it criticizes certain internal operations. The Supreme Court decisions demonstrate that somewhere "up there" justice is served, or that the system does eventually function properly. Wrongs are righted, and the value of the individual in American society is upheld. If the Supreme Court should not provide this service for the system, then operations would be much more open to outside encroachment and interference. Although the police, for example, might object to certain demands from the Court, it is unlikely that they would be more in favor of changes that were fostered by an entirely different source. If the Supreme Court was not a corrective or critical agent, it is possible that change would be delegated to political parties, legislatures, or executives—with some rather unpredictable results. Because the Supreme Court is an *internal* critic, it can steal much of the thunder from external critics and, hence, keep much of the change process within control of the system itself.

Just as the production subsystem can dysfunction by failing to produce the desired changes in offenders, and the maintenance subsystem can dysfunction by making organization either too loose or too rigid, the boundary subsystem can dysfunction by producing the wrong messages. Although people frequently complain that it is "hard to get a straight answer" from a bureaucracy and that executive explanations of the organizational operation are idealistic, it is *not* true that the organization can issue any messages whatever. If the institutional function is to be effective, then the messages from the system to the public must be believed. Thus the constraints on the content of the message involve the ability of the public to receive information about the system from other sources. If the organization is relatively invisible to outside inspection and investigation,

[6] Albert J. Reiss and Donald J. Black, "Interrogation and the Criminal Process," *The Annals of the American Academy of Political and Social Science, 384* (November 1967), 47–57.

then it is more important to the organization that the message should be believed than that the message should be true. However, if the operations of the system are highly visible, then the message had better be true if it is going to be believed. For example, the public may lose respect for the Supreme Court, and the Court's institutional message may have reduced effectiveness to the extent that ideals upheld in the Court are *visibly* denied downward in the system. As more of the system operation is visible to public scrutiny through such means as increased news coverage, competing and conflicting explanations of what is occurring, and what ought to occur, become available. Certain police officials, for example, have been active in challenging the representativeness of appellate court judges as spokesman for the system as a whole. It is likely that there is nearly as much conflict within the system as there is outside it about what its goals and purposes should be and how effective the system is in the achievement of those ends.

Hence, although a decision such as *Miranda* may have considerable effect on the system, the planned effects in a bureaucratic organization often have unplanned or unintended effects as well. For example, there are many policemen who honestly believe that the Supreme Court is hindering them in their work. Why? On the level of actual behavior, very little has changed. However, the *explanations* of that behavior have changed considerably. The Court decision to a certain extent becomes a scapegoat when an arrest "does not stick." Without the Court decision to blame, a "blown" arrest might be interpreted as sloppy policework (i.e., the policeman's responsibility). Hence the common attitude of the police about the Supreme Court protects the police image of craftsmanship.

Furthermore, much of the Supreme Court style and language *does* show an insensitivity to the actual administration of justice. The Court rarely takes police administrators into confidence and asks for advice before a decision is rendered. In *Miranda*, for example, there are probably a number of ways in which the suspect could have been informed of his Fifth and Sixth Amendment rights. Perhaps two main reasons for having the policeman inform the suspects are: (1) so that the first contact of the suspect with the agents of the system is also the location of the announcement of rights, and (2) so that the police (although they complain about it) maintain as much control as possible over the announcement of rights. In contrast, it would have been possible for the Court to order that the suspect be taken directly to a magistrate without questioning, as is the case in Federal procedure, or directly to a lawyer without questioning. Rather than either of those alternatives, the Court allowed something called *cooptation*.

Cooptation is a process by which an outside party is made a member of an organization or is allowed to assume some of the organizational activity so that the organization gains the cooperation of the outside party. In the case of *Miranda,* the court allowed the police to perform an essentially judicial function: stating the rules and rights and hearing the waiver of the right. Allowing the police to take over this judicial function had the consequence of keeping court officials out of the investigative process and keeping police in control of the suspect. The Court gains some cooperation from the police by this inclusion in return for loss of control over the way that the rights were to be announced or whether the waiver of rights was proper.

CONCLUSION: THE POTENTIAL OF SYSTEM MANAGEMENT

Regardless of how poorly the criminal justice system functions today, it probably would improve if there was a common system management. There is now a production process; there are several maintenance centers (such as civil service commissions, training academies, and arbitration boards); and there is some common boundary activity. But there is no common management. There is no simultaneous coordination of system functions. There is no one present to see that the system as a whole achieves results. There is no one with the authority to manipulate one component to change the behavior in another component.

All this and more a system management would have to do. It would, for example, have to coordinate arrest procedure with parole procedure. It would have to be able to evaluate policemen in terms of their contribution to the overall system goals. It would have to be able to summarize the information collected by all patrolmen for use by any judge who wanted to make assessments about real street behavior. It would have to be able to summarize accurately the actual, rather than the intended, activities of correctional centers so that judges would be better informed about possible sentencing alternatives. It would have to be able to gather all information about the success or failure of parolees to give to parole boards, judges, and police officials. It would have to be able to adjust the overall system in keeping with a changing environment. In short, it would have to make sure that information from the boundaries of the system was accurately relayed to production, and that maintenance eased the pressure of production by keeping processes on an even keel. It would also have to increase the accuracy of information sent out to the general public by making sure that all members of the system get along together and abide by agreed-upon rules. Our present system does none of this.

Rather, we now have a deviation from the Integration Model in which all the agencies are independent, or at least we have a Battle Model in which organizational responsibility ends at conviction, and feedback about final results of processing is nonexistent. Each of the agencies, as one can see in the following chapters, has its own peculiar ways of evaluating staff behavior and of judging whether it is accomplishing its goals. The police have clearance rates, ticket quotas, and quiet beats. The district attorney has a batting average of number convicted. The judge has his own clearance rate of number of people processed. The correctional officer has a quiet block. It appears that the primary work in the agencies—as measured by these devices—is not change in offenders, but maintenance of order, predictability, status quo. If this is so, then it must also be so that most officials are not really doing anything really productive. Except for the changes in the labels we place upon him, the suspect, defendant, inmate, parolee, or ex-offender is basically the same, unaltered human being whose passage through the system may be excruciating, but hardly ever worthwhile to himself or society.

In the organizational process, the maintenance subsystem supports production by increasing predictability, reducing conflict, or integrating relationships within the organization. The reverse is not true. Increasing predictability will not automatically increase production. The general tendency in the criminal justice system is the subordination of the change process to maintaining stable sets of relationships among people. In light of the subordination of change to maintenance, the boundary subsystem must control information rather vigorously. Too much visibility, and it is likely that the system will appear to be accomplishing very little.

On a theoretical level, what are we saying?

1. The integration of tasks necessary for a system product is lacking.
2. What we do have is a series of stages and agencies that have their own goals that may or may not contribute to the overall goal.
3. When the agencies follow evaluative criteria that are based on internal measures only, there is no feedback from the environment about final output.
4. The production process becomes ritualized into a series of order-maintenance steps.

If our real goal is the achievement of change in the offender and the community by the entire system, then dependence by any part of the system on any subgoal is replacing the accomplishment of ends with the maintenance of means. For police, generally, there is a dependence on arrests; for courts, a dependence on guilty pleas; and for corrections, a dependence on order. Any of these achievements—or their subparts—are only small stations along the way, and unless they are constantly and consistently approached in relation to an overall system goal, they are themselves worthless in that none of them can change or motivate people to change.

How can we alter this situation? In general we must locate the gauges of "correct" offender behavior where fluctuation in these gauges will also reflect on the official behavior that contributes to offender behavior. We must learn how to gather and use feedback about official performance that will allow us to correct dysfunctional behavior much closer to the original performance (and thus much closer to the organization of the dysfunctional patterns). We must develop much more clearly stated and unambiguous evaluation criteria, so that when the feedback returns to the performers it clearly relates to the performance in questions. It is not always clear to officials now, nor can it be, that they are not effectively producing. And it is much less clear how present performances can be improved.

Much criticism of the system concentrates on the wrong variables. Frequently we concentrate on the difficult variables of community structure and individual psychology that predate an offender's entrance to the system. Or else we concentrate on the same sort of variables after the offender is released from the system. Although these are important questions, it is rare that someone examines the internal relationships of system components. This study is just beginning to happen when people start developing models of the criminal justice system. It would really begin if there were also strategies of system management by which to implement the models developed.

There are, of course, resilient and valuable constraints on present operations that will militate against certain kinds of changes and against certain implementation patterns. It is, for example, impossible to speak of physically and administratively integrating the police, court, and correctional agencies without also speaking of changing the Constitution of the United States. The police and correctional agencies are arms of the executive branch of government, whereas the courts are parts of the judicial branch of government. In other countries, the judicial and executive functions are frequently performed by the same branch of government. But when and where this merging takes place, the possibility of totalitarian, unrepresentative action also occurs. It may be that the present governmental structure is unwieldy and resistant to necessary changes, but changes that would require the merger of executive and judicial activity would be unconstitutional and would fly in the face of all our experience about the maintenance of democratic institutions. Reorganizing the criminal justice system under a common set of managers, although it would create the possibility of more efficient internal operations, is also likely to place broad policy discretion in the hands of an elite managerial group.

Another constraint occurs in the separation of federal, state, and local government. The police generally function under the authority of local executives. Several of these localities are likely to be served by one county prosecutor's office and a set of county judges. Probation is generally a county service, although there may be a state probation office for felony cases. Misdemeanant correctional services are almost always county organizations, whereas felony institutions and parole services are generally organized on the state level. The division of authority between three or more levels of government then cuts across almost all phases of the criminal process and provides for a vertical fractionalization of authority, superimposed on the horizontal division among the three branches of government.

In recent discussions of governmental reorganization such as the systematization of the criminal process, fewer people seem wary of federal, state, and local mergers than they are of legislative, judicial, and executive mergers. There may be, in other words, *less objection* to pooling the authority that presently resides in local, county, and state government than there is to merging the separate functions of judicial and executive agencies. In several places, for example, there have been quite successful experiments with district police forces. There is the Nassau County police force, on Long Island, that serves the entire county. This very large police force, serving over a million people, appears to be much more efficient and effective than separate police forces for each town in the county would be. Similarly, on several occasions there have been prosecuting task forces set up to combat organized crime throughout an entire state or federal region. Such task forces are considerably more effective in investigating and combating criminal activities that cross several legal jurisdictions than cooperating local prosecutors could be. On the correctional side, the Federal Bureau of Prisons and several state correctional departments have contracted with county correctional organizations for the provision of work-release and halfway house services, so that state and federal prisoners can be returned to their communities, under supervision, prior to parole. Reversing this trend toward decentralization of services, serveral other states have done away with county governments and thus have placed *all* correctional activity on the state level. But in either case, the result has been to increase the continuity in services delivery to offenders by breaking down the traditional separation among agencies operating on different executive levels.

It would be both premature and naive, however, to suggest that this flattening of the vertical hierarchy of government can be accomplished on a regional basis. Different levels of governments have always guarded their separate authority jealously, and there are many more instances where the drive toward centralization of authority and unification of services has been defeated than there are instances where it has been successful.

In summary, any model for unification of the criminal justice system must cope not only with the constraints on merger of different governmental functions but also with the constraints on flattening the vertical hierarchy within any one branch of government. Whether such a model is possible is a difficult question, and the implementation of such a model is even more difficult. But both questions should be put off now until we have examined in some detail how the separate organizations of the criminal justice system now operate.

We will try to do this by building four different organizational models: one for the police, one for courts and probation, one for corrections (basically prisons and parole), and one for the juvenile system. We will then analyze the behavior of each component of the criminal justice system in terms of these separate models. Each model has in common a reliance on the theory of organizations as open systems. In other words, each will incorporate the subsystems that we have discussed here in relation to the criminal justice system in its entirety. It must be made clear than even going this far (building an analytical model for police, courts, corrections, the juvenile system—and applying it) involves a considerable abstraction from reality. There is, for example, no one police organization or no one court organization that conforms to all the features of the relevant model.

It is not the purpose of these models to take a photograph of any particular reality. Doing so is a highly inefficient and ineffective exercise for our purposes. *If* we did so, it would involve describing each actual operating agency in considerable detail. Doing so, we would be no further down the road than when we began if our goal is to provide generalizations about the functioning of each type of agency and how each is related to all the others. We elect, then, to build an organizational theory of each component of the justice system. Having done so, we will then have four stepping-stones toward a theory of criminal justice in toto. These models and the use of them become helpful in establishing guidelines for policy and change on a broader level, and for speaking of planning and implementing the integration of services the goals of which are the production of change in the system, in offenders, and in the community.

After the thorough discussion of each component in terms of the four models, we will turn in Part IV to the use of this type of analysis in evaluating the system as it stands and to broader questions of community change—that is, the future of social control in a changing society, and the changes in research and action that the environmental considerations might require.

chapter 9

The Police
as an Organization:
Problems of
Doing What for Whom

Chapter Three provided an overview of the complexity of the organization of policing. Not only are there federal, state, and local police, but within each level of government there are a variety of agencies with law-enforcement power. Some of these agencies, especially at the federal level, are highly specialized in their area of enforcement, whereas others, such as municipal police agencies, have extremely broad responsibilities.

It is not the intent of this analysis to describe organizationally all the various police agencies. Rather we will focus on the municipal police agency because it is the most common agency, has the broadest responsibilities, and most important, is the type of police agency about which we have the most information. Even narrowing the focus of this chapter as much as this, the applicability of the analysis in this chapter may vary, being true of many but not all municipal police agencies.

THE POLICE AND THE CRIMINAL
JUSTICE SYSTEM

There is no such thing as criminal justice administration in the country. Different agencies and different aspects of criminal justice are administered, and there is a system of criminal justice to the extent that different elements influence each other. However, there is not even an established, informal protocol by which conflicting interagency efforts can be controlled or by which necessary interagency cooperation can be maximized.[1] As we stated in the introduction to this section, the absence of centralized management and policy making, in and of itself, is neither good nor bad.

The evaluation of this situation as dysfunctional is heavily dependent on the frame of reference of the analysts. Relying on anything from idiosyncratic hunch to systematic pollings of officials and public, the analyst must decide upon both the functions of criminal law administration and the boundaries of the system he is analyzing, before he can make an evaluation of what structures and processes are beneficial or harmful to the purposes he posits.

In approaching the analysis of the police, there are at least two pitfalls to be avoided. First of all, an analyst who overemphasizes the importance of "latent functions" might argue that any observed structure has evolved into its present state because this structure performs important functions for society. Making this mistake, the analyst could go on to argue quite cogently that the absence of unified justice administration is *functional*. He might say, for example, that existing conflicts between courts and police provide an appropriate check and balance between executive and judicial structures, or that the absence of centralized policy making and resource distribution decisions prevents the criminal justice system from becoming intolerably efficient. Such arguments violate basic scientific principles because they ignore the search for alternative hypotheses and alternative structures.

Another pitfall, and one made more frequently lately, is that the system of *present* analytical focus is the predominant or most naturally important system. Thus, the tradition beginning with the President's Commission on Law Enforcement and the Administration of Justice (1967) has had the effect of inexorably linking police, courts, and corrections as the interagency linkages that *should be* the predominant concern in studying the activity of any one agency. It is obvious that all the agencies who mobilize the criminal process are indeed intertwined with each other. There is little empirical evidence, however, that would support the argument that invoking the criminal process is the overriding concern of the police, or that police interactions with prosecutor and judge outweigh in frequency or significance police interactions with the mayor, the department of education, or the chief financial officer of the municipality. In brief, system identification is always somewhat arbitrary.

[1] Albert J. Reiss, Jr., and Donald Black, "Interrogation and the Criminal Process," *American Academy of Political and Social Science, 374* (1967), 49.

It should always be stated that "for the purposes of X, the relevant system components are . . ." And it should be recognized that those purposes and those components may become insignificant or even change when the particular identified system is then related to larger systems.

In the introduction to Part III, we made an attempt to suggest in skeletal fashion how the analysis of the criminal justice agencies as a system might proceed. In this chapter, we will change our focus, concentrating on the police as a system. Again we will utilize the concepts of boundary, maintenance, and production, but the elements that comprise these subsystems are different for the police system than for the criminal justice system.

THE POLICE AND THE ENVIRONMENT:
A CENTRAL THEME

Several analysts of organizations have suggested that one can identify similar subsystems or activity patterns in all organizations but that certain internal activity patterns tend to predominate, depending on the organization's goals and its relation to its environment.[2] Manufacturing firms, for example, are structured to turn out physical items. Therefore their internal patterns of maintenance and their boundary exchange mechanisms are less emphasized and less carefully designed. In contrast, civil service organizations, whose primary goals seem to concern the regulation of mainenance subsystems in other units of government, are themselves highly structured, maintenance-predominated entities.

The police organization seems to have its own predominating subsystem—that of interaction with varied and often hostile outside units.

Unlike many organizations . . . the police have as their fundamental task the creation and maintenance of, and their participation in, external relationships. Indeed, the central meaning of police authority itself is its significance as a mechanism for "managing" relationships.[3]

Police are not organized to stay home. Even the traditionally dilapidated and unadorned precinct stations suggest more than underfunding; they suggest that most police work is not done from a central location and, given a set amount of resources, an ugly uncomfortable squad room is a lesser deficiency than a patrol car in improper condition.

---

[2] See for example, Amatai Etzioni, *Complex Organizations: A Comparative Analysis* (New York: The Free Press, 1961); and Daniel Katz and Robert Kahn, *The Social Psychology of Organizations* (New York: Wiley, 1966).

[3] Albert J. Reiss, Jr., and David Bordua, "Environment and Organization: A Perspective on the Police," in D. Bordua, ed., *The Police: Six Sociological Essays* (New York: Wiley, 1967), pp. 25–26.

In the following chapters on courts and corrections, we will be emphasizing various production subsystems, and suggesting how maintenance or boundary activities impede or facilitate proficiency in getting specified work done. In this chapter, we will stress the structure of the boundary subsystem, and how production or maintenance activities retard or improve boundary exchanges. We are positing, in other words, that the police are basically a boundary-maintaining organization. And we mean this in several ways. Jonathan Rubenstein, for example, suggests that the police are predominantly concerned with the control or distribution of people and events.[4] For instance, one determinant of how a policeman will respond to even overt law violations is the location of the violation. He is concerned with public rather than private territory, and even more concerned with *his* sector rather than with the adjoining sector. For example, an officer is concerned with where juveniles hang out rather than with whether they hang out at all; he is concerned with the lone black man simply strolling in an all-white neighborhood but may ignore the taunts or suspicious behavior of the same individual if he is seen the next day on a ghetto street. The police, in other words, are extremely preoccupied with observing and maintaining the normative boundaries of community groups and the boundaries of one police group against another.

The boundary-maintenance function of the police explains to a great degree their interpretation of the law, their perception of the community, and their interactions with each other. As the derivation of the term *police* implies, we should expect that many police functions are related to implementation of public policy, to the allocation of events to areas designated as appropriate for those events, and to the distribution of resources in ways and to groups designated as appropriate for the receipt of resources.[5]

The Locality-Relevant Functions of the Police

In Chapter Two we discussed five locality-relevant functions, the performance of which is necessary to the survival of community. In Chapter Three we examined the evolution of the American police, linking the police to the welfare of the state on the one hand and to the Anglo-Saxon concept of community on the other. This double tie is itself significant to the boundary functions of the police. To what extent, for example, can

---

[4] Jonathan Rubenstein, *City Police* (New York: Ballantine Books, 1974).

[5] See Cyril D. Robinson, "The Mayor and the Police," for the argument that the police evolved as a means of keeping the rich and powerful buffered from the poor and aggrieved. In George L. Mosse, ed., *Police Forces in History* (London: Sage, 1975), pp. 277–315.

the police ignore questionable orders from their superiors, such as the late Mayor Daley's order to shoot looters (Chicago, 1967), and rely instead on the directives of the law? Or to what extent can the police ignore the full enforcement of the law, and rely in so doing upon the local normative order of a neighborhood as a basis of deciding what events or activities should be stopped?

In a very small and homogeneous state, where there may be little conflict between what people actually do and what their legislators pronounce as desirable, there may be very little conflict between policing for a community and policing for the state. In complex, heterogeneous situations, however, the police frequently perform a boundary-mediating role, adjusting the prescriptions of the law to the normative patterns of the community.

Jerome Skolnick and Richard Woodworth highlight this mediator role in the case of processing statutory rape—a case where the factual situation of perpetrator-victim status is often fuzzy but where the law provides for no mitigating circumstances in reducing the culpability of the offender.[6] They found that the Westville police assigned to the morals detail universally detested the assignment and actively avoided the initiation of cases, contrary to their behavior in gambling and prostitution cases. Skolnick and Woodworth suggest that the police were assigned an impossible task in this instance—mediating between individuals behaving in relatively normative fashion but in flat violation of legal proscriptions.

Generalizing from such specific instances of conflict, a political science analysis concludes that the police have a very limited hand in reducing clear cases of conflict between community norms and state demands. In these cases of political conflict, solutions require much broader solutions than are available to the police. Either economic-political-social adjustments must be made to accommodate the differences of the group whose norms are out of phase with the law, or the political establishment must escalate the objection to the behavior and repress the group entirely. The normal containment strategies at the disposal of the police for handling marginal or individual deviance will not work as a means of integrating the behavior of deviant groups to externally imposed rules.[7] In American society, the frequency of conflict between the state and various communities should mean that the police occupy a position to which adheres varying degrees of inherent violence. Crime-repressive strategies will inevitably ally the police with groups who control the state, whereas

[6] Jerome H. Skolnick and Richard Woodworth, "Bureaucracy, Information and Social Control: A Study of a Morals Detail," in *The Police: Six Sociological Essays*, pp. 132–133.

[7] H. L. Nieburg, "Violence, Law, and the Informal Polity," *The Journal of Conflict Resolution, 13,* No. 2(June 1969), 192–193.

crime-preventive strategies may place the police in direct disobedience to the law.[8]

Police Ties to the State

According to many commentators, the relationship of the police to the state and the law is far less predictive of their behavior than is their relationship to the local community. Judge Breitel flatly states that whatever the law, the community and its members decide on the policy of enforcement.[9] Michael Banton echoes this sentiment:

> To explain what the policeman actually does it is necessary to see his action as being governed much more by popular morality than by the letter of the law.[10]

These statements, however, are dangerous oversimplifications of fact, and at the same time provide little guidance for police policy makers to deal with the conflict. We made it clear in Chapter Two that statements such as "popular morality" are inaccurate for the variety of community structures and normative combinations that exist. The degree of match between popular morality and the law itself varies in at least two ways. For example, it has been suggested that the British police have become a successful institution in a relatively short time because most citizens are as committed to observance of the law as are the police. Under these circumstances, suggests Charles Reith, the British police have performed an important social reform function by fully enforcing all laws and giving Parliament the responsibility of changing laws whose full enforcement proves detrimental to the public or unpopular with the public. Of added significance is the fact that the English people, according to Reith, have expected this behavior of the police, and they do not protest against the impartial, ministerial police but against the Parliamentary design.[11]

Joseph Goldstein suggests that the American situation is quite different. Goldstein distinguishes *total enforcement, full enforcement,* and *actual enforcement.* Within existing present resource allocations, due process restrictions, and crime investigation technology, Goldstein suggests that total enforcement is impossible. However, full enforcement of the law, within those areas where enforcement is feasible, is a clear

[8] Michael Banton, "Authority and Police Science," *The Police Journal, 43,* No. 8 (August 1970), 368–369.

[9] Charles Breitel, "Controls on Criminal Law Enforcement," *University of Chicago Law Review, 27* (1960), 432.

[10] Michael Banton, *The Policeman in the Community* (New York: Basic Books, 1964), p. 146.

[11] Charles Reith, *The Blind Eye of History: A Study of the Origins of the Present Police Era* (Montclair, N.J.: Patterson Smith, 1974).

legislated mandate. The police have not been granted the discretion to ignore, on an individual or a policy basis, certain opportunities for enforcing the law. However, the police do selectively enforce, and concomitantly selectively dispense with, prosecution on many occasions. For example, police do not prosecute offenders who will serve as informants, felonious assaults in which the victim refuses to prosecute, and gambling cases in which harassment rather than prosecution is the objective of arrest and search and seizure practices.[12]

Goldstein agrees with Reith that a full enforcement policy would be necessary before legislators could determine accurately the beneficial or harmful effects of the law as written. It is clear, says Goldstein, that police usurp legislative power when they decide on selective enforcement programs.[13] The difficulty, however, lies not so much with the police as with a defaulting legislature who would prefer that the police rather than they deal with the conflict between the written law and the technical requirements of certain types of arrests and the norms governing certain groups and behaviors. Overt conflict between police and certain community groups and compromises police make with procedural laws in order to enforce substantive laws must be seen in part as the costs associated with the benefit to the legislature of avoiding political and social conflicts at their level.[14]

Thus, when examining police boundary activity concerning apparently *local* issues and groups, it is important not to underestimate the role of the police as the legitimate coercive power of the state.[15] The police originated as the bureaucratic means of infiltrating society in ways that were unachievable by intermittent military forays. This aspect of the police—their character as an external force sent in to control "the enemy within"—is clearly manifested in police dealings with ghetto blacks.

Blacks and the Police: An Example of State-Originated Conflict

James Baldwin expresses clearly the problems of the policeman in the ghetto:

> The only way to police the ghetto is to be oppressive. None of the police commissioner's men, even with the best will in the world, have any way

---

[12] Joseph Goldstein, "Police Discretion Not to Invoke the Criminal Process: Low Visibility Decisions in the Administration of Justice," in George Cole, ed., *Criminal Justice* (North Scituate, Mass.: Duxbury, 1972), pp. 59–80.

[13] Ibid., p. 78.

[14] Nieburg, "Violence, Law and the Informal Polity, p. 192.

[15] Allan Silver, "The Demand for Order in Civil Society: A Review of Some Themes in the History of Urban Crime, Police, and Riot," in *The Police: Six Sociological Essays*, p. 7.

of understanding the lives led by the people they swagger about in two's and three's controlling. Their very presence is an insult, and it would be, even if they spent their entire day feeding gumdrops to children. . . . The badge, the gun in the holster, and the swinging club make vivid what will happen should his rebellion become overt. . . .[16]

Historically, the police have been an occupying force in the ghetto, and as such, have suffered both from their stereotyping of the black and from the blacks' stereotyping of the police.

In 1970, Louis Harris et al. asked a nationwide sample how they would rate the job done by law-enforcement officials.[17] The responses, when broken down by race, found that 67 percent of the white respondents viewed local police favorably, but only 43 percent of the blacks so perceived the local police. Furthermore, Philip Ennis, in his study of victimization, found that blacks were much more likely to feel that the police were "not so good" in being respectful to people when compared to whites.[18] These and numerous other such surveys have found that blacks consistently are more prone to view the police as disrespectful, less honest, and less objective in their dealings with blacks.

It should not be surprising to find the social distance between the police and blacks greater than between police and whites. Police officers are enforcers of law, which normally places them in a conservative, status quo position. The black, on the other hand, is in a position of wanting or, in some cases, demanding change. The police officer is normally white, upper-lower or lower-middle class—not characteristics of the ghetto black.

Daniel Swett points out that police culture contains five focal values, which may be listed as follows:

1. The institutions of American society must be respected and preserved.
2. Human life generally, and the lives of Americans in particular, must be respected and preserved.
3. Property, both public and private, must be respected and preserved.
4. Authority must be respected and preserved.
5. Order must be respected and preserved.[19]

---

[16] James Baldwin, *Nobody Knows My Name* (New York: Dell, 1962), pp. 65–66.

[17] Louis Harris and Associates.

[18] Philip Ennis, *Criminal Victimization in the United States. Field Surveys II. A Report of a National Survey,* President's Commission on Law Enforcement and the Administration of Justice (Washington, D.C.: Government Printing Office, 1967), p. 56.

[19] David Swett, "Cultural Bias in the American Legal System," in Charles Reasons and Jack Kuykendall, eds., *Race, Crime and Justice* (Pacific Palisades, Calif.: Goodyear Publishing Co., 1972), p. 36.

To the degree that blacks do not accept these values or do not appear to accept them, they are placed in a position of conflict with the police. For example, the first focal value pertains to respect and preservation of societal institutions. Does a lower-class black have strong reason to respect and preserve those institutions that have often worked against his sharing in the bounty of American society? Certainly, many do not share the police's perspective, and those who do not are probably more prone to run into conflict with the law than other people and thus into conflict with the police.

Furthermore, the police are a conservative institution, whereas the black community is demanding social change. It is to be expected that there would be conflictual relations between these two groups. Charles Reasons and Jack Kuykendall note, regarding the irony of the conflict between the two groups: "The police were established to sustain justice through law enforcement, and justice is what minorities seek."[20]

If the degree of conflict between the police and blacks is to be reduced, there must be some mechanism through which system boundaries are altered. Either the state structure must change so that by including blacks in state policy the police become less an occupying force, or the police must reduce their ties to the state and perform more as a local community resource. For example, on the structural level, the courts have dictated that school desegregation is unconstitutional and have attempted to integrate the educational process. When and to the extent that police become protectors of blacks during the integration process, the goals of the blacks and the police acting for the state become congruent.

Police departments have also attempted several strategies to break down the social distance with blacks through various community-relations programs such as team policing, training programs wherein the officer spends extensive amounts of time interacting with citizens in a district to become more familiar with them, and storefront police offices where community members may drop in. Although the objectives of these programs are not limited to improved police-black relationships, such programs may be seen as examples of conflict reduction: making the police a community resource rather than a preserver of status quo in the state.

Robert Trojanowicz and Samuel Dixon classify police-community relations programs into four categories.[21] The first classification is entitled "Communication and Education Program." Within this category, they include such attempts to reduce the social distance between police and public as advisory committees made up of citizen groups that channel

---

[20] Reasons and Kuykendall, *Race, Crime and Justice*, p. 141.

[21] Robert Trojanowicz and Samuel Dixon, *Criminal Justice and the Community* (Englewood Cliffs, N.J.: Prentice-Hall, 1974), pp. 279–326.

input and feedback from community residents to the police; drop-in centers or storefront programs that allow citizens of the neighborhood to drop in and talk with the officers or department representatives; and small-group discussions involving officers and community residents getting together in a relatively informal fashion to discuss law-enforcement issues and problems.[22]

Trojanowicz and Dixon's second category of community relations programs is involvement of citizens in crime-prevention activities.[23] The community-relations aspect of these programs is the assumption that as citizens are involved in law enforcement, they will become more appreciative of the difficulties faced in contemporary law enforcement. Additional advantages may be gained through increased capability of the local citizen to assist in the prevention of crime and apprehension of suspects. One form of citizen involvement is the community service officer. In the President's Commission on Law Enforcement and the Administration of Justice, *Task Force Report: The Police,* it is suggested that police apprentices or police cadets "assist police officers and agents in their work, and improve communication between police departments and the neighborhood as a uniformed member of the working police."[24] Community service officers do not have full enforcement powers and are usually between 17 and 21 years of age. Other citizen-involvement programs are frequently identified as "block watchers," and "block home units," in which members of the community agree to watch children going to and from school to prevent the possibility of child molesting and to inform police of the observance of "suspicious" circumstances.[25]

Third, Trojanowicz and Dixon indicate that there are law-enforcement improvement projects like community-service centers, which, although similar to storefront programs, include welfare, employment, and educational services as well as police services. Teams of officers identified as crisis units trained to deal with and resolve disturbances such as family quarrels also would fall in this category. Since family quarrels and fights are often the most difficult situations for the police officer to deal with, crisis intervention units have the potential for promoting police-community relations by removing less competent officers from crisis situations that they neither understand nor are comfortable in handling. Thus, both this "crisis" program as well as the community-service centers attempt to extend the capability and resources that the police have available. Such

---

[22] Ibid., pp. 279–289.

[23] Ibid., pp. 289–294.

[24] President's Commission on Law Enforcement and the Administration of Justice, *Task Force Report: The Police* (Washington, D.C.: Government Printing Office, 1967), p. 137.

[25] Trojanowicz and Dixon, *Criminal Justice and the Community,* pp. 291–293.

programs are designed to promote the public's perception of the police officers as competent helpers.[26]

The fourth category is youth programs. Programs such as school liaison and educational programs taught or sponsored by police are included in this category. Functions of police-school liaison programs are to induce better working relations between schools and police, and between police and youth, and to improve attitudes of youth and community toward police. Also included in this area are recreational programs sponsored and frequently run by off-duty officers.[27]

Finally, there are a range of programs not so easily labelled as those above. In this area, Trojanowicz and Dixon place training of police officers in human-relations skills or sensitivity training for joint groups of officers and citizens.[28]

Historically, common-law policing began with members of the community taking their turn as law enforcers. Policing has now become such a specialization that special programs, usually initiated by the police, are being developed to build better relations with the public, i.e., to bring the community back into law enforcement, at least to the extent of being more understanding of the policeman's job. Thus, when we examine the boundary subsystem of police and community, we find certain natural barriers that have developed between the police and community, especially when that community is black.

It is interesting to note that the "problem" of police-community relations often becomes bounded itself and is handled as a specialty. In other words, a separate unit of the department is designated as *the* unit to deal with such problems. There is a potential danger in this specialization in that if one unit's responsibility is community relations, then the remainder of the department might become more lax in their dealings with the public.

Other Police-Community Problems

The police department actually has two masters: the community and the state. When the demands of both are congruent, then the officer's job is relatively easy. However, an officer must deal with black-white, young-old, lower class-upper class, and male-female groups. Various combinations of these groups may place different demands on the police. Some may want full enforcement of the law against all but themselves. Others may define the law as a tool of political suppression and the officer as the dupe of the system.

26 Ibid., pp. 295–299.
27 Ibid., pp. 300–308.
28 Ibid., pp. 309–321.

Another problem is that of job status. Generally the public has not attached significant status to the police role. In one study, 98 percent of Denver police officers reported that they had been the victims of verbal or physical abuse from the public.[29] Moreover, the researchers reported that this abuse, especially from poor and minorities, reinforces an officer's already biased opinion and certainly hinders his desire to "communicate" with the people.

Police-community conflict has many sources. We will examine several of these shortly. The significant point at this stage is that the police, as an arm of the state, are bound to conflict with communities, or segments of communities, that are relatively deprived by the structure of the state. The police, in this instance, may not be to blame, but they are the enforcers of the structural, political deprivation if it exists. And the police cannot do much on their own to resolve this sort of problem.

If the state is willing to remove more systematic barriers to the use of public resources, the police can enforce this removal and by so doing can ally themselves, at least temporarily, with disadvantaged groups. In the absence of this political-social-economic change, police amelioration of community problems is probably limited to certain programmatic attempts to reduce the perception of the police as the coercive arm of the state. The police, however, can carry out these programs only at the risk of displeasing other groups who desire to utilize the police as the conservers of established boundaries.[30]

Police Ties to Local Government

Perhaps the major reason for the emphasis on the local- rather than state-related aspects of policing is the executive subordination of the top police official to the community chief executive. In most American cities, the mayor was originally the chief law-enforcement official.[31] One tends to forget that the city itself is chartered by the state and that each individual policeman takes an oath to uphold state law. Legally, the policeman's duty would supersede his administrative duty to the chief executive, should there be a conflict. The problem, of course, is that the policeman's direct link to state authority is not mediated by any supervisory entity except that of the mayor and the head of the police department. Hence, on most occasions where there is a conflict of interest, the police will follow the local prerogatives, personified in their leaders. But the fact that the police need not do so is clear. When the patrolmen see it in *their*

[29] Donald Bayley and Harold Mendelsohn, *Minorities and the Police* (New York: The Free Press, 1969), p. 27.

[30] Nieburg, "Violence, Law, and the Informal Polity," p. 200.

[31] Robinson, "The Mayor and the Police."

interest to rely on state authority, they will do so, as when the New York police went on a full enforcement campaign as a means of gaining bargaining power with the city in contract negotiations.[32]

In very large metropolitan areas, the conflicts between disadvantaged groups and the police, as generated by state political processes, may be very similar to conflicts between these same groups and police, as generated by local politics and resource allocation decisions. Police-community conflict may be functional for city administrators when group frustrations attributable to city politics find outlets as aggressions against the police.[33]

Allan Silver, for example, suggests that the establishment of the police force, as a boundary-maintaining organization, has both (1) removed from the propertied, powerful classes the onus of dealing directly with political insurrection and (2) by doing so has allowed the ruling classes to become less responsive to the demands of the working classes.[34] Prior to the establishment of the police, riots were seen as vehicles for political protest and change. With the introjection of the police between the protestors and those who could implement social change, the government has been able to interpret political dissatisfaction as criminal activity. The confounding of objections to the political status quo with marginal or individual deviance has occurred, in part, because the American police system merges two police functions that were sharply distinguished in Europe. In Europe, the "high police" dealt with political unrest, and the "low police" dealt with traditional street crime. In America, the police boundary function has in effect cut down the viable or effective channels for political change.

Clearly related to these developments are some less rigid but all-important boundaries between police administration and the rest of the city government. The insistence in American cities that the police are independent of political domination is rather closely related to the reality of their subjugation. Even strong mayors, who behind the scenes are quite active in police policy, may insist that the police chief makes his own decisions. In this way the mayor can claim the responsibility for good police work and blame the police for less fortunate outcomes.[35]

Edward Hamilton, an ex-assistant mayor of New York City, states that city administrations have usually perceived the public attitude toward police services as the most crucial factor in political longevity. However,

---

[32] John A. Grimes, "The Police, the Union, and the Productivity Imperative," in Joan L. Wolfe and John F. Heaphey, eds., *Readings on Productivity in Policing* (Washington, D.C.: Police Foundation, 1975) pp. 47–85.

[33] Robinson, "The Mayor and the Police," p. 287.

[34] Silver, "The Demand for Order," pp. 12–15.

[35] Robinson, "The Mayor and the Police," pp. 281–285.

Hamilton states that administrators have traditionally attempted to insulate themselves from the police department because association with it can only cause them trouble: Poor police services could result in political turnover, but satisfactory police services would not guarantee reelection.[36] As a consequence, participation of police leadership in local politics has for years occurred behind closed doors, and police executives have gained little experience or skill in vying with other department heads for power or resources[37] and are unaccustomed to defending their policies or to producing the analytic rationales to support their actions.[38] In other words, part of the inability of the police to enunciate and defend policy in a public forum is a function of the traditional boundary between police services and other aspects of city administration. The police executive has quietly accepted both the mayor's private role in police policy and the mayor's public insistence on police independence—both of which were deemed necessary to political success.

However, the style of political leadership has changed drastically in the last decade. Publics have begun to demand accountability of public agencies for services rendered, and city administrators have discovered that they can utilize data on public services performance to their political advantage. The police executive has been relatively surprised and somewhat trapped by this turn of events because he is usually without the data, the staff, or the personal competence to justify his organization as a public service. His justifications have for years been made in private, to the mayor, and concerned conservation of political order rather than rendering of services in an effective manner.[39]

Thus, the examination of police activities and of the structure of the organization to conduct those activities is presently a complex task. The boundaries that the police are to maintain are rapidly changing—among different community groups, among any of these groups and city administration, between themselves and the administration, and between themselves and the public. But because the police have traditionally been a boundary-maintaining force, the organization has developed little skill in analyzing change or in creating change within itself. These conflicts between boundary maintenance and service delivery to communities with redefined boundaries will be constant themes throughout the rest of our discussion of what the police are organized to do.

---

[36] Edward K. Hamilton, "Police Productivity: The View from City Hall," in *Readings on Productivity in Policing*, pp. 15–17.

[37] Roy Holladay, "The Police Administrator—A Politician?" *Journal of Criminal Law, Criminology, and Police Science*, 53 (1962), 526–529.

[38] Hamilton, "Police Productivity," pp. 21–27.

[39] Ibid., p. 21.

The functions of the police are not easily specified. Is crime control the major purpose? If we were to ask most citizens, this would probably be their response. And if this were the major goal, then we would expect police activities to center on responding to and investigating crimes and patrolling the streets to prevent offenses from occurring.

Another possible goal of the department might be labeled "order maintenance." Order-maintenance functions center on preventing and quieting "behavior that either disturbs or threatens to disturb the public peace or that involves face-to-face conflict among two or more persons."[40] Activities by officers such as quieting loud parties, settling domestic quarrels, sending home a noisy drunk, and separating barroom combatants all fall into an order-maintenance or peace-keeping function. Thus, activities that focus on problems primarily concerned with behavior that disturbs the peace or potentially may do so if not quieted by the officer, are order maintenance in nature.

A third function of the police, and one that has fallen to the police not because it is part of their central functions but because the police are frequently the only agency available 24 hours a day, is serving the public by getting cats out of trees, delivering expectant mothers to the hospital, checking the homes of vacationers, and numerous other service activities. In terms of the *formal* goals of a police agency, the service function is minimized when compared to law-enforcement and order-maintenance duties.[41]

Although the public conceives of the police as a law-enforcement agency, studies suggest that when compared to the formally prescribed activities of the police, the service function accounts for a disproportionate share of calls to the police. For example, James Wilson found that 37.5 percent of the calls to the police in Syracuse, New York, for a six-day period were for service; 30 percent of the calls were for order maintenance; and only 10.3 percent were law-enforcement calls. Thus, calls to the police indicate that citizen requests are frequently for service, not law enforcement or order maintenance.[42]

Paul Whisenand states that the basic mission of the police department

---

[40] James Q. Wilson, *Varieties of Police Behavior* (Cambridge, Mass.: Harvard University Press, 1968), p. 16.

[41] See Herman Goldstein, "Toward a Redefinition of the Police Function," in Alvin Cohn and Emilio C. Viano, eds., *Police-Community Relations: Images, Roles, Realities* (Philadelphia: Lippincott, 1976), pp. 125–130.

[42] Wilson, *Varieties of Police Behavior*, p. 18.

is "to maintain the peace, and to protect life and property."[43] Toward this goal, crime control, order maintenance, and service activities are supposedly directed. For example, the apprehension of offenders preserves the peace in perhaps several ways. First, the apprehended individual may be removed from the streets for a period of time, thus preventing him from committing other offenses. Second, through being apprehended, the offender may be deterred from committing subsequent offenses. Third, the apprehension of offenders may serve as a warning to other would-be violators that there is risk in their committing offenses, and thus they may be deterred from violations. Fourth, by apprehending offenders and punishing them, the morality of the law may be reinforced.

Similarly, even such apparently noncrime-centered activities as removal of cats from trees may serve as a peace-keeping function. One such function might be that good will created by service activities encourages citizens to support and respect the police. This may be demonstrated by their willingness to report crimes to the police, as well as being on the lookout for suspicious activities in their neighborhood that may increase the chances of the police apprehending an offender. Although this may be a circuitous route to peace-keeping, there is still the potential linkage present. Such police activities, although not law enforcement in nature, may permit communications between police and citizens that are noncrime centered and consequently are less threatening to the public than criminal investigations or routine patrol activities.

The police operate in a highly uncertain environment. Uncertainty as to their social status in the community, uncertainty as to their working environment and the dangers within it, and uncertainty as to the function and role with other criminal justice agencies all contribute to the complexity of the operational environment of the police. It is our thesis that, seen as a system on its own, it is the immediate environment and boundary maintenance duties of the police that preoccupy their time and thinking, and that relationships to other criminal justice agencies are determined in large part by the importance the police put on control in the street. There are several ways to examine this hypothesis, but one good starting point is the interaction of the police with other agencies.

The police initiate the filtering of clients into the criminal justice system through the technique of arrest. Their decision to take an individual into custody is normally made in the field without a warrant. An informative study of accused felons in California found that 28.5 percent of the suspects were released without filing of charges and that 21.6 percent had their charges reduced to a misdemeanor. Based on police decisions. 55,994 of the 98,921 felony defendants either had their charges dropped

---

[43] Paul M. Whisenand, *Police Supervision: Theory and Practice* (Englewood Cliffs, N.J.: Prentice-Hall, 1971), p. 80.

entirely or dropped to a misdemeanor.[44] Data such as these point out the power of the police in their dealings with those they suspect of committing an offense. Are these people guilty of an offense? Are they being unjustly arrested and detained? Or do the police handle problems without use of the criminal process?

One may view the system of criminal justice as a series of checks and balances. From this view, it becomes the responsibility of the courts and prosecutor to assess the quality of evidence and the legal admissibility of the evidence gathered by the police to assure that the defendant has not been unjustly handled and accused by the police. Thus, they would "check" on the officer's behavior and measure it against legal standards of appropriateness.

However, most cases do not reach a court trial. As the data presented by Edward Barrett suggest,[45] many cases are dropped by the police themselves before filing of charges in court. Thus, many cases are never reviewed by a judicial officer to assess the appropriateness of the arrest. The data reflect, in some cases, a suspicion that a person has committed an offense but an inability to prove it in court. In other cases, the police may use the arrest to harass the individual. "Harassment is the imposition by the police, acting under color of law, of sanctions prior to conviction as a means of ultimate punishment, rather than as a device for the invocation of criminal proceedings."[46] For example, officers may attempt to disrupt gambling activities by stopping and questioning those they suspect of having gambling paraphernalia. Without legal foundation, they will search a suspect, his car, and perhaps his home, with the hope of finding gambling paraphernalia, which, because of the method of seizure, cannot be admitted into court as evidence against the suspect. However, such police activities permit confiscation and thus disruption of the gambling activities even though the evidence is not legally admissible. Although this activity may be illegal, Joseph Goldstein discovered that these methods had the tacit approval and cooperation of the prosecutor, who agreed with the police that the legal penalties for gambling were too slight to stop the activity, whereas the harassment policy could put a severe crimp in operations.[47]

Furthermore, cases referred to court rarely result in a trial wherein the evidence would be closely scrutinized for admissibility against the ac-

[44] Edward L. Barrett, Jr., "Police Practices and the Law from Arrest to Release or Charge," *California Law Review, 50* (1962), 31.

[45] Ibid., pp. 11–55.

[46] Joseph Goldstein, "Police Discretion Not to Invoke the Criminal Process: Low Visibility Decisions in the Administration of Justice," *Yale Law Journal,* 69 (March 1960), 552.

[47] Ibid.

cused. Many cases are dismissed by the prosecutor; others are negotiated, exchanging a reduction of charge or punishment for a guilty plea; and in other cases, the accused feels little reason for demanding a trial. Of those cases that do happen to reach court, somewhere between 80 and 95 percent are guilty pleas, and only a trifling minority result in the trial process. All of this points out that the operating principles of the justice system are only partially controlled by due-process guidelines, and moreover, that the police are only infrequently constrained by the thought of prosecution at all. For example, the American Bar Foundation survey of criminal justice found that most complaints about police practice arose in areas where police had no intention of going to court, and thus court control of police procedure was negated. Street searches for weapons and drugs were two examples where the police desired to obtain the illegal item itself rather than to prosecute.[48]

When patrolmen in New York City were queried by the Vera Institute of Justice as to the extent, if any, that the *Mapp* and *Miranda* decisions impaired the performance of their duties, 52 percent responded "a great deal" to *Mapp* and 41 percent responded likewise for *Miranda*.[49] An additional 24 percent indicated a fair amount of impairment through *Mapp* and 25 percent indicated the same for *Miranda*. Observations have not always corroborated this perception of impairment. A study in one city found that of 118 suspects questioned, only 25 were given the *Miranda* warnings.[50] Arthur Niederhoffer suggests that the real impact of decisions such as *Miranda* is not in their hindering the law-enforcement process, "but the probable reinforcement of cynicism among policemen."[51] The police use such decisions as evidence of distrust in the police and as demands that if followed, would impair efficiency. Both factors reinforce the already distinct boundary between the police and the remainder of the criminal process. This boundary conflict between the police and the courts would seem to be endemic, with the courts attempting to preserve a moral and normative order and image of justice, whereas the police seek to preserve a behavioral order.[52]

The interaction of the police and prosecutor is probably one of the most frequent of interactions between segments of the criminal justice system. After the police have initiated the criminal justice process by

[48] Laurence Tiffany, Donald M. McIntyre, and David L. Rosenberg, *Detection of Crime* (Boston: Little, Brown, 1967), pp. 11–13.

[49] George P. McManus, "What Does a Policeman Do?" in Alvin Cohn and Emilio C. Vivano, eds., *Police-Community Relations* (Philadelphia: Lippincott, 1976), p. 150.

[50] Reiss and Black, "Interrogation and the Criminal Process," pp. 47–57.

[51] Arthur Niederhoffer, *Behind the Shield* (Garden City, N.Y.: Doubleday, 1969), p. 174.

[52] Reiss and Black, "Interrogation and the Criminal Process," p. 48.

arrest and are ready to have the formal charges filed, they become dependent on the ability and desire of the prosecutor to present "their" case. Likewise, the prosecutor is dependent on the police to serve as his investigators, and without their assistance his job would be considerably more complicated. Although these officials are dependent upon each other, conflicts arise.

The most common point of contention between the police and prosecution office is plea bargaining. Plea bargaining may be a response by the prosecutor to an overly large caseload, or it may be a technique whereby the prosecutor can bargain for a punishment that he feels is more congruent with the offender and/or the particulars of the offense. For example, conviction for burglary may result in a sentence ranging from 10 to 15 years. In a particular case, the prosecutor may feel that the burglar has redeeming qualities such that a lengthy sentence for a particular burglary would be too severe. Therefore, the prosecutor may reduce the charge to breaking and entering or malicious entry, for which the sanctions are much lighter. Obviously, these considerations by the prosecutor may not be in line with the perspective of the police, and they frequently are not. Consequently, officers often feel as though they are being sold out by the prosecutor.

But the prosecutor also plays another role in checking on the procedures used by the police. If an officer performs an illegal search, then it is in part the responsibility of the prosecutor to prevent clear cases of poor police procedure from going to court. He may do this by dropping the charges or negotiating a guilty plea for a reduced charge. In the latter case, the prosecutor is covering up the procedural violations of the officer.

The interaction between the police and prosecutor affects the ability of the police to fulfill their objectives. Although the police frequently complain about the manner and leniency with which the prosecutor handles their cases, to the extent that the prosecutor can educate the officers concerning procedural constraints or how better to collect evidence and present cases, then the ability of the police to utilize the criminal process should improve. However, the impact of such education is muted if officers ignore offenses or use "harassment" tactics rather than appropriate arrest and charge techniques. To some degree, police departments have responded to plea bargaining and dropping of charges against those they have arrested by measuring their "production" not by convictions but by clearance rates (crimes cleared by arrest) when punishment is lacking or too light. Although it is debatable whether or not people are deterred by the amount of punishment or certainty of punishment, it is important to note that many police officers believe that deterrence is effective. Frequently police see the courts as operating with a different agenda in which deterrence is not a high priority. Police officers frequently feel that the court agenda is an overly lenient one. In one study, 82 percent of the responding police officers indicated that less leniency by the courts would be "very helpful."[53]

The police probably interact least frequently with the agencies and agents of correction. Police perception of corrections, however, also contributes to the isolation of the police from the rest of the criminal justice system. To the degree that the corrections system fulfills its responsibilities, the police task should be made easier. And to the extend that the image of prison deters, and/or at least for the length of time that walls separate an offender from new criminal opportunities, there may be some reduction in police workload. Finally, to the extent that corrections can train an individual in legal rather than illegal means of success, the police would be relieved of repeat offenders.

Whereas corrections can make contributions to the police, the police similarly can contribute to the performance of the correctional subsystem, especially in the area of probation and parole services. The police operate 24 hours a day, receive complaints and informatoin from the public, and continuously are patrolling and observing citizens, including probationers and parolees. Consequently, police officers maintain the key to information that is important to the efficient operation of many aspects of the correctional system. When a police officer observes a parolee hanging around a bar and he suspects the parolee should be at work, the police officer can assist the parole officer by informing him of the time and location of his sighting the parolee. Thus the police officer may perform much of the parole officer's surveillance work. It would be inefficient use of resources to have the parole officer routinely patrolling the streets, although there are many things that can only be learned through such activities. It is this working relationship between the police and parole officer that, when it works well, makes the criminal justice system appear to operate as an organized system. Yet, this cooperation does not represent typical interaction between these subsystems. It is more characteristic that the police do not cooperate with parole (perhaps because they believe the parole officer would not do anything anyway), and parole officers frequently fail to work with the police because they believe the police do not understand their role and its inherent problems. Similar conflict between police and probation has also been noted.[54] The police frequently complain that when they rely upon other agencies of the system for the implementation of justice, it is too infrequently done.[55]

---

[53] McManus, "What Does a Policeman Do?" p. 149.

[54] Vincent O'Leary and Donald J. Newman, "Conflict Resolution in Criminal Justice," *Journal of Research in Crime and Delinquency,* 7 (1970), 99–119.

[55] Reiss and Bordua, "Environment and Organization, pp. 37–38.

The "boundary" between the police and the rest of the criminal justice system frequently centers on the issue of control. Do the courts or corrections control the police? A more appropriate description might be "influence." For example, Nathan Goldman found in his study of police handling of juveniles that the differential referral of offenders to court by the police was influenced by the policeman's attitudes toward the juvenile court.[56] His study noted that the police were reluctant to refer a youth to court if the officer in question believed that the court was unfair, too lenient, or might criticize the officer's handling of a particular case.[57] In such cases, the court is not controlling, but indubitably, it is influencing the officer's decisions. Similarly, the correctional system and community standards also influence the judgments of officers, especially in those situations in which the officers have extensive discretion such as in the handling of juvenile suspects.

We are not suggesting in the above review that conflicts between the police and the agencies controlling subsequent stages in the criminal process are the *cause* of police isolation from the rest of the system or the *cause* of their reliance upon immediate control within the confines of their street environment. On the contrary, this isolation would seem to be part of the police tradition of self-reliance in the solution to street situations. Police practice has not changed drastically in 150 years and still evident in today's patrol practices are the characteristics of operation that emerged when the police patrolled 12 hours a day, 7 days a week, with no means to call for assistance and no education in the law.[58] It was during the evolution of the police role that the police, of necessity, developed problem-solving strategies that were not only independent of courts and correctional agencies, but were also independent of central police administration. The policeman depended on his own imagination, physical bearing, and knowledge of the street and its people. Information about persons and behavior inevitably took on different significance for the police than it did for the courts. Police developed informal and direct methods of enforcing behavioral standards, or of managing street situations. The courts, on the other hand, interpreted information about violations as an issue of law.[59] The specific act, as a violation of the law, rather than the total situation as perceived by the policeman, is what is important in court.

[56] Nathan Goldman, "Differential Selection of Juvenile Offenders by Police, in *Police-Community Relations*, pp. 236–246.

[57] Ibid., pp. 243–244.

[58] Mark Haller "Introduction: The 19th Century Police," Mimeographed (Philadelphia: Temple University, n.d.), pp. 1–10.

[59] Reiss and Black, "Interrogation and the Criminal Process," p. 49.

That the police are still oriented to the patrol and control of territory rather than to the enforcement of particular laws is vividly demonstrated by Jonathan Rubenstein's recent study of the Philadelphia police.[60] There is, however, a difference between the policeman's control of his beat today and the control methods that he utilized 70 years ago. The difference, suggests Mark Haller, began with the introduction of call boxes in the 1890s and became highlighted with the introduction of radios and patrol cars in the 1930s.[61] Mobilization and motorization may have increased efficiency and certainly have increased central control over officers, but these steps have reduced significantly the policeman's contact with the citizenry they patrol.[62]

VERTICAL AND HORIZONTAL DIMENSIONS OF POLICE ORGANIZATION

In order to understand more fully the commitment of the police to on-site controls, it is necessary to examine two separate pressures on the police in tandem. On the one hand are those organizational variables that link the police to their superiors, and on the other hand are those situational variables that link the police to their environment. These two sets of variables can be called the *vertical* and *horizontal dimensions* of policing. Although there has been considerable strengthening of the vertical dimension in the last four decades, it would seem to us that the uncertainties of the horizontal connections, that is, the linkages of the policeman to his external environment, are still the most salient factors in determining his role behavior.

The policeman's reliance on informal normative patterns in *his* territory rather than on the legal or executive prescriptions about what he should do is explained to a great degree by the nature of the individual policeman's resource. Because he is alone on the street (and, indeed, there seems to be no other way that he could operate), the patrolman has the power, if not the authority, to negotiate informal solutions to what he perceives as troublesome events rather than to enfrce the law.

The release of offenders at police discretion, for whatever reason, renders ineffective any control system based on limitation of their outputs as inputs. . . .[63]

---

[60] Rubenstein, *City Police*, see especially pp. 129–176.

[61] Haller, "Introduction: The 19th Century Police," p. 18.

[62] National Advisory Commission on Civil Disorders, *Final Report* (New York: Bantam Books, 1969), p. 305; and see James Q. Wilson, "Police Morale, Reform, and Citizen Respect: The Chicago Case," in *The Police: Six Sociological Essays*, pp. 137–162.

[63] Reiss and Black, "Interrogation and the Criminal Process," p. 57.

This characteristic of police work not only reduces court controls to secondary status, as we saw above, it also significantly reduces the power of central police command.[64] Michael Banton argues that a policeman's strict reliance on a legalistic interpretation of his duties would quickly render him ineffective in his duties. In his mediation of disputes in his area, the policeman loses his personal authority to the extent that he relies on his legal authority to act officially.[65] Banton's observations of several American police forces have been validated in a systematic survey of attitudes toward the police by all persons who had called for police service in New Haven in the summer of 1969. This survey found that the great majority of persons were satisfied with police conduct unless the policeman relied on invocation of criminal law.[66]

The policeman is on familiar grounds with many persons in his territory, but he gains voluntary cooperation from few. In order to control his territory adequately, he usually finds the most effective means involves a compromise, trading his potential use (or threat of use) of the criminal law for a satisfactory alteration in behavior or distribution of people in his territory. This situation is very similar to the devices that Gresham Sykes found utilized by prison cell-block guards. Strict enforcement of rules and regulations quickly lost a guard the cooperation of the inmates he guarded. An informal compromise, overlooking certain minor infractions (or even quiet infractions of major rules) at least produced a quiet block.[67] Similarly, the policeman will go to great lengths to break down the barrier between himself and the community. Indeed, argues Banton, much police corruption and violence are most accurately analyzed as attempts (albeit misdirected) to break down police-community boundaries and to establish the informal mediation role.[68]

The predominance of the mediation and dispute-settling tools over the rest of the policeman's repertoire perhaps can be best seen by comparing a normal situation to other situations in which these tools were not available. In these situations one might expect the police to resort to strict law enforcement. However, studies of white southern police patrolling black neighborhoods and British colonial police patrolling African tribes demonstrate that, at least in these particular situations, strict law enforcement does not take place. Deprived by cultural and value differences of their mediator role, the police fall back on a containment policy,

---

[64] This ineffectiveness of executive, bureaucratic control over the police is a recurrent theme in Rubenstein, *City Police.*

[65] Banton, *The Policeman in the Community,* p. 179.

[66] Personal communication with Michael W. O'Neill, field director of the survey for the then Chief Ahern, New Haven police department.

[67] Gresham Sykes, *The Society of Captives* (Princeton, N.J.: Princeton University Press, 1971), Chapter Two.

[68] Banton, *The Policeman in the Community,"* p. 169.

allowing even greater numbers of violations in the areas they cannot penetrate informally than in those that they can.[69]

Several observers have noted that the American police rely even more heavily than British police on informal, personal control rather than on vertically delegated, bureaucratic authority. Reasons for this are complex, but are crucial to an understanding of the American police as boundary maintainers and of the complex means American police have invented for performing the task of street control.

Banton has argued, as we noted earlier, that social control is a product of social relations, not of the police themselve. Social control is higher in small villages and simpler societies than in complex conurbations because people are more dependent on each other.[70] In other words, the information loops, or informal behavior controls, are tighter in social structures where persons have more information about each other and therefore have a greater number of informal avenues by which to check each others' behavior.[71] Under these conditions, according to Banton,

> [t]he policeman obtains public cooperation, and enjoys public esteem, because he enforces standards accepted by the community. This gives his role considerable moral authority and sets him apart from the crowd socially, much as does the role of the minister of religion.[72]

Stated another way, relative homogeneity of values in a community allows the policeman to enjoy special status as well as constrains him to play his official role. The British policeman seems comfortable to play a role symbolic of that social order. The American policeman, in contrast, finds it necessary to intervene actively in situations.[73] The vertical pressure on the policeman to perform according to his office, regardless of the persons or situations he meets, is less viable in the United States because the horizontal, situational pressures are both more heterogeneous and less predictable.[74] Local political and situational pressures are far more pervasive in the United States than in Great Britain. The American policeman is less insulated from varying and contradictory public demands, is exposed to more violence, and withstands more criticism than his English counterpart. The American police have responded by being

---

[69] Ibid., pp. 174–175. See also the excellent vignettes concerning law enforcement in emerging African nations in William J. Chambliss and Robert D. Seidman, *Law, Order, and Power* (Reading, Mass.: Addison-Wesley, 1971).

[70] Banton, *The Policeman in the Community*, pp. 2–3.

[71] See ibid., pp. 86–112; and Leslie Wilkins, *Social Deviance* (Englewood Cliffs, N.J.: Prentice-Hall, 1965), pp. 65–71.

[72] Banton, *The Policeman in the Community*, p. 3.

[73] Reiss and Bordua, "Environment and Organization," p. 35.

[74] Jim L. Munro, *Administrative Behavior and Police Organization* (Cincinnati, Ohio: Anderson, 1971), pp. 42–43.

considerably more attentive and concerned about their external relations than about their relationship to either centralized command or the law.[75]

THE EXTERNAL ENVIRONMENT AND INTERNAL ORGANIZATION

Our major hypothesis has been that the nature of American police work is determined more by the complex, variable, and difficult to predict boundary exchanges than by any other facet of police organization. Put another way, we would hypothesize that internal police organization is primarily dependent on the external environment, rather than the other way around. Although several other studies support this hypothesis,[76] Jerome Skolnick's classic study claims the opposite—that police goals and operational procedures determine what the policeman responds to and how he responds to it.[77] Skolnick suggests that it is the internal bureaucratic pressure on the police to be productive that determines the policeman's interpretation of the law and his response to the public. Although we will attempt no direct refutation of Skolnick's thesis here, we think that the material presented in this section and in the remainder of the chapter is persuasive. Our approach will be to bring together the several observations reviewed above concerning various external relations, and then to display their impact on the internal production and maintenance activities of police organization.

Again, we would caution that this analysis of American municipal police may not be applicable to other countries, or to other specialized police forces in the United States. We believe that our hypothesis holds when the police working environment reaches a certain level of complexity and heterogeneity, and, necessarily, when the police role becomes sufficiently generalist in nature. Since Skolnick's study concentrated heavily on the detective (and principally the vice units) division of one highly "professionalized" department,[78] the apparent conflict between his analysis and ours may be resolvable. Most observers have noted that detectives enjoy considerably higher status, are considerably less vulnerable to community cross pressures, and are considerably more involved in prosecution (and therefore criminal justice) than are officers who routinely patrol the street.

One key to internal police organization is *social density*, a term Banton uses to refer to the degree that community members must interact with

[75] Banton, *The Policeman in the Community*, pp. 100–112.

[76] See ibid.; Reiss and Bordua, "Environment and Organization"; and Wilson, *Varieties of Police Behavior*, and "Police Morale, Reform, and Citizen Respect."

[77] Jerome Skolnick, *Justice Without Trial* (New York: John Wiley, 1967).

[78] Ibid; and Wilson, *Varieties of Police Behavior*, p. 283.

each other in a variety of different roles. Banton argues that the higher the social density, the more sharply and narrowly defined are the different roles. The sharpness of definition allows the British policeman a role as defined by his office and formal stated duties. On the other hand, in the United States both urbanization and high mobility reduce the social density of American communities. As a result, there is less information concerning an individual available in any particular interaction with another, and there is less restriction to particular roles. Therefore, Banton concludes, the police are less protected by office and role in the United States than in Britain. The American police more frequently resort to "settling things individually" because (1) they can place less reliance on the directives structuring their office to be applicable in diverse situations, and (2) they can place less reliance on the manner in which unknown individuals will respond to their symbols of office.[79]

This external situational uncertainty generates two important police organizational characteristics. First, the nature of the work is so varied that such work cannot be adequately performed when guided by a formal set of written principles. (Or at least not by the kinds of principles that heretofore have been the basis of police training!)[80] Second, the police role is largely learned on the job from other police officers. The great part of police socialization, training, or "breaking-in" is performed in an apprenticeship manner, the recruit learning the craft by observation of experienced hands.[81]

The apprentice-master relationship, the policeman's perceived isolation of himself from the criminal jusice system, and the inapplicability of written and formalized standards to highly variable situations all tend to make police officers rely on each other (this is particularly true for those police groups who work most closely together). This reliance is pervasive, including resort for help in times of danger,[82] reference or calls for judgment about appropriate behavior,[83] and in times of deviance, to cover inappropriate and even illegal behavior.[84] An accurate generaliza-

---

[79] Banton, The Policeman in the Community, pp. 224–232.

[80] See John H. McNamara, "Uncertainties in Police Work: The Relevance of Police Recruits' Background and Training," in The Police: Six Sociological Essays, pp. 163–252; and Frank Elmes, "Education or Training?" The Police Journal, 43, No. 2 (February 1970), 55–63.

[81] See Skolnick, Justice Without Trial, pp. 196–199; Wilson, Varieties of Police Behavior, pp. 282–283; and Banton, The Policeman in the Community, pp. 179–181.

[82] Skolnick, Justice Without Trial, pp. 53–54.

[83] See especially Michael W. O'Neill, "The Role of the Police—Normative Role Expectations in a Metropolitan Department," doctoral dissertation, State University of New York at Albany, 1974.

[84] Rubenstein, City Police. For a very analogous situation concerning correctional officers, see Sykes, The Society of Captives; and David Duffee, "The Correction Officer Subculture and Organizational Change," Journal of Research in Crime and Delinquency, 11, No. 4 (July 1974), 155–172.

tion concerning this situation would be that the higher the external pressure on the organizational members, the less these members can accommodate internal organizational strain.[85]

As a result, police administrators are in a difficult situation. The more they demand conformity to departmental policy (and even the more that they rigorously attempt to formulate policies at all), the less are their commands perceived as legitimate by their subordinates. And any overt attempts at internal control are all the more likely to increase the policeman's solidarity with his peers and informal, ad hoc, on-the-street solutions to problems he confronts.[86]

A final factor that pulls the policeman away from centralized authority and the criminal process is, ironically, the very difficulties he encounters in engaging his street environment. Unless the policeman is to be totally reactive, and wait for persons to summon his aid, he must develop ways to observe and obtain information about infractions. But most information useful to policing is not likely to come free for the asking: it flows as exchange relationships are established. The police can rarely buy information or rely on moral demands for its provision. Consequently, most information is gained in channels established by barter: this service for that tip, or this nonenforcement for that more valuable enforcement opportunity. To the extent that a policeman relies on organizational and criminal justice processes for his information, the more likely is it that informal sources will "dry up."[87] Consequently, the policeman is constantly seeking alternatives to formal processing that will both achieve his aims *and* maintain his tenuous ties with the environment. Again, the policeman is pulled away from central authority and formal office, toward his isolated stance in the street. Much police administrative practice, as we shall see, is not a proactive strategy to control and deploy the police effectively, but is a reactive strategy to retain what little observance of office and bureaucratic authority remains.

POLICE GOALS AND PRODUCTIVITY

Although the police never are at a loss for controversy, one can easily wade through the mire of complaint and disagreement one step at a time, dealing with each problem as it appears, and formulating little if any understanding of how these complaints came to coalesce. It is quite possible, of course, that all the controversial issues are separate—that corrup-

---

[85] Banton, *The Policeman in the Community*, pp. 116–119.

[86] Rubenstein, *City Police*, pp. 448–456.

[87] Skolnick and Woodworth, "Bureaucracy, Information and Social Control," pp. 99–100.

tion really is caused by the rotten policeman in the barrel rather than a function of the behavior to be controlled, that riots are really caused by deviants and subversive infiltrators rather than by the distributive priorities of the staff, etc. Although such rationalizations are publicly espoused by police chiefs and politicians alike, we doubt their validity. Regardless of the hottest complaint in circulation, it would appear to us that the core difficulty deals with the articulation of police goals and functions, or, in the current terminology, of making the police productive. Again, the police relationship to their environment is crucial. The modern police were established because changes in social structure made it impossible for informal communal controls on behavior to be sufficient. But what type of activity the police were to introject in the deficient social structure of the nineteenth century is unclear. It would seem that the new entrepreneurial classes and political leaders expected protection from the "dangerous classes."[88] Yet it would also seem that the police were not always willing dupes of the "establishment," but sought to perceive themselves as neutral enforcers of an abstract law that applied equally to all men.[89]

Articulating the functions of police work has always been a problem, and perhaps more of a problem for police administrators than for politicians or academics. As we have seen, it *is* possible to draw broad distinctions in police style, operating principles, and relationships to communities among different cultures. But these broad differences, although informative, are frequently not useful when police are trying to determine policy in any particular city. Administrators have not been very successful in translating broad goal statements into specific objectives—objectives that if met, would, when taken together, lead to the accomplishment of goals.

Most police departments have usually settled for certain measured indicators of activity, but it has always been doubtful whether and how these counted activities relate to desired objectives and goals. Police specialists generally agree that typical private-sector productivity concepts are not applicable to the assessment of police work. There are too few physical analogies in policing to the production of discrete, physical units in industry.[90] There is an apparent consensus that objectification of police work will require multiple measures, relating to different and even conflicting functions. Five functions typically suggested are:

[88] Allan Silver, "The Demand for Order in Civil Society: A Review of Some Themes in the History of Urban Crime, Police, and Riot," in David Bordua ed. *The Police: Six Sociological Essays*, pp. 1–25.

[89] Ibid.

[90] Chambliss and Siedman, *Law, Order, and Power.*

1. The prevention of crime, or the deterrence of crime; reducing in an area the level of crime from what it would have been had the police been absent; or reducing the rate of crime in any policed area from the rate in the same policed area at previous time units.

2. The maintenance of a feeling of security in a community; such a function relates more to the public belief about crime and quality of police service than to actual incidence of criminal events.

3. The apprehension of persons responsible for particular crimes.

4. The performance of a myriad of noncrime services, such as traffic control and response to emergency situations.

5. The maintenance of a certain level of performance quality, or, if not to gain actual support, then at least to perform in ways that do not raise the level of antagonism against the police.[91]

Some of these functions receive more attention than others, and the kinds of attention or emphasis that each receives may differ. For example, although both Rubenstein and Skolnick report that police officers tend to emphasize "real police work," such as the investigative and apprehension roles of detectives, Wilson found a large amount of police time was devoted to noncrime service provision.[92] Of all the functions mentioned, perhaps the most idealized has been that of crime prevention. However, several police specialists, including practitioners, suggest that the police are not organized, trained, or rewarded for doing preventive work.[93] "The preventive function tends to receive attention only when personnel are not otherwise occupied."[94] Or, stated differently, "prevention" may be what either administrators or policeman say is happening when the activity engaged in has no specifiable outcomes.

Because functions such as prevention or maintenance of feelings of security are obviously affected by many more variables than those controlled by the police, they are understandably difficult, hazy concepts. What is perhaps more surprising is the lack of productivity measurement in areas where the police *do* produce identifiable products. But as late as 1976, the former Commissioner of the New York City Police Department could ask:

To what extent do we gather the appropriate data and analyze crime as a means of establishing enforcement priorities? . . . [Are we] bringing to court those cases with the highest priority, or are we loading the sys-

[91] Harry P. Hatry, "Wrestling with Police Crime Control Productivity Measurement," in *Readings on Productivity in Policing*, p. 81.

[92] Jonathan Rubenstein, *City Police* (New York: Ballantine Books, 1973), pp. 398–399; and Jerome Skolnick, *Justice Without Trial* (New York: Wiley, 1967), p. 120.

[93] Hatry, "Wrestling with Police Crime Control," pp. 88–89.

[94] H. Goldstein, "Redefinition of the Police Function," p. 126.

tem with arrests for offenses that are very low on the prosecutor's priority list?[95]

These are important questions, but in light of the nature of police boundary activity, they almost sound naive. To what extent do the police care if cases are important to the prosecutor?

Productivity (or to use the term from our introduction to Part III—*proficiency*) has usually received short shrift from police, primarily because its measurement requires some specification of effectiveness. And effectiveness would require agreement both as to type of function as well as to some conventions for ascertaining (observing) if specified results were accomplished. Effectiveness, however, does not refer to costs incurred during the achievement. Efficiency typically refers to a ratio of output to input, or the extent to which the activities undertaken are as economical as possible.[96] Productivity links or combines effectiveness and efficiency by attaching a quality (or an *outcome*) factor to the counting of outputs (or number of things done.)[97] Because administrators cannot arrive at either an internal or a public consensus on objectives to be accomplished, "we find interest only in the projects which make the current ineffective police operation more efficient."[98]

Former Commissioner Murphy recommends that the most useful starting point in finally developing productivity standards is the kind of analysis we have reviewed—that is, by examining the tremendous variation that now exists in police performance, and in performance indicators, and by doing some plain hard thinking about the underlying reasons for such variations. For example, why do manpower complements, manpower allocation practices, and clearance rates for particular types of crimes vary by as much as 50 percent from city to city, or precinct to precinct?[99]

There are, however, a large number of obstacles to hard thinking about police productivity, many of which can be traced back to boundary or environmental exchange problems. For instance, there is often a political need for short-term success, such as the solution of a particular heinous crime, which reduces the time available for planning and evaluation. There is also the tendency, typical of most bureaucracies, to support traditional programs because officials develop vested interest in what

[95] Patrick Murphy, "Police Accountability," in *Readings on Productivity in Policing*, p. 45.

[96] George H. Kuper, "Productivity: A National Concern," in *Readings on Productivity in Policing*, p. 3.

[97] Ibid.

[98] Al German, "What Is the Developing Mission of the American Police?" *Police Journal, 43,* No. 2 (February 1970), 100.

[99] Murphy, "Police Accountability," pp. 44–45.

they are doing, regardless of the relationship between that activity and total organizational outcomes. Along with the tendency toward tradition and short-term success (or "fire-fighting") is the long-standing absence of technical and analytical in-house employees who are competent to measure objectives, plan their achievement, and evaluate achievement. There is also the belief that police effectiveness, despite all the intervening and external variables that affect it, is measured by crime rates. (Obviously, there is also tremendous vested interest here, such as the effort that goes into F.B.I. *Uniform Crime Reports.*) Also, front-line police, particularly as spurred on by increasingly militant unions, frequently complain that productivity development may threaten job security.[100] Finally, police departments have also been isolated from other departments. With an absence of technical staff, information and idea sharing have been primarily left to police line executives. And police chiefs rarely have the time or proclivity to publish, present papers, or in other ways convene to define roles, functions, or methods of measurement.[101]

In many respects, then, the articulation of police functions, as well as the improvement and stabilization of the police environment, is dependent on the maturity of police management.

The introduction of productivity improvement is a management function and responsibility. It follows that if management does not have a clear concept of what it wants to do and a thorough understanding of how to do it, the rank and file employee is not likely either to greet the program with enthusiasm or carry it out successfully.[102]

Separation of Outcome from Effort

One of the principal difficulties in the improvement of police productivity is the separation or hiatus between the effort of police work and the outcome of that effort. This problem is most significant when the police decide to involve the criminal process, since it is then that the outcome salient to the police is most dependent on processes and decisions made by other agencies.[103] However, the same difficulty may arise when the police do not rely on prosecution, but make referrals or informal street adjustments.

The fact that the information relevant to outcome evaluation is heavily dependent on *some* sector of the environment is another factor that forces the police into bargaining positions with violators, prosecutors, defense

---

[100] James Morgan, "Planning and Implementing a Productivity Program," in *Readings on Productivity in Policing*, pp. 146–147.

[101] Murphy, "Police Accountability," p. 37.

[102] Grimes, "The Police, the Union, and the Productivity Imperative," p. 72.

[103] Reiss and Bordua, "Environment and Organization," p. 38.

attorneys, and courts.[104] Police frequently enter into such negotiations in order to obtain more control over outcome, but they are also distrustful about using subsequent outcomes as reflections of their own work rather than the work of other agencies. This distrust probably increases the tendency of police to utilize informal means of adjustment. Or, as Norval Morris and Gordon Hawkins put it, the police end up making far more judicial decisions than do the courts.[105]

In relation to the measurement of law-enforcement productivity, the separation of police effort from outcome has resulted in the elaboration by all major metropolitan departments of success measures that are manipulable, independent of prosecutorial and judicial decisions.[106] In some cases, such a trend can be seen as a ploy (however unconscious) by the police to avoid qualitative assessments about their work that should be made. For example, the decision to measure arrests per man hour rather than convictions per man hour may be partially based on the desire to avoid a reduction in productivity due to poor evidentiary standards observed by the police. However, it is overly cynical and unfair to the police to attribute this motivation as the sole reason for avoiding use of conviction data. Several police administrators can testify to the difficulty in obtaining appropriate court data. Court and prosecution accounting systems are often not capable of providing police feedback on a case-by-case basis.[107]

Units of Productivity Measurements

Just as there are several police functions that require independent productivity analysis, there are several techniques available by which to measure these functions. And added to the problem of choosing *what* measurements, is the clear indication that little of the appropriate data presently exists.[108] An additional problem in planning what measurements to utilize is the need to predict how the measurement might influence police behavior. For example, although some type of arrest measurement seems indispensable, the use of arrest data, particularly when applied to the productivity of individual officers, seems to encourage officers to make undesirable arrests.[109]

The most common measurement of police effectiveness, or ability to

104 Ibid.

105 Norval Morris and Gordon Hawkins, *The Honest Politician's Guide to Crime Control* (Chicago: University of Chicago Press, 1970).

106 Reiss and Bordua, "Environment and Organization," p. 36.

107 Murphy, "Police Accountability," pp. 40–41.

108 Hatry, "Wrestling with Police Crime Control," pp. 92–98.

109 Ibid., p. 112.

reduce crime, is probably the "clearance rate." Clearance rates are the proportion of offenses known to police that are cleared by an arrest or by other means established by the police (such as death, or refusal to prosecute). *The Uniform Crime Reports* present police clearance rates for the index offenses.[110] The overall clearance rate is 22.2 percent; however, this varies from a low of 14.8 percent for auto theft to a high of 76.9 percent for murder.[111] It is obvious that aggregation of rates across types of crime creates a confusing measurement of effectiveness. Police effectiveness, in this case, is heavily dependent on the seriousness of the crime, the willingness of victims or others to report crime, and the types of technologies available for the investigation of different types of crime.

Police behavior also influences reported rates. For example, Skolnick, in his excellent study of the police, found that "'cleared' merely means that the police believe they know who committed the offense, if they believe an offense has been committed."[112] Furthermore, Skolnick noted that there is wide discretion within police jurisdictions, and striking differences between jurisdictions, concerning how the police decide whether a reported event should actually be handled as a crime. For example, Skolnick discovered that in "Westville" a large proportion of burglary complaints were never recorded as crimes, but instead were listed in a separate file as "suspicious circumstances." Such circumstances were then turned over to the detectives who had the responsibility of determining whether such events actually contained all the elements of a crime or in fact were either inaccurate reports or events that, although troublesome to the "victim," did not actually constitute criminal offenses. Skolnick noted that detectives had wide latitude in making such decisions: not only could they include as offenses, reports of events in which information establishing the fact of a crime was incomplete, but also (and far more frequently) they could refuse to enter and count as a crime, events in which the reported information established a crime but the complainant was not believed or the officer felt the event was insignificant. Although such suspicious circumstances, according to departmental policy, were to receive continued investigation, in reality "suspicious circumstances" were always relegated to last priority by the detectives, who chose to concentrate on "actual crimes." Although there are sound legal and organizational reasons that police must screen reported events prior to classifying them as crimes, the relative freedom of decision making by the Westville investigators left ample opportunity for the police to manipulate their measures of production, rather than changing

---

[110] United States Department of Justice, *Uniform Crime Reports* (Washington, D.C.: Government Printing Office, 1974), p. 176.

[111] Ibid.

[112] Skolnick, *Justice Without Trial*, pp. 168–169.

the actual incidence of crimes. For example, burglaries are widely recognized as extremely difficult crimes to "clear," and consequently there is some organizational pressure to be stringent in classifying minor burglaries, or burglaries in which the evidence is cold or missing, as anything more than suspicious circumstances.[113]

If all police agencies acted in a similar fashion, the uniformity of the practice might make it less of a problem, but Skolnick notes that in a nearly contiguous city, almost every complaint is counted as a real offense.[114] Consequently, it becomes nearly impossible to compare the effectiveness of police in the two cities, or to compare actual incidence of crime, by using official statistics.

A second measurement of the "production" subsystem centers around changes in crime rates. If the rate (crimes per 100,000 people) increases, then it may suggest that the police are failing to "control" crime. If the rate decreases, then one might conclude that the police are functioning to prevent criminal behavior. However, crime rates are only part of the function of police activities. Decisions by the public to report offenses and many other factors may influence these data as much or more than police activities themselves do. Victimization studies have demonstrated that many offenses, even index offenses, are not reported to the police.[115]

Noncrime Productivity

Assessment of police productivity, to the extent that measurements such as clearance rates and crime rates are used, fails to consider other demands placed on the police by the public. For example, we noted earlier, that public requests to the police centered principally on service, and, secondly on order maintenance. It is difficult to assess an officer's performance beyond his arrest record, and consequently few attempts are made to evaluate officers by their performance in order maintenance or service activities. It is a rare department that follows up with citizens who have called on the police, to check the citizens' satisfaction with the manner in which the officer handled the situation. More typically, communities rely on citizens filing a complaint against individual officers if they feel mistreated, thus placing the burden of evaluation on the citizens.

For example, consider the general mission of peace-keeping, and the role of service activities that might contribute toward the attainment of "peace" within the community. Normally, police departments defined service as a necessary evil, but not really linked to the peace-keeping or

---

[113] Ibid., p. 172.

[114] Ibid., p. 178.

[115] United States Department of Justice, *L.E.A.A. Newsletter*, 3 (March 1974), 1.

control of crime functions. Consequently, little assessment is made of police performance in this area, and as long as a citizen does not complain, service activities do not contribute to the officer's performance record. Yet, it may well be that such activities make significant contributions to the public's willingness to report offenses or suspicious circumstances or serve as witnesses.

Order maintenance is another major goal of police agencies, but it also is not a frequent target of measured assessments. Analysis of how officers manage situations that do not result in arrest is rarely conducted. Does the entry of an officer into a family argument reduce the conflict or increase it? Do particular officers repetitively become involved in assaultive situations? Both of these situations could be evaluated to assess the productivity of the officers in their peace-keeping function. Unfortunately, most departments leave such questions uninvestigated, thereby ignoring one of the most important functions of the police officer.[116]

What is a good police officer? In effect, this is the question that we have been raising. At this time, it appears that the main theme centers on crime-control behaviors, especially arrests. However, only a relatively minor part of the police role is crime control in nature. A large share of an officer's time is spent in providing services to the community, although minimal evaluation is alloted to "service delivery." Again, the police have not decided on this crime-control emphasis independently of their environment. Frequent demands for service are likely to give way, in the party politics, to demands for safety. Data on apprehensions are by far the most politically effective data the police have at their disposal, and measurements of other types of productivity have been ignored in favor of political success.[117]

Another difficulty may be that noncrime outcomes are more ambiguous, and processes by which they are provided, harder to observe. Herman Goldstein has listed the following noncrime activities that might be measured: (1) provision of social services, (2) suppression of nuisances, (3) control of traffic, and (4) miscellaneous emergency calls[118] Some of these activities are easily counted; others are not. Those activities that are initiated directly between a patrolman and someone on the street are obviously more difficult to record than those in which a call to the police switchboard results in centralized monitoring of officer responses. But counting, of course, is not sufficient here, any more than it is in the case of arrests. Quality of arrests can probably be indicated in terms of the

---

[116] For an example where such measures were taken, see Hans Toch, J. Douglas Grant, and Raymond T. Galvin, *Agents of Change: A Study in Police Reform* (New York: Schenkman/Halsted, 1975).

[117] Murphy, "Police Accountability," p. 37.

[118] H. Goldstein, "Redefinition of the Police Function," p. 126.

number of arrests that survive the initial judicial hearing, or some other quality checkpoint. However, the quality of services to citizens is another matter. The police or municipal administrators should investigate the feasibility of periodic surveys of citizen satisfaction with police services. Such surveys might be attached to additional questions concerning victimization, if victimization surveys are regularly conducted in a jurisdiction. If not, interviews, or even telephone surveys of samples of people who called for assistance, might be substituted. The police will always have to resolve a question of trade-offs in such assessments. The more thorough and exacting the evaluation procedure, the more accurate and helpful the information is likely to be. But in most cases, increasing methodological precision will also cost more money. In any case, some attempt to apply the methodological standards of social science evaluations is likely to be of more help to policy making than the measures now used, such as numbers of citizen-initiated complaints.

Targets and Tactics

One guiding principle of operations research, but one frequently ignored in police administration, is that of linking the appropriate tactical procedure to each defined target or objective. This principle implies two problems: (1) identifying targets that are really representative of the missions of an organization, and (2) testing the alternate paths to each identified target. For example, Wilkins demonstrates that the tactics utilized to control delinquent gang behavior are often inappropriate to the defined police mission. If the issue at hand is reduction of violent *incidents* among juveniles in a particular area, removal of identified gang members from the area by arrest or by some other means is unlikely to be an effective tactic. If the social conditions in the area remain the same, removal of individuals is likely to result only in change of leadership or membership. The intervention in the lives of particular individuals is an appropriate tactic only when the target is change in *their lives,* and not if the target refers to control of an area. If incidence of crime in an area is the target, then sociophysical change in the environment is the appropriate crime-defensive maneuver.[119]

An extreme example of poor tactical thinking was exhibited by the Chicago police after the ghetto riots in 1966. At that time the police sought to justify the removal of weapons from ghetto residents by illegal searches as a good means of reducing the violence level of the riot.[120] Surely a ghetto resident who has lost a concealed weapon during a field

[119] Wilkins, *Social Deviance,* pp. 200–204.

[120] Wayland D. Pilcher, "The Law and Practice of Interrogation," *Journal of Criminal Law, Criminology, and Police Science,* 58 (1967), 490.

interrogation can and will replace the weapon in a matter of days (or hours). Further, the animosity created by the illegal search and confiscation program may kindle additional riots, or raise the violence level rather than reduce it.

Another problem in the improvement of productivity is the proper identification of the "level" of the target for which different tactics must be designed. It is a relatively straightforward problem, for example, to determine whether or not police vehicles are available for optimum lengths of time. It is quite another matter to determine whether the utilization of motorized patrol contributes to the effectiveness of the department.

At least six different levels of productivity measurement are possible, each one having separate measurement problems and each one relating to different levels of tactical thinking:

1. One can be concerned with the productivity of the individual police official.
2. One can be concerned with the productivity of different police units, such as the productivity of different shifts, different police districts, or different team-policing units.
3. One can be concerned with the productivity of types of units, such as patrol, detective, special, etc.
4. One can be concerned with the productivity of the entire department.
5. One can be concerned with productivity of units larger than the police department, such as the productivity of an entire "crime control system" of public and private efforts to control or reduce offenses.
6. One might be concerned with how the entire crime control network in a community combines with the total community criminal justice system.[121]

Hatry suggests that various interest groups will have a differential concern for these different activity levels. It is probably only within the department that there will be a great deal of concern for the productivity of the individual officer or the productivity of different units. External interest groups, in contrast, are more likely to be concerned with fluctuations in crime rates, or other indicators of how the police, as a department, are contributing to broader community or system goals.[122]

It is a fairly safe assumption that the person or group in question will respond most directly, or emphasize most heavily, those activities about which they are most closely watched and sanctioned. (For example, one would expect a student to place more effort in a course in his major, for which he needs a high grade, than he would in a course that he takes under a pass/fail option.) This being the case, it is also normal to expect

[121] Hatry, "Wrestling with Police Crime Control, p. 90.
[122] Ibid., pp. 90–91.

some conflict between the productivity evaluations conducted at a lower level and the impact of the behavior of the group being evaluated on targets important at a higher level.

For example, if evaluations of productivity on the level of the individual official stress arrests, the individual policeman is more likely to emphasize *arrests* than he is the quality of arrests, which may not be important until we reach the level of the total criminal justice system. Several attempts to correct this problem of interlevel conflict were conducted in the Oakland Police Department, Oakland, California. In one particular project, certain groups of officers were selected and trained to deal with family crisis intervention. According to the police involved, prior to the project, their two most important objectives when answering a family disturbance call were (1) to get out quickly and (2) to make an arrest. After the implementation of the crisis teams, the most important objectives were (1) talking through the problem with the family members and (2) making the most helpful referral to the relevant family-service agency.[123] In effect, the project succeeded in changing the evaluation criteria to which their tactics were directed. Rather than gear their behavior to either self or peer review (getting out quickly) or individual productivity reviews (number of arrests), the officers became concerned with targets defined external to the police department (satisfactory resolution for the family and increased linkage of professional agencies to people in need).

The above example is a good illustration of changing police tactical behavior by redefining or changing the target they were to reach. This type of change is highly necessary in police work, but relatively unlikely to occur until the internal police organization systematically opens itself to inspection or collaboration with outsiders (another aspect of the Oakland program). There are, however, a large number of tactical improvements that can be made without redefining targets and without redefining police boundaries. For example, the *traditional* stated objective of field interrogations was the potential of using the field contact information in later criminal investigations. One police department decided to study whether the characteristics of persons stopped for field interrogations bore any resemblance to the characteristics of persons convicted of crimes. The department found little resemblance: the proportion of blacks and poor people interrogated was far higher than the proportion of these groups convicted of crimes.[124] In other words, not only was the interrogation practice unlikely to achieve the target of gaining informa-

---

[123] Toch, Grant, and Galvin, *Agents of Change*, pp. 273–304, especially 293–296.

[124] Mark O. Morris, *Field Contact Report* (Oakland, Calif.: Oakland Police Department, 1974), p. 18. See also Bruce Terris, "The Police Role," *The Annals of the American Academy of Political and Social Science,* 374 (November 1967), 58–59.

tion about future offenders, but the practice was also likely to exacerbate community relations (or detract from other police objectives). Thus, without changing the target, a decision could be made to change the tactic.

Another relationship between targets and tactics that is important for police to consider deals with the level and complexity of the tactic itself rather than the target. Stated in general terms, operations researchers have frequently discovered that problems can be solved by making them more complex instead of simpler. For example, the Oakland police have a relatively high rate of arrest and conviction for statutory rape because they deal with statutory rape through a complex, interorganizational strategy rather than through the simple strategy of relying on "tips" or individual police reports. In Oakland, the department of public assistance reports to the police any requests for support by pregnant girls who are underage or by their families. This tactic is considerably more effective in enforcing the statutory rape law than lower level tactics utilized by other departments.[125] (Of course, it is another question altogether whether this particular tactic is a desirable one.)

The improvement of productivity in policing will require innovation—both in the nature of the target-defining process and in the nature of the tactical alternatives and measurements employed. Among the many innovations that have now been attempted are team policing, the community safety officer and police cadets, civilianization of many police office duties, specialty units in the booking process, family-crisis intervention, and police violence-reduction, legal screening of cases within the police department, and substitution of summonses or citations for arrests.[126] These and other innovations will create conflicts, and their success may be highly dependent on the ability of the innovators to coopt or negate resistance to change.

Although there may be many ways to deal with resistance to change, many successful innovations have one characteristic that many unsuccessful innovations lack: namely, the persons or groups who could prove most resistant are included in the planning and implementation of the project. For example, the Oakland project for reduction of police violence was designed and staffed by patrolmen with records of frequent violent encounters with citizens.[127] And the innovative studies of patrol productivity in Kansas City were the product of four patrolman-level task forces.[128] Similarly, one of the most effective ways of reducing officer

[125] Skolnick and Woodworth, "Bureaucracy, Information and Social Control," pp. 135–136.

[126] Grimes, "The Police, the Union, and the Productivity Imperative," pp. 80–83.

[127] Toch, Grant, and Galvin, *Agents of Change.*

[128] Grimes, "The Police, the Union, and the Productivity Imperative," p. 75.

resistance to innovation in production activity would be to include union leaders in productivity planning, or to have a union committee draft its own productivity-related demands such as career development, job enrichment, or new types of training.[129] Finally, inclusion of those who might resist is not limited to groups within the police department. Probably the most effective improvements in police-ghetto relations would be accomplished through small action programs and organizations in which both the police and indigents participated.[130]

Productivity and Specialization of Labor

One important aspect of any complex organization is the differentiation made within it in order to accomplish its goals. Some of the major specializations within organizations are both so prevalent and so important to the operation of these organizations that we have identified them as production, maintenance, and boundary subsystems. However, there are also specializations within any of these subsystems. The innovations for productivity improvement are all examples of different ways to organize personnel in order to accomplish production objectives.

Many of the principles still utilized for the division of labor in police are the same as those utilized by the first police commissioners in 1829. Originality has not been a trademark of police organization, and the resiliency of the traditional division of labor patterns in policing is now a major factor in the inability of the police to do their work effectively.

In the assignment of policing responsibilities, three principles of work division are usually used: (1) division by time of day (i.e., into shifts), (2) division by crime or type of service (i.e., into vice or homicide squads), and (3) division by area (i.e., into beats, precincts, and sectors). Division by time would seem necessary in order to provide 24-hour coverage. In small departments, where there may be insufficient personnel to man all shifts, patrol coverage at night may be provided by the state police or some other agency. In larger departments, the decisions as to how to organize coverage into different time periods may become a complex business. There may be problems, for example, in how to maintain coverage during changes in shifts. Or it may seem advisable to introduce overlapping shifts (or adding a fourth shift) to provide double coverage during peak traffic hours or high-crime periods. It may also be possible to decide on the manning of shifts depending on the nature of the crimes or the nature of the service calls generated during particular time periods. Division by type of service is again more complex in metro-

---

[129] Hamilton, "Police Productivity," p. 34.

[130] Chazen, "Participation of the Poor: Section 202(a)(3) Organizations under the Economic Opportunity Act of 1964," *Yale Law Journal* (1968), p. 628.

politan departments than in smaller municipalities. Typical divisions by service would include investigation, operations, and ancillary services. Operations may be further divided into traffic and patrol, and investigation by type of crime. In the largest departments, there will also be divisions into graphic areas, with time and service divisions provided within each of these geographic subdivisions.

In addition to divisions by time, area, and type of service, crime-related labor may be functionally divided. Most investigations are initiated by citizen calls, and usually the first police official on the scene of a crime is a patrolman. In the event of a crime that is not immediately solved, the patrolman's duties are usually limited to scanning the crime scene, noting and identifying all possible witnesses, and then awaiting the arrival of the detectives who will conduct the investigation.

In recent years some police departments have been experimenting with several different alternatives to the standard types of division of labor mentioned above, including different apportionments of management responsibilities. Some departments, for example, have tried four-day, ten-hour shifts rather than traditional five-day, eight-hour shifts. Others have sought to change the usual service or crime specializations. For example, many departments have merged traffic and patrol divisions into one "operations division." Others have reduced the number of investigation specialities. More importantly probably, many police departments are beginning to recognize new target areas, and are developing new specialty units to meet these objectives. Although the police probably have limited ability to alter geographical specialization, some new innovations have also appeared in this area. *Within* departments, basic district services may be supplemented by specialty teams that operate on a citywide basis; and *across* departments, there has been a recent move to regional policing, which either combines several smaller departments into one larger jurisdiction or abolishes small departments, the jurisdictions of which are then patrolled by one larger, nearby department.

Team policing probably deserves special note, as it addresses some problems with both geographic and functional specialization. Team policing gives total policing responsibility within a limited area to one team of officers. These officers not only would carry out all routine patrol, traffic, and service work within their area, but would also be responsible for the investigation of crimes, community relations programs, and many other police matters. In many ways, team policing can be seen as a managerial innovation as well as a new method of dividing police tasks because team policing decentralizes most middle-management decisions and places such decisions in the hands of the patrolmen who are most familiar with their territory.

With the exception of some of these more recent innovations, most police division of labor policies are both antiquated and frequently unrelated to the nature of the tasks policemen have to do. The average police organization clearly emphasizes crime related activities, even though most police products are not crime related. Also most police organization is relatively inflexible, although the police need to deal with a highly unpredictable and rapidly changing environment. In other words, some of the divisions of labor designed in order to get work done tend to militate against effective accomplishment. Many (but not all) of these problems may be understandable in light of police maintenance subsystem, which we will discuss next.

MAINTAINING THE INTERNAL SYSTEM

Banton has hypothesized that American police will develop stronger internal cohesion and solidarity than some other police departments because there is a high level of environmental pressure.[131] Other scholars state that police solidarity, although not a myth, is easily misunderstood. Rubenstein provides a lengthy and detailed report of frequent and intense internal conflicts and dissension, both between front-line patrolmen and managers and on an individual level.[132] Many aspects of police organizational maintenance patterns seem similar to those that are found among prison inmates and guards. There may be high levels of tension and dissention within organizational levels, but there is cohesion or consensus around particular rallying points—such as outside intervention. This final section of the chapter provides an analysis of some of the reasons for this counterculture characteristic, and relates these maintenance patterns to problems of boundary and production. The three aspects of the maintenance subsystem that we will concentrate on are (1) recruitment and training, (2) socialization, and (3) evaluation and sanctioning patterns.

Recruitment and Training

One of the most important determinants of patterns of predictability and stability in policing is the recruitment and training process. The more selective an organization can be, the more it can match its potential personnel to its objectives and goals. Although standards for police recruiting are both more articulated and more demanding now than they used to be, relative to other potential occupations, police work is now less attractive than it used to be. Police salaries and the prestige for police

---

[131] Banton, *The Policeman in the Community*, pp. 195–215; and see pp. 465–476 for discussion of boundary subsystem.

[132] Rubenstein, *City Police*.

work have not kept pace with either the remunerative or the social rewards available in the rapidly expanding field of human service.[133]

The low social status of police work as an occupation in the United States is a major difficulty with recruitment. Since police work is ranked as low as it is in the general American culture, most persons attracted to it are those whose other occupational possibilities are even lower on the status/economic scale.[134] Added to the difficulty of low self-esteem of policemen is the fact that the public respect for police work is also low.[135] Hence many police recruits face a difficult psychological situation, which doubtless influences their attitudes both toward the public and toward the police department. On the one hand, they have selected the most prestigious occupation realistically available to them, and yet they are aware that relative to other occupations, their job has low social prestige. Either these police must accept the proposition that they are presumably inferior to other persons who can obtain higher prestige jobs, or they must reject the validity of the general public rating of police work. The first option is likely to result in apathy on the job and alienation from the department. The second option is likely to result in isolation from the public and development of nonpublic status references (such as their peers), which in turn may justify rejection of the public values and objectives for policing.

Given the position of police work in the American job market, the pool of potential recruits is constricted to persons who place high value on policing and whose value system isolates them from other people.[136] A comparative study of values among police in East Lansing, Michigan, and among black and white males in the general population confirmed these propositions. One of the most telling findings involved police and nonpolice rankings of the value "equality." Whereas blacks ranked equality as the third most important value to themselves, and the white males ranked it twelfth, the police ranked it fourteenth.[137]

Another important result of the position of police work in the American occupational structure is the extreme homogeneity of the persons attracted to such work. According to William Vega, not only are certain classes of persons driven away from police work, but individuals who are likely to retain important commitments to nonpolice groups are either excluded, or, if recruited, are systematically pressured to change their

[133] McNamara, "Uncertainties in Police Work."

[134] Ibid., pp. 197–199.

[135] Ibid.

[136] Milton Rokeach, Martin G. Miller, and John A. Snyder, "The Value Gap Between Police and Policed," *Journal of Social Issues*, 27, No. 2 (1971), 155–171.

[137] Ibid., p. 162.

value orientations or leave policing.[138] The large majority of police recruits, then, will have a tendency to depend on other officers for social judgments about their work, and are *unlikely* to approach police tasks (particularly crime-related ones) in a disinterested, impersonal manner. Thus, both class and psychological factors encourage American police to stress a personal approach to punishment rather than to play the roles suggested by their legal authority and bureaucratic office.[139]

HOMOGENEITY OF RECRUITS AND POTENTIAL POLICE ROLES. A major dysfunction of recruit homogeneity for policing is the low potential for finding among these recruits a variety of skills, value orientation, and career aspirations. The multiple task of police production and the high variety and uncertainty of the environment would seem to require persons with the ability to play many roles and adapt quickly to many different situations. However, the similarities in police recruit social status, value, and experience will limit considerably the ability of departments to conceive and staff new specialty units or to make the police responsive to new or variable evaluation criteria (and targets) rather than traditional ones.[140] For instance, police recruits are very likely to have little previous supervisory experience. As a result, one would expect many policemen to have a low ability to clarify ambiguous and tense street situations to the many potential actors, and also to have low ability to explain to others what they expect of them.[141] These limitations in recruiting structure probably lend to the term *police professionalization* much of its peculiar and nontraditional meaning. Professionalism among police frequently means a reduction rather than an expansion in the types and numbers of tasks police perceive as part of their legitimate repertoire. Professionalism, particularly as enunciated by union leadership, seems a justification of narrowing the police role rather than enriching it, and narrowing their perceived problem-solving strategies rather than increasing them.[142]

Policing in some cultures, particularly in Scandanavia, is beginning to diverge widely from traditional notions of police training and organization. For example, there has been some experimentation with abolishing the police per se altogether, and substituting a public-service agency staff with "safety-welfare" generalists who would perform a wide variety of municipal services.[143] Such innovations are unlikely to work in the

---

[138] William Vega, "The Liberal Policeman: A Contradiction in Terms," *Issues in Criminology, 4,* No. 1 (Fall 1968), 15–33.

[139] McNamara, "Uncertainties in Police Work," p. 203.

[140] Ibid., pp. 199–202.

[141] Ibid., p. 202.

[142] Vega, "The Liberal Policeman," pp. 27–28; see also Bruce Terris, "The Role of the Police," *The Annals of the American Academy of Political and Social Science, 374* (November 1967), 58–59.

[143] Munro, *Administrative Behavior and Police Organization,* pp. 177–178.

United States under present recruiting conditions. Recognizing this problem, one police expert has gone so far as to suggest a police conscription, under which all persons of a certain age would owe their community two years of police service. A police draft, suggests Piliavin would probably provide for better training, more heterogeneous personnel, less self-selection into police work, and a large number of citizens who, as veterans of police service, could reduce considerably the distance between the police and the public.[144]

RECRUITMENT AND TRAINING DELIVERY. The fact that police organizations have limited ability to select personnel is not, by itself, a crippling factor. But, as in all such cases where selectivity power is low, the attention and energy devoted to training and socialization should be high. Not only should police receive *information* during training, there should also be careful attention given to the informal aspects of police work, to value orientations, and to increasing the skill range or behavioral alternatives available to police.[145] A variety of value- and skill-changing techniques are available and effective.[146]

Unfortunately, much police training is unimaginative and narrowly oriented. Even on the issue of law, McNamara found severe deficiencies in one of the best training academies. Most recruit training that he observed in New York City consisted of memorization of laws and memorization of different conditions and situations associated with different laws. McNamara found that few police recruits or patrolmen with two years experience could enunciate three *principles* of law or explain the legality of the police role.[147]

Cognizant of the above problems, an English police executive suggested a distinction between "academy education" and "academy training." Defining *education* as the dissemination of information, and *training* as practice in problem-solving skills and value experimentation, Elmes makes an eloquent (if unusual plea) for decreased emphasis on education and increased emphasis on training. The patrolman, he suggests, is in need of systematic training in how to categorize and gain knowledge and facility in local area culture and conditions—much more than in need of education about particular laws and their application.[148]

The difficulty with this approach is that it requires police administrators, politicians, and communities to acknowledge and affirm publicly that the police are only minimally involved in law-related situations and

---

[144] Irving Piliavin, "Police-Community Alienation: It's Structural Roots and a Proposed Remedy" in *Police-Community Relations*, pp. 589–603.

[145] Rokeach, Miller, and Snyder, "The Value Gap."

[146] See particularly, Toch, Grant, and Galvin, *Agents of Change.*

[147] McNamara, "Uncertainties in Police Work," p. 208.

[148] Elmes, "Education or Training?" pp. 55–63.

that their primary objectives should involve problem-solution techniques that provide alternatives to arrest (as well as to doing nothing!). The explicit admission of this situation was apparently one of the major factors in the success of the Oakland Violence Prevention Unit. Working in small groups on particular, well-defined projects, the VPU officers were able to sell both police administration and significant community groups on the primacy of noncriminal police objectives. Doing so, they were also able to identify and adopt new police performance criteria and formulate strategies by which to incorporate such targets and tactics with Oakland recruit training.[149]

TRAINING AND POLICE PRACTICE. One consequence of typical classroom/lecture/information-giving police training is the increased distance and conflict between training content and the nature of actual police operations. Many police administrators, and particularly the police academy officials, tend to ignore or actively avoid discussion of informal police practices that contradict (or at least do not follow) the legalistic and bureaucratic guidelines enunciated during training. Apparently, academy instructors do not wish to describe actual patrol behaviors, or to analyze the pressures that may lead to informal, on-the-street traditions, because the instructors do not want recruits to interpret such discussions as endorsements of these methods of policing.[150] However, this academy avoidance tends to have effects opposite to those intended. For example, recruits do not receive in their academy training officially sanctioned reasons to *avoid* the adoption of behavioral norms of experienced patrolmen, and therefore they are less likely to break with tradition. Moreover, the recruits are generally given no practice in dealing with the internal and external pressures that would provide possible alternatives to the "locker room" solutions to such pressures. Last, recruits are trained to value, if not revere, the experience of older policemen. As a result, standard academy practices usually increase rather than decrease the likelihood that new police will adopt traditional but informal role behaviors during their probationary period.[151]

Continuing Socialization

Although it would appear that most police values and attitudes are formed in prior socialization experiences, police organization tends to increase the manifestation of certain behavior patterns and orientations that, although potential among police recruits, become actualized through

---

[149] Toch, Grant, and Galvin, *Agents of Change.*
[150] McNamara, "Uncertainties in Police Work," p. 215.
[151] Ibid., pp. 210–215.

police work. If training does little to counteract or control recruit predispositions, the nature of organizational structure and work experience does much to bring them out.

SOCIALIZATION BY WORK ROLE. It is commonly believed that a man's world centers on his work and prescribes his view of the world around him. For example, a doctor enters his medical school to learn how to be a doctor, not just to practice medicine. "Being a doctor" involves learning more than how to remove appendices, diagnosing diseases, and writing prescriptions. It also involves learning how to relate to people, and what expectations are held by others about doctors. Included within this role conception lies the identification of oneself as a professional individual and how to maintain this professional dignity. The police role in our society, although not possessing the status of the doctor's role, is similar in that the police role is defined both by role incumbents and by the persons who interact with the police. As long as the way in which the officer defines his role and the definitions of others are congruent, things move rather smoothly. However, when the self-definition of the officer conflicts with the definitions of others, then the potential for difficulty increases. For example, Figure 9-1 looks at the police officer in his interaction network including his formal, as well as informal, relationships:

Figure 9-1.   Police Interaction Network

Informal		*Formal*
Wife	Police officer	Prosecuting attorney
Children		Courts-judges
Relatives		Offender
Other officers		Probation-parole officers
Members of public		Defense lawyers
		Other officers
		Members of public

It should be noted that the individual police officer interacts with others, some of whom are equals (such as other officers, relatives and friends), some higher in social status and power (such as prosecutors and judges), and some of whom are situationally, at least, inferior in status (such as offenders).

Skolnick argues that in the discharge of the police role, there has evolved a "working personality" of police that involves "distinctive cognitive and behavioral responses" to the environment.[152] It is not only the police role that has this working personality. In fact, the stereotype of university professors as absent-minded reflects the public's description of

[152] Jerome H. Skolnick, "Why the Police Behave the Way They Do," in Jerome Skolnick and T. C. Gray, eds., *Police in America* (Boston: Educational Association, 1975), p. 3.

a working personality. However, Skolnick's description of the police suggests peculiarities in their role that demand special focus. For example, the police are given an authority to carry out their responsibilities that allows and even demands that they command others. This authority based upon law distinguishes the police role from most other roles in society. It not only allows the officer to expect others to obey his lawful commands, but it demands that he do so.

The manner in which the policeman utilizes his authority is extremely important in his relationship with the ordinary citizen. His authority may be expressed by his directing of traffic, by his momentary detention of a person to question him about his identity and intentions, by his decision to arrest an individual and detain him, and finally (in rare situations) by his taking of a life.[153] Perhaps as significant as these situations in which authority is converted into coercive action are those situations in which authority remains on a symbolic level. An officer of the law is vested with an image of authority that carries over into any interaction in which he is involved.

The title of professional in our society is reserved for those occupations having a specialized body of knowledge obtained through education, a license to perform their work, and a code of ethics governing behavior in the profession. It is a term not often given to police officials because their skills are not obtained nor governed in a manner similar to the skills of doctors and lawyers. The police officer does attain an education, but it usually is acquired through working the streets, not in a professional school. Skolnick and Wilson recognized this difference and attached the label of "craftsmanship" to the police position.[154] In other words, the evaluative standards applied to good police work are generally those of other officers knowledgeable in the practice.[155]

"Craftsman" is an excellent description of the policeman. In the previous discussion, we have pointed out that the policeman is socially isolated from the public and there is a divergence between police notions of good police work and the public views of desirable police behavior. Thus, police interact with those who accept their self-definition—other officers. Furthermore, this interaction with other officers feeds the "craftsman" orientation and encourages its development.

The fact that police acquire most of their working knowledge on the street in apprenticeship positions also has implications for training and police supervision. Because academies rarely address the apprenticeship

---

[153] Nelson A. Watson and James W. Sterling, *Police and Their Opinions* (Washington, D.C.: International Chiefs of Police, 1969), p. 12.

[154] Skolnick, *Justice Without Trial*, pp. 231–35; and Wilson, *Varieties of Police Behavior*, p. 283.

[155] Skolnick, *Justice Without Trial*, p. 196.

role that the new policeman will assume during his probationary period, the kinds of knowledge that a policeman gains during the academy period are likely to contrast rather sharply with the techniques and attitudes he will assimilate when learning his craft on the street. And the heavy dependence of the probationer on his more experienced teacher (or craftsman) is likly to reinforce the speed and intensity with which the new police officer will pick up both the style and attitude of his older partner.

SOCIALIZATION AND PERCEPTION OF DANGER. The police are given authority to carry out the peace-keeping functions of society. In carrying out these responsibilities, an officer must exercise his authority to get people to live by the law and to arrest those that have violated the law. That people are less than enthusastic about being arrested goes without saying. The consequence of this is that the police are required to regulate others and in so doing often place themselves in positions of potentially great danger. Thus constantly present, but infrequently occurring, violence is a part of any law-enforcement position. This threat of violence is a second element of the working personality of police and reinforces the relations established through the work role as craftsman.[156]

Moreover, although many occupations are dangerous in our society, such as heavy construction, coal mining or fire fighting, few involve the threat of harm directly from others. Thus, the officer must regard citizens as potentially dangerous. In fact, some training of police officers presents film sequences in which officers must make decisions about whether they would draw their gun and if and when they would fire. Frequently, these scenes are designed to caution the officer that any, even the most innocent setting, can quickly change into a violent altercation. For example, a sequence may show a woman walking down the street with a baby carriage. Threatening? Probably not, but in one such scene the woman draws a gun from the carriage and fires at the officer. Obviously, such a scene does not indicate a likely occurrence; however, it could occur, and officers seeing such a scene are warned about not taking anything for granted, even a woman with a baby carriage. Similar scenes are presented when officers approach a car being stopped for a traffic citation in which, in some cases, very suspicious looking people are courteous, while innocent appearing people commit violent attacks upon the officer.

From 1965 through 1969, 336 law-enforcement officers were killed, whereas from 1970 through 1974, the comparable figure had increased to 611. This indicates a substantial increase in numbers, yet the risk of getting killed, for any particular officer, is small, when one considers the large number of law-enforcement officers who are daily involved in potentially dangerous circumstances.

[156] Ibid., p. 53.

The importance of these data lies not just in the fact that more officers are being killed in the line of duty than previously. The real importance lies in the impact on an individual officer's definition of his working environment. If officers become constantly fearful because of their perception of danger, they may be prone to react to situations in ways that stimulate violent reactions or hostility.[157]

A closer examination of the kinds of activities in which police were killed suggests some reasons why we might expect officers to become more concerned about tasks that commonly are defined as low-risk situations. During the five-year period from 1965–1969, only 13 officers were killed in "traffic pursuits and stops." In the subsequent five years (1970–1974), this figure escalated to 79 killings. The possible impact of this sizable increase is to increase officers' anxiety when involved in traffic situations. Moreover, under the categories of "ambush—entrapment and premeditation" and "ambush—unprovoked attack" there were increases of from 9 deaths in 1965–1970, to 31 deaths in 1970–1974, and from 5 in 1965–1969 to 31 in 1970–1974, respectively. The working environment has apparently become more dangerous in unpredictable times and situations.[158] It should also be pointed out that the number of citizens killed by officers has increased more steeply than the numbers of officers killed.[159]

The police role acknowledges that danger is expected from certain types of people and, in particular, in certain types of situations. Responding to burglaries or pursuing burglary suspects is "known" to be dangerous, and even more danger is involved when the offense is robbery. But it is the unexpected situation in which danger most frequently has violent results. The effect of the increased killing of officers and of the dramatic increases in violence in situations perceived as low risk may have serious implications for the police officer's confidence in his working environment. Perhaps, more importantly, his confidence in his ability to control dangerous situations is somewhat shaken by the apparent randomness of some of the killings. The consequence of danger and of its amplification because of recent increases in killings of police officers is to increase the officers' social distance from large sectors of the public since he sees all people as potentially threating.

The impact of the police perception of danger is broad and influences more aspects of their behavior than on-the-street situations. The belief that danger is ever present, and that the public cannot be relied on for help if it occurs, reinforces the interdependence of officers on each other.

---

[157] Hans Toch, *Violent Men* (Chicago: Aldine, 1969).

[158] Chambliss and Seidman, *Law, Order, and Power*, p. 275.

[159] Ibid., p. 275.

This close relation makes it less likely that policemen will criticize each other publicly, or side with the "prosecution" in inquiries about police misbehavior. Few police officers desire to risk making enemies with their peers in case their help is needed in emergency situations.

Danger has apparently influenced the thinking of police executives as well. Chief Baker of the Berkeley, California, police, devoted the major portion of his article on police options in riots to consideration of the types of weapons that can be utilized against rioters. He did not address the possibility that there may be options to physical suppression, or means to avoid riots or violent confrontations altogether.[160]

More importantly, the police carry over the existence of danger and use its existence as a justification of their actions in many situations that have little to do with danger.[161] For example, a major union charge against productivity innovations is the possibility that changes will reduce safety.[162] Perhaps the most dysfunctional aspect of the policeman's view of danger is the ability to invoke "danger" as a means of gaining police solidarity among officers who otherwise might be willing to innovate.

SOCIALIZATION AND SUPERVISION. Historically, the military style of leadership has been based on the notion that those promoted to positions of leadership are to "direct" the efforts of those under them. In a military-style organization, the discretion of the lower levels of the organization is usually minimal. However, the police officer works in a large geographic area and often must enforce rather vague notions of what is legal or illegal. He has therefore been given extensive freedom in carrying out his responsibilities.

As management of police agencies has recognized the difficulty of closely supervising and regulating the behavior of individual officers, it has attempted to adjust its management to the character of the patrolman's task. Etzioni has suggested that in professional organizations, authority over the primary tasks should remain with the professional handling the problem and that administrators should establish the means by which professionals can carry out their work. In other words, administrators hold authority over staff support-functions but should not dictate how a particular professional problem should be handled.[163] This is to some degree true of police organizations. Given the nature of the police-

[160] Bruce R. Baker, "Riots—What Are the Options," *The Police Journal*, 43, No. 8 (August 1970), 362–366.

[161] Banton, *The Policeman in the Community*, p. 114.

[162] Grimes, The Police, the Union, and the Productivity Imperative," pp. 72–73.

[163] Amitai Etzioni, *Modern Organizations* (Englewood Cliffs, N.J.: Prentice-Hall, 1964), p. 81.

man's task, the front-line officer must have discretion and the authority and skill to use it.[164]

As the management levels of police organizations have recognized the inevitability of patrol-level discretion, management has increasingly abandoned the military style of leadership and moved in the direction of giving greater organizational latitude to the officer. For example, the conception of "team policing" is an explicit attempt to break down the military bureaucracy of police organization, and to change supervision styles so that they are more compatible with the types of tasks that patrolmen must conduct.

One principal difficulty with the strict adherence to a militaristic bureaucracy is the cumbersome length of the formal choice of command, and with it, the difficulty of transmitting or receiving accurate information. A bureaucracy with a large hierarchy frequently has difficulty responding quickly to new environmental problems, and frequently is relatively isolated from its environment. The result, for police, is the reduced ability to achieve socially approved organizational goals.[165] Furthermore, the inflexibility of the organization and the great distance from information sources to decision centers encourage officers on the front line to look for informal means to gain some freedom from rules and regulations. For example, Rubenstein found that many Philadelphia patrolmen guarded their own information sources jealously, and would exchange important bits of information with their supervisors or detectives in exchange for some freedom from supervision, in much the same way as these officers would exchange the opportunity to arrest for some information from a suspect.[166]

The combination of environmental uncertainty, the craftsmanlike structure of the police role, and the inability of police executives to communicate accurately and quickly with the front line not only creates the conditions in which a police subculture can emerge but also produces conditions conducive to its reinforcement and survival.

SOCIALIZATION AND THE COMMUNITY.   The forces impinging on front-line police work do not produce the same kind of solidarity and teamwork that are often eulogized on television or in official police training bulletins. The police are isolated from outsiders, but they are also a highly competitive and distrustful lot.[167] Both selection and training, as well as on-the-job situations, create incongruities between police values and the

---

[164] George F. Cole, *The American System of Criminal Justice* (North Scituate, Mass.: Duxberry, 1975), p. 174.

[165] Munro, *Administrative Behavior and Police Organization,* pp. 76–77.

[166] Rubenstein, *City Police,* pp. 205–217.

[167] Ibid., pp. 438–439.

values of broader American culture.[168] Both police self-image and the police public image would have to change drastically before the police could be considered "as a part of the broad category of occupations which deal with people who are sometimes difficult to handle."[169] Considerably more attention must be given to the development and proper utilization of "gatekeepers" or "group bridgers" in police work. Not only do new types of links need to be formulated with various groups in the community, but gaps between management and front line need to be bridged as well. Experiments in Oakland, California; Kansas City, Missouri; and elsewhere suggest that the police themselves can perform such liaison roles. Other projects suggest that innovative uses of old contacts can be very productive in building linkages with the community. For example, Solomon Kobrin's description of the role of indigent street workers attached to delinquency prevention projects is very similar to the roles played by informants who link police to the underworld.[170] The difference is that newer roles are attached to community service rather than with criminal investigation targets.

Evaluation and Sanctioning Patterns

One of the most important aspects of the maintenance subsystem in any organization is the method utilized for evaluating member performance and rewarding or punishing members, in order that organizational expectations will be met. There are, of course, a great number of ways to evaluate performance, and there are usually a wide variety of sanctioning systems that organizations can adopt. It is typical, however, for organizations to display patterns of organizational control that are congruent with the organizational style in other aspects of its operation.

PUNITIVE BEHAVIOR. As we have seen above, most police operate with only a few vague statements regarding goals. Operational "goal" measures, then, are often arbitrary. Frequently officers are directed away from ill-stated objectives and toward actions which are only counted.[171] Anything better than this situation is unlikely until the police can develop an organizational climate that is conducive to self-examination and open debate.[172] Fostering this set of problems, however, "is the tendency of the

---

[168] Rokeach, Miller, and Snyder, "The Value Gap," pp. 168–169.

[169] Terris, "The Role of the Police," pp. 67–68.

[170] Solomon Kobrin, "The Chicago Area Project—A 25 Year Assessment," *The Annals of the American Academy of Political and Social Science*, 322 (March 1959), 20–29.

[171] Munro, "Administrative Behavior and Police Organization," pp. 119–120.

[172] Michael Banton, "Authority and Police Science," *The Police Journal*, 43, No. 8 (August 1970), 370–375.

department to consider ineffective performance as willful negligence rather than as a technical or judgmental problem."[173] This tendency of some organizations has been labeled "punitive bureaucracy" by Gouldner.[174] Such organizations are characterized by supervisory attempts to punish rather than correct or educate, and to utilize the facts of an event to prove divergence from regulations rather than to analyze the situation so that ineffective behavior can be avoided in the future.

> Thus, supervisors function analogously to judges in that they attempt to match up a patrolman's actions with departmental rules rather than with the consequences anticipated by the patrolman at the time of [patrolmen's] performance. This legalistic orientation influences some supervisors to stress the violation of rules even when the rules . . . lead to ineffective job performance.[175]

The results of such an evaluation pattern are usually detrimental to the organization. For example, personnel are unlikely to relay information about negative outcomes for fear of punishment. And many personnel discover that the safest route is the one of least activity. Finally, because such an orientation assumes that the actors know the *correct* way to behave, little attention is given to analysis of events and planning for future situations.

DEPARTMENTAL POLITICS.   When the police are separated from community morality (or when there are too many community moralities to choose from), the major control of police behavior must come from within the department.[176] Unfortunately, many police control mechanisms are little more than efforts to place blame (and in that respect, quite similar to the notion of "solving" a crime by making an arrest!). When the blame is hard to place, a typical ploy is to suggest conspiracy, as one frustrated police chief seems to express in relation to riots:

> This is the fundamental tragedy in the police service today; it has been given a task for which it was never intended, and yet one that no other group or organization is prepared to assume.[177]

---

[173] McNamara, "Uncertainties in Police Work," p. 185; see also the court cases between the internal investigation units' treatment of police misbehavior and the more educative approach to the police review panels established in the Violence Prevention Unit, in Toch, Grant and Galvin, *Agents of Change.*

[174] Alvin W. Gouldner, *Patterns of Industrial Bureaucracy* (New York: Free Press, 1964).

[175] McNamara, "Uncertainties in Police Work," pp. 184–185.

[176] Banton, *The Policeman in the Community,* pp. 168–169.

[177] Baker, "Riots—What Are the Options?" p. 362. It seems strange that Baker is oblivious to the emergence of police as a middle-class solution to nineteenth-century riots in London and in several American cities; see Silver, "The Demand for Order."

Given the police executives' penchant for avoiding blame and assuming safe responsibilities, it is not surprising to find lower-level officials jealous of formally or informally obtained prerogatives or domains (such as a lieutenant's jealousy with a subordinate "going over his head," or a patrolman's jealousy of his own territory). The culmination of internal police politics is the inability to form true cooperative efforts. Although much of the punitive, defensive nature of internal politics may be the result of external forces, ironically the result of the defensive reactions is an inbuilt incompetence to meet external challenges.

There are, of course, increasing exceptions to these traditional patterns. In Kalamazoo, Michigan, for example, four three-day retreats of sergeants and patrolmen culminated in recommendations adopted as policy changes by the chief. When middle management grew defensive that they were being bypassed, new sessions were set up with them, and the policy review and reformulation continued.[178] In Dayton, Ohio, new police policies were introduced after the formation of the Citizen/Police Policy-Making Project. Front-line patrolmen met with citizens' groups with which there was high police contact in an effort to bring persons usually excluded into the policy formulation arena.[179] As with other types of police innovation, such projects are characterized by shifts in both internal and external boundaries, and by changes in the sanctioning patterns toward reward and away from punishment.

SANCTIONS AND COMMUNITY POLITICS. Many studies have shown that morale, job satisfaction, and other variables important to internal control are affected as much by external factors, such as the status of the occupation, as they are by internal managerial design. No matter how well run the organization, or how professional the police management, police morale and police desire to behave in a socially desirable fashion will be largely dependent on things that police managers cannot directly control.[180]

The kind of policing found in a community will reflect the basic values and priorities of that community.

> If the majority community is more interested in order than liberty, more interested in property than human beings, more interested in community security than personal freedom, more interested in entertainment than in injustices, that community surely is inviting the police state.[181]

One survey of public attitudes toward crime found that 60 percent of the people interviewed favored repressive measures as the best way to deal

---

[178] Grimes, "The Police, the Union, and the Productivity Imperative," p. 76.
[179] Ibid.
[180] Wilson, "Police Morale, Reform, and Citizen Respect," pp. 155–156.
[181] Germann, "Developing Mission of the American Police," p. 99.

with crime, whereas 40 percent favored ameliorative, preventive strategies.[182] The police, then, are not alone in a narrow and conflictual approach to social problems.

Why then the severe criticism of the police from many quarters, and why the firm belief by many police that there is low respect for their authority? Banton provides a complex answer, arguing that the authority of the police has increased not diminished. But the public has also increased its demands that the police behave authoritatively, rather than relying on force or power. The trend toward rational-bureaucratic organization has meant that the exercise of power can and should be questioned. In order to increase their authority, the police need both exposure to criticism and the opportunity to explain their policies publicly.[183]

In other words, the police may be able to gain some control of their environment (and greater internal control) to the extent that they are willing to appear less certain, less rule-bound, and more sensitive to the social conflicts that they either create or must help to control. Becoming less defensive and negotiating openly with the public, however, are not going to be easy tasks.

The fact that the police can no longer take for granted that non-criminal citizens are also non-hostile citizens may be the most important problem which even the technically proficient department must face.[184]

Learning to engage hostile but noncriminal adversaries in productive debate may be one of the most difficult tasks that the police must learn to face. Up to now the police have faced the community using their duty to uphold the law as a crutch. Intent on crime-related duties and safety of the community, the police could excuse themselves from many of the finer points of community interaction. Although enforcing the law will always have its place among police responsibilities, it would seem that for the police to become more productive and more resourceful in community exchange, new service targets must be developed and new evaluation criteria articulated that encourage noncriminal solutions to a wide variety of social problems.[185]

---

182 Jennie McIntyre "Public Attitudes Toward Crime and Law Enforcement," *Annals of the American Academy of Political and Social Science, 374* (November 1967), 41–42.

183 Michael Banton, "Authority in the Mass Society," *The Police Journal, 43,* No. 7 (July 1970), 312–323.

184 Wilson, "Police Morale, Reform, and Citizen Respect," p. 158.

185 H. Goldstein, "Redefinition of the Police Function," p. 130.

chapter 10

An Organizational Model

of the Criminal Courts

The analysis of the criminal justice organization as a system is just beginning. In its infancy, several glaring theoretical deficiencies seem to have been accepted and have become the basis of considerable sociological and legal argument. This chapter deals with sorting out the behavioral patterns observable in a criminal court system into related categories or subsystems that have a theoretical logic. It is suggested that a systematic use of this organizational model may lead to improved court management or to greater understanding of all the complex activities that converge in the processing of defendants from charging through sentencing.[1]

That offenders do progress from intake to output in any particular criminal court and that officials within and among agencies cooperate sufficiently to make this occur a considerable number of times are simple empirical evidence that there is a court system that functions at *some* level of effectiveness with *some* amount of efficiency. The criminal court system may be considered a system in the technical sense if it has the

---

[1] Daniel Katz and Robert Kahn, *Social Psychology of Organizations* (New York: Wiley, 1966), p. 30; on a more general systems level, see Al Angyal, "A Logic of Systems," in F. E. Emery, ed., *Systems Thinking* (Baltimore: Penguin, 1969), pp. 17–29.

basic characteristics displayed by other systems. The central criteria for this decision would be (1) that the components of the court process are set up in such a manner that input, throughput, and output create identifiable pressures coordinating the several organizations; (2) that this coordination is institutionalized through a set of roles, norms, and values common to the entire system; (3) that there are additional mechanisms that relate the system to its environment; and (4) that there is a managerial superstructure coordinating all three of the above.[2]

The criminal court system fulfills these prerequisites, although the ambiguity (or ambivalence) about the purpose of the court system in relation to the larger social system leaves some doubt as to whether the system is merely inefficient or whether it serves multiple functions.

An advantage of open system theory is apparent in the treatment of such ambiguities. Although it may be uncertain as to where to locate the criminal court system in the social system, it is possible to study the internal production of the system in relation to other organizational processes independently of how this production serves society.

This approach should not be mistaken as a purposeful avoidance of the study of system-environment exchange. Rather it is a practical suggestion that the relationships between any system and its environment are better studied empirically. System-environment exchange is generally carried on, in complex organizations, at a level that strains the techniques of social sciences. Thus, one of the best indicators of the significance of a system for society is the study of relationships and operations internal to the system. In the criminal court system, for example, it may be fruitful to consider system values and system structure as they are important to the system itself, rather than conclude that these internal variables are completely controlled by the desires that society or some segment of society holds for the court.[3]

THE SYSTEM OF JUDICIAL ORGANIZATION

Organizations can be found in varying sizes, shapes, and types. The fact that, whatever their differences, they all may be classified as organizations is simplistic but important. All organizations have similarities as well as differences, and selecting the similarities and differences most helpful for our understanding is critical. The theory of the Aryan race, for example, was the inspiration of a madman, although his manipulations of national loyalties and national despair demonstrated the genius of the

[2] Katz and Kahn, *Social Psychology of Organizations.*

[3] For a good analysis of types of organizational goals, see David Street, Robert Vinter, and Charles Perrow, *Organization for Treatment* (New York: Free Press, 1966), pp. 20–21.

insane. Research about the criminal court system may make an error of the former type by classifying all courts together, and may lose the effectiveness of the latter by ignoring similarities between judicial organization and police or correctional organization. The study of judicial organization may begin by locating the organizational behaviors in the court that are common to all social organizations.

Functions of Judicial Organization

As the criminal justice system may be classified as a system if it performs three key system functions, so may the court be treated as a system if it does the same. These three subsystems or functions are: (1) the *production subsystem* that transforms input into output; (2) the *maintenance subsystem* that reduces variability of organizational participants and hence orders the structure for production activity; and (3) the *environmental subsystems* that act upon organizational *boundaries* to (a) increase or improve input, (b) facilitate disposal of output, (c) change organizational or product image for increased effectiveness, or (d) adapt internal structure or throughput to changes in the environment. There must also be a set of managerial activities that intersects and integrates all of the above functions.

THE PRODUCTION SUBSYSTEM.   Whether the throughput is considered as a series of individual defendants or as the manipulation of symbols attached to them, the judicial production subsystem is concerned *only* with transforming input X (say, defendant Jones) into output Y (say, convict Jones). As a productive subsystem, *it is not and cannot be concerned with acquiting inmate Jones.* This may happen, but it signifies a failure in input selection; the production subsystem does not transform unsatisfactory input X into output Y, but into $\bar{X}$, which is rejected.

The courts of the production subsystem are concerned with preliminary appearance, arraignment, trial or reception of guilty plea, and sentencing. In other words, production courts perform operations on a defendant until, as an output, he is transferred to the correctional or probation organization.

The task requirements of transferring defendants from charge to sentence largely dictates the production structure.

The production systems of organizations develop a *dynamic of technical proficiency.* The force field is generated by task requirements, and the ideology is directed toward task accomplishment. The concentration upon getting the task done has the consequences of developing standards of skill and method.[4]

---

[4] Katz and Kahn, *Social Psychology of Organizations,* p. 87.

A typical standard of proficiency is the speed with which a product of a certain quality may be turned out. Criteria of quality, however, may be low in the court system since there is not much competition for the product, which remains internal to the criminal justice system. However, human organizations essentially differ from manufacturing enterprises in that the throughput is human and reactive, and hence gaining agreement of the defendant in the throughput stages is essential to delivering the defendant as output to a correctional agency.[5]

Speed of production is therefore limited in part by the defendant's reaction to his anticipated status as a sentenced convict. Part of the defendant's reaction is prescribed by his previous roles vis-à-vis governmental organizations, by the norms of the organization or social group to which he belonged, and by the values placed on (1) his being treated as a product, and (2) his previous status opposed to his convict status. Because of factors of subculture and social structure, lower-class, poor, black defendants, for example, are more role-ready for both defendant and convict roles than upper-class, rich whites. The productive process will also be lengthened or shortened in correlation to the defendant's objections. He will be classified as output, that is, as a sentenced convict, when (1) he takes on the role, waives a lawyer and pleads guilty; or (2) when the organization demonstrates to him in a trial that (a) it was correct to treat him as producible, (b) his own perception of his previous role and status were incorrect, and (c) he has been divested of his previous status and it is no longer a drawback to taking on a convict status. Naturally, speed of production will change not only from defendant A to defendant B, but also as A is perceived or perceives himself differently.

At the present time, lower-class, poor blacks are becoming less role-ready because their prearrest status is changing. As the concept of pre-arrest status changes, the system has changed its structure by the introduction and greater use of lawyers by whom it is clarified that it is not poverty or race-related roles that make court throughput legitimate, but roles of illegality. And as the popularization of behavioral science studies continues (particularly those studies that advance systems perspectives in various social groups), it will be increasingly difficult to find role-ready defendants, because the social structure of the court environment will be seen as influenced by the boundary subsystems of the court and police processes. As this process occurs, people will complain that the court's use of status designations is not legitimate because these designations are not universally applied at intake—or even further, that the court production process, which is undesirable to the defendant, has actually been

---

[5] See Ibid., pp. 115–117; and Erving Goffman, *Asylums* (Garden City, N.Y.: Doubleday, 1961), p. 17.

performed elsewhere in the social system and not in the proper institutionalized manner. In other words, people will complain that conviction is related to poverty or race rather than to guilt.[6]

The court productive process has been divided into a number of key roles by which the throughput task is achieved. The driving force in the production line is the prosecutor, whose job it is to demonstrate that each unit of input has reached a certain level of acceptability in the court system. His task is structured by the judge, who has the job of enforcing production standards. Defense counsel acts as a quality control device, providing continuing feedback during the throughput phase. The court clerk, the judge, or the court manager schedules the throughput progression by manipulation of the court calendar, announcing the time at which various demonstrations of acceptability will be made. The probation staff, at least in cases of major production units (felons), files a report of final output measure, by which the judge makes conclusions about most likely export or output agencies.

Although this description is, of course, a vast oversimplification, it is probably a more accurate model of production operation than one that looks at defense and prosecution as an adversary model, or does not consider defense counsel as a member of the system or the defendant as a participant in the process. The typical legal arguments, generally revolving around due process, that speak for or against greater defense and defendant participation in the system are debates on a different order. Their general aim is that the defendant has not participated in the *proper way*. As such, these discussions largely involve system change rather than system production.

Criticisms more appropriately discussed in terms of the production subsystem as it stands involve consequences of present production standardization techniques.

> Emphasis on the legalities of organizational control tends in practice to mean that the minimal acceptable standard for quantity and quality of performance becomes the maximal standard. . . . [I]ndividuals may be motivated to exceed the norm for various rewards but not for the satisfaction of properly meeting the rules.[7]

The court production system is heavily dependent on rule enforcement for the motivation of workers. Hence, defendants as a whole will move no faster through the system than the law demands, and decisions about particular defendants will be done only as quickly as the law allows. The result of this form of motivation is paradoxical to the defendant or external critics but makes logical sense within the context of the normative

---

[6] For example, George Jackson, *Soledad Brother* (New York: Bantam Books, 1970).

[7] Katz and Kahn, *Social Psychology of Organizations*, p. 347.

environment of the production system. A defendant may spend considerable time within the throughput process, during which *no* decisions are made about him, whereas the more visible throughput operations will be made with insensitive rapidity. Otherwise stated, the defendant may spend a long time in jail and then have a very rapid guilty-plea hearing. Although, to the defendant, this process may seem unjust because the result to him is generally undesirable, his "warehouse" time in jail is to system operatives very important to output preparations. During the long periods of waiting, the system forces may continually work on the defendant's objection to role performance: (1) by disconnecting him from previous nonsystem roles, (2) by gradually demonstrating that whatever variances differentiated him from other defendants at input have been corrected, and (3) by rewarding him for acceptable role performance with increased horizontal mobility (by moving him rapidly from jail to prison or probation status).

The rule-dominated production standards tend to make officials satisfied with their own performance when they have managed to make the defendant say yes or no at the appropriate times. Feedback about negative consequences of this procedure is limited spacially and temporally from the points of performance. The quality of final criminal justice system output is *usually* attributed to the correctional process rather than to the court process, and correctional officials have not formulated their own input specifications in such a way as to affect the court throughput very greatly. Rather, the correctional system has usually accommodated its own structure to whatever referrals are sent to it by the courts.[8]

Alternative types of motivation for officials' role performance are possible but generally have not been attempted. Monetary rewards for more than minimally acceptable performance are difficult to institute since they would be dependent on taxes, and taxes are dependent on the change of community perception about the importance of system improvement. Value-oriented rewards are largely dominated by various professional organizations, such as bar associations, which are external to the system and the main concerns of which are often *tangential* to the task-related problems of criminal court officials.

THE MAINTENANCE SUBSYSTEM. The maintenance subsystem of an organization is a secondary structure responsible for maintenance of the work structure. This subsystem integrates the needs of organizational members and the demands of the task. The maintenance structure is

---

[8] For example, preconviction jail time is subtracted from prison time. Except in limited cases, such as substituting army service or participation in a welfare program for prosecution, alternatives to a full court processing in view of final output predictions are forbidden.

traditionally conservative in ongoing organizations; it resists changes in the status quo. It does so by institutionalizing activity patterns between organizational members, by creating and distributing system rewards, and by socializing new members into the present organizational state.

The maintenance process is strong in the court system, although its concrete structure is usually less differentiated than in police and correctional organizations. Many court offices are elective rather than competitive, so that the system does not have a strong personnel department that selects new personnel compatible with the status quo. The system must to a degree depend on political parties and law schools to preselect system personnel. Political party selectivity is probably compatible with system needs because successful candidates are typically "practical" rather than "idealistic," or more accurately, they are skilled in the manipulation of values for practical purposes. On the other hand, the selectivity function of law schools is somewhat negative because the law school generally serves to weed out from potential criminal court system applicants, persons who will respond to monetary and value rewards and people who are innovative in their view of the law.

These semiexternal selection patterns may be effective, but they are still outside system control. Consequently, the system must spend considerably more time with socializing their members than police and correctional organizations do. The maintenance structure must work rather strongly and visibly to reduce behavior variations among its personnel.

A first step in this direction is a reduction in official perception of defendant variability. Judge, prosecutor, and defense counsel interactions must be rather standardized, regardless of differences in product units visible to outsiders. A great deal of this perception of variability is controlled by rules of court procedure. With minor variations, all criminals are prosecuted in the same way, through the same decision points.

A second step is the reduction of the time differential in various officials' contacts with defendants. This aids stereotypification. Hence, defense attorneys' time with the majority of clients (poor and uneducated) has been reduced by interpretations of the Fourteenth, Fifth, and Sixth Amendments that fragment and formalize attorney-defendant contact. The alternative of increasing prosecutor time with each defendant has not until recently been explored. This method, however, may be illogical since uniformity of perception seems better guaranteed by uniformity through speed rather than by uniformity through increased care.

A third step is the reduction of time that officials must be in contact with each other. Defense-prosecutor-judge interactions have much less chance of elaboration and diversity under rules of guilty-plea structure rather than rules of trial structure. There is much more variance in trial time than in guilty-plea time; and, to the degree that official interactions are stabilized on predictions of output results, the guilty plea does away with uncertainty factors introduced with the jury.

A fourth step in the maintenance of the stability is the demonstration to all members of the organization that the most available rewards for performance are uniform and systemic rather than individual or valuative. Personnel are rewarded for their mutual cooperation and are harassed for argumentation. Some evidence of conflict with police and correctional agencies probably originates in the maintenance subsystem in terms of the availability of rewards. For example, some personal satisfactions that defense or judges or prosecutors might anticipate by treating defendants in a more personalized and careful manner may be negated by the insistence that police and correctional treatments of defendants nullify whatever beneficial effect court officials might have had on defendants. Court complaints (about other agencies) that originate in this fashion should not necessarily be used as evidence that courts and police and correctional agencies have a great deal of conflict, since many of these complaints are directed inwardly at different court staff rather than at the other agencies. The complaints, indeed, may be so structured that officials will perceive present patterns of police or correctional behavior as unchangeable. Hence, there is little chance that court officials will disagree with each other about the processing of offenders.

The conclusion—somewhat radical, but logical, from a systems perspective—is that the much maligned guilty-plea operation is more necessary to system maintenance (to the predictable and stable interaction of officials) than to the court production process.

BOUNDARY AND ADAPTIVE SUBSYSTEMS.   Boundary structures are located at the perimeter of the organization and are concerned with procurement and disposal for the production subsystem or with obtaining social support for the system as a whole.[9]

Procurement activity is rather well developed in the court system. There are a series of steps and a number of roles designed to obtain for prosecution those persons most likely to complete the production process successfully, and who will give officials the least cause to disagree with each other. At least in some cases, court procurement extends deeply into the police organization. Defense counsel,[10] the magistrate (or his coun-

---

[9] Boundary and adaptive activities are treated as separate subsystems by Katz and Kahn, *Social Psychology of Organizations,* and as divisions of "adjustment to environment" by Chris Argyris, *Integrating the Individual and the Organization* (John Wiley, 1964). These activities are treated together here since both involve an outward environmental perspective, and both take place in the same location.

[10] Particularly at lineup, see U.S. v. Wade, 388 U.S. 219 (1967); and Gilbert v. California, 388 U.S. 263 (1967). At interrogation, see Escobedo v. Illinois, 378 U.S. 478 (1964); and Miranda v. Arizona, 384 U.S. 436 (1966).

terpart),[11] and the prosecutor[12] all have important roles in regulating police activity so that the actual court process is shorter and more predictable. This is done by ensuring that (1) police work standards are compatible with court production standards or (2) the defendant will cooperate regardless of what has actually happened to him by making it appear that objections are futile and standards have been observed.

Where the police object to the thrust of this boundary activity, the court has attempted cooptation by allowing the police to take on some of the court system activity, such as giving the "*Miranda* warning." Whatever the effectiveness of this accommodation upon production standards, under rule-enforcement motivation mechanisms it seems to satisfy both police and court officials: they have all complied with the law.

Disposal activity is less well developed, largely because the throughput process has divested the suspects of their input differences, and disposal alternatives have, until this date, appeared limited. Much of this activity is mechanical, or is even taken on by county or state correctional agencies. The courts have not, until recently, seen the correctional system as open to influence as they have the police organizations. This lack of concern for corrections by the court is interesting in light of the strong procurement activity in the police area of the justice system. Although court extension into other agencies is obviously possible, this activity has seemed organizationally unnecessary. This situation may change as the correctional system and court system are seen to interrelate, or as inmates increasingly perceive themselves as participants in the system and entitled to system "citizenship."

Inmate demand for court attention has in part spurred on and in part followed the increase in the "institutional activity" of the boundary subsystems. In most organizations the institutional activity is carried out at the top of the structure by the warden, the board of directors, the trustees, or the Supreme Court. It is through this activity that the organization obtains social support and legitimation by manipulation of environmental forces. To a considerable extent, appellate activity, at any level, is institutionally oriented. The court organization benefits from the pomp and circumstance of judicial ceremony, from the formality of the opinion handed down, and so on, on an intersystem level. It is in this manner that the court system relates to the public, to other parts of government, and to persons and organizations not involved directly with

---

[11] In the federal system the defendant is taken immediately to a magistrate; see McNabb v. U.S., 318 U.S. 332 (1943; and Mallory v. U.S., 354 U.S. 449 (1957). For issuing warrants (probable cause), see Aguilar v. Texas, 378 U.S. 108 (1964); and Spinelli v. U.S., 394 U.S. *410* (1969); for scope of search, see Chimel v. California, 395 U.S. 752 (1968).

[12] See Frank Remington et al., *Criminal Justice Administration* (Chicago: Bobbs-Merrill, 1968), pp. 413–416.

the system. People are called upon to respect the law and the courts. This plea to potential defendants is particularly important, for it is largely in this symbolic manner that the system attempts to convince its lower participants that on some high level, at any rate, felt wrongs are righted, and that there is indeed one absolute distinction between justice and injustice.

Given that the court maintenance structure is as strong as it is and management of production is weak, successful environmental relationships are largely dependent on this institutional image building, rather than on sound management or research. However, long-run organizational dependence on this subsystem may have dangerous consequences. If this type of system-environmental interaction is to be beneficial to the organization, the boundary spokesmen (1) must have an accurate picture of the environment, (2) must understand what messages from the system will effectively cancel attack on the system, and (3) must receive limited contradiction from other parts of the system. It is becoming more and more evident that these three qualifications are lacking. The environment has become so complex that the Supreme Court or any other appellate court cannot know accurately what the environment is like, without much more research than is carried out now.[13] Also, problems in the lower and trial courts (e.g., in the production subsystem) are sufficiently great at this juncture that other system officials are quite ready to contradict the idealistic messages of the institutional spokesman rather than hide behind the public statements of their superiors. (Thus a district attorney or a well-known trial judge might openly criticize a Supreme Court ruling and suggest that the public should react negatively to it, thus reducing the institutional strength of the court system.)

Lack of effectiveness in institutional activity is a good indicator of deficiencies in the adaptive subsystems. It is through the adaptive enterprise of research, planning, and organizational development that an organization may change its structure so as to better cope with a changing environment. Until recently, adaptive activity in the court system has been almost nonexistent. Most significant recommendations for change are academic and originate with academicians.[14] Many other studies of the court system may bring to light valid criticisms of present operations but seem ineffective as impetus for change.[15] Difficulties in change initia-

---

[13] Shirley Terryberry, "The Evolution of Organizational Environments," *Administrative Science Quarterly, 12*, No. 4 (March 1968), 590–613.

[14] I.e., Joel Handler, "The Juvenile Court and the Adversary System: Problems of Function and Form," *Wisconsin Law Review,* 7 (1965); Abraham Goldstein, "The State and the Accused: Balance of Advantage in Criminal Procedure," *Yale Law Journal, 69* (1960), 1149; and Jerome Skolnick, *Justice Without Trial* (New York: Wiley, 1969).

[15] Samuel Dash, "Cracks in the Foundation of Criminal Justice," *Illinois Law Review, 46* (1951), 385.

tive are multifold, major ones being (1) implicit acceptance of the present adversary structure; (2) lack of insight into organizational structure, with a preponderant emphasis on the production activity; (3) lack of consensus on the goals of the system or ignorance of the relation of goals and operations; and (4) lack of a system-based forum in which to air disagreements and plan change. However, as we saw in Chapter Four, modern court management and information systems are emerging and may address these problems.

Management of the Subsystems

The managerial system coordinates the subsystems of organization, exercises control of hierarchical disputes, and coordinates external and organization requirements. The management system is the decision center of the organization and usually delegates responsibility downward and outward in inverse relation to the structural implications of any decisions that have to be made. The less impact a decision is likely to have upon organizational structure, the more likely it is to be delegated. Thus, as an organization gains complexity, production and maintenance substructures are the first to gain semiautonomy from higher management, and institutional and adaptive structures are the last. In the court system, the highest managerial decisions are made by high court judiciary, where the judge is virtually isolated from the court production process and the operations of maintenance.[16]

Adaptive functions are still largely within the realm of the judicial manager, and his use of poor and insufficient data in adaptive decisions is evident. Most such managers have risen from offices in the production line. Lack of innovation in court structure may largely be attributed to the presence of proficiency—stability-minded men in policy-making positions. The drive for change, which in organizations with well-developed adaptive structures acts as a necessary counterforce to the proficiency and stability dynamics, is, therefore, muted in the court system.

The basic conservatism of judicial management cannot, of course, be divorced from the function of the court system in the social system. Whether its function is one of maintaining order (political subsystem) or one of education (maintenance subsystem), the court system as a whole has acted basically as a repository of precedent and an evocator of tradition. If some decisions of the Warren Court had adaptive overtones, they were made only at a point necessary to the preservation of order, as

---

[16] The radical conclusion of one judge's treatment of guilty-plea mechanics is interesting for its sweep and scope. Obvious is his concern as a manager for court environment. See special concurrence of Judge Levin, in People v. Byrd, 162 N.W. 2nd 777 (1968).

major reaffirmation of American ideals. In this context it may be easier to understand the truncated adaptive structure within the court system. The results of truncation will be dysfunctional to the maintenance and order goals of the social system, to the degree that the court organization is no longer perceived as a legitimate source of order or its precepts no longer perceived as relevant to education.

DILEMMAS IN THE COURT STRUCTURE

The present court structure, as it solves its problems and does its work, generates a number of dilemmas. Four important ones are selected for discussion: (1) a perception of valued functions as those that are valuable, (2) difficulty in changing, (3) role ambiguity, and (4) researcher overload. All of these dilemmas must be subsumed under a larger problem: that social structure has dictated court structure and then has bypassed it as a problem-solving institution.

Functional Imbalance

Obvious in the preceding discussion is the fact that some functions have been emphasized at the expense of others. Although this differential development is typical in organizations, serious flaws may occur if at some point there are no counterweights to the primary dynamics of proficiency and stability. The primary value is based on proficiency. Officials seek to perform their roles satisfactorily, emphasizing a certain quality of case processions, at a definite speed. In doing so, they *may* call upon whatever ideals (such as due process, law'n'order crime control) seem to fit the task requirements. But ideals, it has been demonstrated, are difficult and unlikely measurements of role performance. More concrete criteria are needed in the process of hiring, firing, passing bar exams, or being elected to office. And more concrete criteria are generally used as a measure of personal satisfaction in doing the job well.[17] Particularly in organizations, such as the court system, heavily dependent on rule enforcement, motivation by the evocation of generalized ideals is very unlikely.[18] Officials of the production process are concerned with the *tangible* motion of the case. Defendants have the same consideration, unless they are refusing the role, in which case they have the opposite concern. But in no way are defendants primarily motivated by ideals such as justice, due

[17] James March and Herbert Simon, *Organizations* (New York: Wiley, 1958), pp. 47–52.

[18] W. Keith Warner and A. Eugene Havens, "Goal Displacement and the Intangibility of Organizational Goals," *Administrative Science Quarterly, 12*, No. 4 (March 1968), 539–555.

process, or sanctity of the individual. Instead, they are rewarded in degrees of *tangible* freedom such as dropping of charges, acquital, probation instead of incarceration, reduction of sentence, and so on.

Within the production subsystem, the utility of calling on values such as due process and justice is limited to those substructures wherein the task is dealing with symbols of social stability and worth. This task generally occurs in the larger courts with large budget and higher public visibility, and in appellate courts where precedent and tradition are important to the maintenance of the social order. In other words, these ideals are of primary interest in the boundary substructure to officials who must integrate the court system with other social structures or who must protect the interests of the system against environmental encroachment. It is in the higher courts that the ideals of law enforcement and due process receive constant attention, seemingly with two objectives. First, higher courts may demonstrate that state and individual needs are integrated by the court system and, hence, that an ever-present democratic dilemma between order and freedom is resolved by the judicial institution. Second, higher courts may press upon the environment the high moral awareness of the court organization and, hence, "take the heat off" the production process, where constant attention to these ideals are irrelevant to proficiency and disruptive to stability.

The boundary structure may even act as system critic and, by admitting faults of the productive process publicly, steal much of the thunder from external critics. For example, it is much less disruptive for the system to have the Supreme Court ask for changes than to have a political candidate promise them after the next election. Because what appellate courts usually do is the most *visible* part of the court system, it is not surprising if the public and the court officials also mistakenly perceive this boundary activity as the primary concern of the court. This assumption is a dangerous error, however, in that it yields a very distorted picture of the organization itself. It confuses what is *valued by society* with what is important *to the functioning organization*. Surely ideals such as due process, crime control, law and order, and so on are important to the court system, but as *boundary activities,* not as controlling its production activity. It is the same mistake, for example, by which ancient theologians may have concluded that because man as a whole served God, his ill health was a sign of his lack of faith. Although, as a social animal, his demonstration of faith may have been very important to his personal organization, it was not controlling of malfunctions in his digestive tract.

It may be that the boundary functions of the court system have been overemphasized by the system because they are visible and, as a substructure, have become very powerful. Management structure in the court system, at its highest levels, largely overlaps the boundary structure. The coterminousness of these structures may result in the solidification of the productive process, since the appellate judges, in rising from the production level, take with them a vision of production that is outmoded for present problems and are committed to boundary activity that supports the status quo. Concomitantly, radical restatement of productive problems (which would include, perhaps, a systemic statement of organization and alternate methods of motivating production officials) is systematically precluded. For instance, appellate courts keep issuing decisions about defense counsel activity when there is little data to support the notion that defense counsel really is utilized in the productive subsystem. If defense counsel is utilized, he acts to speed up prosecution or to obtain more guilty pleas rather than to protect the offender.

Counter Trends of Adaptation and Change

To restate the dilemma: overemphasis on the system functions that receive the most attention has precluded the development of system problem-solving functions. Concern for the courts' demonstration of American ideals has beclouded their system location and system function. Organizational conflicts occur because the power and influence of the boundary structure as a managerial structure lock the productive system to solutions of production inefficiency and ineffectiveness that can be formulated and implemented under the status quo of the organization. Since the problems of production are ones of motivation by rule enforcement, differential perceptions of court roles, and the administration of rules in particular cases, solutions generated from the boundary frame of reference are likely to be viewed by all members of the production system as irrelevant, idealistic, and naive.

A goal of organizations faced with a dilemma is the reformulation of the dilemma as a problem with practical solutions.[19] If the dilemmas are a characteristic of present organization, their reduction to the problem level may necessitate a reformulation of policy and a restructuring of organization. This type of change is usually the product of recommendations by an adaptive subsystem. Since the court managerial structure must execute adaptive suggestions and the managerial system is nearly coterminal with boundary structure, the elaboration of an effective adaptive operation is itself an organizational dilemma. A common occurrence in other organizations when the present structure precludes restatement of its insoluble problems is the employment of outside aid.[20] In recent years contracting with consultants on the criminal justice process has

[19] March and Simon, *Organizations,* pp. 154–158.

[20] Problems facing consultants in this relationship will be discussed in the section, "Research Overload."

increased[21] but without many practical changes. The changes have been minimal for a number of reasons. The most significant is that consultants have accepted the basic structural dilemmas—perhaps because much of that structure seems frozen by constitutional and legislative constraints.

The central question that must be put to higher managers is this: What type of communication with the production system will gain the desired response? Equally important is the parallel question: How do production participants view present attempts at policy formulation and implementation? Until now, questions of performance were answered by the examination of existing rules and laws and by the manufacture of new ones. *If rules and laws are themselves part of the problem,* they are ineffective answers, regardless of novel interpretations, as long as they are administered and enforced in traditional ways. Successful adaptation will only begin when higher management is no longer so concerned with rules of procedure that methods of their administration are taken for granted.

Role Ambiguity

The concept of role acts as a link between interpersonal and intrapersonal levels in open system study. The individual in performing a role binds himself to an organization by fulfilling some of its needs in return for some of its benefits. The role is prescribed and related to other roles in such a way that the organization performs the functions necessary for its existence. The rewards are varied, from punishment for role rejection, to money, promotional opportunity, status, and prestige in the community, and including satisfaction in the performance itself.

A major trend in complex organizations has been the fractionalization of roles so that each role consists of one activity. In this way, industrial organizations, particularly, have sought to increase efficiency in lower levels of the organization. However, organizations dealing with people as a unit of production have not been as successful with fractionalization, nor has fractionalization been carried so far, because even the lowest positions in such organizations require considerable discretion.[22] Since this is the case, it would be only natural that the court system would escape the consequences of fractionalization, especially in view of the fact that the court places the demand for a tremendous coordinative effort on higher organizational levels. The court system, in which many activities are present in a single role, increases the need for *intra*role coordination, and demands relatively less coordination between roles.

[21] The President's Commission on Law Enforcement and the Administration of Justice is one such example; the work of the American Bar Foundation field studies may be considered another.

[22] See Donald Cressey, "Contradictory Directives in Complex Organizations: The Case of the Prison," *Administrative Science Quarterly, 4* (June 1959), 1–19.

This is certainly true to an extent. It does not take several judges to write an opinion, just one judge. One defense counsel may perform the many activities of defense, and one prosecutor (although less frequently) may perform all the activities of prosecution. Probation workers also may specialize to a degree, but they perform a wide range of activities with considerable leeway in schedule, technique, and so on. Bailiffs, court clerks, stenographers, etc., may have less varied duties, but the proportion of persons in the system with a minimal number of responsibilities is small.

Whereas industrial managers suffer from role overload, in which the demands of supervising their subordinates are clear but nearly impossible to accomplish simultaneously,[23] court system managers are more likely to suffer from role ambiguity, in which the integration of all activities of the one role is unclear, and the effective hierarchical relationships between roles are not understood.[24] That role ambiguity should occur in an organization structured on rule and law may seem strange. But most of the criminal law defines intake and output, leaving the relationships between official roles rather unclear. Most of the rules delimit the processing of offenders and not the integration of tasks performed by the same official.

Officials in this situation are likely to limit their own discretion and to clarify their own role, but in ways not controlled by policy and organizational structure. The result may be a considerable variation in system product that cannot be attributable to variation in personal skills and capabilities. The influence on the defendant of various officials' decisions about their own roles may be such that the defendant is never sure what has happened to him or what he is to do. And the effect on opinions rendered on similar cases may be so different that one may wonder if the same court has had a hand in both. A rather good example is the case of *Fisher* v. *U.S.*[25] In this case, the majority opinion discussed the principles of allowing or not allowing partial insanity as a defense, in a form typical of boundary activity, whereas Justice Frankfurter, in dissent, argued the facts of the case as if he were part of the productive system. The majority decision had dire consequences for Fisher, as often happens when the man in question is subordinated to ideals he may symbolize, but Frankfurter's approach, if accepted, would have solved nothing about partial insanity. A similar case is *Williams* v. *N.Y.*[26] in which the majority under Justice Black argued the place and stature of probation reports (a managerial activity) with a consequent death sentence for Williams.

Such cases will not be unusual when officials are unclear about the interrelation of subsystem functions, or are unaware that they should be

---

[23] Katz and Kahn, *Social Psychology of Organizations*, p. 185.

[24] Ibid., p. 190.

[25] Fisher v. United States, 328 U.S. 463 (1946).

[26] Williams v. New York, 337 U.S. 241 (1949).

doing several things at once. Naturally, the decision of policy in terms of cases and individual defendants makes the possibility of role clarity considerably more difficult. But the dilemma will have to be approached in terms of system functions and role requirements before it becomes a problem with a solution.

Researcher Overload

Researcher overload is no different than role overload; it is merely a specification of the role that is overloaded. Researcher overload is the condition of the research role in which too many signals are being sent by the organization under study for them all to be recorded and integrated into a cohesive whole. Some general characteristics of researcher overload may be the recording of myriad observations lacking unification by theory, or the expanding of theory that is a distortion or avoidance of observation. Since overload itself seems to be a condition of modern living (e.g., there is a prevalence of noise), the second reaction to overload is probably safer and wiser than the first. Choice between theories, then, becomes an empirical matter of deciding which theory produces least noise and which accounts for the most observations in an orderly manner.

Researcher overload relative to the court system could be studied within the system itself.[27] However, research activity, usually carried out by the adaptive subsystem, is so infrequent in the court system that the more productive discussion of overload concerns the work of outside observers or hired consultants. Although the problems faced by the two types of researchers are different—since the consultant has temporarily joined the organization—the origins of overload are somewhat the same.

The researcher must have at his disposal techniques that can handle the consequences of differential function emphasis and role ambiguity. Lacking these techniques, his research will be no better or worse than the observations of practitioners. In other words, the research may become part of the dilemma and may be viewed by practitioners as irrelevant to the solving of problems.

Most research that has been done in the court system is typical of a certain brand of legal study—novel and sweeping generalizations are drawn from a very personal and subjective (clinical) view of limited cases and conditions. As a method of political argument this type of research may be effective, but as the basis of scientific understanding it is deficient.[28] Although some concern is shown in legal research for the measurement of values and value differences, the usual measurement methods used in court research are very inexact. An appellate court, for

[27] Frankfurter's plurality opinion in *Culombe* v. *Connecticut,* 367 U.S. 578 (1971).

[28] Notably by Marvin Wolfgang and Franco Ferracuti, *Subculture of Violence* (London: Social Science Paperbacks, 1967) and the literature reviewed by them, pp. 113–140.

example, might analyze behavior in terms such as *crime control* or *due process*. In other words, the court tends to label behavior rather than find explanations for it.

Explanations are dynamic and a posteriori. They are generated by theory that can be tested. It is also through a theory that generates testable hypotheses that researchers avoid taking sides on issues whose consequences are not known. The natural tendency in legal research is to champion one side or another because the researcher finds a "saving grace" in a system that evidently favors the "right" or "moral" side. As is common in an age that is schizoid about machinery and technique, the side to be championed in most legal research is the one that seems most human and sensitive. But legal researchers, like most people, are at a loss to assess the humanness and sensitivity of values disembodied from their social context. To the 1960 liberal, the due process cause is just. But it seems in the 1970s that due process symbolizes a machinery insensitive to the needs of the man in the middle. If system planning truly had to fluctuate as rapidly as that, it would not seem to be an effective tool of morality, regardless of who was in power!

The court system as described by the theory of organization is no more tested than the assumptions and hypotheses set forth by appellate judges. But the theory we have used may yield genuine hypotheses such as the following:

1. The greater the number of defendants to be processed, the greater the strain.
2. The greater the strain, the more standardized the procedure.
3. The greater the standardization, the less time in official-official and official-defendant contact.
4. The less the contact, the less different the perceptions.
5. The less different the perceptions, the more predictable the outcome.
6. The more predictable the outcome, the less the strain.

1. The greater the number of defendants to be processed, the greater the interaction with police.
2. The greater the interaction, the greater the strain.
3. The greater the strain, the greater control sought over police action.
4. The greater the control sought, the nearer to arrest will court action begin.
5. The nearer to arrest, the more standardized the procedure.
6. The more standardized the procedure, the less varied the defendant population.
7. The less varied the defendant population, the less differential the perceptions.
8. The less varied the perceptions, the more standardized the procedure.

1. The more standardized the procedure, the lower the relevant hierarchy.
2. The lower the relevant hierarchy, the smaller the systemic vision.
3. The smaller the systemic vision, the less contact with other substructures.
4. The less the contact, the less the managerial impact.
5. The less the impact, the less the change potential.

1. The less the change potential, the less the knowledge of corrections.
2. The less the knowledge of corrections, the less the system integration.
3. The less the system integration, the less varied the decisions about output.
4. The fewer the variations, the smaller the probability of success.

Such propositions can be spun off with rapidity. Some obviously need refinement, and some are more important than others. All are firmly rooted in the system treatment of court organization, and they demonstrate that a systemic treatment of court organization leads easily to studies of police and correctional agencies as well.

This approach, in other words, has the advantage of quantifiability, and statistical techniques are available for its support or demolition. Therefore it may, if carefully approached, be utilized to reduce the noise of simultaneous system signals. It may facilitate the employment of tools that reduce researcher overload. It solves few problems in itself, but findings generated within such a framework can be translated via training and feedback sessions into a language productive of change. If it is adaptive activity, its pursuit may be the basis of an adaptive substructure, since it offers a method of observation that may encompass organizational activity rather than be coopted by one substructure or another.

POLICY MAKING AND ALTERNATIVE SYSTEM STRUCTURES

Open systems, in which there is a high degree of exchange with the environment, are not locked into one structure or another. Both the system and the environment change as they interact with each other. Ths change will take place whether it is observed and accounted for or not. Officials do not need to be aware of system functions or of their roles as system constituents in order to take part in system operations, but whether an understanding of system operation and belonging to a system can make a difference is a matter of debate.[29] Many great changes are surely the product of external forces such as revolution or national catastrophe. But the most observable of these changed inputs have negative consequences for the system in question—such as collapse and disintegration. Changes that produce increased effectiveness most logically have an internal base,

[29] Katz and Kahn, *Social Psychology of Organizations,* pp. 40–47, 73–78.

since most environmental change is unrelated to trends desirable to the organization.

Whether court system managers are aware of system function and of their impact on system structure is probably a moot point. Surely, in some vague and subjective way, personnel at higher echelons must feel a responsibility for what happens at lower levels. But whether their attempts at influence are mere stabs in the dark, or more informed attempts that remain unsuccessful, is not of much consequence to the amount of system education that must take place before internal changes have a chance for increased effectiveness.

UNANSWERED QUESTIONS OF COURT STRUCTURE

It is amazing how much boundary activity is considered managerial at the same time. Although the Supreme Court has questioned how much police activity can be effectively controlled from the bench,[30] the same question is not usually asked of court activity. Perhaps bench-made policy is assumed to affect what goes on below because "it should," or because it is "constitutional." Certainly two birds may be killed with one stone, but not until the correlation of those birds is known. How bench-issued policy that is publicly and externally directed will also affect internal production processes is not known. Indeed, the court system seems to lag behind correctional and police agencies in the very necessary study of its own internal processes.

Managerial decisions about court policy are doubtlessly very low-visibility events, perhaps, at times, bordering on the illegal and improper. The structure of the system nearly mandates this result because hierarchies and roles within hierarchies are generally isolated from each other geographically and administratively. In order for higher courts to affect those under them or for principal role incumbents in any hierarchy to interact with each other, the actors have one of two difficult paths to follow. First, they can interact publicly and very slowly through the rule-bound structures by which cases flow, one by one, through the system. This kind of communication is difficult even in very healthy organizations. Second, they can meet, in a sense, between organizational lines—in that vast area of discretion available in people-processing organizations. This type of interaction has one great advantage over the former; that is, alternative perceptions can be compared and alternative actions can be discussed prior to implementation. The great disadvantage is that differential function emphasis biases the outcome of such meetings, and role

---

[30] Terry v. Ohio, 392 U.S. 1 (1968).

ambiguity increases the effect of nonorganizational and personal factors on the sharing of decision-relevant information.

For example, there are few guidelines available for judges in a chambers meeting over reduction of charge or entering of the guilty plea. The judge may not promise a specific sentence and, hence, coerce the plea, but the question is how should he enter discussion with counsel and prosecutor. May he constructively criticize the perceptions of the other two participants, or may he only supervise a negotiation of which he has no effective part? What kind of judicial style—inscrutable and detached, or friendly and participative—yields best reactions from counsel and prosecutor? Should a judge preface his decision as simply a "matter of law," or should he admit to personal biases and open these to discussion? The same kind of questions are, of course, relevant to the other participants.

On a higher level, the same sort of inquiry is relevant to boundary decisions. Does the court demand certain behavior from police or correctional officials without carefully consulting them beforehand? If the court asks for their opinions, what is the best method? Is the information presented in official briefs and arguments before the bench the most helpful presentation to satisfactory problem solution, or does this formalize opinions to such an extent that only compromises, rather than optimum solutions, are available? Can the various problems of police discretion in stop-and-frisk cases, or of prison control of inmate writ writers effectively be analyzed in the courtroom format? What alternative channels, such as judicial-police or judicial-correctional institutes, are available? If such conferences are undertaken, how are they affected by court battles won and lost, rather than by mutual commitment to system improvement?

Can any question of properly supervised defendant participation in the criminal justice process be seriously addressed without previously studying the types of interaction possible between various system officials?

CONSEQUENCES OF UNANSWERED QUESTIONS

The answers to questions of this type cannot be given in scattershot fashion. They are questions of court policy and have implications for court structure. Obviously changes in court structure will have consequences for the defendants processed by that structure. How any changes will be designed to conform to constitutional process is an important question. Another consideration in this regard is the trend of criminal procedure decisions in relation to the present structures of the system. In many ways, the interaction system of official avoidance of

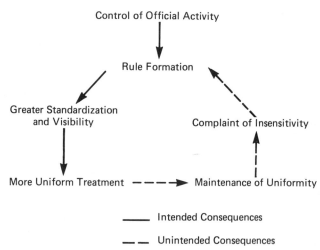

Figure 10-1.   Simplified Court Rule Reaction Model

Control of Official Activity

Rule Formation

Greater Standardization
and Visibility

Complaint of Insensitivity

More Uniform Treatment ----► Maintenance of Uniformity

——— Intended Consequences

— — Unintended Consequences

constitutional structures, the development of the "hard case" (one to which no rule clearly applies), new rules regulating official behavior, and subsequent official deviation all have much in common with the classic organizational deviance models of Robert Merton and Alvin Gouldner.[31] (See Figure 10-1.)

The model shown in Figure 10-1 is not totally accurate because officials do not react to rule formation by purposely avoiding rules or by browbeating defendants. But it would seem that the expanded role of defense counsel, for example, has not drastically altered the court process, because that role expansion, according to the model, merely fits into the court pattern of action, unintended reaction and repeated action. In the particular case of rules introducing lawyers for indigents in noncapital cases (see Gideon V. Wainwright),[32] the innovation may achieve greater standarization and visibility of court decisions and, hence, more uniform treatment (which reinforces the intent of the rule); but it also produces a large indigent clientele who are accommodated in a more or less bureaucratic manner,[33] with increased complaints of inadequate defense by counsel and inadequate support for defense counsel. In other words, although the rule is introduced to cure an ill, it remains a cure

[31] Robert K. Merton, *Social Theory and Social Structure* (Glencoe, Ill.: Free Press, 1957); and Alvin Gouldner, *Patterns of Industrial Bureaucracy* (New York: Free Press, 1964).

[32] Gideon v. Wainwright, 372 U.S. 335 (1963).

[33] See L. Silverstein, *"Defense of the Poor,"* 1, published by The American Bar Foundation, 1965.

subject to the same type of inadequacies and deficiencies that prompted the rule formation.[34] This is not an unusual result of controls imposed upon organizations from an analytic machine-theory viewpoint rather than from an open-system viewpoint. The court process vis-à-vis indigent clientele was deficient with respect to defense opportunity; hence a new rule "corrected" the problem. In the correction, both lawyers and indigent defendants were treated as givens, not interactants. The deficiencies were to be cured by a manipulation of human variables, but none of the variables proved easily satisfied. *Gideon* and other such cases may or may not be improvements, of course. But they are not and cannot be the reduction of the control-by-rule dilemma to a problem of solvable proportions. Such remedies are symptoms of the dilemma itself.

A follow-up on the defense counsel issue does much to verify this view of bench-issued innovation as machine-theory based and dilemma-bound. The usual reaction to conflict in organizational systems is expansion.[35] The managerial reaction to such problems as lack of uniformity or inequality among participants is the elaboration of additional roles and the creation of problem-solving departments. Faced with defendants who were at a disadvantage with more powerful defendants, the organization attempted solution by introducing counsel at trial. Through *Miranda*[36] and *Wade*[37] and other such cases this role expansion gradually seeped into police and correctional activity. In other words, the problem-solving impetus went outward quantitatively without arriving at any decision point with qualitatively satisfactory conclusions. What was, and is, a production-system problem (quality control of defendants processed) became opportunity for boundary activity in two senses. First, the court expanded influence at intake and output. Second, there was tremendous ideological gain, as several famous cases demonstrated the interest of the court in fair treatment for all defendants and emphasized the court system as the renewing font for American ideals. At an earlier date in American history, such side products of a problem might indeed have outweighed the disappointments in failing to resolve production difficulties. But in a decade when defendants in the process are taking on a considerably political stance, the boundary use of defendant-related complaints is an increasingly dangerous activity, since boundary statements without production goal achievement are perceived as damningly hypocritical.

[34] March and Simon, *Organizations*, p. 27.
[35] Katz and Kahn, *Social Psychology of Organizations*, p. 100.
[36] Miranda v. Arizona 384 U.S. 436 (1966).
[37] United States v. Wade 388 U.S. 218 (1967).

The court system may continue in its present structure and become more effective by increasing the scope and intensity of rule enforcement. For example, lawyers, by rule, could be ever-present factors in the process. All decisions could take on an adversary quality of public hearing and deliberation, or at least of counseled bargaining and negotiation. To be earnest in this endeavor, sufficient funds must be allocated to defense work. For example, a problem such as nonindigent middle-class defendants and limited defense funds would have to be settled in favor of providing supplementary finances for nonindigent defenses. Judges would have to be instructed to intervene in any proceeding that did not offer adequate supervision of the production process. If enough lawyers and sufficient funds were not available for this trend, the court could reverse itself and accomplish the same end by denying counsel to all rich and poor, by denying bail to all, whether they could afford it or not, and so on. Since this latter choice seems to conflict with other constitutional demands, the decision to seek greater supervision and more money is more practical.

But continuing this present trend at court elaboration, as has been demonstrated, has its price—a price that is likely to become inflated as elaboration continues. The greatest cost, it seems, is the human reaction by system officials to such regulation, on the one hand, and by the designated regulators, on the other hand, to becoming cogs in a large machine —rather than professionals with serious commitments to particular cases. Present organizational theory is virtually devoid of suggestions that increased supervision and control by rule enforcement have beneficial, long-run consequences.

A second alternative is the development of a unified managerial structure for the courts with a sophisticated adaptive system. Managerial specialists who would have a knowledge of effective function utilization and who would not confuse boundary statements with productive solutions could be trained or hired. A statistically oriented research subsystem that would predict changes necessary in the system to meet changes visible or predicted in the environment could be set up.

In a sense, this approach would professionalize court managerial activity. How such a supervisory office could be superimposed on the existing structure is not entirely clear. There are now administrative judges for local court systems, and administrative decisions are made for the federal system by the Justice Department and the relevant federal judges. But a managerial substructure consciously designed to integrate court activity would necessitate a kind of executive power presently uncommon to the court system. And the legal relationship between the generation of court policy and the results in particular cases for particular defendants would doubtlessly be unclear for years.

A third alternative, at the present no more reality than the second, is the treatment of the court system as part of the criminal justice system. Such a perspective would entail the verbalization of already existent interagency conflicts. It might be decided, for example, that the Supreme Court can only make recommendations for policy which might be rejected or accepted by police and correctional agencies. It might imply the utilization of higher courts as advisory boards to policy makers. It might entail the acceptance that the bench is an inadequate position from which to make generalizations about the intake and output needs of the system. It might, for example, mean that the court productive process should be managed by correctional experts who would have the power to require that certain criteria be met by the court process. For example, there may, as of now, be no legal criteria governing sentence differentials (within maximum-minimum bounds), but correctional officials might be empowered to reject inmates whose court experience would make them unmanageable.

Certainly the intake and output components of a unified criminal justice system would take over much boundary activity that is now court-directed. Policy concerning the community from which defendants come and to which they return would most logically be formulated by the agencies whose officials actively work those communities—as policemen or parole and probation officers. The court system itself would become less concerned with justifying the system's existence or with upholding American ideals, and much more concerned with the actual, routine, but all-important task of processing real people in a variety of different ways. The court system as the central agency has the physical potential of functioning as the throughput agency—as the set of operations that performs the major work on defendants. This is possible, however, only by becoming production- rather than boundary-oriented.

What such unification would do to police and correctional agencies is still unclear. But the change would be as radical as it would be for the courts. As input and output components, rather than individual agencies with individual ideologies, the attempt by either police or correctional officials to work on the individual defendant would cease, and the amount of time they see any particular defendant would decrease.

As an intake agency of a criminal justice system (rather than a peace-keeping organization), the police department has a tremendous amount of social investigation and political action to undertake. The police would have to work upon and with community social structures so that (1) the community itself could come to a unified definition of its criminals, and (2) the persons who did enter the system were indeed role-ready as defendants. The police would actively work to clarify, but not to initiate, the labeling process. Hence, police in this system would not act as upholders of one ideology or subculture, but mediators among many.

The correctional agency, as an output component rather than an independent organization, would need to drop any notion of its peculiar and particular role in punishment and reform. It would be concerned rather with finding and creating jobs, academic opportunities, and practical family improvements. It would have to sell the system product and develop markets for it. In terms of efficient defendant processing, it would have to upgrade the inmate (output) status as the most desirable one in the system—not the most feared and unwanted.

Of course, either of these possibilities, for corrections and police, is impossible without concomitant changes in the central court operation. The court, as the major structure devoted to individual defendants, would be the active throughput agency—the place wherein most energy transformations take place. Although it does not now operate as such, the court structure, not the correctional structure, has the greatest inherent potential for treating defendants individually—for punishment and for reeducation. The dichotomy of such terms, in such a system, might itself become meaningless. Reeducation is difficult for both defendant and officials. But if reeducation is punishing, it is more likely to be accomplished in the court system, by means of extensive debate, deliberation, and confrontation, than in prisons that cannot pretend to embody (for defendants) the meaning of democratic ideals, fair play, understanding, tolerance, and whatever. In other words, elaboration of accusational traditions could be very valuable reeducative and therapeutic tools—if they were defendant-oriented and not organizationally or publicly oriented. To reduce the organization maintenance and public boundary tendencies, system unification would be necessary so that police and correctional agencies could take on those functions. Time and money now devoted to expensive investigatory and incarceratory practices could be transferred to elaboration of courtroom education. Unification would then make systemization practical. Dealing with defendants rather than issues, the courts could indeed become "schools of hard knocks."

chapter 11

An Organizational Model
for the Analysis
of Prisons and Parole

The application of organizational principles to the analysis of prison and parole is fairly straightforward when compared to the analysis of police and court organization. Although parole supervision like police patrol involves considerable discretion of front-line workers, the range of issues in parole work and the range of people that the parole officer deals with are smaller than the range of issues in police work or the range of people that a patrolman must deal with. Both prison and parole organizations, unlike courts, are executive agencies organized in a bureaucratic manner without the complications that arise in the discussion of authority in court organizations. Prisons, unlike any of the organizations that we have analyzed so far, have clearly delineated physical boundaries, and we can speak of events occurring "within" the organization without constantly repeating that the organization is in reality flung out across all parts of a city or county.

THE ETHICS AND THE SCIENCE OF
CHANGING PEOPLE

As we have seen in Chapter Six, changes in people have always been primary goals of prison and parole organizations. Auburn (N.Y.) and the

Eastern State Penitentiary (Pa.) were built to reform offenders, and parole was initiated with the goal of enabling offenders to improve their lot in life. We have also seen that these goals of changing people have rarely been implemented as planned and have frequently caused change in undesired directions.

Nonetheless, it is important to understand some underlying assumptions about changing people if we are to understand the ways in which prison and parole organizations are structured today and if we are to arrive at any helpful suggestions for changing those structures. If the correctional officials who are responsible for running prison and parole organizations have as one of their main goals changing the behavior of offenders, then an important step in understanding why they have organized in particular ways is to understand their assumptions about what makes people change their behavior. For example, there was a strong Christian theme running through the correctional plans that resulted in the Eastern State Penitentiary. If the Quaker reformers had not had so much conviction in the basic strength and goodness of the individual human soul, perhaps they would not have placed so much confidence in the isolation of criminals. And if contemporary legislators were not so ignorant of the original purposes of prisons, perhaps they would not continue to build prisons incorporating the same architectural principles. In other words, much of the custodial emphasis today would seem to be founded on the belief that prisoners are very difficult if not impossible to change, although part of their stubbornness must surely lie in the fact that prison environments militate so strongly against changes in behavior.

Changing behavior is rapidly becoming a specialty, if not a discipline, in itself. Disturbingly prophetic fictional accounts such as Anthony Burgess's *Clockwork Orange* point out the particular change techniques can be alarmingly effective, whereas justifications and controls on their use can be careless or completely dishonest.[1] Changing behavior in people is probably a much more ancient study than modern behavioral scientists will admit. Certainly the ancient Greek philosophers and even more ancient Middle-Eastern and oriental philosophers and religious figures were concerned with changing human behavior. For some reason, many people mark Pavlov's work at the turn of the century as the beginning of scientific explorations in behavior change. Perhaps one of the reasons for this is that contemporary studies usually divorce the techniques of behavior change from the question of whether the change should be undertaken. We now consider how to change people with more energy and concentration than we use in deciding whether or not such changes are ethical. The science of behavior change is growing in sophis-

[1] Anthony Burgess, *Clockwork Orange* (New York: Ballantine Books, 1965).

tication, but the policy decisions about when, why, and with whom the science should be applied have lagged behind in development.

The separation of the scientific from the ethical issues can lead us, presumably, into Orwell's *1984* on schedule.[2] This possibility should make us cautious, but it should not lead us into despair and inaction, for several reasons. One of the major reasons is a conclusion we must draw from one of the primary principles of behavior change: that *change in human interaction and alterations in the basic patterns of social exchange are inevitable.*[3] Change goes on constantly. People and organizations that propose to change behavior cannot lay claim to the creation of change. Instead, they can only plan to utilize the constant forces of change and modify the direction of change for the achievement of some outcomes that are more desired than other possible consequences. Within this view of the inevitability of change, the decision not to act and the default of decisions about action altogether are themselves influential factors in the direction of human interaction. Typically, people who decide that change is impossible or undesirable are actually implying that they prefer the trends that are currently most probable or that they prefer through their inaction to support those forces in society that are presently dominating the promotion of change.[4]

A second major reason that currently is increasing the involvement of people in the promotion of change is the fact that the ethics and the science of change are beginning to separate clearly into distinct issues. As correctional work began in the 1820s, and even as it proceeded through the 1950s, many officials ignored or bypassed the scientific questions in change activity because they mistakenly subsumed these questions under moral or ethical arguments. For example, the reformers who planned the early penitentiaries merely assumed that the institutional structures would work because there was moral justification for the endeavor. Because it was *good* to reform offenders, few people questioned the effectiveness of the relationship between institutional strategies and the desired outcomes in changed behavior of offenders. Now that the science of behavior change has gained strength, the decisions about the goodness or wrongness of the technical applications can be more clearly based on information about the relationships between ends and means rather than based on assumptions about these relationships. Thus, although the science of change has increased the possibilities of its undesired utilization, it has also increased the possibilities of its effective and desired use.

[2] George Orwell, *1984* (New York: Harcourt, Brace, 1949).

[3] Ralf Dahrendorf, *Class and Class Conflict in Industrial Society* (Stanford, Calif.: Stanford University Press, 1959); and Kurt Lewin, *Field Theory in the Social Sciences* (New York: Harper and Row, 1964).

[4] Seymour Halleck, *The Politics of Therapy* (New York: Science House, 1967).

Any kind of chronological recording of important events in the development of planned change is a precarious undertaking. Although planned change has become increasingly scientific, it deals with real people in real situations, and its consequences are value-laden. Whatever scientific findings are included, someone will object that his favorites are not included. With the cautionary note that the following discussion is not an attempt to be complete, we will try to mention briefly the kinds of planned change activities that have become most influential in the correctional area, or show promise of being applied in the future.

One of the most important pioneers in this area was Ivan Petrovich Pavlov, the Russian physiologist. Pavlov conducted a host of laboratory experiments concerning the relationships among sensory stimuli, the transmission of messages to the brain, and the reaction of the brain. He discovered that in many cases, through a careful manipulation of the environment, he could institute a change in the internal response pattern. He could, for example, substitute the conditional reflex of salivation following the ringing of a bell for salivation at the sight of food. In an example with perhaps more practical benefits, he discovered that he could substitute the conditioned reflex of certain breathing patterns for the usually painful response of women to the stimulus of labor contraction during delivery.

It is common in the United States for people who do not know Pavlov's work to make fun of it. "He was the man who made dogs salivate," people laugh. Perhaps in some degree the laughter is brought on by fear. It is frightening to discover that the reactions of one's body—formerly believed to be stable, natural, and fixed—can be changed. It is also frightening to some that the human body, including the mind, which many people have long considered a particular type of independent entity, is in reality a system whose identity is attributable to a dynamic balance with the environment. Perhaps more than anything else, it is this systems characteristic of Pavlovian physiology that makes it so advanced and so relevant to the issues of changing behavior.

Pavlov's influence is certainly too broad to count only certain contemporary developments as his heirs in the field of behavior change. We can, for example, point to his contribution to learning theory and thus to behavior modification. We know an organism learns, as feedback from the environment reinforces negatively or positively the behavioral pattern or the goal-seeking behavior that the organism has engaged in. Most activities that fall under the concept of behavior modification involve altering the negative or positive rewards in systematic fashion until the

behavioral patterns change. It is important to understand that l̦
theory helps to explain why change is difficult as much as it explai̦
change is possible. The longer a person is rewarded for particular behaviors, the more difficult it is to stop that particular behavior. It is
typical in the United States, for example, for a juvenile to commit several
successful crimes before he is apprehended. If punishment follows apprehension, it usually does so with such delay that it is, in learning theory
terms, unlikely for the person to react to the punishment as a consequence of the offense. Furthermore, punishment is typically administered
in such a way that criminal behavior is positively, instead of negatively,
reinforced.

In many ways the criminal justice system might be more effective if
the work of Pavlov and other scientists were taken as more relevant. Most
frequently, however, scientific theory and research have been treated as
irrelevant by officials within the criminal justice system. Many scientists
stop with that comment and then go on to other concerns. When they do
so, in a sense they are ignoring their own findings. If learning theory,
behavior modification, and whatever else has been developed in the scientific community have not caught on swiftly in criminal justice, it may
be that the system and its officials receive no positive reward for doing so.

Another important landmark in the history of planned change was the
work of Kurt Lewin at the University of Iowa during World War II. His
original studies applied principles of behavior change in an area far removed from the correctional field.[5] But, as in all scientific endeavors, the
underlying principles by which systems of people or organizations interact
may remain quite similar even though the situations that cause social
problems change.

Lewin is known as one of the founders of the study of "group
dynamics," which is concerned with such things as leadership, group
participation, task completion by a group, and so on. One of his better-
known projects involved the problem of convincing housewives to use
unpopular cuts of meats during the wartime food shortage. Several
different attempts had been made such as lectures and films on how to
prepare the food, including facts about its high nutritional content. However, housewives attending these presentations, although they absorbed
the information, refused to switch their buying habits. A final attempt to
change behavior took quite a different approach. Rather than have experts stand in front of a passive audience and convince them that certain
changes would be beneficial, small groups of housewives were called
upon to discuss among themselves the reasons why people would not

[5] Kurt Lewin, *Resolving Social Conflicts, Selected Papers on Group Dynamics,* ed.
Gertrud Weiss Lewin (New York: Harper, 1948).

change their buying habits. In other words, these groups were treated as part of the project rather than as recipients of the project. A follow-up study on the buying habits of these housewife-participants discovered that they indeed changed their buying habits and that the change was of long duration. Later, similar studies conducted in other situations confirmed the evidence that one important factor in behavior change was the amount of participation that the changee felt in the project.[6]

Another kind of advance that Lewin was responsible for involved not so much new information about the process of change as suggestions about how to analyze it. Lewin, too, was aware of the interactions between the components in a system, and one of the systems of particular interest to him was the one system set up between the person or group to be changed and the person or group seeking to induce the change. Lewin was one of the first scientists to show real interest in helping other people apply his principles of change in real social situations. What is more admirable, perhaps, is that he attempted to bring the same scientific objectivity to this relationship as to his primary interest in the group to be changed. One example of his interest in the change agent, for example, is a technique for the study of problem situations called "force field analysis." Lewin suggested that in order to change a pattern of activity, it would be helpful to consider that pattern as a "quasi-stationary equilibrium."[7] In order to change that level or pattern of activity, he suggested that we analyze not only the forces that contribute to change, but also the forces that are likely to resist change. If a change agent should seek to promote change without attention to the resisting forces, Lewin suggested that the outcome would be increased resistance rather than change. Although this kind of analytic technique is a simplified version of the complex principles that Lewin might have applied to a theoretical exposition of group dynamics, it has proved to be a highly useful tool to change planners and change agents. It enables them to set out all parts of a change problem in relation to one another, rather than concentrate on narrow factors that are not free to be manipulated independently.

Another set of activities that would seem to be of considerable importance in the correctional area involves the work on juvenile delinquency of Richard Cloward and Lloyd Ohlin. Cloward and Ohlin were two of several people responsible for major theoretical explanations of juvenile delinquency in the early 1960s.[8] Although there was never sufficient

---

[6] Kurt Lewin, *Forces Behind Food Habits and Methods of Change*, Bulletin 108 (Washington, D.C.: National Research Council, 1943).

[7] Ibid.

[8] Richard Cloward and Lloyd Ohlin, *Delinquency and Opportunity* (New York: The Free Press, 1963).

empirical research to explore the usefulness of any of these different theoretical explanations, it was the Cloward and Ohlin theory that caught hold with the Kennedy administration and became the major theoretical foundation for the Office of Juvenile Delinquency and the Office of Economic Opportunity. In the long run it is doubtful how much impact these and related programs had on the incidence of delinquency, but they had considerable impact on our perception of crime and our knowledge of how to deal with it.

One major consequence of these programs has been the realization that action without careful evaluation would be a waste of time in future undertakings. However, due to the failure to complete scientific evaluations that were originally designed to begin simultaneously with the start of each action program, it has been virtually impossible to estimate what effect, if any, was made during the sixties by the billions of dollars spent on social problems.

Certainly not on the same level, but a consequence of some note, have been the notions about who is best equipped to carry out change projects, particularly with minority groups and other persons who are generally alienated from the kind of people who are usually responsible for inducing change. During the sixties, projects in New York City, among others, made use of indigent street workers in order to make contact with "target populations."[9] Although there is still much controversy in using community people rather than college-trained professionals in certain change roles, frequently the indigent workers have demonstrated greater rapport with the target group than the professionals and better ability to track youth down, keep them in a program, know when they were faking, and so on. The use of nonprofessionals in roles that were traditionally reserved for professionals has expanded rapidly, and these roles have become known as "new careers."[10]

It is inaccurate to think of new careers as the development of "aides" to the professionals. Rather than that, this strategy involves a new perception of the professional's role and a recasting of the way in which the "treaters" and the "treated" normally make contact and interact. The new careers strategy interjects a paraprofessional between the client and the professional, allows the professional to concentrate on the managerial tools he has been trained for, and trains the paraprofessional in the communication skills and front-line problem-solving skills that are fre-

[9] Kenneth Clark et al., *Youth in the Ghetto,* final research report (New York: Harlem Youth Opportunity Unlimited, 1963).

[10] *Ex-offenders as a Correctional Manpower Resource,* proceedings of a seminar of the Joint Commission on Correctional Manpower and Training (Washington, D.C.: Government Printing Office, 1966).

quently "trained out of" the professional. The result, when the strategy works properly, is a team approach to problems in which the professional, the new careerists, and the client all meet on more equal terms, rather than on highly authoritarian doctor-client terms.[11]

Perhaps the last development in planned change that needs to be mentioned separately is the advancement and utilization of systems analysis itself. As we mentioned in Chapter Six, one major difference between the President's Crime Commission and the Wickersham Commission is the method of problem analysis. The President's Crime Commission is aware of the interconnection of problems, and of the relationships between treaters, programs, and the treated. No longer is it so likely that problems such as crime will be identified as characteristics of people. It is much more likely for contemporary planners and change agents to approach a problem such as crime as a consequence of behavior patterns that involve a variety of different people. The activity of the government is as important as the activity of the offender in explaining the incidence of crime, and interactions among all components must be accounted for in trying to change behavior. Naturally, not all people in the criminal justice system see things in this complex way.

We now turn our attention to some of the more common change strategies.

THREE DIFFERENT CHANGE STRATEGIES

One way of classifying different change strategies is in terms of (1) the power source of the *change agent,* (2) the reaction of the *changee,* and (3) the reasons for the duration of the induced response. Although there may be a number of combinations of these variables possible, Herbert Kelman suggests that three different combinations are most common. He calls these: (1) *Compliance,* (2) *Identification,* and (3) *Internalization.*[12]

Compliance

Compliance is the change strategy that arises when a change agent has the power to manipulate rewards and punishments. The change agent sets out a particular set of goals that he expects the changee to attain, and the changee conforms—not because he wants to, but because it is required

[11] Dennis Sullivan, *Team Management in Probation* (Hackensack, N.J.: National Council on Crime and Delinquency, 1972).

[12] Herbert Kelman, "Compliance, Identification, and Internalization: Three Processes of Attitude Change," *Journal of Conflict Resolution,* 2 (1958), 51–60.

of him. The change agent maintains the desired responses from the changee by maintaining continual surveillance and administering rewards or punishments in accordance with the behavior. The changee is likely to conform as long as this surveillance can be maintained, or, more precisely, as long as the rewards and punishments remain associated with the behavior.

Identification

Identification is the change strategy that arises when the change agent depends on his social relationship with the changee in order to induce the desired response. The behavior is elicited because of the value of the relationship to the person or group, not because of the value of the behavior itself. The change agent is not as likely to be as specific about the kind of behavior he desires; he is more likely to give the changee some room to maneuver, as long as the changee remains within the "confines" of the relationship that is established. The change agent receives his power through this relationship, whether it be one of friend-to-friend, doctor-patient, father-son, or whatever. The behavior elicited from the changee is likely to be maintained as long as the relationship remains salient. As the relationship grows to have less meaning for the changee, he is less likely to engage in the desired behavior.

Internalization

Internalization is the change strategy that arises when the changee adopts certain behavior patterns that he discovers solve certain problems for him, or are consistent with his values. The power of the change agent lies in his ability to delineate certain alternative opportunities for the changee that the changee had not perceived or thought possible. The changee agent can maintain power if he can demonstrate his expertness in this consultative capacity. The induced response is likely to remain independent of the change agent because the behavior itself has value for the changee and is congruent with the way he views the world.

In the next section, we will put these change strategies into a correctional context and examine the organizational consequences of using one strategy or another as the basis for organizing the correctional "production" process. We will then seek to examine the internal climate of the correctional organizations that might be associated with these three basic production lines. Last, we will see how the three different kinds of organizations relate to the external environment.

FROM ASSUMPTIONS ABOUT CHANGE TO
ORGANIZATIONAL STRUCTURE

Kelman's classification of change strategies is a very helpful device for demonstrating that there are considerable differences in the manner by which one person tries to influence another. Moreover, it is useful in demonstrating that these differences are not just haphazard but are ordered in accordance with changes in key change variables. It is not a simple matter to apply this change strategy classification to prison and parole activity. It is important to understand that Kelman is talking about change strategies in general, whereas prisons and parole offer very particular, often strained settings in which the change process must unfold. It has been argued that all three change strategies can be found in the correctional setting, and that argument will be presented here. It should be remembered, however, that the opportunities in the *present* correctional structure for the identification and internalization strategies are rather limited. Indeed, a frequent utilization of these influence styles and a turn away from the more familiar style of compliance would involve a large change in the entire structure of prison and parole.

Finally, there is a present cultural bias *away* from compliance and toward internalization that makes most leaders in the correctional area speak of internalization as being *more effective* than compliance. This, we must point out, is an error. We do not presently possess research results that would allow reliable conclusions about effectiveness. Furthermore, as we have suggested before, compliance can be a very effective influence style if the culture permits the manipulation of the environment to such an extent that surveillance can be continually maintained and the rewards of punishments administered correctly. In other words, we *cannot,* realistically, compare these change strategies for effectiveness without asking "In what social context?" As we have seen in Chapter Six, prison and parole in the United States have been generally ineffective (in an absolute sense) because the social context includes contradictory elements that make consistent correctional program and structure impossible.

THE SOCIAL CONTEXT OF
THE CORRECTIONAL ADMINISTRATOR

In the last dozen or so years there have been a host of papers and studies that claimed to examine correctional goals. Most of these studies involved a particular aspect of correctional goals—the way in which the administrator in prison and parole settings related to the public.

In one article of particular note, basically because of its simplicity, Donald Cressey studied the differences in the goal of "protecting inmates"—depending on the publics that the prison administrator saw as relevant to support of his other goals.[13] The custodially oriented warden perceived himself as a public servant and state politicians as his greatest asset. Partly as a result of these views, he allowed citizens to tour the prison since the citizens were the tax-paying sponsors of the prison. The prisoners in this facility were always on view, and there were signs throughout the prison instructing visitors not to point out or bother inmates (much as there might be at a zoo). On the other hand, this warden was always careful that inmates were protected physically from other inmates and socially from insults or retorts from officers.

At another institution—a "treatment-oriented" prison—things were very different. The warden did not view himself as a public servant but as a professional. He felt perfectly within his role to shut off his prison from tours and curiosity seekers. On the other hand, this warden sought the aid of university and other treatment professionals in order to advance the work of rehabilitation. As a consequence, inmates were continually involved in research and treatment programs and were virtually unprotected from any of the activities that might be conducted in the name of treatment. Second, this warden believed in relaxing the customary military discipline that could be found at the custody-oriented prison. He felt the strict military discipline was contrary to the treatment climate and inconvenient for treatment professionals. But one unintended consequence of this loosening of discipline was the opportunity for custodial officers to use their informal social relationships as a means of control. For example, Cressey found in the treatment-oriented prison that prisoners were frequently ridiculed and demeaned by the guards. In general, then, Cressey found consequences for inmates very different and dependent on the goals of the institution, which in turn, altered the way in which the outside world impinged upon the prison.[14]

Similar studies have been conducted in parole organizations and in juvenile courts with similar results. For example, the major determinants of a juvenile court judge's detention policy seem to be (1) his concern for the youth and (2) his concern for protecting the community.[15] The behavior of parole officers has been described in a like manner—as the

[13] Donald Cressey, "Achievement of an Unstated Organizational Goal: "An Observation on Prisons," *The Pacific Sociological Review*, 1 (Fall 1967), 43–49.

[14] See also Donald Cressey, "Limitations on Organization of Treatment in the Modern Prison," *Theoretical Studies in Social Organizations of the Prison*, pamphlet 15 (New York: Social Science Research Council, March 1960), pp. 78–110.

[15] Donald Gottfredson, *Measuring Attitudes Toward Detention* (New York: National Council on Crime and Delinquency, 1964).

combination of concern for providing service for the parolee and for reducing danger to the community.[16]

Frequently the administrator's concern for the community and his concern for the offender have been treated as more or less contradictory elements. For example, David Street, Robert Vinter, and Charles Perrow, among others, speak of treatment and custody as the poles of a continuum in which the custodian appears to express concern for the community and the treater appears to express concern for the offender.[17]

MODELS OF CORRECTION POLICY

An organizational policy is an executive goal statement that has *structural* consequences. Policy involves basic ideological components but also operationalizes the goals by determining what will be done in the organization and how, when, and where it will be carried out. A correctional policy, then, is a goal statement that includes executive decisions about how prison and parole organizations should be structured to achieve the specified ends. Policy may begin with certain assumptions about how to change people, but it also includes the nature of the programs in which those assumptions will be manifested.

Four different models of correctional policy can be constructed by juxtaposing the two most commonly mentioned correctional concerns (see Figure 11-1). This diagram may be helpful in establishing what a consistent correctional program would include, and measurements of correctional policy will enable us to discuss the different organizational subsystems in relation to important correctional goals.

The models are formulated by imagining the two dimensions—of emphasis on the community and emphasis on the offender—placed at right angles. If, for simplicity's sake, we limit these continua to the extremes of "high" or "low" emphasis, the result is four different correctional policies. These policies are depicted in Figure 11-1.

With particular attention to key differences in ideology and structure, the four polar policies are described below. One should be careful to understand that, in real life, these polar types are unlikely to be found. One correctional program may incorporate different aspects of several policies, or of all four. Nevertheless, many correctional organizations do tend to take on a flavor or overall character in which one of the policies described below is dominant.

[16] Daniel Glaser, *The Effectiveness of a Prison and Parole System* (Indianapolis, Ind.: Bobbs-Merrill, 1969); and Elliot Studt, *Surveillance and Service in Parole, A Report of the Parole Action Study* (Los Angeles: Institute of Government and Public Affairs, U.C.L.A., 1972).

[17] David Street, Robert Vinter, and Charles Perrow, *Organization for Treatment* (New York: Free Press, 1966).

Figure 11-1. Correctional Policy Models

		REHABILITATION	REINTEGRATION
CONCERN FOR THE OFFENDER	**HIGH**	REHABILITATION Influence style: identification Inmate should become mature man. Treatment for "criminality." Emphasis on self-expression. Parole officers: therapists Custody/treatment split. Parole BD: therapeutic professionals Work release, etc: emphasis on feelings, not actions.	REINTEGRATION Influence style: internalization. Find opportunities for inmates. Change community & inmate simultaneously. Community supervision emphasized. Parole officer: advocate & mediator. Emphasis on team work—all staff are important. Inmates have rights under law.
	LOW	RESTRAINT No influence. Inmate caged for crime. Protection of Institution. "Don't rock the boat." "Serve your own time." Parole officers: observers. Parole board: politicians. Inmates have no rights. Work release, etc.: none.	REFORM Influence style: compliance. Inmate should become a *good* citizen. Instilling right habits. "Firm but fair." Parole officer: police-investigatory type. Offenders have privileges, not rights. Parole Board: community leaders. Work release, etc.: limited to "good" risk.
		LOW	**HIGH**

CONCERN FOR THE COMMUNITY

Restraint

Restraint, in the lower left-hand corner of Figure 11-1, is the policy with a low emphasis on the offender and a low emphasis on the community. Essentially, the organization *itself* seems to be of greatest importance to policy makers. In general, the policy makers who favor restraint believe that little, if any, change is possible with inmates. In other words, none of the change styles described by Kelman are dominant. The correctional administrator is more likely to take the attitude that he is merely providing the program, and the inmate will benefit if he desires. This kind of administrator is likely to justify himself by pointing to rules and regulations. Since he emphasizes neither the community nor the offender, he is unlikely to go out on a limb.

Programmatic features are as follows:

1. Little training is required for staff, except perhaps technical training in the production of certain correctional industries or in maintenance of the facilities.

2. The parole officer is neither an advocate nor a policeman; he merely observes and reports.

3. Legal rights of prisoners are discouraged because the adversary procedure does not contribute to smooth and orderly routine.

4. The parole board is highly sensitive to public opinion, and members are political appointees.

5. Prerelease programs may be used to keep inmates busy or quiet; work release, study release, and halfway house programs are discouraged from "bringing heat on the agency."

Reform

Reform, in the lower right-hand corner of Figure 11-1, is the policy with low emphasis on the offender and high emphasis on the community. This emphasis generally means protection of the community. This policy is frequently highly moralistic: The offender is seen as having *willfully* committed a crime for which he must pay the price. There is the attempt to make the offender "learn his lesson," which means, generally, that all inmates are treated alike and all parolees are treated as if parole were a privilege, easily revoked for poor behavior. Programmatic distinctions are the following: .

1. Training for staff is again not required at a high level; it is more important that staff act as proper models for inmates, presenting correct community attitudes.

2. Vocational skill and proper work habits for offenders are emphasized.

3. Parole officers (and prison officers) tend to be of a police type—they emphasize regulation and investigation.

4. Prisoners have few rights because it is believed that they have lost their rights at conviction. They have privileges that are earned through good behavior.

5. Parole board members, ideally, are upstanding citizens, the best representatives of the dominant social values.

6. Work release, furlough, and other such programs are generally discouraged, unless they can be used as privileges granted inmates who have *already* demonstrated willingness and ability to conform.

7. Basic change strategy is that of *compliance*.

Rehabilitation

Rehabilitation, in the upper left-hand corner of Figure 11-1, is the policy with a high emphasis on the offender and a low emphasis on the community. Generally, there is the ideological viewpoint that criminality is a condition whose major sources lie within the person. The prison is viewed as a "hospital," where therapy for improper socialization, poor family experiences, and so on, may be conducted. Parole is typically seen as the "after-care" from such a therapeutic experience. Major programmatic characteristics are as follows:

1. Training for some staff is highly demanding. Therapy is seen as a job for professionals, and there is a call for counselors, psychologists, psychiatrists, etc., with appropriate college and postgraduate training.
2. There is a major structural bifurcation between custodians, who keep the inmates, and treatment staff, who care for them.
3. The parole officer ideally is a trained counselor with whom the parolee can discuss the problems and pressures of returning to the community.
4. There are major objections to legal interventions in the system because therapy cannot be argued in an adversarial manner. Decisions made by professionals, it is thought, should not be open to legal challenge.
5. The parole board ideally is a clinical review team of behavioral and medical professionals. They emphasize the health of the offender, or, upon revocation, his need for further treatment.
6. Work release and prerelease are used not so much for their practical benefits as to allow the offender to explore the pressures of the community when he is still under supervision of the therapist.
7. The major influence style is one of *identification*.

Reintegration

Reintegration, in the upper right-hand corner of Figure 11-1, is the policy that places high emphasis on the offender and high emphasis on the community. Generally, there is the belief in this policy that criminal behavior has been learned as a means of solving problems, and correctional activity is seen as the provision of opportunities and training for more effective ways of solving problems. There is generally a deemphasis on instructional treatment and an emphasis on community treatment. Programmatic distinctions are listed below:

1. Training for staff is varied, depending on tasks. There is the view that all staff can contribute to the offender's reintegration because they all possess different resources that can be brought to bear on the offender's problems.
2. There is greater use of small institutions close by or within the communities to which offenders will be released.
3. The parole officer is ideally an advocate who can actively help the offender reenter the social structure.
4. There are no objections to the exercises of legal rights by offenders, and the participation of the offender in the design and implementation of his program is encouraged. The parole board is ideally an appellate body reviewing decisions of institutional and field workers. Parole is usually offered as soon as possible, and revocation is seen as a last resort.

5. Prerelease, work release, furlough, and other such programs are close to the core of this policy because it is in these ways that the system can provide alternatives and time for the offender to test them out.

6. The major influence style is that of *internalization.*

FITTING THE POLICY MODELS TO ORGANIZATIONAL REALITIES

As we saw in Chapters Six and Seven, correctional organizations in the United States are not well planned and efficient units in which everyone in the organizations agrees about what should be done and knows his role in doing it. On the contrary, we have seen that corrections evolved over time, that different functions were added at different times (regardless of relationships to other functions), and that the administration of all functions has been complicated by the constitutional and political issues involved in relating different levels of government.

It should go without saying, then, that the correctional policies in the preceding section are scarcely, if ever, found implemented in a consistent fashion from the point of reception to discharge from parole. One of the major splits in the correctional task, for example, is caused by the independent origins of prisons and parole systems. Prison began with the assumption that offender reformation could take place within prison walls, whereas parole frequently emerged from the more contemporary belief that an offender, like any other individual, is affected by the matrix of intersecting roles and social structures in which he lives. Frequently, then, there are major policy differences between prison and parol authorities in one correctional system.

This separation of prison and parole policy is reinforced by the fact that several of these policies do not call for officials to pay much attention to the environment that surrounds their particular segment of operations or that will in the long run affect the offender. For example, if prison officials are firmly in favor of a rehabilitation policy, it is likely that their emphasis on the internal defects in offenders will blind them to contradictory ways that parole officials might behave. It is their job to cure the offender within the prison, rather than integrate their work with the work of the parole officer. To take another example, it is very unlikely that parole officers with a policy of restraint will go about criticizing openly a different policy espoused by prison officials. It is not their responsibility to supervise other officials, and besides they do not hold much hope of change in offenders anyway.

Consequently, it may be quite likely for the offender in his trip through the correctional process to meet, and be required to adjust to, several different staff orientations. In a reception center, for example, he might spend several weeks with psychologists and counselors whose policy is one of rehabilitation, and who take particular care to examine the offender's motivations, attitudes, personal history, relationships with family, and so on. From there, he may be passed on to a prison in which the dominant force is the reform policy of the custodial management. In this setting, offenders are reproved for excusing their behavior or for explaining it in terms of psychological causes, and all offenders are treated alike rather than as individuals with different problems. Toward the end of his prison stay, the same offender may be assigned to a prerelease program that includes group therapy sessions, where the counselor emphasizes that each person can gain help and insight from his peers. Shortly after this experience, the same offender may be placed on parole and told by a reform-oriented parole officer not to consort with any other ex-offenders or parolees!

Frequently the correctional literature has pointed to the advantages inmates take of this kind of situation, by learning which correctional staff will go for what, and then playing different staff factions against each other. Although this state of affairs is true, it deemphasizes the other important aspect that an offender who does seek help of some sort is virtually lost among the inconsistent and contradictory staff orientations that he confronts.

Basically, there would seem to be two different kinds of policy conflict possible. First, there is the possibility of internal dissension within an organization. Second, there is the possibility of conflict between organizations. The conflict in orientations between the custodial force and the prerelease program is an example of intraorganizational conflict. The policy shift between the reception center and the prison would be an example of interorganizational conflict.

Intraorganizational Conflict

A study of policy dissension in one organization was conducted in a minimum security prison in a northeastern state in 1970.[18] The design of the study called for: (1) a measurement of correctional policy by top prison administrators and middle management, (2) a measurement of the policy supported by custodial officer performance, and (3) a measurement from inmates of the policy they perceived as most frequently enforced. The results of this study are given in Table 11-1.

It is clear (from the statistics given in Table 11-1) that top prison administrators were strongly in favor of reintegration and had a close

---

[18] Vincent O'Leary and David Duffee, "Correctional Policy—A Classification of Goals Designed for Change," *Crime and Delinquency*, *17* No. 4 (October 1971) 373–386.

Table 11-1. Policy Scores at Different Prison Levels

Level	Reintegration	Policy Rehabilitation	Reform	Restraint
Top managers	80.0	76.8	57.7	48.2
Middle managers	69.8	80.3	66.0	56.2
Officers	55.2	68.4	77.7	61.5
Inmates	59.7	57.0	80.0	90.0

Note: Data adapted from Vincent O'Leary and David Duffee, "Correctional Policy—A Classification of Goals Designed for Change," *Crime and Delinquency*, 17, No. 4 (October 1971), 384.

second choice of rehabilitation. Middle management, however, had a first preference for rehabilitation and gave reintegration second priority. Although these differences are slight and both groups rated reform third and restraint last, there is some significance in the lack of agreement between these two managerial groups. Generally, it is the top managers who formulate policy and the middle managers who translate policy into action by organizing their subordinates to work in certain ways. If there are divergencies between these two groups, it would make sense to expect this small disagreement to be exacerbated as we continue down the hierarchical levels of the prison. Or, to state it as we did in the introduction to Part III, deviance in the bureaucratic organization tends to be amplified. Small and unimportant differences in one area of organization tend to become large and important differences in other areas of organization. This amplifying effect is evident in the data from the bottom two lines in Table 11-1. Custodial officers reported that the behavior with inmates that they most often engaged in was supportive of a reform policy. Although they reported that the second most frequent behavior would support the rehabilitation policy of middle managers, they reported restraint as more frequent than reintegration. Inmates, as might then be expected, perceived restraint as the policy most frequently enforced, and they reported reform a close second. Reintegration and rehabilitation were equally distant, and, certainly, not in the inmates' perspective, dominant forces in their prison existence.

In prison literature of the past, the kind of divergence noted here between expressed managerial goals and the inmates' perception of reality has usually been analyzed under the concept of the "inmate subculture." For example, Gresham Sykes in the now classic *Society of Captives* argues that the fundamental rift between the staff and the inmates is caused by the inherent flaws in the totalitarian regime.[19] He said that the social and physical deprivations of imprisonment were so great that the

[19] Gresham Sykes, *The Society of Captives* (Princeton, N.J.: Princeton University Press, 1971).

inmates spend a vast amount of energy in organizing an inmate subculture within which they (the inmates) can obtain social rewards such as status and prestige without losing their integrity and bowing down to staff demands. Although there is a great deal to be said for this kind of sociological analysis, the policy data in Table 11-1 and the data of similar studies conducted more recently[20] would suggest that the concept of inmate subculture does not completely or accurately explain the goal conflict that exists in prisons. For example, staff-inmate conflict exists, but it is a generalization that ignores fundamental conflicts at different staff levels. In reality, correctional officers are much closer in their perception of the prison to inmates than they are to top staff levels. In other words, it would seem important to recognize the inmate-staff conflict as *only one manifestation* of intraorganizational conflict in the prison—if we want to reduce that conflict in some way. Clearly, the conflict between inmates and officers is related to conflicts up the line, and it is unlikely that we could reduce the alienation of the inmate group without also reducing simultaneously the divergent behaviors among different staff groups.[21]

Similar kinds of intraorganizational conflicts may be analyzed in parole organizations. There are, however, some major differences based on the fact that parole has a considerably different structure than prisons. Parole organizations, like police and probation organizations, have the characteristics of "front-line organizations." That is, there is considerably more discretion exercised by the parole officer in the discharge of his duties than by members of a prison staff. Parole officers in their supervisory capacity may make decisions about particular parolees when they are miles away from their supervisors and when communication is difficult. Furthermore, the parole officer, regardless of the policy in the organization, is more likely to be seen as a "professional" who has the expertise to make decisions about his caseload without deferring to his superiors. Moreover, parole, unlike prison organization, generally uses the individual parole officer as the key organizing principle. There is less managerial superstructure, and although many parole officers feel bogged down in paperwork, there is also a less complex bureaucracy. Thus, although it makes sense to view prison policy conflict in hierarchical terms, policy conflicts in parole organization tend to be diffused throughout caseloads. Rather than talk about policy differences, we are more apt to

[20] See Daniel Glaser, "The Prospect for Corrections," paper prepared for the Arden House Conference on Manpower Needs in Corrections, mimeo, 1964; and Clarence Schrag, "Contemporary Corrections: An Analytical Model," paper prepared for the President's Commission on Law Enforcement and Administration of Justice, mimeo, 1966.

[21] Vincent O'Leary and David Duffee, "Managerial Behavior and Correctional Policy," *Public Administration Review, 31,* No. 6 (November/December 1971), 603–615.

Figure 11-2.   Glaser's Parole Officer Roles

		LOW	HIGH
ASSISTANCE	HIGH	Welfare	Paternal
	LOW	Passive	Punitive

LOW   HIGH

CONTROL

[Adapted from D. Glaser, *The Effectiveness of a Prison and Parole System* (Indianapolis, Ind.: Bobbs-Merrill, 1969).]

recognize personal differences in parole officers. For example, we might say that they have a different "operating style" or are sensitive to different inmate behavior.

Except in the larger states where the managerial superstructure of parole might be quite large, it frequently seems to make more sense to speak about parole policy conflicts as these conflicts are manifested in the *roles* played by the individual parole officers. One particularly well-known typology of parole-officer roles is the one constructed by Daniel Glaser. It is depicted in Figure 11-2.[22]

Glaser suggests that there are basically four different parole officer types, as distinguished by alternate combinations of the parole officer's activities on the independent dimensions of *assistance* and *control*. Glaser called the officer who was low on both dimensions the *passive* officer. An officer who gave frequent assistance but displayed a low concern for control, he called the *welfare* officer. Officers who display frequent control behaviors but rarely come to the assistance of the parolee, Glaser called the *punitive* officer. Finally, an officer who was high on both concerns, he called the *paternal* officer. Glaser measured these roles in a questionnaire mailed to 510 federal probation officers in 1961. He discovered from their responses considerable differences in the way they handled cases. For example, 90 percent of passive and welfare officers never requested a warrant for parole violation if a parole changes jobs without permission. In contrast, 40 percent of the paternal and punitive officers requested warrants for such violations. Roughly one-third of welfare and paternal officers tried personally to obtain work for parolees, whereas only 13 percent of punitive or passive officers rendered that kind of assistance. In short, Glaser found many significant differences in the ways in which parole officers perceived their role and in the ways that they supervised parolees.[23]

---

[22] Adapted from Glaser, *Effectiveness of a Prison,* pp. 289–297.

[23] Ibid.

Whether or not such differences in role performance contribute to parole organizational conflict is not so clear. Obviously, there might be conflicts involved for a parolee if he were to change parole officers. More difficult to visualize perhaps, but equally important, would be the relationship between the four different roles performed and the activity of the parole board. Glaser states, for example, that the level of assistance provided by federal probation officers was considerably higher than the level of assistance provided in some state organizations he had studied.[24] In other words, there was a trend toward assistance in federal probation and parole policy that was formulated by the parole board and by the district courts that supervise the officers. It is conceivable, then, that this trend created additional conflicts for passive or punitive officers who perceived assistance as unimportant. It is also possible that the parole board may have responded differently to revocation requests made by officers with different styles. Although there is the tendency (and indeed the necessity) in parole organization to grant the officer considerable discretion, the fact that different officers request violation warrants with considerably different frequencies may alter the response of the parole board to such requests. This differential response, in turn, raises the issue of fairness to the parolee. Since the parolee cannot control his assignment to one kind of officer or another, one set of parolees is subject to considerably more control than another set, and some parolees receive considerably more assistance than others. Clearly, the evaluation of a parolee's behavior must include examination of official responses, as well as examination of parolee behavior. Revocation *and* success are both functions of the *interaction* among the parole board, the officer, and the parolee. Assessment of different inmate characteristics by themselves is not sufficient for understanding the correctional process, for predicting what will happen, or for controlling these events.

Interorganizational Conflict

Prison and parole organizations of a particular jurisdiction form a complex system. Understanding what happens in a prison, and understanding what happens in a parole organization, are not sufficient for understanding what happens to an offender who will be processed in both types of organizations. The study of interorganizational relations is just beginning in the social sciences, and we do not possess a great quantity of data at this time. One of the problems is that the social science techniques that are most sophisticated are not capable of handling interorganizational variables with much precision. In other words, we presently are at some-

[24] Ibid.

thing of a loss to conceptualize and quantify the ways in which entire organizations interact with other entire organizations.

One set of concepts that may help us to begin this kind of study are the three organizational subsystems that were developed in the introduction to Part III of this text. We have seen for example that individual organizations are viable to the extent that they integrate the subsystems for production, maintenance, and relations with the environment. Thus it may be possible to study the interrelationships of two organizations by examining the following factors:

1. Production relationships—the extent to which they have joint tasks or production goals and share techniques to accomplish those goals.
2. Maintenance relationships—the extent to which they have personnel and clients who share notions of authority and have common or compatible systems for maintaining internal order through organizational rewards and punishment.
3. Boundary relationships—the extent to which their boundaries are mutually permeable and there are established and effective communication channels between the organizations, and the extent to which the two organizations have a common environment in terms of how they both interact with other organizations.

PRODUCTION RELATIONSHIPS. Because the correctional policy models (Figure 11-1) summarize different goal orientations of organizations, juxtaposing the correctional policies of prison and parole organizations is a handy way of addressing the question of production relationships.

A summary of possible prison and parole policy relationships is depicted in Table 11-2.

In Table 11-2, we have a matrix of possible prison policies and possible parole policies. The main diagonal across the diagram locates identical policy orientations in the two kinds of agencies. The further we travel

Table 11-2. Possible Prison and Parole Policy Combinations

PAROLE POLICY	PRISON POLICY			
	Reintegration	Rehabilitation	Reform	Restraint
Reintegration	—	Rehabilitation/ Reintegration	Reform/ Reintegration	Restraint/ Reintegration
Rehabilitation	Reintegration/ Rehabilitation	—	Reform/ Rehabilitation	Restraint/ Rehabilitation
Reform	Reintegration/ Reform	Rehabilitation/ Reform	—	Restraint/ Reform
Restraint	Reintegration/ Restraint	Rehabilitation/ Restraint	Reform/ Restraint	—

Figure 11-3.   Prediction of Prison—Parole Policy Interactions

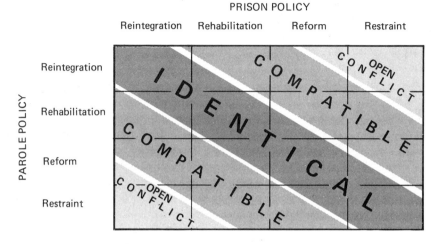

away from that diagonal in either direction, the more incompatible the goals of prison and parole would seem to be. For instance, in the upper right-hand corner we have a prison with a restraint policy coupled with a reintegration-oriented parole office. In the corner diagonally opposite, we have a reintegration prison organization coupled with a restraint parole office. Every combination that occurs above the diagonal represents a policy conflict in which the prison experience can generally be characterized as less flexible or less tailored to the individual inmate than the parole program. Every combination that occurs below the diagonal line represents a policy conflict in which the parole experience can generally be characterized as less flexible or less tailored to the individual inmate than the prison program has been.

Just what the variety of combinations enumerated in Table 11-2 means in terms of consequences for the inmate or consequences for the operation of the agencies is difficult to predict. One suggestion is given in Figure 11-3. In this diagram, the specific policy combinations have been replaced with predictions about the kinds of interactions we might find between agencies and the most likely consequences for the offender who is processed through any one of these combinations. For example, the main diagonal still represents the area of identical policy. In these circumstances there should be (other things being equal) optimum cooperation between prison and parole staff and minimum confusion for the inmate. Of course, each block in this diagonal represents a considerably different world for the inmate. But what each policy entails has been explained above. Here we are only interested in relationships between the two organizations of prison and parole.

In the two diagonals immediately above and immediately below this line of identical policies, we have a line of "compatible policies." In these six cells there would seem to be some conflict between organizations and some "jarring" of the offender. But whether the prison has prepared the inmate for slightly more flexibility than the parole agency can give or the parole agency is more demanding and more energetic than the prison led the offender to anticipate, the differences in these six cells would not seem to be insurmountable.

Last, we have the three cells in the upper right-hand corner, in which the policy clash is such that we should predict disaster. In this group, the prison perceives itself as a public service and perceives individual inmates of small consequence, whereas the parole officers have opposite points of view. The staff will have a difficult time communicating across vast differentials in education, and managerial practices in one agency will seem totally nonsensical to the people in the other organization. The consequence for the inmate is no better. He is likely to be alienated and embittered by his prison experience and completely flabbergasted by the change in orientation when he makes parole. This change is probably so jarring that it will merely add to his adjustment problems rather than aid his return to the community. And in the three cells in the lower left corner, we have the opposite situation. The prison officials have a high concern for the offender, whereas the parole officials have none. The offender will be prepared for the community while in prison, but he will not be prepared for parole officers who treat him as a threat to public safety and who treat his parole as a privilege to be revoked at their discretion. The interorganizational conflicts, again, will be disastrous for the organization, and the consequences will be equally disastrous for the offender.

MAINTENANCE RELATIONSHIPS.   The maintenance functions of organization are a prerequisite for the achievement of high production or for the satisfactory completion of tasks within specified periods of time. Without predictable and stable relationships in an organization, the personnel cannot be expected to expend the optimum amount of energy toward the completion of task assignments. But, as we saw in the introduction, there are some fundamentally different ways of maintaining an organization. A common bureaucratic method, for instance, is to assign particular statuses and roles to organizational members that are more or less permanent. Members are rewarded in terms of how well they perform within these set roles, and the usual means of achieving new status is periodic promotions to new positions based on performance of the old role and the completion of an examination of some sort that supposedly predicts performance in the new role. In prison and parole organizations, status and role are prescribed in civil-service specifications, and promotions are awarded competitively, based on a combination of years in service, scores on examinations, and recommendations. Typical prison organization is generally militaristic, at least in the custodial divisions, and highly hierarchical throughout the organization. Typical parole structures are not much more flexible. The result is that there are relatively few chances of promotion, and a change in job status generally means that a man passes upward in a specific chain of command rather than horizontally to fundamentally different roles. A "good" correctional officer becomes a sergeant, and then a lieutenant. A "good" counselor becomes a counselor supervisor, and a "good" parole officer, a parole supervisor. Typically, then, the people who receive the most organizational rewards are those who demonstrate the greatest staying power within their particular organizational division.[25]

In relation to correctional policy, this kind of maintenance structure is most compatible with restraint and reform. The restraint policy is not founded on any assumption of change in offender behavior, and therefore this orientation toward membership is compatible with the goals of the organization. Reform, with its emphasis on compliance, is dependent for effectiveness on the rigor with which staff adhere to their own rules and enforce rules on inmate behavior. Again, the traditional maintenance patterns seem compatible. When we study the stability requirements of rehabilitation, however, this kind of pattern is less suitable. The change strategy of identification requires that staff who strike the best rapport with inmates or parolees should remain in contact with them, but the typical reward structure promotes the most effective workers to managerial positions and out of contact with offenders. With the reintegration policy there would seem to be even more basic incompatibilities. Change strategies in this policy involve the building of resources and opportunities for offenders and providing systematic evaluation of the consequences of tested alternatives. Furthermore, there is the assumption in this policy that different members will take the lead in different tasks, depending on their interests and capabilities. Otherwise stated, reintegration needs a stable organizational structure, but it requires stability of planned change rather than a structure that is permanently fixed. Permanent status and role assignments will be incompatible with production requirements for shifting responsibilities and shifting communication patterns.

In summary, the maintenance structures that seem compatible with restraint and reform are the most common types, and these structures should aid the coordination of a prison and a parole organization that have restraint or reform goals. The staff in the prison would feel comfortable with the organizational rewards we would find in the parole organi-

[25] See Abraham Blumberg, *Criminal Justice* (Chicago: Quadrangle, 1964), pp. 143–160.

zation, and vice versa. The basic maintenance structures that would seem compatible with rehabilitation policy are not frequently found, but they do exist. They would include (for example) recognition of a staff member's ability to strike up relationships with offenders and to maintain them over time. This quality would have to be valued by the organization, and some mechanism would have to be institutionalized for formalizing the recognition. In several places, for example, pay ranges for counselors have been increased so that they can be financially promoted without changing roles. In related fashion, some institutions have recognized that officers' behavior toward inmates is equally important to the achievement of rehabilitation policy, and new positions have been created that recognize officers' interpersonal skills rather than promote them to the managerial ranks.

Least frequently found in contemporary prison and parole organizations are maintenance structures that facilitate a reintegration policy. One reason for this is that most prisons are physically too large to permit the role flexibility necessary in reintegration. On the parole side, we are beginning to see maintenance structures emerge in which the parole officer's loyalty and responsibility are not directed toward a particular function but toward the overall success of a particular team of individuals. It is this structure that we would expect to find more frequently as the trend toward reintegration continues.

Although there may be greater goal compatibility between reintegration and rehabilitation than between either of these and reform or restraint, the maintenance structures of reintegration and rehabilitation are considerably different, and these differences would probably create certain additional difficulties in terms of cooperation between agencies with these two orientations. The rehabilitation organization is still basically tied to notions of separation of custodial and treatment roles, whereas reintegration-oriented personnel would have a minimum of respect or use for this division. Furthermore, reintegration personnel are not likely to defer quickly enough or with enough ultimate respect for the collegial and professional training that is a major status differential in rehabilitation organizations.

BOUNDARY RELATIONSHIPS.   The last subsystem to be investigated for its contribution to interorganizational cooperation or conflict is the way in which organizations relate to external environments, that is, their boundary relationships. The demarcation of boundaries in restraint and reform organizations is likely to be rather clear, and the passing of staff or offenders through these boundaries is likely to be well controlled. This is true in parole as well as in prison, although in a somewhat different sense. A restraint parole office is likely to protect itself from public criticism. It is likely to do so, not by keeping terribly close surveillance on parolees, but by erecting a wall of paperwork and official regulations between the staff and criticism from the public about behavior of parolees. It can do this, for example, by pointing out that regulations require personnel to be in the office so many hours a week or that regulations require that parolees report so many times a month. Parole is in this sense basically a bookkeeping exercise, and about the only kind of criticism that the office might admit is relevant would be that books are out of order or regulations are not being properly followed. Since it is not seen as the job of the parole staff to obtain jobs for parolees or render other such services, social and physical interaction with the community can be kept to a minimum.

Boundary delineation in reform policy is rather different. The important distinction is that parole officers actively seek out parolees in the community and keep strict requirements enforced about the length and scope of the parolee's travels, his social interaction, and so on.

The prison boundaries of these two policies are rather similar. Restraint has the *least permeable* boundaries, the least contact with outside agencies, the least request for service, etc. The reform prison, as was related in the study by Cressey, may include frequent contact with the public, but of a certain kind.[26] The prison is basically a public enterprise. Its main purpose is the protection of free citizens. The kinds of contact and interaction that are sought are basically the types that will (1) convince the public that a good job is being done, and (2) import to the prison, models of decent values and morals. Thus this kind of prison may seek the support from voluntary service organizations such as the Lions, or they may seek programs in better living that are available in many localities from the Junior Chamber of Commerce, and so on.

The boundaries of the rehabilitation prison are again well delineated in the Cressey study described earlier.[27] There will be little desire on the part of the warden to accommodate the general public, but he will seek support from professional groups, mental health services, and universities. The same is true in a rehabilitation parole office. The office will be active with particular agencies in the community, basically those that can be referral sources for needed counseling, therapy, and so on. This policy focuses on changes within the individual offender, and therefore the kinds of interaction with the environment that are seen as important are limited.

A reintegration policy will imply relatively permeable boundaries. The institutional organization that is ideal under this policy is a small and flexible unit located close to the community of parole release. The rein-

[26] Donald R. Cressey, "The Achievement of an Unstated Organization Goal: An Observation on Prisons," *Pacific Sociological Review, 1* (Fall 1958) 43–49.

[27] Ibid.

tegration organization will seek different kinds of community support for different inmates—depending on inmate values and desires. A major change, however, is that the reintegration organization will actively seek to *give* aid to the community when it has the competence and resources to do so. That is, staff and inmates in these institutions will expect to exchange some services for others. They will go out and invent ways of garnering community support, particularly job offers, housing assistance, and so on.

Now the complicated question becomes the one of how these different approaches to the external environment will facilitate or militate the cooperation between prison and parole organizations with different policies. Generally, we might expect restraint and reform to be compatible, although the reform organization will see the restraint organization as backward and a bit careless. The rehabilitation interaction with the environment will probably seem a waste of energies to the restraint or the reform organization, but the fact that the rehabilitation organization seeks *professional* aid for offenders is likely to carry some weight with the more conservative organization. Reformists might see rehabilitation people as foolish, but generally not as radicals. In some sense the seeking of therapy for offenders carries a "neutral" political aura, although some people would argue it is a conservative stance.

The reintegration organization will be seen as careless by the reformers and organizationally suicidal by the restraint organization. Rehabilitation and reintegration organizations will probably view each other as seeking the wrong kind of community support, but there will be some compatibility between them.

In conclusion, it would seem that the kinds of environmental interactions carried out in relation to different policies will also limit the ability of prison and parole organizations to react to each other. The kinds of community interactions supported by reintegration would probably result in noncooperation from a restraint or reform organization. Reform and restraint organizations would view the environment in a similar light, whereas rehabilitation organizations would focus on the environment in such selective fashion that they might gain *some* cooperation from either reform, restraint, or reintegration agencies.

SPECIFIC ISSUES IN RELATION TO THE ORGANIZATIONAL MODEL

The importance of the policy issues for the coordination of prison and parole organizations should be clear. There are, however, a host of specific issues in the correctional area, the contemporary significance of which requires specific discussion. We have selected six issues here that have received considerable attention in the literature and whose impacts are all interrelated.

1. Issues involved in sentencing, such as choice of sentence option, length of sentence, and the continuation of judicial authority over the incarcerated offender.
2. Issues in classification, such as how offenders are selected for one prison or another, and how it is decided what will happen to them within a prison.
3. Issues in correctional research, such as how it will be conducted and whether the information will be utilized.
4. Issues concerning parole granting and revocation, including the criteria for these decisions and the procedures used for deliberation.
5. Issues in correctional management, such as the relationship between management and research, particular managerial strategies for the implementation of goals and the development of correctional manpower.
6. Finally, a question that is basically an ethical issue—which may make us reexamine our analytical model—Which comes first, the establishment of order or the promotion of change?

This last issue is particularly important because it poses many of the questions we have been addressing in a rather new light. Briefly, there would seem to be some inherent conflicts between any of the influence styles and correctional policies we have discussed and the traditional jurisprudential understanding of retribution. Moreover, although retribution is currently an unpopular justification for the use of the criminal sanction, many of the new legal rights of prisoners would seem to place liberal, legal-rights advocates in the retribution camp and would find them basically opposed to newer correctional strategies that assume there is some compatibility between offenders' desires and the desires of contemporary correctional administrators.

Sentencing

Sentencing at this point in time is a very complex procedure involving the legislature, the sentencing judge, and the parole board. Sentencing has changed its meaning over the years. When the Wickersham Commission reported in 1931, parole was the modal release procedure, but it was still used only in a minority of releases from prison. Over the years, the use of parole has increased and the variety of prisons has increased, and there has been superimposed between the judge and the prison, a department of correction, which, through a reception center, decides on the actual allocation of the prisoner. For these basic reasons, and many more besides, the power that a judge has over the quality of the prison experience for any one offender has decreased steadily. Judicial intervention in correctional decision making is now increasing, but we arrive at that kind of intervention from a different source.

Recent innovations in correctional programs have touched off a series of conflicts between sentencing judges and the correctional authority in Pennsylvania and elsewhere. This conflict was touched off when the Pennsylvania Bureau of Correction began releasing offenders to their homes on temporary furloughs for such purposes as finding jobs, settling family problems, and so on. For some sentencing judges, this seemed to be the last straw. The judges had become accustomed to parole board policies that allowed them (the judges) to more or less control the release time of inmates by increasing or decreasing a sentence in anticipation of what the parole board might do. But suddenly the judges were confronted with releases directly from prison of people they had sentenced to remain incarcerated until paroled. Therefore they enlisted public support against what was in their view the premature return of offenders to the community. Newspapers published stories of furloughed inmates who failed to return to prison at the appointed time or who committed new crimes, and the department had to change its furlough policy so that judges could veto a certain furlough if they so desired.

The apparent conflict was between the correctional policy of the department, which planned to use furloughs as an integrated component in the offender's return to society, and the sentencing policy of some judges, which seemed based on maintaining physical isolation of the offender from society. It is possible, although impossible to be sure at this point, that the judges' objections could have been resolved if there were some other mechanism for policy discussion beside the public press. Although several criminal justice commissions since 1967 have viewed sentencing as part of the correctional process, the actual working relationships between judges and correctional agencies remain poor in many instances. So far we have been able to investigate in a rudimentary fashion the relationships between prison and parole policy. It is obviously of equal importance that we begin to address the issue of sentencing and correctional policy.

Classification

Classification is becoming increasingly sophisticated, and, in more and more states, initial classification is now done at a centralized reception center. As we mentioned in Chapter Seven, reception centers have generally tended to follow a medical model. The idea of classification 20 years ago referred basically to the custodial decisions of cell-block and job assignment. As the policy of rehabilitation has become more popular, this custodial classification has expanded, if not changed, under the concept of "diagnosis." This change in the classification decision meant that officials now decide not only where an inmate is going to reside and work but also what is going to be done with him. Instead of having only his job and cell assignment at stake, an inmate now stands a chance of being sent to entirely different facilities, depending on the initial diagnosis. The Task Force on Corrections of the National Advisory Commission on Criminal Justice Standards and Goals has consequently recognized classification as a decision with major impact on the offender's correctional experience—and thus a decision that calls for the inmate's participation and exercise of legal rights. Indeed, the National Advisory Commission states that classification decisions that are couched in therapeutic terms are frequently custodial decisions in disguise. In other words, the offender is being allocated to particular spaces because someone feels he is dangerous or because someone needs the manpower on a particular prison industry or maintenance assignment. But rather than admit to these criteria for allocation, many reception centers "justify" (or rationalize) the allocation on the grounds that the program will be "good" for the inmate (i.e., help in his rehabilitation).[28]

At least one state has evidently anticipated the National Advisory Commission's criticism by building into the departmental reception-center model procedures for inmate appeal of the classification decision. Whether this model will be implemented remains to be seen.[29]

The important issue here is that there presently seems to be no policy consensus underlying the various ways in which people may be classified. Classifications, in and of themselves, are nonsensical. They are only useful to the extent that: (1) the categories in the classification are theoretically related to some valid purpose; (2) the information that provides the basis for classifying is accurate; and (3) the classifiers are skilled in interpreting data, so that the people classified actually are allocated to the theoretically intended categories.

All three of these prerequisites for classification are obviously related to judicial and correctional policy. If the preconviction system and, ultimately, the sentencing judges are not attuned to and in agreement with the policy of the receiving correctional authority, no useful classifications are possible. If the correctional authority has not achieved consensus about its basic strategies, it is quite possible that the diagnosticians are classifying for one set of goals, while the executives in the various correctional facilities are organized for quite different goals. In this case, the wardens of individual institutions, for example, will be receiving inmates who have been poorly selected for their particular prison structures. Furthermore, classification information is supposedly the accumulation of facts about individuals from which officials make judgments. But facts

---

[28] National Advisory Commission on Criminal Justice Standards and Goals, *Task Force on Correction* (Washington, D.C., 1974), pp. 197–222.

[29] Robert Fitch, *A Model Reception, Planning and Release System*, consultants' report (State of New York: Department of Correctional Services, n.d.).

frequently turn out to be judgments themselves, so that the actual classification is based on generalizations about unknown generalizations about facts. Last, the training that classifiers receive so that they may make categorizations is generally influenced by organizational policy. Either people are hired with particular backgrounds (such as casework or psychology) that reflect the policy of the hiring agency, or training is given to personnel who are already inculcated with the ideology and operational biases of the organization.

In short, there is no chance of neutrality in classification. There is only the chance that all decision makers can be made aware of each other's biases. This is only possible to the extent that policies are overtly stated and openly debated—characteristics of correction that are infrequent due to intraorganizational and interorganizational conflicts.

Research

Research in corrections is increasing in frequency and in sophisication. Much of the original criminological research in the United States was focused on the offender and generally ignored the community and organizational contexts in which the offender lived. This research bias is gradually being corrected, and we are now faced with the equally formidable task of discovering how to measure interactions between people, programs, and officials. As we have said previously, one point of friction between research and correctional administration has been the irrelevance of research findings to correctional managers. This irrelevance can now be more clearly stated in terms of the model we have developed. Correctional structures in the United States have until recently been dominated by reform and restraint policy—each of which has a low emphasis on the interaction of the individual offender and the community and, consequently, is of little use for information about the behavior of individual offenders on parole. Correctional research has also ignored to a great extent, the correctional environment. There have been, as we said in Chapters One and Six, little theoretical or empirical concern about community in terms of its interactions with correctional organizations, and there have been few studies to date that assess the attitude of the general public about criminal justice in general or corrections specifically. Therefore, there would seem to be at this time a dearth of usable information for correctional officials with either reform or reintegration policies.

Correctional organizations will not develop and change significantly without an increase in usable research. Organizations, like other systems, learn by gathering feedback about consequences of actions. But the feedback gathered must be related to the consequences of interest. In other words, the actors in the system and the researchers must bridge a gap in their mutual understanding of correctional goals. Ideally, it would seem that correctional organizations must develop their own research potential in order to maximize the probability of reaching this mutual understanding. In the long run, the recent influx of university-centered research would seem a poor substitute for research conducted within the organization. However, research that is conducted internally has frequently been biased by organizational and political conflicts. Correctional officials are generally unaccustomed to the conduct of research and have frequently demonstrated fear and lack of cooperation with evaluation research. Although this reaction is understandable, given the history of corrections, it points out conflicts that must be resolved.[30] One set of activities that might help would be research into the research process, including, for example, the methods by which administrators and researchers make contact, negotiate projects, and come to agreements. But this is precisely the area where researchers have frequently balked—demonstrating as much fear of evaluation as correctional officials.[31]

Parole Decisions

Why a parole board decides to grant parole and why a parole board decides to ratify an officer's request for revocation are questions that urgently need investigation. The National Council on Crime and Delinquency has undertaken a study of which factors seem to be the most significant to different parole board members.[32] It remains to be seen whether parole boards will use such information to change their parole decision criteria of the processes by which they make decisions.

In a sense the parole board takes on a quasi-judicial capacity when it releases an inmate (and thereby passes judgment on the institution and its ability to influence the inmate) and when it revokes an inmate (and thereby passes judgment on parole and community capacity to readjust to the presence of an inmate). In order to perform either of these tasks effectively, the parole board should have (1) information about institutional-inmate interactions and whether these are predictive of parole behavior and (2) information about the achievement of parole plans and whether the inmate has failed because of the plan or because he ignored it. Either set of information involves the study of correctional policy and organizational structure, and either set of information is generally lack-

[30] David Duffee, "The Use of Organizational Variables in the Periodic Assessment of Correctional System Effectiveness," *Proceedings,* Second International Symposium, Project SEARCH (Sacramento, Calif.: Project SEARCH, 1974), pp. 643–655.

[31] Chris Argyris, *Intervention Theory and Method, A Behavioral Science Approach* (Reading, Mass.: Addison-Wesley, 1970).

[32] D. M. Gottfredson et al., *The Utilization of Experience in Parole Decision Making* and other reports of the Parole Decision-Making Project (Davis, Calif.: National Correction Crime and Delinquency Research Center, 1973).

ing. This lack is at no occasion more evident than when a parole violator is again eligible for parole. If he is granted parole, he is generally being granted the chance to try again the same experiment at which he failed once. Usually there is no systematic evaluation of the original violation and no comparison of that experience with the opportunities that will probably confront the parolee when he is released a second time. If we could learn from the first experience, a second grant of parole should have a greater probability of success. We usually do not learn, and the parole violator usually has a smaller chance of success than when he was paroled the first time.

Correctional Management

Correctional management is changing rapidly in the United States, but many of the changes are rather superficial. By that we mean that changes in correctional managers do not seem to be accompanied by significant changes in the basic structure of prison and parole organizations. One basic reason for this is that correctional management has frequently been conceived as a set of people rather than as a set of activities. Many correctional managers, for example, have come up through the ranks in their respective organizations and are assumed to be capable of management because they have demonstrated the desired qualities in their previous jobs. In this way, a correctional manager is often expected to be the "best" custodian, or the "best" counselor, or the best something else. But in most cases it is assumed that correctional managers should know as much about the other roles in the organization as anyone else and should have demonstrated their skill in performing some of these roles. Frequently this approach to the development of managers works, but there would seem to be little necessary relationship between the process of development and selection and the fact that the manager is successful as a manager.[33]

Correctional management as a set of activities is the operations by which the internal components of an organization are integrated and the organization as an entirety is integrated with the environment. This kind of activity requires equal attention to policy and the development of technical proficiencies; to maintenance and the distribution of rewards for organizational performance; and to boundary functions such as con-

---

[33] The fact that this problem exists in correctional administration certainly does not imply that industrial organizations do not have the same problem. Chester Barnard spoke of functions of the executive as managerial activities, no matter who performed them or where they appeared on the table of organizations; but Barnard clearly recognized that his emphasis on activities (functions) rather than people was a radical perspective. In *Functions of the Executive* (Cambridge, Mass.: Harvard University Press, 1971).

trol over the kinds of inmates received and the way in which they are released, and the marshalling of support from related organizations and the acceptance of the organizational ideology. It has been found in one study that correctional managers frequently concentrate on maintenance functions and lack the power or the willingness to interact with outside groups.[34] This kind of tendency may be a reflection of policy, but it is commonly the result of ignoring policy and its implications. Different maintenance and boundary structures are compatible with different policies. These structures need to be consciously planned and manipulated. But this activity is only possible if policy is clearly stated and strategies for attaining it are purposefully mapped and implemented.

Organization

Much of the conflict and controversy in contemporary corrections has revolved around the desires of different groups for the maintenance of order or for the promotion of change (presumably in desired directions). This is an old controversy, not a new one, and it is found in many other areas besides the correctional one. For example, most people have experienced somewhere along the line a disciplinarian schoolteacher who demands that order be achieved and maintained before lessons are learned. Most people have also experienced the teacher who seems oblivious to order needs and considers education an exciting and noisy process that has its own internal order. The first teacher keeps things quiet, and if there is time left over, the students perform. The second teacher involves students in activities of learning and expects order to be a function of the interest in the learning process.

This difference in perspective pervades the correctional issues that we have discussed, at a deeper level than we have so far addressed. We spoke in Chapter Six about justifications for punishment and contrasted the justification of retribution that seeks to alleviate present dissatisfactions (or prevent anomie) with the justification of deterrence, incapacitation, and rehabilitation, which seek to prevent crime. In this chapter we have presented an organizational model for the analysis of prison and parole that concentrates on the prevention of crime. We are not the only people to select this trend for the goals of the criminal justice system, but we should be aware that retribution is basically irrelevant to any idea of correctional effectiveness. Based as it is on a moral position that a man who wrongs should be wronged, retribution needs no empirical verification of its effectiveness.

---

[34] Elmer K. Nelson and Catherine Lovell, *Developing Correctional Administrators*, final research report to the Joint Commission on Correctional Manpower and Training (Washington, D.C.: Government Printing Office, November 1969).

The tendency to concentrate on different policy alternatives in terms of their effectiveness tends to becloud their similarities. Although reform, rehabilitation, and reintegration are different, they all include strategies for influencing inmates to change their behavior. Adherents of each policy can all be heard to make claims that their strategy is most congruent with the true nature of inmates. Inmates (regardless of how few) who successfully alter their behavior and remain free of additional crime after contact with the correctional process may become proponents for whatever policy and set of programs were of benefit to them. But whatever the differences in the means used to accomplish successful change, the goal of Reform, Restraint and Reintegration is the production of desirable change.

The reader should be aware, however, that production of change in individual offenders and/or in the community is *not* an objective that all people want the criminal justice system (and particularly the correctional system) to direct itself toward. The activities of planned change disturb the social order as it exists. There are a growing number of persons, both within the correctional system and outside it, who believe that the primary emphasis of the system should be the maintenance of order, or the preservation of social norms and interaction patterns as they exist. There are, for example, many offenders who do not desire to change their values, beliefs, or behavior. These offenders might prefer a correctional system that would punish them for their offenses but would not attempt to change them in any way. Many civil libertarians might agree with these offenders—that coerced change, however subtle and however effective, is antagonistic to basic American values concerning the sanctity of the individual. In addition, there are many political leaders and community groups who are threatened by the activities of planned change. They would prefer that the correctional system dispense justice, in the form of retribution.

In other words, a strange set of bedfellows may form a coalition to alter the thrust of correctional policy in the future. Should such a trend develop, it should not be seen as "new." Throughout this chapter we have seen a variety of structural characteristics and social processes of correctional organization that push corrections toward the maintenance of order and away from the production of change. We shall return to the discussion of these competing forces in Chapter 14, as we discuss the future of the criminal justice system.

chapter 12

Organization

of the Juvenile

Justice System

CURRENT TRENDS IN JUVENILE JUSTICE

In Chapter Eight, we discussed the history and development of the juvenile justice system. An attempt was made to identify the major actors in the system as well as to identify their purview of interest. The problems associated with juvenile delinquency have been with us since at least the early 1800s, yet they continue to defy solution in the face of well-intentioned treatment and reform efforts. The juvenile court was identified by its supporters as a meaningful reform, yet three-quarters of a century later we are still groping for the answer of how to respond to the deviance and criminality of youth, and more particularly, how to prevent troublesome youthful behavior. The magnitude of the problem can perhaps be picked up from the tone of the following comments taken from the Juvenile Justice and Delinquency Prevention Act of 1974, in which it was said:

> The high incidence of delinquency in the United States today results in enormous annual cost and immeasurable loss in human life, personal security, and wasted human resources, and . . . juvenile delinquency constitutes a growing threat to the national welfare requiring immediate

and comprehensive action by the federal government to reduce and prevent delinquency. . . .[1]

If one reads this quote keeping in mind early exhortations about juvenile justice, changes in the nature of the problem and appropriate responses to the problem are apparent. There is no mention of saving youth from a downward career, of extending the kindly arm of the state much like a concerned father, or of being concerned with a child's "condition." Instead of such magnanimous and praiseworthy concern, one finds mention of immeasurable loss of life and security, of wasted resources, and threats to the national welfare.

Not only is the tone of the above quote qualitatively different from the benevolent purposes ostensibly served by the juvenile court, but the remedies suggested or implied are wholly antagonistic. The early answer to problems of delinquency was referral to juvenile court and all that that entailed; the answer currently in vogue is to circumvent the juvenile court and its services. This goal is frequently articulated in cries to "divert youth from the system." The conclusion one draws is that we must turn away troubled and troublesome youth from a network of people and services that were purposely established to constructively deal with them.

The point is well illustrated by the steps advocated in the juvenile justice act mentioned above. The law calls for establishing halfway houses and other residential care facilities for youth; community-based programs designed to strengthen the family unit; youth service bureaus to provide work and recreational opportunities; drug and alcohol programs of a preventative as well as treatment nature; programs to keep youths in school; volunteer probation and other volunteer programs; youth-initiated programs; and provision of incentives to use traditional, secure facilities for youths. Judging from this array of alternatives, it would appear that youths diverted from the juvenile court bureaucracy would soon be caught up in another bureaucracy designed to deliver what the first one couldn't, wouldn't, or didn't.

It is generally felt that moving toward community alternatives is a good idea. This judgment is frequently based on the notion that large institutions can systematically dehumanize those that they are supposed to serve; that small community-based operations eliminate many of the degrading aspects of institutional living, and because they are smaller, they are perhaps ipso facto better; and that it is unreasonable to ask anyone to work on his problems and to better himself in an environment apart from the context in which the problems occur. There are many positive aspects to community corrections but there are also liabilities

[1] "APWA analysis of the Juvenile Justice and Delinquency Act of 1974" (Washington, D.C.: American Public Welfare Association, September 10, 1974), p. 1.

that must be dealt with if the ills of the "old" system are not to reoccur in the "new" system.

All of this activity, money, and energy being directed to the development of alternatives to juvenile court and to institutionalization is an indication that delinquency remains a large problem in American society. Without wishing to belabor the point, it might be well to point out that the problem may be a lot more fundamental than may be realized. One must ask whether or not all the halfway houses money can buy, or all the drug and alcohol programs that doctors and social scientists could create, or all the programs imaginable designed to keep children in school would in fact solve the problem. Many studies point out that it is not just a small percentage of youths who are involved in delinquent acts, that it is not just the lower-class youths who are involved in delinquent behavior and trouble, and that it is not only families with a poor structure that produce problem children. On the other hand, we realize that virtually all children commit acts that are or could be defined as delinquent, that delinquency is just as much an activity of the middle class as the lower class, and that good families produce problem children as well. If all this is true, why are we concerned about solving the *problem* of delinquency? The point we want to make is that even though 95 percent of all the youths in America have the problem, and may always have had the problem, we do not define the majority as appropriate targets for our programming. Rather, those who are considered real, genuine delinquents and are in need of attention are probably the more noticeable youths. The National Commission on the Causes and Prevention of Violence (1969) points out that these youths tend to be the poor, the black, and the uneducated. So, although we must talk about the organization of juvenile justice in this chapter, let us remember whom it is really serving.

Not only are the techniques and methodologies of juvenile justice in a state of change, but the principles and underlying purposes of the system are also changing. It was mentioned above, and developed at length in Chapter Eight, that the original juvenile justice movement was designed as a specialized response to children who were troubled or troublesome. We also pointed out that the initial procedure was conceived as a civil, not criminal, matter, and as such was directed toward undesirable as well as criminal behavior. The motive that the court presented to the world can be seen in *Kent v. United States.*

[P]roceedings under this law are in no sense criminal proceedings, nor is the result in any case a conviction or punishment for crime. They are simply statutory proceedings by which the state . . . reaches out its arm in a kindly way and provides for the protection of its children from parental neglect, or from vicious influences and surroundings, either by keeping a watch over the child while in its natural home, or where that seems impracticable, by placing it in an institution designed for that purpose.[2]

The state carried out its benevolent purposes without the procedural due-process requirements developed for adults. Children who were subject to the purview of the justice system were, in a very real sense, the victims of a system that failed to recognize that children, as well as adults, fell under the proscriptions of the Constitution. The height of such sloppy thinking is perhaps represented by those who contend that everything in the juvenile justice process is therapeutic in nature—from being a suspect, through the juvenile court appearance, to incarceration in an institution. However, there seems to be a new day dawning in juvenile justice, a day brought forth by the U.S. Supreme Court. The trend, hinted at the *Kent* decision above, was carried over into the *Gault* decision[3] and is apparent in *Winship*.[4] These cases are discussed below and will show how the juvenile court philosophy of service is being challenged and broken down by these several court cases.

In *Kent* v. *United States,* involving a 16-year-old charged with rape, housebreaking, and robbery, the Supreme Court not only brought under examination the procedures of court officials and police, but it also commented on the quality of treatment being afforded juveniles. Among others, one issue discussed in the *Kent* case was the waiver or transfer of a juvenile case to (adult) criminal court, and denial of access to a social service file to the defendant's attorney. For the purpose of portraying the demise of the service ideology we can offer several of the observations of the Supreme Court without going into the details of the case. One of the major observations was that even though the state operated in *parens patriae,* functioning as a parent did not constitute an invitation to procedural arbitrariness. In this vein, the Court concluded that Kent had a right to a hearing, which he had been denied, on the question of whether or not his case could be transferred to criminal court, and that the counsel had a right to review the social service record and other reports that may be considered by the court. As mentioned above, the Court went on record questioning the effectiveness of correctional measures available to children in saying,

There is evidence, in fact, that there may be grounds for concern that the child receives the worst of both worlds: that he gets neither the protections accorded adults nor the solicitous care and regenerative treatment postulated for children.[5]

[2] Kent v. United States, 383 U.S. 541 (1966).

[3] In re Gault, 387 U.S. 1 (1967).

[4] In re Winship, 397 U.S. 358 (1970).

[5] Kent v. United States; see footnote 2.

The due-process safeguards eventually granted juveniles in the *Gault* decision were only suggested in *Kent*. *Kent* did, however, open up the juvenile justice system to questioning and provided the first legitimate and significant questioning of its philosophy.

The spector of skepticism raised by the Supreme Court in the *Kent* case was operationalized in *In re Gault*.[6] The case involved Gerald Gault, a 15-year-old boy who while still on probation was committed to a state industrial school until the age of majority (21), or sooner if discharged by due process of law. Gerald was charged with "lewd phone calls," which were placed to a woman neighbor. Although juvenile court ideology professes to serve the best interests of the child, the penalty for an adult committing these same acts would have been a fine of from $5 to $50 or imprisonment for not more than two months, rather than the six-year commitment to a training school that Gault received.

The original proceedings against Gault were conducted in the informal tradition of juvenile proceedings. In the light of due process require-ments, the proceedings could be described as somewhat "loose." For instance, Gerald's mother was not notified on the day that he was picked up by the police and taken to a detention home; no formal petition alleging Gerald's delinquency was served on the Gaults; in the petition filed with the court by the probation department, no factual basis for a judgment of delinquency was made; and no transcript or recording of the hearings before the judge was made. As a result, the *Gault* decision granted to juveniles many of the procedural due-process rights available to adults. The basis for this decision is very important in that the Su-preme Court found traditional juvenile court philosophy and procedure lacking in validity and viability. And it is this decision that has forced a fundamental change in the juvenile justice system, changing it from a largely paternalistic system to something akin to an adversary system in which one must prove a case within guidelines of the Constitution. In reaching its decision, the Court took to task the *parens patriae* notion—that the state was a wise parent—and the notion that juveniles have a right to custody and not to liberty, and in so doing, cited the fact that lack of procedural due process has sometimes led to arbitrary and unfair pro-cedures. The Court felt that the performance of juvenile corrections was far outstripped by the rhetoric attendant on it. It asserted that whatever name a juvenile institution had, it was still an institution in which a youth is confined for the greater or lesser time; that his world becomes one of routine, institutionalized behavior; and that rather than having peers and relatives to associate with, the juvenile had state employees, guards, and other delinquents as reference groups. It concluded, "In view of this, it would be extraordinary if our Constitution did not require the procedural

[6] In re Gault; see footnote 3.

regularity and the exercise of care implied in the phrase 'due process.' "[7]
In its decision, the Court awarded the following rights to juveniles:

1. The right to notice of clearly stated charges sufficiently far in advance to allow for preparing for a scheduled court appearance.
2. The right to counsel in hearings in which delinquency will be determined and which may result in institutionalization. Furthermore, the child's parents must be notified of the right to counsel, and they must be provided with counsel if they cannot afford it.
3. The rights to confrontation and cross-examination were granted, and it was determined that juveniles had the constitutional privilege against self-incrimination available to adults.[8]

The *Gault* decision effectively brought an end to an era. The original purpose of the juvenile court was to provide care, regenerative treatment, and leniency to children who were in trouble. This original version of the juvenile court was clearly based on the medical model that assumed that each child could be treated to alleviate his problems. Today the whole idea of individualized treatment minus due process either is nonexistent or is severely mitigated in the juvenile court. Children are given notice of hearings, have a right to counsel, and the questioning of a youth's conduct and ultimate disposition are conducted with an aura of fairness and due process.

The final Supreme Court case to be mentioned, *In re Winship*, examined the evidentiary question of whether or not proof beyond a reasonable doubt" was necessary in the adjudication phase of the juvenile court proceeding. The court had to decide whether "proof beyond a reasonable doubt" was within the essentials of due process and fair treatment as prescribed by *Gault*. Although it was decided that such proof was required in a juvenile case, the dissenting opinions of Justice Burger and Justice Stewart provide an interesting perspective on the possible effects of such a move. The role of law in defining juvenile justice and fulfilling a maintenance function can be seen in the comments of Burger and Stewart: "What the juvenile court system needs is not more but less of the trappings of legal procedure and judicial formalism; the juvenile court system requires breathing room and flexibility in order to survive, if it can survive the repeated assaults from this Court."[9]

REVIEW OF THE SUBSYSTEMS

In this chapter we are faced with analyzing the juvenile justice subsystem in terms of its production subsystem, its maintenance subsystem, and its

[7] Ibid.

[8] Ibid.

[9] In re Winship, see footnote 4.

boundary subsystem. From what has been said already, it should be apparent that this is much more difficult than if we were describing only one aspect of the juvenile justice system. Just in thinking about what constitutes the juvenile justice system, it is clear that we must consider something as abstract as the law and legal precedent; something as concrete as police officers who specialize in juvenile affairs; institutions that are so controversial that they have been eliminated in one state; and a function as complex as that of a probation officer who must serve but who must also maintain surveillance of clients. Due to the specialized roles of each of the components alluded to, it is not possible to discuss the production subsystem as if it were a unified and all pervasive activity. And we have the same problems when dealing with the maintenance and boundary subsystems of the several arms of juvenile justice.

Therefore, before attempting to make sense out of the separate agencies comprising the juvenile systems, it may be helpful to mention again the purpose and functioning of the three organizational subsystems.

Production Subsystem

The production subsystem is concerned with the organization of the agency's work force, or the human resources of an organization, into units to get the organization's work done. The tendency in organizations is to specialize so that the organizational goal of efficiency can be optimized. An example of organizational specialization for the sake of efficiency is the appointment of selected police officers to perform the role of juvenile police specialists. The reason why it makes sense to have specialists in juvenile affairs relates, in part, to the need for specialized training. Juvenile police specialists may need to know more about family dynamics and adolescent psychology and less about polygraph techniques than a detective or a beat patrolman. Thus, to handle juvenile issues, the police choose to train specialists so that juvenile issues can be dealt with as efficiently as possible.

In addition to the "division of labor" issue, the production subsystem involves specifying the nature of an individual's job and developing performance standards. In any organization, a document known as a *job description* will list the tasks and areas of responsibility the individual must cover. The existence of a job description enhances the work of a juvenile specialist because it effectively delineates his activities. He, for instance, is not expected to ticket overparked cars but rather to get down to dealing with those cases involving juveniles that have been brought to police attention.

The maintenance subsystem operates to insure smooth operation and predictability through formalization and institutionalization of procedures. Many activities of an organization are devoted to maintaining a certain equilibrium. These include developing and abiding by a prescribed set of rules that govern organizational behavior, carefully screening potential candidates for the organization, and rewarding seniority in several different ways. Perhaps the most visible examples of maintenance activities that can be found in any organization are those found in criminal justice agencies or closed institutions. For example, the place and status of people in prisons are denoted by the clothes they must wear. In prisons, the inmates, or those who are being processed by the agency's production subsystem, must wear prison garb, which historically consisted of striped uniforms, but more recently consists of khakis or blue denims. On the other hand, custodial personnel such as guards wear military-type uniforms with their status within the orgnization clearly delineated by stripes or other insignia displayed on the uniform. The other members of the staff who do not work in uniform are usually associated with the institutional treatment staff, and would include psychologists, social workers, and vocational counselors.

These examples are rather obvious, so obvious in fact that their purpose is often overlooked; but less obvious, although similar, kinds of activities are being performed in noninstitutional settings. A seemingly trivial but cogent example can be illustrated by thinking about the significance and formality of a suggestion box found in many industries. It is probably natural to assume that a worker in almost any position is interested in making the work he performs as efficient and easy as possible. Furthermore, one might assume that if the worker can think of better ways of doing his job, he would naturally implement them. Such assumptions seem logical and sensible, but they are not as easily dealt with as one might think. The maintenance function is so well developed in many organizations that something as innocuous as a suggested change for the better is institutionalized through the use of the suggestion box. In general, management defines ways in which jobs may and may not be done. Rules are developed that deal with the cans and cannots of the job, and such rules may even be formalized from the worker's point of view through the use of a union contract. In such an environment, a suggested change may exceed the competence of the boss to approve of it; but perhaps more to the point, the supervisor may not have even the authority to consider it. Therefore, employees are requested to put their suggested changes in the suggestion box. The suggestions will then be reviewed by a committee, which may reject, accept, or even reward the individual who suggests the change. Thus, through institutionalizing the procedure for possible changes, the suggestions can be dealt with relatively routinely without interrupting the smooth flow of business. The suggestion box provides a systematic alternative to the way things are done, but it does so in a way that doesn't threaten managerial competence or directly question the way things are done.

Boundary Subsystem

We can see that organizational life may be even more complex and subtle than we have traditionally acknowledged. We have discussed the production subsystem as efficiently organizing the work and the work force so that tasks can easily be done, and the maintenance subsystem as involving moves that are designed to bring regularity and predictability to the organization. We now come to the subject of the boundary subsystem. This is the part of the organization that deals with the environment and the interaction between the organization and the environment. Sales and advertising are typical tasks in a manufacturing operation that are representative of the boundary subsystem. Whenever the boundary subsystem is faced with interacting with the environment, it is more likely for the boundary subsystem to insist that the public adapt to the organization's product than for the organization to adapt its product to the needs and desires of the public. By acting to encourage the organization's public to accept the product as produced, the goals of efficiency, economy, and organizational stability are served.

Examples of the boundary subsystem within juvenile justice are more difficult to provide because of the nature of the system. The boundary subsystem is represented by "exchange relationships" such as taking raw material (deviant or delinquent youngsters) into, and expelling a product from, the system, as well as in obtaining support and legitimation for the functions that constitute the procedures of the juvenile justice system. A less relevant, but nevertheless accurate, example of boundary functioning has to do with statistics heaped on the public concerning success of failure rates, most notably recidivism statistics. The public, to a large degree, may have few vehicles other than delinquency rates or recidivism statistics by which to judge the worthwhileness of the product of the juvenile justice system. Thus, the boundary subsystem can manipulate the opinion, and perhaps the dollars, of the public by putting greater or lesser emphasis on recidivism statistics.

PROBLEMS OF ANALYSIS

The juvenile and criminal justice systems are perhaps somewhat unique in that the general overriding purpose of each component is largely the same: "protection of the public" and "rehabilitation" of the offender. The use of these concepts is problematical in many ways. For instance, some would argue that the issues of community protection and offender rehabilitation are antithetical, whereas others would argue that they are complementary. Still others would contend that the community is protected *through* the vehicle of offender rehabilitation. Further difficulties can be encountered if one attempts to define what these terms really mean. It is not our intent here to resolve or even to discuss these problems. Rather, the main point to be made is that the juvenile police specialist, the probation officer, the institutions and alternatives to institutions, the juvenile court, and the after-care or parole supervisors are all generally interested in community protection and offender reformation. Because of the similarities of purpose of these many components, it is difficult to identify a unique product that each produces or a unique public with which each must interact.

Because the components of the juvenile justice system do not interact frequently and directly with a consuming public, our analysis of these organizations, and particularly of the boundary subsystem, will be different than if we were dealing with a material product. In attempting to identify who or what constitutes the appropriate public with which the boundary subsystem interacts, it becomes apparent that juvenile justice system components frequently interact with *other justice system components*. The interactions engaged in by juvenile justice agencies are frequently with other justice agencies, and therefore there is usually a consistency and predictability to the product that is to be "sold."

In conceptualizing the structure and functioning of juvenile justice agencies, it may be helpful to invoke systems terminology. A *system* may be defined as a collection of entities that are connected through communication. In simple terms, we could assert that the juvenile justice system is made up of "deviant" youth, police, courts, probation officers, institutions, and so forth. All of these separate entities are connected by communication and, perhaps more importantly, by exchange of clients. Even though we can view this collection of agencies as comprising a system, we can also look at each separate component as an individual subsystem. For instance, probation is a system within a system, or a subsystem of the juvenile justice system. For purposes of illustration, we will introduce only a few systems terms: these include *input, process, output, feedback, boundary,* and *environment. Input, process,* and *output* refer to bringing raw material into a system for conversion or processing, and once the raw material is processed, it leaves the system as output. A simplistic example of these three systems components can be offered by analyzing the production of shoes. Leather, cardboard, thread, and other raw materials that come into the factory (input) are operated on to convert them into a new product (process), and the product or shoes are then shipped to a customer as output. If the customer is happy, he may send along with payment for the shoes a complimentary note, letting the factory know they have done a good job. This provides *feedback* on how well the system is doing. We have now dealt with four systems terms and have two left—*boundary* and *environment*. *Boundary* may be a somewhat arbitrary term but can be defined perhaps abstractly as the limits of the system. Anything beyond the boundary or the limits is considered as *environment*. In our example, we could consider the retail store or customer for the shoes as within the system's boundary and the Catholic Church as part of the environment.

We bring up these systems terms because, perhaps uniquely, in criminal justice and in juvenile justice, one system's output is really another system's input. Or perhaps more accurately, the output of the juvenile court subsystem becomes the input of the juvenile institution subsystem. Because of the inbred nature of criminal justice system interactions, boundary relationships within the system are frequently performed with kindred agencies. The system has low visibility with the public at large, in part because of this provincial handling of deviant or dependent youth. It is with this qualification in mind that we can turn to an analysis of the functioning of the three subsystems.

GENERIC FACTORS
IN THE THREE SUBSYSTEMS

One approach to achieving the goals of this chapter is to simply specify which roles or which people perform production, maintenance, or boundary functioning in the juvenile justice system. We could, for instance, indicate that a juvenile probation officer and a juvenile police specialist are involved in production activities in their face-to-face interactions with youth. Similarly, we could indicate that they are involved in boundary interactions when each refers a client to another agency for a needed social service. If this approach were selected, we might leave the reader with the impression that there were particular or unique people performing each of the subsystem functions, or we might give the impression that each person in the system performs each of the functions at particular or unique times. Actually neither of these impressions would be totally incorrect, although both fall short of conveying a universalistic or conceptual understanding of the system. It is important to understand that there are more pervasive or general forces that define and effect subsystem functioning. We shall call these *generic factors,* and they should provide the reader with a conceptual overlay for understanding the system. We shall specify a number of these factors for each of the subsystems.

Maintenance Subsystem

Maintenance activities are those that control internal affairs or regulate activities among organizational members to produce stability and dependability. There are many factors in organizational life that while perhaps serving another function, also serve to increase stability and predictability.

The union contract is one document that serves to regulate work and interpersonal interactions, most notably between employee and employer. Unions exist to give employees a voice in the way the business of an organization will be conducted, to give them some control over benefits and working conditions, and to give them input in the determination of wage levels. One effect of having a union is the solidification of rules, which of course increases predictability of the work place. For instance, coffee breaks or work breaks are a normal part of most nonadministrative jobs and are frequently taken at a time convenient to management and administration. A union contract may, however, specify the length and time of a work break as part of the contract between management and labor. A likely consequence is that if someone wants a specific task done by an employee and it happens to coincide with the work break, the task is likely to wait until the break is over. A typical union contract may regulate hours of work, rest periods, personal leave days, salaries and wages, overtime, medical benefits, uniforms and equipment, and many other aspects of the job. It can be seen that the net effect of unionization. is the establishment of a high degree of regularity and predictability in the work place. Union contracts create a high degree of structure that serves the maintenance function very well.

Another facet contributing to the maintenance subsystem is the existence of a policy and procedures manual that outlines what to do in the general case as well as what to do and how to respond in particular situations. Probation and parole agencies at the federal, state, and frequently at the county level employ a policy and procedural manual that includes: (1) the history and philosophy of probation and parole; (2) a specification of the reports used in an agency such as pre-sentence reports, preparole reports, arrest reports, revocation reports, daily logs of activities, and others; (3) programs and services included in the agency; (4) a statement of goals of supervision, various supervision strategies, and the use of interviews in supervision; (5) casehandling methods and procedures; (6) the use of the interstate compact; and (7) administrative structure, organization, and functioning. These procedural manuals cover many contingencies that a probation/parole officer will face and serve to structure the approach that an officer will take in performing his job. Because the justice system is involved so deeply in the essence of individuals' lives, there is complete documentation and recording of an officer's interactions with clients. This documentation and the recording procedure itself serve to provide an official version of an individual as well as to maintain standard behavior and predictability within probation/parole agencies and between various offices at the same level. The degree of standardization is frequently greater at the state and federal level than at the county level, primarily because state and federal agencies are part of their own bureaucracy, whereas county governments are usually independent of each other.

The union contract and policy and procedures manuals are clearly identifiable and tangible documents that enhance maintenance functioning. There is, however, a more intangible and ideological force that acts to maintain organizational standards, predictability, and interaction. We are speaking about the concept of professionalism, which is invoked in the justice system in ways that would suggest that it is not well understood. Professionalism seems at times to be identified with secrecy, territorial protection, and the need to portray one's competence. Paul Keve has identified the presentence report completed by probation offices as evidence of professionalism. In this regard, Keve indicates.

> [T]he presentence report provides a window to our profession that can help to gain understanding and respect. Through it the judge not only will learn about the defendant, but many learn about the profession of correctional social work.[10]

It is not our task to justify or to denegrate the desire of justice personnel to be regarded as professionals. It is important though to specify the attributes of a profession in order to indicate why we select "professionalism" as a concept that brings order and predictability to the juvenile justice system. The marks or criteria of a profession are said to include the following factors:

1. Possession of a body of specialized knowledge, skills, and attitudes, known and practiced by its members.

---

[10] Paul Keve, "The Professional Character of the Presentence Report," in R. M. Carter and L. T. Wilkins, *Probation and Parole: Selected Readings* (New York: Wiley, 1970), p. 83.

2. This body of specialized knowledge is derived through scientific inquiry and scholarly learning.
3. This body of specialized knowledge, skills, and attitudes is acquired through professional preparation, preferably on the graduate level, in a college or university as well as through continuous in-service training and personal growth after completion of formal education.
4. This body of specialized knowledge, skills, and attitudes is constantly tested and extended through research and scholarly inquiry.
5. A profession has a literature of its own, even though it may, and indeed must, draw portions of its content from other areas of knowledge.
6. A profession exalts service to the individual and society above personal gain. It possesses a philosophy and a code of ethics.
7. Membership in the professional organization and the practices of the profession must be limited to persons meeting stated standards of preparation and competencies.
8. The public recognizes, has confidence in, and is willing to compensate the members of the profession for its services.[11]

The degree to which occupational roles and personnel in the various agencies of the justice system fulfill the citeria of a profession is open to question. It is important to realize that the police *talk* about being professional, that probation officers *feel* they have a vehicle for expressing their professionalism (the pre-sentence report), and that many treatment-oriented staff in an institution *profess* to be professional. Because these various people profess to be "professionals" or strive to be professional in their actions, certain ways of performing duties may be adopted, whereas other ways may be rejected for the same reasons. Behaviors will be more standardized and predictable in an organization because they are perceived as professional, whether or not they are so in fact.

Professionalism is a concern of many justice system personnel. The police exercise "professional autonomy" in making a decision to arrest or to ignore an infraction; probation officers can exercise judgment as to the best counsellng technique to use with a client, if indeed they are professionally trained to the point of knowing more than one strategy; and treatment staff of a training school have a similar degree of latitude. Each of these positions possesses attributes of professionalism, but the occupation itself is frequently cast within a bureaucratic setting.

Bureaucracy is the fourth major factor to be discussed in terms of forces that serve maintenance functioning within an organization. Bureaucracy refers to a type of organization discussed by Max Weber,[12] which

---

[11] Adapted from *Ethical Standards: American Personnel and Guidance Associations. Preamble* (1961).

[12] Max Weber. *The Theory of Social and Economic Organization.* (Glencoe, Ill.: Free Press, 1947).

stresses the ideas of organizational position, authority relationships, and accountability. The essence of bureaucracy entails the following:

1. A hierarchical authority structure based on official position rather than on the individuality of the incumbent. In this type of organization, orders go *down* the hierarchy and information goes *up* the structure.
2. A system of rules governs the rights and duties of these positions. These rules include who may talk with whom about organizational business.
3. A detailed system of rules and regulations for dealing with each particular case. Policy and procedures manuals typically cover what to do given certain specialized circumstances.
4. A clear-cut and highly specialized division of labor.
5. Impersonal social relations with management based on written documents (the files).
6. Recruitment of offiicials to a salaried career with security of tenure on the basis of technical qualifications.[13]

In addition to the features of bureaucracy stated above, we could add the notion of span control, which deals with the ideas that one superior can manage only a finite number of men (frequently said to be seven), and the idea that each person should work for one and only one boss. Bureaucratic organization acts to rigidify and make very predictable the interactions among the personnel of an organization. It would not be unheard of to have a worker at the lowest level in the hierarchy with an office next to a manager two levels above him, and this worker is restricted by regulations about approaching the manager with a question or suggestion. In such a case, the worker would have to speak to his superior, who would, in turn, consult with his boss. This individual might then be able to represent the employee's case, albeit twice removed from the source of the original idea. It is clear that such organizational structure leads to predictability if not inefficiency.

A bureaucratic organization can have a stultifying effect on one who perceives himself as a professional with a recognized area of competence or expertise. The autonomy granted lawyers and doctors frequently does not exist in organizations that are primarily bureaucracies, even though they employ "professional" individuals. The emphasis on responsibility and accountability in bureaucratic organizations can have a pathological effect on those whose job it is to "counsel" or "treat" clients. It is sometimes said, for instance, that probation officers would rather do pre-sentence investigations because they can be counted or quantified, whereas counseling or treating clients is more or less nonquantifiable. Such pres-

---

[13] See Gilbert Smith, *Social Work and the Sociology of Organizations* (London: Routledge and Paul Kegan, 1970), p. 23.

sures acting on the employees of an organization can result in "bureau-pathology" or behavior that (1) exaggerates dependence on regulations, (2) exaggerates impersonality in relations, (3) insists on the petty rights and privileges of office, and (4) resists change.[14]

The factors identified above are rather pervasive and major in their effect on maintenance functioning, although union contracts and procedures manuals are clearly more tangible than are professionalism and bureaucracy. The latter two concepts can be seen as defining the ball park within which union contracts and procedures manuals will be played out, however. There are several other general concepts that can be mentioned as contributing to the maintenance functioning of an organization. They are perhaps not as grand or as all-pervasive as the above factors, but are nevertheless important in maintenance functioning. These factors will be only briefly mentioned.

Training and *education* can be seen as basic requirements for entrance to many positions in the juvenile justice system, but they can also be seen as enhancing maintenance. For instance, it is traditional that probation/parole workers should have a four-year college degree with a preference expressed for a degree in the social or behavioral sciences. Social workers would be more acceptable than those trained in accounting and engineering. Part of social work education involves inculcation of certain values and behavioral styles that are held to be desirable for the profession. Trojanowicz found that social workers have a preference for working independently and for directing their own activity toward goal achievement, that they believe people are best motivated intrinsically, and that they utilize groups for decision making.[15] There would of course be some variation among people trained in social work, but the variation would be much less than that existing between social workers and engineers. Similarity in educational background will obviously act to reduce variability and to increase standardization and predictability. In addition to basic education, continued training programs for police officers or probation/parole workers also act to increase predictability. Continued training programs are also frequently encouraged if not required of those who enter the justice field.

Other unique contributors to maintenance functioning include the operation of a political patronage system, the preferred treatment ideologies, specialization, civil service commission, and job descriptions. *Political patronage* refers to the installation of a politician's preferred people in public service jobs. The maintenance subsystem is served by patronage in that only those acceptable to the politician will be placed,

[14] Ibid., p. 28.

[15] Robert C. Trojanowicz, "The Contrasting Behavioral Styles of Policemen and Social Workers," *Public Personnel Review* (October 1971), p. 248.

and they, in turn, are likely to agree with their benefactors' definition of situations and the preferred mode of responding. Similarly, organizations in general are likely to support *preferred treatment ideologies* that specify what is acceptable and not acceptable with certain boundaries. For instance, if one were employed in a psychoanalytically oriented mental health clinic, manipulation of a patient's environment, such as arranging for different housing, is more akin to a social-structural or social work response and would be implicitly and perhaps explicitly frowned on because it did not attempt to solve the problem with psychotherapy. In the same vein, police officers who *specialize* in juvenile cases are frequently faced with charges of mollycoddling juveniles if they refer a youth to a social agency without first "getting the goods" on the child. The function of the *civil service commission* is, in part, to narrow down the field of applicants for a position by administering tests that are designed to match an individual with a job. Of course one challenge to such testing is that the items in the test are developed by a small number of people and may, therefore, represent only a small sample of the universe of questions that could have been asked. The *job description* determines what a person must do and, in effect, defines a range of behaviors that are appropriate for a particular position. The maintenance subsystem is served because we know, for instance, that a police officer is constrained to search for a youth who runs from an institution and that he doesn't have the option of not searching for the youth, even though freedom might be therapeutically in the best interests of the child.

The Production Subsystem

The discussion of the maintenance subsystem included items that could also be seen as belonging to the production subsystem. For instance, the job description was presented as a maintenance device because it brings predictability to the job. On reading the job description for a juvenile police officer, one can be reasonably sure that the officer will be involved in investigating crimes involving juveniles, that he will evaluate cases for possible referral to a social agency, and that he will become involved with community leaders in designing delinquency prevention programs. It can be seen that the job description as an entity not only regulates activities and increases predictability but it also deals with defining what the officer will do and how he will process those whom he comes in contact with— clearly production activities. It should not be surprising, therefore, that some of the issues or factors presented under the rubric of production subsystems could also be seen as serving some maintenance functions as well. The fact that many of the actors in the juvenile justice system perform so many activities that fall under all three subsystem functions indicates the complexity of their role, and should raise questions about the degree to which they can be or are in fact efficient. Having raised the "efficiency" issue, however, it is also necessary to ask whether the goal of efficiency is or should be a desired goal in a subsystem that processes people instead of material goods.

We will follow the format adopted in the discussion of maintenance in this discussion of the production subsystem. That is, we will attempt to identify activities that are generic to production and then at the end of this section an attempt will be made to discuss the actors in the system that carry out these functions. Specifying activities that constitute the production function in the juvenile justice system is a problem due to lack of consensus. The problem is complicated by the fact that at times certain activities seem to be production activities, and at other times they appear to be surrogates for production activities. Three activities will be presented which appear to be production oriented activities, but which may also act to confuse the issue. Specifically, we will discuss *rate-producing* activities both as production activities and as ways of artificially altering conditions of the system. Secondly, we will discuss the *goal definition* process as one which constitutes production, as well as leading to other production activities. *Preferred ideologies* will be identified as the third factor impacting production functions. It will be pointed out that activities pursued in the system are very heavily influenced by belief systems of the actors in the system.

Many production activities pursued in the juvenile justice system, and in the adult justice system as well, are involved with *rate-producing* behaviors. These may deal with arrest rates, conviction rates, referral rates, diversion rates, or rates of recidivism. Rate-producing behavior in the juvenile system probably takes on less of an evaluative connotation than in the adult system, but the work is nevertheless involved with producing rates, or ratios of youngsters dealt with by choice A as opposed to choice B. In the criminal justice system, the rate of arrests, or the rate of arrests that result in conviction, is probably held out more as an evaluative standard than it is in the juvenile justice system.

The juvenile justice system may be somewhat unusual in the intake phase of the system. In the adult system, the intake function normally involves the police who arrest a criminal whom they have observed in the act of committing a crime, or they may arrest an individual as a result of an investigation, or the grand jury may decide that an individual ought to be arrested and brought into the system for processing. In the juvenile justice system, however, a youth may find himself before the juvenile court as a result of police intervention, or in many states, contrary to the adult system, as a result of a citizen filing a petition (a statement of the reasons why juvenile X ought to go to court) directly with the juvenile court. In essence, the juvenile can be, but probably rarely is, brought before the court by a citizen's complaint without prior screening. In all fairness to the system, it is probably a rarity to find direct referral to a juvenile court judge, but it can happen in states where the law is written.

When a police officer comes into contact with a juvenile who could be charged with delinquency, a number of options are open to that officer. These options include ignoring the offense, negotiating a settlement of the issue between the juvenile and the victim (if there is one), adjusting the offense at the station house, referral to another agency, or referral to juvenile court. The juvenile probation officer may be involved in this because even if a case is referred to court, the court may have the power to reject the referral. In some states, such as Pennsylvania, the probation department has the authority to screen juvenile court referrals. In performing this function, the probation department plays a large part in determining the percentage of cases referred to the court. If the probation department accepts a case, it may still never go before the juvenile court judge. The case may be put on "informal" probation without going to the judge, or, at least in Pennsylvania, the youth may be put on informal probation via a consent decree—an agreement by all parties about supervision without a finding of delinquency being made. Because of their power to manipulate statistics representing various forms of behavior, the police and the probation department can have a lot to say about the amount of existing delinquency activity in an area, and about the number of "delinquent" youths (those judged to be delinquent in court) in a city or county. Due to their ability to manipulate arrest rates, juvenile justice system officials are able to respond appropriately to charges of mollycoddling or even of being overly severe, without changing much about how their clients are substantively dealt with in the system.

Before leaving this discussion of rate-producing behavior, it is necessary to point out the ability of after-care facilities or juvenile parole departments to manipulate success or failure as embodied in recidivism rates. Recidivism statistics involve looking at the number of people who come into contact with the juvenile justice system after having been put on probation or after being released from incarceration. It is relatively easy to manipulate recidivism statistics by changing the definition of recidivism or by altering the period that clients are followed up after completing probation or after incarceration. In the first instance—changing the definition—several options are available. Recidivism can be counted as coming into contact with a police officer, being arrested by a police officer and referred to court (again not implying conviction), being put on probation again, or being reincarcerated. When one considers the substantial "fall out" occurring among the numbers of youths coming into contact with the police and those finally convicted, the degree of manipulation possible is readily apparent. In addition to altering the definition of recidivism, one can simply report recidivism statistics based on follow-up periods of one year, two years, three years, or whatever one desires. The recidivism rate at the end of two years will obviously exceed the one-year follow-up rate.

In essence, the actors in the juvenile justice system spend much of their time on rate-producing behaviors and keeping records of those behaviors. The rates produced may be a result of whim, technical competence, or political pressure, but they are subject to a variety of forces. The production orientation is focused on intake decisions about what to do with a case, and how the case ultimately turns out.

A second consideration in the discussion of generic factors involved in the production subsystem is the area of *goal identification.* Each component of the juvenile justice system must determine what the system is in business to do, despite the feeling that there is probably little, if any, agreement as to the goals of the system. The police keep on arresting youths, probation departments continue to detain youths, juvenile court continues to pass on delinquency, institutions continue to incarcerate, and reformers are busy at work trying to determine how best to divert kids from this system that they see as impotent if not harmful. Nevertheless, each of the components must determine its purpose, mission, and legitimate activities. Confusion over goals and the lack of consistency possible between the various system components can be somewhat alarming, but it seems less so when we stop to consider that in some quarters whatever the juvenile justice system does is considered rehabilitative,[16] but that in other quarters, juveniles are considered to be in an adversarial position with the state and therefore deserve many of the due-process considerations available to an adult.

Problems with goal ambiguity and goal interpretation are not of recent origin in the juvenile justice system. They stem partially from the conflict between the tenets of Classical criminology and its notions of deterrence and the legacy of Positivism, which stressed rehabilitation and cure. In addition, we aren't quite sure what it takes to save a youth from a downward career or to deter him from further criminality. The bind in which we find ourselves can be seen in the findings of Martin Gold's study dealing with delinquents, particularly if we interpret the findings using a labeling perspective.[17] The labeling perspective holds in part that after a behavior has been defined as deviant for an individual, the labeled individual is more likely to continue to emit that behavior than if the individual had not been so labeled. Gold, who posited that delinquency

---

[16] See H. W. Dunham, "The Juvenile Court: Contradictory Orientations in Processing Offenders," *Law and Contemporary Problems,* 23 (1958), 512–525.

[17] Martin Gold, *Delinquent Behavior in an American City* (Belmont, Mass.: Wadsworth Publishing Company, 1970).

was a "pick up game" much like inner-city basketball, found that police apprehension of juveniles leads to the commitment of more delinquent acts. Eleven of 20 matched pairs, differing only on the variable of getting caught, went on to commit more offenses. Gold felt that the apprehension process may set into motion the following dynamics: (1) to stop engaging in delinquency constitutes an agreement that the youth has behaved badly and is therefore bad, (2) if he stops, he's "childish," (3) the original motives are seldom altered by the apprehension process, and (4) apprehension may just make the youth angry and result in his striking out at society. Subsequent studies have verified that apprehended youngsters commit more delinquent acts than similar youths who are not apprehended.

Cast against such a finding, the conflicting messages that juvenile justice officials receive are even more problematical. For instance, police are told that the first and foremost goal of police work is protection of society, and consideration of the best disposition of a youth is secondary. Even if a police officer were to consider referring a youngster to a social service, as opposed to putting him further into the formal system for processing, he (the police officer) may be instructed that such a referral is to be made considering what is best for the youth *and* what is best for society. How does an officer balance or weight what is best for each, particularly if the two factors are seemingly incompatible? For instance it may be in the child's best interest to receive a form of community treatment, but it might seem in the interest of the community to have the child locked away in a secure facility. What is the policeman to do? How is he to decide? Given this kind of struggle, it would not be unlikely for the officer to err on the side of locking up the child. In so doing, he probably minimizes the pressure felt from peers, and the public, and from other components in the system.

Probation departments and courts may be in similar binds in identifying and persuing appropriate goals. They have the power and authority to treat a child's problems, but they also have the responsibility to see that justice or legal issues are dealt with. After all, it's clear that if a youth kicked a kindly old lady and snatched her purse, he will have to be reprimanded in some way. The fact that the youth comes from a multiproblem home and has had few chances in life is a secondary consideration. The law indicates that this kind of behavior demands some kind of punitive action.

The court, in this example, is presented with a clear-cut act of illegal behavior. There is no question that the behavior of the youth qualifies him for a court appearance if for no other reason than the fact that the act constitutes a crime if committed by an adult. Juvenile courts are frequently not presented with such clear-cut cases. In Pennsylvania, the Juvenile Court Act provides for dealing with a second type of problem, kids who are not delinquent but are deprived. Deprived children are those who may lack parental care; who may be deprived of adequate physical, mental, or emotional health; or who, among other things, may be habitually truant. In evaluating the disposition of deprived children, it must be remembered that school truancy generally constitutes a delinquent act,[18] just as it did in Pennsylvania until 1973.[19] The bind that the court finds itself in can be illustrated by certain proscriptions of the Juvenile Court Act. For instance, habitual disobedience to the reasonable and lawful commands of the parent by an ungovernable child is defined as delinquency, whereas school truancy is defined as an attribute of a deprived child. The court must find itself in an exquisite dilemma in fulfilling its production function when faced with the case of a child who is in court for truancy, *and* whose parents continually "commanded" that the child attend school as dictated by law. In this instance, the court is faced with a deprived child if they attend to the truancy problem, and with a delinquent child if they act on the child's habitual disobedience to the parent's lawful commands to attend school. The judge must determine whether punishment in the form of institutionalization is in order, or whether help, treatment, or ameliorative attention is due to the child, the parents, or both. It should be readily apparent that the production function is, at least in this case, completely up to one man (the judge) and his interpretation of the demand characteristics of the situation. Because of the lack of clear and unambiguous definitions of production goals, juvenile justice can indeed be "individualized," with the judge being an omnipotent individual. If you or I were the juvenile in the above example, we would certainly want to appear before a lenient judge as opposed to a "hanging judge," if our fate were so clearly up to one man.

The Juvenile Court Act of Pennsylvania is written in such a manner that conflicts over whether a child is delinquent or deprived can occur, and in a sense, the act institutionalizes such conflict. For instance, Section 20 of the act states the following:

Counsel must be provided for a child unless his parent, guardian, or custodian is present in court and affirmatively waives it. However, the parent, guardian, or custodian may not waive counsel for a child when their interest may be in conflict with the interest or interests of the child.

[18] Juvenile delinquency traditionally includes acts that would be crimes if committed by an adult, or status offenses or acts that are delinquent only because they are committed by a youth, i.e., swearing or truancy.

[19] In 1972, Pennsylvania passed a new Juvenile Court Act which changed the status of truancy from an act constituting delinquency to one constituting an act of a deprived child.

What this section is saying is that if the child's interest and those of his parent are at odds, such as in the above case, a lawyer will be provided to each party. The institutionalization of such conflict probably does not define the production function for the judge any more clearly than previously, but it does imply that production will occur within an arena marked by the legal trappings of an adversarial situation.

From the two examples of the purse-snatching, lady-kicking youth and the school truant, possibly deprived youth, there is a more reasonable chance that the purse-snatcher, rather than the the truant, will be institutionalized. The decision to institutionalize the youth does not, however, carry to the institutional system a clear message as to what it should define its mission to be. In other words, production in the institution is really not much clearer than production in the police, probation, or court phases of the process. Despite the apparent freedom available to the institution in defining what to do with its "clients," it feels compelled to constrain the child's freedom or, more broadly, to protect society from the child. In fact, the simple clarity of this expectation may lead to conflict with those defined as "treatment" staff. However, because institutions must accept juveniles for limited periods of time, and because institutions define the proper target of change to be the individual, the institution will frequently accept an individual adjustment to the institution as evidence of desirable change.

The lack of uniformity in defining the production function allowed David Street, Robert Vinter, and Charles Perrow to develop three organizational models that could be used to classify institutions. The models used were as follows:

1. *Obedience/conformity.* In this type of institution, habits, respect for authority, and conformity training were emphasized. Accommodation to high levels of external control through staff domination was apparent.

2. *Reeducation/development.* Inmates were to change through training in attitude and value change, skill acquisition, development of personal resources, and new social behaviors.

3. *Treatment.* Institutions emphasizing treatment stress psychological reconstitution and strive to accomplish personality change through self-insight and two-person psychotherapy.[20]

The lack of clarity in organizational goals makes it extremely difficult to identify consistent or standard production activities in the juvenile justice system. The lack of standardization yields extreme differences in police practices, probation officer functioning, judicial behavior, and in-

[20] David Street, Robert D. Vinter, and Charles Perrow, *Organization for Treatment* (New York: The Free Press, 1966).

stitutional services. One result of such ambiguity is goal displacement, by which an organization concentrates on the means of doing something rather than on obtaining objectives, which perhaps are not well identified. Thus, in an institution manned by Freudian psychologists, one is likely to find much individual psychotherapy occurring. The result may be an extreme focus on two-person interaction, which necessarily denies that delinquency is a group activity. Although it may be true that the "lone delinquent" is, in fact, the only true "sick" delinquent, there is no guarantee that only sick delinquents are placed in such institutions. Focusing on one's preferred intervention strategy, such as Freudian psychotherapy, leads rather nicely into our next generic production issue, preferred intervention strategy.

PREFERRED INTERVENTION STRATEGY. A third factor influencing the production function, perhaps more directly than the others, is the preferred intervention strategy, or the working ideology adopted by practitioners in the field. The idea relates to the way in which one defines a problem, and to the way one responds once the problem is defined. There are rough corollaries in other professions. For instance, some doctors believe in liberally administering drugs to children, whereas others actively avoid the practice; some mechanics feel that the best way to break in an engine is to baby it, whereas others feel it should be shown no mercy; and some college professors believe that students learn best by doing, whereas others feel that students need to be lectured, in order to gain knowledge. It matters little what area of productivity one considers, people will generally have preferred ways of doing things, even if these ways are based on superstition, someone else's authority, or "tried and true" experiences. The difference between "treatment ideology" and the determination of goals is a subtle one, but treatment ideology will influence the behavior of the worker, irrespective of goal definition.

One of the most fundamental issues that influences treatment ideology, but does not act alone to determine it, is the identification of the problem source. A gross, perhaps overly simplistic way to discuss the identification of the source is to cast the question in a dichotomous way. In doing so, we would ask whether one's delinquency problem, psychiatric problem, or even poverty is attributable to the sickness of the individual, and this represents the individual pathology orientation to the identification of the problem source, or whether the problem is attributable to the society in which the individual finds himself, and this represents the social structural orientation to the identification of the problem source.

The individual approach to delinquency could be represented by B. N. Sanford, who delineates three types of criminals: (1) the presocial criminal who is characterized by an infantile superego and an ego that is weak and unable to cope with the primitive demands of the id, (2) the antisocial criminal who has a severe superego and strong ego who eventually identifies with the underworld, and (3) the social criminal who combines a weak, almost inoperative superego with an ego that is strong and equal to its task.[21] It is clear that Sanford adopts a psychoanalytic orientation in accounting for criminality, and it would be reasonable to assume that any treatment offered by one who adopted this belief system would involve individual psychotherapy.

On the other hand, Richard Cloward and Lloyd Ohlin's work can be seen as representing the social structural orientation.[22] Cloward and Ohlin feel that adolescents who form delinquent subcultures have internalized an emphasis on success goals but resort to noncomformist alternatives when goals are unattainable. Essentially, they see delinquency as a response to frustration arising from discrepancies between economic, social, and educational aspirations and the legitimate means for their attainment. One who embraced the position developed by Cloward and Ohlin might attack the delinquency problem by devoting time and effort to equalizing income distribution, working to equalize job opportunity, and to eliminate the kind of thinking that results in youths being pushed out of school. The social structure is identified as the appropriate target of change, and ameliorative efforts might ignore the delinquent per se.

It is important to see these two positions for what they are—global orientations that provide a framework within which we can cast many efforts of juvenile justice practitioners. Furthermore, neither of these is "right" or "wrong" but are offered as a simple device to enhance the critical analysis ability of those who look at and try to understand the work of others. The fact that these two frameworks exist does not mean that a practitioner's efforts will always represent an orientation to one to the exclusion of the other. For instance, if a policeman were to arrest a purse snatcher with the hope that the offender would be deterred in the future, or perhaps would even learn a lesson, then the police officer's efforts could be seen as reflecting the individual orientation. On the other hand, if the police officer recommended increased recreational and job opportunities for youths in high-crime neighborhoods, then his efforts would be representative of the social structural mode.

One of the more important notions concerning preferred intervention strategy (or treatment ideology) is that the individual's general orientation is likely to be reflected in the majority of his actions, irrespective of the goals of the agency. For instance, if a Freudian psychologist were

---

[21] B. N. Sanford, "A Psychoanalytic Study of Three Criminal Types," *Journal of Criminal Psychotherapy*, 5 (1943), 57–68.

[22] Richard Cloward and Lloyd Ohlin, *Delinquency and Opportunity* (New York: The Free Press, 1960).

employed in a prison that emphasized restraint of inmates, the psychologist's behavior with clients would probably be little different than if the psychologist were found in an institution that stressed rehabilitation or even community reintegration. The psychologist might stress individual adjustment in the reintegration-oriented prison when, in fact, working with the community would be more helpful in the long run. Similarly, a punitive police officer would probably be just as authoritarian in carrying out the role of a juvenile police officer, which is supposed to involve referral to community agencies, as he would be in dealing with an adult offender who had committed a felony.

What, then, are some of the preferred treatment ideologies that could be adopted by people in the juvenile justice field? Probation officers can adopt several styles including that of individual counselor, family caseworker, or community organizer. In other words, the probation officer can carry out his duties by dealing with the individual and his problems, by dealing with the client as a member of social milieu and involving family and perhaps peers in a group treatment process, or by foraging into the community on behalf of his client. In the latter role, he might be trying to alter the situation in which a child finds himself in school, he might be attempting to arrange for jobs for clients, or he might work with a service club to arrange for activities that all youths in a community could utilize. Again, the preferred style of the probation officer may not be equally applicable in all cases, but it will undoubtedly creep into his efforts on the client's behalf. Although an officer who adopts a one-to-one counseling style may find himself attempting to get social services for a particular client, he may not feel as comfortable in that role as the community organization-type worker. It is not likely that one who defines the role as one-to-one counseling will continually pursue contacts with the social service system—it simply is not within the style of a one-to-one counselor.

Treatment personnel in institutions may have the most difficulty implementing their preferred intervention strategy. The expectations of the client and the emphasis on security and control in any juvenile institution, which in turn creates conflict between the treatment staff and the custodial staff, act together to frustrate the best efforts of those who want to transform the client into a better person. In thinking about the likelihood that a treatment person will be able to, in fact, treat, one must keep in mind the outlook of the youth who became institutionalized. There are many factors operating that may negate the impact that is traditionally attributed to institutions. For instance, throughout the period of contact with the juvenile court process, the youth may be threatened with the institutionalization as if it were the worst possible fate, constituting, in effect, civil death. The messages that the youth is receiving in this process do not focus on the wonderful treatment possibilities that exist in the institution, but on how ugly the experience is likely to be. Consequently, the youth must psychically prepare himself to encounter this last, largely unknown, bastion of control that the judge and probation people are holding out to him. If, in fact, it turns out that the youth is to be institutionalized, the message is likely to change to insure a smooth transition from the court to the institution. Once one knows that the youth is to be "sent away," the message he/she gets is that it really is not the worst possible fate and that one will be able to get through the experience with relative ease. The hypocrisy of the competing messages is likely to result in the youth viewing his upcoming institutionalization as not a large problem, and, in the process, the credibility of treatment efforts will be largely negated. One result of this process is that many youths will end up "playing the game" or going through whatever motions are necessary to gain release.

Another factor making difficult the implementation of one's treatment ideology is the constant struggle between treatment and custodial interests. By its very nature, institutionalization involves control and actions that are undertaken in the name of treatment, and vice versa. For instance, being sent to the "hole," the behavioral adjustment unit, or the freedom room—wherever particularly bad kids are sent—may be seen as counter to treatment efforts. Conflicts like this results in continual struggles between treatment and control interests, thereby lessening the likelihood that one's preferred intervention strategy will be meaningfully implemented.

Boundary Subsystem

It may be quite natural to think of the systems and agencies comprising criminal and juvenile justice as having a legitimate role in serving a public need, and therefore, to underestimate the degree to which they must make an effort to stay afloat or viable. It must be emphasized that they too must have clients to serve, money and other resources to operate, and personnel to administer to client needs. Their status as state-supported services does not obviate the need to seek clients that are "in need" of the system's attention. It was indicated above that many of the activities of the juvenile justice system are of a maintenance nature, but the system is also obviously involved in a production process. There is, however, lack of clarity concerning what one is to produce or what change is to be imparted to youth with problems. By the very nature of the way the juvenile justice system is organized, each of its components must interact with other representatives of the system, as well as with people who are external to it or are only tangentially involved. We call the system that controls external affairs, links the organization with others, and deals with the integration of the organization into the environment the *boundary subsystem*. We have here a system of agencies or components whose "conception is of a 'stream of action' in which criminals, like raw material, pass through the organization and have various rehabilitative operations performed on them, each according to his needs."[23] This statement, although alluding to the activities of prison, can be generalized to the whole juvenile justice system that can be conceptualized as a constellation of organizations, each of which renders its particular activities or competencies before passing the "raw material" or youth on to the next organization. Because juvenile justice system clients are passed from one organization to another, by necessity, there must be organizational interactions at the boundary of each segment.

DOMAIN CONSENSUS.   Central to thinking about organizational boundaries and organizational interchange is the concept of domain consensus. "The domain of an organization consists of the specific goals it wishes to pursue and the functions it undertakes in order to implement its goals."[24] Definition of domain aids in understanding the purpose and functioning of an organization, and therefore its members can not only behave in ways that are conducive to effective functioning within their domain, but they can also comfortably structure their interaction with others. Many of the current directions in juvenile justice are having the effect of disrupting definitions of domain, altering the definitions of jobs, and confusing the nature of boundary interactions. For instance, it has been traditionally true that the juvenile court served as a frequent referral source for youth coming to the attention of the police. There was a recognition and acknowledgement of domain—the court didn't try to "catch kids," and the police didn't try to rehabilitate them. If a youth was to be evaluated, and subsequently referred to an appropriate social service agency, the juvenile court was defined as the legitimate component to perform these activities. The current trend toward proliferation and redefinition of services must, however, cause confusion in the definition of domain.

Domain consensus is an important concept to organizations and alludes to staking a claim over a circumscribed realm of activity; it relates to the "right" to operate in that realm and determines, in part, the nature and quality in interactions with other agencies. It would seem until recently that the juvenile justice system as a whole has been relatively insulated from attention, in part because of the geographic isolation of its institutions, but more importantly, because there was relative agreement that dealing with "bad kids" was the legitimate role of the juvenile courts

[23] Donald R. Cressey, "Limitation on Organization of Treatment in the Modern Prison," in R. Quinney, ed., *Crime and Justice in Society* (Boston: Little, Brown, 1968), pp. 469–470.

[24] Sol Levine and Paul White, "Exchange as a Conceptual Framework for the Study of Interorganizational Relationships," in M. B. Brinkerhoff and P. R. Kunz, eds., *Complex Organizations and Their Environments* (Dubuque, Iowa: William C. Brown, 1972), p. 352.

and other juvenile justice units. Furthermore, the legal nature of the justice process mystifies, legitimizes, and formalizes its right to claim the domain over deviant behavior. This is not to say that there have not been critics of the system or even legal attacks on the system, but it does imply that government has a monopoly on the right to establish courts and penal sanctions, and that no private enterprise is likely to infringe on these activities.

As a result of highly developed domain consensus and legitimacy, when a youth is arrested, a highly predictable process will begin. A parent may plead with the arresting officer or, subsequently, may make a special plea to the judge, but that parent knows that the fate of his own son or daughter is now beyond his domain. It is fairly clear that once a juvenile is within the boundaries of "the system" (domain), a predictable processing from police, to court, to probation or institution is likely to occur. Until the *Gault* decision,[25] the legitimacy granted the process was edified by the *parens patriae* notion, or the state as the wise and benevolent parent. The *Gault* decision has allowed certain officials (lawyers) to intrude on the juvenile justice domain by insisting that if the state is to claim the youth as appropriate for its attention, then it must prove its case in an adversariallike setting.

DOMAIN PERMEABILITY. The *Gault* decision leads us into another boundary issue, domain permeability. Boundaries of organizations are more or less permeable to the flow of information, outside influence, and new ideas or new personnel. In pursuing organizational goals, interaction with the environment and, therefore, penetration of the organization's domain are a necessity. Some organizations are more permeable than others, either by nature of the personality of its leaders or by the nature of the type of activity pursued. In thinking about the relationship between environmental interaction and domain permeability, the second Nixon administration presents an enigma. One would normally think of the government as relying on domain permeability to sustain viability and vitality, yet Nixon insulated himself, his office, and his personality. The fact that Watergate happened may in part be accounted for by the extremely impervious boundaries established by the President.

The lack of permeability of the domain of juvenile justice is attested to by the very essence of many of its physical structures. Police stations, courtrooms that exclude spectators, and locked institutions do not indicate that the system welcomes interaction with "outsiders." Many of the factors mentioned in the maintenance section of this chapter seem also to serve a boundary mantenance function. The symbols found in the system such as uniforms, badges, guns, and walls are not conducive to informal

---

[25] In re Gault, see footnote 3.

interaction. The slowness with which reform has come to the juvenile justice system can be partially accounted for by the fact that the system, as designed, interacts with itself and is relatively impervious to domain penetrations.

EXCHANGE RELATIONSHIPS. We have already alluded to the notion of exchange relationships, but this notion deserves to be more fully elaborated. "Organizational exchange is any voluntary activity between two organizations which has consequences, actual or anticipated, for the realization *of their respective goals or objectives.*"[26] Sol Levine and Paul White indicate that exchange relationships in the health field consist of exchanging cases, clients, or patients; giving and receiving labor services; and the sending or receiving of resources other than labor services such as funds, equipment, and other labor services.[27] We can perhaps crudely think of exchange as "you scratch my back and I'll scratch yours," but this need not be the case. Organizational exchanges can be unilateral wherein one organization gives something to another, bilateral wherein two organizations essentially swap resources, and joint exchange wherein two organizations direct resources to a third. In the justice field, state planning agencies (SPA's) and perhaps L.E.A.A. (Law Enforcement Assistance Administration) might be considered examples of organizations that provide unilateral exchanges. For instance, L.E.A.A. may grant an institution $200,000 to determine whether or not the use of paraprofessional parole officers results in lower recidivism rates than the use of regular parole officers. Or, L.E.A.A. might agree to provide special funds to hire new parole officers. Although it would appear that the goals of only one organization are being served, it must be remembered that part of the responsibility of L.E.A.A. is to distribute resources to enhance criminal justice functioning. Therefore, the needs of both organizations are served. Another example of exchange in juvenile justice includes the cooperation of institutional and probation agencies in providing information to the parole authority for consideration in a parole release decision.

Analyzing the nature of exchange relationships may be one fruitful way of understanding the interactions between a juvenile justice system agency and one outside of the system. Robert Emerson invokes notions of exchange relationships very effectively in his study of a large, metropolitan juvenile court.[28] There is much cooperation and exchange between the police, the schools, and the probation officers of the juvenile court. The juvenile court derives its power and influence from its position to review and make decisions about youth whom the schools and police find

---

[26] Levine and White, "Exchange as a Conceptual Framework," p. 344.
[27] Ibid., p. 384.
[28] Robert Emerson, *Judging Delinquents* (Chicago: Aldine, 1969).

troublesome, and in exchange for this power, the court encourages schools and police to function as the eyes and ears of the court. In essence, there is a bilateral exchange in which each organization serves the other. In addition to the surveillance function performed by the police, the police also serve the probation officers as a source of background information concerning cases before the court. Exchange becomes more critical when the court must deal with the Child Welfare Department, which controls money for placing juveniles in expensive, private facilities. The only way the court can get access to these funds is to ask the Child Welfare Department to "bend" the rules, but the price is heavy. The court must respond favorably to Child Welfare in "emergency" situations involving commitment to mental hospitals, bringing the court's power to bear on uncooperative cases of Child Welfare, and finally acting as a "dumping ground" for cases on which Child Welfare has essentially given up. Emerson found that there were reasonably effective exchange relationships with agencies who had a "need" to cooperate, but such was not the case with the children's mental hospital. In this case, the court was unable to be effective in getting hospital services because they could provide little, if anything to the hospital.[29]

Exchange relationships and the very idea of exchange are fruitful ways to think about the boundary functions of an organization. Although many of the boundary interactions occur with other juvenile justice agencies, it is frequently necessary to interact with others outside the system. When one must interact with a person or agency outside the system, it may be helpful to ask the question why the outside contact should cooperate. Organizations, like individuals, have needs and if responding can fulfill a need, then a response seems more likely. Considering the implications of exchange should not be limited to thinking only about agencies beyond the realm of the system. Even though there is a logical sequence to be followed in processing a juvenile through the system, considerations of exchange may help one to understand the nature of problems, or even of helpful interactions. It is possible, for instance, to conceive of juvenile police officers as serving both a production subsystem function as well as a boundary subsystem function in their handling of a particular youth. However, because juvenile officers serve both a production and boundary function, they may be open to charges of inefficiency in the performance of their job.

Perhaps the clearest example of boundary activity in juvenile justice is the referral, made by police or probation and parole workers. In referring a youth to another agency for service, the police or probation officer must be sure that the client fits the description of the type of person or problem served by the referral agency. In essence, the referral must be

---

[29] Ibid., pp. 72–78.

packaged and "sold" to the receiving agency in such a way that the referring agency will be able to maintain its credibility in the future.

An Overview

The juvenile justice system is constituted by many complex units, actions, and decisions. We have really only touched on some of the salient issues and structures that comprise the system and regrettably have had to ignore other issues or perspectives that deserve mention. The chapter has been relatively traditional in scope in that we have discussed the system as it is, and have devoted little discussion to changes that have occurred or are on the horizon. Some changes we are likely to see, or have already seen, include the fact that segments of the juvenile justice system are taking a more active role in diverting kids from the system; they are attempting to encourage schools and the occupational marketplace to treat "unsuccessful" youth and successful youth equally; and they are attempting to interrupt the negative labeling process apparent in our social institutions to interrupt the self-fulfilling prophecies initiated by these labels. Certain organizations, such as Youth Service Bureaus, are being introduced that can be seen by the juvenile justice system either as a resource or a competitor. It is likely that Youth Service Bureaus, which supply direct service to "delinquent" as well as "nondelinquent" youth, will be seen as a resource until and unless there is an insufficient supply of youth coming into the juvenile court to justify the probation personnel and other staff employed by the court. The Youth Service Bureau is just one example of an organization that is penetrating the boundaries of the system, intruding on its domain, taking over some of its production functions, and perhaps, indirectly, redefining organizational maintenance activities. In thinking about juvenile justice, one must determine how the subsystems define and affect the juvenile justice system, but also one must understand that the system is undergoing intrusion and redefinition. Finally, although many changes are seen as laudatory, they also are fundamental threats to the present structure of juvenile justice.

CONCLUDING REMARKS

We have chosen not to go into the composition of police departments, to discuss the role of the defense attorney in juvenile court, to describe the function of probation officers, or to discuss at length the role of institutions in the juvenile justice process. Although all of these are important, we feel that most of these structures have been mentioned elsewhere in the book. There are differences between the adult and juvenile systems, but in terms of traditional structures, the similarities outweigh the differences. The juvenile system is beset with uncertainties about goals and functions, there are ambiguities about what is productive functioning and what is boundary functioning, and the system may be undergoing a significant transition. Again, many of the salient issues have already been identified by a systems perspective that facilitates identification of similar issues and operational patterns in dissimilar agencies.

RESEARCH AND THE FUTURE OF CRIMINAL JUSTICE

part IV

chapter 13

Criminal Justice Research

Research in criminal justice, compared with research in other fields, has a short and undistinguished history. There are no Newtons or Galileos of criminal justice research. No laws have been discovered, and few persons have been unwise enough to have claimed the discovery of them. Few decent theories have been generated, but even more surprising is the fact that few of the existing theories have been empirically tested. Research in criminal justice is just now reaching respectability. Even so, many of the research methods used in the area are laughably unsophisticated when compared to methodologies in other areas of social science. Researchers in criminal justice still make the simple mistakes of generalizing beyond their data, of failing to compare their research groups with the behavior of control groups, or of making comparisons and drawing conclusions based on data concerning noncomparable groups.

The reasons for such problems are many. To begin with, one must undestand that social science research in general deals with the most complex sets of phenomena that can be chosen for study, the interaction of human beings. One can isolate a chemical compound, break it down into its constituent parts, and say something reasonably accurate about the composition. Or one can study an amoeba under a microscope and note its anatomy, physiology, behavior, and so on. But it is extremely difficult to isolate for study the variables of human behavior, and one discovers that behavior of individuals in a laboratory is usually very different from the behavior of the same people at work or play.

Furthermore, the scientific discipline relevant to social study is very young. Psychology and sociology were born as disciplines during the second half of the last century. Economics is an older discipline, but modern economics is just beginning to cope with the problems of evaluating the costs and benefits relevant to the exchanges that occur in a criminal event or in the processing of offenders. History as a discipline is also just beginning to find applications in the criminal justice area. Political science itself is new and has been fragmented into very different components depending on the methodologies applied. Lately, schools of police science and criminal justice have developed. But it is unclear at this point whether they offer anything unique to the study of crime, or whether they merely offer a collection of practitioners and different social scientists who argue among themselves without integrating their different points of view.

THE BACKGROUND OF
CRIMINOLOGICAL RESEARCH

The two schools of thought that have had the most influence over criminal justice research, or have manifested at different points in history most of the major issues in conceptualizing criminal justice research problems, are the Classical and Positive schools of criminology. The Classical school is usually associated with the thinking of Jeremy Bentham and other utilitarians, whose work revolved around the prescription of proper punishment for the severity of particular crimes.[1] One impetus for this work was the thinking about utopian communities and the mechanisms for social control in such societies. Another related impetus was the concern for reforming the eighteenth-century judicial systems, which were notoriously corrupt and riddled with absurdly harsh penalties.

The Classical school was followed by the Positive school, associated with thinkers such as Cesare Lombroso.[2] This school began with attempts to study the biological and physiological characteristics of offenders so that they could be identified, and so that their punishment could be directed toward the particular criminological problems associated with different types of criminals. By and large, the judicial machinery has been most heavily influenced by the Classical school, whereas the correctional

[1] Leon Radzinowicz, *Ideology and Crime* (New York: Columbia University Press, 1966).

[2] Ibid.

agencies have been most heavily influenced by the Positive school. Hence, the judicial cliché is, "Let the punishment fit the crime," whereas the correctional cliché is, "Let the punishment fit the criminal."

The Classical perception of crime causation was basically a deterrent approach, built on a rational, economic model of man. It was assumed in this model that a man's actions were governed by a utilitarian calculus, that he would behave in order to have the benefits for his action exceed the efforts or costs to obtain them. Hence, Bentham suggested that in order to deter a criminal, the punishment for the crime would have to be set at a level that would exceed the possible benefits of the crime but would not be so excessive as to waste state resources or to risk a revolutionary overthrow of the government.

The system of punishments that seemed to fit most adequately into this scheme was an incarceration program: so much time in prison for such and such a crime. The capital and corporal punishments that were common in the judicial system of the time Bentham rejected as too gross and unprecise to act as deterrents. Furthermore, it was clear to him that such punishments included an element of vengeance, which he rejected as not in keeping with a rational order.

The Classical school theory has had many temporal manifestations. Bentham's work was one of the foundations of penal reform in the early 1900s, including the design of penitentiary systems. These reforms have influenced American approaches to crime control ever since. The Classical theories also led to sweeping legislative reform, in which many crimes were defined more clearly and punishments were set out in terms of numbers of years, the most severe crimes leading to life imprisonment or death.

The influence of the Classical school goes much farther than that, however; its influence is evident in all strategies of social control that rely either on a deterrent to the potential offender or on a punishment of the apprehended offender so that he will not commit the same crime again. *General deterrence* is usually the term that connotes the former strategy, in which society attempts to protect itself from the future crime of potential, but as yet unidentified, offenders. *Specific deterrence* is usually the term used to connote the latter strategy, in which the treatment of an apprehended individual is supposed to deter him from committing the same crime again.

In addition to much of the work of judges and prosecutors, a great deal of police operations are structured on the premise that certain displays of force, and hence the promise of apprehension, will highlight the criminal penalities that are supposed to deter. Obviously, it would make no difference what the penalty for a crime was if the offender knew he was not going to be caught and thus could discount the severity of punishment in his calculation of costs and benefits.

Although this theory is widely espoused and has behind it about as long a tradition as any other crime control strategy, it is a theory that has rarely been tested. One difficulty with such a test is the problem of how to measure how many persons are potential offenders, and thus stand a chance of being deterred. Another problem is how to estimate how many persons know the penalty for a crime or perceive a particular criminal act as an offense, and hence can possibly be deterred by their knowledge of the illegality and the penalty attached. Perhaps even more difficult is the opportunity to manipulate deterrents in order to observe the changes in crime rate. And next to impossible, of course, is removing the assumed deterrents altogether, in order to see if there is a rise in crime without them.

The research that has been done usually leads to conclusions that the effects of deterrents are doubtful, and that what deters one group may even spur another group on to more crime! For example, a mayor's decision to wage a "war on graffiti" can provoke teenage groups to even greater artistic heights in alleys and on sidewalks. Or stiffer penalties for gang fighting might encourage gang members to earn tougher reputations by fighting more or more viciously. Or, as has been noted frequently in the literature, deterrents to one kind of crime can lead to rises in another type, so that the actual effect of the deterrent is negligible or negative. For instance, Lewis Yablonsky and Richard Cloward and Lloyd Ohlin have noted that strong social attempts to curb fighting gangs may lead gang members to increased use of drugs.[3]

On the other hand, there is some evidence that particular types of crimes can be deterred by a manipulation of penalties or by stronger enforcement of the existing penalty. These kinds of crimes appear to be ones open to everyone in a particular area and are the types of crimes that are actually calculated as Bentham hypothesized. For example, it has been observed that fewer parking violations occur when officers ticket cars more often. And it has been found that income-tax cheating varies somewhat directly with the citizen's perception of his ability to get away with the fraud.[4]

The Positive school theories are of a different order. Lombroso and Ferri and others began by observing the physical characteristics of known offenders. They studied body weight, height, skull shape, size of ears, and shape of ear lobes, nose, and so on. Although these beginnings doubtless seem primitive now, the studies were based on a fairly revolutionary

[3] Lewis Yablonsky, *The Violent Gang* (New York: Macmillian, 1962); and Richard Cloward and Lloyd Ohlin, *Delinquency and Opportunity* (New York: The Free Press, 1961).

[4] R. D. Schwartz and S. Orleans, "On Legal Sanctions," *University of Chicago Law Review,* 34 (1967), 272.

assumption for the time—that the incidence of crime was related to characteristics of the offender. For many years this kind of physical study continued with the mistaken assumption that we could learn about the characteristics of offenders simply by studying apprehended offenders. When someone finally went out into the general citizenry and discovered the same kinds of characteristics in relatively the same proportion, the bubble burst.[5]

In the meantime, psychology was coming into its own, and the Positive school incorporated the study of psychological characteristics. Again, the mistake was made of assuming that the psychological characteristics of known offenders were a priori different than the psychological characteristics of the general population. But, through all this stumbling, the concept emerged that crime and criminal behavior were related to *something* about or within offenders that could provide at least a partial explanation of why some persons committed crime while others did not.[6]

The greatest influence of the positive school in American criminal justice has probably been in the correctional area. Whereas the judicial system has been largely structured by the rules of evidence, the adversarial balance, and the legislation of proscriptions and deterrents, correctional work was just beginning in earnest when the Positive influence was heaviest. Furthermore, whereas the Quaker penal reform had begun with some utilitarian logic, the penitentiary system always was concerned with reforming the offender. Hence, the Positive school study of the offender replaced the theological theories about penitence and reform.

With the Positive school theory that criminal behavior was related to individual characteristics, it became important to study the individual prisoners and decide how they should be treated so that they might not revert to criminal activity in the future. Hence, classification of offenders became important, along with structuring programs or entire facilities to deal with particular kinds of characteristics. Different kinds of vocational programs were introduced, based on guesses about which offenders were amenable to training and treatment and which were not. As psychoanalytic theory was introduced, from Europe, it influenced social work training, and the counseling of offenders became important, particularly in juvenile institutions.[7]

[5] E. A. Hooton, *Crime and the Man* (Cambridge, Mass.: Harvard University Press, 1939); and L. S. Penrose, "Genetics and the Criminal," *British Journal of Delinquency*, 6 (1955), 15–25.

[6] Edwin H. Sutherland and Donald R. Cressey, *Criminology* (Philadelphia: Lippincott, 1970), pp. 151–171.

[7] Alvin Rudoff, *The PICO Project: A Measure of Casework in Corrections* (Sacramento, Calif.: Department of Corrections, 1959); and "History of Correctional Fieldwork," *Proceedings of the National Probation and Parole Association*, 1941.

Perhaps the greatest influence of the Positive school in corrections, however, was a legislative innovation. Following the assumption that offenders committing the same crime might be different in their motives, character, and reaction to treatment, the indeterminate sentence was introduced in a number of states, notably California. This sentencing practice is an abrupt break with Classical notions about sentencing. It allows judges to sentence in relation to their conception of the potential of the offender and allows parole boards to release in relation to their conception of the improvements that the offender has demonstrated.[8]

Other areas that the Positive school theories have influenced concern particular types of offenders. Some states, such as Maryland, have institutions designated for mentally defective offenders, and other states have special legislation pertaining to dangerous offenders, sexual offenders, or habitual offenders.[9] Certainly the emphasis on the individual has also been very important in the decriminalization of certain behaviors. Diversion from criminal justice is a growing practice, and includes civil commitment to social agencies of alcoholics, drug addicts, and mentally ill offenders.[10]

As sweeping as the influence of the Positive theories has been, it is surprising how meager the research is concerning any theory linking personal characteristics to criminal behavior. Perhaps the best known such research is the work of Marguerite Warren,[11] discussed in Chapter Six. Warren and her associates in California were concerned with classifying juvenile offenders according to maturity level, designing programs of treatment appropriate for each level, and assessing the effects of such treatment. Clearly visible in this research is the emphasis on some attribute or set of attributes about the offenders that presumably contribute to delinquency, and on the attempt to manipulate or change those attributes so that the offender would not repeat the behavior. This research in California has been better than most research of this type in that it attempted to control not only the *persons* but also the *program* and the *treater*. Major findings are that the right combination of person, program,

---

[8] Andrew Alexander Bruce and others, *The Workings of the Indeterminate Sentence Law and the Parole System in Illinois* (Montclair, N.J.: Patterson Smith, 1968), originally published 1928; and Jessica Mifford, "Kind and Usual Punishment in California," *Atlantic Monthly*, 277, No. 3 (March 1971), 45–53.

[9] Daniel Katkin, "Habitual Offender Laws: A Reconsideration," *Buffalo Law Review*, 21, No. 1, F.11 (1971), pp. 99–120; and Nicholas Kittrie, *The Right To Be Different* (Baltimore: Penguin Books, 1971).

[10] Kittrie, *The Right To Be Different*.

[11] Marguerite Warren, "The Community Treatment Project: History and Prospects," *Law Enforcement Science and Technology*, 1 (1967) 191–200; and J. D. Grant and Marguerite Grant, "A Group Dynamics Approach to Treatment of Non-Conformity in The Navy," *Annals of the American Academy of Political and Social Science*, 322 (March 1959), 126–155.

and treater can have beneficial effects, whereas the wrong combination can wipe out the beneficial effects of any one component, or may even result in higher crime rates for some populations.[12]

AREAS OF RESEARCH IN CRIMINAL JUSTICE

There are any number of ways that research in criminology and criminal justice can be classified, such as by discipline, methodology, offender groups, or results. In this section we will look briefly at four different kinds of research, roughly classified by the kinds of problems that the research addresses. These four areas are causation, process, outcome, and evaluation. Obviously, all of these types shade into one another, and one type of research might well be used as a component of a research project with a different purpose. Also, research about the causes for crime may influence research about the processes of crime or the processes of correction. Frequently, evaluation research combines a concern for the process of treatment and the outcome. But in any case, we can discuss many current research topics under these headings with reasonable efficiency in the delineation of method for any one type.

Causative Research

Causes of crime and thinking about them have been age-old problems. One of the charges against Socrates by the Athenian citizens was that he had contributed to delinquency. And the description of the delinquency problem at the trial was very similar to descriptions of the problem in the twentieth century.[13] We have gradually become more sophisticated in thinking about cause, however, and a variety of researches and theoretical constructs have contributed to our notions of crime causation.

DEMOGRAPHIC RESEARCH. One of the prerequisites to thinking about cause is simply to know the extent and dimensions of crime. In the United States, the largest undertaking in this area is the *Uniform Crime Reports* (U.C.R.) issued by the Federal Bureau of Investigation. This reporting system provides a rough measure of incidence of crime reported or known to the police. It includes the "index crimes" usually reported on the news or utilized by executives and political leaders to

---

[12] Although it was written long before the full explication of the "I-Level" theory, we still believe the classic article on interaction between treated, program, and treater is J. Douglas Grant and Marguerite Grant, "A Group Dynamics Approach to the Treatment of Non-Conformity in the Navy," *Annals of the American Academy of Political and Social Science,* 322 (March 1959), 126–155.

[13] Plato's description of Socrates' trial and the claims made at the trial concerning youth crime sound very contemporary.

suggest the overall incidence of crime. These seven index crimes are: murder, manslaughter, rape, robbery, aggravated assault, larceny over $50, and auto theft.

Although the accuracy of the U.C.R. has doubtless increased over the years, it is still dependent on local police cooperation with the F.B.I., is sensitive only to crimes known to the police, and varies with different investigation and reporting policy in each locality.[14]

Another measure of incidence technique is the self-report measures conducted by a variety of sociologists. This technique involves asking persons to respond to questionnaire items about how many times they have committed or been involved in offending behaviors described in the questionnaires. These techniques have been found useful and accurate for certain purposes. For instance, they can be used to discover how many offenses are committed but go undetected or unreported. Invariably such techiques discover considerably more crime than the U.C.R. On the other hand, these techniques have been misused or poorly applied. They can be used, for example, to lead to conclusions that almost 100 percent of the juvenile population is "delinquent" in the sense that they have committed one or more acts defined as acts of delinquency.[15]

Recently the Law Enforcement Assistance Administration (L.E.A.A.), with the cooperation of the U.S. Census Bureau, has engaged in a similar measure of crime incidence designed to measure the extent of victimization in the country. A variety of samples is used to estimate the extent of victimization for particular types of crimes. A major subsample for the five largest cities of New York, Chicago, Los Angeles, Philadelphia, and Detroit is taken more frequently than the entire national sample. This study is called the "Five-City Crime Panel," and it reports every two years the number of victimizations in households or against businesses. The preliminary findings are that for the kinds of crimes reported, there are between three and five times the number of crimes committed as are reported to the police. Major reasons for not reporting were that citizens felt nothing could be done or that the incident was not important enough to generate a police response. While reported, the feeling that the police were antagonistic was infrequent. Moreover, it was discovered that, contrary to popular opinion, the City of New York was the safest of the five cities for a number of different crimes.[16]

Other major findings of any demographic study are that crime rates

---

[14] President's Commission on Law Enforcement and the Administration of Justice, *Task Force Report: Science and Technology* (Washington, D.C.: Government Printing Office, 1967), pp. 55–64.

[15] Martin Gold, "Undetected Delinquency Behavior," *Journal of Research in Crime and Delinquency*, 13, No. 1 (January 1966), 27–46.

[16] See, for example, *Crime in the Nation's Five Largest Cities* (Washington, D.C.: U.S. Department of Justice, April 1974).

differ considerably for different geographical populations and for different offender or victim groups. Lower-class black males are more likely to be victims of murder, assault, and robbery than other groups. In the L.E.A.A. five-city survey, preliminary results show white middle- and upper-class households are least likely to be the victims of any crimes, except larceny over $200.[17]

Such data would suggest that the persons most likely to be involved in criminal incidents are least likely to receive services directed at crime deterrence. And most people with the resources needed to demand better crime protection are relatively safe already. Perhaps the best known such finding is the correlation between lower-class, inner-city conditions and high rates of certain kinds of crimes. Usually forgotten, however, when conclusions are drawn from such data, is that many middle-class kinds of crime are less easy to detect, are less often reported or responded to officially, or are of less concern to the middle-class legislators and executives making and enforcing the law. It seems true that the *kind* of crime varies with social class, wealth, geographical area, and so forth, but it is not evident from present data that lower-class, urban conditions are really causative of *more crime* in an absolute sense.[18]

Ecological research. Closely related to demographic research is research on the ecology of crime. Actually the kinds of variables studied may be synonymous. The distinction we are trying to make is between demographic studies of extent and frequency of crime in wide areas, and the in-depth study of the patterns of crime in a locally focused ecological study. The major figures associated with the ecological approach are Clifford Shaw, Henry McKay, and Frederick Thrasher,[19] of the Chicago school; and Bernard Landers, who did much of his work in the Baltimore area.[20]

An ecological approach to crime is very similar to an ecological approach to any other problem or set of phenomena. The basic goal is to attempt to structure the physical and, in this case, the social segments of a given area into natural subsets and then to examine the extent and nature of crime in each area. The reverse method is to segment the area by crime rates and then work back and designate in each crime-delin-

---

[17] Ibid.

[18] The lack of data demonstrating higher rate of crime for one class than another should be compared with Ramsey Clark's assumption that ghetto conditions breed crime, in his urgent and compelling preface to *Crime in America* (New York: Simon and Schuster, 1970).

[19] Clifford R. Shaw and Henry D. McKay, *Juvenile Delinquency and Urban Areas* (Chicago: University of Chicago Press, 1942); and Frederick Thrasher, *The Gang* (Chicago: University of Chicago Press, 1927).

[20] Bernard Landers, *Towards an Understanding of Juvenile Delinquency* (New York: Columbia University Press, 1954).

eated area the physical and social arrangements. Whether one would work backward from crime rate to area differences or forward from area differences to crime rate depends on the prime concern of the researcher.

A social ecologist, for example, may have criminal incidence as only one factor in a broader design, the main goal of which is the designation of broad social and physical differences. He may use crime rate as one of the manifestations or symptoms of hypothesized broader categories. Thus, he might work from crime rate, birth rate, death rate, etc., back to social and physical designations. Usually, the criminal justice researcher has the reverse hypothesis: He is attempting to locate crime or guess the extent of crime based on other social categories. Hence, he is likely to start dividing a geographical area, such as a city, by type and extent of industry, type and extent of business, type of dwelling, and number of people per square mile. Once he has divided the city into a number of different zones based on such data, he would then look at crime rate, kind of crime, and so on, in order to make statements about the relationship of these physical and social differences and the incidence of crime.

First Shaw and McKay in Chicago, and, later, Landers in Baltimore, became known for excellent studies using this type of methodology.[21] Thrasher's work was related to the Chicago ecological approach, but he emphasized in considerable detail the internal processes and dynamics of each gang he studied, thereby demonstrating the relationships of different gang activity to the cultural, political, social, and economic characteristics of each community.[22]

This kind of study has advantages over the straight demographic approach if the researcher is interested in the sociophysical context in which crime occurs. For example, a demographic study might distinguish between victimization rates for whites and blacks, or among different income levels or different neighborhoods; but frequently the demographer can find neighborhoods very similar in most demographic characteristics that still have very different crime rates or very different kinds of crime. It is at this point that ecological research is helpful in distinguishing why these similar neighborhoods have different crime outputs, even if the reasons discovered are less quantitative in nature and more dependent on clinical or subjective descriptions about neighborhood interactions, strength of local political leadership, family supervision styles, and so on.

The difficulty with both the ecological and demographic approaches is that they are generally insensitive to changes over time. The same researcher can rarely afford to study the same area over several different

---

21 Shaw and McKay, *Juvenile Delinquency and Urban Areas;* and Landers, *Towards an Understanding of Juvenile Delinquency.*

22 Thrasher, *The Gang.*

years in order to examine changes in crime rate as the social or physical conditions change. And without this study of change, one cannot make statements about cause. Clearly, if someone is to speak about ecological variables causing crime, he has to find out if the crime rate varies depending on the variations in the independent variables. Hence, most ecological studies result in conclusions about *association* or *correlation* rather than in conclusions about cause. Even the eloquent arguments by Ramsey Clark at the beginning of *Crime in America* do not demonstrate a causal connection between all the poverty, suffering, and ignorance that he catalogues and the kinds of crime that he mentions as being frequent in these areas.[23] Someone may argue that high crime helped cause these other conditions, or that something else altogether caused *both* crime and these other conditions. Also, such eloquent statements fail to point out that other kinds of crime occur in better neighborhoods, and that there may be some relationship between the economic crimes of the rich and violent crime in the ghetto.[24]

CLINICAL RESEARCH. By clinical research we mean research carried out by psychiatrists, certain kinds of psychologists, and certain kinds of social workers that is oriented to the personal histories, or case studies, of persons involved in crime: Usually included are feelings, emotions, thoughts, psychological history, rationalizations, etc., as these variables relate to the individual's involvement in crime.

Within the criminal justice system, the clinical approach to crime or to the individuals' involvement in crime is still the primary kind of research conducted, because within the system it is decisions about what to do with individuals that have to be made most frequently. One unintended consequence of this emphasis on the individual has been the long-standing inability of the criminal justice system to do anything about the prevention of crime. The reasons for this emphasis, however, are clear. The psychological and psychoanalytic disciplines offered techniques for studying deviance and became respectable professions long before sociological, economic, or political disciplines turned to crime as a major problem. Furthermore, although people both in and out of the system frequently speak about the responsibility of the criminal justice system to prevent crime, the social or organizational responsibility for the failure of prevention is diffuse. Is it the failure of the police? The courts? The correctional agencies? Or, as any of these system agencies would have it, is it the fault of society in general?[25]

---

[23] Ramsey Clark, *Crime in America* (New York: Pocket Books, 1971).

[24] David Gordon, "Capitalism, Class, and Crime in America," *Crime and Delinquency*, 19, No. 2 (1973), 160–175.

[25] See Leslie Wilkins, *Social Deviance* (Englewood Cliffs, N.J.: Prentice-Hall, 1966), Chapter Five.

But even while this useless finger pointing is going on, criminal justice agencies are faced with the responsibility of making decisions about apprehended individuals. At this point, the target is no longer *crime prevention,* but preventing this *person* from causing any more trouble. And since the agencies have done a poor job of collecting a great deal of information about types of crimes, types of neighborhoods, types of programs, and types of treatment results, the only strategy usually available is to amass all the information that can be gained about the one individual in question and to determine what to do with him, based on *his* background.

Naturally, even if we had a great deal of group data, we would still need to make decisions about individuals. But, in most cases, these decisions are now reached without the benefit of any viable and valid information about the performance of control groups and about the performance of groups similar to the individual in question.

Hence, the clinician needs to make decisions about individuals without much to go on. Obviously, as he makes these decisions, he will depend on his memory of similar cases and his recall about success or failure of results in those cases. But he is not likely to have any systematic data base to rely on and by which to control his own biases. For instance, he may recall a couple of very good cases and decisions or recall a couple of real "flops," and be overly liberal or conservative in the present instance because of those biased memories.[26]

CLINICAL STRATEGIES. It is important in speaking of clinical practices to distinguish between *clinical research* and the *conduct of therapy* (clinical strategies). In making the distinction, we will use the term *therapy* to refer to practices that have the *goal of improved conditions or changed character* in the offender, regardless of whether such a goal is achieved. Several different therapeutic programs, such as guided group interaction, group therapy, reality therapy, and so on, have been discussed in Chapter Seven (in relation to adults) and in Chapter Eight (in relation to juveniles). Clinical *research,* on the other hand, has the *goal of discovering information* about the individual, so that decisions about therapy can be made; or of discovering information about the conduct of therapy and the reaction of individuals to therapy, so that we can understand the therapeutic process; or of making more accurate therapeutic decisions in the future by hypothesizing about the causes of deviance in individual cases. Effective therapy uses good clinical research, and most good clinicians will conduct research in the course of therapeutic practice. But the

---

[26] On the general issue of clinical and statistical decision making, see Paul Meehl, *Clinical v. Statistical Prediction* (Minneapolis: University of Minnesota, 1954). For a discussion directly relevant to correctional decisions, see Leslie Wilkins, *The Evaluation of Penal Measures* (New York: Random House, 1969).

two acts are separate in the sense of having separate identifiable goals, even if they are closely connected or simultaneous in time.

Clinical research studies are not really very different from any other research strategy. However, the concepts and the methods differ in relation both to the *stage* of the research inquiry and to the *purposes* of the research. For example, a clinician may spend a long time simply talking to an offender in order to get a picture of the person's emotions, thoughts, social background, etc. This might be described as exploratory research, conducted without hypotheses but leading to hypotheses that may be tested later. Later, a researcher might be interested in comparative questions, and might subject two or more offenders to the same type of questions in order to find similarities and differences. This inquiry might lead to hypotheses about causes in different cases, or to prognoses for different cases. Still later, the clinician might subject a number of different persons to the same therapeutic program in order to examine differential consequences. Or still more complex in design, several similar subjects might be subjected to therapy or to no therapy, on a random basis, in order to ascertain if the therapeutic program has the hypothesized effects.

LABELING RESEARCH. Research stemming from labeling theory has already been described in some detail in Chapter Eight. Basically, this theory suggests a relationship between differential treatment by important influentials and the different behaviors of people subjected to such treatment. For example, it has been hypothesized that the labeling manifest in the public-school "tracking system" for differently classified students determines how these students will act in the school situation. Students chosen for college preparatory classes act the role expected of them, and students chosen for vocational or remedial education act out their respectively assigned roles. Researchers have found, for example, that when they suggested to teachers that a certain student was a potential genius as identified on certain bogus diagnostic tests that they had conducted, that the teachers began to perceive very clever and intelligent responses from the identified student.[27]

Following this theory, delinquency researchers have suggested that juveniles who are labeled as predelinquent or delinquent by school officials, police, judges, and probation officers, will gradually take on a delinquent role in fulfillment of expectations. But otherwise, this action-reaction-reinforcement cycle is simply the old "self-fulfilling prophecy" idea. But it has had great influence on thinking about how to treat delinquents. For example, social welfare departments are now taking a long

[27] J. Brophy and T. Good, "Teachers' Communication of Differential Expectations for Children's Classroom Performance," *Journal of Educational Psychology, 61* (1970), 365–374.

hard look at their foster-parent programs after the discovery that delinquent boys have frequently experienced four or five foster placements. Typically, the response of welfare departments and parents has been that these extremely mobile youth are troublemakers who cannot adjust to family situations. The reverse hypothesis being suggested now is that multiple-placement foster youths are receiving messages from both foster parents and caseworkers that they are expected to be troublemakers and, ultimately, are expected to end up in institutions. Thus, there are plans to train foster parents and social workers to avoid such labeling, so that institutional placement can be avoided rather than prescribed as a therapy.

Perhaps the state where this theory has been researched on the largest scale is Massachusetts, where all the delinquency institutions have been closed down in favor of a variety of community care programs. The evaluation of this change, conducted by Lloyd Ohlin and others, has yielded preliminary findings that the community-treated youth are far less likely to return to delinquency than youth subjected to any sort of institutional placement (positive or "therapeutic").[28] This research tends to support the hypothesis that institutional placement is one of the most drastic labeling practices in use and that it yields the severest and most frequent cases of delinquent behavior.

SUBCULTURAL RESEARCH. Subcultural research began in the 1950s, notably with Albert Cohen's *Delinquent Boys*,[29] and was firmly established in the next decade with the work of Walter Miller,[30] Cloward and Ohlin,[31] and Wolfgang and Ferracuti.[32] The theory, briefly stated, suggests that some deviance may be related to the differentiation of structure in society that leads to a differentiation of behavior, and that the behavior valued and common in certain "value-pockets" or subcultures may be perceived as, and reacted to as, deviant by the dominant cultural group that controls the mechanisms of government and social control.

The various subculture theories are fairly similar in terms of the results that they predict, but they differ in terms of the theorized generation of the subculture. Cohen, for example, suggests that the delinquent subculture is formed as a reaction of lower-class city youth to public-school situations in which they encounter values (such as delayed gratification,

---

[28] Yitzhak Bakal, ed., *Closing Correctional Institutions* (Lexington, Mass.: Lexington Books, 1973).

[29] Albert Cohen, *Delinquent Boys* (New York: The Free Press, 1955).

[30] Walter B. Miller, "Lower Class Culture as a Generating Milieu of Gang Delinquency," *"Journal of Social Issues, 14* (1958), 5–19.

[31] Cloward and Ohlin, *Delinquency and Opportunity.*

[32] Marvin Wolfgang and Franco Ferracuti, *The Subculture of Violence* (London: Tavistock, 1967).

hard work, and intellectual achievement) that they find foreign. The children who are unable to compete for the goals espoused in the schools, as structured by middle-class officials and teachers, find they must either reject such values or live with images of themselves as failures. Cohen suggests that they take the former route, devalue the middle-class precepts, and set up in their place values of immediate gratifications, physical toughness, and material negativism.[33]

In contrast, Cloward and Ohlin emphasize the relationship between opportunity and values. They suggest that the final values of middle-class culture are evenly distributed across society, but that social structure differentiates the opportunities available to different segments of society, and hence, the chance to pursue these values is unevenly distributed. Thus there is a conflict between social goals and the means of obtaining desired ends. Furthermore, they suggest that where stealing does not prove profitable, or in areas where there is little to steal, gangs may turn to fighting as a method of obtaining social status. Finally, when an official crackdown on fighting makes the negative consequences of this means too drastic, or when youth fail in fighting gangs, they may turn to drugs, being then double failures, succeeding neither at legal or illegal means of obtaining status or wealth.[34]

Finally, perhaps the milestone in subculture theory is the study by Wolfgang and Ferracuti.[35] In a broad international study, these authors seek to analyze all the available literature concerning incidence and explanation of violence. They find that violence rates are highest in certain societies where contrasts between wealth and poverty are very great, but where, in contrast to India, the vast contrasts in status and social conditions are not perceived as immutable. They find very similar values placed on the concepts of *omertà* and *machismo* (secrecy concerning revenge and defense of manhood) in Sicily, in portions of Colombia, S.A., Harlem, and the other American ghettos. It is understood in these subcultures that men must protect their physical integrity by accepting challenges to their strength, by protecting their women, etc., at all costs, and that acts of violence conducted in defense of manhood are protected by the silence of all other people in the subculture who know of such incidents.

In addition to their extensive review of the literature, Wolfgang and Ferracuti's work presents a major statement of interdisciplinary research, as it relates to social science investigation of subculture and deviance. They relate anthropological, psychological, and sociological studies of value and culture to political, economic, psychological, and sociological

---

[33] Cohen, *Delinquent Boys.*
[34] Cloward and Ohlin, *Delinquency and Opportunity.*
[35] Wolfgang and Ferracuti, *The Subculture of Violence.*

descriptions of various conditions and hypotheses about deviance causation, and, finally, they attempt to prescribe social actions that accommodate individual, group, organizational, and social levels of strategy.[36]

Given the tremendous influence of subcultural theory on political and
social programs in the Kennedy and Johnson administrations, it is surprising how little research has followed the theorizing. Social scientists have
seemed more interested in formulating different theories than in empirically testing any of them. Lack of research about the theories contributed
to the great drop in the popularity of social action during the first Nixon
administration.[37] The next section will discuss process research, which is
one area where subcultural research has made some headway.

Process Research

Most of the causative research theories and findings that we have discussed so far relate to prearrest social conditions and processes. Although we can certainly speak of causal research in relation to any phenomenon, up to now we have been concentrating on how people have
thought of the problems that give rise to crime. A fairly different research
area concerns what happens within the groups that are identified and
processed as offenders, or what happens in the organizations that are
responsible for processing these offenders.

This kind of research question was posed considerably later than most
of the questions about crime causation, partly because it is a less important question in terms of the numbers of people affected by the answers,
and partly because for many years the organizations that did the processing and the ways that offenders behaved in them were perceived as
natural, unquestionable, and immalleable processes. For example, it was
assumed for many years that inner-city residents would always react
negatively to the police, not because of things that the police might be
doing but because these strange inner-city people were fearful of police
or had no respect for law and order. It was only after a series of riots and
commission reports that people began to understand that negative reactions to the police were variables dependent in part on police recruiting
practices, police perceptions, police operations, and police policy. The
fact that most of the persons processed through the criminal courts were
poor or black or young was for many years perceived as a natural consequence of the characteristics of those groups of people. Only with the
advent of the *Gideon* case,[38] along with social science inquiry into court

---

[36] Ibid.

[37] See the volume *Social Science and the Federal Government, Annals of the American Academy of Political and Social Science, 394* (March 1971).

[38] Gideon v. Wainwright, 372 U.S. 335 (1963).

practices in relation to labeling theory and political and social objections to traditional practices by new legitimate political groups, did people begin to perceive the variability of court policy and practice. Likewise, for many years everyone assumed that all convicts behaved like James Cagney or Humphrey Bogart or, indeed, that broken noses and cauliflower ears were symptomatic of criminality. It was really not until the Supreme Court took a long hard look at the juvenile system in *Gault*[39] that there was widespread questioning of the efficacy of official treatment. And it was not until the uprising and bloody counterrevolt at the Attica prison that there was widespread public acknowledgment that prisoners may not be animals and that research into different means of proceeding might have valuable social outputs.[40]

GROUP DYNAMICS RESEARCH. Work by Kurt Lewin and his associates at the University of Iowa during World War II led to some widely generalized theory about group processes, leadership patterns, and methods of planned change (see the discussion at the beginning of Chapter Eleven). Following this work, any number of group projects sprang up in prisons, probation agencies, and parole offices. Later, the same kinds of projects were introduced in police agencies as a means of changing police attitudes and behaviors, and spread generally to all kinds of organizational development and training projects with police judges and correctional officials.

Again, the same kind of distinction made about clinical research and therapy must be made here between *group work* in the context of managerial change of offender programming and *research about group processes* in criminal justice.

Research has been conducted to suggest that groups of offenders and groups of mental patients can perform many tasks of group living and institutional maintenance that they will not perform when subjected to the totalitarian regime of a set of staff keepers, such as doctors, nurses, orderlies, or prison guards. It has been found that the kinds of groups formed, the kinds of leaders who gain influence, and the product of the groups differ markedly depending on whether the individuals in an organization are each instructed to do a certain task or whether the individuals are asked to decide among themselves how to get particular tasks done and who should do them.[41]

There is a minimal amount of research available that suggests that correctional officers will change their behavior toward inmates so that

---

[39] In re Gault, 387 U.S. 1 (1967).

[40] New York State Special Commission on Attica, *Official Report* (New York: Bantam Books, 1972).

[41] Maxwell Jones, *The Therapeutic Community, A New Treatment Method in Psychiatry* (New York: Basic Books, 1953).

they respect inmates as persons and participate actively in treatment programs when groups of officers are given some leeway about tasks to be completed and goals to be attacked.[42] Conversely, when the affinity of persons to group living is ignored or attacked in the management of the organization, there is evidence that groups will form anyway, but in a subterraneous fashion and with the goal of subverting the goals of the organization.[43] Chester Barnard[44] and Rensis Likert[45] and others have theorized that there is a certain group size that is optimal to the performance of tasks and to the social interactions of the people involved and that the key to effective organization is the creation of such groups or "unit organizations" and their effective arrangement for coordination of purposes. Likert[46] and F. E. Emery and E. L. Trist[47] have conducted research that suggests that organizational production is dependent on whether people are related to overall organizational goals immediately as individuals or immediately through particular types of group organization.

These findings from industry and business have lately been transferred to human service system research. For example, the "new careers" movement in the 1960s was predicated on the theory that offenders would behave differently if they were active in groups of offenders *and* staff with particular common assignments, than when all inmates work in groups consisting of other inmates supervised by a distant and watchful staff.[48]

Most group dynamics research, however, has failed to demonstrate that the group or team approach is necessarily more successful in the short run than typical, pyramidal, individually based management. The success of groups, most of these researchers conclude, is founded in the long-range benefits that are not immediately demonstrable, such as loyalty to the organization, long-run employee satisfaction, and desirabil-

[42] David Duffee, *Using Correctional Officers in Planned Change*, final research report, The National Institute for Law Enforcement and Criminal Justice, September 1972.

[43] Donald Clemmer, *The Prison Community* (Indianapolis: Bobbs-Merrill, 1971); and Gresham Sykes, *The Society of Captives* (Princeton, N.J.: Princeton University Press, 1971).

[44] Chester I. Barnard, *The Functions of the Executive* (Cambridge, Mass.: Harvard University Press, 1967).

[45] Rensis Likert, *New Patterns of Management* (New York: McGraw-Hill, 1961).

[46] Ibid.

[47] F. E. Emery and E. L. Trist, "Socio-Technical Systems," in F. E. Emery, ed., *Systems Thinking* (Baltimore: Penguin Books, 1969), pp. 281–296.

[48] Donald Cressey, "Social Psychological Foundations for Using Criminals in the Rehabilitation of Criminals," *Journal of Research in Crime and Delinquency, 2* (1965), 44–55.

ity of change. These long-range benefits are typically assumed however, and are not as yet empirically supported.

ORGANIZATIONAL RESEARCH. Research on organizations is another recent activity in the criminal justice field, although there are some antecedents that predate the major works of the 1960s. For good reason, organizational research is a newer area of social inquiry than some of the others that we have discussed since organizations of sufficient complexity and magnitude to make them identifiable research enterprises were not very common until the last century. Generally, organizational analysis in sociology is identified with the pioneering work of Max Weber in the latter half of nineteenth-century Germany. Weber's emphasis on organization can be traced to his own moral and religious philosophy and to conflicts and congruences between this particularly German stance toward freedom and responsibility, at the same time that Prussian bureaucracy, both in civil government and military organization, was reaching its full stride. Weber, in other words, was one of the top-flight thinkers of the times with the greatest opportunity to observe and ponder the discovery and building of bureaucracy in full scale. He was both interested in the promise that bureaucratic structure held for large-scale cooperative action and concerned for the dilemmas that bureaucratic life posed for traditional Protestant ethics, including the usual notions of the relationship of the individual to his society and to his moral code, and how concepts of morality and responsibility were altered under the powerful tendency in bureaucracies to subordinate the individual to the goals of organization.[49]

In the United States, it is not surprising that the first earnest scientific interest in organization concerned the operations of industry and business, following the emergence in the 1890s of the vast industrial empires of Ford, Carnegie, and Morgan. One of the first such investigations was F. W. Taylor's *Principles of Scientific Management*.[50] Taylor, Urwick,[51] Gulick and Urwick,[52] and others started with an analysis of ongoing industrial organizations, with particular attention to the most effective methods of structuring physical work in order to obtain the most efficient cost/benefit ratio. Taylor, for example, was the first person to attempt to

---

[49] Max Weber, *The Theory of Social and Economic Organization*, A. M. Henderson, trans., and Talcott Parson, ed. (New York: Oxford, 1947).

[50] F. W. Taylor, *Principles of Scientific Management*, rev. ed. (New York: Norton, 1971).

[51] Lyndall F. Urwick, *The Elements of Administration* (New York: Harper, 1944); and "The Manager's Span of Control," *Harvard Business Review* (May-June 1946).

[52] Luther Gulick and Lyndall Urwick, *Papers on the Science of Administration* (New York: Institute of Public Administration, 1927).

measure the time it took for a particular operator to complete a particular task or set of tasks, and the first to conceptualize managerial performance in terms of the optimum span of control (how many men could a manager supervise personally) and unity of command (how many superiors could a man work under without confusion).[53]

This kind of research progressed rapidly until Elton Mayo, F. S. Roethlisberger, and others began conducting experiments concerning the effect of different physical working conditions of work groups in the Hawthorne plant of the Westinghouse Corporation. During this study in the 1930s, the researchers began with the typical assumption held at the time: that research should answer *for* management how employees could be manipulated for the benefit of the business. One discovery of the Hawthorne project, now widely known as the "Hawthorne effect," was that the social variables in the work setting, such as morale, worker satisfaction, group dynamics, opportunity to make decisions, etc., *also* had a bearing on work output.[54] This discovery in this instance had such a profound effect on the researchers that they broke at least partially from "scientific management" traditions in order to emphasize something that become known as "human relations" in organization. The often-missed anomaly of this new trend, however, is that the researchers did not really break away from their loyalty to management; instead, they began to suggest social rather than physical and economic strategies for maintaining or achieving high production.[55]

Logical shifts in organizational research occurred thereafter. The "human resources" school represented by Likert and others suggested that the goals of the organization and the goals of individuals were not the same, but that the work situation could be structured so that the different goals were congruent. The democratic management trend has emphasized that the goals of organization could be challenged by the organizational participants, and that effective management might entail reformulating organizational goals, or changing organizational structure, or both, so that the organizational climate was more in keeping with the mental health of individual participants and more cognizant of long-range social goals to which organizations should contribute, regardless of short-range unprofitability.[56]

It has not been until recently that much of this organizational theory and research has been transferred to the social service field. For one

[53] Taylor, *Principles of Scientific Management.*

[54] Elton Mayo and George Lombard, *Teamwork and Labor Turnover in the Aircraft Industry of Southern California* (Cambridge, Mass.: Harvard University School of Business, 1944); and F. J. Roethlisberger and W. J. Dickson, *Management and the Worker* (Cambridge, Mass.: Harvard University Press, 1949).

[55] Chris Argyris, *Personality and Organization* (New York: Harper and Row, 1957).

[56] Likert, *New Patterns of Management.*

reason, the social services, such as mental health, mental retardation, social welfare, police, and corrections have long operated without clear conceptions of goals to be achieved and without reliable methodologies for measuring achievement. Rightly or wrongly, research in business and industry could use some short-range measures of success such as waste in production, waiting time on the assembly line, and margin of profit to make some statements about output to which management would respond. But research in police, court, and correctional organization has always been marked by lack of managerial interest in output, rejection by management of any indices of failure that could be collected, and lack of managerial consensus about what the organization should be doing anyway.

Furthermore, in areas of organizational research where the organizations deal with core cultural values such as justice, fairness, crime, and rehabilitation, and where the human products such as suspects, defendants, and convicts are stigmatized and ostracized, there has *always* been the penchant in the organizations involved to explain away unsatisfactory output (such as commission of new crimes) as the failure of the offenders, rather than the failure of the organization.[57] The former governor of Georgia, Lester Maddox, for example, suggested that the problem of correction was not the state of the prisons but the quality of the inmates.[58] This statement led a correctional officer in Connecticut to suggest facetiously that the correctional system should get male and female inmates together and eugenically grow their own inmates. Not so facetiously, "growing their own offenders" in a very real way appears to be one of the problems of our current criminal justice agencies. Beginning with the landmark volume, *Theoretical Studies in Social Organization of the Prison*,[59] Richard Cloward, Donald Cressey, Richard McCleery, and others began to examine the internal structure of various prisons and to observe some rather startling differences in internal management, perception and behavior of staff, and perceptions and values of inmates, depending on the way in which the prison was structured in order to obtain the vague goals of deterrence, reform, and rehabilitation.[60]

In police organization studies, there have been several different trends.

---

[57] Wilkins, *Social Deviance*, pp. 71–86.

[58] *New York Times*, March 17, 1969, AG 24.

[59] Pamphlet No. 15, published by the Social Science Research Council, New York, 1960.

[60] Richard Cloward, "Social Control in a Prison," in Cloward et. al., *Theoretical Studies in Social Organization of the Prison* (New York: Social Science Research Council, March 1960), pp. 20–48; Donald R. Cressey, "Limitations on Organization and Treatment in the Modern Prison," in Cloward et. al., *Theoretical Studies in Social Organization of the Prison*, pp. 78–110; Richard McCleery, "Communication Patterns as Bases of Systems of Authority," in Cloward et. al., *Theoretical Studies in Social Organization of the Prison*, pp. 49–77.

For example, many police studies have retained the interest in scientific management, in part perhaps because of the powerful influence exerted by O. W. Wilson in the volume *Police Administration.*[61] This major statement of police recruiting practice, training, operations, and so on, revived the interest in span of control, unity of command, etc., long after these concepts appeared old and overused in business and industry. On the other hand, operations researchers also became very interested in police work in the 1960s, with scholars such as Alfred Blumstein and Richard Larson producing significant works on computer technology in relation to manpower assignments, cost/benefit analysis of various assignment patterns, prediction of criminal incidence by precinct or block, reduction of police response time, and computerized direction of routine patrol paths.[62]

We can expect this kind of research to continue for quite some time, partly because it appears useful for certain police objectives, and partly because it reduces the need for police executives and others to confront head on and deal with the issues of police policy and goals. If everyone can be busy investigating scientifically the optimization of various police tactics, no one is left to think about whether any of these tactics should be employed in the first place.

A rather different trend in police organization research, and one generally limited to academic circles, is the study of police culture and values and their effect on police behavior. Jerome Skolnick, Arthur Neiderhoffer, and others speak of the "police personality" and of the value placed on "good police work" and "handling the situation" for the operational consequences in terms of intradepartment status differentiations, police-community relations, and police resistance to change.[63] On a broader note, J. Q. Wilson's analysis of police styles relies on a particular brand of political science inquiry in order to establish the reasons for variations in police policy in different communities.[64]

Organizational study in the court area has been considerably slower to develop, but a variety of studies have demonstrated that officials' behavior toward each other and toward defendants varies considerably in relation to the dominant sanctioning patterns in different courts.[65]

[61] O. W. Wilson, *Police Administration,* 3rd ed. (New York: McGraw-Hill, 1972).

[62] Alfred Blumstein and Richard Larson, *Models of a Total Criminal Justice System* (Washington, D.C.: Department of Defense, 1959).

[63] Jerome Skolnick, *Justice Without Trial* (New York: Wiley, 1966); and Arthur Neiderhoffer, *Behind the Shield* (Garden City, N.Y.: Doubleday, 1967).

[64] James Q. Wilson, *Varieties of Police Behavior* (Cambridge, Mass.: Harvard University Press, 1968).

[65] Daniel Katkin and Fred Hussey, "A Review of *In Defense of Youth,* by Stapleton and Teitelbaum, Russell Sage Foundation, 1973," *Buffalo Law Review,* 22, No. 3 (Spring 1973), 1129–1139.

SYSTEMS RESEARCH. On an even broader note than research about organizations, the tendency in criminal justice process research now is toward the perception of systems and the study of intra- and intersystem interaction. Although systems concepts are frequently implicit in organizational study, in group dynamics research, and in some psychological research, systems research as applied to the criminal process can fairly accurately be traced no further back than the President's Commission on Law Enforcement and the Administration of Justice (1967). Prior to that major undertaking, research in the area was generally limited to inquiry about *the police* or *the courts,* or *a prison,* and so on. In other words, there may have been some concern for the variables *within* one organization, but there was little concentration on the connections of these organizations, or on the pattern of cooperation that exists from arrest to final community release. The new systems emphasis has led to questions, for instance, about the effect on police morale of recent Supreme Court decisions,[66] or the effect of variation in police arrest practices on prosecutorial and judicial tasks, or the impact on correctional treatment and administration of judicial sentencing variation.[67]

The methodologies and techniques necessary to such complex investigations have not been available until recently. Without the computer and computer programs capable of sorting and analyzing tremendous amounts of social data, studies of large-scale systems have been highly inefficient if not impossible.

Outcome Research

A particularly important aspect of criminal justice research that has been influenced by systems theory and research and by the technologies invented in the pursuit of system study is outcome research. Indeed, although we have always been able to conceive of *outcomes* (e.g., effects occurring after causes), outcome research has been revolutionized by the system concepts of input, throughout, output, and feedback. The outcome research that has proceeded most vigorously in the last 20 years is research that studies the *outputs* of systems. An output is the transformation of input through the arrangement of a system. In this case, we are dealing with research about arrest, conviction, release, and rearrest as related to criminal justice intake and the arrangements within the system for transformation of input. It is with this change in research perception that researchers began to shy away from studies of individuals or groups

[66] Wayne LaFave and Frank Remington, "Controlling the Police: The Judge's Role in Making and Reviewing Law Enforcement Decisions," *Michigan Law Review,* 63, No. 6 (April 1965), 987–1013.

[67] Robert Dawson, *Sentencing* (Boston: Little, Brown, 1969).

and began to focus instead on the occurrence of events, such as interactions and decisions that relate individuals and groups.

The outcome most frequently counted in criminal justice system is "recidivism." Recidivism, of course, is any number of different things, most of which are really not considered accurately, and none of which is measured very consistently or completely. One might, for example, speak about rearrest given one arrest, or rearrest given a conviction, or another conviction given one conviction, or another arrest/conviction/incarceration given one of any of these, etc. In other words, there is "fall out" from the system at virtually any decision point in the process, and one might then consider reentry into the system from any particular first outcome.

A text such as this is not the place for a detailed discussion of the concept of recidivism nor of its measurement. We must point out, however, that the idea of measuring the return to the system is extremely complex in and of itself, and the problems become multiplied when one actually tries to conduct a recidivism study. At that point the researcher has to confront unwilling and uncooperative officials, or willing but interfering officials, who in trying to help may confound the data, or a cooperative but disjointed system in which the information needed simply does not exist and the channels for retrieving it have to be built from scratch.

We also must point out that the event of a new crime is not the only outcome of the criminal justice system worth investigating, although some of the other outcomes may be equally or even more difficult to measure. The problem with many of the outcomes (and a problem relevant to the recurrence of crime as well) is that their *value* is ambiguous, even if we could measure the incidence of occurrence. For example, what is the *value* of a parolee's performance "on the street," whether or not he commits another crime? Does one measure the amount of money he makes legitimately before returning to crime, or the number of friends he has made, or the amount of taxes he pays, or his renewal of family relations? Is there value to the correctional process beyond numbers of persons returned to the community? Does a high stone wall make persons in town feel safe? Does it count that a mother can point out the wall to her obstreperous son and threaten that he will end up there if he does not behave? In which direction does such a threat count? Does it count as an outcome that the free people believe that the values of their society are upheld in court every time a judge sentences a convict or releases an acquitted person? How could we measure the people's satisfaction with the court system? Which police outcomes are most significant? If the police spend less than 10 percent of their time enforcing the law, why are arrests seen as such an important outcome? Is it because nine hours of doing something else is a price worth paying in return for one hour of law enforcement, or is it because the outcomes of the one hour are easy to measure, whereas the outcomes of the other nine are not? Clearly, we really have much research to do before we can really say a great deal about what the criminal justice system yields.

Evaluation Research

Evaluation research is, in the sense of being research, no different from any of the other researches that we have discussed. The difference is the use of the research in evaluation. Evaluations are made whether one does research or not. Indeed the difficulty of evaluation research is that anyone has a right to evaluate anything, from his own perspective, and the researcher, although attempting to collect information in an unbiased fashion, has probably selected his research strategy or made his basic assumptions in a biased fashion, depending on his own values.

The question is, then, whether there is anything about evaluation research that makes it "better" or more useful than evaluations not based on research. There is probably no clear-cut answer, although most of the literature on evaluation (being written by researchers of course) concludes that evaluation research when properly formulated and conducted can be very valuable to decision makers regarding continuation, modification, or termination of social action programs. There is, however, a great distance between the statement of such potential and the statement of actualities. First, it is very unclear at this point whether evaluation research is really utilized in the decision-making process, even if the decision makers themselves have solicited the research. Frequently it seems that programs may be continued (frequently because a program "has potential" or "shows promise" or "is better than nothing" or "is complying with the evaluator's suggestions as quickly as can be expected") for quite some time, whether the evaluation has been favorable or unfavorable. Also, frequently, programs will then be terminated or modified by decision makers seemingly independently of the evaluation information, because other previously external agents suddenly enter the decision criteria. Furthermore, evaluation research is presumably valuable when the evaluator is aware of his biases or his values, states them explicitly, and then sets up a vigorous research design that will control his own tendencies, as well as any other biasing factors. But an apparently overriding factor in many cases is money. There are many negative findings that can be toned down and many ambiguous findings that turn positive under the assumption that the evaluator with a positive evaluation is retained in the future.

Researchers are, of course, not the only persons corrupted in the criminal justice system. The best control perhaps, for such behavior is the redesign of the evaluation strategies used by the Law Enforcement Assistance Administration and related state planning agencies. In addition to redesign, however, one would presume that another controlling factor would be the recruitment and retention of top-flight researchers as evaluators. Although money is a strong influence, money tends to be an unimportant incentive and a weak counterforce when it can be achieved only in contradiction to core values of a professional group or organization. It is possible to find researchers whose primary value is the quality of their research. The question then becomes, How many of such individuals will be interested in *and* suited for the kind of research involved in the evaluation of criminal justice programs?

There are many different kinds of evaluation studies. Generally, we can say that evaluation starts with an examination of the overall purpose or goal; then it proceeds to the relation of objectives and subobjectives to that goal, to the process of implementing these steps, and, finally, to the outcome from the implementation. The late Edward Suchman divided most evaluative research into *performance evaluation* and *process evaluation*.[68] He suggested that performance could be analyzed in terms of impact, effort, results, and cost/benefit, whereas process evaluation was the attempt to explain how any aspects of performance came about. To look at performance and ignore process is to lose the chance to replicate a program or to modify an existing one in any systematic way; whereas to look at process and ignore performance is, as Suchman put it, to ignore whether the bird is flying or just flapping his wings.[69]

RESEARCH PROCESS AND RESEARCH DIFFICULTIES IN CRIMINAL JUSTICE

We mentioned in the introduction to this chapter that the methodologies in criminal justice are fairly unsophisticated, compared to the social science methodologies used in other kinds of inquiry. The reason for this lag has to do with both the nature of the research process and the nature of criminal justice. A brief look at some of the research problems, other than those we have referred to already, might help to round out the picture of the crimminal justice system.

Perhaps the greatest difficulty, and one that has been implicit throughout this discussion of research, is the difficulty in doing research on a subject so socially controversial as criminal justice. Crime, like birth and death and love, is a subject so common to the core of our cultural values that anyone has a right to express an opinion; these opinions are usually forthcoming; and many of them are so strongly held that they defy almost any empirical evidence to the contrary. Researchers encountering such beliefs have difficulty establishing the importance of their research.

[68] Edward Suchman, *Evaluation Research* (New York: Russell Sage, 1967).
[69] Ibid., p. 61.

If the research does not directly relate to these central beliefs, it probably isn't supported by officials sufficiently to guarantee that the project can be carried out. If the research does directly relate to those core values, then there is no need for the research because "everyone knows this or that to be true (or not true) anyway."

Beyond this very general problem, and a more specific example, is the fact that the subject of research in criminal justice frequently comes loaded with emotional baggage, in terms of stereotypes, symbols, etc., which can be difficult for the researcher to penetrate. The suspect, the defendant, or the convict is considered strange, dangerous, infamous, dirty, clever, etc., by many people, including persons who must legitimate or support the research enterprise. It is difficult for the researcher not to bow to one set of symbols or another that represents to somebody all that is important about crime and criminals. Moreover, the researcher may have considerable difficulty shedding his own preconceptions or holding them in check. For example, apparently one of the major reasons for the delay in research about organization and system in criminal justice is because most researchers and most research utilizers saw the offender as the only problematic issue in the entire complex of interactants that comprise criminal justice. Leslie Wilkins refers to this as the "sinners, saints, and system" problem.[70] He means that as long as the system can define dysfunctions so that remedial action is directed at the individual, it will do so. The system usually makes this attribution by designating the offender as some particular brand of person, whose faults or internal characteristics, in and of themselves, are enough to explain away the system's difficulties.

Another severe problem concerns the necessity of risk, and the measurement of it in the scientific enterprise, and the laws against risk, the avoidance of it, and the strong sanctions for taking chances from the administration side. Research in a scientific fashion is impossible without the acceptance of and the control of risk. Hypotheses are accepted or rejected on the basis that the null hypothesis was or was not able to be rejected at a specified level of risk. Without accepting the hypothesis that something empirical can be known only uncertainly, nothing empirical could be known at all. (The rationale is very similar to the fact that no gambler would be allowed to gamble if he placed his bets *after* the roll of the dice.) Uncertainty, however, unlike ignorance, is the state in which someone goes on to learn. All learning requires variability of opportunity, and all variability implies risk. Hence the researcher sets up conditions in which he can be uncertain and can estimate the degree of uncertainty that he is dealing with.

The administrator, on the other hand, is frequently living in a climate

[70] Wilkins, *Social Deviance.*

that does not permit or condone risk. Uncertainty is generally not comparable with the yes/no answers that make sense at the ballot box or with the legislature. In other words, the room for scientific risk in administration is rather small. And it has proven particularly small in the criminal justice field where one mistake can (or has been known to) cause a riot or cost a life.

Of course, a good administrator is one who intuitively and subjectively acknowledges and deals with risk all the time. Each good decision is based on some sort of estimate of the reliability of the information source, etc. But administrators have difficulty admitting the necessity of uncertainty, particularly to outside groups whose beliefs, values, and feelings about criminal justice are threatened if the expert admits to uncertainty. But it is the open, public, controlled use of uncertainty that allows a scientist to claim for his findings *some* independence from his own state of mind and personal characteristics, because it is through this open and public admission of risk that the scientist is able to control for the tendency toward the subjective certainty of values and beliefs.

Another difference between research and criminal justice administration is the contrast in response to behavior that fails to achieve goals. Frequently, and perhaps most frequently in this particular system, the administrative response to failure is punitive.[71] The assumption is frequently, if implicitly, made that failure was *willful*, a purposeful attack on the rules and well-being of the system. In contrast, the failure for a scientist to obey the rules of science results in a failure to learn, and the usual reaction is to attempt to correct the failing behavior in the future. It is at times difficult for the researcher and the administration to get along when they understand failure so differently and respond so differently to it. Furthermore, whereas the scientist is rewarded for building on valid information, the administrator may be punished for passing on valid information—if it is the "wrong" message. Thus, what the scientist may find out to be true, the administrator may not want to hear.

A last difficulty, perhaps, is not a difference but a similarity. Administrators in the criminal justice system are apt to be autocratic. They are apt to have things their own way because they have thought it out that way. This kind of management style is often prone to produce invalid information about the organization because people will tend to cover up errors or dysfunctions (in order to protect themselves from a punitive response), and they will tend to embellish good and functional action (in order to reap the rewards).

Although researchers often write about finding research to be a "great leveling exercise," or a democratic enterprise, in that everyone is subordi-

[71] See Donald Cressey, "Contradictory Directives in Complex Organizations: The Case of the Prison," *Administrative Science Quarterly, 4* (June 1959), 1–19.

nate to the rules of research, frequently researchers approach criminal justice agencies in the same autocratic, high-handed manner that administrators use. Even though it may be difficult to remain open and persuadable when confronted with suspicion, with lack of cooperation, and at times with outright hostility, the researcher presumably should be aware of the cost of abandoning his democratic approach, whereas the administrator has good reason to doubt the efficacy of abandoning his autocratic manner.

A very good part of this difference in style is a difference in perception of time. Administrators are frequently under pressure to make decisions *now*, regardless of the quantity and quality of information. Obviously, for the two groups to work together, ways must be invented to compromise on the time constraints.

RESEARCH ORGANIZATION IN CRIMINAL JUSTICE

In light of the above difficulties, we must seek new ways of organizing and managing research in the criminal justice area if we are to overcome the impediments to research and the impediments to planned change. There is little in the way of present research activity in criminal justice on which to base a new model. With a few marked exceptions, research conducted by the criminal justice agencies themselves has not been adequately supported. Frequently the "research departments" in an agency are really one or two men and a secretary who together attempt to interest the right kind of outsiders in research in the organization, or attempt to write a sufficient number of grant proposals so they may hire their own outsiders on a subcontract basis. Rarely is research in a criminal justice agency an ongoing activity of major proportions with sufficient budget to carry out activities on its own.

The outsiders who do research in criminal justice are frequently no better as far as the learning of the system is concerned. The criminal justice agencies continually play host to a series of outside scientists who may conduct highly interesting and highly valuable research, all of which is useless to the host agency. And we do not mean "useless" in the sense that the outside researchers come up with "negative" findings. It is more likely that the researchers will continually come up with *neutral* findings; that is, they continually research issues and gather information that does not present to the agency plans of action for the agency. Many things can be of interest to a psychologist or a sociologist about a police department or a prison that do not aid either kind of organization to clarify or more closely approximate its goals.

Then, if the research is to be done by outsiders, the concern is that the research should be done with criminal justice in mind (not simply the managers of a particular organization in mind—they might always remain antagonistic). But the research problem should be structured in such a way that the hypotheses lead to strategic action for the agency. Unfortunately, the outside researchers who advertise specializing in client utilization—that is, the outside consultants—have not appeared up to the task. They frequently charge outrageously for inferior products on the assumption that the unsophisticated organization will not know the difference. But whether good or bad in a commercial sense, the consultants have rarely come up with satisfactory suggestions for system change.

Whether universities can provide the research input needed by the criminal justice system is a matter of conjecture. Many universities have turned to the criminal justice system for undergraduate and some graduate programs, but it is too early to say whether the concomitant research activity will be functional for the system. It is, however, hard to conceive of the university as being the *base* of good criminal justice research, if only because of problems in continuity of program and personnel between the system and the university.

The ideal research organization is probably one *within* the system. But whether there should be one research center for an entire state criminal justice system or whether research might be spread among the larger functional agencies and contracted out to the smaller ones—these are questions that still need a great deal of investigation.

Although we do not see any ideal research organization emerging now, and can not really suggest too much about its structural outlines, there are some *qualities* that such a research undertaking ought to possess.

1. It should have a multidisciplinary staff, and this staff should have special training in interdisciplinary communication.
2. The leadership of the staff might shift from project to project, to prevent any one perspective from becoming dominant, and to maximize the use of resources.
3. Researchers should have free and easy access to operational managers, and, perhaps, should have several operational managers on the staff, perhaps sitting on a rotating basis.
4. The research should not be conducted at the behest of only *one* segment of the system. Front-line workers and offenders, etc., should have easy access to the researchers in order to suggest projects, etc.
5. Research findings should be distributed to all participants in any research, although different forms of dissemination might be used with different groups.
6. The research unit should probably stay together long enough to produce cohesiveness and effectiveness in work but should not stay together so long as to identify with the research staff rather than with the goals of a particular project.

7. The staff should be intimately familiar with the system in question but distant from the worries and pressures of its present operation. They should enjoy enough "ivory tower" distance and leisure to ponder novel solutions, but they should have the experience or the kind of communication that establishes rapport and credibility with research utilizers.

Beyond suggestions such as these it is difficult to go at this point, without introducing our next and last subject, the future of the criminal justice system, which will be discussed in our final chapter.

chapter 14

The Future

of Criminal Justice

Although this has been a lengthy, and at times difficult, introduction to criminal justice, we are sure that much material has been left out, that other scholars would have chosen other points of departure and other means of organizing observations and analytical arguments. However, we are not nearly so concerned that the book is incomplete as we are that the reader understands that it is. Therefore we are particularly desirous of emphasizing the biases and tentativeness of this last chapter.

The future of criminal justice is obviously of great importance to persons planning a career in the criminal justice field, or to persons already engaged in this area. Certainly from their perspective, the future is not so bright now as it may have appeared in the last half of the 1960s. It appeared then to many professionals in the field, as well as to teachers, politicians, textbook editors, and others, that crime was the dominant domestic social problem. Although it is clear that crime will continue as a major concern for quite some time, if not indefinitely, it is startling to observe the rapidity with which priorities have changed. Crime is no longer the most pressing domestic issue. Already it is obvious that it no longer makes sense to separate domestic and international issues. The world's population will starve, run out of energy, and overpopulate all at the same time. Crime may be only one symptom of larger and more troublesome problems.

These newly recognized social problems and the new technologies designed to deal with them will, of course, produce new illegal opportunities and new crime. In some cases the results are likely to be startling. Before we discuss in more detail some potential future differences and similarities, it is necessary to disgress for a few pages about the kinds of predictions we desire to make.

PREDICTION OF FUTURE STATES

Many kinds of predictions or forecasts of future events are possible. Few of them have proven very accurate, although when valid forecasts have been made, they have often been tremendously beneficial—for a particular purpose. Most futurists distinguish between two broad purposes and the kinds of predictions that relate to them. First there are "independent" forecasts or predictions that do not in any practical way attempt a connection of the predicted future and the present. Second there are "contingent futures" or forecasts of alternative future states about which we may have some choice and, accordingly, some hand in shaping.

Obviously, it is this second kind of forecast that we are concerned with in this chapter. But the business of forecasting alternate futures and establishing the connection of those states with the present is obviously more complicated than it might appear in the above paragraph. To make another distinction, this chapter is concerned with long-range rather than short-range predictions. We are not concerned with predicting what might happen tomorrow, or three years from tomorrow. Where one draws the line between short- and long-range forecasts is, of course, arbitrary. But we are not speaking here of predicting the next Supreme Court opinion concerning police practices, or of the rate of recidivism in an offender cohort to be released from prison in the next month. Although even these predictions are hazardous, the techniques employed to make such guesses are fairly standard logical and statistical manipulations, and may be found elsewhere.

On the other hand, the strategies and techniques available for longer-range predictions are much newer endeavors and are therefore likely to be much less accurate. These methods range from the intuition and logic of an expert in the field to the Delphic method, to writing of scenarios of future states, to application of mathematical functions and extrapolating trends from present data.

Although some of the methods are very similar to those employed in short-ranged predictions, others are fairly distinct. Perhaps the major difference involves the attempts by the more sophisticated forecasters to isolate the forecast of future states from present cultural constraints and value preferences. Although this separation of present values from future events cannot be completely accomplished, the attempt generally involves predicting the probable environmental constraints at some time in the future and then positing the logical consequences for the valuation and ideological patterns that will influence how society is structured.

The importance and inevitability of these value level changes cannot be underestimated. It may be foolish to suggest different investigatory, prosecutorial, or correctional practices if we are not willing to acknowledge that social tolerances for deviant acts, and hence the definition of what is criminal, may differ drastically from what is presently the case. Thus, we would suggest that although short-range forecasts about the operation of the system may be adequately made by studying internal operations and trends *within* the system, longer-range predictions about the existence, shape, and operation of criminal justice can only be made by employing knowledge about and predictions about the community within which the criminal justice or other systems will perform certain (and perhaps very different) functions.

Before we attempt even a rudimentary forecast of future community changes in the long-range future of criminal justice, one method is available that will allow us to review some of the most important present issues in criminal justice as well as to provide some familiarity with the interactions between the community and the system. This technique, although it may have sophisticated quantitative counterparts, is the more methodologically simple and substantively oriented method of trend analysis.

CURRENT AND EMERGENT TRENDS IN CRIMINAL JUSTICE

A trend is a cluster of issues and related practices that are seen, at one point in time, as having certain historical commonalities and are presumed to continue in the future in certain directions because of the patterns that are already observed as established. It is important to understand that the "beginning" of a trend cannot be identified prior to, or at the time of, its occurrence, although experts might identify, in retrospect, critical or landmark events that provided impetus to a trend or modified its direction. We may, however, distinguish between clear or *dominant trends*, meaning those that seem already firmly rooted in the values and past actions of a system in question, and *emergent trends*, meaning those whose beginnings are presently more subterranean and whose direction is much more tenuous and controversial.

These two types of system directions should be considered concomitantly since, if they belong to the same system, they will influence each other. Of course, every dominant trend was once emergent, and each will be replaced by other clusters of value and power that become dominant in the future.

Below we will introduce seven interrelated trends and discuss at some length their import for the system as well as their roots in the community environment of the criminal justice system. There is no claim that this listing is representative, let alone complete. But the trends discussed are important in their own right and provide us with an introduction to a more abstract discussion of community change and social control.

New Trends in the Nature of Crime

Although some trends would continue regardless of the kinds of crime committed, certainly the changing nature of crime will have some impact on all the operations of the criminal justice system.[1] When the opportunities for legitimate business are changing as rapidly as they are in the last half of this century, it should surprise no one that the opportunities for illegitimate gain are expanding and changing just as rapidly. Indeed, in many cases the *same* opportunity affords both legitimate and illegitimate profit, depending on which persons in which circumstances perceive a certain confluence of events as advantageous. In other cases it may be rather difficult to determine whether the opportunity seized was used legally or illegally: The lines between legally acceptable and legally unacceptable behavior are rather arbitrarily and vaguely drawn. Although some rather interesting guesses about new and novel crimes might be made, perhaps it is more important to understand that both the character and frequency of crime are likely to change. Crime is likely to be more frequent because there are more and more ways of committing crimes; and crimes are likely to be more complex because almost all patterns of behavior are becoming more complex and increasingly "interrelated" with many other phenomena.[2]

New crimes, as opposed to new ways of doing old ones, are going to appear as a result of the misuse of the vast amount of technology that has appeared in the last 20 years. A great many of the crimes may be related to information or the means of processing and using it. There is no apparent reason why the "information explosion," which has benefited industry, government, and science in numerous ways already, will not also become an object or tool of the clever criminal as well. Information

---

[1] See Leslie T. Wilkins, "Crime and Crime Control in the 1990's," paper presented to the American Academy for the Advancement of Science, San Francisco, February 1974.

[2] Ibid.; Leslie Wilkins, "Crime and Justice at the Turn of the Century," *Annals of American Academy of Political and Social Science*, 408 (July 1973), 13–20; and Seymour Haleck, *The Politics of Therapy* (New York: Jason Aaronson, 1968), pp. 187–195.

may be pirated, forged, destroyed, tampered with, stolen, or folded, spindled, and mutilated—for a price.[3]

New scarcities in raw materials, food, fuel, and other previously plentiful supplies will afford new criminal opportunities. Indeed, legislative reaction in regard to predicted new scarcities is quite slow. If regulation of scarce resources continues to be dependent on the legislators' willingness to risk political unpopularity in order to regulate, then imaginative individuals will have ample opportunity to seize upon the opportunities presented by these new markets long before laws are passed to regulate the distribution of such goods.[4]

It is apparent both in present legal responses to new information technologies and in new resource scarcities, that the criminal law itself is becoming rapidly inappropriate as the vehicle of social control. The new areas of economic opportunity to be seized frequently require complex organizational arrangements and sophisticated production and delivery technologies. Hence, these areas are likely to be controlled by innovative organizations rather than innovative individuals. The application of criminal law to organizations has always encountered difficulty, because criminal law requires proof of individual guilt.[5] In many cases the emerging acts, which may be deemed dysfunctional for social order, will not be the actions of individuals. Even in the rare case where a prosecutor can demonstrate that an individual decision maker was responsible for a criminal act, the alternatives open to the judge will merely punish that particular individual. In most cases, the position the individual occupied in the offending organization will simply be refilled. In the majority of such cases of "organizational crimes," however, there will be no individual responsible. Dysfunctional acts will most frequently be the consequences of large corporate undertakings, rather than the consequences of human perpetrators. As it becomes increasingly absurd to "solve" crimes by identifying individual actors, either there will be fundamental shifts in the nature of the criminal law, or the criminal law will be progressively less important in the array of social control strategies.

Trends in the Due Process of Law

In many respects, the "due-process revolution" is no longer a dominant trend but a dying trend. Many of the procedural changes that could conceivably take place have already occurred. There are, of course, many

---

[3] Leslie Wilkins, "The Information Explosion and Social Control," paper prepared for the National Council on Crime and Delinquency, 1970.

[4] Wilkins, "Crime Control in the 1990's."

[5] For example, one California oil company was placed on probation several years ago for clean air law violations. The probation officer assigned to "the case" was understandably at a loss when he tried to interview and supervise his "client."

areas in the criminal justice process in which the spirit, if not the letter of due-process decisions, has yet to be implemented. On the other hand, the Supreme Court has nearly used up its energy in terms of surveying new decision points or issues in which due process has yet to be applied. For example, the Supreme Court recently shied away from providing prisoners or parole violators with counsel.[6] However, this area might conceivably shift in the next 10 to 15 years, and there are some new practices in the criminal justice field that will be considered. For example, there is no decision as yet that addresses due-process safeguards in several aspects of community-based correction. Return of offenders from halfway house status to prison status for misconduct is one such area.[7] Prosecution of defendants who have allegedly not fulfilled an informal probation contract is another.

Although the due-process evaluation in terms of providing certain guarantees and procedures to defendants and offenders may be nearing completion, there is some evidence that a new understanding of due process may emerge. This area is manifest in decisions such as *Holt* v. *Sarver*[8] and *Jackson* v. *Hendrick*[9] in which entire organizational climates are condemned. Previous to such decisions, the prohibition against cruel and unusual punishment referred to particular acts against particular people by particular people. But the declaration of prison systems as unconstitutional would seemingly provide the kind of flexibility to deal with organizational dysfunctionality that the criminal law itself does not provide. If the organizational form of a prison system may be condemned as having inhumane consequences, conceivably entire court budgets and administrative patterns might be condemned for the inhumane or unfair consequences manifest in both the plea-bargaining process[10] and the money bail system.[11]

Trends in Equal Protection

Up to now, equal protection has been the "weak sister" clause when compared to the impact of due process. Examination of the reasons for

[6] Morrissey v. Brewer, 408 U.S. 471 (1972); and Gagnon v. Scarpelli, 411 U.S. 778 (1972).

[7] David Duffee, Thomas Maher, and Stephen Lagoy, "Administrative and Due Process in Community Pre-Parole Programs, *Criminal Law Bulletin* (September, 1977).

[8] Holt v. Sarver, 309 F. Supp. 362 (E. D. Ark. 1970).

[9] Jackson v. Hendrick, 7 *Law Week 2710* (Ct. Comm. Pls. Pa. 1072).

[10] See special concurrence of Judge Levine in People v. Byrd, 162 N.W. 2nd 777 (1968).

[11] See the Legal Aid Society of New York City, "The Unconstitutional Administration of Bail: Bellamy v. The Judges of New York City, "*Criminal Law Bulletin*, 8, No. 6 (July/August 1972), 459–506.

this status of equal protection makes an arguable, if not convincing, case for the rise in importance of this constitutional clause in the near future. Due process was incrementally applied to more and more aspects of the criminal process as information about the criminal process increased. But the kind of information necessary in order to support due-process claims is relatively simple and direct when compared to the information necessary for valid equal-protection arguments. Whereas due-process contentions rest on a comparison of actual practice to relatively abstract and absolute concepts of fairness and propriety, equal-protection arguments rest on information about *relative* disadvantages of one group compared to another *and* on information about the validity of the governmental purpose in treating these groups differently.[12] For example, although it is true that rich people are required to pay a proportionately higher income tax than poor people, equal protection is not violated so long as there is a valid relation between this differential treatment of income groups and the need for public revenue. In contrast, there was no valid governmental purpose in allowing a rich man to hire an attorney while not providing counsel to the indigent, if the purpose of counsel is the provision of a fair trial.[13]

In many respects, the state of information gathering concerning validity of governmental purpose is just developing. Validity of purpose implies demonstrable effects. Social science, let alone judicial logic, has not yet been terribly effective in this area. For example, what is the purpose in providing aid to dependent children of women who do not live with men but not to children of women who do live with men? The usual argument is that potential wage earners are dissuaded from working if their families can be supported on welfare. Thus, if a potential wage earner is present, no support. But how long can such an argument stand if the demonstrable effects of such a regulation is the encouragement of broken homes? Likewise, can the bail system as the standard means of pretrial release remain in force if it is demonstrated that a greater proportion of bailed defendants abscond than persons released on their own recognizance?

We would predict that equal-protection applications are likely to be increasingly novel as empirical investigations can demonstrate that the purported goals of discrimination have unintended and undesirable consequences.

Divestment of the Criminal Process

Another emergent trend rapidly becoming dominant has been called the "divestment of the criminal process." This term refers to the tendency of

---

[12] In re Antazo, 473 P. 2d 999 (1973) at 1004–1005.

[13] Gideon v. Wainwright, 372 U.S. 335 (1963).

other governmental agencies or of the criminal justice system itself to identify increasing numbers and kinds of behaviors as falling outside the proper sphere of criminal justice intervention.[14] For example, drug and alcohol abuse are increasingly treated by means other than prosecution. Detoxification and treatment centers in a number of cities receive from the police, referrals who previously would have been arrested and prosecuted as petty criminals. There are signs in some states that drug abuse will be treated in similar fashion. Currently there are arguments that other "social problems," such as prostitution, might be legalized and regulated rather than prosecuted.

It is important to realize that although divestment of the criminal process refers to the shrinking scope in the application of the criminal sanction, the alternatives created to handle the "divested" activities might be quite different. For example, Connecticut has abandoned criminal penalities for homosexuality between consenting adults. In other words, such behavior is no longer formally recognized as a social problem. This divestment process is quite different from the coerced civil commitment of drug addicts as an alternative to criminal prosecution.

In this latter case the drug addict is no longer a criminal, and the space he may have occupied in the justice system may be reallocated to other uses. But the drug addict, from his perspective, may be no better—and perhaps may be worse—off. Not only might he still be incarcerated in a civil institution, but the duration of a civil commitment is often of longer duration than a criminal sentence.

The trend of divestment shows every sign of continuing. However, there is little evidence at this point to suggest that the alternative processing of the decriminalized deviant is either more humane or better planned than the criminal justice response had been.

Competency-Based Planning

Clearly related to the above issue of divestment is another emergent trend of "competency-based planning." This is not a formal planning concept; rather it is a term we have invented to cover the growing tendency to focus on the matching of organizational structures and the objectives of social action. In other words, it is a more frequent practice in the 1970s than in prior decades to identify desired social objectives and then to design the agency or system activities to meet these objectives, specifically. At times this new planning practice may merely require an innovative use of an existing agency or a set of practices to accomplish a goal that previously would have been assigned to a different agency. At

[14] Nicolas Kittrie, *The Right to Be Different* (Baltimore: Penguin Books, 1973), pp. 1–12.

other times, competency-based planning may require the creation of a new set of agencies or groups to achieve objectives for which the existing structures appear to be incompetent.[15]

For example, if the objective in the processing of public inebriates is not simply to reduce the extent to which the drunks bother the rest of the public, but, in addition, to provide some modicum of health care to the drunk, then new agencies such as detoxification centers may be more competent than traditional police practices. In this case, a new agency has replaced an older one in order to more adequately match the organizational structure to the specified social objectives. Other such examples include the establishment of R.O.R. (release on recognizance) or 10 percent bail plans to replace the traditional bail bondsman; the establishment of family courts to replace segmented juvenile and domestic relations courts; and the creation of unified criminal justice planning agencies to integrate the activities of police, court, and correctional agencies. Then there are also examples of switching responsibilities from one established agency to another. In these cases, presumably the competency to carry out the objective previously existed, but legislative guidelines or bureaucratic practice withheld the objective from the competent organization. The relatively new practice of social welfare or labor organizations providing vocational training *within* correctional agencies is one such example. Previously either the vocational training experts did not prefer correctional clients, or the correctional agencies, as part of their isolationist stance, sought to provide vocational training internally. A more subtle, but equally important, use of competency-based planning is the innovation of team policing, in which all of the policing duties for one area are delegated to one team of police. Team policing represents a shift in manpower deployment decision making from a centralized agent to a front-line team who are closer to the problems at hand.[16]

This practice of assigning objectives to organizations that seem best designed to achieve the objectives is relatively new. We would anticipate seeing it emerge as a dominant practice in the next 15 years, and to encompass in that time more radical task redistributions. For example, the organizational analysis of the courts in Chapter Ten concludes that the prosecutorial process itself can be rehabilitative if it is managed properly. Therefore, it is possible to see the courts becoming more competent to take on the task of value changing in defendants and leaving to correctional agencies the tasks of placement, training, and reentry support.

[15] The discussion of "designing," as opposed to "planning," is particularly relevant in Harold Bradley, "Designing for Change: Problems of Planned Innovation in Corrections," *Annals of the American Academy of Political and Social Science, 381* (January 1969), 89–98.

[16] Lawrence W. Sherman, Catherine H. Milton, and Thomas V. Kelly, *Team Policing, Seven Case Studies* (Washington, D.C.: Police Foundation, 1973).

An intimately related trend occurs on the other end of the design-planning-implementation-evaluation cycle. As we have seen in the last chapter, evaluation research in criminal justice is in its infancy.

But evaluation methodologies in other kinds of organizational endeavors are relatively sophisticated. As the societal demand for accountability in government continues, we can expect to see these evaluation procedures applied fairly rapidly. "Consequence-based evaluation" is our term to denote, not a technique of evaluation methodology, but rather a guiding assumption: that the scientific evaluation of social programs must include the observation and measurement of actual programmatic outcomes. Although it was not in itself scientific, a major impetus to the emergence of consequence-based evaluations was the change in Supreme Court policy from deciding cases in terms of purposes of intended action to deciding cases in terms of observed effects. If the Supreme Court had not implicitly laid its stamp of approval on the social science techniques that focus on *function* and *consequence* rather than purpose, it is doubtful that such evaluations of criminal justice activity would have emerged so quickly.

Presently the Law Enforcement Assistance Administration, with the aid of the Urban Institute, has inaugurated a new national evaluation program whose entire objective is the implementation of consequence-based evaluation. The evaluation design calls for evaluation methodology in which state planning agencies will (1) collect all existing data on presently funded programs in certain categories, (2) analyze the gaps in the existing knowledge base, (3) standardize evaluation criteria for programs in one category, and (4) implement new evaluation designs that will utilize the standardized criteria.[17] The objective is the systematic investigation of program consequences, which will then be utilized in new program funding, and legislative and social policy decisions.

People-Centered to Event-Centered Action

As one result of the multiple but related trends of divestment, planning, and evaluation, we would anticipate the emergence of entirely new social control strategies. The hallmark of these new strategies will be their

[17] Joe N. Nay, Richard T. Barnes, and Joseph S. Wholey, *Work Description for a Phase I Study under the National Evaluation Program NILE CJ/LEAA*, Working paper 5027–01 (Washington, D.C.: The Urban Institute, November 1974).

emphasis on the structuring of events, rather than an emphasis on processing the people who are related to these events. For example, the New York City police initiated, quite successfully, police training in the handling of family crises. The objectives of this training included reducing the frequency of policy injury in family disputes and the resolution of immediate dangers to the family members involved. The target of police action in this program shifted from the person—such as in the arrest of an offending husband—to the event of the family quarrel. The target was resolution of the difficulty, rather than compounding the difficulty through the use of prosecutorial tactics that could only serve to increase the domestic problem.

There is also a shift from people to events visible in the emerging correctional policy of reintegration. The goals of this policy include provision to the offender of skills necessary to accomplish his objectives legally and to alter the community opportunity structure so that these skills can be utilized. In other words, the target is on reducing the conflux of social interactions that typically exacerbate the conflict between the offender and the community he is reentering. The assumption is that if events can be restructured, persons will no longer need to be treated as problems.

Other examples of event-centered action are the activities of environmental design that make automobiles less stealable or store window displays less vulnerable. On a broader societal dimension, the trends in education to facilitate the inquisitiveness of youngsters by developing new learning environments may replace the more traditional focus on teaching the individual student a prescribed content in prescribed ways. The results of this educational innovation may be a higher probability of learning among students who found the prescriptive teaching culturally foreign or psychologically unacceptable. This event-centered approach to education could reduce the likelihood that "bad students" or "poor students" will later be the focus of criminal justice intervention.

Whether trends such as these can counter or accommodate trends in the changing nature of crime, we do not know. It would appear to us that unless similar adaptive trends are visible in the community as a whole, these important and functional changes in criminal justice will be relatively ineffectual as methods of social control. Therefore, it is extremely important that persons in the criminal justice field be aware of both community structure and the ways in which changes in that structure will not only alter criminal justice effectiveness but the very shape of the system itself.[18]

---

[18] Leslie T. Wilkins, *Social Deviance* (Englewood Cliffs, N.J.: Prentice-Hall, 1965), pp. 78–86; and John M. Martin and Joseph P. Fitzpatrick, *Delinquent Behavior: A Redefinition of the Problem* (New York: Random House, 1969).

The reader should recall from our discussion of community structure in Chapter Two, some basic theses concerning criminal justice that, in our opinion, are not adequately addressed in most discussions of criminal justice goals and functions or in the conceptualization of community by criminal justice experts. *Our first assumption is that the criminal justice system is defined as and operates as a component of the community.* Perhaps more precisely, we must state that various aspects of any particular criminal justice agency must be considered as it functions within a particular community and political structure. Other criminal justice analysts are, of course, aware of the differential impact of varying community connections upon police, court organizations, and correctional agencies.[19] But typically, commentators have analyzed these varying connections as a factor that detracts from the integration of the criminal justice agencies and processes into a system. That most police agencies are local and under executive control, that the prosecutors and judges are county-elected officials, and that felons are handled by state correctional services are all facts that have been emphasized to explain why there are deficiencies in communication in the system, multiple and conflicting goals for the system and its components, and difficulties in standardizing data and evaluation criteria. These data have not been understood as signals or indicators about particularly important and durable characteristics of American community life. Thus, a second related assumption from our point of view is that "fragmentation" of the system—the existence of multiple and conflicting goals, etc.—points to *existence of multiple community functions that must be understood, accommodated, and utilized as designing constraints when people attempt to change criminal justice operations or to implement new programs and management practices within the system.*[20]

A third assumption that we feel necessary to make in order to discuss the future of criminal justice is a comment on the "systems approach" to criminal justice analysis that was adopted by the President's Crime Commission in 1967. This assumption is that *most experts incorrectly have*

[19] In the American Bar Foundation field studies, for example, urban and rural comparisons are made frequently. The President's Commission on Law Enforcement and the Administration of Justice and the National Advisory Commission on Criminal Justice Standards and Goals both acknowledge variations in agencies in different communities. The commissions, in general, however, seem to evaluate such differences negatively.

[20] David Duffee, "Community Structure and Criminal Justice Change," paper prepared for the Association of Criminal Justice Researchers, Northeast and Canada, Dallas, Pa., May 1975.

*assumed that differences and conflicts in criminal justice process are in-
herently dysfunctional or problematic.* We believe that this point of view
has been taken because the systems approach has emphasized the internal processes and problems of criminal justice and has forced a perception of the community as some external "thing" that can be referred to
or ignored but basically taken for granted. More briefly, the "ideal or
analytic model" that people have used most frequently makes internal
management of systems problems the highest priority issues. It relegates
studies of community vis-à-vis criminal justice to the status of a subsystem or subfield that only relatively few administrators and experts will
have to deal with. (For example, police-community relations becomes a
specialty of one police unit, and community-based corrections becomes
one type of correctional program.)

In contrast, our fourth operating assumption is quite the opposite. It
summarizes our entire frame of reference regarding the understanding of
present system operations and future trends: *namely, the primary
analytic or ideal model should provide a valid and systematic understanding of the community and the criminal justice system should be
understood as it performs a variety of community functions.*

As we demonstrated in Chapter Two, the various criminal justice
agencies are integrated into a variety of different community structures of
subsystems. Criminal justice organizations contribute in various ways to
all five locality-relevant functions:

1. *Production-distribution-consumption.*
2. *Socialization.*
3. *Social control.*
4. *Social participation.*
5. *Mutual support.*

Several conclusions were supported by this analysis of criminal justice as a component of community structure. First, it would seem that
both individual agencies of justice and the agencies of justice taken together must perform several different goal-achieving activities at once.
Second, it would seem that the predominant or controlling influences
upon any particular justice organization in one community may not be
the predominant or controlling influence upon the same type of agency in
another community. Third, it seems likely that the pressures for a unified
and integrated criminal justice system emerge primarily from experts and
agencies who are most concerned with the community function of social
control.[21]

---

[21] Wilkins raises this point in the final footnote of "Crime and Crime Control in
the 1990's"—see footnote 1.

Even considering the function of social control alone, we also saw that there may be disagreement about the best methods of providing social control and the role that criminal justice agencies might perform along this dimension. For those who are concerned primarily with public safety through reduction in crime by particular individuals, legalistic police work, highly formal and equal judicial decisions, and professional rehabilitative correctional processes seem most important. The vertical articulation or organization of criminal justice processes, manpower, and resources seems to be a necessity. For these individuals, it is only through the increased systematization of operations, information, and management objectives, and the increased support and expertise of state and federal government that such social control activity can be performed.

To other persons who are concerned with the impact of crime on the maintenance of community norms and values, this highly professional, highly integrated system is perceived as a threat to the achievement of social control. The emphasis on this side is not on the specific outcome for individual violators of the law. Instead the emphasis is on how the visible portions of the criminal process impact on and support the belief that law-abiding citizens are relatively rewarded for achieving their personal objectives while conforming to legal prescriptions.

We have also seen that there are powerful conflicting beliefs concerning the achievement of the *social participation* function in community life. Some persons assume that social participation is supported to the extent that the criminal process, and other visible means of identifying and reaffirming community norms, clearly draw the line at behavior that excludes people from the conforming group. Kai T. Erikson[22] and Émile Durkheim,[23] for instance, argue that the invocation of the criminal sanction, or the formal identification of criminal behavior, is functional because it strengthens the group feeling within the community. Other persons argue that the value placed on the individual in American society, or the irreducible worth of any actor as a human being, is so strong that social participation is supported by social processes that dramatize that criminal offenders are valued as human beings or individuals and that they are included in the community, even as they are identified and punished.[24] From this point of view, due-process issues are extremely important as a social statement that there are only very limited and special circumstances under which an individual, regardless of his behavior, will be isolated or cast out of the group.

[22] Kai T. Erikson, *The Wayward Puritans* (New York: Wiley, 1965).

[23] Émile Durkheim, *The Division of Labor in Society* (New York: The Free Press, 1964), pp. 96–110.

[24] John Griffiths, "Ideology in Criminal Procedure or a Third "Model" of the Criminal Process," *Yale Law Journal*, 79 (January 1970), 359–417.

It was our intention in Part I of this book (Chapters One and Two) to describe very briefly the present operational processes and issues in the criminal justice system and to relate this presentation to a complex but unified model of community. In Part II (Chapters Three through Eight) we attempted to describe the present goals and operations of various parts of the system and to explain the present state of the system in terms of historical development of both the agencies themselves and the changing face of American political and social life. In Part III (Chapters Nine through Twelve) we applied one system model of organization to the operations of various agencies. In Part IV, Chapter Thirteen, we discussed some of the difficulties in researching criminal justice. In this final chapter of Part IV we hope to place these descriptive and analytic exercises in perspective by integrating both our descriptive and analytic pictures of the system into the broader model of community. This is not to say that we will provide final answers about the future of the system or pat suggestions about the ways in which the system ought to move. What we mean to suggest is that the internal management models and decisions about internal operations are not valid if they are made in a vacuum. And, in our opinion, the entire analysis of the system is something of a vacuous intellectual game unless it is grounded in the realities of the changing social milieu without which the criminal justice system would not exist in the first place.

What we are asking of both ourselves and the reader in this last chapter, therefore, is to take a hard look at the present goals and operations of criminal justice as these may be reformulated or specified from an "outsider's" perspective. Rather than assume that the justice system as it exists should be maintained and improved, let us assume that important social values and end-states should be achieved. To the extent that these objectives may be partially or completely achieved by the criminal justice apparatus, we then have the organizational knowledge and expertise to direct, or redirect, the system toward these ends. On the other hand, to the extent that important social values and end-states seem more feasibly obtained through other social arrangements, we then have the knowledge of organizational characteristics and dynamics in criminal justice agencies that may impede these achievements and may deal with them accordingly.

Changes in Vertical and Horizontal Dimensions of Community Structure

A more fundamental question about the American social system than the questions concerning criminal justice per se, is the question of whether the American community, defined by any currently common means, may continue to exist as a significant social entity. Acute problems of world population, food supply, international relations, and the ecology of important natural resources (no matter how the problems are resolved) carry important implications for the structure of human interaction, as we anticipate the turn of the century. One conclusion based on such world problems is that many "natural" or long-accepted boundaries between human groups are no longer helpful delineations of personal or group interest. For example, the need for energy conservation or energy creation is so critical to any group of human beings that no organized groups of people can attempt to maintain and utilize their share of world energy without considering how other groups will respond to that expenditure or cultivation of the supply. And no nation can afford to decide how to raise and distribute its own food supply without considering the food needs of other groups of people.

In short, there are many fundamental issues for which a particular town line, county boundary, ethnic group, or nationality can no longer provide useful reference points. Stated another way, if significant locality-relevant functions must increasingly be characterized as worldwide concerns, communities may also become worldwide in scope.

Although issues of social control and justice have perhaps less frequently been couched in the framework of international concerns, there are certainly many instances to the contrary. For example, there was frequent mention of Third World powers during the 1971 Attica revolt.[25] Marxian economists would analyze all criminal justice activities of capitalistic societies as one means of controlling the manipulated working class. Also, organized criminal activities apparently include international cooperation and exchange, if not international "syndicates." The entire notion of *mens rea* or criminal responsibility is dependent on the concept of individual culpability, which does not seem appropriate to the modern world community of international organizations and conglomerate enterprise.

But even though the increasing scope of travel and communication technology and the increasing immediacy of foreign problems to local affairs do raise doubts about the endurance of cultural and political definitions of community boundaries, it is important to notice that the notion of worldwide community does *not* alter the distinction between "community" and state or national government. Nor does it do away with the distinction between horizontal and vertical dimensions of community structure.

We noted in Chapter Two that one major trend in twentieth-century community structure was the increasing importance of vertical connections for the performance of community functions and likewise the d

---

[25] Tom Wicker, *A Time to Die* (New York: Quadrangle, 1975).

creasing importance of horizontal connections. There seem to be fewer and fewer kinds of social activities that one geographically or politically bounded group of people can carry out on their own. As examples, the financial fate of New York City involves decisions at both the state and federal levels; the findings of community-based correctional programs frequently involve state and/or federal funds; and state and federal monies are increasingly important to the delivery of education in local school districts.

Although there are myriad examples now of vertical connections between local and state organizations for the delivery of certain social services and performance of locality-relevant functions, there are as yet few indications that the dissolution of horizontal connections at the local level are being replaced by horizontal connections of broader segments of society. In other words, there are few indications that the social integration of functions that once existed on the local level (and may still exist in smaller and more rural and more homogeneous communities) are re-emerging at the state, national, or some transnational level.

Some social commentators have termed this absence of horizontal articulation, or the lack of integration of various community functions, as the emergence of the "mass society." Mass society is perhaps a sloppy term, connoting different things in different contexts. As it is used by David Riesman[26] or Daniel Bell[27] or Amitai Etzioni,[28] however, mass society seems to connote the absence of significant social groupings within which individuals obtain a social identity. Stated differently, mass society connotes the lack of group moorings or membership that mediate between the individual and the political state.

There have been in the last few years several attempts to reengineer this lost sense of community. Pennsylvania, Illinois, and Minnesota, for example, have been experimenting lately with the regionalization of particular social services. For example, in Pennsylvania, ten "common human service regions" have been delineated, at least on paper, and attempts have been made to reorganize social service policy and service provision to meet social needs as they exist in each region, rather than make social policy from Harrisburg that would apply uniformly across the state. All three states have attempted to regionalize correctional services so that each region would contain its own set of correctional institutions and field services. The idea is that continuity of social service can be better managed on this regional level than on a state level and that all offenders would remain fairly close to their home communities. These recent experiments in the decentralization of state bureaucracies for social service

[26] David Riesman, *The Lonely Crowd* (New Haven: Yale University Press, 1969).

[27] Daniel Bell, *The End of Ideology* (New York: The Free Press, 1960).

[28] Amitai Etzioni, *The Active Society* (New York: The Free Press, 1968).

delivery may have demonstrated some ability to reduce the number of stepping stones between fiscal and social policy decisions and the delivery of certain social services. However, these devices have not as yet demonstrated much effectiveness in doing so. Nor have they been able yet to integrate the variety of social services within a region. In Pennsylvania, for example, there has been considerable difficulty getting all public and private agencies with similar objectives to work together, let alone integrate matters of transportation with those of education or social welfare or criminal justice. The Pennsylvania correctional system is now reverting to a more centralized system.

Perhaps one exception to this horizontal articulation problem is the several federal revenue-sharing programs. In this instance, local governmental units have some control over where money will be spent. Hence, to the extent that local government bodies are representative of all factions of a community and are cognizant of the multiplicity of local needs, revenue sharing may provide some integration by allowing different communities to distribute these funds according to local needs.

Nevertheless, the present acknowledgment that local communities and individuals no longer feel able to marshall sufficient resources to meet their needs and no longer feel adequately represented in decisions that will have impact on community-level activity is qualitatively different than an acknowledgment that communities need to provide coordination across different community functions. Regionalized social services, revenue sharing, and the like, are programs that seem primarily geared to providing more effectively a cafeteria line of social services in a more palatable manner. These programs, in other words, are attempts to implement more effectively vertically organized and separate functions. The "consumer" or client of such services is still seen as the individual who passes through an array of social services, picking his education here, and his employment counseling there, and his legal aid at yet another stop. The decision to create "one-stop, integrated social service centers" is really no different: indeed, the unified center may actually be the epitome of the depersonalized and community-less model of gathering the social means of survival.

In contrast to this model of social living, both the disappearing cohesive community and the notion of worldwide community point to something quite different. That difference has to do with the recognition that not individuals, but social groups, are the basic social unit, and that these groups are defined by the interrelationships that hold the individuals together, rather than by the analytic categories that break them apart.

To examine this difference very concretely, we might examine the differences in role of the local parish constable or the local justice of the peace versus the role of the urban policeman or the legally trained urban court judge. The constable and the local magistrate had some dues similar to those of their modern counterparts. For example, the constable might apprehend an offender and hold him until the magistrate determined if a wrong had been done and how the matter should be dealt with. But although the modern urban policeman and judge now seem to concentrate on these and related matters, the earlier officials had significant positions and duties of another sort. The community magistrate and the constable typically had to earn a living by doing something else, and they were typically commoners who were known throughout the town prior to their assumption of their official capacities, and their appointment or election to these duties was a significant statement of social prestige. Their basic expertise was not in matters of criminal law and criminal procedure, but in their social knowledge both of the values and norms of their community and in their personal knowledge of the human beings they dealt with. And, as socially important members of their community, they also had significant contact and interaction with other important community leaders, such as the mayor, the minister, the schoolteacher. Perhaps the most important difference in role, then, between these local community officials and the modern urban policeman and judge was that what they (the local constable or justice of the peace) did in an official capacity had to be done in accordance with their knowledge of how other officials were performing, and more importantly, with the knowledge that what they did by way of maintaining order could be, and was, done as well by people with other leadership positions. The town physician, minister, or schoolteacher, or any particular citizen had both ideas about, and impact upon, the way that justice was meted out. Any particular Saturday-night altercation was potentially just as much a part of Sunday's sermon as it might be Monday's trial. Likewise, the town doctor probably did as much marriage counseling as the minister, or the schoolteacher may have had as much of a hand in the orderliness of the town youth as the constable.

The purpose of this examination of community integration is *not* to call for "turning back the clock." One cannot create small towns out of vast metropolitan systems. The key point is that some social functions performed in horizontally articulated communities have been lost as particular community activities have become specialities, and these specialities have been supported by complex organizations, each with its own set of higher-level constraints, controls, and resources. The defense usually made in the comparison of the local magistrate with the urban judge, or the local constable with the modern policeman, is that the modern officials are more professional, more educated, and more competent to perform in their own particular areas. Our point is that this higher competence, better education, etc., are valid only from the perspective of vertically organized, fragmented community functions. We would suggest that the modern specialists have also lost some resources and some competencies; most significantly, whole sets of information have been lost about the community in its entirety and about any of its citizens as complete human beings rather than role-incumbents eligible for particular kinds of social services.

Leslie Wilkins proposed that the problem of reintroducing the functions of social participation and mutual support into a highly bureaucratized and urbanized set of social service systems requires an examination of the information flow that seems to exist in more homogeneous and horizontally articulated groups. In order to begin this examination, he utilizes the examples of a small British village and a small primary group.[29] In both of these examples, Wilkins asserts, the information system functions to retain deviants within the group, rather than to exclude them. Both the village idiot and the town squire in the village example, and the group clown in the peer-group example, are deviant compared to the norms of the group. But such groups suffer if such actors are removed, and both kinds of groups resist the removal of these unusual members to special facilities or specialized status. The importance of these group members to the small village, for example, is both recognized and accepted by the town constable or justice of the peace, to introduce our own examples of small-town actors. It is understood by these community officials that deviant events must be kept within bounds, but that isolating the deviant actors from the group is not an available control option because removal in order to achieve social control conflicts with the achievement of social participation (group membership) and mutual support (provision of services, refuge, understanding to community members who are in dependent situations).

John Griffiths, a legal scholar, has addressed the question of how the criminal process would operate, what it would look like, and what its guiding philosophy would be if the aim of the contemporary criminal justice system were to maintain offenders in the community rather than to remove them.[30] He calls the criminal process manifesting this objective the "*family model* of the Criminal Process."[31] His rationale for the term *family model* is that social discipline through the criminal process can function analogously to discipline in a family. The wrongdoer in the family situation is punished for behavior that violates family rules, but the offending member of the group is *not* cast out of the family. The objective of the family disciplinary procedure is to maintain the family group.

In a similar fashion, Griffiths suggests, the criminal process can be utilized to achieve the same objective of group membership maintenance.

---

[29] Wilkins, *Social Deviance*, pp. 62–71.

[30] Griffiths, "Ideology in Criminal Procedure."

[31] Ibid., p. 371.

He acknowledges that implementation of such objectives through the criminal process would require both very different thinking and very different behavior on the part of all participants. The officials would have to behave as mediators of social norms, and as representatives of all aggrieved parties (the victim and the state, and the offender).[32]

Griffiths argues that the one grand social experiment with the family model was the juvenile justice system established in 1899. However, he admits, and as we have seen in Chapters Eight and Twelve, that the juvenile system never achieved the objectives of social reconciliation. Griffiths maintains that the juvenile movement was a failure because the operations and guiding ideology of the criminal process were so influential that the behavior required of officials and offenders was never adequately structured or rewarded. The social participation and mutual support functions that the juvenile justice system were to perform were reduced to lip-service rationales and reexplanations of the social control strategies that were actually employed.[33]

Griffiths' family model and the realities of the juvenile justice experience highlight both the particular social dynamics that support our contentions concerning community functions and the legal system contribution to their performance. For example, it was explicitly stated in the Illinois Juvenile Court Act of 1899 (and in other similar acts that followed) that protection of the community (i.e., a social control function) and rehabilitation or ameliorization of the juvenile's condition were one and the same activity. Warren's model of locality-relevant functions and our analysis of the justice system role in these functions would suggest that the identification of social control functions and social participation and mutual support are *not* the same. The social technologies and the vertical, highly specialized systems that contribute to deterrence require different official education, training, and orientation than the horizontal articulation of groups that contribute to social participation and mutual support.

From 1900 until the present, a dominant trend in community structure has been the increased importance, intensity, and complexity of social control efforts through the elaboration of specialized vertical systems for remediation and management of identified deviants.[34] A correlated trend has been the reduction of importance and intensity of social participation and mutual support (i.e., the decreasing duration and salience of family and primary group relations). Many social scientists and social program administrators have rationalized bureaucratic and vertically arranged human service systems as substitutes for or replacements of the previ-

---

[32] Ibid., pp. 380–386.
[33] Ibid., pp. 399–404.
[34] Kittrie, *The Right To Be Different*, pp. 39–49.

ously institutionalized forms of social participation and mutual support.

Our suggestion is that this substitution has not yet been effective, or, more probably, that it has never really taken place. The juvenile court and its related organizations did not provide substitutes for cohesive primary groups. The "paternalistic juvenile judge" is not a father substitute, but merely patronizing.[35] The introduction of due-process constraints on this "paternalism" has not altered the system's primary role in handling the juvenile in ways commensurate with social control criteria. The criminal process for adults has faired no better in this sense. The primary emphasis is on what to do with the individual who is not a member of the community, rather than on what to do with him because he is. Thus, we suspect that the long-range shape and objectives of criminal justice will be determined by the future trends in communiy structure along vertical and horizontal dimensions, and by the relative emphasis on social control, social participation, and mutual support.

THE SOCIAL CONTROL FUNCTION

As we demonstrated in Chapter Two, the criminal justice system traditionally has been *assumed* to contribute to the social control functions of community structure. Although we agree that the system probably does do so, we have no way of measuring whether indeed this is the primary function of the system, or one that it performs effectively. We were more concerned, in Chapter Two, with trying to analyze the various ways in which the system attempts to achieve social control objectives, and whether these various ways were compatible with each other. Our conclusion was that, in all probability, several strategies conflict with each other, and that particular criminal justice systems will emphasize one set of strategies more than another, depending on the relevant community structure. (See Figure 2-1.) Briefly, we see conflict between strategies of deterrence and strategies of retribution (or the prevention of anomie). If demand for deterrence and demand for retribution are both weak, we suspect that the community itself is very weak. If demand for retribution is strong but demand for deterrence weak, we suspect that the horizontal associations in the community are strong and vertical associations weak. If the demand for deterrence is strong and the demand for retribution is weak, we suspect that the vertical dimensions of community structure are strong and the horizontal dimension is relatively latent. If both demands are strong, we assume that the community structure is highly heterogeneous and unstable, that conflicting social groups are attempting to

[35] David Duffee and Vincent O'Leary, "Models of Correction: An Entry in the Packer Griffiths Debate," *Criminal Law Bulletin, 7*, No. 4 (May 1971), 329–352.

gain control of the criminal justice apparatus, and that either massive public reeducation or civil disorder will result.

The future of the criminal justice system is dependent on the future demand for retribution versus the demand for deterrence activities. If deterrence continues to be stressed (as in the capacity of police to respond quickly or to patrol more widely, or in the case of more effective correctional programming, to change offenders' behavior), then the criminal justice system will become a more sophisticated, complex, and expensive version of what it presently is. Agency cooperation and integration, systemwide management, and information systems will be employed, and the criminal justice agencies will be increasingly less influenced by various external community groups. Instead, the agencies will be increasingly influenced by each other, and particularly by higher-level state and federal decision-making groups and expert staffs. It would seem to the authors that it is this type of criminal justice system toward which most criminal justice programs in colleges and universities are now geared.

If this type of system prevails, it is also likely that communities as significant social units will continue to become less important. The long-range impact of a deterrence-directed criminal justice system will be to move from the maintenance of community order to the provision of selected, specialized services or interventions directly for individual offenders through the agency of large bureaucratic systems.

Concomitantly, some other changes will also ensue. Wilkins predicts that if this sort of criminal justice system continues to elaborate, ultimately it will collapse altogether.[36] It is his suggestion that the legal system, because it can be invoked only at the point that a law is violated, cannot adapt quickly enough to the changing nature of crime. New behavior that merits deterrence will be invented long before laws can proscribe it and before means can be invented to police and/or treat it. However, we think there is another option. This would be that on the point of collapse, the constitutional constraints on the operational system of deterrence would be either changed or relaxed. If this happens, the deterrence system may continue to function, but the citizenry would be increasingly subjected to more intrusive and encompassing forms of investigatory and supervisory activity.

If retribution rather than deterrence becomes the principal demand, or the dominant social control strategy, the criminal justice system is likely to look quite different than would be the case if deterrence strategies are followed. Implementation of retributive objectives would require a criminal justice apparatus that demonstrated to the nonoffending public that the norms and values of the community are upheld. As we argued in Chapter Two, prevention of anomie and deterrence may well be nega-

---

[36] Wilkins, "Crime and Justice at the Turn of the Century."

tively correlated in several ways. The retributive model is not concerned with the future behavior of offenders, but with whether offenders are recognized as persons who have violated accepted patterns of group interaction. Perhaps more problematic is the point that a community with strong group norms and high group observance of norms is likely to be one in which crime is less frequent. Because it is less frequent, each incident of crime is likely to be perceived as more important. Each incident will be seen as threatening more fundamentally the structure of the community, and there is likely to be broader interest and greater community involvement in the handling of the event. In other words, the crime and the criminal are less likely to be delegated to criminal justice specialists—the retributive reactions will be communitywide reactions.

The "criminal justice system" in such a community would *not* be a system per se, as that term is used to delineate the linkages of the agencies that administer the criminal process. The criminal justice system, in this instance, would be more accurately described as an informal community communication and decision network that sets the general tenor and texture of the community. It may *include* certain criminal justice officials. But the system in this instance would be the linkages between these persons and other important community representatives (who may or may not be government officials) who are both the major spokesmen of community values and the leaders in the time of other kinds of community crises.

It would seem dubious that this kind of criminal justice system is viable in the future—because it is doubtful that this sort of "community" is viable in the future. Indeed, as we have stated, it is because this sort of informal cohesive and homogeneous community structure has broken down that it has been replaced with the vertical, deterrence-oriented system. There have been, of course, examples of "backlash" and "reactionary politics" that may manifest at least tentative returns to this sort of community structure in some instances. For example, cases of vigilantism have been reported in which certain citizen groups "have taken the law into their own hands." Serving similar functions, perhaps, are cases of block organizations or even local gangs who have decided to crack down on drug pushers or keep outside troublemakers out of a neighborhood.

Many such activities are, obviously, on tenuous legal ground—or are even illegal. At least such activities and community organizing are frequently frowned upon by the police who complain that untrained and unauthorized persons are usurping their legal powers. This kind of incident demonstrates the conflict between the professional, deterrence-directed system and the informal retribution-directed system. The history of the criminal process would indicate that the officials of the vertically organized deterrence system were originally delegated authority from elected officials of the citizenry who are *now* claiming that the criminal justice system no longer supports the community norms and values.

We would predict that a return to relatively isolated, autonomous, and cohesive communities is highly unlikely to occur. Hence, about the only two ways in which a retributive system would again become dominant are the following. First, new social values that are widely accepted by nearly all the various community factions, classes, ethnic groups, etc., may become dominant in the future. If this phenomenon occurred, it would be conceivable that a new type of community might emerge, unified by a new set of cohesive factors. The worldwide community of man is perhaps the limiting case. Certain social critics have argued that such new values are now present and may ascend in scope and importance. The cliché "Do your own thing" may be one such example—in which the particular personal objectives of people widely vary, but they hold in common the idea that doing one's own thing can only be accomplished if others are also able to pursue their own objectives. Activities that coerce groups or individuals to behave in certain ways so that others could achieve their aims would receive communitywide approbation. In other words, crimes would be those behaviors that treated other persons as means rather than ends. Wilkins calls such a value orientation "enlightened self-interest,"[37] and Etzioni speaks of similar notions as "beyond tribalism" and "the active society."[38] Although it sounds like a desirable outcome, George Jackson's vision of achieving the same type of community includes the requirement of doing away with the "pigs" first.[39] If pigs are persons who manipulate others to their own gain, indeed, such animals would not be included in the new community. But it would appear that the criminal justice system as it presently operates (which would also be unnecessary in such a community) would both protect the pigs from bodily harm and continue to decrease the horizontal articulation necessary to produce such a community.

The second possibility for a future retributive justice system would be the usurpation of all governmental functions, including the justice system, by a dominant minority group who would then enforce its own norms and values upon every other community group. Although some Marxists may argue that this takeover has already taken place, other commentators, such as Dahrendorf, have argued that society has become too complex and too pluralistic in authority structure for such totalistic regimes to occur.[40] In contrast, Etzioni states that new totalitarian

---

[37] Ibid.

[38] Etzioni, *The Active Society,* pp. 550–552.

[39] George Jackson, *Soledad Brother* (New York: Bantam Books, 1970).

[40] Ralf Dohrendorf, *Class and Class Conflict in Industrial Society* (Stanford: Stanford University Press, 1959), pp. 215–218.

regimes may well emerge but that such a regime is inherently unstable. Either the controlling minority successfully reeducates the controlled groups to the one set of values, or the regime dissolves or is overthrown.[41]

The criminal justice system in such a social structure is nothing more or less than the military branch of government: The enemy within is perceived to be as threatening as is the enemy without. While the police control the captive population, the army invades other countries.

None of these futures for criminal justice appears very desirable (or if desirable, then rather unlikely). The reason for this, we suggest, lies in the nature of the tasks assigned to criminal justice within a social control area. Criminal justice, utilized as a primary form of social control, is inherently oppressive, expensive, and violent. Criminal justice utilized as a secondary or remedial form of social control can never substitute for forms of community self-control that arise from common values and accepted human interaction patterns that all community groups abide by. In short, criminal justice as a major social enterprise is either a signal that community itself is in a state of dissolution or that the community is an armed encampment in which the group in power protects itself from the captive groups.

SOCIAL PARTICIPATION AND MUTUAL SUPPORT

There are, of course, other uses, or other possible uses, of criminal justice. The major ones, we would suggest, occur in the areas of social participation and mutual support. These are the two locality-relevant functions in American communities that have typically been performed by religious institutions and the family. Social participation refers to the community structures that provide for a sense of membership and belonging through informal interaction and ritual. Mutual support refers to the community structures that provide assistance to group members in time of need, when emergencies or crisis situations call for either instrumental goods and services or emotional support.

Within the last century, the major trends in community dynamics have formalized these two functions of community. Formal organizations, both of a voluntary and a bureaucratic nature, have taken over the performance of mutual support in a number of areas. Charitable organizations have replaced, to a large extent, the informal family or community efforts to meet welfare or health needs for large portions of the American population.

Some confusion, or some dual functionality, exists in the areas of welfare and mental health, which are similar to the multiple functions per-

41 Etzioni, *The Active Society*, pp. 442–446.

formed by the criminal justice system. It is arguable (if not convincing), for example, that institutionalized welfare, unlike its more informal and voluntary predecessors, is equally relevant as a social control function. Services are provided to the poor or to families with emergency needs, but regulations must also be met, and families receiving services must be deemed eligible because they fit into some preestablished need category. Some social critics have argued that this routinized provision of minimal support to the chronically poor is a means of maintaining control over the economically disadvantaged and dispossessed. Likewise, mental health services, although increasingly perceived and administered as another set of health needs for many members of society, have traditionally functioned as an alternative system to criminal justice that processes and controls persons who are perceived as deviant or troublemakers.

A fundamental question in the analysis of the current trend toward the divestment of the criminal process would be whether the offender groups that are now being reallocated to other human service systems are merely being subjected to new forms of social control or whether the services rendered under the new systems represent a shift in community function being performed. This question is also crucial to analysis of the due-process trend. Typically the divesting systems are under less stringent constitutional control than the criminal justice system. One of the reasons for lesser stringency is that the alternate processes, typically falling within the health or welfare complex, have labels that designate them as benefits to the client rather than as punishments for an offense. Of course, the juvenile justice system also long withstood constitutional challenges and judicial scrutiny of administrative decisions and processes under the rubric of acting in the child's behalf. The Supreme Court finally rejected this rationale in 1967 and went on to examine the actual conditions and consequences of the supposedly beneficial service.[42] The same judicial intervention will probably occur in the health and welfare systems, especially if these systems are actually performing social control functions rather than providing mutual support.

These trends of divestment and due process lead us, then, to the crucial question: How does one tell the difference between activities of social control and the activities of mutual support?

There are at present no ways to define the social impacts and measure the degree of contribution to one function rather than another. The reader must also remember the point made in Chapter Two, that the criminal justice system undoubtedly does contribute even now to social participation and mutual support functions.

The present dominance of crime and "crook catching" on the television is some evidence of the fundamental symbolic or cultural significance of

[42] In re Gault, 387 U.S. 1 (1967).

crime and criminal justice to the American community. Citizens participate vicariously or actually in the ritual of investigation, prosecution, and public trial. Social participation is one function of the criminal process because it brings various community groups together in reaction to a particular offense, in sympathy for a particular victim, or in empathy for a particular defendant.

The criminal justice system also performs many activities that are clearly of a mutual support nature. As mentioned earlier, the majority of police calls in any police jurisdiction are requests for some type of service that are unconnected to criminal events. Further, judicial dispositions frequently include as factors in the decision the extremities forced on an offender's family, or the kinds of probation or institutional services that might serve to improve the offender's psychological or social skills and competencies. And many correctional services, particularly in the newer community-based programs, include job training, education, vocational or physical rehabilitation, corrective surgery, etc., which are provided not as a condition or means of punishment but because the services are needed (and frequently requested) by the offender.

But, as we have pointed out in both the descriptive and analytical chapters of this book, both social participation, from the offender's viewpoint, and mutual support, from the offender's viewpoint, are frequently ineffective or damaging because they are functions disturbed and distorted by the primary emphasis on social control. The court system, for example, as it currently operates, serves to separate systematically the defendant from his membership in the community. Although the present court process may serve a community social participation function, it does so at the expense of the offender. If, instead of the present system, Griffiths' "Family model" of the criminal process were to be implemented,[43] the objective of the court process would be to determine how the offender could be retained in the community rather than a series of determinations that lead to extracting him from the community. Our conclusions about court structure in Chapter Ten are consistent with this family model. The court system, if it focused on the moral obligations of the defendant, might become an educational process in which the defendant's membership in the community was renegotiated.

If the police and correctional systems, as well, were to emphasize mutual support activities rather than social control activities, in terms of their impact on the offender, then other significant changes in agency operations would have to occur. These changes would be fundamental shifts in operating style, in policy, and in key indicators of effective personnel performance. The basic change, from our point of view, would

---

[43] John Griffiths, "Ideology in Criminal Procedure, or a Third 'Model' of the Criminal Process," *Yale Law Journal*, 79, No. 3 (January 1970), 371–376.

involve elevating to a dominant position the emergent trend away from people-centered and toward event-centered action. The police organization would have to concentrate on social services, in the sense that social disturbances be handled, when at all possible, on the street or in the community, by negotiating disagreements between antagonistic parties or by referring people to other social service agencies. Correctional agencies would have to concentrate on linking persons with particular social needs to either formal or informal groups who could deliver such services, not on the rationale that such service was part of the offender's "treatment plan," but simply on the rationale that such a service was needed by a member of the community.

Changes such as these probably would require different structural changes in different parts of the system. The social service activities of the police, and the skills, particularly of patrolmen, for handling social conflicts on the street without resorting to the prosecution process, have always been recognized but rarely have been rewarded and seldom have been legitimized as parts of the training and promotional system. Such changes, therefore, would require elevating some of the informal peer-group sanctions for "good police work" to formal organizational demands and would require alterations in recruitment and evaluation policy.

In correctional agencies, on the other hand, the skills of social support have frequently been sought and recognized formally. However, the bureaucratic organization of correction has frequently pressured the most innovative social service providers to move on to other organizations because the professional helping skills are difficult if not impossible to employ within the environment set up by the coercive situation. If mutual support activities are to be provided effectively by correctional agencies, the structural emphasis on isolating the offender-client from the community has to be drastically reduced, and the stigma of the convict has to be discarded as a criterion of eligibility for the social services in question.

The net effect, then, of a criminal justice system in which social participation and mutual support are dominant functions is probably the dissolution of the criminal justice system as we know it and the strengthening of the social and political commitment to provision of mutual support within the community. The more likely outcome, although it probably amounts to the same thing, is the total divestment by the criminal process of its mutual support functions, in order to reallocate these functions to other community systems and to retain a minimal criminal justice apparatus that would intervene more surely and more swiftly, but for considerably shorter periods of time, into the lives of proportionately fewer American citizens.

Name Index

Subject Index

The Criminal Justice System

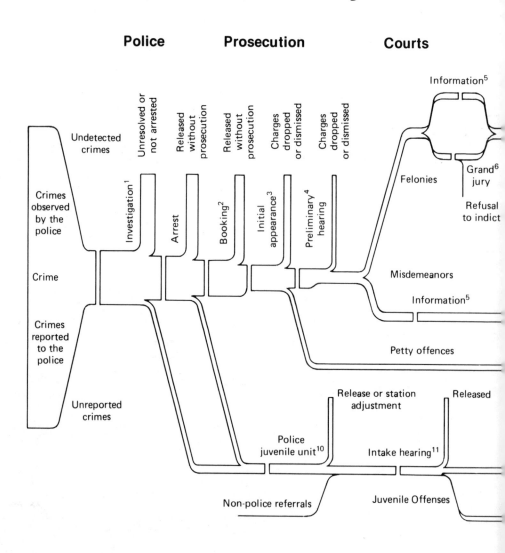

Police **Prosecution** **Courts**

Information[5]

Undetected crimes

Unresolved or not arrested

Released without prosecution

Released without prosecution

Charges dropped or dismissed

Charges dropped or dismissed

Felonies Grand[6] jury

Refusal to indict

Crimes observed by the police

Investigation[1]

Arrest

Booking[2]

Initial appearance[3]

Preliminary[4] hearing

Crime

Misdemeanors

Information[5]

Crimes reported to the police

Petty offences

Release or station adjustment Released

Unreported crimes

Police juvenile unit[10]

Intake hearing[11]

Non-police referrals

Juvenile Offenses

---

1 May continue until trial.

2 Administrative record of arrest first stage at which temporary release on bail may be available.

3 Before magistrate, commissioner, or justice of peace, formal notice of charge, advice of rights, Budget Summary trials for party offenses usually conducted here without further processing.

4 Preliminary testing of evidence against defendent. Charge may be reduced. No separate pre-liminary hearing for misdemeanors in some systems.

5 Charge filed by prosecuto basis of information subm by police or citizens. Alte tive to grand jury indictm often used in felonies, alm always in misdemeanors.

6 Reviews whether governm evidence sufficient to just trial. Some states have no grand jury system, others seldom use it.